CONSTITUTION FOR A DISUNITED NATION

CONSTITUTION FOR A DISUNITED NATION

On Hungary's 2011 Fundamental Law

Edited by
Gábor Attila Tóth

CEU PRESS

Central European University Press
Budapest–New York

Published in 2012 by

Central European University Press
An imprint of the
Central European University Limited Liability Company
Nádor utca 11, H-1051 Budapest, Hungary
Tel: +36-1-327-3138 or 327-3000
Fax: +36-1-327-3183
E-mail: ceupress@ceu.hu
Website: www.ceupress.com

400 West 59th Street, New York NY 10019, USA
Tel: +1-212-547-6932
Fax: +1-646-557-2416
E-mail: mgreenwald@sorosny.org

ISBN 978-615-5225-18-5

LIBRARY OF CONGRESS CATALOGING-IN-PUBLICATION DATA

Constitution for a disunited nation : on Hungary's 2011 fundamental law / edited by Gábor Attila Tóth.
pages cm
Includes bibliographical references and index.
ISBN 978-6155225185 (hardbound)
1. Hungary. Alaptörvény. 2. Constitutional law—Hungary—Congresses. I. Tóth, Gábor Attila, 1970- editor of compilation.

KKF2064.52011.C66 2012
342.439—dc23

2012031829

Table of Contents

IV. INSTITUTIONAL DESIGN

V. EUROPEAN PERSPECTIVES

VI. APPENDIX

Preface

More than two decades after the post-communist constitutional transition, Hungary entered the spotlight again. The winner of the 2010 elections gained two-thirds of the seats in Parliament, which made constitutional revision exceptionally easy—bypassing political and social deliberation. On April 25, 2011 (Easter Monday), on the first anniversary of the 2010 election, the president promulgated a new constitution, called the Fundamental Law. The new document has attracted the attention of scholars, politicians, media and the general public, both at home and abroad. While it is the first newly made constitution to originate from a democratically elected parliament in Hungary, the way the text was drafted as well as the content of the text itself, according to many views, are in conflict with some of the basic features of democratic constitutionalism.

This is a book about the new Hungarian constitution. It is meant as a comprehensive account of the Fundamental Law's main attributes and its underlying principles. Focusing on both the constitution-making procedure and the substance of the text, the authors outline and analyze how the current constitutional changes are altering the basic structure of the Hungarian state. This is a particular story, but it is of global relevance. The aim of the contributors is to examine a constitutional transition from the perspectives of comparative constitutional law, legal theory and political philosophy.

One of the crucial judgments emerging from this volume is that the Fundamental Law of Hungary does not fulfill the integrative function of modern constitutions. It is biased in favor of the winners of the 2010 elections and against everybody else. It provides a mythical historical narrative that goes against the grain of republican traditions. It prefers Catholics to non-believers and followers of other faiths. Of course, Hungary is not exceptional in being a disunited nation. For an important analogy, the so-called red (Republican) and blue (Democratic) political cultures deeply divide the people of the United States of America. In Northern Ireland nationalists and unionists disagree on no less than under which state (the United Kingdom or Republic of Ireland) the country's territory should be governed. In Belgium the Flemish and Walloon communities not only speak different languages, but are unable to find a common political language. Every modern political society with a plurality of moral convictions, world views, and interests must face the question of whether there are principles that all the parties can share despite their deep disagreements; if there are, what kind of institutional design can help to implement their common political and constitutional goals. In this respect the Hungarian case provides sad lessons on the consequences of a delusive constitutional majoritarianism.

The volume's title refers to a further aspect of the new Hungarian constitution's conception of the nation. The Fundamental Law does not identify the "people" with citizens as subjects of the same legal system; it rather insists that there is "one single Hungarian nation that belongs together," a nation including all ethnic Hungarians regardless of their habitual residence and effective link to the state. According to the Fundamental Law, the "nation [was] torn apart in the storms of the last century." This refers to the historical Hungary as believed to have existed in the Middle Ages, and certainly to those neighboring territories where some two and a half million Hungarians are still living today as a consequence of the post-world-war treaties of 1920 and 1947. Therefore, Hungarians living beyond the borders are treated by the Fundamental Law as members of a nation disunited by the international legal and political order. The constitution that identifies the nation as an "intellectual and spiritual" constitutional community can be understood as a descendant of the East-Central European nationalist ideas and movements from the last two centuries. The authors of this book not only examine what the Hungarians have achieved or failed to achieve, but, implicitly, also call attention to what modern societies can learn from the Hungarian trauma.

János Kis's introductory article tells the story of Hungarian constitutionalism from the 1989 Constitution to the 2011 Fundamental Law. He presents the historical and political causes that explain the transition from the former's demise to its replacement by the latter. Kis anticipates that Hungary can solve its own constitutional crisis only if the Fundamental Law is replaced by a constitution that is suitable to unite society into a political community of equals and has the joint support of rival political sides.

Part One contains theoretical inquiries about legitimacy. The key concepts are majoritarian and partnership approaches to democracy, sociological and normative legitimacy, procedural and substantive elements of constitutionalism. In his opening essay *Ronald Dworkin* combines main insights from his recent works with reflections on the current state of democracy in Hungary. He argues that majoritarian decision-making in itself gives the government no legitimacy at all. The government sets the country on a road to the disintegration of democracy if it subverts the most basic principles that would enable the community as a whole to claim that it's a partnership of self-government. *Andrew Arato* establishes a conceptual framework and a global typology of democratic transition with forms of constitutional-making, and, based on this, examines the legitimacy problems of the 1989–90 and 2010–11 constitutional transformations. Arato also examines the possible scenarios of a legitimate future conclusion of the process from a change in accordance with the procedures of legality to revolutionary outcomes. *Zoltán Miklósi* raises a normative issue that applies not only to the 2011 constitution-making, but also to the prospective alteration of the constitution's identity: may a constitution-making majority legitimately pass a constitution without any support from its political rivals? Miklósi holds that rival parties have a shared responsibility to cooperate in sustaining the constitutional arrangement that regulates the political competition. What's more, in case of disagreement, no party should act alone in fundamental constitutional matters, even if it is fully convinced of the rightness of its position.

Part Two turns to historical narratives. *Sándor Radnóti* contrasts the revival of a historical constitution with the traditional English constitutionalism and, more generally, examines the role of symbolism in the modern constitutional era. In his view, first, the correct home for the Holy Crown of the Hungarian Kingdom is in the National Museum, instead of the Parliament, where it resides now. Second, although the crown is one of the historical symbols of Hungarian statehood could justifiably be mentioned in a constitution, the Fundamental Law puts the reference to the crown in a religious context, which is not acceptable to a significant part of the nation. *Zsolt Körtvélyesi*'s contribution gives a detailed account of the lasting constitutional troubles to be expected as a result of the Fundamental Law's equivocating between the political and ethnic conceptions of the nation. The author analyzes the Hungarian external citizenship and voting rights in connection with international standards and regional trends.

The articles in Part Three are dedicated to the issues of human rights, the principles of dignity, equality, and civil liberties. *Catherine Dupré* compares the Fundamental Law's dignity provisions with similar provisions of other European constitutions. On the face of it, the Fundamental Law's conception of human dignity seems to be quite open and inclusive. But a contextual and systematic reading of the text brings to light some critical elements in its understanding of rights. *Kriszta Kovács* provides an in-depth analysis of the ban on discrimination and affirmative action provisions comparing them with the 1989 Constitution. She offers an evaluation of how egalitarian the new constitutional regime is. *Renáta Uitz* places herself in a quasi-originalist position by uncovering the original intent of the drafters and the original meaning of the text on freedom of religion and churches. Uitz's chapter also reflects on whether the venture of making a new constitution was justified and on what are its most important consequences, first in the Hungarian context, and then from an international human rights perspective.

Part Four focuses on the institutional design. The title of the chapter from *Miklós Bánkuti*, *Gábor Halmai* and *Kim Lane Scheppele* (From Separation of Powers to Government without Checks) suggests a strong position on the nature and direction of the constitutional change. *Oliver W. Lembcke* and *Christian Boulanger* discuss the fate of the Constitutional Court. They invite their readers on a journey into the domain of classical theorists from Juvenal to Sieyès with the aim of contextualizing the limitation of the independence and competences of the Court. *Márton Varju* examines the constitutional issues of governmental accountability and the relationship between the state and the market from a different perspective by taking into account modern societies in the age of governance or the so-called post-regulatory state.

Part Five contains two articles on European perspectives of the Hungarian constitutionalism. *András Bragyova* examines the effect of the Fundamental Law to the relationship between the domestic legal system and the law of the European Union, whereas *Jeremy McBride* considers the constitutional changes from the viewpoint of the mandate given to the European Court of Human Rights by the European Convention. The two authors draw slightly different conclusions: Bragyova argues that there is no reason to expect important changes in the constitutional status of the European law, even if the Fundamental Law expresses preference for national sovereignty against a further federalization of the European Union. McBride's analysis shows that several provisions in the Fundamental Law are framed in a manner suggesting that they either will not reach the level of protection required by the European Convention or will require conduct that is incompatible with the requirements of that instrument. Both authors emphasize, however, and we can agree, that much depends on interpretation and application of the Fundamental Law. But the question remains: How can an interpretation favorable to basic human rights, civil equality, democracy, separation of powers, and the rule of law prevail given the Fundamental Law's aim, as many contributors of this volume suggest, to safeguard and promote the interests of a particular political force and its constituency rather than integrating the nation as a political community?

I hope that readers of these essays will share the inspirational and intellectual rewards that I have found in collecting them.

GÁBOR ATTILA TÓTH
September, 2012

Acknowledgements

The authors wrote their chapters for the purpose of this volume. Earlier, most of the contributors had discussed the Hungarian constitutional transformation at international conferences and workshops. They learned a great deal from the papers, presentations, and comments that, hopefully, have much improved their chapters.

Christian Boulanger organized a workshop at the Law and Society Institute of Humboldt University, Berlin (January 19, 2011), entitled *The Hungarian Constitutional Crisis and European Constitutional Standards*, where Christoph Möllers and Catherine Dupré commented the lectures from Kriszta Kovács and Gábor Attila Tóth.

The German Sociology of Law Associations held their 2nd Congress at the University of Vienna (September 9, 2011), where Oliver W. Lembcke, Kriszta Kovács, Tamás Szigeti, and Gábor Attila Tóth discussed the topic in the panel *Kampf um die Ungarische Verfassung* (Struggle for the Hungarian Constitution).

Gábor Attila Tóth gave a lecture entitled *Hungary's Constitutional Transformation from a Central European Comparative Perspective* at the conference of the German-Southeast Asian Center of Excellence for Public Policy and Good Governance and Thammasat University, Bangkok (February 25, 2012).

The Foundation for Law, Justice and Society and the Centre for Socio-legal Studies, University of Oxford organized a lecture of János Kis with the title *Constitution-making in Two Stages* held at the Central European University (March 24, 2011). The Rule of Law Center and Humboldt University, Berlin invited Kis for a lecture and discussion about the Hungarian constitutional change (May 12, 2011).

Kim Lane Scheppele examined the legality of Hungary's new constitution in her lecture *The Unconstitutional Constitution* at the Central

European University (January 31, 2012) with a comment from Renáta Uitz.

The Princeton University Woodrow Wilson School of Public and International Affairs organized a discussion on *Hungary's Constitutional Revolution* with the panelists Kim Lane Scheppele, Jan-Werner Müller, Paul Krugman, Gábor Halmai, Miklós Haraszti, and Miklós Bánkuti (February 14, 2012).

Ronald Dworkin's essay is a lightly edited transcript of his talk given at the Central European University (January 27, 2011).

Zsolt Körtvélyesi thanks all those who commented on his paper during the preparation: Mónika Ganczer, Balázs Majtényi, Szabolcs Pogonyi, and Anny Stoikova.

Catherine Dupré acknowledges the important support of the Leverhulme Trust which awarded her a Research Fellowship in 2010-2011. She thanks Kriszta Kovács, Atina Krajewska, and Stephen Skinner for their comments, suggestions, and clarification of a number of footnotes.

Christian Boulanger and Oliver W. Lembcke are grateful to Virág Zsugyó for her research assistance. Their German paper was translated into English by Jim C. Wagner.

Sándor Radnóti's chapter is a translation from Hungarian by Judit Pokoly.

Miklós Bánkuti translated the Transitional Provisions and the Second Amendment of the Fundamental Law.

Kriszta Kovács translated the First Amendment of the Fundamental Law.

Gábor Attila Tóth is grateful to Susanne Baer for valuable suggestions during his DAAD research fellowship at Humboldt University. He thanks Nenad Dimitrijevic, Jacques Ziller, and one anonymous reader who reviewed the manuscripts and offered very beneficial critical comments. He thanks, also, Christopher Marcisz for acting as copy editor for this volume.

INTRODUCTION

From the 1989 Constitution to the 2011 Fundamental Law

JÁNOS KIS

On January 1, 2012 the new constitution of Hungary, called the Fundamental Law, came into effect, and on January 2, the government held a gala in its honor at the Opera House in Budapest. In response, tens of thousands gathered in front of the building to demonstrate their anger at what they saw as a subversion of the democratic constitution of the republic. The guests at the gala decided to leave by the back door. It is hard to imagine a better illustration of the claim implicit in the title of this volume. Democratic constitutions aim to unite the nation they are meant to govern by expressing the consensus of principles and procedures to which citizens are committed to together. But the new Fundamental Law divides the Hungarian nation. Its aim is to entrench a sweeping but momentary victory of the right over the left into symbolic hegemony and institutional domination.

The Fundamental Law identifies the sovereign people as the totality of ethnic Hungarians, excluding Hungarian citizens of a non-Hungarian ethnicity and including individuals of Hungarian ethnicity not living under Hungarian law. It attributes a constitutive role to Christianity for the Hungarian political nation. It venerates the Holy Crown, a symbol of the Greater Hungary that was ruled for a millennium by the ethnic Hungarian nobility. It declares its continuity with the prewar authoritarian regime while stigmatizing the socialist party—which was three times elected to govern the country in free and fair elections—as the successor of a criminal organization.

It flies in the face of the principle of basic rights held by everybody by virtue of their personhood, and makes those rights conditional on satisfying duties. It betrays the principle of representative government by entrenching the current government's policy preferences into constitutional provisions and by providing for an electoral law tailored to the interests of the party now in majority in the Parliament. It undermines the rule of law by providing for retroactive imposition of disadvantage, by allowing the parliamentary majority to pass any law in an accelerated procedure while leaving no room for discussion, and in other ways. It violates the principle of separation of powers by limiting the powers of the Constitutional Court, by increasing the number of constitutional justices and by allowing the present majority to appoint new justices without the concurrence of the opposition; by mandating early retirement to judges and granting the power to appoint their replacements to one person, the head of the National Judicial Office; by allowing the chief prosecutor (himself elected by the present majority) to choose the court that shall try a criminal case whether or not the particular court chosen by him is competent to try that case, and so on. Critics of the Fundamental Law claim that it removes Hungary from the family of liberal democracies. This is a serious charge which the articles collected here aim to better assess.

Before addressing the Fundamental Law itself, however, it may help to ask a prior question. In 1989, Hungary was a leader in the post-communist transition. Already during the run-up to the first free elections, it gave itself a constitution that was exemplary in many ways and worked for more than two decades. What caused the demise of that constitution, and its replacement by the controversial Fundamental Law? This introduction focuses on this question.

Constitution-making in Two Stages

The year 1989 has entered history books as the year of "velvet revolutions" in Eastern Europe. With the exception of Romania, the dismantling of communist regimes proceeded peacefully, involving at some point roundtable negotiations between delegates of the state party and those of the opposition-in-the-making. The negotiations sought an agreement on the ground rules for free (in the case of Poland, semi-free) elections, and insofar as the constitutions in force threatened to block the process leading up to the elections, the agreement included some constitutional amendments as well. Partial as these amendments have been in most cases, they had foundational significance. Rather than merely reforming the old regime, they put an end to it and laid the basis for a new one.

The roundtables were not taken themselves, however, to have had a mandate for constitution-making. They invariably understood their task to be limited to facilitating the run-up to free, competitive elections, and were determined to leave the task of creating a new constitution to an elected assembly.

They had no more formal authorization to make law for the old regime as they had popular authorization to make law for the new one. In order for their decisions to come into legal effect, those decisions must have been sent for enactment to the communist legislature—an institution whose claim to legitimacy suffered a definitive blow from the very roundtable decisions. And so the agreements commanded no legitimate authority except insofar as they were meant to regulate the transition from the old regime to a new one and to provide assurance that both the holders of power and their opponents were to abide by those rules.

To conclude: the roundtables were exceptional bodies having the capacity to start a coordinated process of constitutional change but leaving, out of necessity, the completion of the process to an assembly that had the democratic mandate they lacked.

The constitution-making profile of the "velvet revolutions" can, thus, be characterized as consisting of two stages. In the first stage, a roundtable agreement is struck on the ground rules of preparing and holding free elections. The second stage takes place when a body of freely elected representatives adopts, in the sovereign people's name, a new constitution.

In Bulgaria and Romania, the new constitution was made in 1991. In the Czech Republic and Slovakia, it was made in 1992. Poland gave itself a "small constitution" in 1992, eliminating the remnants of the communist system after the first fully competitive election in that country, while the final constitution was adopted in 1997.

The Hungarian Anomaly

Hungary, too, made its attempt to bring the post-communist constitution-making process to a conclusion. That attempt, made in 1995–1996, went astray, however, and there was no follow-up for fifteen years. When, in 2011, it finally came to adopting the Fundamental

Law, its authors refused to see it as the second stage of the process started in 1989. The Fundamental Law claims continuity with what is called the "historical constitution" of the Hungarian Kingdom but it is conspicuously silent about any relationship to the constitutional changes of 1989. The other post-communist constitutions were adopted in the spirit of the "velvet revolutions" of 1989, and the polities informed by them never turned against that tradition, except for the brief episode of the Law and Justice Party government in Poland that announced a project of founding a "Fourth Republic" but fell without carrying out that project. Finally, with all their deficiencies, the constitutions of the other post-communist countries command a reasonably wide consensus as the shared supreme law of the political community. No such consensus is enjoyed or even sought by the Fundamental Law of Hungary.

Contrary to common belief, the constitution in force in 2011 could not be replaced by a new one with a mere two-thirds majority. Article 24(5) of that constitution provided that "[t]he parliamentary resolution about the rules of detail of preparing a constitution shall be adopted by the four-fifth of the members of parliament." The preparations of the constitution-making work were started by repealing the four-fifth provision—controversially, with a mere two-thirds majority. In this manner, the opposition—representing even in the short run a significant minority of the citizenry and, in the long term, the other half of the country—was deprived of any standing as a party to the process.

In sum, the anomaly of Hungary's post-communist constitution-making has three important aspects to it. First, it was concluded with an unusual delay. Second, its concluding stage did not come as a completion but rather as a negation of the initial constitution-making process. And, third, by breaking with the political principles that guided the 1989 Constitution, it divides the nation rather than unites it.

Taken together, these characteristics raise a number of distinct questions. Why was the post-transition constitutional moment missed in Hungary? How could the country live for two entire decades under the amended constitution of the old regime? If that constitution proved to be apt to serve as the supreme law of the country for such a long time, why was it swept away instead of being formally confirmed as the final constitution of the republic?

The 1989 Constitution

The Hungarian roundtable had, similarly to its peers in Eastern Europe, limited its ambition to revise the communist constitution to what seemed necessary for removing the obstacles to free elections. It was unique, however, in that it understood those obstacles in a highly expansive manner. To the surprise of the participants themselves, the amendment process took on a momentum that did not relent before it yielded a constitution that was new in all but its name. Pace its preamble asserting that it was adopted "in order *to facilitate the transition* to a legal state based on multi-party system, parliamentary democracy, and social market economy" (my emphasis), it included no interim provisions. While, technically, the amended constitution remained Act XX of 1949, it is not misleading to call it the 1989 Constitution.

Thanks to a combination of political wisdom, fortunate circumstances and unforeseen effects of procedure and strategy, the constitution issued from the roundtable talks met all the standards that a modern, democratic constitution is expected to meet. It recognized the equal status of all as bearers of human and civil rights just in virtue of their personhood, and provided for the institutional protection of basic rights through separation of powers. It allowed the parliamentary majority to conduct the ordinary business of government with the smallest coalition of representatives still larger than the opposition factions combined, while giving the opposition a say in the issues of long-term significance by requiring a qualified majority for deciding such issues. It changed the constitutional requirements from a set of desiderata into binding norms by giving wide powers of judicial review to the Constitutional Court and by enabling ordinary citizens to petition the Court on legislation they deemed unconstitutional. The Court was empowered to resolve controversial matters of procedure and principle through interpretation, offering determinate solutions, binding for all, to unforeseen constitutional disagreements. Finally, the constitution provided for a separation of state and church and for state neutrality in matters of religion, world view and ways of life, thereby enabling a society characterized by religious, cultural, and sociological pluralism to form a political community of equals living with each other in mutual respect. It allowed the minority-that-be to recognize the right of the majority to govern without giving up their own autonomy and self-esteem.

So a short answer to our question is that there was no pressure to write a new constitution in the years that immediately followed the transition. While in the other post-communist countries, the amended constitutions of the old regimes were utterly unsuitable as a framework for liberal democracy and a capitalist market economy, and had to be replaced by a new constitution at the earliest convenience, the 1989 Constitution of the Hungarian Republic could do the job of regulating the workings of a democratic polity very well. (Even the Fundamental Law recognizes this. Its reasoning says that the 1989 Constitution was "workable.")

This cannot be the full story.

Ambiguity of the Constitutional Agreement

The freely elected Hungarian parliaments consisted, from 1990 through 2010, of the same parties that played a decisive role in the roundtable talks, and those parties had come to an agreement on the constitutional essentials of the new regime at the roundtable. Why have they missed the opportunity to confirm that agreement, once they had the democratic mandate to do this?

The 1989 Constitution provided for a unicameral legislature with the government answerable to the legislature, and the president of the republic having no executive powers and elected by the legislature. This constitutional design continued the liberal-democratic stream of the country's political history. There was an alternative conception on the table, one foreseeing a corporatist upper house of delegates of the clergy, the Academy of Science, major interest groups and local governments, and a president to be elected by direct popular vote, endowed with executive powers. The roots of the alternative conception go back to the authoritarian stream of Hungarian political history. Surprisingly, the division between the liberal-democratic and the authoritarian conceptions of the basic institutional structure departed from the left-right cleavage with which one would expect it to be correlated. This was partly due to the fact that the Hungarian Democratic Forum, the then leading party on the right, was itself divided on the issue, whereas only the two minor right-wing parties—the Smallholders and the Christian Democrats—were non-ambiguously committed to the authoritarian conception. On the other hand, it was the state-party, whose successor was to become the major party of the left in the following two decades, that sponsored the authoritarian option at the roundtbale, its conduct motivated less by ideology than by a certain hope to preserve at least part of its hegemonic power. Only the left-liberal Alliance of Free Democrats and Fidesz (then itself a left-liberal party) stood up without reservations for the liberal-democratic conception.

In the previous section, I referred to a combination of political wisdom, fortunate circumstances and unforeseen effects of procedure and strategy as an explanation of how the liberal-democratic option prevailed in the political struggles of 1989. This formula is but a shorthand for a complex story the intricacies of which cannot be dealt with in this Introduction. Let me mention only that the state-party, eager to have its candidate, highly popular at that time, elected president before the parliamentary elections, made a separate deal with the Democratic Forum on adopting the parliamentary regime for the long run but having direct presidential elections as a one-time exception at the start. (As it transpires from the protocols of the Politburo, the hope was to amend the constitution soon in order to consolidate the exception into the rule.) The form of the deal made it easy for the liberals to carry the parliamentary system to victory by initiating a referendum aiming to veto the exceptional measure. Once the popular majority rejected the early presidential elections, what remained was a pure parliamentary regime. As to the corporatist upper house: the delegation of the state-party felt they had to choose between their two aims, and they made a strategic decision to focus on the issue of the presidency, and to postpone the issue of the corporatist second chamber for later. Since the communist constitution provided for a unicameral parliament, continuing the "small constitution" of 1946 that abolished the aristocratic upper house of the pre-war authoritarian regime, the decision to remove the issue from the table left the country with a unicameral parliament elected by popular vote.

Thus, on the one hand, an agreement was made in which all the parliamentary parties of the following twenty years participated in making and the outcome, as finalized by the November 1989 referendum, was respected by all. On the other hand, the outcome failed to command unanimous consent. Furthermore, neither the liberal-democratic option nor its authoritarian alternative commanded, in any of the parliaments elected between 1990 and 2010, a qualified majority of two-thirds that would have been necessary for adopting a new constitution. So the constitutional status quo defined by the victorious liberal-democratic tradition could not gain confirmation at the hands of a freely elected legislature, but neither could it be subverted in the spirit of its authoritarian alternative. The constitutional moment passed without seeing the enactment of a final constitution.

A Precarious Balance

The ambiguity of the constitutional agreement was, thus, inherited by the resulting constitutional status quo. On the one hand, the 1989 Constitution satisfied the principles that confer normative legitimacy on a constitution duly respecting and protecting them. On the other hand, the very same principles that justified the content of the constitution failed the way it was created. It was a constitution democratic in its nature but lacking democratic confirmation. This was a serious symbolic defect that proved fatal in the long run.

The roundtable legitimized itself by identifying the post-election years as the moment when a new constitution can and should be made. A failure to live up to that promise appeared as a serious flaw; it suggested that post-communist society was unfit for constituting itself into a political community.

Modern, pluralistic societies are torn by unavoidable conflicts of interest and pervasive disagreements. For such divided societies to form a political community nevertheless, their members must agree on a shared constitution that can resolve their conflicts and disagreements. True, there can be no guarantee that the disagreements stop at the gate of the constitution: disagreements of policy easily translate into disagreements on how the conflicting policy positions are to be judged in the light of the constitution. But a society constituted into a political community agrees to understand its constitutional controversies as consisting, typically, in conflicting interpretations of the shared constitutional principles and procedures. It agrees, for example, that the state should extend equal protection of the law to all, even if it is divided on what equal protection of the law requires in a particular context. Or it agrees that the state should respect and protect freedom of expression, even if it is divided on whether hate speech or speech expressing contempt for national or religious symbols is constitutionally protected. It, thus, treats the disagreements in question as turning around the correct interpretation of the agreed-upon general principles of freedom and equality.

The failure of the constitutional moment casts doubt on whether Hungary had a constitution confirmed by all, consequently allowing the constitutional controversies to spill over into attacks on the authority of the constitutional provisions themselves. As evidence of this spillover tendency, consider the prevalence of constitutional amendments. Between the elections of 1990 and 2010, there were twenty-three constitutional amendments in Hungary (in roughly the same period, the Bulgarian constitution was amended four times, the Czech constitution five times, the Polish and the Romanian constitutions once). Another way in which the interpretive disagreements spill over into a weak allegiance to the constitution is a low degree of respect for the constitutional provisions in force. In a republic where the shared constitution enjoys high authority, those holding and competing for public power act within the constitution's bounds out of respect for it. The lower the authority of a constitution, the less it is complied with as a matter of respect, and the more compliance becomes a matter of weighing the costs of disobedience against its benefits. With the weakening of respect for the constitution, the possessors of and competitors for public power become increasingly prone to depart from the constitution's requirements any time they can expect to remain unpunished. Once underway, this tendency risks getting out of control: the rival political sides begin to see each other as ready to set aside the constitution whenever they can, they get an additional incentive to act so themselves, the mutual expectation working in the way of a self-fulfilling prophecy. This tendency gathered momentum during the first decade of the democratic republic.

It was, however, contained by a countervailing tendency, due to the stabilizing role played by the Constitutional Court. The Court could not but treat the 1989 Constitution as if it had been the shared constitution of the republic whose provisions may have been open to conflicting interpretations but not to fundamental challenges to their authority. This was the only way for it to impose its own authority as the ultimate arbiter on controversies of constitutional significance. Being remarkably successful at imposing its authority, it helped to consolidate the authority of the constitution itself.

And so the first decade of the republic was dominated by a precarious balance between the forces of erosion inherent in the precarious status of the constitution and the forces of consolidation concentrated mainly in the stabilizing role of the Court.

The Balance Subverted

The balance was precarious because it depended on the readiness of the rival political forces to accept the Court's authority to decide their controversies, and that readiness was weakening over time.

The democratic republic was established in the spirit of the best traditions of liberal democracy. It is in this spirit that the Court began its ambitious project of specifying the abstract principles of the constitution. Its interpretive practice bore a particular imprint: it was marked by the political conception of the Second Vatican Council, a progressive Catholic view accepting to a large degree the secular character of the modern state without being a secular view itself. So the Court's position on issues concerning the separation of church and state and on some issues of personal morality such as abortion or gay rights was problematic, but it provided a remarkably strong reading of political liberties (such as freedom of expression and freedom of assembly) and of certain personal rights (such as the right of control over one's sensitive data or the due process rights), as well as of the procedural guarantees of the rule of law. So long as the spirit of 1989 was fresh and alive the holders of and competitors for public power were more or less prepared to accept the authority of the constitution as specified in this manner.

With the moment of the "velvet revolution" submerging into the historical past, however, this willingness was gradually weakening. The Court's practice itself was not insensitive to the changes in the general political climate, but its changes were moderated by the normative force of precedents and the requirements of consistency of judicial reasoning, the gap between the constitution as specified by the Court and the views of the main political forces were ever widening. The political class became progressively estranged from the constitution that was supposed to regulate its internal conflicts and its use of the state vis-à-vis the citizens. Right-wing advocates of persecuting the crimes of the communist regime turned against the prohibition of retroactive criminal legislation. Others on the right rejected the Equal Treatment Article allowing for affirmative action. Left-wing supporters of racial equality, alarmed by the rise of racism, objected to the interpretation of the Free Speech Article as extending constitutional protection to hate speech. They began to argue that constitutional liberties were drawn too broadly in 1989: such a broad understanding, they insisted, was appropriate in face of communist power hegemony, but once that hegemony was broken, it became an obstacle to the consolidation of democracy. Politicians of all stripes converged on attacking the constitutional hurdles on majority decision as incompatible with efficient governance.

Ironically, by the time the estrangement from the constitution in force reached a critical level, the disagreement on presidential powers and the structure of the legislature lost its political significance. In about fifteen years, the support for the semi-presidential and semi-corporatist system by and large vanished. The Socialists, after half-hearted—and failed—attempts to initiate, in 2003 and 2004, a change in the structure of the 1989 Constitution, finally made their peace with it. As to the constitution's right-wing enemies, the Smallholders dropped out of Parliament in 2002, and so did the Christian Democrats (to return in 2010 on the list of Fidesz), while the Forum shrank into a small party and disappeared in 2010. By that date, the semi-presidentialist and semi-corporatist blueprint became the constitutional ideal of the lunatic fringe.

All things being equal, the conditions for a consolidation of the constitution vastly improved.

But other things were not equal. The middle of the second decade of the republic brought not the consolidation of the 1989 Constitution with it but its end.

The Demise of the Constitution

The estrangement of the political class from the constitution went on embedded in a wider political process called by political observers the "populist backlash."

In many ways, the transition to liberal democracy and a capitalist market economy was a unique success. Within only a couple of years, Hungary achieved a more perfect and more durable democratic polity than it ever had in its history. It had parliamentary government issuing from regular, competitive, free and fair elections based on universal and equal ballot, it raised the level of protection of personal and political rights very significantly, it established a reasonably secure system of ownership rights, and in some respects it became a more tolerant country.

At the same time, the tectonic changes of the transition to a capitalist market economy and liberal democracy, condensed into a mere couple of years, brought severe shocks with them. First, a "basic rights shock": for many, it was extremely hard to come to terms with the discovery that freedom of speech does not mean just freedom to criticize the government but also freedom to mock on others' sacred beliefs or to vent hate on vulnerable groups; that equal protection of the law involves the coming out of gays and lesbians and their demand for access to the institution of marriage; that the due process of law protects not just the innocent but also the criminal, and so on. It came, second, to a "capitalism shock." The collapse of the socialist economy left a large part of the workforce structurally unemployed and incapable of re-entering the labor market. Entire regions were left behind by the economic take-off that followed the transformation crisis. Heavy overrepresentation of the Roma minority among the underemployed and in the decaying regions added racial overtones to the emerging social conflicts. Third, there came a "weak institutions shock." The new democratic institutions proved to be inept against anomalies such as the rising tide of corruption. To these three shocks was added a "globalization shock": the sudden appearance of transnational corporations, by the vulnerability of the domestic economy to the vagaries of the global financial and investment markets beyond the control of the Hungarian state, and by the impact of transnational political integration, especially in the form of the European Union.

Together, these shocks generated a cumulative process that eroded the public's tolerance of economic losses, of social solidarity, of the trust in the political class, and of the confidence that the new regime could make its promises true.

At the beginning of the 1990s, the overwhelming majority of Hungarian citizens nourished great expectations concerning liberal democracy and the capitalist market economy. By 2010, however, a significant minority turned against the system as such, and the majority, while still accepting the system, grew rather skeptical about its capacity to deliver. Anti-Semitic and, in particular, anti-Roma sentiments were sadly prevalent in post-transition Hungary from the beginning on, but as a political platform, racism remained by and large marginal until the last years of the previous decade when the anti-system extreme right made its surge after a long period of incubation. Similarly, trust in the political class, always relatively weak, reached a record low level towards 2010; on the anti-system right, it was crowded out by vehement anti-establishment emotions. This shift went parallel to a dramatic reduction of tolerance for the economic losses large segments of society had to suffer as a consequence of the transformation crisis of the post-communist economy—losses significantly increased by the policy mistakes of the successive governments in the early years of the second decade and, then, by the global credit crunch and of the recession followed by it.

The "populist backlash" is a phenomenon any society predictably undergoes in the wake of tectonic social, economic, and political changes, and it was registered, to a greater or lesser degree, in all post-communist countries of Eastern Europe. As evidence of that backlash, the receptivity for anti-system ideas was raising everywhere in the region. Hungary was not special in this regard. Around 2005, the index of the demand for right-wing political extremism as constructed and measured by political scientists was roughly the same in Poland and in Hungary. By the end of 2009, however, that index was halved in Poland while it doubled in Hungary. By that time, the government of the Law and Justice Party fell in disgrace in Poland, while the socialist-liberal coalition, running the country from 2002 until 2010, was in full crisis in Hungary.

When it came to the 2010 elections, there was growing agreement, shared even by some columnists and pundits on the left that the constitution was somehow responsible for what was perceived as weakness and inefficiency of the state on the one hand and disintegration of social solidarity on the other and, that, the country needed a thoroughgoing constitutional reform in order to escape the political deadlock.

We have now most of the key elements that explain the Hungarian anomaly. We have a story of how the second stage of the constitution-making was indefinitely postponed in the years directly following the transition. It could be postponed because the 1989 Constitution was capable of governing a democratic society with a capitalist market economy, and it had to be postponed because neither the institutional structure instantiated by the constitution in force nor its alternative commanded a constitutional majority in the Parliament. We also have a story of how the 1989 Constitution failed to get consolidated even as the support for the semi-presidentialist and semi-corporatist system was slowly eroding. The consolidation was frustrated by a coincidence of this erosion with a "populist backlash" to the processes started in 1989 and a progressive estrangement of the political class from the constitution.

Something is missing, though, from this account. As it stands so far, it is able to explain how the 1989 Constitution became vulnerable to attacks on its basic principles. It does not explain the nature of the attacks themselves. It does not explain what we earlier described as one political side's attempt symbolically and institutionally to entrench its temporary victory over the other. It is this attempt that translates Hungary's post-communist constitutional history into a genuine anomaly. In order to account for it, we have to consider an aspect of that history that up to this point has been left in the dark.

Constitutional Partnership

I said earlier that the 1989 Constitution was suitable to provide a framework for a political community of equals living with each other in mutual respect. However, the suitability of the constitution is only a necessary, but not a sufficient condition for the promise of such a community to come true. A number of further conditions must be obtained. The vast majority of the citizenry must accept the political and economic system laid out by the constitution. Citizens belonging to diverse groups—religious, ethnic, cultural, sociological and other—must accept each other as part of the sovereign people declared by the constitution to be the ultimate source of all public power. Since modern political communities govern themselves through representatives, the citizenry must accept the political class as legitimate holders of the delegated powers defined by the constitution. The previous section offered a cursory view of how these conditions eroded over time. There is a fourth condition though that we have not considered yet.

Representative democracy is inseparable from the struggle for power between rival political factions. It divides the body of legislators into government and opposition, and it gives the opposition incentives to attack the government, to criticize its mistakes, to unmask its vices, and to reveal the sectional interests motivating its decisions, the reward of effective criticism being a better chance for gaining in the next election. The agonistic processes of modern democracy direct the struggle for power into peaceful channels, and turn it into a means of promoting the common good. But they cannot function as such a means unless the rival forces that, together, make up the class of competitors for political power under a common constitution accept each other as legitimate partners in upholding, protecting and perfecting the constitution, the shared framework of their power struggles.

When the major political forces accept each other as constitutional partners, and when they know this about each other, the party in opposition can safely expect the party in government to refrain from taking advantage of its majority in order to permanently exclude its rival from power, while the party in government can safely expect the party in opposition not to strive toward debilitating day-to-day governance. Constitutional partnership involves mutual self-restraint: neither the government nor the opposition does everything the law permits them to do against the will of the other. For its part, mutual self-restraint has a dual impact. On the one hand, it contributes to building trust and co-operation between political rivals; on the other hand, it stabilizes the constitution itself by reducing the likelihood of political moves that one side believes to be constitutional but that seem blatantly unconstitutional to the other side. Under such conditions, the room for constitutional disagreement requiring the intervention of the Constitutional Court is significantly narrowed: the Court's interpretations can build on a prior interpretive texture woven by the practices of mutual self-restraint of the participants of power struggles.

However, where constitutional partnership fails to develop or unravels, democracy is unstable and inefficient. The competitors for power do not see the prospect of an electoral defeat as involving partial and reversible losses but as carrying with it the threat of total and permanent annihilation. Since they expect the other side to do whatever it can against them, they themselves are motivated to do the same. Under such conditions, local conflicts easily translate into clashes over the constitution itself; policies stretching over more than one electoral cycle tend to fall apart, and politics becomes reduced to a race for short-term sectional gains. Furthermore, the Constitutional Court, deprived of the advantages of mutual self-restraint, may find it ever harder to preserve its capacity of impartially adjudicating on the divisive issues and of appearing to all the parties to the conflicts as an impartial adjudicator.

Building and maintaining the practices of constitutional partnership is an intricate matter everywhere; as the example of the United States shows such practices can erode with serious consequences even after a long history of their cumulative growth. The relationship between competitors for public power in the new Hungarian democracy, however, started out from a particularly inauspicious historical background.

"Cold Civil War" Between the Right and the Left

Hungary's twentieth-century history was marked by cataclysmic collisions between the political right and left of the country. Before World War I, the modern social democratic and radical-left found itself in the position of political pariahs. The war, ending in a military catastrophe, swept away the traditional ruling class, allowing the former pariahs to fill the power vacuum. The revolutionary government engaged in land reform, introduced universal suffrage, secured freedom of the press and of assembly and issued social legislation, but it was politically weak, and was further weakened by the victorious Entente's territorial demands. Having no military force to resist the Entente, the president, in a desperate move, invited the Social Democrats to form a purely working-class government. The Social Democrats, however, united with the newly found Communist Party, and declared a Republic of Councils hoping for military assistance from Soviet Russia. They introduced red terror to consolidate their power and engaged in armed action to defend Hungary's traditional boundaries.

The collapse of the short-lived Republic of Councils led, after a period of counter-revolutionary turmoil and white terror, to the establishment of an authoritarian regime. The regime had for its basis a self-professed "Christian middle class," a social group whose male members sought their career mainly in the public bureaucracy and the military, and identified themselves through their religious affiliation. They interpreted the short episode of left-wing revolutionary governments as the rule of usurpers, of Jews, and lower-class people unfit to lead the nation, while they took themselves to be its natural leaders. They laid the blame for the disastrous outcome of the war on the pre-war liberal establishment, the revolutionary left and the Jewry whom they associated with the two mythical enemies of the Hungarians: international Bolshevism and international financial capital. Although their anti-Bolshevism, anti-capitalism and anti-Semitism were more of a traditionalist than of a radical character, these attitudes, combined with their territorial revisionism made them an easy target for Nazi Germany looking for satellites in Eastern Europe. The rulers of the country accepted corrections of the Treaty of Versailles at the hands of Hitler, and they brought Hungary into the war on his side; they progressively deprived Hungarians identified as Jewish of their rights and possessions, and co-operated with the Nazis in deporting hundreds of thousands of Jews to Auschwitz and other concentration camps.

The war ended in a physical and moral disaster for Hungary and for its right-wing establishment. But the debacle could not become the moment of truth for the right. Already during the 1945–1946 experiment with a lopsided democracy, the so-called "Christian middle-class" found itself excluded from political life. Following the communist takeover, its members were dispossessed, disenfranchised, and faced educational and job discrimination, forced relocation, or imprisonment. They played no leading role in the 1956 Revolution, but were made the main culprit for it during the years of repression and reprisals that followed. In the decades following the "consolidation" of the 1960s, the political stigma was gradually removed and they were allowed, as everyone else, to seek personal prosperity in exchange for leaving politics to the party-state. But although it was favorable for private advancement, the "consolidation" failed to create appropriate conditions for public historical self-examination. And so when it came to the disintegration of the regime, the right re-emerged on the political scene without ever taking critical distance from its ideological and political heritage. The decades of communist rule not only prevented it from critically engaging with its own past: they seemed to provide *ex post* justification for the right-wing politics between the two wars heavily colored by anti-communism.

The right correctly insisted on the necessity of a moral break with the communist regime: the principles that justified the new regime condemned the old one. However, condemning the communist regime for them involved rehabilitating the pre-war authoritarian one. In its rhetoric, anti-communism went hand in hand with coded anti-Semitism and not so coded anti-liberalism.

The successors of the communist state party had their own historical liabilities. They condemned the Stalinist terror without ambiguity, but were at best ambiguous about the 1956 Revolution and the military crackdown on it followed by massive reprisals. They rather wanted to think as if the revolution was immediately followed by "consolidation;" they remembered the concessions that made life more comfortable for most people but forgot about continuing censorship, religious persecution, imprisonments for beer-house anti-communist talk, and the network of secret informants actively reporting on hundreds of thousands until the very end. In their account, the post-1956 regime was characterized by a cumulative process of reforms that finally culminated in the 1989 transition. Right-wing nostalgia for the pre-war authoritarian regime allowed the left to remain apologetic about the later periods of the communist regime, and to present the tradition of the left as always being on the side of democracy and humanism while left-wing nostalgia for the "consolidated" communist regime allowed the right to remain apologetic about the pre-war authoritarian regime. Furthermore, the revival of right-wing anti-liberalism, of coded anti-Semitism and of the ambiguous relationship to capitalism drew a deep wedge between the liberals and the right, and contributed to a rapprochement between the socialist successors of the state party and the liberal successors of the democratic opposition to the communist regime. In less than two years, the mutual alienation of the right and the left was complete. For the right, the term "left" regained its meaning as a synonym for aliens to the nation, while the term "right" regained, for the left, its meaning as a synonym for hostile to democracy.

The reactions to this polarization were not symmetrical. The right began to see itself, as it had between the two wars, as the natural leader of the country, and to regard the electoral victories of the left as results of fraud. The left never denied the legitimacy of the right's electoral victories, and made no attempts to exclude the right from the common constitution. But its failure to modernize and to dissociate itself from the communist past allowed the right to present it as communism surviving under the surface of the new regime, and the right's virulent anti-communism allowed the left to see themselves as defenders of democracy.

It is against this tendency that cooperation under a shared constitution should have built the practices uniting the right and the left in constitutional partnership. Was the outcome a forgone conclusion? I don't think so. After all, the semi-feudal social structure underlying the ideological cleavages inherited from earlier times was not there anymore. After almost half a century of communist rule, Hungarian society was much better educated, it was much more urbanized and secular, its occupational stratification was much more modern than it had been before the war. In many ways, the right's self-image and the corresponding self-image of the left were anachronisms. And so there was some hope for cooperation under a shared constitution to prevail over the shadows of the past.

This is not what happened. Instead of constitutional partnership developing between them, the left and the right ended up involved in a "cold civil war" with each other. When, in its turn, the right won a decisive battle in the "cold civil war," it used its electoral victory to entrench it in a constitution designed to symbolically confirm and institutionally perpetuate its hegemony.

Summary

To repeat: 1989 gave Hungary a constitution suitable for a political community of equals living in mutual respect with each other. It should be added that the social structure of the country was apt to bear such a constitution. From a long-run perspective, the chances for the 1989 Constitution to get consolidated were not bad after all. Its defective origins, casting doubts on its legitimacy in the short run, could be expected to progressively lose their significance as time goes by. A constitution commanding and seen as commanding legitimate authority over a sufficiently extended period of time is not compromised anymore by the illegitimate circumstances of its creation. Consider the post-war constitution of Japan. It was drafted by U.S. army officers with a legal degree and it was imposed on the reluctant emperor and his government by General Douglas MacArthur, commander-in-chief of the occupying forces. It is hard to imagine more inauspicious conditions for a constitution's birth. And yet more than half century later this circumstance has no impact whatsoever on the legitimacy of that document.

In the short run, however, a constitution's authority is weakened by its questionable origins, and this circumstance fatally affected the 1989 Constitution's capacity to resist to the double pressure of the "populist backlash" and the "cold civil war." If the "populist backlash" had been less dramatic, the "cold civil war" would have been easier to tame, and the right would have been much less likely to win a constitution-making majority. On the other hand, without the "cold civil war" the processes of the "populist backlash" would have been less likely to escalate as they did. But even together, these two tendencies could have been contained, perhaps, by a constitution with a more solid initial authority. The 1989 Constitution, bearing the stigma of consisting, technically, in an amended version of the 1949 Constitution and lacking democratic confirmation by a freely elected parliament, proved insufficiently resistant to the disruptive forces generated by the social, economic, and political transition.

This Introduction started with the question of the demise of the 1989 Constitution, which was so well suited to integrate a pluralistic society into a political community. Now we have a story of its demise, and this story suggests a different question: How could the 1989 Constitution survive so long against such powerful odds against it? Its great internal virtues provide a major part of the answer. But there is another part to it. To be sure, only a minority of the political agents was ready to own the constitution. But no significant political agent could explicitly disown it. Nobody could claim that it was imposed on the country against their will. Nor could anybody claim that it excludes them from the political community or treats them as dispreferred competitors for public power.

This is definitely not true about the Fundamental Law. It is (and it is meant by its authors to be) a constitution of one half of the nation imposed on the other half against their will. It deepens the constitutional crisis of Hungary instead of resolving it.

If the story told in this Introduction suggests a prediction, that prediction is that Hungary's constitutional crisis will not come to a resolution until the Fundamental Law is replaced by a constitution not only suitable to unite the Hungarian society into a political community of equals but having the joint support of the two political sides for such a union. Such a constitution cannot be the gift of a regenerated right to the left. Nor can it be the gift of a victorious left to the right. It either will come true as a common creation of the two sides or will not come true at all.

I. LEGITIMACY

What Is Democracy?

RONALD DWORKIN

I'm going to tell you an imaginary story. And I'm going to ask this question: is the story that I will imagine the triumph of democracy or its ruin?

The story begins with a country which has painfully emerged from terrible periods of tyranny, established what looks like a path to a mature democracy. It has free elections, with near universal suffrage, it has a free and independent press representing opinions across the range of the political spectrum, it has a constitution which embeds fundamental rights of individuals against the majority, it has constitutional court active, indeed from time to time zealous, in its enforcement of this constitution. The constitution itself is regarded as the fundamental law, and it provides that it cannot be amended except through a vote of two-thirds of the Parliament.

Then one day this rather agreeable story is broken by the election of a government which through a large majority, but also through the structure of districting, does elect two-thirds of the Parliament and sets about to change the character of the nation. It enacts a press law establishing a council whose members are entirely appointed by the government with the power to determine on its own that an article in a journal is offensive or derogatory of the nation, and to impose serious, indeed punitive fines in so doing. It enacts that law in spite of the fact that the law is patently unconstitutional. It enacts other unconstitutional laws, for example in violation of property rights for pension funds. It changes the jurisdiction of the constitutional court again by parliamentary vote in order retrospectively validate its unconstitutional legislation. Worse, it proposes to call a constitutional convention to thoroughly rewrite the constitution so as to solidify its own power.

Is this the triumph or the ruin of democracy? Legitimacy in the modern world means democracy. Democracy means government by the people, or rather government by a majority of the people. Let me add one further fact to my imaginary story: the government which has enacted this legislation, the government which seeks to impose these radical changes, was and remains popular (this may be a departure from any story you know, but I'm imagining it) and would be elected with an even greater majority if an election were called today and held in three months. What the people want, that is, the people have. If the government allowed unelected judges in the constitutional court to deprive the people of what they want, if the government in that way yielded to history and convention, then it would have forfeited democratic legitimacy.

I ask again: is that really the triumph of democracy? It depends on what we should mean by democracy. I imagined just now a concrete account of what democracy is—it is government by majority. That is a procedural matter, government by majority may be unjust, it may be unfair to a minority, but it's nonetheless democratic. And that's important because it means that if we want to correct the injustice as we see it, than we must do so in democratic politics. We must argue with the people to try to change enough minds to make a difference. And if we were to sponsor the idea that a panel of unelected judges should do the job for us, then even if in that way we achieve greater justice, we would forfeit legitimacy. That is the majoritarian conception of democracy.

I suggest an alternate conception of democracy, which I would call the partnership conception. This argues that democracy is government by the people as a whole acting as partners in a joint venture of self-government. That sounds a bit wooly, doesn't it? I'll try to make it clearer later. But what I propose to do is to ask, which of these two conceptions of democracy, one of which would endure what my imaginary government has done, and the other which as I'll try to show would condemn it, which of these two is superior as a conception of democracy? What kind of a question is that? It plainly isn't a question we can answer by looking in a dictionary for the word "democracy." It isn't a question we can answer in the fashion of some philosophers who seek to unpack a concept by discovering the hidden rules that people follow when they apply that concept. From Beijing to Caracas, from Minneapolis to Moscow people call their own form of government democracy, in spite of the fact that there are great differences. They use different tests to identify democracy, and we learn nothing by asking what are the shared tests. There are no shared tests.

So I suggest a different methodology, and indeed a different philosophical project. This begins with the idea that some of our concepts—democracy, justice, liberty, law—are contested, or as I prefer to say, interpretive concepts. I mean we share those concepts, they live in our forms of lives, as Wittgenstein put it, that we inhabit as values. And we share an interpretive concept, because we share the idea that it stands for some value, but we disagree as to exactly what value this is. There are values in that neighborhood named "democracy," we agree. We strive to make our government democratic, but we disagree as to what that means, and our disagreement is therefore a disagreement about value. It is a disagreement about democracy, because it's a disagreement about much else. It's a disagreement about dignity, about justice, and much else. So, I suggest to you that the way we proceed to choose between our two model conceptions of democracy, or others you might wish to propose when we discuss these matters together, we proceed by asking what's good about each conception? What would recommend choosing one conception over an other? And that means that we can't confine our attention to traditional concept of democracy—we must look to see what other values we can suppose that would lead us to designate one conception of democracy as bad and another good.

I'm going to start with what I call the majoritarian conception, because that's very familiar, and has a great deal of academic support. So I'm going to ask what's good about the idea that when a political community disagrees about what to do, its leaders should follow the greatest number of people. Why is that a good thing to do? What recommends it? Supporters of this conception would have a very quick answer: it's a fundamental principle of fairness. When a group, not just a political group, any group, has to make a collective decision, when it has to decide what a group should do, rather than individuals, and the group disagrees, it is a fundamental, inherent principle of fairness that the largest number should be followed. And that designates the majoritarian conception of democracy, because that's only the application to politics of a more fundamental, very basic principle of fairness. But when we look again, we find that this isn't a general principle of fairness at all. We very quickly think of situations in which the fact that the greater number favors a decision of one sort or another, counts morally for nothing in its favor.

A case I like to use to make this point is the case of the overcrowded lifeboat at sea. One person must be thrown overboard in order to save all the rest. How do we decide? The worst way, or practically the worst way would be to take a vote. Because that would mean that the least popular, perhaps a member of a disliked race, would be chosen. The choice would be made on the basis of grounds that really have nothing to do with the decision to be made. Now we would prefer a lottery or some other method that makes it a matter of chance, rather than a matter of popularity, who lives and who dies. And we see that in politics as well. When nations used to fight wars with conscripted armies, the question arose who should be drafted to fight and perhaps die on a foreign field. And nobody thought that there should be local votes to choose this. It was thought that the only fair way to do it was by lot, or by a test of who would be the best soldier, or some other fact. The consideration that a great many people in a particular village wanted "x" to go and fight would be morally irrelevant to the selection. Now, I'm not—I want to make clear—saying, that a majority vote is never appropriate in politics. Of course it is, very often. Very often it is the only defensible method of choosing. So far I mean only to say that it is not because there is fundamental principle of fairness that says that's always the way to decide. If that is the right way, I should rather say, when that's the right way to decide in politics it's because there are other considerations which in those circumstances make it the right way. It is not a fundamental principle that's always applicable.

What else can be said? There is a version of an argument in the political science literature that says that democracy is best because majority vote is best, because the greater number are more likely to find the truth about what should be done. People who make this argument appeal to a mathematical proof by a French philosopher and mathematician, Condorcet, who showed by demonstration that if each individual person in a group has a greater than 50 percent chance of being right about some matter then the view of the largest number is more likely to be the correct view. The premise however, that each person is more than 50 percent likely to be right about a matter of political morality is hardly self evident, and I put it to you that history shows exactly the opposite. There are other arguments. People say that majority vote gives us political stability. If a majority is pleased by a decision there's likely less likely to be any kind of insurrection or fraction within the community. Again, that hardly discriminates between the majoritarian and the partnership conception, which says everyone must be treated as having an equal stake in the decision, and which seems to me at least as likely to give stability to a political community.

Consequentialists say the right decision is just a matter of what will please the most people, because justice consist of the greatest happiness of the greatest number. That's highly contestable, I think it's wrong. But even if it were right, majority vote is not the best test of what's conducive to the greatest happiness of the greatest number, because majority vote doesn't take into account the intensity of a preference, or the degree to which people gain or suffer. It just counts heads.

We have cleared away a number of arguments that people might make as to why there is any moral virtue at all in a majority vote. But I've so far left the argument that seems to me the strongest, and has indeed seemed to people generally the strongest. And that is this: One of the essential virtues of legitimacy in the modern world is political equality. Each person must be thought to have, and provided with, as much power over collective decision as anybody else. It's hard to manage equal power over a large political community but majority rule plainly comes closer than any alternative would do. Because majority rule just means everybody has the same power, and we see how adding together equal power leads to a majority decision. If we would take the view of minority, obviously, political equality would be compromised.

We need at this point to focus on the concept of political equality. What does it mean? When are people in a political community equal? We can distinguish two answers to that question and they lead to very different results. One is equality of political impact. Your political impact is measured as the difference that you can make just by your vote or choice alone. We have to distinguish that from political influence, which is the difference you can make not just by the impact of your own vote, but because of your influence over the way other people vote, and these are plainly very different matters. Now, once we've made that distinction I would suggest it seems irresistible that political influence is more important than political impact. How can I say that I have equal political power in the Unites States compared to a billionaire who gives money to political campaigns, or to a sports hero, or to a television personality, or to a charismatic preacher? All of these people have exponentially more influence than I do, because others are moved to do what they suggest.

So we should accept that political equality means equality of influence. But as soon as we say that we see that if so, political equality is not a desirable goal. Yes, we want money not to matter as much as it does in my country, but we want other things to matter. We want a great preacher like Martin Luther King to have influence on the civil rights movement, we want moral leaders, we want brilliant statesman to have a greater influence. If we were to set out to make everyone's influence in politics the same, we'd have to forbid speech altogether, because with speech comes influence, and differential influence. So after all we have to turn back to equality of political impact. But as soon as we say that, then we realize that in anything larger than a small town meeting equal political impact is absolutely impossible. Representative government means that some people, a few people, will have exponentially more impact on decisions through their choice than you and I have. And this is true not just of elected people but administrative appointees, people in charge of making economic decisions for the community, or judges in a constitutional court.

If equality of political impact is impossible anyway, why should it matter? In a country the size of Hungary the political impact of any ordinary citizen is so small that it can sensibly be rounded off only to zero. And if political impact is in anyway infinitesimal, why should it be a major goal of political institutions to make that infinitesimally small impact equally infinitesimally small?

Now, you may well have begun to think that my argument has gone out of control. I've gone too far. I seem to be challenging the very idea of political equality. Then why not dictatorship, if we can find a decent dictator? If everything I said up to now is right, why should we care about political equality? Because we have a better idea of what political equality is. It's not mathematical, it's a matter of status. Political equality means, each person in the community is regarded as equally important in two dimensions: what happens to that person is equally important, and that person's voice and opinion is equally demanding of attention. Now, that means that some denials of equality in the political process really are intolerable, because of their assaults on dignity. When almost everywhere women could not vote there was no interpretation of that denial available except the assumption that their views were less worthy of attention. That was the only conclusion, the only kind of justification that could be available, and that's a justification that is outlawed by the idea of political equality. But there are many kinds of gross inequality in political impact that carry no such implication, for example—to repeat—representative government. The fact that we elect some people and give them massive power doesn't mean that the rest of us are challenged in our dignity or importance. It's simply a means of sensibly accommodating, and seeking the goals that we all share. And that is also true, whatever else may be said about it, of a constitutional court. Judicial review gives a small number of unelected judges much more power. That may be a bad idea, it may be a good idea, but there is nothing in it that challenges political equality as a status, because there is nothing in the design of that institution that calls into question the dignity of any citizen. So, political equality is indispensable, but political equality must be understood as a matter of equal concern and respect for people, not any striving for a mathematical equality in the impact, still less in the influence, people have in politics.

I want to summarize the argument thus far, but mainly to make clear what I am not arguing. I am not arguing that the principle of majority vote has great importance, but must sometime be compromised because other things like justice or individual rights are important. I'm arguing for a much stronger conclusion, namely that majority preference in and of itself has no value whatsoever. When we come to the discussion, I hope some of you will try to show me that I'm wrong. But I iterate that strong conclusion: we should reject the majoritarian conception of democracy because it doesn't state anything of intrinsic value. When it's appropriate it's appropriate because of something else.

Now, I turn to the partnership conception. I said rather glibly and even cryptically that the partnership conception is a matter of self-government by a community acting as a partnership. Now, what do I mean? I have to take a step back again into the bitter history of political morality. In the 17th century, roughly, there was a seismic change in political morality, because the old principles of divine authority were no longer satisfactory. The question became urgent, it became the modern question of political philosophy, what justifies coercive government? Obviously, coercive government backed by steel, police and army is indispensable to civilization, but what could justify it? Why isn't coercive government, the might of the community trained against an individual, why isn't that subjugation, subordination, a form of slavery? That is the question which political philosophy strived to answer. It is the question that the long and honorable tradition of social contract theory tries to answer. The answer it gives is that coercive government is consistent with individual dignity because it's based upon the consent of the governed. Still, every form of social contract theory, understood as a real attempt to base government on the actual consent of the governed, has failed and the idea cannot be revived. There never was a historical contract by our ancestors. And even if there was, what's that got to do with us? The theory that we give implied consent to our government because we don't leave is too ridiculous even to permit anybody to defend it without a smirk. The most sophisticated form of this theory, put most effectively in our time by John Rawls, is that government is based on a hypothetical consent: what people would consent to, if they were rational under certain conditions. But that's not an argument from consent, because a hypothetical consent is no consent at all, and the circumstances that a philosophy like Rawls' has to imagine in order to say what would be rational consent has nothing to do with our circumstances. Now, Rawls doesn't mean to rely on an actual or hypothetical consent doing any important work, but that just emphasizes that consent is not an idea that we can any longer use to answer what I call the modern question: What justifies coercive government?

A different tradition of defining and defending democracy is based on the idea that democracy is self-government. We are governing ourselves. But that's an idea that so far only compounds the mystery. Clearly, government by majority is not self-government by everyone, indeed it isn't even self-government by members of the majority one by one. Abraham Lincoln at a very dark point in our civil war said that government must be not only for the people, and of the people, it must be by the people. He was appealing to an assumption of self-government that has yet to be redeemed. Now, I think it can be redeemed, if we think of action what is genuinely action by a collective group. The question of when it is right to say that a group is taking some action rather than an individual has occupied philosophers a good deal in recent decades.

We can sensibly think of self-government by a group, if certain assumptions hold within that group and these assumptions seem to be true in cardinal number. First, that everyone has an equal stake in a political decision. That everyone's fate matters just as much as anybody else's in that decision. You can't have partnership without that assumption. But secondly, that everyone enjoys equal respect within that association, and equal respect requires among other things not just that each person have a vote, but that each person's opinion be deemed worthy of attention. Respect in the sense of having a hearing.

Those seem to me among, not exclusive, but among the dramatic requirements of anything that could be regarded as politics by partnership, by a joint venture in self-government. Majority government does not supply either of these. If we want a partnership conception of democracy, we need more. What more? Plainly—you see I'm returning to my imaginary government—plainly we need free speech, uninhibited free speech, and we need a free press, uninhibited and independent free press. If we take seriously the idea that every opinion is entitled to attention and consideration we need an understanding that government may not decide what should be said and who should hear what. Free speech is the nerve of a partnership democracy. A partnership democracy also demands a structure, it demands a form of principle, in which partners who find themselves in the minority can challenge whether the requirements of association have been met. That is, whether their fate has been counted properly, whether their own ethical, religious and political convictions have received an opportunity for attention, and that can only be done through a structure of government in which there is a forum of principle as a check on majority parliamentary decisions. If free speech is the nerve of partnership government, judicial review and an independent constitutional court is in my opinion the essential skeleton.

Now, back to my imaginary government. I asked whether the government in my story had achieved the triumph of democracy. Well, it has on the majoritarian conception. But the majoritarian conception is so impoverished if I'm right that it gives that government no legitimacy at all. That government has set the country on a road to the ruin of democracy because it has subverted the most basic principles that would entitle the community to claim that it's a partnership of self-government. In the worst days of the Second World War, Learned

Hand, a very great judge for whom I once worked, addressed a large throng of people in Central Park in New York. He said when the spirit of liberty dies in the hearts of men no law, no court, no constitution can put it back. I think that's true. But there's something we have to add, which is that when the spirit of liberty still lives in the hearts of men and women then law, courts, and constitution are the indispensable oxygen, indispensable to keep that flame of liberty still alive.

Regime Change, Revolution, and Legitimacy

ANDREW ARATO

Transitions to Democracy and Constitution-Making Forms

Ever since 1989, the question whether the transitions to democracy in Central Europe were revolutions has been an intense subject of debate. Behind this debate lies a rigid alternative between revolution or reform. Since the transformations were not reforms compatible with, or preserving systemic identities, they had to be, supposedly, revolutions—an idea confirmed by the presence of large masses on the scene in some, but only some countries. For a long time I have found a schema introduced by Janos Kis to be the most productive way of transcending the reform-revolution dichotomy, which was extremely misleading for many of these important cases.[1] Using the double polarity of legality and legitimacy, and continuity and rupture, Kis was able to outline

[1] This scheme was in part a result of a productive dialogue between us, that made me replace the framework I originally introduced. Similar readings of Kelsen, and the need to go beyond him, played an important role in our discussions. The key to the solution that led to a simpler framework than mine was the explicit abandonment of Kelsen's identification of legality and legitimacy. See Kelsen, H. *General Theory of Law and State,* trans. Wedberg, A. (Cambridge, Mass.: Harvard University Press, 1945); Weber, M. *Economy and Society,* trans. Fischoff, E. at al, Roth, G. and C. Wittich, eds. (New York: Bedminster Press, 1968); Schmitt, C. *Legality and Legitimacy,* trans. Seitzer J. (Durham: Duke University Press, 2004). For our main pieces see: Kis, J. "Between Reform and Revolution," *East European Politics and Society* (Spring 1998); Arato, A. *Civil Society, Constitution and Legitimacy* (Lanham: Rowman and Littlefield, 2000) Chapter 3; Arato, A. *Constitution Making under Occupation: the Politics of Imposed Revolution in Iraq* (New York: Columbia, 2009) Chapter 1. I want to briefly indicate below that my original framework, more hermeneutic than ideal typical still has some uses.

three major forms of transition, reform, revolution, and "coordinated transition," to which I added a fourth that I now call, following Bruce Ackerman, revolutionary reform.[2] Subsequently, I maintained that one specific type of constitution-making (two in the case of the last)[3] corresponds to each transition type. The result is the following scheme:

Major Types of Democratic[4] Transition with Forms of Constitution Making

	LEGITIMACY CONTINUOUS	LEGITIMACY RUPTURED
LEGALITY CONTINUOUS	*Reform*: Normal amending process: Major amendments or new constitution within same regime. Sweden 1974 Turkey (between 1983 and present)	*Regime Change*: Roundtable with Interim Constitution(s) and non-sovereign constitutional assembly. Poland 1989–1997, Bulgaria 1990 Hungary 1989–1996 (failure) South Africa 1993–1996
LEGALITY RUPTURED	Type 1. "Revolutionary Reform": *Convention* Massachusetts and New Hampshire 1780s; U.S. Federal Convention 1787; (West) Germany 1948 Type 2. Plebiscitary "democratic" version: (auto) coup with plebiscitary legitimacy. *Plebiscite* 18th Brumaire's of Napoleon Bonaparte 1799 + Louis Napoleon 1852; Argentina 1949; Peru 1993; Russia 1993]	Revolutionary Constitution Making: *Constituent Assembly* Pennsylvania 1776, France 1789–1791; 1793–1795; 1848; 1945–1946, Weimar 1919; India 1948–1950; Venezuela 1999 Arab Revolts 2011–2012

This table can use some commentary. First, the link between transition type and constitution-making method is strong, but not absolute. In principle, in a particular form of transition there can be ways of using any of the constitution-making methods. I myself made a suggestion to that effect with respect to the Turkish reform process,[5] and argued elsewhere that in Iraq the roundtable, two-stage model was grafted into a revolutionary overthrow of the previous regime.[6] Whether such grafting can succeed is an open question, as the Iraqi example shows. Usually, it is particularly serious legitimation problems with a type of transformation in a particular context that lead to such attempts, but the generation of legitimacy by using a non-characteristic constitution-making model may not succeed.[7] There is at the very least an elective affinity if not causality between transition type and form of constitution-making that is difficult to set aside.[8] Second, and closely related, as I show below there can be a constitution-making process

[2] Ackerman, B. *We the People, Transformations* Vol. 2 (Cambridge, Mass.: Harvard University Press, 1998).

[3] There are two depending on which type of legitimacy is continuous. Ackerman collapses these two, plebiscitary and republican forms into a single type. He has however recently become a critic of plebiscitary forms, that should have necessitated another look at his scheme.

[4] Democratic in the broadest sense, including plebiscitary types. I do not consider plebiscitary democracy in its pure form as in the relevant cases to be democratic, on normative grounds. The fact is that plebiscitary and even caesarist leaders argue for their leadership on democratic grounds.

[5] Arato, A. "Democratic Constitution Making and Unfreezing the Turkish Process," *Philosophy and Social Criticism* 36, 3–4 (2010).

[6] Arato, *Constitution Making under Occupation.*

[7] Thus in Iraq the externally imposed revolution, as I have discovered and argued, could not generate revolutionary legitimacy for the agent, the United States and its forces. As a result the constitution-making method was adopted from the paradigm of regime change, but with limited success that did not overcome the legitimation problems. Arato, *Constitution Making under Occupation.*

[8] Thus I argue, learning across types, and especially from the new type should work on the level of principles rather than concrete method. See Arato, *Civil Society, Constitution, and Legitimacy,* Chapter 7; and "Conventions, Constituent Assemblies and Round Tables: Models, principles and elements of democratic constitutional-making," *Global Constitutionalism* 1, no. 1 (2012).

that proceeds for a time one way and turns into another. Several Latin American cases, like Argentina (1949) and Venezuela (1999) started as conventions, and wound up as plebiscitary coups or as revolutionary constituent assemblies (or their combination). Reform[9] too can fail and turn into roundtable led transitions, as in most relevant cases here, but also into revolutionary constituent processes as in India and other post-colonial cases.[10] Third, classification cannot be absolutely neat because one major element can be missing from a form that nevertheless is classified with others that are largely similar. For example the conventions of Massachusetts and New Hampshire were legally established (there was no legal rupture) and so were some Latin American cases (Argentina 1994), where this was provided for by the amendment rules. (Other Latin American cases involve later ruptures, leading to the plebiscitary or revolutionary types). The prototypical case of regime change (*ruptura pactada, reforma pactada!*) Spain involving an interim constitution, followed by elections and a second round of constitution-making. It did not have a roundtable, and its interim rules, confirmed by a referendum, were established from above. Fourth and finally: substance may be different than form; the real process may be different than the formal process. Thus for example Carlos Menem led a constitution-making effort in Argentina in 1993–1994 that was based on the American convention (without illegality) in form, but plebiscitary in substance. The question arises as to whether the transition in a roundtable country, like Czechoslovakia, was not simply hiding what was in effect a revolutionary collapse or even overthrow of the old regime. The fact that the constitution-making effort through the

---

9 These pervasive authoritarian attempts at reform do not belong in my typology. Regarding them, Przeworski, A. *Democracy and Market: Political and Economic Reforms in Eastern Europe and Latin America* (New York: Columbia University Press, 1991) maintained that "liberalization," a broader category, always fails. I consider the Mexican reforms under the PRI, focusing on electoral rule change, successful for a very long period. See Arato, *Civil Society, Constitution and Legitimacy,* Chapter 1.

10 Or it can succeed, as did the initial top down reform in Spain, by turning into a multi-stage process with an interim constitution, the law of reform. Spain for this reason is a marginal case of the post-sovereign model, achievable because of the rare democratic commitment of some of the initial regime protagonists. Prime Minister Suárez proceeded to establish forums of negotiation later than customary in this model.

roundtable failed, and was replaced by processes carried out by normal parliaments assuming sovereign powers in both Slovakia and the Czech Republic sustains this hypothesis.[11]

That outcome also indicates that a form can fail, something that my table notes in the Hungarian case. Such a failure can be argued empirically, by the fact that a process was either replaced by another one or led to political chaos or a new form of authoritarianism with or without a paper constitution. Thus the replacement of reform by roundtables in Poland, Hungary (1989) and South Africa, the replacement of revolutionary reform by revolution as in Venezuela, or the roundtable model by an illegitimate reform as I will argue in Hungary in 2011, all represent failures of the previous model, if not of constitution-making in general. Alternately, failure can be ascertained by a comparison to a fully developed, normatively attractive mode. In the case of roundtable-led regime change, that model in my view is that of South Africa.[12] While it is hazardous to judge in terms of this normative comparison alone, when both empirical and normative[13] approaches converge, we are justified to speak of failure. Even then, a process can always be redeemed by a subsequent one. Whether that will be possible and likely in Hungary now is the ultimate interest of this paper.

---

[11] Technically the failure was caused by the existence of an inherited amendment rule with strong minority vetoes that was difficult for a multistage roundtable-led process. But the amendment rule could have been replaced in the beginning, under the veil of ignorance. Most likely, the reason for failure was the absence of a communist partner strong enough to force the negotiation of an interim constitution that was workable. And this means that one sociological precondition of the model was absent.

[12] See Arato, A. "Constitution-Making as a Learning Process: Andrew Arato's model of post-sovereign constitution-making: editor's introduction," *South African Journal on Human Rights: Constitution-Making as a Learning Process* 1, 26 (2010) 1–18; Arato, A. "Post-Sovereign Constitution-Making in Hungary: After Success, Partial Failure, and Now What?" *South African Journal on Human Rights: Constitution-Making as a Learning Process* 1, 26 (2010) 19–44.

[13] Here I do not mean a normative evaluation of the result, but of the process. Again my method is the same, as other reflections on empirical legitimacy. I use the normative model to discover what may be empirical problems, and then test my initial hypotheses by looking at the discourse of conflict on the same issues.

Legitimacy Problems of Democratic Change

In my mind, the core gain of the roundtable-led regime change model has to do with the generation of political legitimacy.[14] However, this gain is not always actualized. I have in mind legitimation in the sociological, rather than the philosophical sense, even if the two cannot be separated entirely.[15] Thus it is a matter of justifications of rule empirically available, one that the citizens, groups and administrative staffs are likely to find valid, under the given historical circumstances. This should not be confused with either legality, or legitimacy as a normative matter, from the point of view of moral philosophical reflection. By legality I mean the following of existing procedural rules, that admittedly also carries, on its own, a relatively weak legitimation potential, as the critics of Weber's rational legal legitimacy rightly noted. Matters are more complex concerning the distinction of the sociological and the philosophical. One perspective is from the observer's point of view, the other focuses on the probable views of the participants: the legitimacy offerings of elites and the chances of acceptance by others. While legitimacy from a philosophical point of view can be imputed to constitutions on the bases of their content,[16] legitimacy from the sociological point of view is much more likely to depend in part at least on the process of constitution-making. Even an otherwise acceptable liberal democratic constitution is open to challenge based on the manner in which it was made. While the philosophical meaning of legitimacy of constitutions can perhaps be ascertained from the liberal point of view, the sociological has an internal relationship to the democratic one. However, as Habermas realized[17] an analysis focusing on sociological

[14] Thus this model is the best candidate for what I called grafting in the case of legitimation problems with other types of transition, or earlier forms of constitution-making.

[15] See Arato, *Civil Society Constitution and Legitimacy,* 69 and 74; Kis, J. "Between Reform and Revolution."

[16] See for example John Rawls, both in *A Theory of Justice* (Cambridge: Belknap Press of Harvard University Press, 1971) and *Political Liberalism* (New York: Columbia University Press, 2005).

[17] Habermas, J. *Legitimation Crisis,* trans. McCarthy, C. (Boston: Beacon Press, 1975).

legitimacy (unless it is to work through unreliable surveys) cannot entirely dispense with normative considerations. This has however an epistemic or hermeneutic rather than normative function, in helping to identify the norms in society or in a process that are meant to play and can play a legitimation role in the sociological sense. The task however is not to substitute the analyst's own views of what is legitimate and illegitimate for the views of relevant actors, but to use these as the bases of interpretation to discover what empirically can and cannot be made legitimate. But only the existence of social contestation concerning legitimacy can confirm that the analyst's discovery of legitimation problems is based on empirical insight rather than normative projection.

According to the logic of the scheme here introduced, of the four forms only revolution and regime change involve ruptures of legitimacy, and thus, it may seem, have problems of legitimation to solve. To the extent however that a new constitution is to be made, in my view all the forms have significant legitimation problems even if the protagonists of roundtables seem to be the only ones aware of these. In the case of reform, a simple mechanical constitutional amendment by a legally established legislature, using the existing revision rule, admittedly has no legitimation problems. Here legal legitimacy is sufficient. When however that rule is used to replace a whole constitution, especially where such an option was not explicitly provided for[18] raises important normative questions among participants. Written constitutions and the distinction between constituent and constituted powers have been historically introduced to limit the ability of incumbent governing authorities to change the fundamental rules of the game, and a reform that does so is *prima facie* problematic. This was the great insight of the Indian judges of the basic doctrine fame, who did not even have codified eternity rules to rely on.[19] The problem is only exacerbated when the ease of replacement is facilitated by highly disproportional electoral outcomes and an easy, one dimensional amendment rule.

[18] As in the current Spanish and Bulgarian constitutions, and arguably Article 146 of the Grundgesetz.

[19] Granville, A. *Working a Democratic Constitution: The Indian Experience* (New Delhi: Oxford University Press, 1999).

In the case of revolutions to be sure new revolutionary legitimacy is generated, linked to the processes of liberation by an often charismatic elite or leadership. Here the high level involvement of the masses in the overthrow of an old regime can establish a kind of identity between liberating elites and large population sectors. Nevertheless in a complex society, there may be large scale agreement concerning what should be replaced but not likely concerning what should be put in its place. The friend-enemy relations thus change quickly in the midst of revolution. When an elite imagines that its earlier credit earns it the right to dominate the constituent process, and to impose a constitution through either minority will or even a narrow majority there is likely to be broad opposition to these efforts. Revolutions not only start in civil war but can also lead to new ones as in France in the 1790s and Russia after the dissolution of the constituent assembly in 1918–1919. This is a sign of a contest around legitimacy, and the repressive nature of post-revolutionary regimes is a tacit admission of a fundamental legitimation problem, of the need to replace hegemony by domination, using Gramsci's terms.

With exception of the American cases, and West Germany, it is variously systemic and normative problems that undermine legitimacy for revolutionary reforms. The plebiscitary mode shares its normative problems with revolution. Moreover given the instability of plebiscitary democratic support, resting on momentary states of will, and the weakness of its representative capacity, the model is likely to suffer from an aggrieved version of the problem of dual democratic legitimacy analyzed by Juan Linz in the case of presidential regimes.[20] Even when democratic legislatures are suspended, many citizens are likely to find alternative and more plausible instances of representation in civil society, often religious elites. The repressive nature of such politics is again the likely testimony to this. But even the republican option centering on constitutional conventions has a serious difficulty when legal rules are ruptured, as it was clear around the time of the adoption of the U.S. Federal Constitution. Moreover, unless there is great normative and even sociological homogeneity among the republican institutions, as in that one case, the alternative claims of popular sovereignty by

---

[20] Linz, J.J. "Presidential or Parliamentary Democracy: Does it Make a Difference?" in Linz, J.J. and A. Valenzuela, *The Failure of Presidential Democracy* (Baltimore: Johns Hopkins University Press, 1994).

competing institutions, the normal legislature(s) and the constitutional convention can easily lead to dual power, new ruptures of legality and serious challenges to the legitimacy of the body that wins this struggle. Not surprisingly, these conflicts have been managed historically either by over-arching (or underlying) federal arrangements or, as in West Germany, by an external occupation. Elsewhere, the outcome can easily be a constitution without legitimacy as in Russia after 1993, or one whose legitimacy is constantly challenged.

Finally, in the case of regime change the actors themselves are generally aware of their legitimation problems. This is a great advantage, and leads I believe to the normative superiority of this model, admittedly from an external point of view. Negotiating with old regime actors who have lost their legitimacy, including new ones in agreement with the old, excluding others, making agreements whose *quid pro quo* character can be justified only in terms a strategic modus vivendi, are all problematic from the point of view of democratic legitimacy, and the main actors recognize it as such. This is why, at its best this model turns out to be a factory of legitimation, introducing elements like *public* openness, *inclusion* of new participants, fully *consensual* decision rules, as well as treating the fictional *legality* of old regimes as actual, as if they could be made elements of the rule of law. And even this is not enough. The participants also tend to affirm the merely provisional nature of their constitutional product, their inability to completely substitute for free elections, and the making of the final constitution by those elected under these rules. These steps add the missing democratic component in the legitimation of the paradigm. While it is not only unproblematic, but necessary to establish an independent body enforcing the initial agreement, it is equally important to make these agreements in such a way that the final process retains its open and democratic quality. Thus in general, the enforcement is limited only to procedural aspects.[21]

[21] The 34 substantive constitutional principles, agreed upon at the Multi-Party Negotiating Forum in South Africa apparently contradict this last claim. They were necessary under the circumstances of extreme societal division, and possible in my view, because of the charismatic nature of the ANC and its leadership. Even in South Africa, fundamentally entrenching by principles consociational democracy would not have been possible, or desirable.

The Hungarian Case, 1989–1990 and its Relationship to the New Paradigm

There have been several types of challenges, difficult to reconcile with one another, of treating the Hungarian process as an example of a new paradigm of transition and constitution-making. The first points to its uniquely fragmented or patchwork character. Another to the achievement of what seemed to be a permanent constitution already in 1989. Yet another, looking at this document formalistically as the amendment of the 1949 Constitution, denies that there has been constitutional replacement at all.[22] Finally, another challenge, compatible with the previous, treats the roundtable agreements as a corrupt bargain in which the previous elite dominated. This is incidentally a point of view also present in the previous elite, with reverse evaluation, choosing to regard the new as the result of mere reform.

The study of the history of what was achieved and how it was done, which is fortunately possible based on available sources, leads to the rejection of these claims.[23] Nevertheless the Hungarian case is unique. As I have argued elsewhere, of the major components of the developed model[24] it has satisfied all but one: the completion of the second stage, in terms of the free election of a (non-sovereign) con-

---

[22] This can happen in Western scholarship even, however mistaken, as in Elkins, Z., T. Ginsburg, J. Melton, *The Endurance of Constitutions* (Cambridge: Cambridge University Press, 2009).

[23] See Bozóki, A. ed. *The Roundtable Talks of 1989. The Genesis of Hungarian Democracy* (Budapest: Central European University Press, 2002).

[24] See Arato, A. "*Post-Sovereign Constitution-Making in Hungary: After Success, Partial Failure, and Now What?*" Briefly enumerated: 1. Two stage process 2. Legal Continuity 3. Roundtable agreements 4. Interim constitution fully breaking, in substance, with old one 5. Enforcement of interim constitution by a constitutional court. 6. Free election of a non-sovereign constitutional assembly, and 7. Production of a final constitution. The idea of two stages was implicitly present in Kis, J. " Between Reform and Revolution" and explicitly in "A rendszerváltást lezáró alkotmány" [Constitution closing the transition] *Népszabadság* August 19, 1994. We have both articulated this view at the Budapest EKINT conference in 2003, where former Chief Justice Sólyom argued that the constitution was then fine as it was. Majtényi, L. and Z. Miklósi eds. *És mi lesz az alkotmánnyal?* [And what will be with the constitution?] (Budapest: Eötvös Károly Intézet, 2004).

stitutional assembly, and the production of a final constitution. The effort to make the final constitution in 1994–1996 failed. Nor do I regard the Fundamental Law recently enacted as the conclusion and completion of the model, but as I will explain, its subversion by a process of illegitimate reform.

This to me is a serious matter from the point of view of empirical legitimacy. The Hungarian model, as many participants of the roundtable realized, has all the legitimation difficulties of this model in general, but with some specific Hungarian additions. None of the participants were democratically elected. The old ruling party played an important role. The new participants, though they established their credentials in the oppositional roundtable, were formally present on the invitation of the ruling party, except for Fidesz, who was brought in against the will of that party. Others like the Hungarian October Party were excluded and demonstrated against this exclusion. Public visibility and accountability were weak, due especially to the wishes of the old ruling party. The presence of the old Parliament in the process was too active, repeatedly modifying some of the agreements. (It changed the electoral rule, and the mode of presidential elections according to the positions of the then still-ruling Communist Party). There were well-founded rumors of private deals between leaders of the old ruling party, and new party leaders that violated the consensual nature of the agreements. Subsequently, the process allowed a relatively large scale conversion of the previous political power to new economic ones. While a program of retributive justice was rightly excluded, nothing like a truth and reconciliation process was provided for.

Most seriously, while the new constitution was formally pronounced as provisional, no procedures were enacted concerning the creation of a final constitution. Thus the illusion was created that a non-democratic, only partially legitimated instance, the roundtable created Hungary's final constitution. At the same time, leaving the single chamber amendment rule of the 1949 constitution in place, the expectation was created that governments in power will repeatedly modify the new constitution according to their shifting interests as incumbents. This idea was confirmed by the pact of 1990 of two opposing parties with less than 50 percent of the popular vote, but over two-thirds of the seats, that modified the constitution substantially, without however producing a new one. Fidesz, I should admit, was at that time rightly critical of the pact between the Alliance of Free Democrats and the Hungarian Democratic Forum.

I do not say that the process was therefore not legitimated at all. From what I called the normative or philosophical perspective, the 1989–1990 Constitution was a liberal democratic one, that despite its flaws[25] deserved acceptance and support.[26] Thus, it was possible for such a constitution to earn empirical support over time. Moreover, even during the process of its making, conditions capable of generating legitimacy in the sociological sense were by no means disregarded. The inclusion of nine very different participants in the roundtable was a wide one. The plenary sessions, at least, were public. The rule of law was rigorously maintained. Moreover, the referendum of 1989 overcame the corrupt bargain concerning the election of the president of the republic. That was the only moment of popular participation in the process, important for that very reason. But to produce the full political legitimacy associated with the model, especially in the short and middle term,[27] its completion was absolutely necessary. This could have been done even without the initial enactment of the necessary rules, by using the existing amendment rule to produce new rules. It was important however in this process to avoid even the appearance that a new constitution would be expressing merely incumbent advantage, and the desire for political preservation of power.

The imposition of a new constitution by electoral winners was indeed avoided from 1995 to 1996, with a coalition having over 70 percent of the seats enacting highly consensual rules for constitution-making.[28] These rules provided that 80 percent of Parliament had to

---

[25] Mainly: strong tendency toward parliamentary sovereignty, one that was however balanced by a very strong constitutional court.

[26] While I consider the process of the making of this constitution also open to criticism from a normative point of view, I believe that on balance the result should have outweighed the flaws in the process.

[27] In the long term, constitutions made in processes with legitimation problems, real as in the case of the 5th Republic in France and perceived as in the case of the Grundgesetz, can be compensated for by successful functioning and popular understanding of the impartial nature of the enforcement of important rights.

[28] See Arato, *Civil Society, Constitution and Legitimacy* Chapter 6; and Arato, A. and Z. Miklósi, "Constitution Making in Hungary 1989-1996" in Miller, L. E. and L. Aucoin eds. *Framing the State in Times of Transition: Case Studies in Constitution Making* (Washington DC.: United States Institute for Peace, 2010).

agree to new procedural rules of constitution-making. Also a parliamentary Constitutional Committee was created, one based on inclusion and consensual principles (disregarding parliamentary composition, each of six parties had an equal number of members; five would have to agree to any provision). This was indeed a potentially successful way of ending the process, adding new democratic and pluralistic legitimacy to the result, enabling the actors to establish a new amendment rule that would close the process unless very large majorities of both legislatures and the population chose to reopen it in the future. That this process failed was a very serious blow to constitutional legitimacy in Hungary. The fact that it failed because of the initiative and obstruction of leaders of the old ruling party, again controlling the government,[29] only increased the (false) impression that the roundtable constitution was their achievement, one that they would seek to preserve.

In this context, as far as the political right was concerned, even the constitution interpreting and defending role of the Constitutional Court could be seen as supporting what was ultimately a corrupt arrangement, a perception re-enforced by the fact that key members of the Court were not at all enthusiastic about the legislature completing the process by enacting a new constitution. Of course the more radical right-wing parties of that time helped to bring the project down, but this did not stop their attacks on the constitution in place.

Thus, on balance, I believe that the Hungarian constitution-making process never overcame its legitimation problems. Only the consensual conclusion of the process, by a democratically elected assembly could have done so. There are two ways of denying this diagnosis. The first, identifying legality and legitimacy, would maintain that because of the rigorous legal continuity in the process, and its admitted enforcement and development by the Constitutional Court, there never was a legitimation problem. This view however would reduce the roundtable

[29] A draft proposed by the constitutional committee had to be approved by two-thirds of Parliament. This could not happen because many leaders of the socialists, whose representatives supported the draft in committee, did not vote for their own draft, in alliance with right-wing deputies. The coalition partner, the liberal party, was firm in its support of the process and the draft, but so was Fidesz at the time.

model to a case of mere reform, confirming if unintentionally the criticism that the old system was preserved, and its beneficiaries were protected under new colors.

The second, identifying legitimacy in the sociological sense with its philosophical meaning, would argue that since the 1989–1990 constitution fully satisfies democratic and liberal norms it is therefore legitimate. I agree with the philosophical judgment here. But I am skeptical about the implicit assumption, that on these bases legitimate origins too can be ascribed to it through mere imputation. The fact that these origins are then described as a rule of law revolution (*jogállami forradalom*) shows the assimilation of the roundtable model to revolution, a perspective not favored by the fact that in 1989 the population did not experience the process as any kind of revolution. Moreover, the main actors specifically avoided interpreting it in terms that evoked the traditions of revolutions of 1848 and 1956.[30]

The 2011 Fundamental Law, and the Legitimacy Problem

In my interpretation, the sociological legitimacy of the constitution was not satisfied by either the appeal to legality, or to fundamental liberal and democratic norms incorporated in the document. I am pretty confident that the survey literature from a now 20-year period, dealing with constitutional values and their acceptance, would sustain this judgment. What I focus on instead and did in the early 1990s[31] is the challenge from the right that I considered partly unjustified because it misconstructed the facts and achievements of the roundtable-led process. Such challenges were justified, however, to the extent that the defenders of the new regime did not satisfy their initial promises, explicit in the constitutional text as well as implicit in their very procedures in both 1989 and 1995–1996. This promise was one to replace the bargained constitution by a democratic as well as consensual one. Such is the heart of the sociological legitimacy problem, and it opened

[30] Aside from the symbolic act of the reburial of Imre Nagy, that said nothing about the process going on. See Arato, *Civil Society, Constitution and Legitimacy* Chapter 3.

[31] Ibid.

the door to István Csurka's critique in the 1990s, as well as Viktor Orbán's in 2010. Thus the so-called "revolution in the polling booth" is the true inheritor of the earlier demand for a second revolution. The existence of the disproportional electoral rule, along with the old amendment rule of the constitution implying parliamentary sovereignty only made the job of the new "revolutionaries" easier.

Let us look at the process the Fidesz-led government engaged in when making of the new Fundamental Law.[32] I will use my earlier typology here not to make a fetish of classification, but in order to pinpoint the legitimation problems in making the new Fundamental Law. While some will argue[33] that this process represents the missing completion of the roundtable paradigm, I very strongly disagree with this, and wish to provide the interpretive grounds for the disagreement based on comparative and theoretical considerations. I believe that it is essential to the constitution-making method linked to the new paradigm of transition stressed here that it is *post-organ sovereign* in all of its stages and as a whole, that none of the protagonists of the several stages—the roundtable, the Parliament and the Constitutional Court—claim to fully embody the will of the sovereign people. No organ of state or government is supposed to be sovereign, without limitations. Here one organ, Parliament, did explicitly claim to fully embody the sovereign constituent power of the Hungarian people. While not elected as such, nor given any kind of mandate to produce a new constitution, Parliament became a sovereign constituent assembly on the basis of barely more than 50 percent of the votes to its majority.[34] Consistently with that conception, the rule established in 1995–96, the four-fifths rule requiring consensus among some par-

[32] For its general critique, both in terms of process and result, see the three part article of János Kis, "Alkotmányozás - mi végre?" I-III. [Why constitution-making?] *Élet és Irodalom*, 55, 12. 13. and 14; as well as Arato, A., G. Halmai, and J. Kis eds. *Opinion on the Fundamental Law in Hungary* in this volume.

[33] This was explicitly claimed in the original explanation appended to the Fundamental Law, when first sent to the Parliament.

[34] This was explicitly asserted when the regular Parliament converted itself into a National Constituent Assembly by a mere declaration that was disregarded by all accept the Fidesz parliamentarians. It was however a correct statement of what they had actually done, without any legal provision supporting the step.

ties beyond the government alone, was not only disregarded, but was explicitly repealed by two-thirds of the vote. That move would have been unconstitutional, but was not really vulnerable to invalidation because of the previous, in my view mistaken, declarations of the Constitutional Court rejecting amendment review.[35] In any case, the Fidesz government made impossible its litigation through packing the Constitutional Court by eventually seven new members. This, along with a new majoritarian appointment scheme, removed the only check of parliamentary sovereignty in the Hungarian system, the Court, whose jurisdiction was already curtailed by amendment earlier in the year. Comparison with the 1995 process, that remained under the jurisdiction of the Court, is again instructive.

Was it a process that while not completing the earlier regime change, re-enacted its logic? The use of the old amendment rule, and the challenge to the existing constitution's legitimacy in the preamble of the new Fundamental Law, as inconsistent as it was, points in the direction marked by legal continuity/legitimation break. With respect to the constitution-making procedure however, this Fidesz led process, unlike the one started in 1989, had only one stage, only one major agent, and as already said original sovereignty was asserted. Thus not only one but many features of the new paradigm were not present, and thus we cannot even speak of a marginal case here.[36]

There can also not be a question here of recourse to two other transition types, the options of revolutionary reform and revolution. Both require ruptures of legality, and I do not think that the limited illegalities involved can be interpreted as a legal rupture. Revolution also requires ruptures of legitimacy, which was (inconsistently) claimed here, but without serious foundations. Not only was the legitimation rupture not as complete as in revolutions, whatever the claims made by the preamble, there was no other legitimation principle proposed

---

[35] Decision 61/2011. (VII. 13.)

[36] I will admit that the process satisfied a very abstract interpretation of the Kis scheme (note 1). But Kis in the substance of his article, outlined the parameters of a negotiated transition within legal continuity that point to a very different process than the one involved here. As for my own version, it is clear that the constitution-making process itself was as far as possible, within the broadest meaning of democratic politics, from the constituent process characteristic of regime change.

than parliamentary sovereignty, embodying popular sovereignty, and this (alas) was already established in the 1989–1990 regime, if inconsistently given the creation of such a strong constitutional court.[37]

Accordingly, the new Fundamental Law, after pronouncing in its preamble the invalidity of its predecessor, in its final provisions claims authority for its makers on the basis of the very amendment rule in place since 1949, something that was not done in 1989 when the rule was used without such claims. The roundtable did not claim its authority to recommend from any provision of the 1949 Constitution, to which it was "unknown" as an institution. It is true, as in 1989, this amendment rule was used to produce a completely new constitutional text, but this time there were significantly fewer substantive changes. If 1989 was not a revolution, and it was not, then neither was 2010. It was not even a counter-revolution, despite the presence of a genuine counter-revolutionary force, Jobbik, in Parliament, a party that did not support the new draft. At most it is a contrary revolution in the sense of Joseph de Maistre, that is reversing revolutionary results by methods other than a revolution. Other possible criteria of revolutions that I list in my 2000 book[38] (a complete replacement of regime, revolutionary experience, and hermeneutic appeals to a revolutionary tradition) were also absent. So far there has not been any attempt to establish revolutionary retroactive justice, and in Europe that would be now quite unthinkable. Only the process of purges in many institutions recalls a revolutionary logic. But purges of key institutions alone do not make a revolution, as the 19th century U.S. spoils system indicates.

In spite of legal continuity, it can still be asked whether, on the level of constitution-making, the process represented a revolutionary reform in either of its types, republican or plebiscitary. Was it at least a marginal case of one of these types? On the level of constitution-making, there was however nothing here that resembled the classical American republican model, nor even the informal one based on a plural-

---

[37] At that time the principle was new, in spite of the fact that it was formally present in the 1949 Constitution. The sovereignty of the Communist regime, in the material sense, was exercised by the Political Bureau of the Central Committee of the Communist Party. This body could give legally (or politically and sociologically) binding orders to Parliament.

[38] Arato, *Civil Society, Constitution and Legitimacy,* 86–103.

ity of institutions and stages stressed by Ackerman.[39] This goes for the New Deal version, that was borderline plebiscitary in his depiction, but where Roosevelt also depended on other institutions that retained their independence (Congress and Court) and on at least two crucial elections, with his constitutional plans clear in the second. The one project anticipating Orbán's moves, the attempt to pack the Supreme Court resoundingly failed. Nor did the new Roosevelt Court, after regular appointments, become merely an instrument of the executive. As to the full plebiscitary type, there was neither a *coup d'état* carried out in Hungary, nor even an auto *golpe*. Significantly not only was plebiscitary confirmation in a referendum not used; it was aggressively avoided by the governing party. Plebiscitary claims were made, but these remained entirely untested. All this means above all that not only the forms of legitimation characteristic of the roundtable form as well as revolutions were missing, but continuous republican or plebiscitary legitimations were not relied upon nor generated.

So reform is left as the main possibility. Accordingly, I first interpreted the Fundamental Law as a particularly large amendment package, similar to one enacted in Turkey in the previous year that also involved court packing. But it was also pointed out to me that the Fundamental Law threatens many aspects of the rule of state law, and thus involves the potential replacement of regimes. That would be incompatible with reform. But I add: only with legitimate reform.[40] As under the basic structure doctrine, ordinary amendments that threaten fundamental components and therefore the identity of the constitution are indeed illegitimate. In India they are also illegal, or have been made

---

39 Ackerman, *We the People*, Vol. 1 and 2.

40 Why don't I make the same argument in terms of an illegitimate form of the regime change type, that involves a break in legitimacy without generating a new form? I admit that here the two possibilities of illegitimate reform and illegitimate regime change converge. I choose the first because the process lacked all major components (e.g. the negotiated character) necessary for regime change. But the choice could equally depend on whether there is literally a change of regimes or not. In my view this is not yet decided, as it already was in October 1989. The decision will depend on the interpretation of the Fundamental Law, and the kind of role the Constitutional Court assumes under it. One end result could be a corrupted version of constitutional democracy, and another, a semi-authoritarian system. I am not ready to say that the second is necessarily going to be actualized.

illegal by a long tradition of court precedents even without explicit textual guidance, as by the eternity clauses of the Grundgesetz, and the Turkish constitution of 1983. The problem: in Hungary there is neither a relevant set of precedents, nor appropriate codification entrenching parts or principles of the constitution on a higher level than the rest.[41] Thus what remains to be said, is that the Fundamental Law and its enactment were legal but illegitimate, or in a peculiar British usage: unconstitutional but legal.[42]

Thus the process Fidesz pushed through was on the whole legal. That is why I call it reform. But again it was not legitimate, in part because of its own claims rejecting the legitimacy of its own ground, and in part because of how it was done. More exactly the legitimacy problems of this process have to do with how it was done in light of what was done. Or, what was done could have been done legitimately only through a different process than the one used. (Such a better process of course may not have produced the same result, and thus it was avoided).

It is not only from my external point of view that the process had serious legitimacy problems. The fact that it was non-consensually adopted without even the use of referendum has been continually pointed out by all other political actors. The contrast with 1994–1996 was obvious. So were the inconsistencies of many new elements adopted with the basic structure of constitutionalism as well as parliamentary government. To the first group belong the attacks on the Constitutional and other courts: the removal of jurisdiction, the court packing and the forcible retirement of ordinary judges. The second group includes first and foremost the establishment of long term offices and tenures, and the multiplication of cardinal laws, both restricting the policy options of future freely elected governments. One set will

---

41 The only exception was arguably the implicit self-entrenchment of Article 24(5), the four-fifth rule, repealed unconstitutionally by Fidesz this year, by using the two-thirds rule, according to Article 24(3) of the 1989 Constitution.

42 In the UK this possibility is inherent in the constitution having important conventions that have not been legally codified. A court, as in Canada in 1982, or a constitutional amendment like the 23rd in the U.S. can legalize such conventions, but unless and before that is done the violations of convention remain legal. Roosevelt's election to third and fourth terms, violating existing conventions, was legal.

make the protection of rule of law more difficult. The other will make democratic government weaker and less accountable. The electoral law is even more disproportional than the previous one, implying a calculation (right or wrong) that Fidesz will get an equal number of seats even with much fewer votes the next time around.[43] This is an incumbent protection measure incompatible with the essence of written democratic constitutions that seek to protect the polity against the self-preservation of incumbents. While the calculation behind introducing the new electoral law may be wrong, its normative problems do not thereby disappear.

Again, all these normative qualms are constantly articulated empirically in Hungarian and even European politics. With the exception of the governmental party, to those who care, inside and outside Hungary, the legitimacy of the enterprise has been seriously damaged. A constitutional reform that usurped radical constituent powers could perhaps be made legitimate if at issue were only its procedural origins. Then, with the passing of time, and serious constitutional jurisprudence by a Court, a secondary level of legitimacy could emerge. But here it is also a matter of content, whose illegitimacy is likely to become clearer and clearer as the new provisions actually go into effect, and as for example a packed and intimidated Constitutional Court visibly surrenders its earlier role of protecting fundamental rights.[44]

How Can the Process be Now Legitimately Concluded?

In one respect Fidesz itself may have implicitly recognized the legitimacy problems of what it has done. Contrary to an early idea of adopting the Spanish-Dutch type of amendment rule in the Fundamental Law that would have required the assent of two parliaments, in different sessions, voting by two-thirds, it has preserved the old parliamentary single chamber single session two-thirds rule for the future.

[43] Act CCIII of 2011 on the Elections of Members of Parliament.

[44] Of course it may not. Even packed courts sometimes surprise their packers, as happened after the first packing (with two justices) in Hungary. With seven new justices such a turn is unlikely.

This was under the impact of criticisms that claimed (rightly in the given case, wrongly in the abstract) that such a new rule would cast the Fundamental Law "in cement," depriving future parliaments of the very samc power that Fidesz has used now. Such an argument however belongs to the tradition of parliamentary sovereignty, in one particular interpretation (refuted by H.L.A Hart for example) that a parliament cannot bind another parliament exactly of the same type. The powers of one, accordingly, belong among the powers of the other. The argument is inconsistent with written constitutions and its entrenchment, thus with what Kelsen called a constitution in the formal sense. In practice it is overcome not with the other possibility inherent in the idea of omnipotence (namely that God is so powerful, that he can create a stone that even he cannot lift) but with constituent and constitutional assemblies generating higher legitimacy than available to ordinary parliaments. In the United States this was done e.g. by involving ratification through special assemblies, that was not a requirement in the case of ordinary lawmaking. There are other ways of accomplishing the same surplus of legitimacy, as already discussed. My point is however that Fidesz did not avail itself of any of them. Thus it was particularly vulnerable to the charge that it did not have the right to bind future parliaments to a greater extent that the present one was bound. It did not wish to expose its product to ratification by either a referendum or by a two-thirds vote of the next parliament. Instead, Fidesz backed down and left the existing amendment rule in place.

This fact is highly significant for the future. If the process was left open in 1989–1990, and was open in 2010–2011, it remains open exactly the same way now. What was a bad amendment rule under a fairly reasonable constitution, is now a token of possible improvement under a bad one. Even the Fidesz electoral rule as currently proposed is a double-edged weapon: with a shift in the electoral arithmetic the opponents of the Fundamental Law could have the constitution-making qualified majority. Of course that is only one possible scenario. Another is Fidesz retaining two-thirds with fewer votes. We cannot know what they would do to the rule of law, separation of powers and democratic accountability if they had a second, so-called mandate, but there is reason to fear.

In spite of the disproportionality of the likely electoral rule, or if it is in the end made much more proportional on the bases of new calculations, there is also a likelihood that no party will gain constitution-making majority even in coalition with others. In that case, given the number of new two-thirds laws the country can become ungovernable as the constitution makers of 1989–1990 already feared. Moreover, with the long term appointments already made by Fidesz, the dead hand of the past could continue to govern especially if there is a new majority. The Constitutional Court made by Fidesz, which is currently meant to be quiescent, might reassert activism to control a new and different government.

Those dissatisfied with such outcomes have the choice to wait for the opening provided by the amendment rule. Under fortunate conditions, they would not have long to wait. The nightmare may then be over after the election of 2014. But in the case of the other two scenarios things would be different. If Fidesz achieves a new large majority under rules of its own creation, with a minority of votes, especially in an alliance with the far right Jobbik, only extraparliamentary movements and protests can protect the remnants of constitutionalism and democracy reliably. The option then is either a color revolution even at the cost of illegality, or acquiescence in whatever Fidesz does. I am happy that I will not be called upon to make that unpleasant choice. Others however may have to. A revolution of course would not obey the constraints illegitimately put into the constitution by Fidesz.

Fortunately, much more likely is the outcome of a fragmented party picture, with Fidesz no longer able to form government (even with Jobbik). A new coalition government would still have to face the hurdles established in the Fundamental Law, and thus the problem of ungovernability. Under these conditions, much would depend on the availability of a right-wing force, outside of Fidesz or emerging from its midst, capable of making a new constitutional compromise with other parties. That could take the form of a new roundtable, a constitutional convention or even a return to the rules of 1994–1996 to produce a new constitution. All this can be done legally by using the amendment rule of the Fundamental Law, that is the same as the old Article 24(3) or even older Article 15(3), to produce new constitution-making and ratification rules. Such a legal regime change would however assume that two-thirds of the votes in Parliament are available or attainable; there will be no Communists or Socialists to insure the compliance of the required number of deputies. Many on the right will have to be convinced, and even here extraparliamentary movements and pressure would have a role to play. The problem would be less serious of course by far if the new government had the two-thirds, though even then a wide as possible inclusion of other forces, as against the effort of 2011, would still be highly desirable.

The difficulty arises only if there is neither two-thirds nor a right-wing partner. In that case the unpleasant choice of revolution, the republican form of revolutionary reform or passive acceptance of ungovernability remain three options for a new government in place. I do not know what would be my choice. The best of these three options would be perhaps revolutionary reform involving a break in legality (probably in the form of the temporary restoration of the Constitution of 1989–1990 and the Court as it was before the Fundamental Law) and entrusting a new body, a convention or a roundtable to recommend a new draft that could be passed by a referendum if the parliamentary votes are unavailable. I am afraid however such a "double differentiation" of constitution drafting and legislative bodies has little tradition outside the United States and some Latin American countries. A democratically elected parliament cannot defer as easily or to the extent to another elected body as did the Communist parliament of 1989, that also did so rather unwillingly. Thus revolution or a radical version of revolutionary reform are more probable scenarios, with a parliament again taking constituent power for itself, this time under a legal break, with the full repudiation of a constitution, the Fundamental Law.

Unfortunately, revolutions, even the colored ones, are only exceptionally the foundations for constitutional democracy. But even revolution could in its stages subsequent to legal break adopt the legitimation principles generated by the process of regime change in Hungary and especially elsewhere, e.g. Poland and South Africa: inclusion, publicity, and (subsequent) legality, and perhaps ratification by either a new constituent body, or the next parliament. If there has to be an illegality in Hungary, the process of replacing the Fundamental Law should nevertheless be one that in the end still earns the adjectives of the rule of law, Rechtsstaat and jogállam.

Constitution-Making, Competition, and Cooperation

ZOLTÁN MIKLÓSI

In April 2010, Fidesz, one of Hungary's major parties, achieved a decisive victory in free and fair legislative elections. Due mainly to the splintering of the opposition and quirks of the nation's electoral rules, Fidesz's sizable advantage at the polls translated into a two-thirds majority in the Parliament, slightly over the qualified majority needed to amend or replace the constitution. In due course, the party announced its plan to adopt a wholly new constitution, and despite the protests of opposition parties and a lukewarm public, it indeed passed the new Fundamental Law on a party-line vote exactly one year after it came to power.

The constitution that has now been replaced was adopted in 1989 during Hungary's transition from one-party rule to democracy, as a result of a cooperative effort between the then-new democratic parties and the outgoing Communist party. The common understanding at the time was that the participants of this process lacked democratic authorization to establish a permanent constitution, and therefore adopted what was officially an interim constitution, to be finalized or replaced after the first free and democratic elections. However, this was not to be; the broad consensus that had been achieved in 1989 and which would have been necessary to complete the work started in that year could not be recaptured, and all subsequent attempts to pass a new Fundamental Law fell short. Eventually, even though some prescient observers warned that in the absence of such a constitutional closure the 1989 Constitution would be open to challenges on legitimacy grounds,[1] the idea of a final and permanent foundational law receded from the public agenda, and despite some criticism, no one in

---

1 See e.g. Andrew Arato's contribution in this volume.

the political mainstream seemed to question the legitimacy of the existing one, which provided for a reasonably well-functioning framework of governance, as well as adequate protection for individual rights.

It was in this context that, without much advance notice, Fidesz rammed through the Parliament its own constitutional plan, without any support from the other parties in the legislature. The content of the new Fundamental Law as well as the process of its adoption have been the target of intense criticism, most of it well founded. Nonetheless, in this paper I am not going to engage in those controversies. Instead, my aim is to raise a more general and arguably more fundamental issue: is it permissible for a constitution-making majority, wholly convinced of the need for a new constitution and fully certain about what its content ought to be, to pass a constitution for the whole nation without any support from its political rivals? Or rather, is it the case that some decisions require consensus even if it is hard to achieve, and even if one side controls the procedurally required majority? I will limit my focus to constitutional changes that alter the identity of the constitution and thus amount to adopting a new one, and will disregard simple amendments.[2]

***

The term "constitution" is used in two different manners. In a looser sense, it is used to refer to just any set of rules that specifies the basic operating procedures of a nation's government, regardless of the content of the rules. In a stricter sense, the concept identifies an ideal to which existing constitutions aspire and may realize to a greater or lesser extent, and which may be used as a vantage point from which to evaluate actual constitutional arrangements. In the present paper I use the concept in the stricter sense. However, it is not my aim to elaborate and defend the ideal itself. I merely state what I take to be the core of the ideal, and examine what norms apply to the making of constitutions that are understood as aspiring to realize it.

The ideal is that of the collective self-governance of free and equal persons who each pursue their own personal projects and goals, under the conditions of pervasive disagreement and scarcity of resources.

---

[2] For a clarification of the difference between the two types of changes, see below in the text.

The characterization of persons as equal and free in pursuit of their own goals, as well as the conditions of scarcity and disagreement, imply specific constraints that the system of collective self-government must satisfy if it is to count as legitimate. Freedom suggests that the system of collective self-government must provide individuals with very large latitude in developing and pursuing their own preferred view of a worthy life. Scarcity implies that often it will not be possible for everyone to fully realize their goals, and therefore collective decisions will be necessary about resource distribution. The equality of persons supports the requirement that in making such collective decisions, each person's relevant interests be given the same weight. Finally, pervasive disagreement regarding the desirable content of collective decisions gives rise to the demand that binding collective decisions be made in such a manner that each individual has an appropriate opportunity to influence the outcome in a variety of ways, including voting and publicly discussing and criticizing the available alternatives. A constitution is legitimate if it establishes a system of collective decision-making that reasonably approximates these requirements.

In what follows, I will simply assume that the substantive properties that a constitution must aspire to realize are sufficiently well-understood, and also that we have clear standards to determine whether an existing constitution passes the test of legitimacy. Leaving aside these issues, I will instead focus on the process of constitution-making, and examine what norms apply to this process under the circumstances of democratic politics, chief among them disagreement regarding desirable constitutional provisions.

It is a rare event when an entirely new constitution is adopted in a country, and when it happens the primary reason is usually the result of the basic illegitimacy of the previous system. The problem of what conditions must be met in order for the constitution-making process that serves as the bridge between the previous, illegitimate state of affairs and the new, legitimate arrangement to be itself a legitimate one has received quite a bit of attention from political theorists lately, though not quite as much as the substantive issues of what makes the new, steady-state condition legitimate. Yet it is an even rarer event, and raises different issues regarding the legitimacy of the transition process, when a new constitution is adopted under conditions that themselves fulfill the requirements of legitimacy. What requirements should govern the adoption of a new constitution that replaces a constitution that is itself legitimate?

This question has received less attention, possibly because the answer appears so obvious: the existing legitimate constitution provides the rules of its own amendment, as well as the procedure in which a new constitution might be approved. Whereas in the case of a transition from an illegitimate regime there cannot be, by hypothesis, any legitimate formal procedure of making a new constitution, and therefore the problem of how to achieve a legitimate process and avoid tainting the legitimacy of the new regime as a consequence of its necessarily less-than-immaculate conception is a pressing and urgent one. It might be thought that this question has no analogue in the admittedly rare event of a transition from one legitimate regime to another. As there are detailed procedures regulating the adoption of a new constitution that are presumed to be legitimate, all the constitution-makers need to do, it might be suggested, is to follow these procedures carefully and conscientiously.

I will try to raise doubts about this seemingly obvious suggestion. Once we consider what a constitution is, and what basic functions it serves, it cannot be the case that strictly following the written requirements that are included in the constitution in force is always sufficient to guarantee the legitimacy of the outcome. But before engaging those questions, however, I need to diffuse two interrelated worries that might make someone think that the issue addressed here lacks any practical significance. The first worry is that the question raised here lacks any actual application, because there can be no valid reason for adopting a new constitution to replace a legitimate constitution that is in force. The second worry is that the adoption of a new constitution on the basis of an existing, legitimate one is not a distinct problem, but simply a special limiting case of amending the existing constitution. After all, the exact same outcome could be reached in substantive terms by a series of amendments as by adopting a new constitution in one step. The first worry may be formulated in the form of a dilemma: it is either the case that there was a valid reason to adopt a new constitution, in which case the old one in force could not be legitimate; or it is the case that there was no valid reason to adopt a new constitution, in which case the new one cannot be legitimate. The second worry raises the possibility that there is no principled way of distinguishing between the adoption of a new constitution and of merely amending an existing one.

Adequate Reasons for Constitution-making under Legitimate Conditions

The two worries are related in that they may be diffused with reference to the same set of considerations. Here, I will give only a brief and abstract description of these considerations; substantially more will be said about them in the main discussion. The idea is that all constitutions must discharge a few fundamental functions, such as establishing an effective governmental organization and providing for the appropriate protection of basic rights and liberties. These functions, however, may be discharged in several different institutional arrangements, all of which are equivalent or at least satisfactory as measured by the standards of the political ideal that all constitutions, properly so-called, are meant to realize. In other words, the political ideal in question significantly underdetermines the precise institutional features of acceptable constitutions.

The political ideal fixes the conditions of legitimacy of constitutions (as far as their content is concerned), but there are several legitimate arrangements within the acceptable set. This raises the interesting question of which among the acceptable alternatives is most suitable for adoption by any particular country, and the answer probably lies in the specific circumstances of that country: the particular political risks that its history makes it especially susceptible to, the distinctive resources that its existing social practices endows it with, and so on. We should note, though, more generally, that the fact that there are several different constitutional arrangements that equally satisfy the demands of the political ideal means that every political community faces a choice when it is adopting a constitution, a choice that must be settled in the light of various reasons that apply to it. And this also raises the possibility that after a political community has adopted in a legitimate process a constitution that is within the acceptable set and is therefore legitimate, it may come to discover reasons that were either unnoticed or too easily dismissed at the time of the original choice, reasons that suggest an alternative arrangement would be preferable given the distinctive circumstances of the community in question. And of course, given that the political ideal itself underdetermines this choice, and the sorts of considerations that bear on the more limited question of which alternative within the acceptable set ought to be chosen are of such a nature that they are unlikely to provide conclusive evidence in favor of any alternative, it is quite plausible that at least sometimes the newly noticed considerations constitute valid reasons for adopting another constitution. Therefore, it can be the case that it is both true that the existing constitution is a legitimate one and that there are valid (though not necessarily decisive) reasons for adopting a new one.

Joseph Raz has suggested a further set of potentially valid reasons to change the legitimate constitutional structure of a state that do not bear on its distinctive historical circumstances and socio-political resources. He raises the possibility that from time to time a political community may have adequate reasons to shake up its constitution just because such change is likely to shift power relations between different social groups, and this may be beneficial in order to avoid some groups cementing their power advantage.[3]

Such changes are acceptable or even desirable, he suggests, but only if the new provisions are also in themselves legitimate. Raz distinguishes such reasons from "merit reasons," which are based on the moral desirability of some particular constitutional provision, given its content. The reasons he considers here, by contrast, do not derive their strength, if any, from the content of the change, but simply from the desirability of change itself. Therefore, we may call them simple reasons for change, to distinguish them from the circumstantial reasons for change that I discussed.

The circumstantial reasons for change derive their validity, if any, not merely from the content of the proposed change or from the fact of change itself but from the combination of the distinctive historical circumstances of the political community in question and the content of the proposed provision. They do suggest, in contrast with simple reasons for change, that under the circumstances the proposed content is morally more desirable than the one that it seeks to replace, whereas

---

[3] See Raz, J. "On the Authority and Interpretation of Constitutions" in *Between Authority and Interpretation* (Oxford: Oxford University Press, 2009), 323–350, esp. 349–352.

simple reasons for change might be indifferent between many new provisions with different content, as long as they are within the acceptable set.[4] In Raz's terms, merit reasons are what determine the legitimacy of constitutions, and the further reasons, either the circumstantial reasons for change discussed above or the simple reasons for change suggested by him, are only considerations that may determine the choice between different legitimate constitutions.

It is possible to clarify the difference between amending a constitution and adopting a new one with reference to some of the same observations. There are certain basic functions that all constitutions, properly so-called, must discharge, and the provisions and rules responsible for discharging them are the legitimacy-enabling parts of the constitution. These parts together may be called the basic structure of the constitution, which supplies its distinct identity. To anticipate the discussion to follow later, the legitimacy-enabling functions include the institutions that provide for the effective protection of individual rights, the governmental organization that is necessary for the state to provide basic justice, and the rules that provide for a fair and effective political competition. But all constitutions contain other provisions that do not belong to their basic structure, and which are arguably not strictly necessary for them to be legitimate, even though they perform important roles. The proposal submitted here is that any change that affects the basic structure of a constitution also affects its identity, and therefore counts as adopting what is substantially a new constitution. By contrast, changes that do not concern the basic structure are properly regarded as mere amendments.[5]

Given the clarifications provided in the previous paragraphs, I am now in a position to formulate the problem in a more exact manner.

---

[4] Of course, there also exist countervailing reasons of stability and continuity as well, which may defeat both circumstantial reasons for change and "simple" reasons of change. There are also, as I shall argue, further reasons, independent of stability and continuity, which may defeat reasons for change.

[5] To be sure, not all changes that are related to the basic structure alter their fundamental mode of operation. Therefore, it is more appropriate to say changes that modify the fundamental way the basic structure operates count as adopting a new constitution. I realize that this formulation leaves it as an open question what constitutes the fundamental way of operation, but I have to leave it at that.

Are there any circumstances that may defeat the legitimacy of replacing a legitimate constitution by another legitimate one, given that the new one was approved in the correct procedure and there were adequate, valid reasons for changing the basic structure of the replaced one?

The problem as stated assumes that three requirements are satisfied. First, the process of replacement is appropriate as stipulated by the constitution to be replaced. Second, the content of the replacement itself satisfies the conditions of legitimacy. And third, there are valid, adequate reasons to replace the existing legitimate structure with another legitimate structure.[6] I will argue that indeed, there may be circumstances that may defeat the newly adopted constitution's legitimacy. As this formulation makes it clear, I am concerned here only with the legitimacy conditions of adopting a new constitution to replace a constitution that is itself legitimate. When it comes to replacing an illegitimate constitution, the reasons for doing that may override the considerations elaborated here.

Second-order Reasons and the Circumstances of Politics

Another way of formulating the question is this: given that there are valid reasons to replace the existing constitution, and a legitimate procedure to do so, are there any valid second-order reasons for refraining from acting on the valid first-order reasons? In this context, first-order

[6] These questions were inspired by political developments in Hungary in 2010 and 2011, as described at the beginning of this paper. However, I do not believe that in Hungary's case the conditions referred to in the formulation above were met: the process of adoption was not flawless, there were no adequate reasons to change the basic structure, and in terms of content, the new product is arguably deficient from the point of view of legitimacy. The Venice Commission, the advisory body of the Council of Europe responsible for monitoring constitutional matters in member states, criticized the rapidity, inflexibility, and lack of transparency of the process (see Venice Commission, *Opinion 614/2011 on three legal questions arising in the process of drafting the new Constitution of Hungary*), as well as several aspects of the outcome (see Venice Commission, *Opinion 621/2011 on the new Constitution of Hungary* in this volume). However, rather than engaging with the specific controversies surrounding Hungary's new constitution, I intend to raise the more general problem specified above.

reasons are reasons regarding the desirability of replacing the existing constitution with a new one, in light of its content, the circumstances, and the simple reasons for change, stability, and so on, whereas second-order reasons are reasons to act or to refrain from acting on the balance of first-order reasons.[7] Let's assume that after careful consideration and deliberation of all the merit reasons, circumstantial and simple reasons for change, and reasons for stability and continuity, a governing majority with constitution-making powers has come to the conclusion that a specific change in the basic structure is morally desirable on the balance of such first-order considerations. Might there be any valid second-order reasons to apply to the situation that may require it not to act on the balance of first-order constitutional considerations?

Where should we look for such possible reasons? In order to get a start on this issue, we may consider an analogous problem that is widely discussed in democratic theory. The problem in question concerns the reasons applying to collective decision-making under what came to be known as the "circumstances of politics." The circumstances of politics are constituted by (1) the existence of very pressing moral reasons to make collective decisions that are binding for every member of the political community, and (2) pervasive and deep disagreement among members of the community regarding the content of the collective decisions that are to be made.

The deepness of the disagreement means that it is not a sign of imperfect information, inadequate reflection, or a failure to deliberate and reason in good faith. On the contrary, it is assumed to be one of the fundamental facts of politics that people may still disagree about central issues of political morality even after carefully reflecting in good faith on all the relevant considerations. One of the central problems of democratic theory is to show how is it possible to make such legitimate decisions against the background of deep disagreement that purport

---

[7] For the idea of first-order and second-order reasons, see Raz, J. *Practical Reason and Norms* (Princeton, N.J.: Princeton University Press, 1990), 39. The interaction between first-order and second-order reasons is different from that between competing first-order reasons. Competing first-order reasons may *override* one another, whereas second-order reasons may be *exclusionary*: they not simply override conflicting first-order reasons but exclude them from the consideration.

to speak in the name of all of the governed. Let us assume that justice requires that the community make one or another collective political decision, but members of the community disagree about what justice requires the decision to be. Under the circumstances of politics, it is argued, in light of pervasive and deep disagreement, individuals, even those in positions of public authority, may have second-order reasons to refrain from acting on what they take to be the balance of first-order reasons regarding justice, and instead to act on the decision that was the outcome of a fair procedure, such as a majority vote following a fair deliberative phase, with equal opportunity for all members to have an input.[8] Thus, the political community as a whole, insofar that it follows some fair procedure, acts on "reasons that are second-order in relation to the reasons that people properly act on in forming their substantive views (and in deciding how to vote)."[9]

What the analogy is meant to show is that under the circumstances of pervasive disagreement, there may be second-order reasons for any individual to refrain from acting on his or her first-order reasons about some matter of public importance. But of course it may be objected that the analogy is misleading, because it describes what any individual has reason to do, in his or her individual capacity (either as a private citizen required to comply with collective decisions or as an official required to enforce them), in relation to society's collective decision. It is assumed that society must adopt a single course of action concerning some issue, and that individuals disagree about what that course ought to be (in terms of first-order reasons). Given that society must take a single course and individuals disagree about it, there is inevitably a conflict between what that course will turn out to be and at least some people's judgment about what it ought to be, as society cannot act on all individuals' reasons. By contrast, in the context discussed in this paper, such conflict is not inevitable, as we are considering whether a constitution-making majority should act *on its own* view of the balance of reasons. It is assumed that the majority in question has come to a

[8] The significance of disagreement is comprehensively discussed e.g. by Waldron, J. *Law and Disagreement* (Oxford: Oxford University Press, 1999), and Christiano, T. *The Constitution of Equality* (Oxford: Oxford University Press, 2008).

[9] Waldron, *Law and Disagreement,* 196.

unified view of the merits of the issue, and it is procedurally possible for it to enact that view.

The objection may be further elaborated in the following manner. When society must take a single course of action and its members disagree about what that ought to be, it is inevitable that the outcome will be settled by what are second-order reasons (such as majority-rule) in relation to the issue to be decided. The fair procedures of decision-making themselves embody the second-order reasons that arise out of reflecting on the circumstances of politics. But once a certain view has emerged as the winner in the fair process, the majority representing it has no *further* second-order reason to refrain from enacting it.

To be sure, constitution-making is different from ordinary political decision-making. Significantly, an important part of what is involved in constitution-making is changing the rules of ordinary political decision-making. Therefore, one might want to resist the objection that is being contemplated here by suggesting that even though democratic procedures capture all second-order reasons arising out of considering the circumstances of politics when it comes to ordinary decision-making, this is not so with changing the democratic procedures themselves. Even if a majority thinks the balance of first-order reasons supports changing the democratic procedures, there might be second-order reasons to refrain from acting on the balance of first-order reasons.

But now a modified version of the objection may be proposed. Almost everywhere, amending or replacing the existing constitution requires a special procedure that is more demanding than the procedure of ordinary decision-making. Indeed, some regard it as one of the defining marks of constitutions that they cannot be changed in the ordinary legislative procedure.[10] Therefore, the revised objection could be as follows: the special procedures pertaining to changing the constitution capture all second-order reasons that may apply to the question of whether an appropriately authorized majority should act on its view of what the balance of first-order reasons recommends. Thus, if there are adequate (first-order) reasons to replace the constitution, and it can be done in accordance with the special requirements of consti-

[10] See Raz, "On the Authority and Interpretation of Constitutions," 325. Where it not so entrenched, the constitution could not be superior law with respect to ordinary law.

tution-making, then there are no *further* second-order reasons for the constitution-making majority not to replace it.

In order to assess the force of this objection it is necessary to examine these special procedures as well as the usual justifications for them, to see whether they indeed capture all possible second-order reasons.

Second-order Reasons and Special Requirements

What may be the nature of the possible second-order reasons to refrain from acting on one's first-order reasons in constitutional matters, and in what way can existing practices of special constitutional procedures be understood to capture those reasons? Special constitutional procedures depart from ordinary law-making by requiring the approval of the change by more than a one-off, simple majority of lawmakers. The departure usually takes one or both of two different forms: either a one-time supermajority (two-thirds, four-fifths, etc.) of the members of the relevant body is required, or the constitutional change must be approved on two or more occasions by the relevant body or bodies, where the subsequent occasions are separated by general elections to these bodies.[11]

I will refer to all such requirements as supermajoritarian practices. These are sometimes applied for purposes other than changing the constitution, such as juries, and the rationale underlying these practices may also be relevant for identifying possible second-order reasons of the type I am searching for. What kind of considerations might these practices be seen as expressing? I will first look at customary justifications for supermajority requirements to see if they may provide residual reasons not to act on the balance of first-order reasons even when the required supermajority is obtained. Then I will attempt to find second-order-reasons that are only partially captured by supermajoritarian practices.

[11] In the case of changing the U.S. Constitution, the amendment needs to pass both Houses of Congress by a two-thirds majority, and it has to be approved by the legislatures or conventions of three-fourths of the states.

Supermajoritarian practices are often seen as enforcing simple reasons of stability. In the case we are considering, a simple reason of stability holds that the constitutional structure that is in force (and which is within the legitimate set) should be favored over other acceptable alternatives just because it happens to be in force. Simple reasons of stability, like the simple reasons of change discussed above, are not attached to the specific content of the constitutional provisions that they protect (or intend to replace, in the case of simple reasons of change). They do not hold that the content of the provisions in force (just by itself or in combination with the historical circumstances) selects them over their legitimate alternatives. Rather, they hold that being in force (and presumably, having been in force for some time) represents a distinct advantage of the existing structure insofar that the relevant actors whose behavior it is designed to regulate are already familiar with it, and they have their settled, reasonable expectations about it, and so on.

Therefore, a transition to another legitimate structure would involve significant transaction costs that may outweigh any expected benefit from the change. While simple reasons of stability may have some weight in many areas of ordinary legislation as well (such as taxes, etc.), they may be especially pressing in constitutional matters, and therefore may be legitimately enforced by supermajoritarian practices. Such a simple reason of stability may even count against a constitutional change that would introduce a structure that is acknowledged to be superior to the existing one by every relevant actor.

However, simple reasons of stability belong to the class of first-order reasons regarding the desirability or undesirability of the proposed change. They must be appropriately weighed against the competing first-order reasons for change (simple or circumstantial), and their role in the practical deliberation is exhausted by the weight assigned to them in the accounting of first-order reasons. In the problem I am considering, however, it has been assumed that the balance of all first-order reasons favors replacing the existing constitutional arrangement, and the only question remaining is whether there are any second-order reasons left not to act on the balance of all first-order reasons. In other words, it is assumed that simple reasons of stability have already been accounted for and outweighed by first-order reasons for change. It would be illicit double-counting if we still took them into account at this later stage as second-order reasons. Therefore, we may conclude that considerations of stability are not of the type of reasons I am trying to identify.

Another possible justification for supermajority that has been frequently suggested proceeds on epistemic grounds. It holds that supermajority decisions have superior truth-tracking capacity, i.e. they have a higher probability of getting the correct answer on the problem to be decided than simple majority decisions, under some standard assumptions about the rationality of the actors.[12] Coupled with the assumption that in constitutional matters it is more important to get the right answer than in matters belonging to ordinary law-making, supermajoritarian practices may be seen as reasonable even if they render decision-making normally more difficult and costly in these matters. If, as is assumed in the problem discussed here, the *status quo* represents a legitimate situation, then the conservative *status quo* bias of supermajority requirements can be justified on the ground that a departure from a legitimate state of affairs in matters of such grave importance is permissible only if there is a very high chance that the outcome will itself be legitimate.

In light of supermajorities' purported superior truth-tracking capacity, are there any truth-tracking-related reasons for a supermajority to refrain from enacting its view of the balance of first-order reasons? A procedure's truth-tracking capacity is, in the context under consideration, its ability to identify the first-order reasons that apply to the situation and to come to the right conclusion about what decision the totality of such considerations supports. Given that in the problem discussed here it is assumed that the supermajority in fact identified a valid answer, there can be no more truth-tracking-related reasons not to enact that answer. Therefore, we may conclude again that this consideration in favor of supermajoritarian practices does not spill over to a residual second-order reason to refrain from acting in possession of the required supermajority.

A third possible epistemic ground for supermajority requirements is provided by cases in which it is morally more important to avoid certain types of errors (type one, let's say) than other types (type two), even if by reducing the chance of avoiding type one errors we increase

---

[12] Supermajority requirements are discussed in the context of truth-tracking by Goodin, R.E. and C. List, "Special Majorities Rationalized," *British Journal of Political Science* 36 (2006): 213–241 at 223–225.

the chance of making type two errors. In other words, the aim of the supermajoritarian practice here is not to minimize error overall but to minimize certain types of error only. To this extent, this ground is only a special version of the truth-tracking rationale discussed in the previous paragraphs.

A well-known example is the case of guilty verdicts in criminal trials. Court proceedings are in general supposed to be optimized to reach the correct answer in the facts of the matter, but it is usually accepted that as long as some errors are unavoidable, it is better to err on the side of innocence. It is better to let a guilty person go free than to convict an innocent person to a prison sentence. Therefore, guilty verdicts require a special majority of the jury, in some cases even unanimity. (Other safeguards in the criminal procedure, regarding restrictions on admissible evidence, etc., also make it less likely to convict an innocent while at the same time making it marginally more likely to acquit a guilty person). It is at least logically possible that one could devise an alternative system that would reach the right verdict with a higher probability than procedures with these features, but that would lead to a higher likelihood of the wrong kind of error. Given the assumption about the asymmetrical significance of the two types of error, therefore, the supermajority requirement can be justified.

It is certainly possible to find analogues to this case in political decision-making, i.e. when there is more reason to avoid some type of errors than other types, and that this could justify supermajority requirements in political decision-making. However, this rationale for supermajoritarian practices does not lend support to the idea that in our example there may be second-order reasons for the party that controls the required majority not to act on its view of the balance of first-order reasons. This is so because in the cases considered here, it was assumed that the constitution-making majority has identified a legitimate alternative to the existing arrangement, and therefore the possibility of making the wrong kind of error is not present.

Let's take a step back and generalize the conclusions reached thus far. Democratic procedures, whether supermajoritarian or otherwise, are usually justified on intrinsic or instrumental grounds, or both.[13]

---

[13] Christiano, T. "Authority and Democracy," *Journal of Political Philosophy* 12 (3) (2004): 266–290.

Instrumental justifications hold that democratic procedures are more likely to produce outcomes that are substantively good (just, efficient, rational, etc.) than nondemocratic ones. Intrinsic justifications hold that democratic procedures are inherently fair, whether or not they are also more likely to produce objectively desirable outcomes, e.g. because they treat everyone as equals, and give every relevant party an appropriate chance to influence the outcome. In the terms of the present discussion, then, instrumental justifications hold that democratic procedures are more likely to capture and correctly weigh the valid first-order reasons that apply to a decision than nondemocratic ones. By implication, an instrumental justification of supermajoritarian practices of constitution-making hold that such practices are more likely to capture the correct balance of valid first-order reasons about a specific constitutional change than their alternatives.

All of the rationales for supermajoritarian practices considered so far (stability, truth-tracking, asymmetry of errors) are of an instrumental nature. They all suggest that such practices are more likely to get the right outcome (or to avoid the worst outcome). Now, from an instrumental perspective of course supermajoritarian requirements are only imperfect approximations of an ideally truth-tracking procedure, and they always leave open the possibility of producing a wrong answer. To this extent, in every actual instance of a proposed constitutional change, there is a lingering second-order reason, borne out of uncertainty about the quality of one's deliberation, not to act on what one takes to be the balance of all first-order reasons. But in the situation I am now considering, such uncertainty has been assumed away: it has been stipulated that the constitutional change that is being contemplated is within the legitimate set. Therefore, as far as instrumental justifications are concerned, we should not expect that any contrary second-order reasons remain once the required supermajority is achieved. In this light it is not surprising that this is exactly what we found in the case of the justifications considered so far. That leaves us to examine whether some justification of supermajority requirements that claims their intrinsic fairness produces some second-order reason for a constitution-making majority to refrain from acting on its view of the balance of first-order reasons in the matter.

What kinds of justifications are available for supermajoritarian practices that do not rely on their likely consequences, but rather on their intrinsic fairness? In order to get an answer, we need first to see first what intrinsic justifications of democracy in general are available. Intrinsic justifications of democratic procedures claim that quite apart from their likely outcomes, they are superior to their alternatives because they provide everyone who is subjected to them with an appropriate opportunity to influence the decisions that are made in them; furthermore, everyone has a reason to *see* that they have such opportunities, and therefore that they are publicly treated as equals.[14] Within this context, simple majority decisions are regarded as intrinsically fair because they (and only they) display a combination of properties that can be seen, if specific factual conditions are present, as necessary for equal treatment. First, simple majority decisions satisfy the requirement of *anonymity*, which means that the identity of the persons who cast the votes do not influence the decision: for any particular distribution of votes over the alternatives to be decided, any two voters could swap their vote and the outcome would still remain the same. In other words, simple majority rule does not give more weight to any vote just on the ground of the identity of the person who made it. Second, simple majority decisions satisfy the requirement of *symmetry*, i.e. they treat not only the voters but also the alternatives that are voted on alike. Any alternative, independent of its content, is chosen just in case it gets one vote more than the other (in binary choices). Therefore, no voter is disadvantaged even indirectly because of the content of his preference regarding the alternatives.[15]

Now, supermajoritarian practices depart from the requirement of symmetry and therefore privilege one alternative (the status quo) over the others.[16] This may be justified in terms of intrinsic fairness once one recognizes that simple majority rule treats every person fairly only under very restrictive and special assumptions. If every member of the

---

[14] An intrinsic justification of democracy along these lines is worked out in great detail by Christiano, *The Constitution of Equality*.

[15] See Goodin & List, "Special Majorities Rationalized."

[16] Indirect departures from anonymity are also common. For instance, federalist arrangements frequently give more weight to the votes cast in less populous jurisdictions, as in the U.S. Senate, where all states have the same number of seats, regardless of population size, or the German Bundesrat, where votes are allocated on the basis of a formula of regressive proportionality.

political community has an equal probability over her lifetime to be on the winning side of a vote as everyone else, and the votes in which she is on the winning side are on average not significantly less important for her than the ones in which she is on the losing side, then the simple majority rule distributes the benefits and burdens of collective decision-making roughly equally over all members.[17]

On the other hand, if there are persistent minorities in the community, so that some people are on the losing side of all votes, or all the votes that are really important for them, then the simple majority rule does not treat them as equals. Or, even in the absence of persistent minorities, if some decisions are so exceptionally important for some persons that being on the losing side in them would necessarily imply that they are treated unequally by the community regardless of the distribution of winning and losing over the other decisions, then again applying simple majority rule in such decisions violates the requirement of equal treatment. Such issues include individual choices regarding personal life plans, which are therefore usually protected by individual rights. The institution of individual rights essentially gives each individual a veto over collective decisions in such matters, thus technically requiring unanimity for any collective decision to be made in them. In sum, if there are persistent minorities in the community or if there are issues of such outstanding significance for individuals, then supermajoritarian practices are intrinsically justified as fair.[18]

Can this intrinsic justification of supermajority requirements give the party that controls the required majority a second-order reason not to act on its considered view of the balance of first-order reasons, given the special assumptions that were made about the choice? Recall that it was assumed that the party with the required supermajority is about to make a constitutional decision that is itself legitimate, i.e. it would not impose an unfair burden on anyone, nor would it introduce a decision rule that increases the future probability of unfair collective decisions. So if there are such intrinsic reasons for supermajority requirements that survive the existence of the required supermajority, then the reasons must be related not to how the decisions treat any of the mem-

[17] Kis, J. *Constitutional Democracy* (Budapest: Central European University Press, 2003), 71–74.

[18] Christiano, *The Constitution of Equality*, 288–299.

bers of the community, but to inherently procedural norms. Inherently procedural norms hold that certain ways of making a decision automatically disqualify the outcome, regardless of its content. One such family of inherently procedural norms is represented by rules designed to eliminate conflicts of interest, i.e. the possibility of an actor having a disproportionate impact on a decision in which he, together with some others, has some significant stake.

Such norms indeed may explain why a party with the required supermajority has decisive second-order reasons not to implement a constitutional change under the conditions discussed here.

Competition, Cooperation, and Second-order Reasons

In order to motivate this argument, it is useful to take a somewhat closer look at the kinds of matters that constitutions regulate, to see if something analogous to a conflict-of-interest strategy could be available here. It is usually understood that constitutions discharge two fundamental functions. First, they provide the ground rules of the governmental organization, making sure that the community has the institutions necessary for fair and effective collective self-governance, with the appropriate division of labor among the various organs of government. Second, they provide for a framework of fundamental rights as well as the means of effectively protecting them. As far as these functions are concerned, it is difficult to see how a conflict-of-interest argument may get a foothold to show that the party controlling the required supermajority should refrain from enacting a legitimate constitution.

However, constitutions do more than just regulate the governmental organization and provide for a scheme of basic rights and liberties. At least in modern democracies, they also outline a competitive political process that serves as the main vehicle of individual and collective political judgment-formation, of political accountability, and of filling in a variety of the most important offices of public authority. Moreover, the process of political competition is instrumental not only in the citizens' forming judgments about the performance of various political actors or the merits of different public policies, but it is also crucially involved in the development of their political self-understanding. The process of political competition is not exhausted by the electoral process, but comprises all the institutions and practices that structure the relations between those controlling the executive and legislative branches of government and those who are in the opposition, from parliamentary procedures to media practices and other mechanisms of political accountability. The practices of political competition are therefore central to the issues that are covered by the basic structures of constitutions.

There are two key points that must be kept in mind to understand the relevance of political competition for the argument that is being explored here. First, as with the other fundamental matters that are regulated by constitutions, the political ideal that all constitutions aspire to realize admits of several different legitimate ways of organizing the practices of political competition. Second, however, these different practices, legitimate though they are if viewed in the abstract, weigh the various concerns that are affected by the system of political competition—stability, responsiveness to voters' views, flexibility, decisive impact, and so on[19]—in different ways and thus distribute advantages and disadvantages among the various partisan competitors in divergent manners.

If there were a single feasible system of political competition that satisfies these disparate concerns to a perfect extent, then there would be no difficulty, since in that case this feasible system would be the only fully legitimate one and there would be only one fully legitimate manner of distributing the costs and benefits of competition between existing competitors. Since these concerns are systematically in tension with each other, however, there are several legitimate but imperfect systems of political competition that cater to the various interests of existing competitors to different degrees. There is only one way a scheme of competition may be perfect, but all imperfect schemes are imperfect in their own ways, and accordingly, they will inevitably advantage certain parties over others. The parties will therefore inevitably disagree about which legitimate but imperfect scheme to adopt.

---

[19] For different theories of political competition and the interests they serve, see Pildes, R. "The Theory of Political Competition," *Virginia Law Review* 85:8 (1999), 1605–1626, and Schleicher, D. "'Politics as Markets' Reconsidered: Natural Monopolies, Competitive Democratic Philosophy and Primary Ballot Access in American Elections," *Supreme Court Economic Review* 14 (2006), 1–26.

Now, if the choice of the scheme of political competition could be carried out behind a veil of ignorance, so that the parties do not know how their specific interests will be impacted, then it would be permissible for one competitor alone to pick the rules of the game. (But then this choice might be wholly underdetermined among the legitimate alternatives). However, this is of course never the case, as actually existing parties always have at least some ideas regarding how they would be affected under different rules. Therefore, in the absence of the possibility of choosing the rules under uncertainty, joint decision by the rival competitors appears to be the only acceptable option, since the partisan competitors deciding together ensures that no rival may alone pick that scheme from among the acceptable alternatives that advantages it alone at the expense of its rivals.[20]

Let us attempt to bring the insights of this analysis to bear on the problem under discussion. One party with the required supermajority comes to the conclusion that the balance of first-order reasons (under the specific historical circumstances) supports the replacement of the existing constitutional arrangement (with its scheme of political competition) with another legitimate arrangement, and that this can be done in a flawless procedure. However, despite the presence of the required majority and the validity of the reasons supporting the change, the other partisan competitors are not convinced and insist (perhaps foolishly) on keeping the existing arrangement. Given that different legitimate schemes allocate advantages and disadvantages in different ways, it will be impossible to put the suspicion to rest that the party with the supermajority acted simply to advance its own partisan advantage, even if all admit that the proposed arrangement is legitimate as far as its content is concerned. If the suspicion is widespread enough, it may hurt social trust in the political institutions, thereby weakening the conditions necessary for their adequate functioning. If the preceding analysis is correct, then the party with the supermajority has a decisive second-order reason based in a norm of procedural

[20] This is so only if, as in the problem discussed in this paper, there is already a legitimate alternative in place, and therefore there is no shortfall in legitimacy. If there is an illegitimate situation, then adopting a legitimate arrangement may be morally necessary even if joint decision by the rivals is not possible.

fairness not to implement the change unilaterally, even though this would be feasible given the institutional procedures. The supermajority requirement in this case expresses the underlying ideal of co-decision by the rivals, and the force of this ideal remains intact even if the required majority is obtained.

The analysis provided in the preceding paragraphs may be expanded by connecting it to a related observation about the functioning of political institutions. Political institutions and democratic ones in particular, require a degree of social confidence in their adequate functioning and capacity for self-correction. This trust is not self-sustaining, but is in fact continually sustained to varying degrees by the main political actors through their conduct. A paradox of democratic institutions is that vigorous, often confrontational political competition is indispensable for preserving the capacity of self-correction, and citizens must perceive the political process as competitive in order to sustain their belief in its potential for adequate functioning and achieving worthy collective goals. At the same time, while partisan competitors engage in robust confrontation *within* the existing political arrangement, they must cooperate with each other in *maintaining* the framework itself within which they compete. If they don't cooperate in sustaining the basic framework, and are not *seen* as cooperating to sustain it, then the suspicion will be irresistible that what the framework itself serves is not the common good but merely partisan advantage, and therefore the requisite public trust will erode. Thus, both competition and cooperation are necessary to preserve the adequate functioning of democratic institutions, and the public's confidence in them. Therefore, maintaining the necessary public trust requires that the partisan rivals act together in certain matters, or if joint action is not possible and the status quo is legitimate, that they refrain from acting.

Conclusion

The preceding analysis shows that political actors who are normally engaged in political competition and confrontation with each other within the rules of the constitutional arrangement have a joint responsibility to cooperate to sustain the arrangement itself. This responsibility means that whenever possible, they act together if some change becomes necessary to the constitutional fundamentals. If, on the other hand, even though there are adequate reasons supporting such change, but it is not strictly necessary, acting together represents such a constraint that precludes acting unilaterally on the reasons that support the change.

The supermajority requirements that apply to constitution-making may be seen in this regard as expressing the demand of joint action by the partisan rivals as a norm based in procedural fairness. The stipulated supermajority is specified in such a way so as to reasonably ensure joint action while at the same time not to make decision prohibitively costly. But such rules are only rough approximations of the ideal, and it is sometimes possible for the required supermajority to obtain even though there is disagreement among the main political actors about the desirability of the constitutional change. Whenever this is the case, the party with the supermajority has a second-order reason not to act on its view of what the balance of first-order reasons supports.

Adopting a whole new constitution is an act to which the requirement of partisan cooperation applies with special force. In light of the analysis presented in this paper, no partisan actor should act on its own in such matters if the others disagree, even if it enjoys the required special majority and is fully convinced of the rightness of its position.

II. HISTORY AND COMMUNITY

A Sacred Symbol in a Secular Country: The Holy Crown

SÁNDOR RADNÓTI

The Dignified Part of a Constitution

In his classic work, *The English Constitution*, Walter Bagehot differentiates between the efficient and dignified parts of the constitution. "Every constitution must first gain authority, and then use authority." The dignified part of the constitution "excites and preserves the reverence of the population," while the efficient part "works and rules."[1]

Bagehot was a conservative liberal, a "Whig" who understood the crown (the queen) and in part the aristocratic House of Lords as the dignified part of the constitution. Although the boundaries are fairly fluid, the efficient part—in Bagehot's interpretation—is predominantly embodied by the Lower House. The dignified leader of the state is the king/queen, the efficient leader is the prime minister. This is the apology of the English establishment in opposition to the American constitution. The precondition is that although the efficient part is modern and simple, the constitution must "contain likewise historical, complex, august, theatrical parts, which it has inherited from a long past."[2]

Bagehot's book used to be the manual of princes (the future George V had to read it, too), and even as late as the end of the last century it was put down that nothing had superseded *Bagehot's* views on the monarchy according to the Royal Encyclopedia.[3]

---

[1] Bagehot, W. *The English Constitution* (Boston: Little, Brown, and Company 1873, 2nd Edition), 44. My attention was directed at Bagehot's distinction in connection with the Holy Crown by György Bence. "Barátsággal váltunk el" [We parted in friendship], Philosopher György Bence on Fidesz, the nature of the political parties and the crown. *Népszabadság*, January 15, 2000, 19.

[2] Bagehot, *The English Constitution,* 47.

[3] See Taylor, J. A. *British Monarchy, English Church Establishment, and Civil Liberty* (Westport, Conn.: Greenwood Press, 1996), 123.

Notwithstanding the uniqueness of the English constitution it is convincing that every constitution must have a dignified foundation that can be accepted by the people. A constitution is the embodiment of the people's agreement. To quote the title of a constitution of 1647–49: *Agreement of the People*. But what is dignity? We must agree with Bagehot that it is more than a mere trinket or symbolic ornament hung on the constitution. In my view, it may stem from two independent sources. One is a long past or antiquity that issues from the stories of foundation and continuity of a historical nation, the other is the agreement of the people, a broad-scale consensus. Thus, the dignified part is divided into a past and a present component. (If not antiquity, durability does have a role in efficiency, as it creates calculable conditions.)

The founder of modern political conservatism Edmund Burke explained the significance of antiquity by claiming that a state is a partnership: "As the end of such a partnership cannot be obtained in many generations, it becomes a partnership not only between those who are living, but between those who are living, those who are dead, and those who are to be born."[4] This organic view of the joint undertaking of many—past, present and future—generations is modern insomuch that the prerogatives of the past ("of the dead") are not based on unalterable, a-historical and obligatory dogmas but on far weaker, more incidental and historical traditions. The past, present and future are no longer encompassed by a single common historical horizon.[5]

Obviously, even this interpretation of the past can be the basis for conflict, as Tom Paine's famous response to this conception proves: "Every age and generation must be as free to act for itself in all cases as the age and generations which preceded it. The vanity and presumption of governing beyond the grave is the most ridiculous and insolent of all tyrannies."[6]

The hidden conflict, however, need not necessarily emerge sharply between right-wing and left-wing, regressive and progressive models.

---

4 Burke, E. *Reflections on the French Revolution* (London: J. M. Dent & Sons Ltd., New York: E. P. Dutton & Co. Inc., 1951 [1910]), 93.

5 See Koselleck, R. "A kora újkor elmúlt jövője" [The past future of the early modern age] in Koselleck, *Elmúlt jövő. A történeti idők szemantikája* [The past future. A semantic of historical times] (Budapest: Atlantisz, 2003), 18.

6 Paine, T. "Rights of Men" in *The Great Works of Thomas Paine* (New York: D. M. Bennett Liberals and Scientific Publishing House, 1878.) Vol. II. 7.

The constitution is the basic law of the collective and political functioning of the state acknowledged by its citizens, and hence by definition it cannot be biased. If the aspect of the broad consensus of "the living" is considered, then we ought to have—logically—the *minimalism* of the present member and the *musealization* of the past member of the "dignified part."

Minimalism

The aim of the dignified part of the constitution must be to achieve the broadest possible agreement which is still meaningful; in modern secularized societies with a plurality of moral convictions, world-views, and interests this cannot be more than a minimum. Mention can be made of the rule of law, freedom, righteousness, equality, political pluralism, national sovereignty (Spain's constitution, 1978), unity, liberty, world peace and equal membership in united Europe (Germany's basic law, 1949/1990), self-determination of the people, liberty, equality and fraternity (France's constitution, 1958/2008), etc.

The classic preamble of the American constitution wishes to establish justice, insure domestic tranquility, provide common defense, promote general welfare and secure the blessings of liberty. It is actually astonishing that God is mentioned but once: in the date ("done… the Seventeenth Day of September in the Year of our Lord 1787"). The Declaration of Independence, written twelve years earlier, makes the point that the equality of people is God's creation, and the rights of man to life, freedom and happiness all derive from it. While there is consensus on the validity of these rights, we also realize that their source of origin has become musealized. That means to say that even those who doubt the divine origin of these values may appreciate them as respectable and acknowledge them as theirs on the basis of historical memory.

In the text of some 20th century constitutions, the *invocatio dei* has generated debates in the name of the freedom of thought, but it is precisely its museality that can justify it broadly, for everybody. For example, the first sentence of the preamble of the Swiss constitution—"In the name of God Almighty!"—refers to the starting words of the "Bundesbrief" confirming the allegiance of Schwyz, Uri and Unterwalden and repeated in several subsequent constitutional documents.

The solution in the Hungarian Fundamental Law is the quotation of the first line of the national anthem written in 1823 ("God bless the Hungarians") which has been sung by Hungarians of most diverse world views for over a century and a half at all festive occasions, without attempts by any movement to monopolize it. (True, in the closing formula of the preamble the phrase "our responsibility before God and man" is also included.)

Musealization

Even effective constitutions may get musealized on account of their antiquity, historic significance or identity-creating influence. The historical past of a constitution is a considerable value, but it may also be a source of tensions—between efficiency and dignity. This problem is solved in the American constitution through the practice of amendments and interpretation. The second oldest constitution in the world—Norway's, from 1814—has had several of its articles annulled over time, but as a good indication of the historicizing-musealizing tendency the numbering has been preserved: it has sections to which no text belongs any more. Section 2—itself a relic of earlier laws—is even more peculiar. The original text ran as follows: "The Evangelical-Lutheran religion shall remain the official religion of the State. The inhabitants professing it are bound to bring up their children in the same. The Jesuits and monastic orders are prohibited. Jews may not settle in the state." The ban on Jews was repealed in 1851, that of the monastic orders in 1897, while the prohibition of Jesuits was not cancelled until 1956. The first two sentences are still included in the constitution, but a preceding sentence more or less invalidates them: "All inhabitants of the Realm shall have the right to free exercise of their religion."

The musealization of traditions means the relaxation of their strict content and compelling force without a loss of dignity. The simile of the museum is illuminating because the musealization of objects implies both the shedding of their original functions and their revaluation. Getting into a museum means the polar opposite of devaluation; while the aim of an altarpiece is no longer to inspire devotion, it does not still exclude it. Respect for the work unites those who perceive it without imposing upon them a definite connotation or a certain direction of this respect.

The Hungarian crown implies several definitions (historical art work, accessory, jewel, badge, historical relic) on which everyone can agree. Undoubtedly, this consensus has little inflaming potential. There are other ideas about the sacral nature of the crown which may have great exciting potential but at the same time hopelessly divide those who perceive it (Catholic relic, pagan talisman, magic historical object). These ideas imply strong symbolical–theological, or political–theological connotations, some of which can be sharply differing, even incompatible, while others can be combined with each other: unity of the king and country, unity of Hungary or the one-time territories of Hungary, unity of the Hungarians against "foreigners," unity of Christian Hungarians as against non-religious people or Jews, unity of Catholic Hungarians against heretics, prerogatives of the nobility, ennobling effect of the faith in the crown, independence and continuity of the Hungarian state, source of legislation, and many other implications.

The sacral definition of the Hungarian crown tied to faith cannot become consensual, and attempts at syncretization disrupt tradition. The holy crown doctrine causes a fundamental split in tradition, for some of the great personages of Hungarian history arguing against archaic, corporate Hungary and serfdom or directly fighting for the republic (István Széchenyi, Sándor Petőfi, Bertalan Szemere) were mortal foes of this doctrine. It is however possible to have symbolic (but not sacral) interpretations of the crown which may inspire patriotic feelings as a material relic of Hungarian history.

The Visible and Invisible Crown

The crown as fiction was raised by Ernst H. Kantorowicz in his classic book, *The King's Two Bodies*. Baldus de Ubaldis (1332–1400) recalled that in days of yore the emperor in Rome had a material and visible crown, a diadem, and an invisible one that he had got from God. He concludes from this that the crown inherited by an heir from his father by hereditary right is also dual. What in Kantorowicz's view this means to say is the following: "There was a visible, material, exterior gold circle or diadem with which the Prince was vested and adorned at his coronation, and there was an invisible and immaterial Crown—encompassing all the royal rights and privileges indispensable for the government and the body politic—which was perpetual and descended either from God directly or by the right of inheritance. And of this visible Crown it may well be said: Corona non moritur."[7] Continuity is represented by the invisible crown.

Presumably, Hungary also had an invisible crown. The assumed name of our first crowned king—István: Stephanus—also means crown. In the 13th century the definition of *corona* by the chancellery was not "jewel used when transferring power, but the symbol of the exercise of state power,"[8] a symbol of monarchic might separated from the material crown. In the 14th century, it symbolized the territory of the state and the state as legal person.[9] Josef Karpat opined that in the 13th century the crown was a prevalent concept of political law yet its material form hardly occurred in the sources. It was named as *dyadema* in the latter sense.[10] The conspicuous insistence on the material crown began with the last offspring of the Árpád dynasty. From then on, continuity was represented by the material crown.

One may argue, of course, that the Hungarian crown is not only a royal insignia but also a relic. In connection with the French crown, which included a piece of Christ's wreath of thorns, Kantorowicz says: "It seems however, that in this case material and immaterial crowns were merged into another, and the borderline between the visible object of worship and the invisible idea was as hazy here as it was at once the visible holy relic of St. Stephen, Hungary's first Christian king, and the invisible symbol and lord paramount of the Hungarian monarchy."[11] That, however, is only partially satisfactory because the reliquary crowns could also be replaced, material sanctity could be

---

[7] Kantorowicz, E. H. *The King's Two Bodies. A Study in Medieval Political Theology* (Princeton, N.J.: Princeton Univerity Press, 1957), 337.

[8] Eckhart, F. *A Szentkorona-eszme története* [A history of the holy crown doctrine] (Budapest: Magyar Tudományos Akadémia, 1941), 44.

[9] Karpat, J. "Corona regni Hungariae im Zeitalter der Arpaden" [1937] in Hellmann, M. ed. *Corona regni. Studien über die Krone als Symbol des Staates im späteren Mittelalter* (Weimar: Hermann Böhlaus Nachf., 1971), 231.

[10] Ibid., 340.

[11] Kantorowicz, *The King's Two Bodies,* 339.

relativized. It is more important still that the relatively late reliquary crown of Saint Louis, the Sainte Couronne, is not analogous with St Stephen's Holy Crown: its legends do not include the definition that its character as reliquary was assumed via contact with the founding king. The analogies must be found more to the east.

From Percy Ernst Schramm's essays[12] one can make out a Western–Eastern Europe dividing line where continuity was represented by the invisible/immaterial crown—that is why the material crown could be given away or buried after a king's death, that is why a king could have more than one crown. In East and Central Europe—towards the end of the High Middle Ages and in the late Middle Ages—continuity was represented by the visible crown: the crown of the Holy Roman Emperor, the crown of Charlemagne (dated most probably to some time between 967–983; Charlemagne died in 814; the special veneration of the crown began at the turn of the 12th and 13th centuries), the crown of Saint Wenceslas of Bohemia (made, or at least transformed, more than 400 years after the saint's death, in 1345), the crown of Polish Boleslaw the Champion (venerated as a relic since 1320 as the crown of the coronation in 1025) and St. Stephen's crown (called holy from the second half of the 13th century) belong here. In France, the concept of invisible crown was introduced around 1150, in England during Henry I, more or less at the same time, but its complicated theology evolved in the late Middle Ages.

So it seems that the more sophisticated attitude with a distance from the material characteristics, the body of the regalia itself became distinct from a more barbarian attitude clinging to the material presence of the definite jewel, the latter being closely tied up with political uncertainty, the emergence of pretenders to the throne, the country's threatened survival. The more uncertain the power, the more materially present its tokens must be. When—as happened in the first five years of the 1300s—three prominent foreign gentlemen are crowned kings of Hungary (Charles Robert of Anjou, Wenceslas of Bohemia and Bavarian Otto Wittelsbach), it is not immaterial who is crowned with the "true" crown. "That was the moment," Pál Engel writes,

---

[12] See Schramm, P.E. mit Beiträgen verschiedener Verfasser: *Herrschaftszeichen und Staatssymbolik. Beiträge zu ihrer Geschichte vom dritten bis zum sechszehnten Jahrhundert* I–III. (Stuttgart: Anton Hiersemann, 1956).

"when the crown became a politically charged relic, and before long it was surrounded by an almost religious devotion and a mysterious idea of the state, the holy crown doctrine, became associated with it."[13]

The archaic and modern normal cases of keeping material crowns can clearly be differentiated. The archaic place of the crown is a sacral space or treasury locked away from the common people or the outsiders, while the modern place of a crown is a museum or historic site functioning as a museum. The turbulent history of the Hungarian crown begins with vicissitudes being tossed from treasury to treasury in Székesfehérvár, Visegrád, Buda, Esztergom, Vienna, Prague, Eger and Pozsony.[14] The adventures it underwent include cases of—Hungarian, Czech, Austrian, Turkish, American—alienation (theft, custody, pawning, etc.), loss, burial underground. For some time in 1944 it was kept in a coal cellar in Budapest. After the world war it was kept in Fort Knox, where the American federal gold reserves are stored, locked away from the public. Its return on January 6, 1978 was preceded by complicated diplomatic negotiations, and the optimal solution—placing it in the National Museum—was only slow to crystallize.

The Holy Crown Doctrine

In the 16th century, István Werbőczy retrospectively codified the "crown of the nobles" tying the medieval organological idea of the body of the state with the crown in his work *Tripartitium,* which was a de facto law-book until 1848.[15] To confront two slightly deviant interpretations of his teaching: "the king and the nobleman are somehow

[13] Engel, P. *Beilleszkedés Európába, a kezdetektől 1440-ig* [Adaptation to Europe, from the beginnings to 1440] (Budapest: Háttér, 1990), 264.

[14] The most recent summary of the coronations of Hungarian kings and preservation of the crown is given by Endre Tóth, in Tóth, E. and K. Szelényi, *A magyar Szent Korona. Királyok és koronázások* [The Hungarian Holy Crown. Kings and coronations] (Budapest: Kossuth, 2002), 69ff.

[15] See "The Customary Law of the Renowned Kingdom of Hungary: A Work in Three Parts Rendered by Stephen Werbőczy (The 'Tripartitum')" in *The Laws of the Medieval Kingdom in Hungary* Vol. 5, trans. and eds. Bak, J.M. and P. Banyó and M. Rady, (Idyllwild, CA: Charles Schlacks, Jr. and Budapest: Central European University Press, 2008).

united in the Holy Crown and the noblemen are equal, that is the peculiar aristocratic democracy,"[16] and "the crown is the symbol of the community of nobles, its members are the noblemen and as non-nobles are excluded, so is the king rather a passive contributor to the working of the noblemen's communitas originally possessing the Holy Crown."[17] Werbőczy's concept of the Holy Crown was the legal source against despotic rulers, in place of powerless kings, and during the frequent periods of interregnum. It was a pragmatic counterweight to the dynastic ambitions of non-Hungarian kings, the legal foundation of the incessantly repeatable free election of kings.

The holy crown doctrine began to assume a political and constitutional role towards the end of the 18th century, uniting the ideas of the nobility's resistance to enlightened absolutism. This was the period when the modernizing reforms and the independence of Hungary became the two poles. The holy crown doctrine became a contributory factor to the new Hungarian catastrophe which is usually described as the conflict between independence and progress, "this tendency culminated in Joseph II, who upturned the status quo radically, had no respect for national character and the achievements of historical development, and wished to bestow upon Hungary the benefits of a providential state caring for the welfare of all its subjects equally."[18]

When as a result of the reshuffling of the roles, the ruler became ultraconservative and the Hungarian noblemen (and middle-class citizens) became reformists, and a rare opportunity arose for patriotism (national independence) and progress (modernization) to reconcile—that was the most fascinating period of Hungarian history, the Age of Reforms—the timeliness of Werbőczy decreased and the veneration of the crown was encouraged in protection of the Throne and the Altar by the court. The holy crown doctrine of the Tripartitum cannot have been popular among our great national politicians who wanted to lift and enfranchise the millions of the peasantry, who fought for political equality. Membership of the Holy Crown was a partition wall

16 Eckhart, F. *A Szentkorona-eszme története,* 290.

17 Hóman, B. and Gy. Szekfű. *Magyar történet* [A History of Hungary] Vol. II. (Budapest: Királyi Magyar Egyetemi Nyomda, 1936), 590.

18 Grünwald, B. *A régi Magyarország 1711-1825* [Old Hungary 1711–1825] (Budapest: Osiris, 2001), 48.

between nobles and serfs. It was not a whimsical statement but one of inner conviction when count István Széchenyi noted almost sarcastically at the time of writing *Stadium* that the Hungarian nobleman was not the real owner of his land: "The great honour that I am a member of the Holy Crown or a piece of Saint Stephen's robe—is neither *de facto physice* nor *moraliter* true, whereas I am no owner, but simply user—*usufructarius*."[19]

The construction of corporate political law, the holy crown doctrine became topical in the latter half of the 19th and especially the first half of the 20th century. Josef Karpat is right in saying that the euphemistic stylization of the holy crown doctrine by the Hungarian law historians was in relation to romantic historicism and romantic nationalism.[20] What they declared to be an ancient Hungarian idea was mostly the intellectual creation of late 19th–early 20th century legal historicism. However, the teachings of Győző Concha, Imre Hajnik, Ákos Timon and other law historians would never have won the prestige of official ideology, had it not been useful for the daily political developments.

We may track down the possibility of actualization if we return to the two kinds of interpretation of the holy crown doctrine cited above. The idea of political power shared by the king and the nation could be revived by the consolidation of the Austro-Hungarian Compromise of 1867. With the help of the doctrine the requirement that the integrity of historical Hungary be preserved and "the territory belonging under the scepter of the common ruler as Hungarian king be separated from the area ruled in his capacity of Austrian emperor; in other words, no part of Hungary should become or remain in foreign constitutional relation."[21]

The Holy Crown conceived of as the symbol of the noblemen's community "eventually allows for a kingdom without a king."[22] This historistic postulation was a godsend to Miklós Horthy's kingdom without a king (1920–1944), since the restoration of the monarchy or a free election of a king were out of the question, and neither could a

[19] Eckhart, *A Szentkorona-eszme története,* 294.

[20] Karpat, J. "Die idee der heilegen Krone Ungarns in neuer Beleuchtung" (1943-44) in Hellmann, M. ed. *Corona regni*, 349.

[21] Eckhart, *A Szentkorona-eszme története,* 282.

[22] Hóman & Szekfű, *Magyar történet,* 590.

republic be proclaimed since it defined itself in opposition to the short-lived republic which was established after the so-called "revolution of asters" (1918). After the resolutions of the Trianon peace pact divided the country's territory, "the unity of state and the body of the nation" had revisionist significance. Nor can the actualization of the lines be overlooked: "there stood the great symbol of nation and state visible from afar, the Holy Crown which incorporated all enfranchised persons and which was, and could rightly be, believed by every nobleman, every member of the populus Werbőczyanus, to be each one's own property as well."[23]

The holy crown doctrine, which placed the mystic "membership" ahead of the idea of constitutional patriotism[24] and citizenship, which extended its frontiers far beyond the political borders of the state with reference to *irredenta* based on historical law, and which, on the other side, selectively and arbitrarily ranged the people within the borders into nobles ("Hungarians") who could partake of the membership and into ignoble ("non-Hungarians") excluded from it, entailed peculiar consequences as to the Holy Crown as an object. On the one hand, it became the target of overheated, fetishistic worship in which Catholicism of a baroque flavor mixed inorganically with pagan idolatry.[25] It was looked upon as a sort of lucky charm, its image was the most widespread symbol of the Horthy era. On the other hand, the medieval idea went together with the medieval storage of the object: locked up, invisible. The regalia were inaccessible not only to the public but also to scholars. That is absolutely logical: if the unbroken continuity and the fiction of belonging to the absolute present are to be upkept, the critical spirit of scholarship must be kept away. If the selective and initiating character of the mystery is to be preserved, equality-promoting publicity must be shut out, and visibility must be privileged and/or ritualized.

[23] Ibid., 591.

[24] See e.g. Müller, J-W. *Constitutional Patriotism* (Princeton, NJ.: Princeton University Press, 2007).

[25] On the "fully 'pagan' charismatic experience" of the holy crown doctrine perfectly alien to Christianity, see Rugási, Gy. "Szellemképek. Töredékek a közelmúlt vallástörténetéből" [Apparitions. Fragments from the religious history of the recent past] *Holmi* 11 (2000), 1338.

Modernization of the Crown

Scientific aspect

Modernization means, on the one hand, that the crown becomes the subject of scientific examination, and on the other, as a work of art—viewed both scientifically and relished as a source of delight—it ceases to be untouchable, questions can be put and doubts can be formulated about it. Besides, the need of the visibility of the crown, its public display and permanent exhibition also arises.

The decision to place the crown jewels in the National Museum after their return from America in 1978 solved the question of publicity and researchability for twenty-two years. The regalia had found their adequate modern place. Instead of crown guards and their corps, a scientific crown committee was established. The decision was not to the credit of the political phronesis of the "existing socialist" system, nor to that of the party who returned it. The joint communiqué of the two governments merely spelled out that the Hungarian party "shall exhibit the crown and the crown jewels in Budapest permanently in an adequate historical place so that the country's population, Hungarians living abroad and foreigners can all see it."[26] In the tension between the desire to expropriate the cultural memory and the fear of the connotations of the Holy Crown still living vividly in communicative memory, Hungarian decision-makers were forced to make a comparatively wise decision. It was only comparatively wise because while they converted the stateroom of the museum into a sort of sanctuary, they tried to belittle and neutralize the crown with the "museum item" label.

At the same time, they satisfied both the modern preconditions of visibility and the selection of the right historical place. It is a specific problem of the Hungarian crown jewels that they have no traditional place that is visible or could be rendered visible. Some of the similar historical relics are preserved in museums (e.g., the Louvre, the German National Museum in Nuremberg) and some others are stored in historical venues that have been musealized themselves. Such are—to

[26] Cited in Gant, T. *A Szent Korona amerikai kalandja 1945–1978* [The American adventure of the Holy Crown] (Debrecen: Kossuth Egyetemi Kiadó 1997), 107.

mention the two most important ones—the Schatzkammer in Vienna and the Tower in London. The Danish regalia are preserved in the treasury of Rosenborg Castle. The place with the greatest past is of course the Tower of London: the (changing) set of crown jewels has been preserved there since 1303. All these places are public like museums or gradually became museums. Those visiting the Tower were allowed to see the crown jewels in the 18th century. King of Denmark Frederick VII made his treasury in Rosenborg public in 1859. The Czech regalia is the only major set of crown insignia which is invisible to this day—it was only put on display eight times in the 20th century—and access to them is ritualized: they can only be opened in the crown hall of Prague Castle in the presence of the president of the state, the prime minister, the archbishop of Prague, the president of the chamber of deputies, the president of the senate, the head of the cathedral chapter of St. Vitus church, and the lord mayor of Prague.

Since no place has survived in Hungary that could historically be connected to the crown, it was quite correct to place it in a museum, which is not only suitable on account of the profile of its collections—Hungarian historical remains—but it is one of the major Hungarian historical monuments itself. The Hungarian National Museum (and library) is the manifestation of a crystal-clear idea from the Age of Reform, which was realized along side the early Modern European trend of founding museums and organizations. It was started with generous patriotic donations (first of all by the founder, Count Ferenc Széchényi in 1802) and from squeezed-out state patronage, and pursued a high level of scholarship, in pursuit of egalitarian cultural goals and at the same time eminent national interests. Mihály Pollack's building, erected in 1837–47, is in a dry but inspired neo-classical style. Similarly to other museum buildings of the age—Smike's British Museum, Schinkel's Altes Museum (Berlin), von Klenze's Glyptothek (Munich) or William Wilkins' National Gallery (London)—Pollack reinterpreted the Greek temple for a temple of culture. It is part and outstanding example of the set of urban stylistic signs which made the museums in the towns of Europe, America and Australia recognizable over the 19th century.

As soon as it was built, the National Museum became the site of a crucial event in Hungarian history, the public meeting on March 15, 1848. There is a legend also associated with the event: that Sándor

Petőfi recited his *National Song* (one of the best-known patriotic poems in Hungary) standing on the sidewall of the stairs. The real historical event tied to the venue is no less significant: the insurgents approved of the 12 points here, including these three demands: "equality before the law as to religion and human rights," "sharing of burdens by all," and "abolition of corvée." With these (and their implementation by law) Hungary became the homeland of all its citizens, the privileges of the membership of the Holy Crown, the *populus Werbőczyanus*, was put to an end. Prerogatives were replaced by equal rights.

The National Museum was an optimal place for the preservation of the Hungarian regalia in a triple sense: 1) by its function, cultural-historical and political-historical symbolism, 2) as a museum, as one of the finest relics of Hungarian culture, and 3) as an important memorial of the transformation from corporate Hungary to the Hungary of all its citizens it could receive the art object—one of the most important artistic and historical relics of early Hungarian history, the symbol of old Hungary—in an objective and reconciliatory manner.

True, the reconciliation of the republic with its historical precedent, the kingdom, via peace-creating remembrance could of course only become topical after the change of systems in 1989–90 in the name of the new historical self-interpretation and tradition-creation. Nevertheless, the crown's museum career, though begun late, had its positive results: the crown jewels were visible and ready to be investigated.

Political aspect

The other important tradition of the modernization of the Hungarian crown is of a political character. After the defeat in the 1848–49 war of liberation, prime minister and minister of the interior Bertalan Szemere had to choose the crown's future. He had it buried near Orsova while he deliberated three possible ways forward: destroying the crown; putting it up as the subject of an undefined political bargain; or musealization. It speaks for Szemere's elevated character that the fourth customary possibility of a revolution—the sale of the precious metal and the gems—did not tempt him.

The annihilation of the regalia is a typical republican revolutionary act. In 1649 Cromwell issued the order to crush the English crown jewels for symbolizing the "heinous reign of kings"; most of the crown jewels on display in the Tower today were made upon Charles II's order for his coronation in 1661, during the restoration. On July 31, 1793, Bertrand de Barère recommended the annihilation of "the frightful souvenirs of the former kings."[27] Corollarily to the revolutionary events, the royal tombs at St. Denis' were ravaged, and together with several other regalia including Bourbon crowns, the crown of St. Louis and another old crown associated with Charles the Great—Couronne de Charlemagne—also perished.[28] This line of tradition was followed by Szemere when he thought of annihilation, which he discarded, understanding the crown as a "historical souvenir."

Prior to the burial, a sacrilegious thing happened which however fitted well the protestant and republican tradition: as his memoirs reveal, Szemere tried on the crown. "Having heard once that [King] Ferdinand [V] could hardly wear it on his head for its weight, I put it on my head and became convinced that this headgear was not meant for a human head. I have faith in God that crowns will soon go out of fashion."[29] Crowns may get on unauthorized heads for two reasons: someone flirts with the possible role of the "false monarch," or he declares everybody's incompetency. A classic example of the former is Napoleon, who seriously considered having himself crowned with the Reichskrone, the crown of the Holy Roman Empire. Since it was inaccessible to him (it was rescued from Nurnberg, where it had been kept since the times of Sigismund of Luxemburg, king of Hungary and Holy Roman Emperor, through Regensburg to Vienna to be saved from the French, and it can still be seen there), he decided upon another historicist reference:

---

[27] See Twining, Lord E. *A History of the Crown Jewels of Europe* (London: B. T. Batsford, 1960), xxxii and 261. See also McClellan, A. *Inventing the Louvre. Art, Politics, and the Origins of the Modern Museum in Eighteenth Century Paris* (Cambridge: Cambridge University Press, 1994), 158.

[28] Not only revolutionary vandalism but also the tradition of museal preservation is in connection with the French Revolution. A few days after the destruction of the royal graves, on August 10, 1793, the former royal castle—the Louvre—opened its gates as a public museum and in Louis XIV's Apollon gallery several (surviving) crowns were also put on display in celebration of the fall of despotism. See Duncan, C. *Civilising rituals inside public art museums* (London and New York: Routledge, 1995), 22.

[29] Szemere, B. *Naplóm* [My diary] Vol. I. (Pest: Ráth Mór, 1869), 198.

instead of the crown attributed to Charlemagne and passed down materially, he crowned himself emperor in 1804, in the presence of Pope Pius VII, with the symbolically inherited (and materially remade) crown of the Roman emperors, the golden wreath of laurels.

The other option—that no one, or everyone, has authority to wear the crown, this full-blooded democratic carnival of idol shattering—has its latter-day descendant: in the art shop of the Viennese Treasury anyone can buy a cardboard copy of the Reichskrone fitting his or her head and, turning the viewing of the holy relic into a festival of fools, all can enter the street with crowned heads. Szemere's trying on the crown reveals the same as the poems of the great Hungarian republican poet, Sándor Petőfi: "There is no beloved king any more!" "The crown is very expensive, / It doesn't become a king. / A king! what's a velvet saddle good for / on an ass? / Long live, / Long live the republic!"

The legitimate place of the crown in a republic was first worded by Szemere: "I wish I had shattered it, I had the power to do so, yet I thought, if it was no subject of bargaining, so when we had won, which I still thought certain, it would be good for the national museum," he wrote in his diary entry for September–October 1853, in response to the fact that the Habsburg authorities found the cache on September 8.[30]

The Contemporary Status of the Crown

No matter what the scientific or political analysis of the symbolic contents of the crown alive or resuscitated in connection with the holy crown doctrine, there are people who believe in them, and therefore most of these meanings demand respect. If there are—as there are—foolish, harmful and even dangerous implications in it, their representation cannot be hindered under the freedom of thought and speech.

[30] Ibid., 205. It is to be noted that the recovery of the crown also inspired another important writing, a satire, a part of Count István Széchenyi's *Ein Blick* entitled "The circus about the crown" in *Széchenyi István válogatott művei* [István Széchenyi's selected works] Vol. II. (Budapest: Szépirodalmi, 1991), 713.

Art object

First of all, the crown is an art object, "an object of artistic value." It belongs to the group of art works that were made as decorated artifacts for use. Its being an artifact no longer belongs to its current status, but its implications for use must be known if we want to understand it as an art work. In this sense, the crown is an accessory of coronation, exercise of power, ceremony. Its ornament is not external, as it is a headdress and as such, it is a jewel. Being an accessory of the exercise of power, it is a badge of royal power. Also, it is a historical art object, which was made long ago and preserves, though refuses to fully expose, the stylistic history or histories of its genesis. It has an extraordinary historical role that is normally missing from art objects, as most of them live their own history. That is what causes the difficulty in the research history of the Hungarian crown: "it is impossible to consistently separate the historical and art historical-archeological problems."[31] In such cases we can speak of historical souvenirs—in a slightly outdated sense which identifies the memorable acts of the past tied mostly to historic personages (wars, ruler changes, emergence and demise of states, etc.).

There is therefore a set of definitions—historical artwork, accessory, jewel, badge, historical souvenir—which describe the real status of the crown and about which, in my view, everyone can agree. All can agree, but not all rest content with that, since it is an objective and not emotional approach.

Symbol

The crown also has a fervent symbolical status employing strong commitment, also having different definitions, but at this point no consensus can be expected. The crown is a Christian (catholic) relic on account of its physical contact with the confessor founding king, and as such, it is the symbol of Christianity and Christian Hungarians. The crown is a pagan charm, a magic symbol of the survival of the Hungarians. It is a historical relic, a historical souvenir venerated as sacred which has

[31] Von Bogyay, T. "Über die Forschungsgeschichte der heiligen Krone" in *Insignia regni Hungariae I*, 66.

strong symbolic—theological and political theological—connotations in connection with the state, the nation and Christianity. These are often sharply contrasted, often blendable and often incompatible connotations: the unity of king and country, unity of Hungary and the former territories of Hungary, unity of Hungarians versus "foreigners," unity of Christian Hungarians versus heretics, faith in the nobility's prerogatives, the ennobling selection of the crown, the independence and continuity of the Hungarian state, a source of law, and so on and so forth. These definitions derive from various strata of tradition and differ even on the basis of the religious belief. An attempt to syncretize them may lead to the breakup of tradition, to featuring new customs as ancient. To refer back to Walter Bagehot's differentiation between the effective and dignified parts of a constitution, the trouble with the forced innovations of tradition is that they are so little dignified.

Historical souvenir

Between the "fervent" and necessarily impatient symbolic status and the real status that appears cold from the former viewpoint there may be a third as well, the one that associates warm feelings to the crown as a historical souvenir and a highly generalized symbol that can be verbalized somehow like this: this object was witness to the history—with its disasters and successes, disgraces and glories—to which I am heir and participant. Since this is a feeling, notably the national feeling, it is not something that can be made compulsory, nor can there be consensus about it, and it is not even declarable that it is the unfailing criterion of Hungarian patriotism, since quite a lot of the greatest Hungarian patriots spared few words for the Holy Crown, or if they did, they sometimes did it sarcastically.

Re-sacralization of the Crown

Museums do not always satisfy those who ascribe sacrality to an art object. Once, however, an object became incorporated in a museum context, it can only be torn from it and re-sacralized quite arbitrarily. The most powerful and alarming example of removing objects from the museum context, re-sacralizing and re-symbolizing them took place after the Anschluss when the imperial insignia preserved in the Vienna Treasury were moved back to Nuremberg to validate the town's right granted to it by Sigismund. The imperial insignia were meant to signify that the Third Reich preserved and restored the continuity with the medieval empire. "Creditable testimonies revealed that the most expressive insignia—centered round the imperial crown—were planned to be exhibited on the imperial party precincts, in the staircase of the congress building of the NSDAP, at least temporarily, for the period of party congresses."[32] The Americans found them in Nuremberg and unlike the Hungarian crown, they returned them: they have been on display in the treasury of Vienna since 1954.

When in the 1980s a German museum of history was being planned in West Berlin, it was raised in the project debate to exhibit in the new museum a replica of the imperial crown. The idea, rooted partly in the typically 19th century museum differentiation between objects of esthetic value and objects of historic value, and partly in the exaggerated need for all-round museum presentation for education purposes, triggered off a polemic. In this debate, it was correctly argued that the defects of a museum might also have historical meaning, just as the whereabouts of an important object has.

In the second half of the 20th century the efforts at re-sacralization usually went together with restitution demands. The restoration of the former proprietary rights, of the original status became the most pressing problem of museum policy. Not that it was unknown earlier: the extensive seizure of art works by Napoleon forced the Vienna Congress to decide on some regulation. After World War II this process was precipitated by the German and Soviet art thefts, the state requisitioning of art works in the socialist global empire, the bills presented by the liberated colonies. The restitutive demands often have strong emotional motives, and only a subcategory of the claims implies religious, national, or tribal type re-sacralization.

The sacred stone of the Scots, the "Stone of Scone" was returned by England to Scotland in 1996, after 700 years. This hardly wrought heavy sandstone slab was the seat of the Scottish kings; after seizing it, the English had a gothic throne of oakwood incorporating the stone

---

32 Fillitz, H. *Die Schatzkammer in Wien. Symbole abendländischen Kaisertums* (Salzburg und Wien: Residenz, 1986), 13.

made in honor of it, and the kings of England were crowned on it, including the last.[33] The throne was a strong political symbol: signifying the annexation of Scotland. It was also a reliquary, since legend has it that Jacob leant his head against it when he saw his dream of the ladder, and awakening, he made a memorial pillar out of it.[34] The national symbolism of the stone has been kept alive; in 1950 Scottish nationalist students even managed to steal it for some months. Its return now was a political gesture, with the aim of influencing the outcome of the first elections held for the restored Scottish parliament. A debate flared up about where to place it: instead of the ancient locality Scone, ardently advocated by some, it was placed in the throne room of Edinburgh Castle next to the Scottish crown jewels, the *Honours of Scotland*, which have been on public display since 1819.[35]

The specific situation here is that the unity of an historical art object was disrupted, the historical souvenir of great emotional and symbolical value which is not an art object was removed from the "holder" of significant artistic and historical value and returned in what was a symbolic gesture to the nation which considers it as the mythological token of its fate by tradition; there it was placed under museum circumstances and exhibited.

Act I of 2000

The Parliament passed Act I of 2000 *on Commemoration of Saint Stephen's State Foundation and the Holy Crown* during the first premiership of Viktor Orbán. As its preamble states, "the Holy Crown is a relic embodying the continuity and independence of the Hungarian state in the nation's mind and in the Hungarian political tradition. On the 1000th anniversary of the foundation of the state Hungary elevates the Holy Crown to a due place, removing it from the nation's museum

---

[33] Schramm, P.E. "Geschichte des Throns in England und Schottland" in Schramm, *Kaiser Königen und Päpste. Gesammelte Aufsätze zur Geschichte des Mittelalters* IV, 1. (Stuttgart: Anton Hiersemann, 1970), 274ff.

[34] Genesis 29, 10–22.

[35] From a nationalist perspective see Hamilton, I.R. *The Taking of the Stone of Destiny* (Moffat: Lochar Publishing, 1991). See also Keating, M. *The Independence of Scotland, Self-Government and the Shifting Politics of Union* (Oxford: Oxford University Press, 2009).

and putting it under the aegis of the Parliament representing the nation." Article 2(2) spells out that "the Holy Crown and the belonging insignia except for the coronation mantle are to be kept in the building of the Parliament." According to section 3, "the Holy Crown and the belonging insignia can be viewed by anyone according to the visiting rules of the building in which they are preserved."

The act was preceded by a social and parliamentary debate which had no result, thus the act reflects no consensus but some compromise. The protagonist of the dispute was the question of the site, and this time the conservatives wanted to innovate, the anti-conservatives wanted to conserve the status quo. The modern position (retaining the museum preservation) confronted the historicist position which was divided at first. The media raised the idea of placing the objects into church custody, into the Matthias Church in Buda castle. The idea to house it in the royal palace of Buda held its ground for quite some time—with a keener sense of history than his colleagues, deputy Miklós Csapody (Hungarian Democratic Forum) adhered to this idea to the end, looking upon the parliamentary display as temporary.

Eventually, the transfer to the Parliament won. None of the recommended new places were based on firm and convincing tradition, while the idea of the Parliament rested on no tradition whatsoever. The final voting showed a divided parliament: the proposition of Tamás Bauer (Alliance of Free Democrats) supporting the original—museum—preservation was turned down by 60 percent of the votes, which is by no means a convincing majority in case of a "commemorative act." Much of the discussion featured the modernized revitalization of the holy crown doctrine: the symbolic significance of the regalia was metaphorically established in this way. Although formally the act was not meant to resuscitate this doctrine and did not ascribe the crown legal personality or a constitutional role, this interpretation was activated in the symbolical space, as the dispute clearly demonstrated.[36]

---

[36] Decision 26/2000. (VII. 6.) of the Constitutional Court rejected—in my view mistakenly—the motion which emphasized that the legal status of the crown could only be changed by a two-thirds majority. In its justification it differentiated the crown in the coat of arms from the crown as an object being a property of the state. The latter, it argued, had no constitutional function and therefore the proprietary state could decide about its place with a simple majority.

Since no reference to the tradition of the locality could be made in support of the historicist suggestion, since no historical grievance could be seen as redressed by the new location, the reasons given remained highly abstract. "Why did we choose the building of the Parliament for the place of the Holy Crown? Because the parliament embodies sovereignty, and the crown stand for the foundation and continuity of the Hungarian state," Ibolya Dávid, Justice Minister (Hungarian Democratic Forum) said. "The Holy Crown... symbolizes Hungarian statehood, hence it is not a museum item and its most appropriate place is indeed here in the Parliament," said László Salamon (Fidesz). Surprisingly enough, the motif of creating a tradition did not occur.

While focusing on criticizing the symbolical contents of the bill, the opposition mobilized adequate professional—museological—arguments against the transfer and expressed their worries that the visibility of the crown jewels would thereby be limited. The MP's of the opposition (led by Tamás Bauer, Iván Pető and György Wiener) failed to adduce the argument that one of the functions of the parliamentary display of the crown was to decrease and relativize the importance of the National Assembly. One of the fundamental elements of the Crown's historical symbolism still preserved by communicative memory (e.g., in the form of law courts passing judgment in the name of the Holy Crown)[37]—the Holy Crown as the source of law—is in contradiction with the modern symbolism of the parliament—popular sovereignty as the source of law.

The pragmatic aim of pressing for the codification of the noble romantic nationalist conception of history certainly represented by a few deputies with inner conviction in a festive, commemorative act was demonstrated by the irreconcilable division in a politically insignificant question (what the crown symbolizes and where to keep it). Several pro-government deputies "blurted it out" in the heat of dispute, and the spokesman of the extreme right István Csurka downright declared: "now secularization, liberalism is waging a desperate battle with faith, a Hungarian identity and a sense of history."

---

[37] Under Act 1930:34 the courts passed judgment in the name of the Holy Crown and not the Hungarian state. Eckhart, *A Szentkorona-eszme története,* 265.

The removal of the crown from its museum context which was created at long last, and its placement in a representative and commemorative setting ill suited for both thorough study and taking delight in it as an art work is by no means a return to some good old tradition, but is an arbitrary innovation. The banal conclusion can be drawn from the scientific history of the Hungarian crown that the deeply anti-traditionalist, forceful resuscitation or historicist construction of the tradition of the crown as a symbol of the adoption of Christianity or the body politic, that is, the revival of its theological or political sacrality has always hindered unbiased scientific examinations.

In typical foreign examples re-sacralization went together with restitution, whereas this is not the case with the Hungarian crown. The restitution of the crown was its return by the United States. The need for its re-sacralization appeared independently of it and resulted in a clumsy solution: torn from its museum context it was put in a place which is not verified by any tradition, while conversely, it does not fulfill the three fundamental tasks of a museum: preservation, researchability and presentation. The museum is the place where (in theory) the visitor who reveres an object as sacred can peacefully coexist with one who does not.

The Hungarian case is unparalleled: I do not know of a single analogy in the civilized world to a significant historical souvenir and exceptionally valuable art work being re-sacralized out of pragmatic political considerations so that it is removed from its museum context, "to be put under the aegis of the Parliament representing the nation, removed from the museum of the nation."

The Crown in the Fundamental Law

The place of the crown is in the museum—but is it justified to mention the crown in the constitution? Musealization means disideologization and desacralization of the tradition. The musealized object does not impose claims from the past upon the living but it fills them with respectable memories. Of course, conflicts may occur in a real museum, too. The idol of a tribe as a museum object may be painful for members of the tribe who may demand restitution to be able to perform the procedures of re-sacralization. After all, the Hungarian crown is no longer in the National Museum, although the Hungarian society is not a homogeneous tribe but a heterogeneous secular society. Since the art work itself couldn't escape being undeservedly dragged around and in 2000 the "commemorative act" defined its new place, it is obvious that the concept of the crown would be even more controversial about which even less agreement can be expected.

The legislators writing the constitution made attempts at some minimalization by reducing the number of words in the preamble from that of Act I of 2000: "We honor the achievements of our historical constitution and we honor the Holy Crown, which embodies the constitutional continuity of Hungary's statehood and the unity of the nation." That, however, immediately incurred the rightful criticism that the crown might not symbolize, let alone embody the non-existing constitutional continuity of the Hungarian state, while on the other side the only other party that took part in the process of creating a new constitution—the extreme right—was quick to announce that the content was insufficient as it would have to be based on the holy crown doctrine. Too much on one side—too little on the other.

Of course, it would be quite different if Hungary had an old constitution continuously kept in effect, in which the crown could also be an honorable historic relic. The Holy Crown would belong to the dignified historical part of that constitution. But in the new constitution its function is to make up for the lack of a constitutional continuity. Falsifying history, this *restitutio in integrum* is not reconciliatory but upsetting because it makes a provocative parade of archaic, corporate, gentry Hungary. In that Hungary, there was no "equality before the law as regards religion and human rights" as compared to the laws of 1848, and Werbőczy's aristocratic democracy was the symbol of feudal inequality. Since in other parts of the new constitution the rights are offset by or emphatically conditional on obligations, this entails the chance to differentiate the more equal and the less equal, thereby reproducing the inequality implied by the membership of the Holy Crown, even if this inequality may depend on merit and not on descent. And that is but a single sentence of the unusually verbose—thirty sentences long—preamble re-baptized National Avowal heading the new constitution. But, *pars pro toto*.

The dignified part of a constitution is usually and mainly contained by the preamble of a written constitution. Already the new name of the preamble precludes that the new Hungarian constitution could be dignified, for the members of a modern secularized society cannot be united by any National Avowal. The new constitution adopts Burke's formula on which modern political conservatism is based: "Our Fundamental Law shall be the basis of our legal order: it shall be a covenant among Hungarians past, present and future"—but when this is reinforced with an avowal, it deprives Burke's thought of its modernity by re-dogmatizing the tradition.

It blabbers and rants about the past and as for the present, it does not seek as wide a constitutional consensus as possible but resembles an agitating, homogenizing, activist pledge that excludes those who think differently. Instead of pluralism it is based on—and mainly aims at—a sort of monolithism; national consensus in this sense means that "individual freedom can only be unfolded through cooperation with others." It gives up the ideological neutrality of the state. The normative way of life it formulates is such that "the family and the nation provide the most important framework of our coexistence, and that our fundamental cohesive values are fidelity, faith and love," and the constitution "expresses the nation's will and the form in which we wish to live."

Nevertheless, it is not the easily reconstructed anti-liberal, meritocratic, anti-egalitarian, Christian-national, nationalistic ideology that is important about this constitution, an ideology does not apply to the entire nation while at the same time it stretches beyond it (naming the "members of the Hungarian nation" as its subjects and not the citizens of the state).[38] The most important aspect is its voluntarist aggressiveness that alone obliterates conservative elevation and degrades ideology into power arrogance.[39] It cannot lay claim to legitimacy despite the two-thirds majority, and it will surely be recorded in the history books as another imposed constitution. It increases the chance "that the public good is disregarded in the conflicts of rival parties, and that measures are too often decided, not according to the rules of justice and the rights of the minor party, but by the superior force of an interested and overbearing majority."[40]

---

[38] See Zsolt Körtvélyesi's contribution in this volume.

[39] See Renáta Uitz's contribution in this volume.

[40] Madison, J. "The Federalist No. 10" in Hamilton, Madison, Jay, *The Federalist Papers* (New York: Bantam, 1982), 43.

From 'We the People' to 'We the Nation'

Zsolt Körtvélyesi

Introduction

In Hungary, as in the region in general, the distinction between the nation in the political sense and the cultural nation is far from clear-cut. While the former describes the community of citizens regardless of their ethnicity, the latter unites those of the same ethnicity or cultural family[1] (most notably those who speak the same language) regardless of their country of residence or citizenship. While the 1989 Constitution mostly used the more neutral notion of "the people," the Fundamental Law only adds to the confusion around the two understandings. A recent change in the naturalization rules has also significantly supplanted nation in the ethnic sense over the political nation.

As a part of this trend, the Parliament of Hungary adopted an important amendment[2] to the Citizenship Act in 2010,[3] allowing preferential naturalization for ethnic Hungarians living in neighboring states by removing the requirement of residence in Hungary. This marks a significant shift towards ethnicity and de-territorialization of

---

[1] Where not stated otherwise, I will use "ethnic" and "cultural" interchangeably. As the new preferential naturalization rule shows (see the discussion of the most recent Hungarian amendment later) even the legal framework applies a mixture of cultural conditions, territory and descent. According to the classification applied by the European Union Democracy Observatory on Citizenship of the European Union Institute, ethnic preference will qualify as "cultural affinity." The notion of the cultural nation, based on a shared vision of common origin, seems wide enough to include, for our discussion here, the concept building largely on ethnicity.

[2] Act IVXV of 2010 on amendment of the Act on Hungarian Citizenship.

[3] Act LV of 1993 on Hungarian Citizenship.

citizenship. The extension of voting rights followed this step, the new Electoral Act was adopted in December 2011,[4] eliminating the requirement of permanent residence in Hungary for voting. This further blurs the boundaries of the nation and the people, i.e. the cultural, ethnic community and the political one. The extension of citizenship and of voting rights can be seen as the execution of the vision enshrined in the Fundamental Law about what the nation is.

This chapter will argue that the concept of the ethnic nation took over the concept of the political nation in the legal sphere, and will present two areas where this happened: the Fundamental Law, mainly its preamble, and a recent amendment of the Act on Hungarian Citizenship. First, I will analyze the text of the Fundamental Law to reconstruct the vision of who the source of the new constitution is, and show why the new constitution reflects an ethnic turn, compared to the earlier constitution that built largely on the concept of the political nation.

The second thematic study of the chapter will focus on the boundaries of the citizenry. This section gives a historical overview, without which it is hard to understand the concept of nation in the Fundamental Law, reflecting the legacy of the twentieth century, namely the existence of ethnic Hungarian communities in neighboring countries. External kin play a central role in Hungarian citizenship policy as well. I will review the history of Hungarian citizenship policies, the recent changes, and the new boundaries of citizenship.

In the third part, I analyze the current regulation on external citizenship from various aspects. The fact that this is a contested territory where no clear standards apply—neither in domestic laws, nor in international or European law, and diverse theoretical and practical arguments and considerations can be invoked—makes it hard to give a concise account on citizenship offered to co-ethnics living abroad. The chapter proceeds to provide an overview of the possible international and European constraints. The regional trends, bilateral relations, security concerns and political considerations are discussed. Some of the arguments for external citizenship have strong resemblance to the minority rights claims. This connection is examined in a separate section. The conclusion suggests that there is no binding standard that would clearly ban similar regulations, although the practical applica-

[4] Act CCIII of 2011 on the Election of the Members of Parliament.

tion will be limited by established rules of international law (sovereignty of the other states concerned and the requirement of genuine link for enforcement under international law). Furthermore, the concept of external ethnic citizenship marks a regional trend, and the Hungarian move can be seen as a part of this "Balkanization of citizenship policies."

After reviewing these contexts, I turn to the question of what citizenship is or should be about, and how external citizenship fits this framework. A short summary is given on the extension of voting rights that is closely connected to the extension of the citizenry. The concluding part gives a short account on how citizenship policy is used for the purposes of nation-building.

Starting from the top of the legal hierarchy, in the following section, I review the new constitutional text, what it says and implies about the concept of the nation—a notion that seems so central for the drafters of the Fundamental Law.

The Source of the Fundamental Law—The Nation According to the Preamble

Constitutions often define the community from which they derive their legitimacy, and that is, at the same time, the main subject of their provisions. The preamble ("National Avowal") of the new Fundamental Law starts with the following statement: "We, members of the Hungarian nation… with a sense of responsibility for every Hungarian, hereby proclaim the following." The text does not use the term "people," ("peuple," "Volk") unlike the U.S., the French or the German constitutions, nor does it refer to "citizens of Hungary," as suggested by the Venice Commission,[5] but uses the term "nation" which is very much a charged notion in the Central and Eastern European region.

There are constitutions that refer to the (titular) nation as *the* sovereign entity in the country, but most of them go on to add the nonethnic element as well. The Constitution of the Republic of Poland uses both the term "nation" and "all the citizens," the Constitution of the Slovak Republic contains reference both to "the Slovak nation"

[5] See Venice Commission, *Opinion 621/2011 on the new Constitution of Hungary*, in this volume.

and to "citizens of the Slovak Republic." While the Constitution of Romania establishes Romania as a "National State," it refers to the "Romanian people" as the source of national sovereignty, to Romania as "homeland of all its citizens." The Constitution of the Republic of Croatia not only adds "members of other nations and minorities who are... citizens" to "Croatian people," but also enumerates the most important national minorities living in the country, one by one. This does not mean that all these constitutions reflect an adequately civic, non-ethnic vision of the nation, and work with a notion of the political nation that is neutral to the origin of its citizens. But it certainly means that the nationalities, non-titular ethnic groups are also mentioned as authors, at least co-authors, of the basic text of the country. The Fundamental Law is unique in this sense, but to show this, we have to engage in a more thorough reading of the text itself.

The National Avowal[6] sends a strong message with its very title, a mix of religious devotion and national sentiments.[7] This return to the nineteenth century national movements is emphasized with the motto taken from the national anthem: "God bless the Hungarians." The preamble uses the word "nation" (*nemzet*) ten times, while the term "people" (*nép*) appears in the preamble only four times: two occurrences simply refer to democracy, or *popular* representation; in one case, it is about "other peoples"; and in one occasion, where it is truly about the Hungarian people, it is a mere historical statement about Hungarians defending Europe for centuries.

The first sentence of the preamble refers to members of the Hungarian nation, as the source of the "proclamation." So it is not the people, the citizens, but those belonging to the "nation." The question then is who the members of this nation are, which of the two usages is relevant here: is it the nation in the political sense, as suggested by the last sentence of the preamble, "we, the citizens of Hungary?" (Although here, too, the original Hungarian term *polgár* is not

[6] Majtényi argues that the title ("Nemzeti hitvallás") can also be understood as a reference to the well-known irredentist poem of the inter-war period, "Nemzeti hiszekegy." Majtényi, B. "'Vár állott, most kőhalom'—Alaptörvény és irodalom" ['Castle stood, a ruin now'—Fundamental Law and literature] *Fundamentum* no. 4 (2011): 97–105, 103.

[7] See the full text of the preamble in Appendix I.

the legal term for nationals, those holding Hungarian citizenship, but a notion that is central to the rhetorics of the governing political party Fidesz, using it as a reference to the ideal, middle class citizen, or "bourgeois.") The first sentence suggests that the nation does not include every Hungarian: after declaring that "We, the members of the Hungarian nation…" are the ultimate constituent power, it mentions a "sense of responsibility for every Hungarian." The subject and the object of the sentence cannot be one and the same, and the term "responsibility" appears later (in Article D) in the context of ethnic Hungarians. This might imply that this "nation" is the neutral expression, without the ethnic component.

However, the text, overall, rather than refuting the claim that it is adopted in the name of the Hungarian nation in the cultural, or ethnic, sense, reinforces this feeling, although not in clear terms. Some remnants of the old text (the 1989 Constitution) appear in the preamble, as the reference to the nationalities as "constituent parts of the State," but this does not alter the fact that there is an important shift towards the ethnic concept. While the text contains both civic and ethnic elements, nevertheless builds largely on the ethnic concept. It is certainly true that the use of the term "nation" in the preamble is not creating, only reflecting the widespread confusion about this term, but by doing this it reinforces this phenomenon.

The Fundamental Law engages in a doublespeak that seems to give the necessary concessions to the neutral or civic version of the nation, while in its heart, it builds on the ethnic community. The preamble talks about an "intellectual and spiritual unity of our nation torn apart," which is hard not to be read as a reference to peace treaties and the loss of territories and of ethnic Hungarians as citizens. As János Kis argues, people is replaced by nation in the ethnic sense, while the text does not exclude the possibility of a revisionist interpretation.[8] Similarly, the Venice Commission talked about "potentially problematic statements" in the Fundamental Law, "on the protection of the rights of Hungarians abroad contained in the preamble and other related provisions of the new Constitution, which may be found problematic and engender concern in the framework of inter-state relations."[9] The

[8] See the introductory chapter by János Kis in this volume.

[9] Venice Commission, *Opinion 621/2011*, para 149.

European Parliament in its resolution stressed, among other things, the need to "explicitly guarantee in the Constitution, including its preamble, that Hungary will respect the territorial integrity of other countries when seeking the support of ethnic Hungarians living abroad."[10] Note that the earlier constitution included a specific clause on this.[11]

Furthermore, the National Avowal makes a controversial reference to the Carpathian Basin. This geographical term is known as a reference to the territory of the "historical Hungary," including the territories now belonging to the neighboring countries (plus Poland). This sentence, however, also refers to "the languages and cultures of nationalities living in Hungary, along with all man-made and natural assets of the Carpathian Basin." One might wonder what is the place of the other "man-made... assets" outside Hungary, belonging to the cultures of other nationalities, in the preamble of the Hungarian constitution, even from an ethno-national point of view.

If we look beyond the preamble and turn to the body of the text for guidance on the meaning of the term "nation," we find a straightforward statement in Article D: "there is one single Hungarian nation that belongs together." And one has no doubt that this is the ethnic nation: this article elaborates on the responsibilities due to the ethnic Hungarian communities abroad. If we accept this, and there is only "one single Hungarian nation," also source of the text, what is the place of non-ethnic Hungarians but Hungarian citizens in the new constitutional order? The preamble is unambiguous on this question: "The nationalities [*nemzetiségek* in the original, so non-ethnic Hungarians] living with *us* [i.e. with the Hungarian nation] form part of the Hungarian *political community*." (emphasis added) Not only are they, the nationalities, not "us," they are also not members of the Hungarian nation. The Slovakian and Croatian texts, as we saw, add the neutral, non-ethnic component to the constituent power. The Hungarian Fundamental Law seems to rest on a distinction between the *source* of the constitution-making authority (*pouvoir constituant*), the source of the

---

10 European Parliament, *Resolution on the Revised Hungarian Constitution*, July 5, 2011, Article 1(d), http://www.europarl.europa.eu/sides/getDoc.do?type=TA&reference=P7-TA-2011-0315&language=EN&ring=P7-RC-2011-0379.

11 1989 Constitution, Article 6(3).

constitution on the one hand, and those entitled to exercise political rights, on the other. Ethnic Hungarians are part of the "nation," under the terms of the Fundamental Law, while non-ethnic Hungarians who are nonetheless citizens of Hungary are part of the "political community" only. This—excluding non-ethnic Hungarians from the source of the constitution—is certainly a novelty in the new text, and it is hard to see how this reflects the idea of "one single Hungarian nation." The Venice Commission concludes in the same vein that "the Preamble has been written in the name of 'we the members of the Hungarian nation,' intimating that members of the 'nationalities living with us' are not part of the people behind the enactment of the Constitution."[12]

One might argue that the sometimes fuzzy phrasing of a preamble has nothing to do with the actual situation of minorities in the country, that of kinship ties, or the relationship with neighboring states where co-ethnics live. Some would also add that the confusion that we have seen are inherent to all texts that use high principles and elevated statements. While maintaining that the preamble does matter—it has legal force, as the Fundamental Law clearly says,[13] although it remains to be seen how it will influence the interpretation of the law—it is probably more important how this reflects a general attitude towards the constituting community by those at the heights of power, e.g. in the form of shaping citizenship policies.

To understand what is behind this ethnicizing trend, we will have to go back, and review the history of who belonged to the nation, more specifically the history of citizenship policies in Hungary, the political decisions that have been forming the legal reality behind the concept of the (now: one single) "Hungarian nation."

Redefining the Citizenry—Boundaries of the 'Nation'

Ever since the regime change of 1989–90, Hungarian legislation on citizenship has been preoccupied with Hungarians living in neighboring countries. While this is not the only area affected by the fact that important number of ethnic Hungarians live in neighboring states—it

---

[12] Venice Commission, *Opinion 621/2011*, para 40.

[13] Article R(3).

had a crucial influence on the domestic regulation applying to minority self-governments, for instance[14]—it is certainly one of the domains where this was the most prominent force behind legislative changes. And the existence of sizable Hungarian minorities abroad, in turn, was a result of historical developments in the region. While history is not explaining all that we have seen in the last two decades' legislation on nationality, the existence of kin-minorities is a predetermining factor that accounts for most of the important trends and changes.

I will briefly review the changing concepts and rules of Hungarian citizenship. In doing so, I will use "citizenship" and "nationality" interchangeably.

Hungarian citizenship up to 1990

As with the term "nation," the contested boundaries of citizenry are loaded with history. Hungary adopted its first Act on Citizenship in 1879.[15] Applied in a multi-ethnic country, with Hungarians constituting only a relative majority (48 per cent in 1910),[16] this Act did not make any reference to ethnicity. This does not mean that ethnicity at that time did not play a role at all in naturalization. A law from 1886,[17] while making no clear reference to origin, was based on the intent to apply ethnic preference: allowing easy naturalization to Csango groups (*Csángók*, Hungarian, or *Ceangăi*, Romanian, considered Hungarians but living on the Eastern border of Romania).[18] An interesting parallel is that the ethnic preference rule of the 2010 amendment reflects the specificities of the Csango community.

---

[14] See e.g. Majtényi, B. *A nemzetállam új ruhája* [The nationstate's new cloth] (Budapest: Gondolat, 2007).

[15] Act 1879:L on the Acquisition and Loss of Hungarian Citizenship.

[16] Romsics, I. *A trianoni békeszerződés* [The peace treaty of Trianon] (Budapest: Osiris, 2001).

[17] Act 1886:IV on Mass Repatriation.

[18] Parragi, M. "A magyar állampolgársági jog és a külföldön élő magyarság" [The Hungarian Law of Citizenship and the Hungarians living abroad], *Kisebbségkutatás* no. 1 (2000), http://www.hhrf.org/kisebbsegkutatas/kk_2000_01/cikk.php?id=195.

The Treaty of Trianon of 1920[19] and its consequences have a central role in discussions around ethnicity in Hungary. The Hungarian Kingdom lost, through the Treaty, two-thirds of its territory and half of its population, and more than three million ethnic Hungarians ended up outside Hungary.[20] The Treaty contains important provisions on nationality. Article 61 prescribes the automatic loss of Hungarian citizenship and acquisition of the state formed on or acquiring the new territory for all those living on territories lost by Hungary. Those concerned with this regulation had, by virtue of Article 63, a choice ("right to opt") between their "old" citizenship and the new (territorial) one. In the former case they had the obligation to leave the country, for the state of which they chose the citizenship. More importantly, all those belonging to a (racial or linguistic, in the terminology of the Treaty) minority in any of the states concerned by the Treaty—"Austria, Hungary, Italy, Poland, Romania, the Serb–Croat–Slovene State, or the Czech–Slovak State"—had this option of either leaving their homeland for the state where they belong to the ethnic majority and hold citizenship, or staying in their homes, but acquiring and losing their citizenships according to the territorial changes (Article 64). While both regulations reflect the goal of avoiding statelessness—like the European convention adopted on this issue almost a century later[21]—the first is, at first sight, neutral, the second rests on the ethnic principle. The Treaty envisaged a window of twelve or six months, respectirely, for exercising the right to opt, but later Hungarian regulations[22] applied a more preferential rule, granting easier access to citizenship for those who ended up in a country other than Hungary, but moved to Hungary because of the border changes.

The next series of events that influenced the citizenship status of many were the border changes of 1938 and 1940, the two Vienna Awards (on transferring the Southern, then the Eastern part

[19] Treaty of Peace Between The Allied and Associated Powers and Hungary And Protocol and Declaration, Signed at Trianon on June 4, 1920.

[20] Romsics, *A trianoni békeszerződés*, 201.

[21] Council of Europe, *Convention on the avoidance of statelessness in relation to State succession*, ETS no. 200, 19 May 2006, http://conventions.coe.int/Treaty/EN/Treaties/Html/200.htm

[22] Act 1922:XVII on Common Charges and State Expenses in the First Six Months of the Fiscal Year of 1922/23.

of Czechoslovakia, and Northern Transylvania, Romania to Hungary) and of 1941, annexation of Voivodina (Yugoslavia). As a result, Hungary regained part of the territories lost after the First World War. The Moscow Armistice Agreement annulled these acquisitions, and although neither this Agreement, nor the Paris Peace Treaty of 1947[23] specifically mentioned the issue of citizenship, the post-war regulations usually followed the same logic as we saw after the First World War, based on the territorial principle.[24]

The law that finally replaced the first Citizenship Act was adopted in 1948. This and later laws applied and apply a rule of unlimited "inheritance" of citizenship. As a result, there is a large number of "latent citizens" who do not know that they are Hungarian citizens, probably do not speak the language, and might be second, third or even fourth generation immigrants in a distant country. Hungary does not have any information on people holding this "dormant nationality." In the decades of socialism, the question of ethnic Hungarians in neighboring countries vanished from the official agenda.

Hungarian citizenship from 1990 to 2004

The first government after the change of regime in 1990 had to address the complex legacy of the twentieth century. The new Citizenship Law of 1993 applied an overall restriction on access to citizenship.[25] However, most of the naturalizations did not follow these general rules, the large majority of cases were dealt with under the exceptional regulations based on ethnic preference. For these cases, the law prescribed relaxed conditions for naturalization, e.g. a one-year residency requirement instead of the general eight-year rule. Debaters over Hungarian citizenship regulations have been more obsessed with co-ethnics living abroad than with non-kin immigrants—a tendency often described in

[23] Treaty of peace with Hungary: Union of Soviet Socialist Republics, United Kingdom of Great Britain and Northern Ireland, United States of America, Australia, Byelorussian Soviet Socialist Republic, etc., and Hungary. Signed at Paris, on February 10, 1947.

[24] Parragi, "A magyar állampolgársági jog és a külföldön élő magyarság."

[25] Maatsch, A. *Ethnic Citizenship Regimes. Europeanization, Post-war Migration and Redressing Past Wrongs*, Palgrave Politics of Identity and Citizenship Series (Great Britain: Palgrave Macmillan, 2011), 63.

the literature as an East/West divide.[26] The final adopted text required ethnic Hungarians to have been residing in Hungary for one year, and to have an ancestor who was a Hungarian citizen.[27] Although most of the additional conditions (criminal record, security threat, burden on the social welfare system, state interest, citizenship test, etc.) also applied, the residency requirement of one year was still very favorable compared to the general rule of eight years.

As already mentioned, the text incorporated the repatriation formula that granted automatic access to citizenship for those who had lost Hungarian citizenship in the past, and in three groups of cases, this could happen without taking up residency in Hungary.[28] A recent case[29] where an ethnic Hungarian living in Serbia claimed to be a citizen shows the difficulties with the application of the above regulations. The claimant, Zoltán Sőregi[30] was born in 1926 in Zenta, a town that used to belong to Hungary but was ceded to the Serb–Croat–Slovene Kingdom. Following the Second Vienna Award, the territory became once again part of Hungary, and the claimant became Hungarian citizen. He argued that no specific provision canceled this move, after the borders shifted back in 1945, and Zenta became part of Yugoslavia. The Hungarian authorities declined to recognize Mr. Sőregi as a Hungarian citizen.

The Supreme Court acknowledged that the claimant's parents were Hungarian citizens, and that the claimant himself was granted Hungarian citizenship in 1941. However, based on the citizenship rules adopted after the war, the claimant would have retained his Hungarian

[26] Not without controversy, see the debate in Bauböck, R. and A. Liebich, eds. "Is There (Still) an East-West Divide in the Conception of Citizenship in Europe?" *EUI Working Papers,* RSCAS 2010/19 (Florence: European University Institute, 2010).

[27] Act LV of 1993 on Hungarian Citizenship, Article 4(3).

[28] Ibid., Article 5 and 5/A.

[29] Supreme Court of the Republic of Hungary, Judgment No. Kfv. IV.37.129/2010/5. (November 10, 2010).

[30] The claimant was represented by Tamás Gaudi-Nagy, MP of Jobbik, an extreme right wing party, who mentioned the name of the claimant in the Parliament, http://www.mkogy.hu/internet/plsql/ogy_naplo.naplo_fadat?p_ckl=39&p_uln=43&p_felsz=300&p_szoveg=&p_felszig=300 (the name is otherwise erased from the judgment available for the public).

citizenship only if he had been residing on Hungarian territory.[31] As he stayed in Zenta, in Yugoslavia, he lost his Hungarian citizenship. The judgment thus concluded that although Mr. Sőregi has no right to be recognized as Hungarian citizen or has no automatic access to citizenship, he can apply for citizenship under the preferential rule designed to benefit ethnic Hungarians. This case can be seen as representative of the situation that the debates over extending Hungarian citizenship to ethnic Hungarians living beyond the state borders addressed.

After the new law was adopted in 1993, a consensus (rarely seen in Hungarian political life) seemed to emerge: parliamentary parties did not challenge the requirement of residency in Hungary for the naturalization of ethnic Hungarians. Moreover, Fidesz politicians in the debates over the 2001 Status Act argued that the Hungarian Card and the benefits attached to it are a substitute for citizenship—as this latter would risk going counter to the main goal of the Hungarian diaspora policy, namely helping members of the Hungarian communities abroad on the territory where they are residing, and not encouraging them to leave their homeland for Hungary. As one Hungarian official—then Government Office for Hungarian Minorities Abroad vice-president, now Fidesz MEP—pointed out, referring to the then (2001) and now foreign minister János Martonyi: "The Hungarian Foreign Minister also rejected any idea related to granting dual citizenship to ethnic Hungarians living abroad—this would be almost impossible also because of the accession negotiations with the EU,"[32] and dual citizenship would be "a very delicate issue for Hungary on both the domestic and the international level." Furthermore, the "issue of dual citizenship would be meaningful for the smaller minority communities in Vojvodina, Croatia, Slovenia or Ukraine—but would have no reality in the case of the large minorities, such as the Hungarians living in Romania.'[33]

---

[31] Prime Minister's Decree 5070/1945 and Act LX of 1948.

[32] Gál, K. "The Hungarian Legislation on Hungarians Living in Neighboring Countries" in *The Protection of National Minorities by their Kin-State,* Science and technique of democracy, No. 32 (Strasbourg: Council of Europe, 2002), 157.

[33] Gál, K. "The Hungarian Legislation on Hungarians Living in Neighboring Countries" in Kántor, Z. et al. eds. *The Hungarian Status Law: Nation Building and/or Minority Protection* (Sapporo: Slavic Research Center, Hokkaido University, 2004), 309–400.

Debates on 'dual citizenship' from 2004

It was against this background that a political organization (the "World Association of Hungarians") with no democratic support in Hungary, maintaining connections with Hungarian communities abroad initiated a referendum on the "dual citizenship" of ethnic Hungarians in 2003. Hence the preferential naturalization of co-ethnics without the residency requirement became known as the question of "dual citizenship."

The Electoral Commission or the Constitutional Court could have blocked the initiative, but both bodies decided that the question could be put to referendum. The Constitutional Court decided that there is no interference with constitutional or international norms, most importantly with the non-discrimination principle and previously undertaken international obligations.[34]

The 2004 referendum campaign was endorsed by the then leading opposition party Fidesz. The question created much controversy and—as the results have shown—division in society. The socialist party played the welfare card in a xenophobic way[35] and argued that new ("dual") citizens—naturalized ethnic Hungarians living in the neighboring states—would pose a huge burden on the Hungarian social benefits and health care system. Although the number of those supporting the idea of external citizenship for co-ethnics was higher than those opposing it, the difference was very slight, 51.57 per cent against 48.43 per cent. Furthermore, the turnout was low, 37.49 per cent, falling below the threshold for a referendum to be conclusive. The results were often interpreted as the majority of Hungarian voters (voting against and absenting) said "no" to their fellow Hungarians' inclusion into the nation.

[34] Decision 5/2004. (III. 2.) For an extensive critique of the decision, see Tóth, J. "Kettős állampolgárságot népszavazással?" [Dual Citizenship via referendum?] *Fundamentum*, no. 2 (2004): 88–96.

[35] Feischmidt, M. "A kettős állampolgárságról" [On dual citizenship] *Kisebbségkutatás* no. 1 (2005), http://www.hhrf.org/kisebbsegkutatas/kk_2005_01/cikk.php?id=910.

It came as no great surprise, then, that when Fidesz gained a two-thirds majority in the 2010 general elections, the Parliament adopted a modification of Article 4 (3) of the Act, canceling the one year-residency requirement and extending the application of the preferential rule. The amendment was followed by institutional changes, reflecting the conceptual shift: the government set up a new department within the already existing office for nationality affairs, with new staff, for the execution of the amendment, and also, breaking with a tradition of 130 years, separate nationality affairs from immigration issues, and move them under the authority of a different ministry. An additional 200 civil servants were recruited, while the original staff of the Office for Immigration and Nationality and the ministerial citizenship section is 70 civil servants.[36]

The regulation in force

Unlike a constitutional preamble, a legal text that seeks application on the ground cannot avoid a definition of its target group. The Act on Hungarians Living in Neighboring Countries ("Status Act") rests on the principle of self-identification ("persons declaring themselves to be of Hungarian nationality," here in the ethnic sense); additional conditions include residency in one of the listed neighboring states and the lack of Hungarian citizenship.[37] This latter was erased following the extension of citizenship.

The 2010 preferential naturalization rule operates with three distinct conditions. In all cases, the applicant has to speak Hungarian. From the two further conditions, only one has to be met: either one has to have at least one ancestor who was a Hungarian citizen (the old rule), or has to demonstrate the *likelihood* of "origins from Hungary."[38] The latter requirement is a strange mixture of origin and territory.

---

[36] EUDO Citizenship Observatory, *Changes in the Hungarian Citizenship Law adapted on 26 May 2010,* http://eudo—citizenship.eu/docs/CountryReports/recentChanges/Hungary.pdf.

[37] Article 1(1) of the Act LXII of 2001 on Hungarians Living in the Neighboring Countries. See in English in Kántor, Z. et al., eds. *The Hungarian Legislation on Hungarians Living in Neighbouring Countries* (Sapporo: Slavic Research Center, Hokkaido University, 2004).

[38] Article 4(3) of the Act on Hungarian Citizenship as amended by Act IVXL of 2010, entered into force on January 1, 2011.

According to the government official responsible for the execution of the new regulation, this targeted the Csangos.[39] A close reading will show that not only ethnic Hungarians will qualify: if a mere plausibility of an origin from Hungary is enough, and it can go back as far as the Csangos' links with the country, this will include all those who have at least one descendant who at some point lived on Hungarian territory—so most of those who live on a territory once encompassed by historical borders of the Hungarian Kingdom. The only further condition is the knowledge of the Hungarian language. But, as explained in the Government Decree implementing the legislative changes,[40] linguistic skills are not assessed in a systematic manner.

Those defending the new clause point out that it does not rest on an ethnic principle, nor does it grant citizenship collectively, regardless of the intentions of the individuals. The new regulation, however, does lead to mass naturalization of ethnic Hungarians living in neighboring countries. Furthermore, this is not some side effect, it is indeed the core and original intent behind the amendment: uniting the nation (again, the ethnic one) across borders. As the explanatory notes of the amendment state, the goal of the new regulation is to offer a simplified naturalization procedure for "Hungarians living beyond the borders."[41]

Given the vague formulation, a lot depends on the application of this clause, and for this, one should look at how the new rule is applied in individual cases. The European Convention on Nationality guarantees both the right to get, in writing, the reasons of the decision and the right to administrative or judicial review.[42] Hungary entered reservations to both articles. The official interpretation of the preferential conditions remains unknown both to the applicants and to the public in general. We will not learn the applied standards, which would resolve the dilemma on what the content of the clause is.

---

39 Forró, G. "Kettős állampolgárság: készülnek az ügyfélfogadásra" [Dual citizenship: getting ready for applicants] *Krónika.ro*, September 20, 2010, http://kronika.ro/index.php?action=open&res=42510.

40 Governmental Decree 224/2010 (VIII. 4.) on the implementation of the Act on Hungarian Citizenship.

41 Bill T/29, submitted on May 17, 2010, on the amendment of the Act on Hungarian Citizenship, 4.

42 Council of Europe, *European Convention on Nationality*, ETS no. 166, November 6, 1997, Article 11 and 12.

We have seen that Hungary officially and legally derogated from the established European minimum requirements of a fair and transparent procedure. However, there are external, legal and non-legal, constraints to the project of redefining the boundaries of the nation.

Possible External Limitations and Legal Considerations

International constraints

An obvious limit to the application of preferential rules based on ethnicity is the non-discrimination principle, enshrined in practically all human rights documents. The European Convention on Nationality, the European Convention on Human Rights, and the EU Treaties all include a reference to non-discrimination. Protocol No. 12 to the European Convention on Human Rights—not yet ratified, but signed by Hungary—puts a general ban on discrimination, regardless of a connection with rights protected under the Convention or its Protocols.

The European Convention on Nationality expressly prohibits discrimination based on "national or ethnic origin."[43] However, its Explanatory Report[44] says that "knowledge of the national language" or specific "descent or place of birth" "are justified grounds for differentiation." Furthermore, more favorable treatment to nationals of other states, e.g. preferential treatment of citizens of other EU states, is acceptable. The question remains, what the limits of such preference are, what is necessary and proportionate, and what is already beyond that.

In the Hungarian case, even without the last amendment, naturalizations based on ethnic preference clearly outnumbered all other cases.[45] This means that, in practice, the exception became the rule. With the new amendment, the average number of naturalizations per month is higher than the yearly average from earlier years (3–6,000 per

[43] Ibid., Article 5(1).

[44] Council of Europe, *Explanatory Report to the European Convention on Nationality*, ETS no. 166, 1997, para 40–41.

[45] For an overview, see Tóth, J. and Z. Körtvélyesi, "Naturalisation in Hungary: Exclusion by Ethnic Preference," *Open Citizenship* 2, no. 1 (October 25, 2011): 69, Table 2.

year against 5–10,000 per month[46]). Is this beyond the legitimate margin for applying an ethnic preference, according to the Convention on Nationality and the Explanatory Report? The 2010 amendment widened the gap between the general rule (eight year residency with other conditions) and the preferential case (no residency) too much. The difference is not proportionate when contrasted to the basis of the distinction ("cultural affinity"). Although, as we do not have related case law, it is hard to assess what standard the European Convention on Nationality prescribes. We have, however, other European standards, set by European courts.

While jurisprudence of the European Court of Human Rights and the Court of Justice of the EU both address issues of discrimination and nationality, there are only a few cases where cases of ethnicity based preferential naturalizations—and not of statelessness[47] or of distinctions between groups of citizens[48]—are at stake. The recent case on the Slovenian "erasure"[49] demonstrates how allegedly neutral conditions (i.e. erasure from register of permanent citizens) could amount to ethnic discrimination—although the European Court of Human Rights, in this case, did not discuss the discrimination argument (as it already found a violation of Article 8). The jurisprudence of the Court of Justice of the EU also underlines the national discretion in defining who is their national. This is indeed a principle of international law, too, the principle that nationality belongs to *domaine réservé*. It was the *Nottebohm* decision[50] of the International Court of Justice that showed an important limitation to this, namely, the criteria of "effective nationality." This means that a nationality is only valid under international law if it reflects

---

46 Wetzel, T. "Eddig mintegy 160 ezren éltek a könnyített honosítás lehetőségével" [So far 160,000 persons took the opportunity to naturalize under the preferential rules] *Vajdaság Ma,* November 5, 2011, http://www.vajma.info/cikk/vajdasag/12560/.

47 *Andrejeva v. Latvia* [GC], no. 55707/00, February 18, 2009.

48 *East African Asians v. United Kingdom,* no.'s 4403/70-4419/70, 4422/70, 4423/70, 4434/70, 4443/70, 4476/70-4478/70, 4486/70, 4501/70 and 4526/70-4530/70 (joined), December 14, 1973; *Abdulaziz, Cabales and Balkandali v. United Kingdom,* no.'s 9214/80, 9473/81, 9474/81, May 28, 1985.

49 *Kurić and Others v. Slovenia* [GC], no. 26828/06, July 13, 2010.

50 *Nottebohm Case (Liechtenstein v. Guatemala),* 1955 I.C.J. 4 (April 6, 1995).

a genuine connection between the state and its citizen, a factual situation. As in that case citizenship "was granted without regard to the concept of nationality adopted in international relations," the concerned state (Liechtenstein) could not invoke the right to diplomatic protection vis-à-vis the other state (Guatemala). National sovereignty, accordingly, means both that a state can decide who is its citizen and that other states can take actions that go against such decision—and this latter will prevail if the acquisition of citizenship violated a principle of international law. This does not preclude the state from continuing to regard its national as a citizen under national law—but it cannot invoke this fact under international law. We can add that a mere reference to ethnicity would certainly not fulfill the requirement of effectiveness.

Still, the *Nottebohm* principle does not seem to work on the European level. In the Micheletti case[51] the European Court of Justice stressed that member states have exclusive competence to define who is their citizen—and, consequently, who should be treated as EU citizens in all other member states. While the Nottebohm decision suggests that no obligation will flow (on the international level) from a non-effective nationality, this is not so in the European cooperation: a member state will have to give all the benefits an EU citizen rightfully gets even if the underlying national citizenship is not effective. The importance of this case lies partly in the fact that it found community law violation in case of a Spanish (civil code) regulation that rested on the genuine link principle, treating dual nationals as nationals only of that state where they habitually resided before arriving to Spain.

This shows that external citizenship appears in a complex multilayer system where international law (in some cases requiring genuine link for enforcement), EU law (so far with an approach closer to the "reserved domain" principle) and the national laws of both countries (tolerating multiple citizenship or not) can play out in completely different ways. Hungary failed to consider this complexity, as the cases and considerations in the next section show.

---

[51] *Mario Vicente Micheletti and Others v. Delegación del Gobierno en Cantabria*, C-369/90.

Responses from other states, security and political considerations

The attitude of neighboring countries shows the limits of what the Hungarian government can achieve. Austria, Slovakia and Ukraine forbid dual citizenship (although not without ambiguities), Slovakia specifically adopted the relevant amendment to counter the Hungarian law. Romania and Serbia, on their part, cannot genuinely oppose the Hungarian move, as they are playing the same card with regards to their co-ethnics living near their borders.[52]

It is not by chance that the OSCE High Commissioner on National Minorities in his Bolzano Recommendations,[53] not independently from his original role, stresses the security aspect of granting citizenship *en masse* to groups living in other states. His recommendation No. 12 suggests that it is legitimate to take "preferred linguistic competencies and cultural, historical or familial ties into account in their decision to grant citizenship to individuals abroad. States should, however, ensure that such a conferral of citizenship respects the principles of friendly, including good neighborly, relations and territorial sovereignty, and should refrain from conferring citizenship *en masse*, even if dual citizenship is allowed by the State of residence." I would emphasize the last point, about avoiding naturalization of persons living abroad *en masse*, even with the consent of the concerned state. (It is not clear, however, how a state can make numerical adjustments once it has decided that a certain category of people are entitled to citizenship. It can certainly determine the pace, but not the final outcome, if it remains faithful to its own regulation.)

The Explanatory Note attached to the Recommendations adds that granting citizenship to persons residing abroad "can be a highly sensitive issue" because of the potential tensions arising from "[c]ontested claims or competing attempts" over conflicting jurisdic-

[52] See, respectively, Iordachi, C. *Country Report: Romania* (Florence: European University Institute, 2010); and Rava, N. *Country Report: Serbia*, (Florence: European University Institute, 2010).

[53] Organization for Security and Co-operation in Europe High Commissioner on National Minorities, *The Bolzano/Bozen Recommendations on National Minorities in Inter-State Relations & Explanatory Note*, http://www.osce.org/hcnm/33633

tions, especially if this happens at a substantial number, relative to the population of the home state. Accordingly, the Note suggests that "[s]tates should... refrain from granting citizenship without the existence of a genuine link between the State and the individual upon whom it is conferred,"[54] as stated in the *Nottebohm* judgment.

If we consider the case of Georgia, it is easy to see the point the High Commissioner made: in the 2008 war Russia argued that it had to intervene to protect its citizens who became citizens exactly because of the liberal naturalization policy disregarding territoriality. Hopefully no similar threats exist in the case of countries who are members of the same alliance (NATO, EU), but it is the same tendency that we see in the Balkans: using citizenship policies to question the existing borders and the sovereignty of neighboring states, applying a more or less clear ethnic criteria.

As ethnicity in itself will not fulfill the requirement of a genuine link, and considering that 200,000 applications were submitted at the end of the first year of the new regulation, Hungary is clearly going against this recommendation. This number will continue to grow, and as citizenship cannot be revoked and the unlimited application of *ius sanguinis* ("inheritance" of citizenship) is guaranteed by the Fundamental Law,[55] the existence of large number of external citizens will be a continuing reality for Hungary.

It is the quantitative factor that is raised by Hans Ulrich Jessurun d'Oliveira, too, who reckons that granting external citizenship *en masse* in the case of an EU member state can violate the principle of solidarity of the EU.[56] Somewhat similarly to the national budgetary steps taken that weakened the eurozone, but allowed more leeway to certain national governments, granting citizenship *en masse* can serve the goals of national governments, but it is often other member states that carry the burden of this—as demonstrated by the *Micheletti* case. It is not by chance that the Hungarian government around 2001, led by the same prime minister who became later the promoter of external citizenship, opposed the idea

---

54 Ibid., 19.

55 Article G(1).

56 D'Oliveira, H. "Nationality and the European Union after Amsterdam" in *Legal issues of the Amsterdam Treaty*, ed. O'Keeffe, D. and P. M. Tworney (Oxford and Portland, Oregon: Hart Publishing, 1999), 406 and 407.

of granting nationality to external kin in public, and the definitive shift came after the EU accession was a done deal. (Hungary joined the EU on May 1, 2004, and the referendum took place on December 5, 2004.)

While the above factors may advise us that granting external citizenship targeting co-ethnics is not the best idea, there are two arguments appearing in the debates over external citizenship again and again that seem to suggest otherwise.

Arguments for external citizenship and minority rights

The first argument is that granting citizenship to ethnic Hungarians living in the neighboring countries was a duty. This was a necessary step to remedy the situation after the world wars, to acknowledge the sufferings of those who ended up on the other side of the border, and also to end discrimination between those who lost their Hungarian nationality as a result of the peace treaties and those losing their nationality by other means (and, in both cases, their descendants). This comparison uses a mistaken standard. The unlimited inheritableness of Hungarian citizenship is an anomaly, resulting in more than a million latent citizens who do not know of their being Hungarian nationals, and vice versa, Hungary does not know of them, either. So if one seeks to eliminate the distinction (which is not a necessity, because the distinction is based on a relevant difference, the fact that jurisdictions moved over a large number of people), the inheritance rule should be limited, and the residency requirement could be added in all cases.

The other propositions (about remedying an unjust situation and helping Hungarian communities abroad) relate to the second argument, namely the issue of minority rights. According to this, granting Hungarian citizenship to external kin is a way of furthering their claims as members of a national minority. In the literature it seems established that granting citizenship *en masse* to external kin is not a tool of minority protection.[57]

Article D of the Fundamental Law—the "Responsibility Clause," see above—also follows the minority rights logic. According to this,

---

[57] Halász, I. "A kettős állampolgárság mint a magyar nemzetpolitika eszköze?" [Dual citizenship as a tool of the Hungarian nation-policy?] *Regio: kisebbség, politika, társadalom* 15 (2004): 18–35.

Hungary "shall facilitate the survival and development of their communities; it shall support their efforts to preserve their Hungarian identity, the assertion of their individual and collective rights, the establishment of their community self-governments, and their prosperity in their native lands, and shall promote their cooperation with each other and with Hungary." Of this, the preservation of identity and the promotion of cooperation with Hungary can be seen as relevant for citizenship, the other, and probably more important goals are not. Citizenship and minority rights follow different logics that eventually contradict each other; it is enough to think of how large blocks of Hungarian citizens will be less likely to succeed in their struggle for territorial autonomy, the ultimate goal for most political leaders of these communities. Nobody could seriously consider that this cause is furthered in any way by granting citizenship. On the other hand, it is easy to see how it can go against such attempts.

It is a basic principle of minority rights that minority protection is primarily the responsibility of the home state. Offering minority members the citizenship of the kin-state without residency will send the message that the primary connections of these people link them to this country, and not to their home state. Which is, of course, not true, it will be this latter that will be responsible for building roads, infrastructure, adopting civil, labor and company law regulations, social policy etc. that apply on that territory and that are relevant for the everyday life of these dual citizens. Given the heated debates about loyalty in this region, defining co-ethnics in the Hungarian nation will have the consequence of defining them out of the (political) nation in the account of the neighboring states. Sadly enough, Slovakia took the message seriously, and introduced a ban on multiple citizenship.

The problem is that these moves are fully in line with established principles of nationality. Austria could react the same way if one of its citizens acted against the ban on multiple citizenship. The Austrian Nationality Law prescribes that upon "acquisition of foreign nationality" citizens lose their Austrian nationality.[58] The loss of citizenship in case of "voluntary acquisition of another nationality" is a legitimate condition, specifically mentioned in the European Convention

[58] Federal Law on Austrian Citizenship, 1985, Articles 26 and 27(1).

on Nationality; it is the first of the allowed grounds of loss *ex lege*.[59] The Slovakian amendment complies with the only exception in the Convention,[60] namely the goal of avoiding statelessness.

Up to now, there were no such practical issues with Romania and Serbia, who themselves are playing a similar game with their respective kin-minority communities. In the case of Ukraine, the situation is less clear. While there is a constitutional clause outlawing multiple citizenship, the execution of this is far from being unambiguous. There is pressure against Ukrainian citizens taking foreign citizenships, but no established legal procedure is in place.

We can wonder if this is what we understand by supporting minorities, among others, by helping them to live where they reside and to maintain contacts with the kin-state; which are all legitimate concerns for the minority rights approach.[61] Tensions are growing with the extension of voting rights, which came next. It is not easy to discern the limits of legitimate measures from both sides. This was an area of concern in the case of the Status Act which was analyzed and criticized by the Venice Commission for applying extraterritorial elements.[62] But while minority rights protection is a duty primarily of the home state, decisions about citizenship and exercising voting rights from abroad are a legitimate use of the sovereignty of the other state. Practical considerations will also play a role, and one cannot emphasize enough how much numbers count in this case. If several hundreds of thousands vote from Romania and Serbia, it will require organization and certain cooperation with these states. The traditional solution of using embassies for this purpose might not be sufficient. Using the post offices—state owned companies in both concerned countries—can also be a delicate issue. Imagine a case where one side of the political spectrum is leading by a small margin. Would it be the same struggle, harsh political declarations from both sides, with a rising nationalist tone, as it happened with the loss of nationality of Hungarians

59 Council of Europe, *European Convention on Nationality*, Article 7(1)a).

60 Ibid., Article 7(3).

61 See e.g. Council of Europe, *Framework Convention for the Protection of National Minorities*, ETS no. 157, 1 February 1995, Articles 17 and 18.

62 Venice Commission, *Reports on the Protection of National Minorities by their Kin-State.*

in Slovakia? Hungary navigated itself into a situation where its legal and constitutional responsibilities towards ethnic Hungarians living abroad—external citizenship, voting rights and the duty to promote the case of autonomy—go largely beyond its competences, beyond what it can realistically achieve. This can be seen as the exact opposite of what the prominent political and legal thinker, minister of the 1956 revolutionary government, István Bibó said, in 1946, as if talking for the entire country: Hungary "cannot give up its political interest in the fate of Hungarian minorities, but it will apply this by securing the realistic interests of Hungarian minorities, and not through loud demonstrations."[63]

The results of the new legislation show both the limits of Hungarian competence to act and the reasonableness behind the principle of cooperation. The requirement to sit down and discuss the responsibilities of the concerned governments is more than just a security concern, it reflects practical considerations. This was largely neglected by the Hungarian government, which failed to start negotiations before introducing external citizenship unilaterally.

It is not just that the time has not come for the full toleration of dual identities and translating them to dual citizenship, accepting dual loyalties, duties, affiliations. This does not seem to be the case even with South Tirol. But more importantly, it does not seem to be a necessity. For that, we have to overview briefly what nationality/citizenship is about.

Confusions and elements of nationality

If we take a look at the core components of what, constitutionally, nationality entails—diplomatic and consular protection, the right to return "home" (what would that mean for a citizen who never came to that territory?)—we can see that the arguments for external citizenship often reflect a confusion about the meaning of citizenship.

The British Institute of International and Comparative Law (BIICL) compiled a list with the components of citizenship. They enu-

---

[63] Bibó, I. "A békeszerződés és a magyar demokrácia" [The peace treaty and the Hungarian democracy] in *Válogatott tanulmányok* [Selected studies], Vol. 2 (Budapest: Magvető, 1986), 296.

merated fourteen rights and four duties.[64] Some items refer to rights and duties that are becoming more and more detached from citizenship, like the duty to pay taxes and national insurance contributions, the right to welfare benefits, health care, education, employment and housing, or linguistic rights and non-discrimination. EU law covers even more areas, also mentioned in the report, including the right to vote, petition, and stand as a candidate, or free movement—while, obviously, the right to have a passport remains dependent on nationality. (That is why free movement rights for citizens of non-EU countries require special attention, and in the context of Hungarian external citizenship, after the visa liberalization for the Western Balkans, it is only those living in Ukraine who would need targeted measures. And as we have seen, for them, dual citizenship is not a solution, it violates the Constitution of Ukraine.)

The right to protection also became a common responsibility of EU member states, based on Article 20(2)c) of the Treaty on the Functioning of the European Union. If we do not consider the case where protection should be provided against another member state, this will not make a difference for external citizens. If we envisage such a scenario—a serious conflict between two member states—dual citizenship will not help, again, as the "external" state (in the present case, Hungary) will not be able to provide diplomatic or consular protection, against the will of the other state, for a national who is at the same time a national of the other concerned state and lives in that state.

Access to public office and public service and political rights in the national arena remain dependent on nationality. The BIICL Report mentions the duty of allegiance and military (or alternative) service as well. The latter is (if we exclude the possibility of war) not relevant for Hungary which abolished compulsory military service in 2004. The interrelated questions of allegiance, political rights and public office and service remain a contested territory.[65] This sensitivity further underlines that citizenship is not an apt tool for creating a common

---

[64] Medjouba, F. and J. Stefanelli, and M. Sánchez, *The Rights and Responsibilities of Citizenship* (London: British Institute of International and Comparative Law, 2008).

[65] See e.g. *Tănase v. Moldova* [GC], no. 7/08, April 27, 2010.

platform that Hungarians living in Hungary and those in neighboring countries could share.

In the account of the European Convention on Nationality, "'nationality' means the legal bond between a person and a State and does not indicate the person's ethnic origin."[66] It does not follow from this, however, that ethnicity can play no role. Taking "cultural affinity" into account is a legitimate part of naturalization procedures. However, at least in international documents, citizenship is a neutral political concept, making no reference to ethnicity, which is reassuring for members of national minorities. Challenging this framework has unintended but logical consequences: if *they* belong to *you, they* don't belong to *us*. Despite the arguments that external citizenship is only an expression of the multiple identities one might have (thus being a truly multicultural measure), this is how the said policy plays out in the Central and Eastern European region. The intentions behind the law are not devoid of traditional ideas of nation-building, together with the goal of remaining in power with an extended citizenry. The next section briefly discusses the changes in the electoral system that concern external citizens.

Extension of Voting Rights

The Fundamental Law removes the earlier constitutional link between voting rights and residency, and allows that a cardinal act detaches active suffrage and the requirement of residence in Hungary.[67] The Parliament adopted the 2011 Electoral Act accordingly, granting voting rights to citizens who do not have registered address in the country. Taken together with the extension of citizenship described above, this move risks creating a serious mismatch between those who vote and those who bear the consequences of political decisions.[68] According to the new law, non-resident citizens can only

[66] Article 2.

[67] Article XXIII(4).

[68] See e.g. Bauböck arguing for grating voting rights to those who are "stakeholders," a concept addressing both the issue of immigrants and émigrés. Bauböck, R. "Stakeholder Citizenship and Transnational Political Participation: A Normative Evaluation of External Voting," *Fordham Law Review* 75, no. 5 (2007): 2393–2447.

vote for party lists, in contrast to resident citizens who can also elect individual local candidates.[69]

The Venice Commission makes an important distinction between the legitimate goal that Hungary support Hungarians living in neighboring states to preserve their identity and something that goes beyond this, what the Commission calls "extra-territorial decision-making."[70] This threat is present from both sides. Kin minority members—at least those with citizenship—can see their attachment to Hungary reinforced (having the right to vote) while this reorientation might mark a move away from their home country's political life. This, again, questions the validity of such principles as the goal of integration and the basic tenet of minority protection about the primary responsibility of the home state.

Seen the widespread practices of voting from abroad, it is hard to argue that this phenomenon would go against established rules or international principles. As the Venice Commission found, "[t]he principle of the right to vote from abroad of citizens who are permanently resident abroad or temporarily out of the country is [...] recognized in a broad majority of" the 57 member states.[71] E.g. all other V-4 countries (Czech Republic, Slovakia and Poland) allow non-residents to vote. In Slovakia (a country of around 5.5 million) this concerns, according to estimates, around 200,000 citizens not living in the country, but those actually casting a vote remained below 6,000.[72] In Bulgaria, external votes in the 2009 elections were above 150,000[73]—in a country of 7 million. Romania is applying an external dual citizenship policy towards Moldova, somewhat similarly to what Hungary is now doing. The some 300,000 Romanian citizens living in Moldova can

[69] Article 12 of the Act CCIII of 2011 on the Election of the Members of Parliament.

[70] Venice Commission, *Reports on the Protection of National Minorities*, para 44.

[71] Venice Commission, *Report on out-of-country voting*, para 20.

[72] Halász, I. "Választások és kisebbségek 2010. A 2010. évi közép-európai választások tapasztalatai kisebbségi szemszögből" [Elections and minorities 2010. The experiences of Central-European elections of 2010 from the viewpoint of the minorities] *Pro Minoritate*, Spring (2011): 120.

[73] Kovács, M. and J. Tóth, "Kin-state responsibility and ethnic citizenship: The Hungarian case" in *Citizenship Policies in the New Europe*, R. Baubock, B. Perchinig, and W. Sievers eds. (Amsterdam: Amsterdam University Press, 2010), 15.

participate in Romanian elections, and their votes proved to be decisive in the presidential elections of 2009.[74] In Croatia, nearly a tenth of all voters are external citizens, so it is not surprising that their votes were crucial at the parliamentary elections in 2007, and actually changed the balance.[75]

These are experiences from countries in the region, which can inform the next elections in Hungary. After the elections, although politically less realistic, legally it is possible to revoke voting rights from external citizens. The Fundamental Law also allows that the Parliament adopt a cardinal act reestablishing the connection between permanent residency and the right to vote. This is not the case with citizenship. The unlimited "inheritance" of citizenship, the unconditional application of the *ius sanguinis* principle—which is, in addition, guaranteed by the Fundamental Law—will make sure that the extended citizenry will remain with us for a longer time.

Final remarks—Nationality as a hostage

The Fundamental Law marks a significant shift in the constitutional concept of the nation, and is reflected in practice in the extension of citizenship and voting rights. All this is not to say that this phenomenon—using citizenship policies for the project of nation-building, or "uniting the nation across borders"—is unique. On the contrary, it seems to constitute a regional trend. If we take a closer look, it actually marks a trend of "Balkanization of citizenship policies," treating citizenship as the hostage of nation-building, which can contribute to destabilization in the region.[76] The stated trans-border goals, of "virtualizing borders," turn out not to work in the ideal liberal way, as originally envisaged with the spread of multiple citizenships.

---

[74] Kovács M., S. Pogonyi, and Z. Körtvélyesi, *The Politics of External Kin-State Citizenship in East Central Europe* (Florence, European University Institute, 2010).

[75] Kovács M. and J. Tóth, "Kin-state responsibility and ethnic citizenship: The Hungarian case," 14.

[76] As in the case of Bosnia with around 500,000 Croatian citizens, see Sarajlić, E. *Country Report: Bosnia and Herzegovina* (Florence: European University Institute, 2010).

Francesco Ragazzi and Kristina Balalovska make an important distinction between post-territorial, in contrast to post-national, citizenship policies.[77] External citizenship policies that apply an ethnic preference are not virtualizing borders, but drawing new borders, based on ethnicity, and these borders are at least as dangerous and undesired as the borders we seek to overcome by a common European framework. Furthermore, it can create new borders within the Hungarian communities it seeks to gather under the umbrella of the "one single Hungarian nation." Some will both acquire Hungarian citizenship and the Hungarian Card (and become a "Status Hungarian"), some will only get one of the two, while others will continue to live without either (and they seem to constitute a majority, for now).

Hijacking nationality for the purposes of nation-building is both a bad idea and marks a regional trend. It is hard not to see the political opportunities behind these steps: extending the electorate and portraying supporters of the external citizenship as the only true proponents of "the national cause." Granting co-ethnics external citizenship is sending a false message, raising false hopes among members of the diaspora communities about where to turn if they want a better life. This can go counter the goal of integration, even without considering that some of the concerned countries do not tolerate multiple citizenship. In this way the legitimate goal of supporting Hungarian communities—providing means to maintain their language, culture and connection with Hungary—ends up working out in the exact opposite direction. The results so far raise doubts as for how much it benefited the kin minorities who are supposed to be in the focus of this legislative move.

Ethnic preference has been present in the Hungarian citizenship policy since 1993. Due to the lack of rule of law guarantees in the naturalization procedure and the common interest of both sides, it could have been easy to apply the existing conditions in a way that would have allowed an easy naturalization of those ethnic Hungarians who have at least some connection with the country (e.g. registered

---

[77] Ragazzi, F. and K. Balalovska, "Diaspora Politics and Post-Territorial Citizenship in Croatia, Serbia and Macedonia" *CITSEE Working Paper Series,* 2011/18 (Edinburg: University of Edinburg, 2011).

address). It is also clear that Hungarian communities in neighboring countries need different policy measures that reflect the local specificities; there is no “one size fits all” response to their concerns. Of course, a nuanced approach might have gone against the projected image of this “one single Hungarian nation,” a vision that has constitutional force now.

III. HUMAN RIGHTS

Human Dignity: Rhetoric, Protection, and Instrumentalisation

CATHERINE DUPRÉ

Introduction

The commitment to constitutional protection of human dignity was a prominent feature of the Hungarian 1989 post-communist constitution, where it was enshrined under Article 54(1), as the first Article of chapter XII on fundamental rights.[1] The 2011 Fundamental Law also enshrines human dignity and does so in several places: it is firstly mentioned in the preamble ("We hold that human existence is based on human dignity"), secondly in Article II, the second provision of the "freedom and responsibility" section ("Human dignity shall be inviolable. Every human being shall have the right to life and human dignity; embryonic and fetal life shall be subject to protection from the moment of conception"), in Article XVII(3) ("Every employee shall have the right to working conditions which respect his or her health, safety and dignity.") and finally in the first sentence of Article 37(4) (see below).

---

[1] Article 54(1): "In the Republic of Hungary everyone has the inherent right to life and to human dignity. No one shall be arbitrarily deprived of these rights." See: Dupré, C. *Importing the Law in Post-communist Transitions, The Hungarian Constitutional Court and the Right to Human Dignity* (Oxford: Hart Publishing, 2003). A selection of constitutional case-law in English translation can be found in Sólyom, L. and G. Brunner eds. *Constitutional Judiciary in a New Democracy: The Hungarian Constitutional Court* (Ann Arbor: University of Michigan Press, 2000) and Erdei, Á. and A. Holló eds. *Selected Decisions on the Constitutional Court of Hungary (1998-2000)* (Budapest: Akadémiai Kiadó, 2005).

This chapter aims to critically comment on these provisions and to assess the extent to which they contribute to the democratic quality of the Fundamental Law, an object of Hungarian and international concern from the moment the government started outlining its constitutional project.[2] The underlying assumption is that the democratic quality of a constitution does not automatically flow from being adopted through a democratic process,[3] but that it also requires compliance with a number of substantive standards. In Europe, these include the principles of separation of powers and the rule of law together with a particular quality of human rights protection, the hallmark of which is human dignity, which has arguably become one of the paradigmatic features of European constitutionalism since 1949.[4] Dignity's central role was confirmed by the Lisbon Treaty in December 2009, which identifies dignity as the first foundational value of the European Union under its Article 2 and further deploys it in the Charter on Fundamental Rights, particularly under its first title. The Charter broadly endorses the commitment to human dignity developed by the European Court of Human Rights under a number of its Articles, particularly 2 (right to life), 3 (prohibition of torture, inhuman or degrading treatment or punishment), 4 (prohibition of slavery, servitude and forced labor) and 8 (right to privacy).[5]

---

[2] Kovács, K. and G.A. Tóth, "Hungary's Constitutional Transformation," *European Constitutional Law Review* 7 (2011), 183–203. See also the web-based petition: http://verfassungsblog.de/hungarys-constitution-worry/.

[3] Also problematic in the Hungarian context, see Kovács, K. and G.A. Tóth, Ibid., and Arato, A., G. Halmai , J. Kis eds. *Opinion on the Fundamental Law of the Hungary,* para 1–3 in this volume.

[4] Häberle, P. *Europäische Verfassungslehre* [European constitutional doctrine] (Baden-Baden: Nomos, 2009), 295–330 and *The Principle of Respect for Human Dignity* (Strasbourg: Council of Europe Publishing, 1999). Weinrib, L. "Human Dignity as a Rights-Protecting Principle," *National Journal of Constitutional Law* 17 (2004) 325–345. Habermas, J. "Das utopische Gefälle, das Konzept der Menschenwürde und die realistische Utopie der Menschenrechte [The utopian gradiant, the concept of human dignity and the realistic utopia] *Blätter für Deutsche und Internationale Politik* 8 (2010), 43–53.

[5] As a result of not being enshrined in the European Convention on Human Rights, human dignity is protected by the European Court of Human Rights in a diffuse manner: see Maurer, B. *Le Principe de Respect de la Dignité Humaine et la CEDH* [The principle of respect for human dignity and the European Convention on Human Rights] (Paris: La documentation française, 1999).

It is suggested that the supranational commitment to dignity protection has therefore become a requirement of European constitutionalism, confirming thus the commitment to dignity to be found in most member state constitutions. Therefore constitutional protection of dignity in Europe is arguably embedded in a substantial and consistent (if not uniform) set of European standards[6] against which the constitutional and democratic quality of individual constitution may be usefully discussed.

The chapter first argues that while the drafting of the dignity provisions appears to be quite open and inclusive, a contextual and systematic reading of the Fundamental Law highlights the determinism of this concept, which pushes it out of line with European constitutionalism. The second part explores the scope of dignity protection, which explicitly includes "every human being," "life of the fetus" and "workers" and discusses some of the issues arising out of such drafting. Third, the chapter discusses how protection of human dignity explicitly shapes the competences of the constitutional court, which are much reduced by the Fundamental Law compared to the 1989 Constitution. Finally, comparing the Fundamental Law with other European constitutional norms brings to light some disturbing omissions in the design of rights and dignity protection.

Determinism

At first sight, dignity is defined as a right under Article II but beyond the mention of "human," it is not defined in terms of substance: "Every human being shall have the right to life and human dignity." This is *prima facie* broadly in line with the European (and international) approach to dignity, where this concept is understood as an essentially human attribute, left conceptually open so as to embrace and protect the whole range of human activities and identities. In par-

[6] Di Ciommo, M. *Dignità umana e Stato costitutional, la dignità umana nel costituzionalismo europeo, nella Costituzione italiana e nelle jurisprudenze europee* [Human dignity and constitutional state, human dignity in European constitutionalism, in the Italian constitution and in European case law] (Firenze: Passigli Editore, 2010) and Burgogne-Larsen, L. ed. *La dignité saisie par les juges en Europe* [Dignity applied by judges in Europe] (Bruxelles: Bruylant, 2010).

ticular, it is not generally understood by reference to supra-constitutional references to God or ideology. As a result, the commitment to dignity which lies at the heart of European constitutions therefore acknowledges and protects the essential freedom to self-determine and to shape one's own destiny.[7]

However, a combined reading of the Hungarian dignity provisions, particularly of the primary provision under Article II, with Article R(3) reveals that the constitution drafters opted for what can be called here a deterministic approach to dignity. This results from the particular rule of interpretation enshrined under Article R(3) which provides that the provisions of the Fundamental Law shall be interpreted in accordance with their purposes, the Avowal of National Faith and the achievements of our historical constitution. Consequently, if this were to be implemented as such, this rule of interpretation would arguably affect the concept of human dignity, which has to be read in compliance with the "National Avowal" (preamble). This approach to dignity, which—explicitly and normatively—ties the concept's interpretations to the preamble, is unique in European constitutions and problematic for several reasons.

First, it endows the preamble with an unusual normative strength, i.e. an explicit requirement to interpret the constitution in conformity with its values.[8] The second issue raised is one of substance, namely the type of values that make up the National Avowal. The emphasis on Christianity ("We are proud that our King Saint Stephen built the Hungarian State on solid grounds and made our country a part of Christian Europe," "the role of Christianity in preserving nationhood" as well as the "God bless the Hungarians" in the opening line of the constitution) and in particular on Catholicism (the reference to "King Saint Stephen" right at the beginning and to the "Holy Crown which embodies the constitutional continuity of Hungary's statehood and unity of the nation" towards the middle of the preamble) is remark-

---

[7] Häberle, P. *Das Menschenbild im Verfassungsstaat* [The image of man in the constitutional state] (Berlin: Duncker und Humblot, 2008 4th ed.), 38.

[8] Some preambles have been used in constitutional adjudication to provide some hermeneutic guidance, but their normative strength remains rare and subject to discussion, see Orgad, L. "The Preamble in Constitutional Interpretation," *International Journal of Constitutional Law* 8 (2010): 714–738.

able in European constitutionalism. Giving normative strength to these religious references under Article R(3) is arguably out of line with post WWII-European constitutionalism.

If some constitutions in Europe refer to "God," the connection between the religious and the constitutional domains was arguably severed in post-WWII European constitutions.[9] Significantly, the connection between God and dignity was considered in the German Basic Law and explicitly rejected by a vote at the drafting stage. Moreover, in Ireland, where the preamble of the 1947 constitution refers to the authority of the "Holy Trinity," academics have argued that "the case law has long since broken loose of that particular inspirational source."[10] Much more recently and at the supranational level, the Lisbon Treaty only mentions the "religious inheritance" of Europe in its preamble with no specific identification of one prevailing religion and as part of a whole set of other inheritances (cultural and humanist), and "universal values of the inviolable and inalienable rights of the human person, freedom, democracy, equality and the rule of law."[11] In short, as the Venice Commission points out in its Opinion on the Fundamental Law, "a separation between state and churches is an inevitable consequence of the rule of law, respect of human rights and the idea of democracy."[12]

Consequently, in Europe, human rights (like other constitutional aspects) are not interpreted by reference to religious values. Instead, they are often read against the backdrop of a range of values as is eloquently illustrated by Article 2 of the Lisbon Treaty, which lists the EU foundational values as including "respect for human dignity, freedom,

---

[9] Häberle, P. "Gott im Verfassungstaat" [God in the constitutional state] Häberle, P. ed. *Rechtsvergleichung im Kraftfeld des Verfassungsrechts* [Comparative law in the field of constitutional law] (Berlin: Duncker und Humblot, 1992), 216–222.

[10] Hogan, G. "How Catholic was the Constitution?" (paper presented at *The Constitution at 70*, Trinity College Dublin Centre for Law and Democracy June 8–9, 2007), and Hogan G., G. Whyte, and J. M. Kelly: *The Irish Constitution* (London, Butterworths, 1994).

[11] Von Bogdandy, A. "The European Constitution and European Identity: Text and Subtext establishing a Constitution for Europe," *International Journal of Constitutional Law* 3 (2005): 295.

[12] See Venice Commission, *Opinion 621/2011 on the new Constitution of Hungary*, para 72 in this volume.

democracy, equality, the rule of law and respect for human rights, including for the rights of persons belonging to minorities." In comparison, the values contained in the Hungarian preamble are quite different with a unique emphasis on:

> Family and nation provide the most important framework of our coexistence, and that our fundamental cohesive values are fidelity, faith and love. We hold that the strength of community and honor of each person are based on work... [T]he common goal of the citizens and the State is to achieve the highest possible measure of well-being, safety, order, justice and liberty.

This cluster of key words—family, nation, work, order—is a chilling echo of Europe's darker constitutional past.[13] If read strictly, it is suggested that the Article R(3) rule of interpretation could put the Hungarian Fundamental Law significantly at odds with the liberal and pluralist approach to rights such as dignity (Article II), privacy and family life (Article VI), freedom of thought, conscience and religion (Article VII), equality (Article XV) or marriage (Article L) that has been developed since WWII in Europe.[14]

Scope of Dignity: Construction and Confusions

The Fundamental Law constructs dignity as a human quality, shared by everyone, with a special mention of workers under Article XVII(3). Even though this provision appears quite inclusive, it deserves close

---

[13] Joerges, Ch. and N.S.L. Ghaleigh eds. *The Darker Legacies of Law in Europe* (Oxford: Hart Publishing, 2003). In particular, see the French constitutional statute of July 10, 1940 (never enacted, but encapsulating the foundations of the Vichy regime): "*Cette Constitution devra garantir les droits du Travail, de la Famille et de la Patrie*" [This constitution will guarantee the right of work, family and fatherland] (preamble). See also Franco's constitution: Article 1, *Fuero de los Españoles* [Statute law of the Spanish people], July 17, 1945.

[14] The Venice Commission identifies some problematic issues in relation to freedom of religion, freedom to marry, freedom of thought and equality. See *Opinion 621/2011*, para 71–73 in this volume. See also the contribution of Renata Uitz in this volume.

critical scrutiny. Moreover, the drafting of Article II with its emphasis on the protection of "life of the fetus from the moment of conception" stands out in European constitutionalism and raises a number of issues.

'Human dignity shall be inviolable'

Under Article II, "human dignity shall be inviolable." The claim of dignity's inviolability is typical of post-WWII European constitutionalism, from the 1949 German Basic Law (Article 1) to the EU Charter of Fundamental Rights (Article 1), and including the latest constitution adopted by an EU member state, Finland in 2000 (Article 1).[15] This does not mean that in everyday life Europe is a sort of paradise, where human dignity is never breached. Rather, it is submitted that this is more helpfully understood as an axiomatic statement which structures a constitutional order and indicates European constitutionalism's priority to protect dignity.[16] This was eloquently put by the European Court of Human Rights, which held in the marital rape ruling that "the very essence [of the European Convention of Human Rights] is respect for human dignity and human freedom."[17]

In the 2011 Fundamental Law, a similar claim can be found under Article I ("The inviolable and inalienable fundamental rights of MAN shall be respected. It shall be the primary obligation of the State to protect these rights").[18] However, when read in the light of Article

---

[15] "Human dignity is inviolable. To protect and to respect it shall be the duty of all state authority." (Article 1, 1949 German Basic Law); "The constitution shall guarantee the inviolability of human dignity and the freedoms and rights of individuals and promote justice in society." (Article 1(2), 2000 Finnish Constitution); "Human dignity is inviolable. It must be respected and protected." (Article 1, EU Charter of Fundamental Rights).

[16] On German dignity case law see Kommers, D. *The Constitutional Jurisprudence of the Federal Republic of Germany* (Durham: Duke University Press, 1997) and Häberle, P. *The Principle of Respect for Human Dignity* (Strasbourg: Council of Europe Publishing, 1999).

[17] *S. W. v. United Kingdom*, no. 20166/92, October 27, 1995, para 44.

[18] Article 8(1) of the 1989 Hungarian Constitution read: "The Republic of Hungary shall recognize the inviolable and inalienable fundamental human rights; respecting and protecting these rights are primary obligations of the State."

R(3), this commitment is arguably no longer in line with European constitutionalism, as the priority appears to be given to the National Avowal and its problematic values discussed above (subject to confirmation by judicial interpretation). If taken literally, this rule of interpretation would alter the constitutional hierarchy, by prioritizing the values expressed in the preamble over "inviolable dignity." This may result in an instrumentalisation of the concept of dignity, which would no longer serve the protection of human identities and freedoms, but rather serve the purpose of enforcing some or all of the values identified in the preamble. In this scenario, the constitutional axiom of inviolable dignity is devoid of meaning.

'Every human being'

The 2011 Fundamental Law makes it clear that dignity is a human quality (Article I and II) and in this, it is completely in line with post-WWII constitutionalism and echoes the 1989 Hungarian constitution. The phrase is inclusive, in Hungarian "all human persons" and arguably builds on the equality of dignity drawn from the fact that we are all equally human.[19]

However, the ontological humanity of dignity is arguably qualified by Article I(4) ("Legal entities established by an Act shall also have the fundamental rights, and they shall also be bound by the obligations which, by their nature, apply not only to human beings"), which makes it possible to extend the protection of rights to a range of non-human and unspecified "legal entities." Leaving aside the issue of letting matters of such constitutional importance be decided by ordinary statute (not even a "cardinal act"),[20] it is suggested that this provision can potentially upset the foundations of liberal democracy, where rights were historically defined as human attributes, ever since the 1789 French Declaration on the Rights of Man and the Citizen and the 1948 United Nations Universal Declaration of Human Rights. It is not quite clear what the drafters had in mind, nor is it clear that they were aware of the confusion that Article I(4) may trigger. Legal persons may

---

[19] See Kriszta Kovács's contribution in this volume.

[20] On cardinal laws, see Venice Commission, *Opinion 621/2011,* para 22–25; on special acts see para 59.

be granted some entitlements—as well as responsibilities—but it is suggested that these should clearly be distinguished from human rights, in theoretical, practical and drafting terms.

Finally, it has to be noted that under Article I(2) fundamental rights may be exercised by "individuals and communities." This provision introduces a communitarian dimension of rights, unknown to post-1989 Hungarian constitutionalism, which had been constructed on the basis of a strong emphasis on *individual* rights as an attempt to rebalance and counter the communist focus on collective rights.[21] Moreover, this communitarian approach to rights is arguably atypical of European constitutionalism, which has promoted and constructed a society made of equal individuals and where individuals' rights cannot be subsumed and dissolved in society or in a group. This approach was strengthened after WWII as a reaction against totalitarian regimes, which subjected the individuality of human beings to that of the community to which they were said to belong, defined by their race and religion. Finally and importantly, this choice of drafting arguably evades the key issue of minority (rather than community) rights, which as noted by the Venice Commission, is not fully addressed by the 2011 Fundamental Law.[22]

The 'right to life and dignity'

As under the 1989 constitution, the "right to life and to human dignity" forms one semantic and normative unit in the 2011 Fundamental Law. This phrase proved problematic in the euthanasia ruling[23] as

---

[21] Dupré, *Importing the Law in Post-communist Transitions,* 122–127.

[22] Venice Commission, *Opinion 621/2011*, para 42–44. 1989. See also Amnesty International 2010 Report, "Racism, violent attacks and discrimination against gypsies," 165–166.

[23] Bárd, P. "The Hungarian Constitutional Court Decision on Euthanasia. A Half Hearted Ruling, Case Study of the Decision 22/2003. (IV. 28.) of the Hungarian Constitutional Court," *Revue de Justice Constitutionnelle Est-Européenne* 4 (2004): 105–121; Halmai, G. "Birth and Death—A Constitutional Approach. Constitutional Court on Abortion and Euthanasia," *Revue de Justice Constitutionnelle Est-Européenne* 4 (2004): 87–104 and Jakab, A. "Die Euthanasieentscheidung des ungarischen Verfassungsgerichts vom 28 April 2003" [The Hungarian constitutional ruling on euthanasia of April 28, 2003] *OsteuropaRecht* 50 (2004): 31–40.

the two concepts are arguably not coterminous. While they may be mutually supportive, they may also conflict with each other and, for instance, transform the right to life into an obligation to live (even without dignity). Distinguishing life from dignity in constitutional drafting would arguably have not only clarified the scope of each right, but would also have left all options open (to the judge or law-maker), thus making it possible for the Fundamental Law to adjust to social and scientific developments that cannot be anticipated at the time of drafting.

Also, had the drafters wanted to protect "life in dignity," a number of alternative formulae would have been possible as indicated by other European constitutions, such as "an existence free and dignified" as guaranteed by work,[24] "a life in conformity with human dignity"[25] or "a life in dignity and independence."[26] These choices reflect a more comprehensive approach both to the right to life and to dignity, which are arguably more in tune with the standards and sophistication of human rights protection in twenty-first century Europe.[27] Moreover, they are not incompatible with the general commitment to dignity (as under Article II) or the acknowledgement of dignity protection for specific human beings (i.e. the elderly and workers under the EU Charter). The Hungarian drafters, however, apparently chose not to approach dignity in this way, and the second part of Article II focuses on protecting "the life of the fetus" in a way that arguably highlights what may have been their main dignity agenda.

Protection of 'life of the fetus'

This is the third component of Article II and it focuses on "life of the fetus." Despite this provision's clear focus on life and not on dignity,

---

[24] Article 36, Italian constitution.

[25] Article 23, Belgian constitution.

[26] Article 25, EU Charter: "The Union recognizes and respects the rights of the elderly to lead a life in dignity and independence and to participate in social and cultural life."

[27] More generally, see Nussbaum, M. and A. Sen, eds. *The Quality of Life* (Oxford: Clarendon Press, 1993).

this study would not be complete if it did not address even briefly the more salient issues raised by this phrase.[28]

First, Article II is arguably at odds with provisions on life and/ or dignity in European constitutions, which are concerned with protecting human rights *after* birth. The closest provision is perhaps the Irish constitution,[29] which explicitly enshrined "the right to life of the unborn" following the 1983 reform.[30] Moreover, constitutional case law on fetal and embryonic life varies, and the European Court of Human Rights has acknowledged this diversity, using it as an argument not to decide in the abstract "whether the unborn child is a person for the purpose of Article 2 of the Convention."[31] What is clear, however, is that European constitutions do not explicitly protect fetal and embryonic life "from the moment of conception."[32] It may be inferred from this wording that the drafters of the Fundamental Law intended to grant a particularly and unusually strong protection to life before birth.

---

[28] The concept of dignity can be and has been used in relation to bioethics: Andorno, R. "Human Dignity and Human Rights as a Common Ground for a Global Ethics" *Journal of Medicine and Philosophy* (2009): 1–18 and Plomer, A. *The Law of Ethics and Medical Research* (London: Cavendish, 2007), 67–93.

[29] Article 6(1) of the Czech Charter of Fundamental Rights and Basic Freedoms reads: "Everyone has the right to life. Human life is worthy of protection even before birth" and the Slovak constitution contains a similar provision under Article 15. It has to be noted that these provisions do not guarantee a right to life and that "protection of life before birth" does not necessarily overlap with "protection from the moment of conception."

[30] Article 40(3)(iii). Following this provision, introduced in 1983, unless the pregnant woman's life in danger, the fetus's right takes priority and abortion is illegal. Advice on arranging an abortion was also illegal until the ruling of the European Court of Human Rights in *Open Door and Dublin Well Woman Centre v. Ireland*, no. 14234-5/88, October 29, 1992. Lawful advice can now be provided as long as it does not promote or advocate a termination. Jackson, E. *Medical Law. Texts, Cases and Materials* (Oxford: Oxford University Press, 2010), 701–702. See also *A., B. and C. v. Ireland* [GC], no. 25579/05, December 16, 2010.

[31] *Vo v. France*, no. 53924/00, July 8, 2004, para 84 and 85.

[32] This choice of wording might to have been influenced by the American Convention of Human Rights, Article 4(1) of which reads: "Every person has the right to have his life respected. The right shall be protected by law and, *in general*, from the moment of conception. No one shall be arbitrarily deprived of his life." (emphasis added).

This is in line with the constitutional "encouragement of the commitment to have children" under Article L, and the preamble's emphasis on the family "as the most important framework of our coexistence [together with the nation]."

It is suggested here that the emphasis on a constitutional right to life "from the moment of conception" may neither be necessary, nor effective, to protect unborn life. Under the case law of the European Court of Human Rights, while the fetus is not explicitly defined as a person for the purpose of Article 2, it is clearly protected through positive obligations.[33] States may not therefore treat fetuses and embryos as mere objects of experimentation or trade. In particular, embryos enjoy explicit protection under the Convention for the Protection of Human Rights and Dignity of the Human Being with regard to the Application of Biology and Medicine signed at Oviedo in 1997 and ratified by Hungary in January 2002.[34] Moreover, it is argued that while Article II seems to support a particularly restrictive approach to abortion, so far allowed under the 1989 constitution and regulated by statute law (following Decisions 64/1991 and 48/1998),[35] it may turn out to be less effective than perhaps intended as it introduces a problematic confusion in relation to the constitutional rights and protection before birth. As the Hungarian language distinguishes between "embryo" (*embrió*) and "fetus" (*magzat*), the first official translation with both terms in English for the original *magzat* is confusing but might be understood as making explicit the drafters' intention to grant the same constitutional status and protection to prenatal life throughout the pregnancy. By protecting the "life of the fetus" ..."from the moment of conception" (i.e. before the fetal stage), the Fundamental Law arguably disregards the biological reality of the development of prenatal life in various stages, thus depriving lawmakers of the flexibility to reflect these different developmental stages, and this may be particularly problematic in relation to *in vitro* embryos. This leads to the

[33] *Tysiąc v. Poland*, no. 5410/03, March 20, 2007, para 110–112.

[34] Articles 11-14, Article 18 and Article 21.

[35] Küpper, H. "Das zweite Abtreibungsurteil des ungarischen Verfassungsgerichts" [The Second Abortion Ruling of the Hungarian Constitutional Court] *OsteuropaRecht* (1999): 155–169.

second difficulty of Article II, namely the lack of distinction between *in vitro* and *in utero* embryos. It is therefore suggested that the Fundamental Law may provide limited guidance in relation to surplus or defective embryos.

Furthermore, strictly speaking, protection of embryonic and fetal life does not imply a right to be born alive, but the protection of life *in utero* and presumably *in vitro* too. The most problematic issue of this emphasis on prenatal life is that it completely ignores the fundamental reality that this life cannot develop outside a woman's uterus, and protecting it without considering this fact appears futile.[36] This points to the glaring absence of the key character, the pregnant woman.[37] It is suggested that it is not possible to consider the constitutional status of prenatal life (whatever it may be) without considering that of the woman carrying that life in her womb.[38] The difficulty is of course to strike the balance between the pregnant woman's clearly defined constitutional rights, notably to life and dignity (Article II), and to privacy (Article VI)[39] and the interests of prenatal life. It is submitted that the Fundamental Law constructs a very questionable picture of women's dignity and this is where the deterministic definition of dignity discussed above becomes particularly problematic. Considering the heavy emphasis on family in the National Avowal and the requirement to interpret the Fundamental Law in compliance with it, in the worst case scenario women's dignity may therefore be interpreted as related to maternity and motherhood, an interpretation which might be strengthened by Article L which protects "marriage understood to

---

[36] In vitro life has no future if not implanted in a woman's womb. It at best be suspended by freezing in vitro embryos.

[37] Even the Irish constitution acknowledges the existence of the pregnant woman: "The State acknowledges the right to life of the unborn, and with due regard of the equal right to life of the mother, guarantees in its laws to respect, and, as far as practicable, by its laws to defend and vindicate that right."

[38] "It follows from this recapitulation of the case-law… that the unborn child is not regarded as a 'person' directly protected by Article 2 of the Convention and that if the unborn do have a 'right' to 'life,' it is implicitly limited by the mother's rights and interests." *Vo v. France*, para 80.

[39] As is discussed below, the Fundamental Law does not enshrine a right to physical and mental integrity.

be the conjugal union of a man and a woman... and the family" and "[encourages] the commitment to have children."[40] Therefore the Fundamental Law arguably identifies women primarily as wives and mothers. This identity is so deeply embedded in the values and fabric of the Fundamental Law that no space is left to question women's wishes for maternity under Article II.

If this is the reason for the omission of women's dignity under Article II in the specific relation to fetal life, then we are faced with a gross breach of human rights and of dignity in particular as women become a means to an end: to marry, found a family, produce children and implement governmental demography policy.[41] The Venice Commission saw these risks and urged that Article II "cannot be read as considering the life of the unborn child to be of higher value than the life of the mother and does not necessarily imply an obligation for the Hungarian State to penalize abortion."[42]

Workers' dignity

Article XVII(3) is generally about employment rights, i.e. national economic policy, collective bargaining and right to strike. The Fundamental Law emphasizes the importance of work in the National Avowal and several provisions are about work.[43] Article XVII(3) is

---

[40] The Venice Commission expressed some reservation on the restrictive approach to the concept of family and marriage, *Opinion 621/2011*, para 46–50. The Commission focuses on the (im)possible recognition of same sex marriage or unions. What has to be added is that under Article 8 (right to private and family life), the European Court of Human Rights has protected a very wide concept of family, in comparison to which Article L is extremely restrictive. Moreover, Article VI(1), which is phrased in minimalist terms and does not reflect the Court's case law.

[41] Stolz, J. "Angoissée par son déclin démographique, la Hongrie renvoie les mères au foyer" [Anxious about her demographic decline, Hungary sends mothers back home] *Le Monde,* January 6, 2011 and Stolz, J. "La Hongrie 'a besoin de chaque vie'" [Hungary 'needs every single life'] *Le Monde,* May 20, 2011.

[42] Venice Commission, *Opinion 621/2011*, para 66.

[43] See also Article XII (free choice of occupation) and Article XVIII (prohibition of child labor).

overtly modeled on the EU Charter.[44] This raises some issues of clarity and consistency as explained by the Venice Commission in its first opinion on the Hungarian constitutional transformation.[45] Moreover, in the EU Charter "dignity" is a new addition to the well-established requirements of health and safety and its significance is not fully understood yet. The explanations of the Charter mention Article 26 of the revised Social Charter, which is largely about prevention of sexual harassment in the workplace.[46] While this is an important aspect of workers' rights, the protection of dignity at work is not reduced to this one aspect.

It is suggested that the Kantian imperative never to treat a human being as a means to an end but as an end as such, which is the philosophical foundation of human dignity in European constitutionalism,[47] is not limited to the public and private spheres, but that it extends to the work sphere too.[48] Therefore within the constraints of the unequal work relationship (the hierarchic imbalance between employer and employee), dignity protection arguably means

---

[44] Article 31(1) reads: "Every worker shall have the right to working conditions respecting their health, safety and dignity."

[45] Venice Commission, *Opinion 614/2011 on three legal questions arising in the process of drafting the new constitution of Hungary*, para 25–26.

[46] Article 26, Revised Social Charter: "With a view to ensuring the effective exercise of the right of all workers to protection of their dignity at work, the Parties undertake, in consultation with employers' and workers' organizations: 1. to promote awareness, information and prevention of sexual harassment in the workplace or in relation to work and to take all appropriate measures to protect workers from such conduct; 2. to promote awareness, information and prevention of recurrent reprehensible or distinctly negative and offensive actions directed against individual workers in the workplace or in relation to work and to take all appropriate measures to protect workers from such conduct."

[47] Fletcher, G.P. "Human Dignity as a Constitutional Value," *University of Western Ontario Law Review* 22 (1984): 171–182 and Weinrib, L.E. "Human Dignity as a Rights-Protecting Principle," *National Journal of Constitutional Law* 17 (2004): 325–345.

[48] De Tissot, O. "Pour une analyse juridique du concept de dignité du salarié" [A legal analysis of the concept of the employee's dignity] *Droit Social* (1995): 972–977. Héas, F. "Observations sur le concept de dignité appliqué aux relations du travail" [Observations on the concept of dignity as applied to work relationships] *Le Droit Ouvrier* 746 (2010): 1–8.

that workers should not be reduced to mere objects at the complete disposal of the employer and instrumentalised in order to achieve certain ends (e.g. in twenty-first century management-speak targets imposed by the employer). The connections between work, workers' rights and dignity raise many complex issues and three points can be highlighted here.

First, human beings arguably do not lose their dignity (and the related rights) in their identity and activity as workers in the workplace. Therefore all the constitutional rights also arguably apply in the workplace: particularly relevant in this respect are workers' autonomy, the right to self-determine and to participate in work-related decisions, and the right to privacy. Second, even if the constitutional dimensions of the work sphere are not fully articulated (unlike the private and public spheres) in Europe, it remains entirely clear that forced labor, slavery and human trafficking are absolutely prohibited by European constitutionalism. The first two prohibitions are explicitly listed under Article 4 of the European Convention on Human Rights[49] and all three of them are confirmed by the EU Charter.[50] Intriguingly, the 2011 Fundamental Law does not enshrine the prohibition of forced labor.[51] As will be discussed below, this is not the only missing right, but its absence is particularly striking considering the general EU Charter flavor that permeates the Hungarian provisions and in particular the verbatim copy of Article 31 EU Charter in relation to dignity at work. It can only be hoped that this is due to absentmindedness at the time of drafting and does not point to any particular agenda.[52] Finally, some constitutions in Europe have elaborated connections between work and dignity and can be mentioned here to place Article XVII(3) in

---

[49] The case law is limited largely due to victims' difficulty of accessing courts. See *Siliadin v. France*, no. 73316/01, July 26, 2005 and *Rantsev v. Cyprus and Russia*, no. 25965/04, January 7, 2010.

[50] Article 5, EU Charter: "1. No one shall be held in slavery or servitude. 2. No one shall be required to perform forced or compulsory labour. 3. Trafficking in human beings is prohibited."

[51] The prohibitions of slavery and human trafficking are enshrined under Article III(1).

[52] Stolz, J. "A Gyöngyöspata, vitrine de l'extrême droite" [At Gyöngyöspata, show case of the far right] *Le Monde*, August 16, 2011.

a wider comparative perspective in order to show the possibilities of constitutional drafting in this respect. The Italian constitution provides that remuneration for work has to "be sufficient to ensure [workers] and their families a free existence in dignity [*un'esistenza libera e dignitosa*]."[53] Article 59 of the Portuguese constitution provides that "the organization of work in keeping with dignity and personal self-fulfillment, while reconciling the needs of vocational activity and family life." Under Article 23, the Belgian constitution enshrines dignity at work in an even more comprehensive manner: "the right to employment and to free choice of a professional activity in the framework of a general employment policy... the right to fair terms of employment to fair remuneration, as well as the right to information, consultation and collective negotiation."

It is not possible here to comment on these approaches in detail, but it is clear from the mere wording that constitutional provisions on dignity at work and workers' dignity can create very different designs and rights from the Fundamental Law, which offers, by comparison, a restrictive and conservative protection of workers' dignity.[54]

The Eye of the Storm: the Constitutional Court's Competencies

The Fundamental Law contains one last mention of dignity in a unique location, as part of the definition of the Constitutional Court's competencies under Article 37(4):

> As long as the level of state debt exceeds half of the Gross Domestic Product, the Constitutional Court may, within its competence pursuant to points b) to e) of paragraph (2) of Article

[53] Article 36(1) reads: "Workers are entitled to remuneration commensurate with the quantity and quality of their work, and in any case sufficient to ensure to them and their families a free and honorable [dignified] existence."

[54] Cieslar, A., A. Nayer, and B. Smeesters, *Le droit à l'épanouissement de l'être humain au travail, Métamorphoses du droit social* [The right to self-fulfillment in the workplace. Transformations of Labor Law] (Bruxelles: Bruylant, 2007).

> 24,[55] review the Acts on the central budget, on the implementation of the budget, on central taxes, on duties and on contributions, on customs duties, and on the central conditions for local taxes as to their conformity with the Fundamental Law exclusively in connection with the rights to life and human dignity, to the protection of personal data, to freedom of thought, conscience and religion, or in connection with the rights related to Hungarian citizenship, and it may only annul these Acts for the violation of these rights.

The explanation for the inclusion of dignity in this provision is to be found in the clash between the Constitutional Court and the Orbán government.[56] As a result of the court's adverse ruling on retroactive taxation, the government reformed the 1989 Constitution in November 2010,[57] so as to by-pass this ruling and to restrict the court's competencies, seemingly to avoid similar rulings in the future.[58] As expected (or feared), the court's competencies have remained restricted in the Fundamental Law.[59] Protection of human dignity together with a number of rights (right to life, protection of personal data, freedom of thought, religion and conscience, and rights related to Hungarian citizenship) act as an exception to the restrictions on the court's competencies in reviewing "Acts of the central budget."

---

[55] Article 24(2) reads: "The Constitutional Court shall... b) review, at the initiative of a judge, the conformity with the Fundamental Law of rules of law applicable in a particular case; c) review, on the basis of a constitutional complaint, the conformity with the Fundamental Law of the rules of law applied in a particular case; d) review, on the basis of a constitutional complaint, the conformity with the Fundamental Law of a judicial decision; e) review, at the initiative of the Government, of one fourth of all Members of Parliament or of the Commissioner for Fundamental Rights, the conformity of rules of law with the Fundamental Law..."

[56] Decision 184/2010. (X. 28.) See Kovács, K. and G.A. Tóth, "Hungary's Constitutional Transformation," 192–195.

[57] Venice Commission, *Opinion 614/2011*, para 9.

[58] The Constitutional Court delivered a further ruling reiterating that retroactive taxation violates human dignity. Decision 37/2011. (V. 10.)

[59] Venice Commission, *Opinion 614/*2011, para 34–64, and *Opinion 621/2011*, para 91–101 and 120–127. See also the chapter of Christian Boulanger and Oliver W. Lembcke in this volume.

Restricting a constitutional court's power based on the subject of the statute (i.e. the national budget) reduces the protective scope of all the other rights as they are excluded from constitutional review.

In particular a number of essential rights that contribute to dignity protection are excluded from constitutional review, such as privacy (Article VI), prohibition of torture and inhuman and degrading treatment and punishment, prohibition of slavery and human trafficking (Article III), and crucially, equality before the law and non-discrimination (Article XV). The rationale for the exclusion of these rights (and inclusion of those protected) is not clear.[60] In any event, it does not appear to follow the exclusion from derogation under Article 15 of the European Convention of Human Rights, i.e. Article 2 (except in respect of deaths resulting from lawful acts of war), 3, 4(1) and 7 (no retroactivity of criminal punishment). Moreover reading Article 37(4) in the light of Article 54(1) of the Fundamental Law,[61] which maintains some constitutional protection for key rights "in special legal orders," highlights a paradoxical discrepancy between routine constitutional operation and emergency situations. Namely, under Article 37(4) (routine constitutional operation), the prohibition of torture, medical and scientific experiment, eugenics practices, presumption of innocence and the right to a fair trial cannot be subjected to constitutional review if they are affected by a budgetary statute, whereas they are protected "in special legal orders." Finally, the drafters seem to have been oblivious of the fact that, under Article 51 of the Charter of

[60] "In order to understand the motivation behind the selection, there is little point in searching for principled reason. Hungarian case law reflects that the Constitutional Court has annulled tax and other financial measures by referring to those rights and principles which are missing from the list." Kovács, K. and G.A. Tóth, "Hungary's Constitutional Transformation," 194.

[61] The protection of rights in "special legal orders" is much reduced in comparison to the 1989 Constitution, which maintained protection for a wide range of rights under Article 8(4), including life and dignity, personal security, legal capacity (Articles 54-56), the presumption of innocence (Article 57), freedom of thought, conscience and religion (Article 60), the rights to equality, education, protection of minorities, citizenship (Articles 66–69) and the right to social security (Article 70/E). Generally, see: Ferejohn, J. and P. Pasquale, "The Law of Exception: A Typology of Emergency Powers," *International Journal of Constitutional Law* 2 (2004): 210–239.

Fundamental Rights, member states of the European Union are bound by the Charter "when they are implementing Union law." As a result, it is suggested that the restriction under Article 37(4) of the Fundamental Law may cease to be relevant if the Acts of the Budget involve "implementation of EU law."

This restrictive approach is however clearly in line with a general tightening of governmental control over the Constitutional Court, primarily through a reform of the rules on judicial appointment, which does away with the requirement of cross party consensus in Parliament and deprives constitutional judges of the power to select their own president.[62] The Constitutional Court was a new institution of the 1989 Constitution which played a very active role in the construction of democracy after the end of communism, particularly, but not exclusively, through its review of constitutional rights.[63] This restriction of the Constitutional Court's competencies forms part of a general picture of greater control over the ordinary judiciary[64] and the replacement of the four ombudsmen established under the 1989 Constitution by a single one under the Fundamental Law.[65]

In short, the inclusion of dignity under Article 37(4) is a formal acknowledgement of this concept's constitutional importance, but a closer look reveals that it may be no more than that. Moreover, as discussed below, the Fundamental Law has arguably omitted a number of mentions and rights which form an essential part of dignity's normative construction in European constitutionalism.

---

[62] The Venice Commission has expressed concerns about this, *Opinion 621/2011*, para 24–101.

[63] Halmai, G. ed. *The Constitution Found? The First Nine Years of Hungarian Constitutional Review of Human Rights* (Budapest: INDOK, 2000); Paczolay, P. ed. *Twenty Years of the Hungarian Constitutional Court* (Budapest: Constitutional Court of the Republic of Hungary, 2009).

[64] Articles 25–28, Fundamental Law, see Venice Commission, *Opinion 621/2011*, para 102–110.

[65] Article 30 creates one single commissioner for fundamental rights. See Venice Commission, *Opinion 621/2011*, para 114–115.

Eloquent Silences

This section argues that the Fundamental Law lacks a number of rights that make up a more comprehensive definition of human dignity in European constitutionalism, namely some components of the normative core of this concept under the European Convention on Human Rights and the EU Charter of Rights, the definition of dignity as being an "inherent" quality to humanity, and perhaps more problematic of all, the connections between dignity and the foundations of democracy.

Missing components of the European Core of Human Dignity

The EU Charter of Fundamental Rights defines human dignity as being made up of a cluster of particularly fundamental rights, which are listed under its first title: the right to life and the abolition of the death penalty (Article 2), the respect for physical and mental integrity (Article 3(1)), the prohibition of torture, inhuman and degrading treatment or punishment (Article 4), and the prohibition of slavery, forced labor and human trafficking (Article 5). In comparison, the Fundamental Law provides a very patchy picture of human dignity. In addition to the lack of a prohibition on forced labor discussed above, a clear mention of the abolition of the death penalty is arguably absent and the Venice Commission expressed concerns about this:

> The Venice Commission would like to add that, in the light of Protocol 6 ("Restriction of the Death Penalty") and to Protocol 13 ("Complete abolition of the death penalty") to the ECHR, both ratified by Hungary, and taking into account that the will of the Hungarian authorities is to give high protection to human life, it is regrettable that neither Article II nor any other Article in the Constitution mentions explicitly the complete abolition of the death penalty.[66]

[66] *Opinion 621/2011*, para 68. The Venice Commission is further concerned by the provision of life imprisonment without parole (para 69–70) under Article IV(2) which reads: "No one shall be deprived of their liberty, except for

Moreover, a general right to physical and mental integrity (Article 3 EU Charter) is arguably lacking in the Fundamental Law. It appears as an odd omission considering the Fundamental Law's obvious awareness of the EU Charter approach to dignity in other respects, such as work. This is particularly the case in relation to Article 3 of EU Charter from which the Fundamental Law retains some of the key components, such as the prohibition on medical and scientific experiments on human beings without their free and informed consent[67] and prohibition of all eugenics practices, use of the human body or any of its part for financial gain and human cloning.[68]

The omission of the general right to physical and mental integrity therefore appears to be deliberate. It is arguably significant too. Article 3(1) EU Charter is phrased in very broad and inclusive terms: "Everyone has the right to respect for his or her physical and mental integrity" and it applies to a much wider range of cases than the very specific ones listed under Article III of the Fundamental Law. Moreover, the phrase "physical and mental integrity" is often understood as a legal synonym of human dignity, which is sometimes easier to use in the context judicial adjudication, as it retains dignity's versatility, while its meaning is perhaps more immediately understandable by judges and lawyers.

Furthermore, protection of "physical and mental integrity" has been well developed by the European Court of Human Rights at the crossroads of Article 8 (privacy, self-determination and autonomy) and Article 3 (prohibition of torture and inhuman and degrading treatment or punishment). Since the minimum threshold of severity does not apply, a breach of "physical and mental integrity" can be much more easily ascertained under the Convention, thus leading to more far-reaching protection than is possible in the (fortunately) rare cases of actual torture. Finally, reliance on the right to physical and mental

reasons stipulated in an Act and only in accordance with the procedure stipulated in an Act. Life imprisonment without parole may only be imposed for the commission of a willful and violent criminal offence."

67 Article III(2): "It shall be prohibited to perform any medical or scientific experiment on human beings without their informed and voluntary consent."

68 Article III(3): "Practices aimed at eugenics, the use of the human body or its parts for financial gain, and the cloning of human beings shall be prohibited." See also Article 13 and Articles 21–22 and of the Oviedo Convention.

integrity can be used to complement other rights (such as privacy) and may be instrumental in tilting the balance in their favor (as may be the case with women seeking a termination of pregnancy).

As a result, out of the rights that make up the core normative definition of human dignity under the EU Charter, the Fundamental Law only recognizes a selection, leaving out some of its most fundamental aspects, i.e. prohibition of the death penalty, prohibition of forced labor and the right to physical and mental integrity.

Inherent dignity

Under the Fundamental Law, dignity is no longer an inherent or innate human quality. The omission is apparent with reference to Article 54 of the 1989 Constitution, which refers to human dignity as being an innate quality. The inherent quality of human rights and dignity was one of the essential post-WWII commitments to building a better world, as reflected in Article 1 of 1948 Universal Declaration of Human Rights ("All human beings are born free and equal in dignity and in rights"). Moreover, European constitutions have generally enshrined dignity as being explicitly or implicitly inherent.[69] Therefore, following European constitutionalism and post-WWII international human rights protection conventions, dignity is arguably the concept that defines humanity and triggers constitutional protection. This acts as a timely reminder that dignity is not something we have to deserve by meeting certain obligations or may lose through, for instance, particular types of behavior·

The Fundamental Law seems to point to a different understanding of dignity and constitutional rights, according to which full protection of rights and dignity depends on compliance with the values set by the constitution's drafters, made compulsory through Article R(3).[70] This constitutional approach to rights, combining the subordination to

---

[69] E.g. Article 10, Constitution of Spain; Article 6, Constitution of Bulgaria; Article 12, Constitution of Slovakia; Article 1, Charter of Fundamental Rights of Czech Republic, Article 30, Constitution of Poland.

[70] Article XIX(3) makes this clear in relation to social security which provides that, "The nature and extent of social measures may be determined by an Act also in accordance with the usefulness to the community of the beneficiary's activities."

ideologically imposed values and ignorance of the inherent dimension of human rights and human dignity might bring back times that one hoped had been relegated to the totalitarian and anti-democratic past of Europe.

Foundation of democracy

The Fundamental Law establishes Hungary as a democracy under Article B(1),[71] which confirms the commitment to democracy stated in the National Avowal,[72] and appears at first to be in line with European constitutionalism. What is more intriguing however are the ways in which the Fundamental Law constructs the foundations of democracy. The Fundamental Law's approach to its past proceeds from a deliberate and explicit editing of Hungarian constitutional history in the National Avowal:

> We do not recognize the communist constitution of 1949, since it was the basis of a tyrannical rule; therefore we proclaim it to be invalid… We date the restoration of the self-determination of our State, lost on the nineteenth day of March 1944, from the second day of May 1990, when the first freely elected popular representation was formed. We shall consider this date to be the beginning of our country's new democracy and constitutional order.

The invalidation of the 1949 Constitution proclaimed above, together with the decision to identify the birth of the "new democracy and constitutional order" with the first free elections in May 1990, negates the essential role of the post-communist constitution, formally an amendment to the 1949 Constitution and adopted in October 1989. This creates a number of paradoxes, one of which is of a technical nature: the procedural rules following which the Fundamental Law was adopted have therefore no valid constitutional basis.[73] Moreover, as the

71 "Hungary shall be an independent, democratic state under the rule of law."

72 "We hold that democracy exists only where the State serves it citizens and administers their affairs in an equitable manner and without abuse or partiality."

73 See *Opinion on the Fundamental Law of Hungary*, para 1–3.

1989 constitutional revision was arguably the first and most fundamental step towards the establishment of liberal democracy in Hungary, it is surprising that the Fundamental Law does not acknowledge this historical fact. Having negated those crucial months of democratic and constitutional foundation, the National Avowal reaches back to a much more ancient past encapsulated by the phrase "historical constitution" with a questionable and uncertain definition,[74] and, more to the point, of arguably remote relevance for twenty-first century constitutionalism in Hungary.

In addition, the Fundamental Law does not lay the foundations of democracy in its commitment to protect human dignity and human rights and therefore differs from European constitutional practice after WWII and dictatorships in Southern and Central Europe. The foundational connections between dignity and democracy are explicitly made in some constitutions, notably the Portuguese constitution which ties the definition of republic with the concept of dignity;[75] the Spanish constitution, according to which dignity is a foundation of "the political order and social peace"[76] and the Romanian constitution which elaborates on these connections in very explicit terms.[77] This approach to founding and defining democracy by relating it to the protection of dignity has also been adopted at the supranational level, both by the European Court of Human Rights as discussed above and explicitly in the Lisbon Treaty (Article 2). This omission seems to be deliberate as the Fundamental Law does not contain a clause linking Hungary's

---

[74] Bak, J.M. and A. Gara-Bak, "The Ideology of a 'Millennial Constitution' in Hungary," *East European Quarterly* 3 (1981): 307–323.

[75] Article 1 reads: "Portugal is a sovereign Republic, that is based on dignity of the human person and the will of the people and is committed to building a free and just society united in its common purposes."

[76] Article 10(1) reads: "The dignity of the person, the inviolable rights which are inherent, the free development of the personality, the respect for the law for the rights of others are the foundations of the political order and social peace."

[77] Article 1(3) reads: "Romania is a democratic and social state, governed by the rule of law, in which human dignity, the citizen's rights and freedoms, the free development of human personality, justice and political pluralism represent supreme values, in the spirit of the democratic traditions of the Romanian people and the ideals of the Revolution of December 1989 and shall be guaranteed."

respect of fundamental rights to international and European human rights instruments.[78]

The constitutional foundations of the new Fundamental Law are arguably of a negative nature: they are not to be found in dignity and human rights, they are not to be derived from the 1989 Constitution and they are not to be traced back to the transformation that took place between 1988 (to use an indicative date) and May 1, 1990. It is not quite clear how the National Avowal's re-construction of Hungarian history may affect the regime established by the Fundamental Law and its human rights practice in particular. It seems however certain that such selective memory and exclusive reconstruction of the constitutional foundations of the Fundamental Law taints its overt commitment to democracy.

Conclusion

The picture of human dignity that emerges out of a closer analysis of the 2011 Hungarian Fundamental Law is unusual with regard to European constitutionalism: instead of being an inherent quality acknowledged for all human beings equally, it is loaded with religious and family values and it focuses on embryonic and fetal right to life while forgetting pregnant women. Moreover, there is a gap between the apparent effort to respect some European standards in relation to human rights, demonstrated in the choice of terminology and inclusion of certain rights, primarily (but not exclusively) from the EU Charter on Fundamental Rights, and the constitutional reality as constructed by the Fundamental Law. Some aspects are more concerning than others, such as the apparent restriction on women's dignity, autonomy and privacy, lack of explicit protection of minorities and perhaps above all uncertain democratic foundations resting on a selective and exclusive construction of history.

[78] Venice Commission, *Opinion 621/2011*, para 30. The Fundamental Law has two general clauses: Article Q, recognition of international law and commitment to fulfill its obligations and Article E which relates to Hungary's EU membership.

Constitutionalism and democracy cannot be reduced to the sole text of the constitutional fundamental norm and good practice and culture sometimes arise out of constitutional drafting of an uncertain democratic quality. The Fundamental Law came in force in January 2012 and has already been complemented by a number of cardinal acts. Moreover, the Fundamental Law remains to be refined and further constructed by judges and in particular by the Constitutional Court. Therefore, this commentary can only offer a partial picture of the concept of dignity as it arises out of the text of the Fundamental Law. Some of the points above may appear in retrospect to be severe and mistaken, and it can only be hoped that the more alarming points of this analysis will be proved wrong.

Equality: The Missing Link

KRISZTA KOVÁCS

A constitution is much more than a fundamental legal document. It is the basic charter of the political community, which draws on the experience of the past and expresses hopes for the future to create a set of principles that are beyond the power of ordinary legislative majorities to change. The 1989 Constitution of Hungary was a good example of this. It had the potential to facilitate democracy and free markets and to ensure equal protection to all persons. In April 2011 a brand new constitution was promulgated, named the Fundamental Law. It changes the characteristics of Hungarian constitutionalism, abandoning the idea of a secular state based upon liberty, equality and democracy.

This article evaluates the equality clause of the 1989 Constitution and the anti-discrimination jurisprudence of the last two decades, and compares the equality provision in the 1989 Constitution with the corresponding part of the Fundamental Law, thereby offering a measure for assessment of the place of equality in the Fundamental Law.

The first part of this article provides a detailed analysis of the 1989 Constitution and examines the interpretive practice of the Constitutional Court concerning the three dimensions of the equality clause: prohibition of arbitrariness, a ban on discrimination and affirmative action. The second part describes the main features of the Fundamental Law that focus on the problem of equality, and how the wording of it in many aspects has an anti-egalitarian character. Further, the ban on discrimination marks, like the affirmative action clause, a step back from the level of equality guaranteed by the 1989 Constitution.

The 1989 Constitution

The concept of equality

The 1989 Constitution did not contain a general equality clause.[1] Despite this, it was based upon the concept of a political community of equal persons. This was manifested directly in several constitutional provisions. Article 54(1) ensured the right to human dignity, and Article 70/A(1) stipulated the ban on discrimination. According to this, the Republic of Hungary should ensure the human rights and civil rights of everyone on its territory without any form of discrimination, such as on the basis of race, color, gender, language, religion, political or other opinion, national or social origin, financial situation, birth or any other grounds whatsoever. Paragraph (2) said: "Any kind of discrimination described in paragraph (1) shall be strictly penalized by law."

In addition, the 1989 Constitution expressly ensured equal legal capacity; it provided for equality before the courts and it guaranteed equality of men and women in respect of all civil and political as well as economic, social and cultural rights. Furthermore, the constitution had an "equal pay for equal work" provision, it contained the principle of general and proportionate sharing of taxation, it ensured universal and equal suffrage, and last but not least it had an affirmative action clause.[2] The Constitutional Court applied these constitutional norms

---

[1] In constitutional law the general equality clause is a subsidiary rule, which applies when the specific, enumerated fundamental constitutional rights cannot be invoked. A general equality clause does not specify the content of the equality guaranteed, rather it states the postulate that whatever the content of the norms of the legal system, they should treat the subjects of law equally. A good example of this is Article 3 (1) of the German Constitution, according to which "all persons shall be equal before the law." For more on this see Bragyova, A. "Equality and Constitution" in *The Constitution Found? The First Nine Years of the Hungarian Constitutional Review on Fundamental Rights*, ed. Halmai, G. (Budapest: INDOK, 2000), 257. It should be mentioned that the Hungarian Constitutional Court used the notion of the general equality clause differently; it construed such a clause to serve as the basis of all constitutional rights. In the present article I am using the term general equality clause in the latter sense.

[2] Articles 56(1), 57(1), 66(1), 70/B(2), 70/I, 71(1), 70/A(3). The Hungarian Constitutional Court uses the term "positive discrimination." In the

to elaborate the "general equality rule," according to which the law should treat every person with equal respect and assess their characteristics with equal concern.[3]

Certainly, rival conceptions of equality provide rival answers to the question of exactly what kind of regulation and distribution the principle of equal respect and concern requires. Libertarian conceptions stipulate that treating people with equal concern means that the state should protect the people's possessions and their enjoyment of that property. Material equality requires the state to make the material wealth of all citizens as nearly as equal as possible throughout their lives. The concept of equality of welfare requires the state to distribute property so as to make the welfare of all citizens roughly equal. Equality of resources, in contrast, recognizes that differences in talent are differences in resources; therefore it seeks to compensate the less talented. This concept holds individuals responsible for their decisions and actions, though not for circumstances beyond their control—race, sex, disability, but also intelligence and social position—which thus are excluded as distributive criteria.

The 1989 Constitution did not set out a particular conception of equality that the state institutions must follow. And rightly so. The constitution could insist, however, that the jurisdiction accepted some plausible conception of equality in each of its decisions about property and other matters of policy.[4] It was possible to choose between better and worse background concepts.

It seems that the Constitutional Court did not endorse the pluralism of readings, rather it implicitly opted for a specific reading of equal-

European Union it is "positive action," and in the United States it is called "reverse discrimination," "affirmative action" or "preferential treatment." In order to avoid some of the (intended or unintended) pejorative connotations associated with the alternatives, in the present article I am using the terms affirmative action and positive measures/actions. These terms mean those measures that assist individuals on the basis of their belonging to certain minorities or a social group in a special situation to enable them to take advantage of opportunities open to everyone. See McHarg, A. and D. Nicolson, "Justifying Affirmative Action: Perception and Reality" in *Debating Affirmative Action: Conceptual, Contextual and Comparative Perspectives,* eds. McHarg, A. and D. Nicolson (Oxford: Blackwell, 2006), 2.

[3] Decision 9/1990. (IV. 25.)

[4] Dworkin, R. *Law's Empire* (Oxford: Hart Publishing, 1998), 382.

ity. One of the main reasons could be that the constitutional text [Article 70/A(3)] itself suggested that it was the duty of the state to improve the social and economic position of the members of disadvantaged groups so that their opportunities are equal.[5] Libertarian and neoliberal concepts were not in harmony with the wording of the constitution. Therefore other background theories such as equality of welfare or resources could serve as pillars for the constitutional adjudication concerning equality. In the early nineties the Court's understanding of equality was on the most important points very close to the Dworkinian theory of equality of resources. This can be traced for example in Decision 9/1990. In this case the Court examined the provision of the Act on Income Tax that granted special tax benefits to families with at least three children or to single parents with two children. The Court held the rule constitutional, arguing that "the ban on discrimination does not mean that any discrimination, including even discrimination intended to achieve a greater social equality, is forbidden." It established that "the ban on discrimination means all people must be treated as equal (as persons with equal dignity) by law—i.e., the fundamental right to human dignity may not be impaired, and the criteria for the distribution of the entitlements and benefits shall be determined with the same respect and prudence, and with the same degree of consideration of individual interests." The language of the Court's argument was clearly related[6] to Ronald Dworkin's conception of the right to treatment as an equal.[7] It seems therefore that for constitutional jurisprudence, equality of resources served as a background theory even if the Court did not refer to it expressly.[8] Although there have been significant alterations over the years within this relatively solid framework, the concept can still be applied for evaluating the jurisprudence connected to

[5] See more on this in the "Affirmative action" subsection of this article.

[6] As, among others, Péter Paczolay pointed out. Paczolay, P. "Judicial Review of the Compensation Law in Hungary," *Michigan Journal of International Law* 13 (1992): 815.

[7] Dworkin, R. *Taking Rights Seriously* (London: Duckworth, 1977).

[8] For instance, the Court when interpreting the affirmative action clause of the Constitution, argued that "[i]f a social purpose is not in conflict with the Constitution, or a constitutional right may only be achieved if equality in the narrower sense is not met, then such a positive discrimination shall not be declared unconstitutional." Decision 9/1990. (IV. 25.)

the constitutional ban on direct and indirect discrimination as well as for the constitutional affirmative action clause.

The purpose of the 1989 Constitution was to ensure equal protection to all. However, the constitution did not disclose which kind of treatment of an individual violated the requirement of equal treatment. Constitutional case law on the equality clause comprised three dimensions: prohibition of arbitrariness, a ban on discrimination and affirmative action.

Prohibition of arbitrariness

The first of these three dimensions involves ensuring equal treatment of equal situations and prohibiting the equal treatment of manifestly unequal situations. According to Article 70/A(1) of the constitution, strict equality was called for in the legal sphere of civil freedoms, requiring that all citizens of the society must have equal basic rights and fundamental liberties. Certainly, discrimination concerning fundamental rights is the most grievous. However, there are cases when not such rights are at stake, but statutory rights or even interests that are not protected by rights. Under the constitutional case law "the ban on discrimination, according to Article 70/A(1) of the constitution—in the case of a violation of the right to human dignity—extends to the entire legal order." That is, this principle extended beyond the text of the constitution regarding "human and civil rights" and also includes other rights and interests.[9] It was true, however, that Article 70/A(1) governed the whole legal system only if the discrimination eventually violated human dignity. If there was a challenge to the validity of the government's policy choices, the Court judged the issue (e.g. the tax and finance provisions) applying the reasonableness test. There should have been a "constitutional basis" (objective reason) of the distinction. The arbitrary restriction of a non-fundamental right was unconstitutional, since in such cases the affected persons were certainly not treated as persons with equal dignity.

[9] Decision 61/1992. (XI. 20.) This standpoint led to the extension of the scope of the constitution towards private relations. Gárdos-Orosz, F. "Constitutional Rights: Horizontal Effect and Anti-Discrimination Law in Hungary," *Acta Juridica Hungarica* 49 no. 1 (2008).

Ban on discrimination

The second dimension of the case law concerning the equality principle, the ban on discrimination, presupposes the illegitimacy of any differentiated treatment based upon irrelevant criteria. The reason for this is that it is highly probable that wrongfully differentiating among citizens based upon inter alia race, color, gender, language, religion, political or other opinion, national or social origin, financial situation, birth or any other similar grounds violates the right to be treated as an equal. Therefore the ban on discrimination seeks to help prevent racist, sexist, homophobic, etc. sentiments from being used as a justification for public decisions.

The legislation certainly does not treat persons equally, if the legislative act could only be justified by prejudice or partiality. This happens when the legislator consciously tries to exclude persons from a community or block them from an opportunity on the basis of an essential characteristic or capacity of theirs. In this case this vicious aim itself does harm. The same is true if the legislator is guided by the conviction that doing harm for a non-discriminative purpose is acceptable, since the person can be considered inferior because of belonging to a certain group.

The 1989 Constitution had a list containing forbidden discrimination, such as those based on racial criteria or sex. Discrimination on grounds of ethnic origin is seen to be the most widespread form of discrimination not only in the European Union, but also in Hungary.[10] The groups that are subject to systematic discrimination, and are identified as "racial" groups in Hungary, are the communities of Roma people. They continue to face discrimination in access to education and employment. Roma families are deprived of access to social housing by discriminatory rules and practices of local authorities; and Roma children are still confronted with segregation in schools.[11]

[10] Discrimination in the EU, Special Eurobarometer 317, http://ec.europa.eu/public_opinion/archives/ebs/ebs_317_en.pdf, 11, 60.

[11] European Commission against Racism and Intolerance, *Report on Hungary*, CRI 2009(3) 8. See also the judgment of the European Court of Human Rights in *D.H. and Others v. Czech Republic,* no. 57325/00, November 13, 2007, para 143, 182, 205.

Despite this the Constitutional Court has not so far examined the law from the perspective of racial discrimination. Although the Constitutional Court had to tackle some of these issues, it has not openly addressed the problems affecting Roma. Below I illustrate this with two examples.

The principal source of the discrimination experienced in everyday life by Roma in the field of housing is, in most cases, not the contents of legislation enacted at a central level, but appears rather to be the manner in which local authorities exercise their powers. For example around 2,000 local governments have enacted provisions barring persons caught squatting in property from having access to social housing for a number of years, generally between three and five years. These provisions result in a disadvantage for Roma, who are proportionally far more often unable to afford even nominal housing costs, forcing them into occupying homes without legal authorization. Although the Constitutional Court struck down one such provision as unconstitutional, the decision did not deal with the discrimination issue. The Court annulled the provision on formal grounds arguing that it contradicted the Act on Flat Rentals.[12]

The same has happened in the field of social benefits. The local representatives of Monok, a village in an underdeveloped region in the north of Hungary, stipulated that child protection support is only to be paid to parents who enroll their children in kindergarten or school and refused to pay the regular social benefits financed by central government to the unemployed, unless they participated in public works.[13] Later several local governments followed the "Monok Model" and tightened the payment of regular social benefits and the child protection support. The parliamentary commissioner for minority rights found such a modification of the child welfare and social benefit system worrying from a constitutional perspective. The commissioner argued that although the local decrees do not expressly mention individuals of Roma origin, the decrees are ethnically motivated and directed toward the Roma population. They are the ones who, lacking proper qualifications, are qualified only for unskilled or low-skilled

[12] Decision 4/2005. (IX. 28.)

[13] For more on this see Szabó, Y. "Work for Benefits?" *The Hungarian Quarterly* 191 (Autumn 2008).

labor. The demand for such work, however, has decreased in Hungary. Therefore they are in greater need of living almost solely from social benefits. The case then reached the Constitutional Court, and the Court, although it declared the local decree on tightening the child protection support of Monok as unconstitutional, did not address the equality issue. The Court annulled the local decree on formal grounds, arguing that the provisions contradicted the Child Protection Act.[14]

Neither of these decisions dealt explicitly with the conflict between the local governments and arbitrary squatters and those who live mostly on social benefits, who are mainly Roma. The Court refrained from examining the actual situation of Roma, therefore the problems relating to their discrimination have remain largely hidden.[15]

Traditionally one of the most frequent classification laws applied is the classification based upon sex or gender. While equality among members of different ethnic communities calls for equal treatment in almost all cases, equality of men and women requires a much more varied approach. Sex and gender appear irrelevant in some circumstances but not in others.[16]

In the Hungarian constitutional jurisprudence, issues regarding the equality of women were typically examined not upon the constitutional provision declaring a general ban on discrimination, but upon Article 66(3), according to which "during work the protection of women and youth is ensured also by separate rules." As a consequence, cases regarding female equality appeared as affirmative action issues in the case law, and therefore these cases will be discussed later in this article. The Court, however, examined issues regarding the equality of men based on Article 70/A(1). In the absence of objective reasons, the Court held it to be unjustified discrimination between genders that the pension scheme provided credits toward a pension for the years that a male worker spent out of employment while caring for young children at home only if he had raised his child alone,[17] that only spinsters were

[14] Decision 20/2010. (II. 18.)

[15] See Tóth, G. A. "Unequal Protection: Historical Churches and Roma People in the Hungarian Constitutional Jurisprudence," *Acta Juridica Hungarica* 51 no. 2 (2010).

[16] Dorsen, N. and M. Rosenfeld, A. Sajó, and S. Baer, *Comparative Constitutionalism, Cases and Materials* (St. Paul, MN: West, 2010), 723.

[17] Decision 32/1997. (V. 16.)

granted the right to early retirement pension,[18] and furthermore, that following marriage men could not bear their wife's name.[19]

As we can see, characteristic sex and racial discrimination judgments are missing from the Court's jurisprudence. The main reason for this could be the tests developed by the Court for the assessment of discrimination. Laws suspected of discrimination must meet the strong test of necessity/proportionality in the case of discriminations concerning fundamental rights. In cases where no such rights are at stake, it is sufficient to apply the weaker test of reasonable goal, as discussed above. However, this could not be applicable for many widespread cases of discrimination based upon race and gender. Roma and women typically suffer such discriminations as do not concern fundamental rights.[20] Therefore it seems necessary to elaborate detailed tests for the assessment of discrimination based upon suspect classification.

The list of reasons for discrimination prohibited in Article 70/A(1) of the constitution was not exhaustive. Extension of the list was possible by reference to the notion of discrimination "on any other grounds." Certainly, any other grounds could mean only such situations in which it is highly probable that the person's disadvantage is caused by the legal system's or the social customs' built-in prejudices.

Discrimination on the ground of age was qualified as such a situation at the very beginning of the Court's jurisprudence.[21] At the same time, however, the Court very clearly stated that age requirements attached to certain jobs and positions, provided they apply for all persons belonging into the certain category and are not arbitrary, do not violate Article 70/A(1) of the constitution.[22]

---

[18] Decision 7/1998. (III. 18.)

[19] Decision 58/2001. (XII. 7.)

[20] Kis, J. *Constitutional Democracy* (Budapest: Central European University Press, 2003), 279.

[21] Decision 1596/B/1990. (May 6, 1991). In the concrete case the Court held a petition unjustified that considered discriminatory the termination of a constitutional justice position when turning 70.

[22] Upon these requirements the Court held constitutional the 45 year age limit necessary for the nomination as a constitutional justice (Decision 1350/B/1992. (February 23, 1993)), the upper age limit regarding heads of university departments (Decision 857/B/1994. (February 20, 1995)), and rules regulating the upper age limit for professional service performed in the armed forces (Decision 1280/B/1992. (March 27, 1995)).

Other grounds, such as disability, have also recently emerged for special treatment under the non-discrimination clause. Although the 1989 Constitution provided for the general ban on discrimination, did not name specifically disability-based discrimination. According to the ordinary courts' and the Constitutional Court's case law, however, this type of discrimination should also be classified as discrimination "on any other ground."[23]

"Any other grounds" in the constitutional text also included discrimination on grounds of sexual orientation. In 1995 the Constitutional Court considered same sex relationships legally protectable.[24] In 1999 a decision clarified that discrimination upon sexual orientation was qualified as discrimination "on any other ground" under Article 70/A(1).[25] Later the Court used this argument to annul a provision of the Criminal Code which criminalized an adult who established a consensual sexual relationship with a minor of the same sex, while a consensual sexual relationship was not punishable if the two persons of the same age were of different sexes. The Court argued that the distinction based on sexual orientation of persons was unjustifiable on the basis of objective facts.[26] A further step was taken in 2008 when the Court held

[23] Additionally, the Act CXXV of 2003 on Equal Treatment and Promotion of Equal Opportunities clearly defines disability-based discrimination.

[24] Decision 14/1995. (III. 13.) "On the other hand, the applicants failed in their challenge of the notion of marriage as a union exclusively of a man and a woman." Sólyom, L. and G. Brunner, *Constitutional Judiciary in a New Democracy. The Hungarian Constitutional Court* (Ann Arbor: The University of Michigan Press, 2000), 45, 316. In the opinion of Tamás Lábady (at that time Constitutional Justice), there is no need to accord special constitutional protection to life-partnership and to cohabitation of same sex persons. The persons concerned do not have the right to make use of the same institution (of marriage), but to be treated as persons enjoying equal rights. Lábady, T. "Constitutional protection of privacy: Protection of marriage and the family, right to privacy," *Acta Juridica Hungarica* 45–46, 1–2 (1995–1996).

[25] Decision 20/1999. (VI. 25.)

[26] Decision 37/2002. (IX. 4.) The decision was based upon the established case law of the European Court of Human Rights on the prohibition of homosexual relations between adults (*Dudgeon v. United Kingdom*, no. 7525/76, October 22, 1981; *Norris v. Ireland*, no. 10581/83, October 26, 1988; *Modinos v. Cyprus*, no. 15070/89, April 22, 1993). See also the judgment of the European Court of Human Rights concerning the different age

that the establishment of the institution of registered partnership for same-sex couples was not unconstitutional.[27]

When dealing with discrimination on account of sexual orientation the Hungarian courts and the legislators were largely bound by the case law of the European Court of Human Rights and the relevant EU law.[28] However, this influence could be traced not only in the field of discrimination on ground of sexual orientation but also in other fields of anti-discrimination law.

For instance, provisions banning indirect discrimination have appeared in the Hungarian legal system. First, the Act on Equal Treatment and Promotion of Equal Opportunities declared that indirect discrimination means a violation of the principle of equal treatment.[29] Recently the Constitutional Court declared a local government decree forbidding rummaging through garbage in the town's territory to be

---

consent under criminal law for homosexual relations. *L. and V. v. Austria*, no. 39392/98, 39829/98, January 9, 2003.

[27] The Act, instead of opening up marriage for same sex couples, introduced the possibility of registered partnership which was open both for same sex and different sex couples. The Court annulled the Act saying that regarding different sex couples, a registered partnership very similar to marriage would duplicate the institution of marriage, which would result in the "devaluation" of the institution of marriage. Decision 154/2008. (XII. 17.) In line with the Court's decision, Parliament adopted a new Act on Registered Partnership, under which registered partnerships are only open to same-sex couples. All the rules of marriage apply; notable exceptions are the right to take the partners' name, the right to adopt children and the right to participate in assisted reproduction.

[28] The European Court of Human Rights has dealt with several aspects of the equality of LGBT persons. See *Salgueiro da Silva Mouta v. Portugal*, no. 33290/96, December 21, 1999 on parental rights, *Fretté v. France*, no. 36515/97, February 26, 2002 on the permission of adopting a child, *Karner v. Austria*, no. 40016/98, July 24, 2003 on the right to succeed to the deceased partner's tenancy, and *Schalk and Kopf v. Austria*, no. *30141/04*, June 24, 2010 arguing that cohabiting same-sex couples, living in a stable de facto partnership, fall within the notion of "family life." See also the Council Directive 2000/78/EC and the judgment of the Court of Justice of the EU in the case of *Jürgen Römer v. Freie und Hansestadt Hamburg*, C-147/08, on May 10, 2011 concerning a discriminative pension favoring married recipients over those living in a registered life partnership.

[29] Article 7 and 9 of the Act CXXV of 2003 on Equal Treatment and Promotion of Equal Opportunities.

a violation of the ban on indirect discrimination. Hundreds of homeless people have been subjected to short-term arrest by the police on grounds of the decree. The Constitutional Court found the decree unconstitutional, arguing that indirect discrimination is a covert violation of equal treatment by the use of apparently neutral provisions and practices, the consequences of which are detrimental for members of disadvantaged groups. Although the decree did not expressly and exclusively affect the homeless people, it did, however, raise a well-founded suspicion of indirect discrimination against them.[30]

Although the concept of indirect discrimination was not explicitly available at a constitutional level, the legislators and the courts imported the doctrine of indirect discrimination from the relevant EU Directives and the case law of the Court of Justice of the EU.[31]

Affirmative action

The third dimension of equality helps to offset situations of unequal opportunity. Article 70/A(3) was the affirmative action clause of the 1989 Constitution which read that "the Republic of Hungary shall promote the equality of rights for everyone through measures aimed at eliminating the inequality of opportunity." The constitutional text itself suggested that it was the duty of the state to improve the social and economic position of the members of socially disadvantaged groups so that their opportunities were equal. The constitutional term "eliminating the inequality of opportunity" directly referred to the social context, and to the fact that there are people for whom status differentiation is correlated with disadvantage, which required the legislators to evaluate from time to time the situation of social groups forming within society. In this way, the legislator could identify who the beneficiaries of affirmative action should be. Article 70/A(3) of the 1989 Constitution did not name those persons whose interests demand state

[30] Decision 176/2011. (X. 12.)

[31] It should be noted that the "effect test" developed by the U.S. courts was the basis of the indirect discrimination policy in Britain. McCrudden, C. "Institutional Discrimination," *Oxford Journal of Legal Studies* 2, (1982): 328, 336. The EU law (for instance Council Directive 2000/43/EC) imported this policy from the American and British legal system.

intervention. It was the duty of the legislator to recognize and to examine which social groups could not take part equally in the life of the political community, possibly but not necessarily because of structural discrimination.

What qualified as a positive measure? The 1989 Constitution did not give details of positive measures. This was mainly because the means of preferential treatment can be of several types. They could include training programs, job advertisements, or scholarships published expressly in forums where they are most likely to be read by those concerned. Affirmative action could also involve internal regulations which demand that employers in certain companies, or the entrance examiners of universities should give some advantage to those applicants who are from disadvantageous groups. Another positive measure is when for example women expecting a child, persons raising children, or people with disabilities are given special benefits. Clearly, quotas are the strictest measures because they usually do not allow a departure from the numbers they prescribe.

In the two decades since the political transition, Hungarian authorities have tried to introduce milder measures and numerical goals as well as rigid quotas.[32] Government decrees introduced the policy of automatically granting extra points in the admission process to those who were disadvantaged (e.g. to disabled applicants, to applicants of undereducated parents who lived in difficult financial situations, to applicants who formerly lived in permanent custody, and to those on maternity leave).[33] These governmental decrees had a legitimate aim, they did not violate individual rights, and were suitable for reaching the set aim, but they were not adequate. The decrees helped people living in difficult financial conditions in such a way that, say, Roma students themselves did not come any closer to passing the university entrance exam. The decrees should have aimed to help specifi-

---

[32] Result quotas set the goal to be achieved, but not the ways to do it. For example they determine the rate of representation of a target group in a given area of employment or education. A rigid quota requires the employees or universities to keep certain amount of places for the members of the disadvantaged group, and it may happen that these places are left vacant due to lack of applicants.

[33] Governmental Decree 246/2003. (XII. 18.), Governmental Decree 237/2006. (XI. 27.)

cally the higher education of seriously disadvantaged Roma students. The definition of disadvantaged applicants did not cover all people of Roma origin; in this way the decrees achieved less than they could have according to the Constitution.

The legislators introduced measures aiming to amend the social position of women. For instance in 2008 quotas were proposed by members of Parliament in order to help women get onto party lists and thereby have a greater share in politics. The bill would have determined the rate of men and women present on the party lists entering elections. According to the proposal, both sexes should have been present in equal numbers.[34] Since the bill did not receive the required majority vote of the members of Parliament, the parity provision has not become part of the Hungarian legal system.

Up to this point I have been trying to present the positive measures applied by the Hungarian legislature. Some of them were subject to constitutional review. For instance, petitioners questioned the constitutionality of affirmative action employed in higher education. The Constitutional Court therefore examined the constitutionality of the Governmental Decree automatically ensuring extra points in the admission process to those who were disadvantaged, and upheld the contested provision by saying that the social purpose of helping to get admission to universities was in accord with the constitution, and giving extra points did not infringe the equal dignity of those people detrimentally affected by the system.[35]

In addition, Constitutional Court decisions examined welfare benefits and traffic allowances of disabled people, as rules facilitating equal opportunities of those concerned.[36] And there is a decision according to which the special situation of psychiatric patients required positive measures.[37]

---

[34] Bill T/3066, Section 1. Together with this proposal the Bill T/3060. would have amended the Constitution in such a way that it would have required the prime minister to present women and men as at least one-third of the candidates when appointing ministers. The bill did not receive the required two-thirds majority vote of the members of Parliament.

[35] Decision 635/B/2007. (July 5, 2010).

[36] Decision 462/B/2002. (December 17, 2002), Decision 553/B/1994. (June 23, 1997).

[37] Decision 36/2000. (X. 27.)

One noteworthy point with regard to preferential treatment concerns Article 66(3) of the 1989 Constitution, which was based, according to the interpretation of the Court, on "the recognition of differences resulting from the natural, biological and physical differences of men and women; the biological characteristics of women, especially the biological and psychological dimensions of motherhood, and the weaker physical force of women, as a result of which they react to certain environmental harms earlier and with more severe consequences."[38] In consideration of these biological reasons the Court held constitutional a provision restricting compulsory military service obligation to men,[39] the application of different age limits for civil protection obligation and call of duty,[40] a provision providing for the request of retirement pension for women earlier than for men,[41] and transitional pension regulations favoring women.[42] It should be noted though, that these measures are to be explained not necessarily by biological differences between men and women, but by inequalities in the social position of men and women, and by women's double burden of family and work. These were provisions that in the long run served the achievement of a greater social equality between men and women.

The 1989 Constitution was written in the language of abstract moral principles. It guaranteed equal human dignity and it contained an open-ended ban on discrimination as well as an inclusive affirmative action clause. The constitutional text left room for maneuver for the Court to interpret the equality principle. In some cases it worked well, however, a number of highly important areas of anti-discrimination law were not addressed by the Court. There is no decision about racial discrimination, and the Court has yet to address the issue of suspect classifications. Can the new constitution serve as a basis for this?

---

38 Decision 7/1998. (III. 18.)
39 Decision 46/1994. (X. 21.)
40 Decision 28/2000. (IX. 8.)
41 Decision 32/1997. (V. 16.)
42 Decision 28/2000. (IX. 8.)

The 2011 Fundamental Law

Anti-egalitarian character

The Fundamental Law has been criticized for the manner in which it was framed, and several aspects of its content are widely disputed. I will focus on the Fundamental Law and the principle of equality.

The Fundamental Law and especially its preamble, called the National Avowal, change the characteristics of the Hungarian constitutionalism. The 1989 Constitution established a secular state based upon a pluralist society. The leading principles were liberty, equality and democracy. The Fundamental Law does not follow the idea of a secular state. It has its foundations in historical and religious considerations. The National Avowal places special emphasis on values such as family, nation, loyalty, faith and love, and is dominated by religious references. One cannot find the principle of equality in the long list of values on which the Fundamental Law is based;[43] on the contrary, many provisions have an anti-egalitarian character.

1. Although there was no clear mention of the constituting people as such in the 1989 Constitution, it implicitly identified the constituting "people" with those citizens who reside in the country, and who are the subjects of the legal rights and obligations; that is, who fall under the scope of the acts adopted by Parliament, and who take the consequences of the political decisions.[44]

On the other hand, the Fundamental Law seems premised on a distinction between the Hungarian nation and (other) nationalities liv-

[43] The word "equality" is not included among the 509 words of the National Avowal; and occurs three times in the main text of the Fundamental Law: in Articles 2, 35 and in Article XV. Equality under the law is missing from among the guiding principles pertaining of the operation of the judicial system. Furthermore, the Fundamental Law contains no provisions concerning the "equal pay for equal work" principle and the omission of the proclamation of the equality of public and private property is also revealing.

[44] According to Article 70(1) of the 1989 Constitution all adult Hungarian citizens residing in the territory of the Republic of Hungary had the right to be elected and the right to vote in parliamentary elections; they had the right, furthermore, to participate in national referenda and popular initiatives.

ing in Hungary. The Hungarian nation, in turn, also includes ethnic Hungarians living in other states. The National Avowal does not have the original "We the people" formula, but rather, "We the members of the Hungarian nation." It states that there is "one single Hungarian nation that belongs together" and it consists of all ethnic Hungarians, regardless of their habitual residence and the center of their interests. Although the Fundamental Law does not define explicitly the notion of the nation, it follows from its provisions that "the members of the Hungarian nation" include Hungarians living abroad, even without an effective link to the state. Therefore, it seems that the "original people," those who established the constitution, consist of not only those who live in the territory of Hungary, but also ethnic Hungarians around the world.[45] The document therefore enshrines an ethnic vision of the "we the people" concept.[46]

The provisions concerning elections and the right to vote also mirror this. Although Article 2 of the Fundamental Law provides that members of Parliament shall be elected by direct and secret ballot by citizens eligible to vote, on the basis of universal and equal suffrage. In a similar manner, Article 35 reads that local government representatives and mayors shall be elected by direct and secret ballot by citizens eligible to vote, on the basis of universal and equal suffrage. Despite this, the Fundamental Law does not provide universal and equal suffrage for Hungarian adults. Article XXIII(4) reads that a cardinal act may subject the right to vote or its completeness to residence in Hungary, and it may prescribe additional criteria for eligibility to stand as a candidate in elections. Based upon this constitutional provision, Act CCIII of 2011 on the General Elections grants voting rights to Hungarian citizens abroad, including ethnic Hungarians residing in neighboring countries, however, in violation of the principle of equal suffrage, ethnic Hungarians abroad will only cast a single vote, on a national party list.

It also goes against the egalitarian principle that under Article XXIII(6) of the Fundamental Law, those disenfranchised by a court

---

[45] Hungary is a country with approximately 10 million inhabitants, and the populations of Hungarian communities abroad amount to several million people.

[46] See more on this in Zsolt Körtvélyesi's contribution in this volume.

for limited mental capacity shall not have the right to vote and to stand as candidates in elections. Clearly, this provision places those under guardianship in a better position than the 1989 Constitution did. According to the 1989 Constitution, persons under guardianship automatically lost their right to vote. In 2010 the European Court of Human Rights argued that such an indiscriminate removal of voting rights, without an individualized judicial evaluation and solely based on a mental disability necessitating partial guardianship, cannot be considered compatible with the Convention.[47] However, the European Court of Human Rights did not entirely close the possibility to restrict the right to vote in order to ensure that only citizens capable of assessing the consequences of their decisions and making conscious and judicious decisions should participate in public affairs.

Although the Fundamental Law may be an improvement on the relevant provision of the 1989 Constitution, the current rules still fall short of international human rights standards by saying that judges will decide whether people have the required "mental ability" to vote. First, Article 29 of the UN Convention on the Rights of Persons with Disabilities obliges Hungary as a state party to the Convention that "persons with disabilities can effectively and fully participate in political and public life on an equal basis with others, directly or through freely chosen representatives, including the right and opportunity for persons with disabilities to vote and be elected." Furthermore, the Venice Commission emphasizes that "universal suffrage is a fundamental principle of the European Electoral Heritage. People with disabilities may not be discriminated against in this regard… Voting procedures and facilities should be accessible to people with disabilities so that they are able to exercise their democratic rights, and allow, where necessary, the provision of assistance in voting, with respect to the principle that voting must be individual."[48]

Second, the mental ability clause seems to be a covert discrimination on the ground of disability, as it will likely only be applied to people with intellectual disabilities and people with psycho-social (mental

[47] *Alajos Kiss v. Hungary*, no. 38832/06, May 20, 2010, para 44.

[48] Venice Commission, *Revised Interpretative Declaration to the Code of Good Practice in Electoral Matters on the Participation of People with Disabilities in Elections*, CDL-AD(2011)045, 2.

health) disabilities.[49] Therefore, the universal accessibility of elections has not been realized by the Fundamental Law.

2. The Fundamental Law does not take seriously the equal recognition of the plurality of forms of life and the neutrality of the state. According to the third sentence of Article VII(2), the state shall cooperate with the churches for community goals. Article VII(3) authorizes Parliament to adopt an Act on Churches. Under Article 21(1) of the Transitional Provisions[50] the Act on Churches lists the recognized churches and defines the condition for recognizing further churches. The act may prescribe that recognizing an organization as a church should require that the organization has been in existence for a given length of time with a certain number of members, and that the state take into account the general historic traditions and societal support for the organization.

The act passed by Parliament in December 2011 grants formal recognition to only 14 of 358 already registered religious organizations in Hungary. Under the Act, the term "church" is to be interpreted not to include religious denominations and religious communities. The churches are equal, but not all of the religious organizations. The act recognizes predominant churches including Reformed, Roman Catholic, Lutheran and Orthodox, along with a few Jewish organizations. The excluded groups (including, for example, Anglicans, Buddhists, and Islamic communities) automatically lost their legal status as a church on January 1, 2012, thereby losing the ability to maintain schools and social institutions with state subsidies as well as tax breaks from the government. Although these churches had the possibility to apply for re-registration, it was up to the two-thirds majority of the members of Parliament to decide upon their request.[51]

---

[49] Mental Disability Advocacy Center, Disability Discrimination Enshrined in New Hungarian Constitution, http://mdac.info/news/disability-discrimination-enshrined-new-hungarian-constitution

[50] The Transitional Provisions of the Fundamental Law form a part of the Fundamental Law. [Article 31(2)] The Transitional Provisions and the First Amendment see in this volume.

[51] On February 29, 2012 Parliament amended the Act on Churches to extend the list of churches to include thirteen more religious communities. See more on this in Renáta Uitz's contribution in this volume.

Under the 1989 Constitution it was within the competence of the judiciary to register churches. For the acquisition of the legal status of "church" the former act imposed the only requirement that the church must have at least one hundred founding members. In this normative system the courts did not have the possibility to evaluate the principles of faith or other characteristics of the religious association. According to the new Act on Churches politicians decide on which organization qualifies as a church, based upon their membership, tradition and societal support. This method does not take seriously the right to freedom of religion of the believers whose churches are not recognized by the state, which means that the legal provisions in question do not display equal concern for the fate of all believers and non-believers.

3. As I mentioned earlier, Roma are the largest ethnic minority group in Hungary. Despite this the Roma minority is not explicitly mentioned in the Fundamental Law, let alone among the target groups of affirmative action. On the contrary, there are provisions that implicitly target the most vulnerable Roma population. They are the ones who, living in great poverty and lacking sufficient food are more often caught in the act of taking, e.g., fruits and vegetables from their neighbors' garden. This could be the "reason" why Article V guarantees everyone's right to repel any unlawful attack against his or her person or property, or one that poses a direct threat to the same. The article is about a right to self-defense in the state of nature described by Hobbes, and not a basic right in a constitutional state.[52]

Article M identifies the foundations of the economy: these are value-creating work and freedom of enterprise; and Article XII(1) prescribes the obligation to perform work to the best of the individual's ability and potential, which means that that work is no longer a right but an obligation.

According to Article XIX(1) the state only needs to concern itself with creating social security for the groups included in the list (and not people unemployed through "their own fault," for example). Another change is reflected in the fact that the assistance to be provided is no lon-

---

[52] It may remind us of the old constitutions of southern states of the United States of America that served to protect the property of farmers from native and black Americans.

ger of the extent "necessary for subsistence," but just the extent "determined by law." In addition, under Article XIX(3) the nature and extent of social measures may be determined by law in accordance with the usefulness to the community of the beneficiary's activity. If one wants social benefit, he/she must work within the framework of community service.

Last but not least the Fundamental Law abolishes the position of an independent specialized parliamentary commissioner for minority rights established by the 1989 Constitution. In the future a vice ombudsperson will be in charge of protecting the "interests of ethnic groups" living in Hungary. This can be evaluated as a step back from the model of the 1989 Constitution.

Although the above-mentioned, unusual provisions are not evidently problematic in themselves, they implicitly target Roma, who are the most prominent victims of racial discrimination and social exclusion in present day Hungary. The Fundamental Law does not treat the most vulnerable ethnic minorities with equal concern; instead it echoes particular social attitudes and prejudices.

4. The Fundamental Law's Transitional Provisions break with the tradition of the equal recognition of individuals in other regards as well. They include a rule stigmatizing the governing majority's political rivals. According to point 4 of the Transitional Provisions, the Hungarian Socialist Party shares the responsibility of the state party as the legal successor of the then state party, "as the inheritor of the illegally amassed wealth, and as the benefactor of the illegitimate advantages acquired during the transition."

I now turn specifically to Article XV, which contains the general equality rule, the ban on discrimination, the requirement that women and men shall have equal rights and the affirmative action clause.

Ban on discrimination

According to Article XV(2) "Hungary shall ensure fundamental rights to everyone without any kind of discrimination, such as on the basis of race, color, gender, disability, language, religion, political or other opinion, national or social origin, financial situation, birth or any other grounds whatsoever." In addition, there is a special provision requiring that "women and men shall have equal rights" in Article XV(3).

The wording of Article XV(2) speaks of "fundamental rights" instead of "human and civil rights." Although under fundamental rights we understand only those human rights protected by the constitution, it is very unlikely that the constitutional jurisprudence will change in a way that it refuses the protection of the ban on discrimination on rights beyond the group of fundamental rights.

It should be laudable that "disability" is listed as a prohibited ground of discrimination in the Fundamental Law. However, as discussed above, Article XXIII(6) undermines this principle by stating that a judge can take away the right to vote from those with limited mental ability.

The other problematic point of the non-discrimination clause is that Article XV(2) lacks any mention of the ban on discrimination on grounds of sexual orientation, which is a noteworthy omission in a recently worded legal document. For instance, the Directive 2000/78/EC explicitly protects against discrimination on grounds of sexual orientation,[53] and Article 21 of the Charter of Fundamental Rights of the EU similarly prohibits discrimination based on sexual orientation.[54] As for example the case law of the European Court of Human Rights shows, cases concerning discrimination on the ground of sexual orientation have become particularly important in today's societies as compared with the time of drafting of the 1989 Constitution. Recently, the European Court of Human Rights has dealt with several aspects of sexual orientation as a prohibited distinctive feature under Article 14 of the Convention.[55]

The Venice Commission therefore drew the attention of the Hungarian authorities to the relevant case law of the European Court of Human Rights and proceeded from the assumption that the Constitutional Court would interpret the ground for discrimination in such a

[53] Council Directive 2000/78/EC (November 27, 2000) establishing a general framework for equal treatment in employment and occupation.

[54] And for example Article 6 of the proposal for a new constitution for the Republic of Iceland (2011) expressly includes the ban on discrimination on account of sexual orientation.

[55] See footnotes 24 and 28.

manner that Article XV(2) prohibits also discrimination on grounds of sexual orientation.[56]

Although it is possible that the Constitutional Court will interpret Article XV(2) in such a way, nevertheless, including physical or mental disability, sexual orientation or age as certain additional non-discrimination grounds cannot be considered unnecessary from a legal point of view. Article XV(2) is, of course, an open-ended provision in the sense that the list of non-discrimination grounds is not exhaustive, therefore judges can and should apply Article XV(2) in relation to discrimination grounds not explicitly mentioned in that provision. This would be in line with the general equality rule enshrined in Article XV(1), according to which "[e]veryone shall be equal before the law" and with international human rights standards. Yet the constitution-makers failed to make an important symbolic step by not including sexual orientation as an additional non-discrimination ground. Sexual orientation constitutes one of the most important parts of the personal integrity which requires the highest level of legal protection, namely constitutional protection.

It seems, however, that was not a simple failure, but there is an ideology behind not protecting sexual minorities explicitly. It is important to note in this context that Article L(1) itself enshrines discrimination based on sexual orientation by defining and protecting "the institution of marriage as the union of a man and a woman" and leaving open the possibility that such a marriage could be the basis for the only type of family protected by the state and which serves as "the basis of the nation's survival." As the Venice Commission pointed out, there are no established European standards in this respect, therefore the definition of marriage belongs to the Hungarian state.[57] However, a definition excluding personal relationships from constitutional protection based on the persons' sexual identity and orientation would go

[56] It should be noted that Article 8 of the Act CXXV of 2003 on Equal Treatment and Promotion of Equal Opportunities forbids discrimination based on factors that include sexual orientation and sexual identity. However, it is a simple majority act, therefore as a guarantee it would be needed if the legislation acknowledged protection against discrimination on the ground of sexual orientation at the highest level, in the text of the constitution.

[57] See Venice Commission, *Opinion 621/2011 on the new Constitution of Hungary* in this volume.

against the fundamental principle concerning equal human dignity. In addition, with this definition the constitution-makers have ruled out the future ability of the Hungarian legislature, following the worldwide tendency, to make the institution of marriage available to same-sex couples.[58]

Affirmative action

Mere rules banning discrimination have not proved to be sufficient when facing discrimination. This is why recently worded constitutions and international human rights documents accept that it is not enough for the state to apply sanctions against discrimination; it has to take positive measures to improve the opportunities of the disadvantaged. The Fundamental Law accepts this by requiring that special measures shall be taken to promote effective implementation of the equality principle. Article XV(4) provides that Hungary shall facilitate the realization of equal opportunity with special measures.

On the one hand, Article XV(4) rightly defines the purpose of applying special measures in facilitating the realization of equal opportunity. According to Article 70/A(3) of the 1989 Constitution, the state promoted the equality of rights through positive measures. However, the aim of the positive measures is not the equality of rights, but the elimination of inequality of opportunity.

On the other hand, however, Article XV amounts to a set-back from the 1989 Constitution. Article XV(5) states that "Hungary shall take special measures to protect children, women, the elderly and persons living with disabilities." By expressly identifying the possible "beneficiaries," there is a danger of introducing a restricted affirmative action policy. The wording of the Fundamental Law excludes the vulnerable social groups most often victims of prejudice (e.g. Roma people, religious, sexual minorities) from the possibility of being subject to positive measures. It is problematic, because affirmative action is needed to help all of those who are, from no fault of their own, in a constantly regenerated disadvantageous situation because of their real or conceived membership of a social group. For instance, education, employment and public services are still spheres where the color

[58] See the *Opinion on the Fundamental Law of Hungary* in this volume.

of a person's skin or their ethnicity makes a difference. In public life openly LGBT persons still rarely achieve a leading role. Therefore Article XV(5) will be in line with the general affirmative action clause enshrined in Article XV(4) only if it is interpreted in such a way that it will not limit the beneficiaries to those less-advantaged specified in Paragraph (5).

Conclusion

Equality should be one of the essential foundational values of a constitution, the foundation on which the political community can build its future and come to terms with its past. One of the most important background principles of the 1989 Constitution was that everyone has an equal right to human dignity; therefore the state must treat all its citizens as equals, in the sense that political decisions must display equal concern for the fate of all. This moral principle could serve as a starting point for rights adjudication. Taking into account the discrepancies and loopholes of the Fundamental Law and its Transitional Provisions concerning equality, one can conclude that the Fundamental Law turns its back on the egalitarian principle and the idea of a pluralistic and secular state. It is not designed to transmit the best constitutional traditions to future generations, but rather, with its historical and religious references, it leads back to a misty past.

Freedom of Religion and Churches: Archeology in a Constitution-making Assembly

RENÁTA UITZ

Many aspects of the new Hungarian constitution are difficult to assess, as its key provisions need to be entrenched by further statutes, the so-called cardinal laws, to be passed by a qualified majority in Parliament.[1] This means that Parliament could delay strategic decisions concerning the content and details of most key constitutional provisions, and this delay also allows for some fine tuning of key details, thus essentially extending the constitution-making process: the Hungarian parliament passing legislation with qualified majority is essentially a vastly expanded constitution-making assembly. By the end of 2011, i.e. before the Fundamental Law's entry into force, most cardinal laws were yet to be made. Nonetheless on freedom of conscience, religion or belief and church-state relations the Hungarian parliament has already passed not only a provision in the Fundamental Law (Article VII), but also a supplement to this provision (Article 21(1) of the Transitional Provisions of the Fundamental Law), and not one, but altogether two cardinal laws.

The first cardinal law to entrench the new constitution's religion provision was passed in the summer of 2011.[2] In mid-December 2011 it was rumored in the press that the Constitutional Court will invalidate the first cardinal law due to irregularities in the legislative pro-

[1] Article T(4): "'Cardinal Act' shall mean an Act, the adoption or amendment of which requires the votes of two-thirds of the members of Parliament present." Note that the 1989 Constitution also required the further regulation of fundamental rights issues to be in acts of Parliament passed by a qualified majority. The main difference was that such statutes did not have a special name and status in the hierarchy of norms.

[2] Act C of 2011 on freedom of conscience and religion, and the legal status of churches, religious congregations and religious communities.

cess. On December 19, 2011 when the Constitutional Court decision was read out (but not yet published in the Official Journal),[3] Parliament withdrew the first cardinal law in an amendment appended to the act on national minorities.[4] Soon afterwards, the second cardinal law on church-state relations was introduced in Parliament. The bill was first read on December 23, 2011 and was passed on December 30, 2011.[5] The latest cardinal law on freedom of religion and churches entered into force at the same time as the new constitution and the Transitional Provisions, on January 1, 2012. In addition to setting the conditions for registration, and re-registration of churches, the cardinal law also recognized the status of 14 churches. Parliament amended the new cardinal law in February 2012, adding altogether 18 previously registered religious churches to the new list of recognized churches,[6] at the same time a parliamentary resolution refused to re-recognize 66 previously registered churches.[7]

This chapter is an attempt to reflect on the provisions of the Fundamental Law (Part I) in light of centuries of evolving (i.e. moderate) religious tolerance in Hungary (Part II), and vantage point of twenty years of the Constitutional Court's jurisprudence (Part III). A detailed analysis of the latest cardinal law on freedom of religion and churches (Part IV) and its debate in a constitution-making Parliament (Part V) reveals some novel claims about the powers of Parliament under the new constitution, and the vision of Parliament about the political community the constitution is meant to guide. The chapter also reflects on the justification and consequences of the legislation, first in the Hungarian context (Part VI), and then from an international human rights perspective (Part VII).

The picture of the new constitution and its architects thus revealed and reconstructed is not a pleasing one. What emerges from the haze of self-congratulatory laudations and the shadows of dated symbols

---

[3] Decision 164/2011. (XII. 20.)

[4] Article 241, Act CLXXIX of 2011.

[5] Act CCVI of 2011 on freedom of conscience and religion, and the legal status of churches, religious congregations and religious communities.

[6] Act VII of 2012 amending the act on freedom of conscience and religion, and the legal status of churches, religious congregations and religious communities.

[7] Parliamentary Resolution 8/2012 (II. 29.) on the refusal of church registration.

suggests a faded commitment to fundamental rights, non-discrimination and the rule of law at the expense of a reinforcement of national symbols and a rhetoric of sovereignty. And while this story is reason for concern in itself, when the key provisions of the new law on freedom of religion and churches springing from the fertile soil of the new constitution are examined in light of European human rights jurisprudence, the new Hungarian constitution, with its insistence on the uniqueness of the Hungarian endeavor, becomes a true monument to the lack of respect for the constitutional project inspired by the Enlightenment in a free and democratic Europe. Reservations about the new church registration regime were confirmed the Venice Commission in March 2012, when it found that several provisions of the new Hungarian cardinal law violate European human rights standards.[8]

I. The Fundamental Law: An Ode to Christianity and a Reluctance to Separate Church and State

On Easter Monday of 2011, the president of the republic signed into law a new constitution for Hungary, a document which was passed during Seder, an observer caring about the pluralistic religious history of Hungary may care to add. The Fundamental Law was adopted by a Parliament where a Christian-Conservative coalition of Fidesz and the Christian Democratic People's Party holds a more than two-thirds majority of the seats.

The Fundamental Law appears to bring little change to the existing church-state regime on its face. Article VII(1) continues to guarantee the right to freedom of thought, conscience and religion as an individual right,[9] and paragraph (2) provides for the continued separa-

---

[8] Venice Commission, *Opinion 664/2012 on Act CCVI of 2001 on the right to freedom of conscience and religion and the legal status of churches, denominations and religious communities of Hungary.*

[9] Article VII(1): "Everyone shall have the right to freedom of thought, conscience and religion. This right shall include the freedom to choose or change one's religion or other conviction, and the freedom to manifest or abstain from manifesting, to practice or teach, either alone or in community with others, in public or in private, one's religion or other conviction through religious acts or ceremonies, or in any other way."

tion of church and state, proclaiming that "The churches and the state shall operate separately. Churches shall be autonomous. The state shall cooperate with the churches for the attainment of community goals."

The formulation on church-state relations is a clear departure from the provision in the 1989 Constitution in the Hungarian, which is easily lost in translation. Article 60(3) of the 1989 Constitution talked about the separate zones of operation for churches and state (*'elválasztva' működés*), and not the separated operation of churches as state (*'különváltan' működés*) as if these actors were meant to belong together nonetheless.[10] This latter nuance is furthered by the expressed reference in Article VII(2) of the Fundamental Law to the cooperation of churches and state in order to achieve "community goals." Despite the nuances in terminology, one has to admit that the express reference to "cooperation for community goals" in the new provision simply accounts for the *status quo* of the last twenty years which emerged as a result of the Constitutional Court's silent yet firm leadership under the 1989 Constitution.[11]

A more visible departure from the 1989 Constitution is traceable in the entrenchment clause: Article VII(3) provides that the "detailed rules relating to churches shall be laid down in a cardinal Act." In contrast, Article 60(4) of the constitution used to provide that limitations on freedom of religion as an individual right be set by an act of Parliament passed by a qualified majority. Thus, the new constitution does not retain a supermajority requirement to safeguard religious liberty. Acts of Parliament passed by a simple majority may well impose original limitations on this fundamental human right. In contrast, Parliament may regulate church-state affairs with a supermajority, thus, the current Parliament is in a position to fix its preferences regarding churches which future governments controlling a simple majority in Parliament will not be able to alter.

---

[10] See András Jakab arguing that the new formulation is less confrontational than the old one. Jakab, A. *Az új Alaptörvény keletkezése és gyakorlati következményei* [The evolution and practical consequences of the new Fundamental Law] (Budapest: HVG ORAC, 2011), 211.

[11] On this see in English Tóth, G.A. "Unequal Protection: Historical Churches and Roma People in the Hungarian Constitutional Jurisprudence," *Acta Iuridica* 51, no. 2 (2010): 122–135; see also my "Aiming for State Neutrality in Matters of Religion, The Hungarian Record," *University of Detroit Mercy Law Review* 83 (2006): 761–788.

As to the possible content of legislation on church-state relations, the Transitional Provisions provide further guidance. Article 21(1) expressly authorizes Parliament to identify so-called recognized churches in a cardinal law, thus clearly empowering Parliament to offer a privileged position *ex lege* to certain churches. The same provision expressly provides that a cardinal law on church status may require for recognition of churches a certain length of operations, membership, historical traditions and societal support. This is a clear departure from the preceding legal regime in which the constitution did not distinguish between churches recognized as such by the state. Thus, Article 21(1) of the Transitional Provisions clearly creates a possibility to discriminate between religious communities, despite the prohibition of discrimination on the basis of religion (Article XV(2)). As if seeking to insulate this clearly discriminatory provision from a constitutional challenge, in May 2012 the Parliament adopted a constitutional amendment to confirm the constitutional stature of the Transitional Provisions which were added to the new constitution in December 2011, as an afterthought.[12]

In addition, unlike its predecessor, the Fundamental Law has several segments which read like an ode to Christianity. The new constitution proclaims in its introductory segment, entitled the National Avowal, that: "We are proud that our king Saint Stephen built the Hungarian State on solid ground and made our country a part of Christian Europe one thousand years ago;" "We recognize the role Christianity has played in preserving nationhood. We value our country's different religious traditions;" "We promise to preserve the intellectual and spiritual unity of our nation torn apart in the storms of the last century," and that "We honor the achievements of our historical constitution and we honor the Holy Crown, which embodies the constitutional continuity of Hungary's statehood and the unity of the nation."

The language of the National Avowal is heavy with symbols and sweeping statements. The status of these pronouncements is clarified by Article R(3) of the new constitution which makes it clear that the provisions of the constitution shall be interpreted according to their aims, the language of the National Avowal and the achievements of the

[12] See the Transitional Provisions and the First Amendment of the Fundamental Law in this volume.

historic constitution. If the language of the National Avowal is vague, there is even less guidance on what one shall regard as "an achievement of the historic constitution" of Hungary. For instance, the regulation of religious toleration and church-state affairs in Hungary certainly forms a thick record, and the selection of achievements from this record is a clearly value-driven exercise. One may point to periods of increased toleration as much as to periods of re-Catholicization as an example of an achievement, depending on one's personal preferences. The extent to which a strong constitutional attachment to a particular strain of Christianity will allow for the recognition of pluralism and tolerance in practice in a neutral fashion under the new constitution is not clear. Therefore, before reflecting on more recent developments, it is imperative to explore how such laudatory words resonate in the broader context of Hungarian religious affairs, in somewhat remote history as well as in recent constitutional jurisprudence.

II. Support for Leaving Religious Diversity Behind? Reflections on the Historical Record

The constitutional language which places an apparent emphasis on the importance of one strain of Christianity which was instrumental to preserve Hungarian nationhood, should be disturbing even among Hungarian Christians. After all, the strain of Christianity which can be credited for preserving nationhood is that of Roman Catholicism. Thus, the National Avowal's formulation—despite a gesture towards "different religious traditions"—fails to acknowledge the religious diversity of Hungarian society which has prevailed most visibly at least since the Reformation. With this gesture the Fundamental Law, and the new law on freedom of religion and churches is not based on the protection of religious liberty, but rather fits the well-known, pre-Enlightenment pattern wherein the scope of religious toleration reflects the state of power struggles of competing political elites. This approach, closely connected with a logic of sovereignty in the Hungarian context, is antithetical to the protection of religious liberty as a fundamental right.

It is not to be disputed or undervalued that Hungary has long established ties with the Roman Catholic Church, going back to its foundation as an independent state and the coronation of its first monarch. Although the Catholic Church remained dominant in Hungary as a key component in a well embedded Habsburg state ideology,[13] an account on religious freedom also has to reflect the cycles of struggles between Catholics and Protestants[14] where periods of open violence were followed by periods of relative peace and toleration. With the pendulum of toleration and re-Catholicization swinging back and forth for centuries. As an often mentioned achievement, Act 1895: LIII introduced a three-tier system of church recognition wherein so-called "recognized religions" remained at the top trier. Below this level the 1895 law introduced the category of "acknowledged" religions, whilst at the bottom of the hierarchy were those faiths which did not belong to either class which were simply "tolerated," i.e. not persecuted. For its time it was a considerable achievement that the 1895 act allowed for the state recognition of further religious communities, even if in a lesser class, and established legal rules for their recognition. This three-tier system was described as an intermediate solution between retaining an established church and separating churches from the state.[15]

The difference between "recognized" and "acknowledged" churches was only abolished after WWII, with Act XXXIII of 1947. As far as it applied to recognition of churches, however, the 1895 law stayed in force until transition to democracy. In the 1980's—before the transition to democracy began—the communist government recognized as a proper church the Hungarian Evangelical Brotherhood, the Congregation of Faith, the New Hungarian Apostolic Church, the Hungarian Community of Jehovah's Witnesses and the Hungarian Commu-

---

[13] On this aspect see recently Ducreux, M-E., "Emperors, Kingdoms, Territories: Multiple Versions of the Pietas Austriaca?" *The Catholic Historical Review* 97, no. 2 (2011): 276–304.

[14] In contemporary statutes Calvinists are referred to as "Helvets," while Lutherans are mentioned as "Augsburgians." Contemporary Hungarian terminology mentions Calvinists as "Reformed" protestants, while Lutherans are "Evangelicals." My text keeps with Lutheran and Calvinist to the extent practicable, while Protestant refers exclusively to "old / traditional European" Reformation denominations.

[15] Differences between accepted (*bevett*) and acknowledged (*elismert*) religions are spelled out in Szathmáry, B. *Fejezetek az állami vallás- és egyházjogból, Tanulmányi segédlet az V. évfolyamos joghallgatók számára* [Chapters from state religion and church law, Study aid for 5th year law students] (Budapest: Károli Gáspár Református Egyetem, 2006), 36–38.

nity of Krishna Consciousness still under the 1947 act.[16] After Act IV of 1990 had been adopted by the outgoing Communist parliament,[17] for the last twenty years over 300 religious communities (among them representatives of world religions, new religious movements and home-grown movements) operated undisturbed under the law.[18]

In Hungary the development of the legal framework on church-state relations was gradual, and any achievement towards greater toleration was highly dependent on the religious affiliation or personal philosophy of key decision-makers. Historic developments stand as clear testament on behalf of toleration in the increasing richness and plurality of the Hungarian religious scene. At the same time, it is not an exaggeration to say that before the entry into force of the first democratic constitution in 1989, and the 1990 law on religious freedom the Hungarian legal system did not recognize full legal equality of religious communities, and preserved a prominent position for the Catholic Church throughout much of Hungarian history. Recognition for other religious communities depended on the whims of the political process, and at least historically, major backlashes were not unusual. Therefore, the new constitution's determination to privilege the strain of Christianity which was instrumental to preserving Hungarian nationhood is highly suspect from the perspective of the protection of religious freedom and equality. As a side note, ironically, its privileged position did not leave the Catholic Church unharmed either. The power of the monarch to interfere with the internal affairs of the Catholic Church and other churches went to such an extent which is clearly incompatible with basic percepts of current human rights standards applicable to any church but an established church.

---

16 Here I follow Schanda, B. in *Az Alkotmány kommentárja* [Commentary to the Hungarian Constitution], ed. Jakab, A. (Budapest: Századvég, 2009), Vol. 3, 2244, fn 1.

17 For an English translation of the Hungarian law see Durham C. and S. Ferrari eds., *Laws on Religion and the State in Post-Communist Europe* (Leuven: Peeters, 2004) 153 et seq. For a comprehensive English language account on the law see Schanda, B. *Religion and Law in Hungary* (The Hague: Kluwer, 2011).

18 For the latest data in English see U.S. State Department / International Religious Freedom Report 2010–Hungary, as available at: http://www.state.gov/g/drl/rls/irf/2010/148942.htm. As it was also reflected in the parliamentary debate there are no firm data on the number of registered (and still operating) churches.

III. The Contributions of the Constitutional Court under the 1989 Constitution: Inventing 'Historic Churches'

The 1989 Constitution provided for religious freedom, separation of church and state, and also for the prohibition of discrimination on the basis of religion. The first democratic law on religious freedom introduced a general church registration system, making registration open for all religious communities with one hundred members.[19] With its relatively low threshold and undemanding formal requirements, the old Hungarian law used to be rather permissive in its genre, allowing for unprecedented religious diversity and opportunities for new faith-based initiatives.

Despite strong separationist language in the constitution, and an easily accessible registration system, over the years the post-1989 Hungarian governments became known for their willingness to distinguish between "historic churches" and others (the so-called "small churches"[20]) without a formal legal definition of "historic" and "small" churches. For instance, Hungarian governments maintained a concordat-based regime of cooperation with a select few registered churches, while other similarly registered churches fell under the generally applicable legal rules.[21] A Concordat was concluded between the state and the Catholic Church, was promulgated in an act of Parliament, and has the status of an international agreement.[22] Other agreements between the government (so, no the state) and the respective churches

[19] Article 9(1)(a), Act IV of 1990.

[20] See Sajó, A. "A 'kisegyház' mint alkotmányjogi képtelenség" ['Small church' as a constitutional non-sense] *Fundamentum* no. 2 (1999): 87–98 (showing the discriminatory impact of the distinction between historic churches and small churches).

[21] The qualitatively different nature of the lesser agreements and the Concordat with the Roman Catholic Church is clear from Schanda, Religion and Law in Hungary, 40–49.

[22] The Concordat between the Holy See on behalf of the Catholic Church and the Hungarian state was signed in Vatican City on June 20, 1997 (i.e. under a Socialist government) and was promulgated in Act LXX of 1999 during the next, Conservative term, as an international agreement. On the status of the Concordat as an international agreement see Constitutional Court Decision 15/2004. (V. 14.) and Decision 99/2008. (VII. 3.).

were subsequently promulgated in a lesser legal norm (a Cabinet decree) and not in an act of Parliament.[23]

The Constitutional Court had a massive role in inspiring and then perpetuating this differentiation, despite the clear prohibition of discrimination on the basis of religion in the Constitution (Article 70/A). In its foundational decision on church-state relations in 1993 the Constitutional Court held that legal equality allows for taking the social status of individual churches into account.[24] According to the prevailing scholarly opinion on church-state relations, the concept of state neutrality shall be understood in the context of cooperation between the state and the churches, with regard to the nature of the particular instances of such cooperation (e.g. education, health care).[25]

Take the case of the Cabinet decree on the Army Chaplaincy which requires the army chaplains to come from four specified denominations (Roman Catholic, Calvinist, Lutheran and Jewish).[26] The preamble of the Cabinet decree explains that the chaplaincy was established in this particular manner upon agreements concluded by the government and these "historic churches." The Constitutional Court upheld the scheme introduced by the government.[27] The justices were satisfied with seeing that the establishment of the chaplaincy was pre-

23 The agreement between the government and the Lutherans was concluded on December 7, 1998 and was promulgated in Governmental Decree 1056/1999. (V. 26.); with Calvinists it was concluded on December 8, 1998 and was promulgated in Governmental Decree 1057/1999. (V. 26.). The Baptist Church entered into an agreement on December 10, 1998 and was promulgated in Governmental Decree 1044/2001. (IV. 20.). The Serbian Orthodox Parish of Buda entered the agreement on December 9, 1998 and was promulgated in Governmental Decree 1043/2001. (IV. 20.). The Hungarian Association of Jewish Congregations entered an agreement with the Hungarian government somewhat later, on December 21, 2000, which was promulgated as Governmental Decree 1045/2001. (IV. 20.). In addition, the Jewish community has a separate agreement on the maintenance of closed Jewish cemeteries. See Governmental Decree 1140/2001. (XII. 26.). Since 2006 a government decree required the minister of education to enter into agreements with all churches which maintain a higher education institution. See Governmental Decree 2066/2006. (IV. 3.).

24 Decision 4/1993. (II. 12.)

25 Schanda, in *Az Alkotmány kommentárja*, 2262.

26 Article 2(2), Governmental Decree 61/1994. (IV. 20.)

27 Decision 970/B/1994. (February 20, 1995).

ceded by a voluntary opinion poll in the armed forces concerning religious affiliation. Moreover, the Constitutional Court found that "'historical' for a group of churches is a reference to the actual national history of the formation of churches. Therefore, the designation alone does not constitute impermissible discrimination."[28] The Constitutional Court also emphasized that in the composition of the Army Chaplaincy churches are accounted for according to their "actual role."[29] Thereupon the Constitutional Court found that singling out particular denominations does not constitute unconstitutional discrimination or any other violation of freedom of religion. In the aftermath of the decision, a chaplaincy for prisons was established along similar lines.[30]

The Constitutional Court became the true master of the historical record in a lesser known case concerning national and public holidays.[31] In the case petitioners of Jewish faith challenged the provisions of the Labor Code prescribing the official days of rest. Petitioners submitted that while Hungarian official holidays include such Christian festivals as Christmas, Easter or Pentecost, even the most central holidays of the Jewish faith are not official holidays. Petitioners claimed this regulation is discriminatory and prevents them from the proper exercise of freedom of religion. The Constitutional Court rejected the petition, finding that the roster of official holidays matches societal practices on days of rest, and does not have a religious connotation anymore. Jewish holidays are not included among national holidays because they are not part of a wider national tradition. While seemingly the decision is phrased in neutral terms, the Constitutional Court's construction of the historical record is hardly free of value judgments when it decides who belongs to the mainstream of proper tradition, and who is excluded from it.

Despite a separationist constitutional language which also was supported by an anti-discrimination rule, the church-state regime under the 1989 Constitution, as supplemented by further statutes, is best described as cooperationist, with significant (mostly political

---

[28] Decision 970/B/1994. (February 20, 1995).
[29] Decision 970/B/1994. (February 20, 1995).
[30] Decree of the justice minister 13/2000. (VII. 14.).
[31] Decision 10/1993. (II. 27.)

and financial) advantages to the "historic churches" over the "small churches"—tags which are based on political distinctions beyond the neutral façade of the even-handed regulatory framework. The contribution of the Constitutional Court in devising and legitimizing this regime from the early days of its operation would be difficult to deny.

IV. The 2011 Cardinal Act on Freedom of Religion and Churches Enters the Scene

Although the Fundamental Law calls for a cardinal act on church-state relations (Article VII (3)), it does not provide detailed further direction on the matter. The first (and later withdrawn) cardinal law on freedom of religion and churches was among the very first ones, it preceded the cardinal act on the Constitutional Court or the reform of the judiciary also foreseen in the new constitution. The reason for the rush is not entirely easy to find as religious freedom issues were not in the public eye, until the autumn of 2010—around the same time when the making of the new constitution was starting to catch up—when the fight against "business sects" became a dominant topic in the Hungarian media space. In the middle of November 2010 a television documentary claimed that hundreds of millions of forints of government funding were channeled to business sects. In December 2010 the secretary of state for the Ministry of National Resources, Imre Nyitrai, told the press that the budget could save 3 billion forints on making church registration less accessible. In early 2011—i.e. before the new constitution was passed and ratified—the secretary of state in the Ministry of Public Administration and Justice, László Szászfalvi, promised a new church law, indicating that the optimal threshold of registration would be around 10,000 founding members.

The concept of the new church law finally arrived in the spring of 2011. According to Szászfalvi, the aim of the new law is "to reinforce communities which engage in credible church and religious activities, and to remove from the scope of the law those organizations which were formed expressly for business purposes." This concept sought to divide churches into three classes. The top class was meant to include "historic churches" with a 100 years presence or 25,000 members. This concept resembled in essence the church registration regime in the 1895 law, while considerably raising the formal conditions required for registration compared to the conditions set forth in the 1990 law. From its inception the concept took it for granted that churches registered under the 1990 law will need to seek re-registration under the new law in case they intend to continue their operation as a church.

A fine tuned version of the concept was revealed in early April 2011 when the government announced that under the new law the Catholic, the Reformed, the Lutheran and the Evangelical churches, as well as the Unitarian and the Orthodox communities will be recognized as historic churches.

Following an eventful spring, the bill finally emerged in June 2011. Despite its title listing three types of religious organizations, the bill submitted to Parliament introduced one level of registration for churches only, and required 20 years and 1,000 founding members for registration.[32] Others, who did not qualify for church status were meant to become associations. Courts were meant to be assisted by a body of experts in deciding about church status. Although the three-tier system of registration as foreseen in the concept was not introduced, the appendix to the bill included the names of 44 churches (registered under the 1990 law) in three clusters which were meant to be continued in their church status by the force of the statute, and without undergoing separate re-registration. In a number of other respects, like in offering a definition for religious activities, or listing activities which do not qualify as "primarily religious" the 2011 bill was clearly reminiscent of the bill which was introduced unsuccessfully in Parliament by the previous government lead by prime minister Viktor Orbán between 1998 and 2002.[33]

In less than a month, at the end of an extraordinary session in a working day that ended way after midnight, Parliament passed an altered version of the bill, adopting amendments to the bill proposed by

[32] Bill T/3507.

[33] For a description of the previous bill see Schanda, B. "Religion and State in the Candidate Countries to the European Union: Issues concerning Religion and State in Hungary," *Sociology of Religion* 64, no. 3 (2003): 333–348, 343. For a critical commentary on the bill from an international human rights perspective see e.g. Buda, P. "Állam és egyház: A polgári átalakulás eredményeinek leépítése" [State and church. Demolishing the achievements of civic reforms] *Fundamentum* no. 2 (2001): 127–142, 131 et sec.

the parliamentary committee on constitutional affairs. Under the new law,[34] churches which have operated in Hungary for at least 20 years and have at least 1,000 founding members were meant to be registered not by a court of law, but by a qualified (two-thirds) majority of Parliament upon the initiative of the responsible minister. The appendix to the law listed 14 churches (registered under the 1990 law) while the others—among them Christians, Buddhists and Muslims—were meant to seek re-registration with a Parliament after the entry into force of the new law on January 1, 2012. As a transitory measure, churches fated to lose their church status until their re-registration could expect to enter into a separate agreement with the government concerning the continued financing of their public interest tasks.

After the adoption of the new law, churches threatened by the sudden loss of their legal entity status petitioned various governmental actors, invariably, challenging the new law or their being left off the list of recognized churches.[35] Altogether some 72 churches requested re-registration under the new law, well before its entry into force. Finally it became apparent that Parliament was not planning to amend the new church law significantly when it took steps to open up the famously strict Hungarian ownership rules for arable land before associations. This gesture was meant to ensure that the church of Krishna Consciousness does not lose title over its farm, housing many believers of the community to whom the land is of spiritual significance, once—upon the loss of their church status—it becomes an association under the new church law.[36]

When Parliament withdrew the first cardinal law in order to prevent its invalidation by the Constitutional Court, a private members'

---

[34] Act C of 2011 on freedom of conscience and religion, and the legal status of churches, religious congregations and religious communities.

[35] The new law on churches attracted such international attention that on September 6, 2011 a secretary for Parliament in the Ministry of Public Administration and Justice, Bence Rétvári attended a videoconference on the Hungarian law convened by Johns Hopkins University. Available with the website of the Hungarian Embassy in Washington at http://washington.kormany.hu/videoconference-on-hungary-s-new-law-on-churches.

[36] The motion was first tabled by the human rights committee of Parliament as rider no. 31 to Bill T/5001. The amendment finally became part of the latest cardinal law on churches (Article 42).

bill quickly followed from the Fidesz and Christian Democratic People's Party.[37] Much of the bill was an apparent match of the law which was withdrawn a few days before. As a major change, the recognition of churches by a qualified majority decision of Parliament was replaced by a procedure based upon the procedure for a people's initiative. As a departure from the previous cardinal law, the conditions of recognition were also altered, welcoming only those churches which had a record of presence for at least a century on the international scene. This latter condition would have clearly meant that in addition to the Church of Scientology, the Krishna Consciousness community would also be excluded from among the envisioned church status recipients.

The latest cardinal law on churches,[38] as adopted in one week's time in the final days of December 2011, departs from the withdrawn law in several important respects. Unlike its predecessor, it clearly introduces a three-tier system, with 14 churches recognized by Parliament in an appendix to the law, other churches which may be recognized by parliament subsequently, and the third layer of religious associations (to which rules on associations apply). In the end, church status may be requested on behalf of religious associations by 1,000 signatures through a people's initiative. As a departure from the bill, the presence requirement was extended to include not only to centennial foreign churches, but also churches which had operated in Hungary for at least twenty years. As another novelty compared to the withdrawn law, the chairman of the Academy of Sciences may be requested by Parliament to issue an opinion on the presence requirement, as well as on the religious nature of the activities of the applicant association, and on the nature of its creeds and rites. It is a new condition that the creeds and rites of the applicant cannot violate the right to physical and mental health, the protection of human life and human dignity.

Interestingly, the number of churches recognized by Parliament *ex lege* did not change, although since the summer of 2011 it became apparent that several churches meet statutory requirements. Under the latest cardinal law Parliament is obliged to decide on applications filed under the previous law until the end of February 2012. Other churches

---

37 Bill T/5315.

38 Act CCVI of 2011 on freedom of conscience and religion, and the legal status of churches, religious congregations and religious communities.

which were registered under the 1990 law qualify as associations after January 1, 2012.

In February 2012 Parliament decided on the fate of the applications for church status which had been submitted in the summer of 2011, under the law which had never come into force. As required by the new cardinal law an experts' committee was established in the Academy of Sciences to assist Parliament in determining the religious qualities of applicant associations. The Academy, however, refused to assess the religious qualities of the churches under consideration: to the dismay of the sponsor of the amendment, who was in charge of the recognition process, the Academy concluded that this was not a matter for scholarly assessment or judgment. Thus, instead of following the procedure set forth in the new cardinal law, Parliament simply amended the appendix of the cardinal law which was passed in December 2011. Neither the amendment of the cardinal law in which church status was granted *ex lege* to some previously registered churches, nor the resolution in which 66 churches were turned down offer insights into the reasons behind Parliament's decisions.

V. Parliamentary Archeology: Uncovering the Intent of the Legislator

After twenty years of stability the latest Hungarian law on freedom of religion and churches brings radical changes: it affects all previously registered churches, their believers, supporters and wards, it impairs the rights of the vast majority of registered churches at least for a transitional period (the length of which is not known) and is expected to deprive a number of previously registered churches from their church status altogether. It is worth recalling that at the time when the latest church law was adopted, Transitional Provisions were added to the Fundamental Law in order to provide a sound foundation for the new church registration regime.[39] As the latest law entrenches the provisions of the new constitution, it is crucial to pay more attention to the reasons advanced by key governmental actors in support of such grave limitations of fundamental human rights at a time, when such

[39] See Article 21 of the Transitional Provisions in this volume.

a limitation of rights was not even allegedly required due to pressing external forces. The parliamentary record reveals that the final turn of events, wherein the task of church registration was removed from the competence of courts and transferred to Parliament, was the result of a conscious and calculated decision. This major (and unusual) decision corresponds to a conception of freedom of religion, church-state relations as well as the role of courts vis-à-vis the elected representatives of the people. The debate leading to a surprising grand finale presents a grim picture of a Parliament which just produced a new constitution for a European democracy.

The record on the debate on the Fundamental Law and its relevant Transitional Provisions reveals little, as religious liberty and church-state relations were not a matter of central concern in Parliament at the time. As might be expected, the debate in December 2011, over the resubmitted bill offered less insight on key issues (such as transferring the power of registration to Parliament) than the parliamentary debate of the summer of 2011 when the bill was first introduced. In order to reveal the logic of the constitution-making process, it is crucial to explore the key themes of the debate on the two bills.

Although mindfulness of conformity with the new constitution was mentioned in the parliamentary debate of the new cardinal law both in the summer and in the winter of 2011, the need to live up to the new constitution was not the prevalent justification for the new regulation of church-state relations.[40] Instead of framing the purpose of the new law in terms of constitutional change, in his opening statement introducing the bill, Tamás Lukács the sponsor of the summer bill for the Christian Democratic People's Party took it for granted that "it is not necessary to prove an abuse of rights on a sensitive field, when Hungary has 343, or according to others, 362 religious organizations registered. It is not the topic of a parliamentary exposé to list the numerous types of abuses, but compared to the church numbers of

[40] As if to confirm the practical significance of the National Avowal, in order to indicate the place and purpose of the new law on religious freedom and churches in the legal system, secretary of state László Szászfalvi referred to the National Avowal at the start of the parliamentary debate. Journal of Parliament, June 23, 2011, Day no. 103, Speech no. 4 (general debate). The records of parliamentary debates are available in Hungarian at http://www.mkogy.hu/internet/plsql/ogy_naplo.naplo_ujnapok_ckl?p_ckl=39

other European countries it is not an exaggeration to say that abuse of rights in our country obtained increasingly large domains in the last 20 years."[41] Indeed, the need to suppress business-sects was a key theme in December 2011 as well.[42]

It is certainly not inconceivable that several entities which were registered under the old law did misuse the advantageous economic (predominantly tax) status which church registration entailed. Under the 1990 it was clearly possible to dissolve churches which operated in violation of the law, as this opportunity could have been sufficient to remove the so-called business sects.[43] It would not have been impossible in the last 20 years to review the tax records of not only alleged business sects, but of all registered churches using the avenues of monitoring available under the 1990 law. This avenue would have been all the more advisable to take as church status became so appealing as a legal form of operation for certain non-religious actors exactly due to the wide range of economic advantages attached to it by the state. It is important to emphasize, therefore, that granting legal entity status to religious communities does not automatically mean that the state should also award tax exemptions to such organizations, or provide them with public funds. It was the peculiarity of the Hungarian law that certain economic benefits were automatically granted to churches, and with a permissive church registration regime under the 1990 law church status became easy to obtain, and ultimately to abuse. Nonetheless, despite occasional waves of outbursts against business sects and new religious movements, we have little idea on the true extent of this problem. If anyone is to blame for widespread sect-business in Hungary, the culprit must be the government.

In the parliamentary debate the struggle against business sects was invariably turned into the expression of a genuine need to introduce some order or discipline in the church sphere. As the lead speaker of

[41] Journal of Parliament, June 23, 2011, Day no. 103, Speech no. 2 (general debate).

[42] See e.g. László Varga (Christian Democratic People's Party), Journal of Parliament, December 23, 2011, Day no. 158, Speech no. 78; László Szászfalvi, Journal of Parliament, December 23, 2011, Day no. 158, Speech no. 142 (general debate); Zoltán Demeter (Fidesz), Journal of Parliament, December 23, 2011, Day no. 158, Speech no. 152 (general debate).

[43] Article 20(2), Act IV of 1990.

the Socialist party on the opposition side, István Nyakó noted in the general debate of the first bill in the summer: "[Fidesz] faction leader [János Lázár] had said in the meeting of the committee of constitutional affairs that these 350 churches—and this is recorded [in the Journal of Parliament]—operated in a legal manner, or at least we do not see any legal precedent, court decision indicating that they might have operated in an illegal way. [According to the sponsors of the bill] the boundless and untransparent flourishing of various communities, denominations, churches devalued the existence and operation of churches which meet a real social demand."[44] The need to reduce the number of churches as a key regulatory goal was confirmed in the debate on the new bill in December 2011 by secretary Szászfalvi, and repeated by others.[45] As Christian Democrat deputy László Varga eloquently put in the heat of the general debate in December: "it is impossible to let a thousand flowers bloom all over the place."[46]

Furthermore, it seems that in addition to an objection against the sheer number of churches, the government-supported legislators also had value preferences concerning which churches are acceptable in the Hungary of the new constitution. Apparently, pluralism, or at least religious diversity, is not a welcome phenomenon as the need to protect Hungarian identity takes over. In this respect, in the summer the desire to serve justice over centuries was a prevalent theme offered to justify the new law. The exposé of MP Lukács noted several times that the purpose of the new law was to ensure that a new legal order is introduced reflecting the historical role of and injustices suffered by certain churches. Zoltán Demeter who was the lead speaker for Fidesz in the debate proclaimed that "due to her unique history Hungary is entitled to a unique church-state model,"[47] which he named as a model of "supportive separation."

[44] Journal of Parliament, July 11, 2011, Day no. 108, Speech no. 367 (closing debate).

[45] Journal of Parliament, December 28, 2011, Day no. 160, Speech no. 280 (second reading).

[46] Journal of Parliament, December 23, 2011, Day no. 158, Speech no. 116 (general debate).

[47] Journal of Parliament, June 23, 2011, Day no. 103, Speech no. 14 (general debate).

References to history and traditions took a different form in the debate over the second bill in December. The bill initially offered recognition by Parliament only to those additional churches not listed in the appendix of the law, which could show 100 years of international presence. In the parliamentary debate the Christian Democrat sponsor of the summer's bill, Tamás Lukács, argued in favor of this new requirement claiming that "in the European legal regime the definition of originality is defined by 100 years for nationalities." Therefore the same should apply for churches.[48] Others suggested that 100 years is a "fair historical measure."[49]

The parliamentary debate in December 2011 was even more underscored by the need to tailor church registration to a manner which reflects Hungarian identity, understood as a means of responding to "real social needs." After all, the Transitional Provisions appended to the new constitution identifies social support for churches as a basis for permissible governmental discrimination between them (Article 21(1)). In this spirit, in December 2011 secretary Szászfalvi justified the latest bill with a new argument, by pointing out that the list of 14 recognized churches indeed corresponds to the religious affiliations of 99 per cent of the population as represented for the 2001 census, adding that in 2010, 91 per cent of the redirected transfers of one percent tax donations to churches went to those 14 churches which were on the list of recognized churches.[50] This almost mechanical argument about responding to the religious makeup of the population was flavored by the need to recognize those churches only which the population identifies as real churches,[51] and, invariably, emphasizing that the task of Parliament was to register only those churches which correspond to the value system of the new constitution.[52] These strains

48 Journal of Parliament, December 23, 2011, Day no. 158, Speech no. 126 (general debate).

49 Péter Hoppál (Fidesz), Journal of Parliament, December 23, 2011, Day no. 158, Speech no. 180 (general debate).

50 Journal of Parliament, December 23, 2011, Day 158, Speech no. 80 (general debate).

51 Béla Turi-Kovács (Fidesz), Journal of Parliament, December 23, 2011, Day no. 158, Speech no. 146 (general debate).

52 János Kővári (Fidesz), Journal of Parliament, December 28, 2011, Day no. 160, Speech no 244 (second reading).

of argument revolving around the religious identity of Hungarians were finally connected by Szászfalvi in December 2011 when he said that under the new law the decision about registration does not even really rest with Parliament, as along the new criteria the decision on church status "was made by the people during previous centuries."[53]

Despite the above statements, for a long time it seemed that the debate in Parliament would not reveal the real purpose behind the new law, and we would be left with the need to suppress business sects and to respect historic churches. Among the expositions of legislative intent it was sad to see the extremely personal nature of the debate, heavy with frequent character attacks, attempting to out deputies as disguised lobbyists of sect interests. In retrospect, however, such attacks appear still less unpleasant than the rampant anti-Semitic laments of the far-right radical party, Jobbik. The style and tone of thc parliamentary debate is only worth to pay attention to, because as Ildikó Lendvai of the opposition Hungarian Socialist Party noted about the new regime, since Parliament is entrusted with registering churches, "from now on we could have this debate repeated every week. We might be discussing initiatives regarding a church or a religious community now, and these undignified stories are not likely going to get more rare, but despite all your good will, they will get more frequent."[54]

The debate in Parliament finally took an exciting turn in the summer during the adoption of the first cardinal law, when the committee on constitutional affairs, upon the proposal of the faction leader of the governing party, János Lázár, introduced an amendment to make the registration of churches the task of a qualified majority in Parliament. Although the qualified majority rule was eventually dropped from the law in December, since Parliament remains in charge of church registration, this contribution is highly relevant in understanding how the new regulation of church-state affairs fits in the new constitution and the self-understanding of the constitution-making assembly.

When responding to some nagging by András Schiffer, faction leader for the smaller opposition party Politics Can Be Different, Lázár

[53] Journal of Parliament, December 28, 2011, Day no. 160, Speech no. 250 (second reading).

[54] Journal of Parliament, July 11, 2011, Day no. 108, Speech no. 407 (closing debate).

justified the amendment putting Parliament in charge of church registration by submitting that similarly to the recognition of national minorities, the recognition of churches was an act of sovereignty. Lázár continued by saying:

> You should not delude yourselves with trying to transfer the responsibility for the decision to judges, because you are the ones who make the law on the basis of which the judges will decide who is a church and who is not. In 1990 the law on the basis of which it was determined who is a church and who is not was also made by deputies in Parliament. This time we will make this law, and the responsibility is on us, whether we are ready to name in concrete terms who do we find as worthy and befitting for church status in 2011, or whether we are not... Why could we not offer to churches, depending on whether the government concludes an agreement with them or not, to decide whether they want to maintain their church status, or not, as this will not prevent them from exercising their freedom of religion. This law opens the way for them to exercise their religious freedom. This much you have to admit. I believe that it is much more transparent, more open; and—starting from the responsibility we have towards national minorities—I believe that following from their oath all members of Parliament are willing to undertake the responsibility for churches, to make decisions in the case of people who wish to exercise their religious freedom.[55]

In this logic freedom of religion is granted to communities of believers on the basis of their commendable qualities and contributions, depending on the government's assessment. Note how the basis of this exercise is detached from freedom of religion as an individual right, and depends on the decision of the government to conclude a concordat, and ultimately, on the decision of Parliament to grant church status. In this logic, therefore, it is the government or Parliament (thus, ultimately, a gesture of the sovereign) that distributes a privilege to practice freedom of religion, pending further qualifications. This logic was further strengthened by Tamás Lukács in the debate in December

[55] Journal of Parliament, July 11, 2011, Day no. 108, Speech no. 403 (closing debate).

2011, when he said that Parliament has to be in charge of church registration as this gesture provides churches as public institutions of special significance with additional dignity and legitimacy beyond the protection of fundamental rights.[56] This conceptual framework presents a clear departure from the one emphasizing the utmost importance of fundamental rights, and left behind with the 1989 Constitution. The elements of this novel approach will be analyzed later, in the hopes of bringing further clarity into the vision the state is expected to play under the new Hungarian constitution.

Without entering into details on a connected point, before concluding this section it is worth pointing out the Fidesz faction leader's account of the responsibilities of parliamentary deputies and the respective roles of Parliament and the judiciary, and their relationship in a curious conceptual framework. According to the classic division, the task of Parliament is to make general rules, which will be enforced by the executive and applied by the judiciary in individual cases. One of the fundamental sources of trust in the judiciary is the professional competency of the judges, another one is the process of judicial selection along with safeguards protecting the judicial career, while a third one—closely connected with the previous two—is the nature of the judicial process. The above distinction together with the qualities mentioned before make the independent and impartial judiciary one of the most important instruments of preventing the arbitrary exercise (abuse) of governmental power and ensuring the protection of human rights in a constitutional democracy committed to the rule of law. Access to court is one of the best-know safeguards of fundamental rights.

It appears, however, that Lázár's logic rests on different premises. His point of departure is that if Parliament does not decide a particular matter itself, then the deputies transfer responsibility for the decision to the courts, an action which constitutes a relinquishment of a parliamentarian's basic duties. According to the approach quoted above at length in the church registration context the real decision is not about setting the proper conditions for seeking legal entity status, but determining "who is a church and who is not." In the context of freedom of

[56] Journal of Parliament, December 23, 2011, Day no. 158, Speech nos. 98-100 (general debate).

religion the latter is the decision for the sovereign to take, and not for a court of law.[57]

From this unorthodox perspective it all of a sudden becomes crystal clear how Parliament—the heir of a revolution which took place in the polling booth—received the power to register churches with a qualified majority. What happened in February 2012, with the first round of additional church registrations cozily fits in this logic, as some of the churches which were added to the appendix of the cardinal law clearly do not meet the statutory criteria for church status as they undisputedly did not appear to have 1,000 believers in Hungary, while among the rejections one finds communities which clearly should have qualified. For instance, when recognizing the Anglican Church, the chairman of the human rights committee of Parliament openly admitted that the motivation for the decision was that four ambassadors belong to the church.[58] When recognizing the Coptic Church, the same chairman reasoned that in order to prevent the persecution of Christians in the world, it was important to recognize the oldest Christian churches and also the churches of world religions, in the hope of reciprocity in international relations. At the same time, the Hungarian Evangelical Brotherhood, although it undisputedly met the statutory conditions, was turned down in February, with the committee finding that they can apply next time, in the round when Parliament is not taking a discretionary decision, but follows the recognition procedure (complete with popular initiative) as prescribed by the law.

Thus, in February 2012 Parliament was making pure discretionary decisions when selecting additional "acknowledged churches," as openly admitted by Gergely Gulyás (one of the chief architects of the Fundamental Law) in a meeting of Parliament's human rights committee.[59] Furthermore, it was confirmed several times in the parlia-

[57] Due to the limitations of this chapter, I will not explore the relationship of the legislature and the judiciary in further detail.

[58] Tamás Lukács, Committee on Human Rights, Minorities, Civic and Religious Affairs, February 13, 2012. The record of the committee meeting is available at http://www.parlament.hu/biz39/bizjkv39/EMB/1202131.pdf

[59] Committee on Human Rights, Minorities, Civic and Religious Affairs, February 14, 2012. The record of the committee meeting is available at http://www.parlament.hu/biz39/bizjkv39/EMB/1202141.pdf

mentary debate that the conditions for church recognition in the new cardinal law do not grant church status as a matter of a right, so Parliament retains its discretion in grating church status even if an applicant clearly meets statutory criteria.[60] With these lessons about parliamentary intentions and procedure in mind it makes good sense to reflect on the premises of the justification and its consequences, first in the Hungarian context, and then from a human rights perspective.

VI. The Power of the State

The take on church registration as an exercise of state sovereignty is unusual, yet it adequately illustrates that the current constitution-making majority in the Hungarian Parliament does not regard church recognition as a matter of freedom of religion, but rather they view it as a question of the exercise of state power.

In the Hungarian constitutional tradition if the language of sovereignty is invoked in relation to religious manifestations in general, or to churches in particular, it is best understood as a reference to the powers of the monarch to closely manage and govern churches. Despite its contested origins, according to tradition, the Hungarian kings since the beginning of the state are to be regarded as "apostolic."[61] This quality—which is usually granted to kings responsible for historic conversions of their subjects, but not to entire dynasties—coupled with the holy crown doctrine permitted the Hungarian monarchs to retain significant influence over the Catholic Church. Historically, royal powers over the Catholic Church expanded to creating the internal organization of the Catholic Church (seats of bishops and archbishops), appointments of church leaders as well as lesser positions, the distribution of church property and the power to assent to the communication of church letters and circulars to the

[60] See e.g. Tamás Lukács, Journal of Parliament, February 13, 2012, Day no. 162, Speech no 361 (general debate).

[61] Balogh, M. "Regnum et sacerdotium. Állam és egyház történetileg változó viszonyai Magyarországon" [Regnum et sacerdotium, The historically changing relations of church and state in Hungary], *Vallástudományi Szemle* 6, no. 4 (2010): 9–24, 11–15.

general public. Somewhat surprisingly, the doctrine was consolidated by the early 16th century in the collection of the laws of the domain (Werbőczy's *Tripartitum*).

By the 17th century it was common wisdom that the apostolic Hungarian king retains powers equivalent to those of the first king, St Stephen.[62] When other religions were recognized by the Hungarian government over the centuries, an equivalent of similar powers was extended to the newly recognized religious communities. The Hungarian government kept exercising its control powers over the internal affairs and governance of the Catholic Church until 1918. The Hungarian monarchs had their conflicts with Rome in order to preserve their own powers. It was a Catholic Church tightly controlled by the monarch which then could have a say in the affairs of the state through formal procedures and informal channels.

The holy crown doctrine is expressly referred to in the National Avowal as the physical embodiment of the continuity of Hungarian statehood: "We honor the achievements of our historical constitution and we honor the Holy Crown, which embodies the constitutional continuity of Hungary's statehood and the unity of the nation." The unambiguous reference to the Holy Crown strengthened by the constitutional requirement in Article R(3) to interpret the new constitution in light of the historical achievements of Hungarian constitutional development arguably opens the possibility to resurrect the millennial powers of the Hungarian sovereign over the organization, property and governance of churches, down to determining details of leadership. The exercise of this power visibly violates the autonomy of religious communities, and is antithetical to the separation of church and state, a requirements which is maintained in the new constitution itself.[63] Therefore, the concept of sovereignty as reheated in the parliamentary debate of the new church law is an extremely dangerous and inadequate instrument, which also happens to violate fundamental human rights. A sovereignty-based regulatory model which distributes the

[62] Ibid., 12, fn 5.

[63] See András Jakab arguing that the application of Article R(3) is acceptable to the extent it does not lead to absurdities, and to the extent it is in compliance with international human rights obligations. Jakab, *Az új Alaptörvény keletkezése és gyakorlati következményei*, 184–185.

opportunity to exercise religious freedom according to the discretionary decision of the sovereign is by definition unfit for a constitutional democracy entrusted with preserving religious diversity.

VII. The Hungarian Law in Light of International Human Rights Standards

In the parliamentary debate considerable time was spent on estimating how the new Hungarian law on freedom of religion and churches will fare in international comparison. In his exposé opening the general debate on the bill, Tamás Lukács submitted that "among countries where registration is tied to a threshold requirement, the 1,000 persons we are proposing here belongs within the lower requirements."[64] Secretary Szászfalvi—as if to prevent further comparisons—added in the beginning of the general debate: "Regarding the membership requirement, let me note that 1,000 persons is a rather low requirement compared to the church regulation in a number of EU countries, such as in Slovakia, which has fewer inhabitants than our country and its threshold is 20,000 persons."[65]

In contrast, even a brief and superficial analysis finds that the new Hungarian law violates a number of established rules of human rights jurisprudence and as such, is highly problematic. This was also acknowledged by the Venice Commission's opinion on the Hungarian cardinal law in March 2012. As a preliminary issue, it is important to briefly reflect on the relationship of freedom of religion and church registration, especially since in the parliamentary debate it was suggested that through regulation the state may define the acceptable manifestations of religious freedom. It is well known that freedom of religion as a human right is protected in Article 18 of the Universal Declaration, Article 18 of the International Covenant for Civil and Political Rights, Article 9 of the European Convention on Human Rights, and most recently, in Article 10 of the EU Charter on Funda-

---

64 Journal of Parliament, June 23, 2011, Day no. 103, Speech no. 2 (general debate).

65 Journal of Parliament, June 23, 2011, Day no. 103, Speech no. 4 (general debate).

mental Rights. It is also widely accepted that freedom of religion has individual, as well as collective aspects, and that the desire to operate in an organized manner and to seek legal entity status in order to assist this organized operation is a protected manifestation of the right. Churches are not worthy of protection because of their mere existence, but because they serve as a mean and the framework of the enjoyment of one of the oldest fundamental human rights. Despite suggestions to this effect in the Hungarian parliamentary debate, freedom of religion is a human right recognized in international and human rights law the exercise of which does not (and cannot) depend on the good will or benevolence of the government.

The European Court of Human Rights has been consistent in reaffirming that although the member states may regulate the exercise of freedom of religion, this may only be performed in a neutral fashion, in a manner which promotes religious diversity and pluralism, features which the Court regards to be key characteristics of European democracies.[66] The state is not expected, and is clearly not required, to act as an umpire between competing religious communities, and cannot become involved in settling intra-faith disputes.[67] The Hungarian parliamentary debate was heavy with discussing the need to reduce religious diversity in Hungary, to select legitimate churches and to bring order into the church sphere. Although the Venice Commission did not find fault with the primary goal of the Hungarian cardinal law in reducing the number of registered churches and in responding to the abuse of church status via suppressing business sects,[68] since Article 9(2) of the European Convention does not list such objectives among the grounds of permissible limitation of religious freedom, these legislative aims continue to appear *prima facie* suspect in light of applicable European standards.

As it was emphasized both by the European Court of Human Rights and the Office for Democratic Institutions and Human Rights' (OSCE/ODIHR) advisory panel of experts on freedom of religion or belief, the

---

[66] *Hasan and Chaush v. Bulgaria*, no. 30985/96, October 26, 2000, para 78; *Metropolitan Church of Bessarabia v. Moldova,* no. 45701/99, December 13, 2001, paras 116–117.

[67] *Metropolitan Church of Bessarabia v. Moldova*, paras 118 and 123; *Hasan and Chaush v. Bulgaria*, para 62.

[68] Venice Commission, *Opinion 664/2012*, paras 15–17.

legal registration of a religious community as a church cannot become the precondition or prerequisite of the free exercise of religion as an individual right.[69] As the following analysis will also demonstrate, it is also accepted that access to legal entity status may be subject to certain conditions, as it is appropriate for the state to keep record of various entities to which it grants legal personality.[70] Furthermore, due to the specificities of the Hungarian context it might be important to add a point which is well known in Hungarian legal academia, i.e. that granting legal entity status to religious communities does not automatically guarantee state funding for the same organizations. The state is entitled to make the funding of religious communities subject to further conditions.[71]

The relationship of churches and states is described by many models in the literature, admitting that the wide array of national variations is due to the historical circumstances of each country. Therefore, a careless international comparison may easily yield to misleading conclusions, since several national legal systems might not have straightforward comparators. The Guidelines of the OSCE/ODIHR panel of experts emphasize that the primary reason to provide legal entity status to religious communities is to facilitate their religious life, and not to install state control over them. As a result, the Guidelines in line with the jurisprudence of the European Court of Human Rights urge the member states to make such solutions available for religious communities which permit "at a minimum, access to the basic rights associated with legal personality—for example, opening a bank account, renting or acquiring property for a place of worship or for other religious uses, entering into contracts, and the right to sue and be sued—should be available without excessive difficulty."[72]

---

69 *Masaev v. Moldova,* no. 6303/05, May 12, 2009, para 26. See also OSCE/ODIHR, *Guidelines for Review of Legislation Pertaining to Religion or Belief* (2003), 17. http://www.osce.org/odihr/13993

70 OSCE/ODIHR, *Guidelines for Review of Legislation Pertaining to Religion or Belief*, 17.

71 Confirming this point in general for the Hungarian context see Schanda, B. *Magyar állami egyházjog* [Hungarian State Church Law] (Budapest: Pázmány Péter Katolikus Egyetem Kánonjogi Posztgraduális Intézet – Szent István Társulat, 2000), 71.

72 OSCE/ODIHR, *Guidelines for Review of Legislation Pertaining to Religion or Belief*, 17–18.

The Court regards legal personality acquired as a result of governmental registration as a prominent aspect of freedom of religion protected by Article 9 of the Convention.[73] Denial of access to legal entity status to a group of believers amounts to a violation of freedom of religion and freedom of association (Article 11) of the Convention.[74] The Court pays special attention to multi-tier systems wherein recognition at the lowest level does not provide access to legal personality. This is due to the fact that lack of access to legal personality deprives religious communities of those rights and opportunities without which these religious communities clearly suffer disadvantage. In one case the Court found a violation because "the applicants were unable to obtain recognition and effective enjoyment of their rights to freedom of religion and association in any organizational form."[75]

Arguably, under the latest Hungarian church registration regime entry level legal entity status is provided to religious communities in the form of so-called religious associations operating under the Civil Code and the new cardinal act on associations.[76] Such religious associations differ in one respect only from other associations: resolutions of religious associations passed in connection with their religious operation are exempt from judicial review.[77] Since registered associations are required to operate with a registered membership under Hungarian law,[78] this format is unfit for the exercise of religious freedom as the

[73] *Religionsgemeinschaft der Zeugen Jehovas and Others v. Austria*, no. 40825/98, July 31, 2008, para 66; *Metropolitan Church of Bessarabia v. Moldova*, para 118; and also *Koretskyy and Others v. Ukraine*, no. 40269/02, 3 April, 2008, para 40; and *Canea Catholic Church v. Greece*, no. 25528/94, December 16, 1997, paras 30 and 40–41, *Kimlya and Others v Russia*, no. 76836/01 and 32782/03, October 1, 2009, para 85.

[74] *Kimlya and Others v. Russia*, para 84 et seq.

[75] *Kimlya and Others v. Russia*, para 87.

[76] Act CLXXV of 2011 on the freedom of association, on public purpose status, and the operation of civic organizations replaces Act II of 1989 on the freedom of association. The Venice Commission did not assess whether religious associations in this form met the requirements for entry level entity status, as the legal rules governing this status were not referred to it. See *Opinion 664/2012*, paras 41 and 42.

[77] See Article 62(7) of the Civil Code, and Article 62(7) of Act CLXXV of 2011 on the freedom of association.

[78] Article 61(1) of the Civil Code, also Article 5 of Act CLXXV of 2011 on the freedom of association.

registration requirement runs counter to the right to the freely choose one's religion. In addition, under Hungarian law associations are expected to operate in a democratic, self-governing fashion. It is highly questionable whether this mode of operation is suitable for religious communities under spiritual leadership.

As was mentioned before, the latest Hungarian church law is based on the premise that churches which were registered under the 1990 law need to seek re-registration for church status under considerably more stringent criteria, or continue to operate as religious associations. In the last 15 years the European Court of Human Rights decided a number of cases on registration and re-registration of churches which shed light on European standards. Most of the cases originated in Russia after a 1997 law introduced a burdensome re-registration procedure for already recognized churches.[79] The most important lesson from these Court cases is that re-registration of churches does not *per se* violate the Convention. In the re-registration procedures the Court, however, emphasized that—since re-registration requirements affect churches which have already obtained legal entity status—in the new procedure the state shall provide very weighty reasons for denying registration if the affected church had not otherwise violated the law (i.e. apart from operating without the required new registration while waiting for their re-registration process to conclude).[80] The jurisprudence suggests that the delays of the re-registration process may themselves violate the Convention, as during the transitional period the state forces previously registered churches to operate in a less advantageous (and befitting) legal framework. This conclusion is in line with other components of the Court's jurisprudence, as the Court also considers it to be a violation if delays imposed by a member state force a religious community to operate without registration.[81]

The Court also examines the length of the mandatory waiting period, and the government has to justify the length of the waiting

---

[79] *Church of Scientology Moscow v. Russia*, no. 18147/02, April 5, 2007; *Moscow Branch of the Salvation Army v. Russia*, no. 72881/01, October 5, 2006; *Jehovah's Witnesses of Moscow and Others v. Russia*, no. 302/02, June 10, 2010.

[80] *Church of Scientology Moscow v. Russia*, para 96; *Moscow Branch of the Salvation Army v. Russia*, para 96.

[81] *Religionsgemeinschaft der Zeugen Jehovas and Others v. Austria*, para 66–67.

period prescribed in national law. Not long after finding that a 15-year waiting period (required for re-registration) violated the Convention in the Russian context,[82] in the Austrian context the Court also found a 10-year waiting period (required for upper-tier registration) in violation of the Convention. In the Austrian case the Court took into account that the affected religious community had already operated in the country for over half a century on a lower level of registration, and it also considered that the government decided to enter into a concordat with another religious community which had operated in Austria for a shorter period than the applicant.[83] Thereupon it is reasonable to conclude that the 20 year waiting period imposed in the Hungarian law does not meet the level of protection expected by the Court. The Venice Commission found this duration requirement clearly excessive.[84]

Although the Court has examined the length of the statutory waiting period a number of times, somewhat surprisingly, so far it has not gotten around to assessing the threshold membership requirements. Since the Hungarian parliament decided to raise the number of founding members required for registration significantly (more precisely: by ten times) it is expected that in case the law is challenged in Strasbourg, the Court will wish to hear about the reasons behind this measure. Since the Court has been consistent—if not persistent—in reminding the member states that under Article 9 it was their task to preserve religious diversity and pluralism, the Hungarian justification according to which Parliament wished to curb the number of registered churches is unlikely to be accepted under Article 9(2).

As was mentioned in the parliamentary debate, currently only Slovakia requires more founding members for a registered church with its infamous 20,000 threshold. After the Hungarian law the second highest requirement is in Croatia (500),[85] followed by the Czech Republic (300)[86] and Austrian (300 at entry level[87]). Therefore, despite the

---

[82] *Kimlya and Others v. Russia.*

[83] *Religionsgemeinschaft der Zeugen Jehovas and Others v. Austria*, paras 96–98.

[84] *Opinion 664/2012*, paras 57–64.

[85] See *Laws on Religion and the State in Post-Communist Europe*, 93 et seq.

[86] See *Laws on Religion and the State in Post-Communist Europe*,105 et seq.

[87] For a recent description of the Austrian law see e.g. Schima, S. "Focus: Freedom of Religion in Austria," *Vienna Journal on International Constitutional Law* 3, no. 3 (2009):199–209, 202.

optimism in the parliamentary debate, the new Hungarian requirement became the second highest in Europe. With such a high requirement the Hungarian government certainly did not live up to the OSCE/ODIHR guidelines suggesting to abandon high minimum membership requirements.[88] Note that with regard to 1,000 signatures required for the popular initiative for a petition on church registration, the Venice Commission took a stance, which treats this requirement not as a minimum membership condition, but suggests that the signatures essentially may come from anyone from a population of 10 million who is in support of the registration request of even the smallest congregation.[89] The Venice Commission however warned that this requirement is acceptable only to the extent that "it does not deprive religious groups from access to legal personality."[90]

International comparison matters not only for national pride and self-respect, but also because the European Court of Human Rights is known to regularly take into account European trends and consensus (where it exists) when it determines the level and intensity of rights protection.[91] Recently in a party registration case the Court compared national rules on minimum membership requirements, and found that although 13 countries prescribed a threshold, the Russian requirement of 50,000 founding members for party registration is considerably higher than any other rule in Europe.[92] This Russian setting is similar to the one of the new Hungarian religion law to the extent that the Russian law raised the existing threshold requirement by five times, and required the re-registration of already registered and functioning political parties. The Court consulted the parliamentary record, and also arguments submitted before the Russian Constitutional Court in prior proceedings to find that with this adjustment the Russian government intended "to strengthen political parties and limit their number in order to avoid disproportionate expenditure from the budget during

[88] OSCE/ODIHR, *Guidelines for Review of Legislation Pertaining to Religion or Belief*, 17.
[89] *Opinion 664/2012*, para 55.
[90] *Opinion 664/2012*, para 56.
[91] For a recent, famous example of consensus analysis in the religion domain see *Lautsi and Others v. Italy* (GC), no. 30814/06, March 18, 2011.
[92] *Republican Party of Russia v. Russia*, no. 12976/07, April 12, 2011, para 110.

electoral campaigns and prevent excessive parliamentary fragmentation and, in so doing, promote stability of the political system."[93] Upon a thorough analysis the Court rejected these justifications in light of the facts on the ground.[94] Considering key similarities between the Russian and the Hungarian laws it would be rather surprising to see the Court depart from the stance it took about an unnecessarily high registration threshold preventing the meaningful exercise of a Convention right.

Regarding religious communities awaiting re-registration it is clear that the Court leaves the member states considerable discretion in deciding which faiths to accept. At the same time, it is easy to detect a certain impatience in the jurisprudence when the member states appear to delay the registration or recognition of communities which have an established record of unproblematic presence in the country (especially when the case involves registration on a higher level in a multi-tier system), and also of churches which are known to freely operate in other member states.[95] Therefore, it is reasonable to expect that a potential refusal to re-register internationally well-known and respected congregations which functioned smoothly for twenty years (such as the communities of Muslims and Buddhists, and also several Christian groups) will be met with disapproval in Strasbourg.

As the above analysis already indicated, in addition to the conditions of church registration the Court also examines the nature of the proceedings. It is a well-established requirement in the jurisprudence that the protection of rights cannot be illusory, and that the procedures associated with the exercise of various rights cannot become an obstacle to the enjoyment of the right. In the context of church registration it does not only mean that the requirements of the registration process have to be clear and predictable, but it also follows that the conditions for registration have to be such that they could be met realistically.[96] The Court also expects the state to be consistent throughout the registration process, as it amounts to a violation if the state makes self-con-

---

93 *Republican Party of Russia v. Russia*, para 111.

94 *Republican Party of Russia v. Russia*, para 112–114.

95 *Jehovah's Witnesses of Moscow and Others v. Russia*, para 155; *Religionsgemeinschaft der Zeugen Jehovas and Others v. Austria*, para 98.

96 *Church of Scientology of Moscow v. Russia,* para 92 (e.g. requiring the submission of numerous originals of documents, in multiple proceedings).

tradictory representations at different stages of the same registration process.[97]

The Achilles heel of the new Hungarian law is certainly the provision which hands over the recognition of churches to a discretionary decision of Parliament. The lack of due process safeguards was criticized by the Venice Commission at length.[98] The new law does not indicate any opportunity for appeal or judicial review of a rejection. Indeed, the fact the Parliament's refusal of recognizing 66 churches was in the form of a parliamentary resolution also suggests that judicial review was not envisioned as a part of this process, since parliamentary resolutions are not evidently amenable to judicial review under Fundamental Law. This is clearly in contravention of Court's jurisprudence which requires under Article 6(1) access to court outside the criminal process since its decision in *Golder v. United Kingdom* in 1975.[99] More specifically, in the freedom of religion context the Court found that lack of access to court in a property dispute over church property violated the Convention.[100] Considering that the Court found that the absence of a judicial avenue violated Articles 9 and 6 of the Convention in case where the applicants sought to contest much less than a refusal to register a church, it is reasonable to conclude that the Court will find the Hungarian law to violate the Convention.

As was mentioned already, it is a fundamental requirement of Court's jurisprudence that member states strive to preserving religious diversity, as an aspect of democracy, in a neutral and impartial fashion. The requirement of neutrality, also expressed in the form of the principle of non-discrimination (Article 14) applies irrespective of the histories and national traditions of the member states. It is an important caveat for the Hungarian legislature that the decisions which the state takes regarding particular churches also fall within the general human rights framework established by the Convention and developed by the Court. In practice, this means that concordats and similar bilat-

---

97 *Moscow Branch of the Salvation Army v. Russia*, para 91.

98 *Opinion 664/2012*, paras. 71–79.

99 *Golder v. United Kingdom,* no. 4451/70, February 21, 1975, para 34.

100 *Sâmbata Bihor Greek Catholic Church v. Romania*, no. 48107/99, January 12, 2011. In the case petitioners had to turn to a commission (but not an independent court) to settle their dispute.

eral agreements with churches are assessed within the legal framework applicable to the exercise of freedom of religion and to church-state relations.

For instance, in addition to its multi-tier church registration system Austria maintains a concordat regime with select churches. Thus, while the Austrian authorities were unwilling to register Jehovah's Witnesses at a higher tier, the government concluded a concordat with the Coptic church. Since the latter have operated in Austria for a much shorter time than the Witnesses, the Court took the concordat as an evidence of discrimination in the application of the waiting period requirement imposed by Austrian law.[101] The Court followed a similar track in a Croatian case where the government refused to conclude concordats (required for access to hospitals and prisons) with certain Protestant communities. Since the applicant communities met the statutory requirements on the basis of which other churches were selected for their concordats, the Court rejected the government's justification claiming that the other churches performed a historic role, and found Croatia in violation.[102]

In closing, note that this brief overview reflects only on those features of the new Hungarian law which raise concerns even before the law enters into force and is applied in practice. It is difficult to predict how the law will function when claims for registration start to reach Parliament. Nonetheless, as even such a short overview reveals, the Hungarian law clearly falls short of the applicable international and European human rights standards.

Conclusion

This chapter aimed to seize a unique opportunity and analyzed closely the record of Hungary's constitution-making Parliament on freedom of religion, a fundamental right of great significance. The symbol-heavy language of the new Hungarian constitution's National Avowal came alive in the parliamentary debate. For the first time it became really

---

[101] *Religionsgemeinschaft der Zeugen Jehovas and Others v. Austria*, para 91.

[102] *Savez Crkava "Riječ života" and Others v. Croatia*, no. 7798/08, December 9, 2010.

traceable how arguments from this mystical corner of the new constitution will work, and what they may entail. The image of limited government was clearly not traceable in the parliamentary debate on the new cardinal law. Instead, one often found references to sovereignty, discretionary powers and the need to express proper values through legislation. The references to the unlimited powers of the sovereign, the vision of Parliament as an ultimate arbiter of matters of identity and distributor of privileges of engagement in matters of civil and political rights, together with an utter distrust in the judiciary as voiced in the parliamentary debate are equally problematic from the perspective or respect for constitutionalism, rule of law and human rights. These propositions suggest that the Parliament of constitution-making majority clearly does not view the new constitution as a constraint on their own powers and present or future decisions.

The exercise in this chapter revealed that the Hungarian parliament was not constrained by international and human rights commitments when it decided to fundamentally alter the legal regime applicable to the exercise of freedom of religion in Hungary. Many aspects of the newly enacted cardinal law on freedom of religion and churches, such as the mandatory 20 year waiting period, the 1,000 threshold supporter requirement, the recognition of churches based on a discretionary decision of Parliament and the lack of access to court are most clearly in violation of the European Convention. It certainly does not make a good impression on the new Hungarian constitution that its articles are believed to be best entrenched in a cardinal law of such quality. It remains to be seen whether the actors of the political scene (while activating the full force of their constitution-making potential) are willing to realize the unintended consequences of their words and actions, and decide to offer a retreat towards contemporary standards in order to complement historic achievements. Otherwise ultimately some 300 churches are expected to lose meaningful legal entity status in Hungary altogether.

Although rather tempting, it would, however, be a serious mistake to blame the new cardinal law completely on the language of the new constitution, on the National Avowal, or the Transitional Provisions. The new cardinal law cozily fits within the pattern of centuries of religious toleration laws in Hungary. In this pattern periods of toleration are taken over by periods of repression and intolerance. The enemy of the day is chosen according to political conveniences and interests of key stakeholders. The elegant understatement courteously adopted to describe this situation refers to historic players and traditions, in order to make us forget that it is discrimination on the basis of religion that the speaker is attempting to mask. It is sad but apparent that the Constitutional Court's jurisprudence became instrumental in perpetuating exactly those propensities of the Hungarian political community which the 1989 Constitution was meant to counteract.

At least the 2011 Fundamental Law is not burdened with such high expectations to protect fundamental liberties and to build a constitutional democracy, as its predecessor from 1989 was. The new constitution's National Avowal commits Hungarians to add their rich national culture to European diversity. In order to do so, the new constitution's Hungary is not expected to be diverse and European, it is sufficient for it to be unique. As this chapter demonstrates, Hungary with its new constitution and new cardinal law on freedom of religion and churches is on the track of departing far away from the European standard, and building a unique, if unusual, regime of its own.

IV. INSTITUTIONAL DESIGN

From Separation of Powers to a Government without Checks: Hungary's Old and New Constitutions

MIKLÓS BÁNKUTI, GÁBOR HALMAI and
KIM LANE SCHEPPELE

On April 24, 2011, Hungary adopted a new constitution that entered into effect on January 1, 2012. With a great deal of public fanfare,[1] symbolic flourish[2] and even a new iPad App,[3] the new Fundamental Law promised to end the Hungarian transition begun in 1989 by completely replacing the constitution established at that time.[4] The new government, led by the center-right political party Fidesz,[5] won a con-

---

[1] Among other things, the new Hungarian constitution was accompanied by an op-ed piece in *The Wall Street Journal* by Hungary's deputy prime minister, Tibor Navracsics, see "A New Constitution for Hungary: Locking in the Values of the 1989–1990 Transition, At Last," *The Wall Street Journal*, April 19, 2011.

[2] The constitution was officially signed by the president of the republic on Easter Monday, making it the "Easter Constitution." That highlights the aspirations expressed in the constitution itself to make Hungary a Christian nation.

[3] The app can be seen at http://www.napiapp.com/2011/05/12/magyarorszag-alaptorvenye/.

[4] The government argued that too much of the communist 1949 Constitution remained in place during the 1989 constitutional transformation: "The new constitution has great symbolic and practical significance. It provides a foundation for the spiritual and intellectual renewal of Hungary. It reflects the past, present and future of the nation, and the fundamental values of the Hungarian people. On a practical level, it will revise and update a legal framework that was formulated under the communists in 1949. Despite revisions since 1989, large parts of the original text remained until yesterday." Navracsics, Ibid.

[5] Fidesz ran a joint party list with the Christian Democrats in the 2010 election and they together got 53 percent of the vote. Under the disproportionate Hungarian electoral law, this translated into 68 percent of the seats in the Parliament. Though this is formally a coalition government, the current government acts as a supermajoritarian single-party formation.

stitution-making majority in parliamentary elections in 2010, and they decided to use all of the power that they had to completely remake the Hungarian political order.

A closer look at the 2011 Fundamental Law, however, reveals that it is not the final entrenchment of a previously constitutional democratic state in Hungary, but it is instead something altogether more troubling. Nowhere is this more visible than in the structure of government that the new constitution creates. Under the 1989 Constitution, Hungary had a constitutional framework that ensured checks on power, multi-party participation and a substantial role for minority parties. Under the 2011 Fundamental Law, this delicate system has been dismantled and Hungary has become a constitutional democracy in name only.

This is a harsh assessment, and in this chapter, we will provide evidence that the system of checked power that characterized the Hungarian government from 1990 to 2010 has been gutted under the new constitution. In its place, a new governmental form has been created in which the current prime minister, Viktor Orbán, can operate with a free hand. In addition, the Fidesz government—the very government that brought in the new constitution—can continue to control policy far beyond any electoral mandate it may have, constraining future governments with the decisions that it makes now. In fact, the primary constraints on power in the new constitution are those imposed on future governments that might want to disagree with the current one. They are not constraints on what the current government can do.

The new constitution *appears* to still contain the key features of constitutional constraint imposed by checked and balanced powers. But, as we will show, those constraints are largely illusory. They are illusory because key veto points have been abolished or seriously weakened. Appointments to key offices, like Constitutional Court judgeships, parliamentary commissioner, the head of the State Audit Office and the chief prosecutor, no longer require minority party input. Independent boards regulating crucial institutions necessary for democracy, like the Electoral Commission and the Media Authority, no longer ensure multi-party representation. The Constitutional Court itself has been weakened because its jurisdiction has been limited and the self-governing judges' organization that once supervised the ordinary judiciary has been reduced to an empty shell with no power. Under the new constitution, the president of the Constitutional Court, formerly elected by his fellow judges, is now elected by the Parliament, injecting a more political note into this previously apolitical office. Under the new law on the judiciary, the sitting president of the Supreme Court was deemed unqualified and had to step down. His 17 years of experience as a judge on the European Court of Human Rights did not count when the new law set five years of judicial experience *in Hungary* as a minimum qualification for the post. And then the Fidesz Parliament elected his replacement with their two-thirds majority vote.

The constraints on power that appear in the new constitution are also illusory because the specific people who occupy crucial positions can be appointed for extraordinarily long terms, thus maintaining the current government's control over any foreseeable future government. Loyalists to the current government can stay in power through multiple election cycles, thereby making it almost impossible for a future government dominated by different political parties to carry out new policy initiatives. Offices like the chief prosecutor (nine years), the president of the Supreme Court (named the "Kúria," nine years), the president of the National Judicial Office (nine years), the head of the Budget Council (six years), the head of the State Audit Office (twelve years), Constitutional Court judges (twelve years), the president of the National Media and Infocommunications Authority (nine years) are being filled by the current government, but the people in those powerful offices—all party loyalists of the Fidesz government—will remain through multiple election cycles. This "dead hand" control over future governments is exacerbated because most of these key positions require a two-thirds vote of the Parliament for election to the post, and the holders of these offices are now allowed by law to stay beyond the end of their terms if a new parliamentary supermajority cannot muster support for a new candidate. In the case of the presidents of the National Bank (i.e. the central bank) and the Budget Council, the appointments are made by the president of the republic. But the presidents of the republic (Pál Schmitt, János Áder), then and now, are also former Fidesz party leaders put into that spot by the current governing supermajority. In those cases, there is only one degree of separation between a direct and indirect Fidesz party vote.

While there appear to be some important veto points in the new constitutional order, those veto points are controlled by precisely this cadre of long-serving officials. As a result, elaborate procedures in the new constitutional order that appear to guarantee constitutional constraint on these officials are disconnected from the real sites of power. For example, the new system for appointing judges, lodged in the National Judicial Office, almost completely disconnects the actual selection process from the system of expert vetting. While existing judges have some role in the screening of new judges, in fact, all new judges are ultimately chosen by the head of the National Judicial Office, an official who will serve for nine years following a two-thirds parliamentary vote, before these judges are then formally appointed by the president of the republic. Under the new constitution, any national budget approved by the Parliament can be vetoed by a newly created Budget Council. But if the Parliament and the Budget Council fail to agree on a budget by March 31 of each year, then the president of the republic can dissolve the Parliament and call new elections. This process can be repeated until the Budget Council is satisfied with the Parliament it has gotten. To make matters worse, the Budget Council and the new National Judicial Office operate with very few constitutionally grounded standards about when they can exercise their powerful vetoes. It appears that these checks on power are in reality only checks on the possibility of a future government of a different political stripe being able to do much of anything at all.

As we will show, under this new constitution, it will be difficult to consider Hungary a constitutional-democratic state, even as it retains the outer appearances of both constitutionalism and democracy. Instead, the new constitution gives the Fidesz government the power to do whatever it wants without constraint, and then entrenches the Fidesz government, its policy preferences (like the pension system, the family welfare support system, the basic rules of taxation, all assigned to cardinal laws) and its personnel off into a distant constitutional future.

To see how the new constitution fails to live up to a system of checked and balanced power, we must first understand how the 1989–90 Constitution in fact did set up a constitutional democracy in Hungary. Only then can we understand how the 2011 Fundamental Law undermines the constitutional guarantees that were once both present and working.

Revolution of the Rule of Law: Separation of Powers in the 1989–1990 Constitution

Three pillars

The 1989–1990 Constitution was completed in a series of stages and was contained in a variety of different legal sources. The constitution consisted of three pillars: 1) the 1989 text as amended substantially in 1990 with smaller amendments that occurred up through 2010, 2) the two-thirds laws required under the constitution and 3) the interpretive decisions of the Constitutional Court. Let us take each of these in turn.

Pillar 1: The constitutional text. In 1989, the national roundtable provided a framework for negotiations between the state-party and the democratic opposition. Through the roundtable, the parties agreed to change the existing constitution: Act XX of 1949, a Stalinist-era constitution.[6] The participants in the roundtable negotiations decided to use the existing constitutional amendment rule, which required an absolute two-thirds vote of the members of the Parliament, to bring the almost wholly new constitution into existence. In October 1989, the communist Parliament changed the 1949 Constitution through more than 100 individual amendments, incorporating these new constitutional features agreed in the roundtable process.

After the democratic multiparty elections in 1990, the constitutional text was amended again, this time in an agreement between the two largest vote-getters, the one that anchored a coalition government and the other that was the largest party in the opposition at the time. These amendments removed the last remaining elements that marked the communist pedigree of the text. The resulting 1989–1990 Constitution was based on a broad consensus of the parties involved in the transition and served as the foundation of the Hungarian government for 20 years. But it was brought about through a "rule of law

6 There were two political parties that dissented from this agreement: Alliance of Free Democrats and Fidesz, both of whom wanted to avoid a semi-presidential system featuring a president from the former state party, the Hungarian Socialist Workers' Party.

revolution"[7] in which there was never a sharp break with the old order. The old amendment rule of the 1949 Constitution, requiring an absolute two-thirds vote of the Parliament for any constitutional change, was kept in effect in order to avoid entrenching the constitution too early in the young life of the new republic.

Pillar 2: The two-thirds laws. At the roundtable and again after the 1990 elections, both the government and opposition parties agreed that crucial features of institutional design not specified in the constitution would be decided through laws requiring a relative two-thirds vote of the members of the Parliament.[8] In the 1989 agreement made as part of the roundtable process, any law pertaining to the structure of government or any law touching on fundamental rights required a two-thirds vote of the Parliament. The 1990 agreement reduced the number of such supermajority laws.[9] As a result of this agreement, key laws on the Constitutional Court, the judiciary, elections, political parties, media regulation, nationalities protection, the police, the military, the Prosecution Office, the State Audit Office and citizenship had to be passed with a parliamentary supermajority. Given that these laws filled in the blanks in the constitutional text about how the constitutional order would be structured, they should be considered constituent parts of the constitutional order, even though the two-thirds laws were all subordinate to the constitutional text itself. The procedures used to adopt the two-thirds laws distinguished them from ordinary laws and entrenched them almost as much as the constitution.

---

[7] See the phrase *jogállami forradalom* (rule of law revolution) in the Hungarian Constitutional Court's Decision 11/1992. (III. 5.) on retroactive justice.

[8] A constitutional amendment in Hungary requires a one-time two-thirds vote of all of the members of Parliament, an "absolute" two-thirds majority. A two-thirds law requires a one-time two-thirds vote of the members of Parliament who are present in a particular session, subject to a quorum rule, a "relative" two-thirds majority.

[9] As part of this agreement the opposition party received the right to nominate a president of the republic and the governing party got the acceptance of the constructive vote of confidence in the constitution. See Halmai, G. "The Transformation of Hungarian Constitutional Law from 1985 to 2005" in *The Transformation of Hungarian Legal Order 1985–2005*, eds. Jakab, A., P. Takács and A. Tatham (The Hague: Kluwer Law International, 2007), 1–19.

Pillar 3: The decisions of the Constitutional Court. The 1989 amendments and the two-thirds Act on the Constitutional Court set up a very powerful body as the key expositor and guardian of the constitution. The Constitutional Court not only had the power to nullify any unconstitutional law upon request, but it had the power to review any law for its constitutionality at multiple stages of the legislative process. Once a law was enacted, *anyone* could challenge its constitutionality in an abstract proceeding, which meant that virtually all major laws were reviewed by the Constitutional Court. In the early years in particular, the Court struck down as unconstitutional roughly one-third of all of the laws it reviewed.[10] Moreover, it often declared that the Parliament was acting unconstitutionally "by omission" when the Parliament had failed to pass a law that the constitution required the Parliament to enact.[11] The Court's decisions had particular influence in the area of human rights. But the Court also had many things to say about the competencies and constitutional limits of various state institutions, as well as about the separation of powers. Given that the constitutional text itself was often rather vague about the organization of state power in the Hungarian Third Republic,[12] the Constitutional Court often filled in the details.

These three pillars combined to hold up a robust Hungarian constitutional democracy in which checks on power were plentiful and leg-

---

[10] Between 1990–1993, the Constitutional Court annulled 35 percent of the normative acts it reviewed that were passed before May 1990 and 31 percent of the normative acts it reviewed that were passed after May 1990. In 1994–1995, the Constitutional Court annulled 24 percent of the normative acts it reviewed that were passed before May 1990 and 28 percent of the normative acts it reviewed that were passed after May 1990. *The Constitutional Court of Hungary* (Budapest: Constitutional Court, 1996).

[11] About the jurisdiction and the practice of the Constitutional Court see Halmai, G. "The Hungarian Approach to Constitutional Review: The End of Activism? The First Decade of the Hungarian Constitutional Court" in *Constitutional Justice, East and West, Democratic Legitimacy and Constitutional Courts in Post-Communist Europe in a Comparative Perspective*, ed. Sadurski, W. (The Hague: Kluwer Law International, 2002), 226–253.

[12] Hungary has had three republics in its history. The first was declared in 1918 when Hungary regained its independence after World War I. The second was declared in 1946, when the Parliament again declared itself a republic following the expulsion of a Nazi puppet government. The 1989 Constitution created the Hungarian Third Republic.

islative minorities were given a major voice. While the single-text constitution was rather thin on substance in key respects and had many missing pieces, these other two sources of constitutional law filled in the gaps to create a workable and successful new constitution for Hungary.

As we can see, therefore, the central features of the old constitutional framework involved a trio of interrelated choices: a) to create a parliamentary rather than presidential system of government, b) to establish a president and a Constitutional Court who were to be a constitutional check on the government's actions and c) to retain the 1949 Constitution's unicameral Parliament.[13]

In this tripartite constitutional framework, where the constitutional text, constitutional laws and decisions of the Constitutional Court operated together, how were the major institutions of state designed—and how were they supposed to work? In the next section, we will explore these three sources of Hungarian constitutional law to explain the system of checked powers that characterized the 1989–1990 Constitution.

The features of the parliamentary system

Most of the states in post-communist Europe chose a parliamentary system of government after the transitions of 1989.[14] Parliamentarism typically has the strength that the central source of power rests in the popularly elected body, based on representation of the expressed preferences of the voters. If one wants to diffuse power after an authoritarian period, parliamentarism seems the best method for doing so because it avoids the excessive concentration of powers one finds in a presidential system. In a parliamentary system, the head of government, the prime minster, is accountable to the Parliament. He must command a majority in the Parliament to be elected and he may be replaced after a no confidence vote by a parliamentary majority as well. In Hungary, the Parliament was elected using a complex system

[13] Hungary had had a bicameral Parliament from 1848 to 1945.

[14] O'Neal, P. "Presidential Power in Post Communist Europe: The Hungarian Case in Comparative Perspective," *Journal of Communist Studies* 9 no. 3 (1993): 177–201.

of individual mandates and proportional representation of party lists, and the prime minister had to command a working majority from the group that resulted. But the German style of vote of no confidence introduced in the Hungarian system through the 1990 agreement required that no prime minister could be replaced unless there was a candidate with majority support to govern in his place. This has made Hungarian government quite stable since the transition and has practically guaranteed that elections will occur at regular intervals of four years.

Parliamentary systems often feature a president who stands above politics as a head of state and as a referee among competing sources of power in times of crisis. In the Hungarian Third Republic, the presidency of the Republic is an office that possesses substantial "neutral" powers—like the power to send laws the president disagrees with back to the Parliament for revision or send laws the president deems unconstitutional to the Constitutional Court for review—so he is more powerful than most head-of-state presidents. As such, he belongs neither to the executive, nor to the legislative branch, but rather has a balancing role between them. In the old (and also in the new) constitution, the president is elected by the Parliament for a five-year term of office, which means that the president does not serve on the same electoral cycle as the four-year Parliament. The selection mechanism for the presidency and the timing of it was one of the most controversial questions at the roundtable, and in the end, the parliamentary election of the president was determined in a popular referendum by establishing whether the president should be elected before or after the Parliament.[15]

The Hungarian president possessed a number of important competencies that acted to check the government. In a crucial decision on the powers of the president with respect to his commander-in-chief and appointment capacities, the Constitutional Court ruled that the president had limited powers under the constitution, powers that the president must share with the government. That did not mean, however, that the president was merely ornamental. Instead, the president was responsible for ensuring that the legal requirements for appoint-

[15] See ibid., for a detailed account of the negotiations over the role of the president in the 1989–1990 Constitution.

ments and the constitutional requirements for laws were met before he could sign off on them. He could refuse his agreement if he felt that the government was not following the constitution or the laws in its actions. This could be a substantial power if the president and the government of the day had different views about what the constitution required. The petitions to the Constitutional Court that resulted in these decisions on the interpretation of the constitutional powers of the president were submitted by the prime minister, along with his ministers and the members of the Parliament that supported the government at the time. They went to the Constitutional Court in order to resolve the political conflict that had erupted between the prime minister and the president. The Court narrowly tailored the presidential competences, but nonetheless established that the president had the obligation to protect the constitutional order by checking the government's actions for constitutionality.[16]

Parliamentary procedure and independent bodies

Hungary's type of parliamentarism was unusual in one other respect. Hungary has a *unicameral* Parliament. While unicameral parliaments are not unheard of, especially in non-federal states, they are also a distinct minority among constitutional states in Europe. Unicameral parliamentary systems have the advantage of permitting responsiveness and rapid action; they have the disadvantage of not building in many checks on legislation. A study by the Constitution Unit at University College, London[17] reviewed unicameral systems in Europe and found that most had developed other structures (besides an upper house) to slow down the almost surely guaranteed passage of any law that the government of the day wanted. The UCL study shows that most unicameral parliaments build in extensive opportunities for minorities to participate in legislative procedure and various administrative checks

[16] Decision 48/1991. (IX. 26.), Decision 8/1992. (I. 30.), and Decision 36/1992. (VI. 10.)

[17] The Constitution Unit at the School of Public Policy of the University College of London, *Checks and Balances in a Single-Chamber Parliament: A Comparative Study* (London: University College, 1998). http://www.ucl.ac.uk/spp/publications/unit-publications/24.pdf.

(like ombudspersons and audit offices) as well as constitutional checks (robust judicial review) to overcome the limitations of unicameral chambers.

Hungary's 1989–1990 Constitution entrenched quite a few of the recommended checks on unicameral parliamentarism. For example, through a crucial two-thirds law specifying the rules of parliamentary procedure, otherwise known as the "house rules," the Parliament expressed its commitment to having important internal checks on all important acts.[18] The parliamentary house rules gave a substantial voice to minority parties. Every parliamentary party was entitled to have seats on every parliamentary committee, no matter how small their fraction.[19] In addition, to ensure that laws would be publicly debated over a reasonably long period of time, every bill was required to go through a general and a detailed debate on the floor after a mandatory report was published by the designated committee of the Parliament. The law on legislation also legally required that sponsors of legislation consult with the national and local governments as well as with interested groups outside the Parliament. Sponsors of legislation were also required to provide an impact assessment of the planned legislation.[20] These many procedural requirements gave minority parties, interest groups and the general public many opportunities to see what was going on in the Parliament and to participate in the process of drafting and debating laws.

For appointments of justices to the Constitutional Court, parliamentary procedure required a two-stage process: a) getting through a nominations committee in which each party in the Parliament was able to cast one vote regardless of the size of their fraction and in which a

---

[18] Parliamentary Resolution 46/1994 (IX.30.) on the Standing Orders of the Parliament of the Republic of Hungary.

[19] In its Decision 27/1998. (VI. 16.), the Constitutional Court ruled that when a political party reaches the minimum five percent threshold in the parliamentary election, it can have its own parliamentary faction, and consequently representation on every committee in the Parliament even if its number of MPs is below the minimum required for establishing a fraction according to the house rules.

[20] Formerly it was required by the Act XI of 1987 on legislation. Now the following acts regulate the law-making procedure and the requirements concerning the consultation: Act CXXX of 2010 and Act CXXXI of 2010.

majority vote in that body established who the nominees should be and b) running in a second-stage election process on the floor of the Parliament where a two-thirds majority would be required for election. This process obviously gave minorities in the Parliament a disproportionate voice and made it impossible for most governments to just push their own nominees onto the Constitutional Court, even with a parliamentary supermajority. Compromise, and even log-rolling, became normal, which meant that the Constitutional Court could not easily be captured by a single political party.

In addition to the two-thirds rule that required parliamentary procedure to be determined by a supermajority, other two-thirds laws set up important checks on the governing party (parties) where they might be tempted to use their parliamentary majority and sympathetic prime minister to run roughshod over the opposition. In independent boards like the National Radio and Television Commission, a two-thirds law required that the seats on the board be filled by a two-thirds majority decision of the Parliament. But even in boards that were elected by a *simple* majority of the Parliament, the previous governments nominated not only representatives of their own side, but also candidates from the opposition parties. For example, the National Electoral Commission in every previous parliamentary term, except under the first Orbán government between 1998 and 2002, always had members that came from both governing and opposition parties among its five-member core membership.[21] Regardless of the balance of power in the Parliament, then, these crucial watchdogs of the democratic process were not generally packed with loyalists by the party in power given this combination of written and customary rules.

Other key state offices whose independence was important in the constitutional design also featured supermajority election procedures. The 1989–1990 Constitution, together with the two-thirds law on the national ombudsperson system, created four parliamentary commis-

[21] In addition to five seats nominated by the government and elected by the Parliament, the Electoral Commission also has one member delegated from each political party in the Parliament. This rule always guarantees diversity on the Electoral Commission but in all governments except the first Fidesz government, there was also party diversity among the five members that the government could propose.

sioners (ombudspersons) charged with both examining potential violations of human rights and making public reports about their work.[22] Ombudspersons were elected by a two-thirds vote of the Parliament.

With all of these checks on the shape of major political institutions as well as on the selection of the occupants of key offices in the Hungarian state, the 1989–1990 Constitution deliberately made the unicameral parliamentary system subject to a whole series of internal checks on the power of temporary majorities. Repeatedly, the Hungarian Parliament after 1989 tied its own hands by putting fundamental aspects of the constitutional order beyond majority rule, creating the requirement of a two-thirds supermajority on crucial topics of constitutional concern. When the possibility of writing a new constitution emerged in 1995 to complete the transition, the Parliament amended the constitution to require that *four-fifths* of the members of Parliament approve the rules for drafting a new constitution. This super-supermajority rule was designed to ensure that any new constitution would have very broad political acceptance.

Legal checks on power: The Constitutional Court, the ordinary judiciary, and the Prosecution Office

All of this said, the most crucial check on power in this unicameral parliamentary system was the Constitutional Court. The Court played a prominent role under the 1989–1990 Constitution in ensuring that Parliament both respected constitutional principles in legislation and properly created the institutional framework for implementing the constitution. The Court was given the jurisdiction to review laws during the legislative process upon request by the president of the republic.[23] In addition, the Court had the power to rule on the constitutionality of laws that were referred to it for review by ordinary judges who wanted guidance.

---

[22] Besides the general parliamentary commissioner and his deputy, the original ombudsman system consisted of ombudspersons for data protection and freedom of information, for minority rights, and later also for the rights of future generations.

[23] In the original text of the Act on the Constitutional Court, it had the power to engage in preliminary control of pending laws if initiated by a substantial minority of MPs, but in 1997 this possibility was abolished by the Parlament.

But the *actio popularis* jurisdiction of the Court was perhaps the most crucial constraint on the powers of the unicameral Parliament. The *actio popularis* allowed *anyone* to petition the Court to review any law after it went into effect. This broad access to the Court gave the Court many opportunities to test the constitutionality of laws without a requirement that the petitioner have standing or any other overt connection to the matter under review. This feature created the opportunity for extensive abstract review of legislation; virtually every major law came up for review at the Constitutional Court. As a result, the Constitutional Court was actively involved in almost all aspects of the transition and provided a constant check to ensure that the Hungarian government stayed within the 1989–1990 Constitution. Of course, variations in the appointments of justices to the Court meant that it was not always equally aggressive in carrying out these responsibilities. But the Court generally rose to the occasion and kept the government under the constraint of the constitution. This was particularly true during the first several years of the Court's existence, while President László Sólyom served as the most visible face of the Court in public life.

The ordinary judiciary took longer than the other branches to establish itself as a fully independent institution under the 1989–1990 Constitution. At the start of the transition, the Ministry of Justice controlled the process through which judges were hired, disciplined and managed, even though the president of the republic formally named the judges. The Constitutional Court upheld this system as constitutional in a decision in 1991,[24] though with substantial dissent. When the act on the judiciary was redrafted taking the decision into account, it permitted the justice minister to appoint the court leaders, including the president and the vice-president of the appellate courts. These and other powers were contested again before the Constitutional Court on the grounds that this arrangement violated judicial independence. In particular, the petitions challenged the justice minister's interpretation of the provisions setting the rules that determined the role of different judicial bodies in the nomination procedures. The law required support from the court before a person could be named as its president. The justice minister at the time argued that a person could be appointed as the court president if a single judge within that court agreed. The

[24] Decision 53/1991. (X. 31.)

Constitutional Court ruled that "support" in the law meant majority support, so the vote of a single judge was not enough to appoint a court president.[25] This served as a powerful check on the justice minister who could then not appoint just any judge to any court.

In 1997, Parliament changed the constitution and adopted a new judicial act[26] that stripped the justice minister of all of his powers and created self-administering courts. After that point, even though the president of the republic maintained the formal power of appointing judges, the process leading up to the recommendation to the president was controlled by judges.

The legal status of the prosecutor remained almost unchanged from the Soviet period even though the constitution was otherwise changed almost completely in the meantime. According to Article 52, the president nominated the chief prosecutor for approval by Parliament for a six-year term. The chief prosecutor was accountable to the Parliament and had to report on his activities to them. All governments tried to bring the office of the prosecutor under their influence, but each failed without the necessary supermajority to amend the constitution.

Repeated tensions between the Prosecution Office (often elected by a prior government) and the governing majority of the day resulted in a major decision of the Constitutional Court on the independence of that office. While the Court found that the Parliament had the right to inquire about specific cases handled by the Prosecution Office, the Court also blocked the Parliament from issuing directives to the chief prosecutor. Because the prosecutor's term of office was fixed and did not depend on the support of the Parliament, however, the Court ruled that the Parliament could not remove the chief prosecutor from office.[27]

As you can see, the structure of the post-1989 Hungarian government was more constitutionally constrained than one might guess from reading the constitution alone. While some of the powers of the Constitutional Court could be discerned directly in the 1989–1990 Con-

[25] Decision 38/1993. (VI. 11.) This was the first case when the Court applied the German approach of interpretation in conformity with the Constitution.

[26] Act LXVI of 1997 on the Organization and Administration of Courts.

[27] Decision 4/2004. (II. 20.)

stitutional text, much about the Constitutional Court's extraordinary role in the constitutional system could only be worked out from understanding the two-thirds law that set up the Constitutional Court and from seeing the respect accorded the decisions of the Court among the political branches. But even beyond the Constitutional Court Act, the discussion among the Court's various members as to the legally guaranteed jurisdiction of the Constitutional Court and whether the Court should engage in strict or expansive readings of the constitution were also important. The Court's "extended interpretation" also frequently burst open the framework of the clearly assigned jurisdiction of the Court, and in fact resulted in the institutionalization of a new sphere of authority. This is what the first Constitutional Court President Sólyom has somewhat euphemistically termed "jurisdiction alteration." Sólyom himself claimed to have borrowed the concept from the Italian Constitutional Court's position on "living law." In addition, Sólyom also viewed the transplantation of the exercise of "interpretation in conformity with the Constitution (*Verfassungskonforme Auslegung*)" imported from Germany.[28]

While a unicameral parliamentary system may appear dangerous because there are so few apparent checks on the power of the majority, the house rules, appointment procedures, composition of independent boards, and even the requirements of the two-thirds laws themselves required parliamentary majorities to "read in" the opposition parties at almost every turn. In addition, the robust jurisprudence of the Constitutional Court ensured that there was a review of virtually all legislation by an independent body. Hungary, as a result, developed a vibrant and robust constitutional democracy in which both constitutionalism and democracy were honored.

Unfortunately, the Achilles' heel in the Hungarian constitutional system was the two-thirds rule for amending the constitution which only lightly entrenched the whole constitutional structure. And this is where our story of the 2011 Fundamental Law begins.

---

[28] In Germany, the Constitutional Court tends to interpret the legal regulations to be examined in light of the demands deduced from the constitution in order to define an abstract "province of constitutional interpretation."

"Revolution in the Polling Booth" Separation of Powers in the 2011 Fundamental Law

The overwhelming victory by Fidesz in the 2010 elections has been presented by Fidesz as a revolution, implying that citizens called for a major change in the organization of the government. But their supermajority is a trick of the existing election law which gave Fidesz 68 percent of the seats in the Parliament after the party received 53 percent of the popular vote. In addition, the size of the Fidesz vote was due also to the collapse of their primary opponents in the election, the Socialists, who held the parliamentary majority from 2002–2010. The bottom fell out of the Hungarian economy on the Socialists' watch, and the party was mired in scandal. No wonder, then that the Socialists gained only 19 percent of the popular vote in the 2010 election.

Because of these two factors, it is hard to interpret the victory Fidesz won in the 2010 elections as a positive mandate for a constitutional revolution. In fact, Fidesz never promised during the election campaign to rewrite the constitution if it were elected. Rather it promised the reverse. When asked directly before the election whether Fidesz would use a supermajority to change the Hungarian constitution, Tibor Navracsics, now justice minister in the Fidesz government, explicitly denied that such a development was planned.[29] Though Viktor Orbán promised "big changes" if his party was to come to power, *constitutional* change did not seem to be what he had in mind. So while it is true that many citizens decisively rejected the Socialist party, that is not the same as voting for a constitutional revolution. Yet, in the nineteen months from taking office in May 2010 to January 1, 2012 when the new constitution took effect, Fidesz enacted the most significant constitutional reforms since 1990.

---

[29] Tibor Navracsics stated in April 2010 to the German newspaper *Die Presse* that Fidesz did not plan on changing the constitution even if it won a two-thirds majority. "Ungarn: Haben kein Drehbuch für Zweidrittelmehrheit" [Hungary: 'There is no screenplay for a two-thirds majority'], *Die Presse*, April 8, 2010.

Flow of constitutional amendments to the 1989–1990 Constitution

Even before enacting a new constitution, Parliament passed a series of constitutional amendments between May 2010 and April 2011 which suspended key constitutional checks on legislation and facilitated a constitution-drafting process that could proceed without opposition involvement.

In one of its earliest constitutional amendments when it took office, Fidesz made it easier to change the constitution without having to consult any of the opposition parties. The government amended the constitution to remove a provision that required a four-fifths vote of Parliament to approve the rules for drafting a new constitution. Amending the constitution requires only a two-thirds vote, yet this four-fifths provision was put in place to protect the interest of minority parties. But Fidesz did not have four-fifths of the Parliament, so it used its two-thirds vote to remove the four-fifths requirement. This change enabled it to revise the entire constitution using the votes of only its own parliamentary bloc.

This change was followed by other major institutional changes that made it more difficult for the opposition to gain any traction in objecting to the constitutional revolution while it was going on.

The Constitutional Court weakened

In an effort to limit the Constitutional Court's ability to check the major changes as they were being enacted, Fidesz pushed through three crucial constitutional amendments that crippled the Constitutional Court. First, the procedure for electing judges to the Court was changed in June 2010 so that a candidate no longer had to be nominated by a majority of parties in the Parliament before being elected by a two-thirds vote. Instead, a single two-thirds parliamentary vote was all that was necessary. Given the composition of the Parliament, this meant that Fidesz had the votes to put anyone it wanted onto the Court.

Then, the jurisdiction of the Constitutional Court was limited so that the justices could no longer review fiscal laws. In October 2010, Parliament passed an amendment to limit judicial review of budget and tax measures after the Constitutional Court found that a 98 percent retroactive tax on state employee compensation was unconstitutional. After the amendment, the Court could only review budgets, implementation of budgets, tax laws, and laws regulating local government taxation if those laws violated certain listed rights (the right to life and human dignity, protection of personal data, freedom of thought, conscience and religion, or the right to Hungarian citizenship). Conspicuously, the Constitutional Court is not allowed to review these laws if they infringe other rights, like the right to property, equality under the law or fair judicial procedure, all rights much easier to infringe with fiscal measures. By making it nearly impossible for the Court to second-guess budget and tax policy, the Fidesz government could act in the financial arena without having to pay attention to the usual constitutional constraints.

For example, when the government effectively nationalized private pensions by establishing a large penalty for those who refused to move their private pensions into state coffers, a prior Constitutional Court decision was directly violated. In this prior decision,[30] the Court had held that people had property interests in the money they had paid into public pension funds, so that it was unconstitutional for the government to threaten to cut these pensions if people didn't move their private pension funds into the public accounts. But the new limitation on the Court's jurisdiction was designed to eliminate judicial scrutiny of such policies, effectively making the Court's prior decision unenforceable.

Finally, a constitutional amendment increased the number of judges on the bench from 11 to 15, giving the Fidesz government the chance to name four additional judges and thereby ensure a majority of friendly faces on the Court. Because the government was also able to fill vacancies on the Court that had opened up after it took office, Fidesz named a total of seven new judges to the Court in its first 15 months in office. These new judges added to the reliable votes that Fidesz could already count on from appointments made when the prior rules guaranteed that all major parties had some of their candidates on the bench, thereby giving Fidesz a new and reliable majority on the Court. This majority made it highly unlikely that any important element of the new constitutional program would be derailed.

---

[30] On social security benefits, see Decision 43/1995. (VI. 30.)

The Electoral Commission captured

The Fidesz government also took quick action to revise the composition of the Electoral Commission. The new electoral law abolished the fixed terms of office, and with it abruptly ended the terms of office of the members of the Commission who were elected in February 2010 for four years. Instead, starting with the parliamentary elections in April 2010, the members of Electoral Commission were to be elected after each general election by a majority vote of the Parliament, with the first time occurring before the fall 2010 self-governmental elections. This ended the mandates of those elected earlier even though their terms of office had not expired. While this move left the delegated seats (through which each parliamentary fraction could send a delegate to the Commission) unchanged, the new system for electing members to the Commission enabled the government to gain supermajority control of the Commission almost immediately. As a result, the government had seven votes out of 10 on the Electoral Commission filled with its loyalists.

Gaining control of the Electoral Commission was important not just because of role of the Commission in elections, but also because the Electoral Commission is the institution through which all public referenda have to pass before they can be certified for a public vote. Had any part of the public, or any organized opposition group, wanted to challenge part of the Fidesz program through a referendum, a majority vote on the Electoral Commission could block it. As Fidesz well understood, the referendum option could be used to destabilize a government and even cause it to collapse.[31]

[31] Previously, in 2008, the Electoral Commission tried to block the Fidesz's so-called "social referendum" that offered three questions for public input pertaining to fees for doctor's visits, hospital stays and university tuition, all of which were plans of the Socialist-Liberal government. Although the Electoral Commission refused the request for a referendum, the Constitutional Court overturned the Electoral Commission and approved the questions. When the referendum was finally held and the plans of the government in power were defeated, it caused the fall of government and the replacement of the prime minister. See Halmai, G. "Referendum and Representative Democracy," *Fundamentum* no. 5 (2008): 5–21.

Media control established

In a set of changes that brought the media under its control, Fidesz used its supermajority to rewrite constitutional laws on the oversight of both public and private media. The reforms created a five-member Media Council that was granted authority to review media content, including the content of news outlets. While the jurisdiction of the Media Council was at first limited to public media, a later change in the law extended its jurisdiction to private media as well, including not just broadcast and print media, but online media too. Most crucially, the Media Council has been tasked with ensuring that news organizations adhere to a principle of "balanced" news coverage, backed with the power to levy substantial fines if media organizations violate this vague principle. In addition, all public media outlets are required to use the version of the news produced by the Hungarian News Agency, which is itself under the control of Fidesz and which rarely reports criticism of the government.

While council members are elected by Parliament for nine-year terms by a two-thirds majority, the chair of the Media Council is nominated by the prime minister for a term of nine years.[32] However, the only possible candidate for the chair of the Media Council is the president of the National Media and Infocommunications Authority,[33] the administrative agency created by Media Act, who in turn is directly named by the prime minister.[34] With respect to the rest of the Media Council, however, a two-thirds vote for election of its members means that the current government can fill all of the seats with members of the ruling party, as indeed it already has. Their nine-year terms mean that these Fidesz loyalists will be in power into a third election cycle. Moreover, even if the Parliament refuses to elect the prime minister's candidate as chair of the Media Council, that person can still exer-

32 "The president of the Authority, who is appointed by the prime minister, shall become a candidate for the chairmanship of the Media Council by virtue and from the moment of appointment."Article 124(1) of the Act CLXXXV of 2010 on media services and mass media (Media Act) amended by the Act XIX of 2011.

33 Article 109(1) of the Media Act.

34 Article 125(1) of the Media Act.

cise the powers of the office.[35] These changes were strongly criticized by the European Union, the Council of Europe, as well as the United States and Germany for constituting a serious infringement on the freedom of press,[36] because the one-party nature of the Media Council composition is not in line with Council of Europe recommendations.[37] This fact is further aggravated by the long term of office of nine years[38] which is unprecedented in Europe.[39]

The constitutional role of public media is to serve the public interest through ensuring cultural and political diversity in news coverage. But under this new system of management and organization of public media organizations, public media will likely fall short of this objective. Between April 2010 and December 2011, after Fidesz had consolidated its hold over the Media Council, the government laid off hundreds of employees of public media organizations, many of whom claim to have sympathies elsewhere on the political spectrum. While the govern-

---

35 "Even if Parliament does not elect the president of the Authority as chairman of the Media Council, the president of the Authority shall still convene meetings of the Media Council, which (s)he shall attend with consultative powers and with a right to chair those meetings but without being involved in the decision-making process. The power of the president of the Authority to convene and chair meetings shall prevail from the moment of his/her appointment by the prime minister and until elected as chairman of the Media Council with full powers." Article 125(4) of the Media Act; the Act however fails to be explicit whether the chairman's powers, e. g. the nomination of the director generals of the public service broadcaster [Article 102(2) of the Media Act] persist upon failure of election.

36 See for instance, European Parliament, *Resolution on the media law in Hungary* (10 March 2011), P7_TA(2011)009; Commissioner for Human Rights, *Opinion on Hungary's media legislation in light of Council of Europe standards on freedom of the media*, CommDH (2011) 10, or the German government's response to a question of MPs of the faction Die Linke in the Parliament (Bundestag) in November 9, 2011 http://dipbt.bundestag.de/dip21/btd/17/077/1707704.pdf.

37 *Recommendation Rec(2000)23 of the Committee of Ministers to member states on the independence and functions of regulatory authorities for the broadcasting sector*, Appendix, Point 3; Commissioner of Human Rights, *Opinion on Hungary's media legislation in light of Council of Europe standards on freedom of the media*, para 39.

38 Article 124(1) of the Media Act.

39 OSCE, *Analysis and Assessment of a Package of Hungarian Legislation and Draft Legislation on Media and Telecommunications* (September 2010), 41.

ment claims it was engaged in austerity measures in firing these public employees, critics saw a purge of those who disagreed with the government. As part of this effort to restructure public media organizations, several long-running cultural and political shows were cut while a number of visible TV and radio personnel opposing Fidesz' policies were fired. At the end of 2011, several journalists who had been fired from state television—because, they say, they disagreed with Fidesz—went on hunger strike to protest what had happened.

But the changes to the Constitutional Court, the Electoral Commission and the Media Council all occurred before the new constitution went into effect. In many ways, the changes disabled these formerly independent bodies so that they could no longer provide a check on the constitutional revolution that then occurred. Signed into law on April 25, 2011, the new Fundamental Law constituted a radical overhaul of the constitution and brought many additional changes to the system of separation of powers. But these earlier constitutional changes meant that the previously robust constitutional system could not defend itself.

The content of the 2011 Fundamental Law

The preamble, called the "National Avowal," sets the tone for this new constitution: "We do not recognise the communist constitution of 1949, since it was the basis of a tyrannical rule; therefore we proclaim it to be invalid." This invalidation of the 1949 Constitution not only repudiates that text, but it also casts doubt on the validity of the first post-communist constitution, which was formally a 1989 amendment to the 1949 Constitution. Because the 2011 Fundamental Law was adopted following the procedural rules of the 1989–1990 Constitution, the repudiation of the 1949 Constitution also raises questions about whether the procedural rules under which the new constitution was adopted are valid as well. [40] In following the amendment rules of the 1989–1990 Constitution, which had followed the amendment rules of the 1949 Constitution, the new Fidesz constitution is not different in kind in its attachment to the 1949 constitution from the one it seeks to replace. In short, in its attempt to repudiate the

[40] See *Opinion on the Fundamental Law of Hungary* in this volume.

"communist constitution," the Fidesz government has created a theoretical mess without purging the underlying continuity with the communist constitution.

One of the features of the 1949 Constitution that the new Fundamental Law retains is the unicameral Parliament, though the number of representatives will be reduced from 386 to around 200 after the cardinal law on elections comes into effect. Borrowing from the 1989–1990 Constitution, the new Fundamental Law also continues the prior configuration of many other political institutions. The president of the republic will continue to be elected by the Parliament for five years, as under the old constitution. The prime minister, also, must maintain the confidence of a simple majority of the Parliament and can only be replaced by a constructive vote of no confidence, as under the old constitution. The president continues to be the figure who formally appoints members of the cabinet, the president of the National Bank and the members of most of the independent regulatory bodies, upon the nomination of the prime minister, as under the old constitution.

But the judiciary, up through and including the Constitutional Court, has been massively changed. The Fundamental Law and the new law on the Constitutional Court[41] significantly limited abstract review of legislation by eliminating *actio popularis* review which allowed any individual to petition the Court for abstract review of any law. Abstract posterior review may now only be initiated by one-fourth of members of Parliament, the commissioner for fundamental rights, or the government. Even the president no longer has this power.

At the moment, there is no unified one-fourth opposition bloc in the Parliament that could come together around such a petition, so one can imagine that the power will not be used as long as this particular composition of the Parliament holds sway. The government is highly unlikely to challenge its own laws before the Court. The commissioner for fundamental rights so far has chosen to exercise this competency to send laws to the Court not only within the sphere of his competence but also with respect to general structural issues of the sort that abstract review used to reach. The response of the Court to this practice is not yet known.

[41] Act CLI of 2011 on the Constitutional Court.

In addition, the Court has been further reduced in its role in the constitutional order because the limits on judicial review of fiscal policies put into effect before the new constitution was enacted were extended in the Fundamental Law. Now the restriction on the Court's jurisdiction will disappear when public debt drops below 50 percent of the Gross Domestic Product, something that no one expects will happen for the foreseeable future. The new constitutional amendment, enacted on December 30, 2011, however, purports to prohibit the Constitutional Court from *ever* reviewing fiscal laws enacted during the period when public debt is more than 50 percent of the GDP. Only *new* fiscal laws enacted after the debt drops below 50 percent may be reviewed by the Court under this last-minute constitutional change.[42]

In a significant change for the better, however, the Constitutional Court will now be able to review the constitutionality of judicial procedures and decisions through the mechanism of the "constitutional complaint." In a constitutional complaint, a person whose rights have been affected by the concrete application of a law may go to the Constitutional Court for redress. The Constitutional Court may decide either that there has been no violation of rights, or that a violation of rights was caused by the unconstitutional interpretation of a constitutional law, or that a violation of rights was caused by the application of an unconstitutional law. The Constitutional Court now has a mechanism short of the declaration of the unconstitutionality of a law to fix unconstitutional interpretations of law, even as it retains the power to find laws unconstitutional as well. But the elimination of the *actio popularis* will mean that citizens will be limited to bringing actions in cases involving only infringements of their own rights, or in cases where the law does not provide the possibility for a legal remedy. Judges from the ordinary courts will continue to be able to petition the Constitutional Court to review a law that the ordinary judge believes may be unconstitutional before it is applied in a concrete case, as they have been able to do since 1990.

While this expansion of Constitutional Court jurisdiction to cover constitutional complaints is to be commended, it does not really substitute completely for the *actio popularis* review. That is because constitutional problems that do not involve immediate violations of rights cannot be reached by the constitutional complaint. Challenges to state

[42] Article 27 of the Transitional Provisions of the Fundamental Law.

structures, for example, are very hard to make in this sort of case. Whole areas of the constitution will therefore not be easily defended by the Constitutional Court any longer, nor can many new aspects of the constitutional order that violate constitutional principles, for example the cardinal laws, be easily challenged under this new system.

The constitutional reforms have also seriously undermined the independence of the ordinary judiciary through changing the appointment and reassignment process for judges. According to the cardinal acts on the structure of the judiciary and the legal status of judges,[43] the head of the National Judicial Office can select either any judge from among the top three candidates recommended by the judicial council of the court where the appointment would be made or none of them at all. If she decides against the top candidate, her decision may, under amendments to the law in 2012, be vetoed by the National Judicial Council, an elected panel of judges. She may then call for a new tender, so she still has substantial power. And, in any event, by the time these limits were placed on her powers, she had already replaced nearly 10% of the judiciary without this check. While formally, the president of the republic must sign off on all new judicial appointments, the decision of the head of the National Judicial Office alone is necessary in order to promote or demote a judge presently sitting anywhere in the judiciary.

The nomination process for new judges became quite salient because the Fundamental Law reduced the retirement ages for judges on ordinary courts from 70 to 62, starting on the day the new constitution went into effect. This change forced 274 judges into early retirement in 2012 alone. Those judges include eight of the 20 court presidents at the county level, two of the five appeals court presidents and 20 of the 80 Supreme Court judges. Those positions were then opened up for replacement by the current government. In addition to these judgeships, the government had even more new judgeships to fill because the usual procedure for appointing judges was suspended for the six months before the new constitution came into effect. In an act adopted in June 2011, the Parliament halted all appointment procedures for judges between that date and January 1, 2012. The combined effect of two laws, one lowering the retirement age for judges and the

[43] Act CLXI of 2011 on the Organization and Administration of the Judiciary and Act CLXII of 2011 on the Legal Status and Remuneration of Judges.

other suspending the appointment procedure, was to give the Fidesz government the power to appoint hundreds of new judges.

The head of the National Judicial Office, who has the power to choose the judges, is elected by a two-thirds supermajority in Parliament to a nine-year term. The first occupant of that office is a sitting judge who is a close personal friend with the prime minister and also married to the one of the chief authors of the new constitution, so many were dismayed that she didn't appear to be a neutral person. With these new appointments, Fidesz will be able to control judicial philosophy on the courts for the foreseeable future, especially as there are now plans to raise the retirement age of the judges who are left and who will be hand-picked by this one party loyalist.

The Act on the Transitional Provisions of the Fundamental Law, an omnibus constitutional amendment passed at the very end of 2011, allows both the head of the National Judicial Office and the chief prosecutor to assign specific cases to specific courts according to their assessment of the relative workloads of these courts.[44] The impact of this provision on the independence of judicial decisions could be crucial and possibly seriously damaging. The head of the National Judicial Office and the chief prosecutor now have the power to shop around for favorable judges to hear each case. While the government's rationale for this change is that they want to improve the efficiency of courts, there is nothing in the law to preclude or even evaluate whether the prosecutor or the head of the National Judicial Office are using this new power for choosing judges favorable to the side of the government.

In addition to this serious assault on judicial independence, Parliament's ability to manage the budget has been severely reduced by the Fundamental Law. The Fundamental Law creates a Budget Council with the power to veto any budget proposal by the legislature, if the budget adds to the national debt. Again, given Hungary's difficult financial picture, it is hard to imagine any foreseeable budget that does *not* add to the debt. The intent of giving this power to the Budget Council is to enforce fiscal discipline on Parliament in line with the requirement of the Fundamental Law so that Parliament does not increase government spending as long as the debt/GDP ratio exceeds 50 percent. But even though the Council's constitutional objective is to

[44] Article 11 of the Transitional Provisions of the Fundamental Law.

enforce these debt limits, the Council will likely have much discretion in defining whether a budget meets these requirements because budget projections depend on contestable figures like the rates of future growth and inflation. The veto power of the Budget Council means that Parliament will have to satisfy the political and economic objectives of Council members, effectively reducing citizen influence over crucial public spending measures.

That is not the only problem with the Budget Council. With the three members of the Budget Council elected for long terms of office (two six-year terms and one twelve-year term), the Budget Council will also outlast the life of any specific Parliament. The government that has the ability to appoint these members will have "dead hand control" over the budget process even if that government leaves office. Combined with another constitutional provision, the Budget Council raises even more serious dangers. The president of the republic is given the power to dissolve Parliament and call for new elections if a budget is not passed by March 31 of each year. A fight between Parliament and the Budget Council can result in the Parliament's dissolution and in a call for early elections—and the process can theoretically repeat until the Budget Council gets the Parliament it wants.

The issues of institutional independence go beyond the constitutional reforms and concern the appointments to key government positions. With its supermajority, Fidesz elected party loyalists to most government positions with terms that extend to multiple election cycles. Fidesz has now appointed the chief prosecutor (for a nine-year term), the president of the Supreme Court (for a nine-year term), the head of the State Audit Office (for a twelve-year term), the head of the new National Judicial Office (for a nine-year term), and the new judges on the Constitutional Court (for twelve-year terms). In addition, the new Media Council has nine-year terms for its chair and members. In 2013, Fidesz will also be able to select a new president for the National Bank for a six-year term. All of these office-holders may remain in office until Parliament can agree by a two-thirds vote to replace the office-holders at the end of their term, which could mean in practice that these terms of office could extend even further into the future.

Under the old constitution, long terms of office for these independent state officials were the norm as well, so the problem here isn't just with the length of time that these officials spend in office. The problem is that the current government is filling those jobs with people whose backgrounds are more political than expert. For example, the appointment of a former Fidesz MP instead of a person with auditing experience as the head of the State Audit Office is especially worrying given the extended powers granted to this office. The State Audit Office is a powerful agency with the authority to audit any government agency, local or national, or any publicly funded project. It has the power to freeze state funding if a local government has failed to implement a financial management plan drafted by the Office. In addition, the State Audit Office has the power to conduct investigations into the misuse of government money, which gives it powers more like those of a chief prosecutor. Given these powers and given that they are carried out on the basis of investigations done by auditors under the direction of the head of the Office, it is worrisome that this person can demote or promote any auditor without any justification, or reassign any auditor from one project to another.[45] The lack of standards of independence for the auditors who will conduct these investigations is disturbing.

With the new constitution, virtually every independent institution is coming under political control. The cardinal act on the National Bank[46] and the Transitional Provisions of the Fundamental Law have increased the possibility of government influence over monetary policy. The Act on the National Bank increased the number of vice-presidents from two to three and gave the prime minister the authority to choose directly the individuals who will fill these positions. Previously, the president of the Bank selected the vice-presidents and the president of the republic appointed them, but now the prime minister has a central role. The National Bank vice-presidents are all members of the Monetary Council, which decides on interest rate policy. The act will also increase the number of Monetary Council members from seven to nine. Indeed, Fidesz will be able to appoint another member in 2012 when normal rotation in office occurs.

The system of ombudspersons has also been radically changed under the 2011 Fundamental Law. While the old system had four ombudspersons with separate offices for human rights, minorities protection, data protection and future generations, the new system com-

---

[45] Act LXVI of 2011 on the State Audit Office.

[46] Act CCVIII of 2011 on the National Bank.

bines three formerly separate offices into one and moves the fourth out of the ombuds system altogether. The position of the ombudsperson for data protection has been eliminated and its function moved into an agency without the guarantees of independence that the prior office had. According to the Act on Informational Self-Determination and Freedom of Information, which was adopted in November 2011 and which entered into force on January 1, 2012, a National Agency for Data Protection and Freedom of Information replaced the ombudsperson. The current data protection ombudsperson in office was not grandfathered into this new scheme but was instead required to leave office immediately, even though he had just been appointed in 2008 for a six-year fixed term. The head of the new data protection authority, a substitute for the prior independent ombudsperson, is nominated by the prime minister and appointed by the president of the republic for a period of nine years,[47] through multiple election cycles.

But lifting data protection out of the independent ombuds system was not all that happened. The offices of the three remaining ombudspersons were also rearranged. With the new Fundamental Law, Parliament elects the commissioner for fundamental rights and that ombudsperson has two deputies—one for the protection of the future generations and the other for the protection of minorities. No new ombudsperson can be added without amending the constitution. Moreover, the two deputies are under the control of the general ombudsperson rather than having independent mandates, offices and staffs as was true in the old system. The ombuds system has therefore been radically shrunk and made more dependent on one person. In the place of the separate and independent ombudspersons with separate staffs, there is one general ombudsman and two deputies, all sharing one staff.

---

[47] Viviane Reding, vice-president of the European Commission, in a letter to the Hungarian government dated December 12, 2011, as well as the statement of the European Commission issued on January 11, 2012 expressed concerns about the independence of the national data protection authority. On January 17, 2012 the European Commission launched accelerated infringement proceedings against Hungary over the independence of its data protection authority (*European Commission v. Hungary*, C-288/12.), as well as over measures affecting the judiciary (*European Commission v. Hungary*, C-286/12.).

In rewriting the Fundamental Law, the role of the Parliament itself has also been affected. The sheer number of cardinal laws that must be passed by *this Parliament* with its two-thirds majority limits what any *future* Parliament can do in a number of substantive areas where majority decisions were previously the norm. For the first time, cardinal laws regulate, among other things taxation, family protection, and pensions. The Economic Stability Act, a cardinal law passed by Parliament at the end of December 2011, defines the basic principles of taxation and the structure of the pension system.[48] With this act, Parliament adopted a universal flat tax on personal income and business income. From here on out, any change to the tax system would require a subsequent two-thirds vote in Parliament.

The requirement that pension policy be set by a cardinal law means that it will be more difficult for future governments to implement reforms to the Hungarian pension system. Due to an aging and declining population in Hungary, the ratio of workers to retirees continues to shrink. The Hungarian pension system could face a serious deficit that would require substantive reforms to the system. Addressing a looming deficit in the pension system is an urgent task for future Parliaments and political parties, yet the constitution will limit Parliament's ability to implement change to those provisions that can be agreed by a supermajority. The number and scope of the new cardinal laws means that future Parliaments cannot engage in ordinary legislation in areas that are typically decided by majority vote. Instead, huge swaths of policy are put beyond any mere majority.

The number of supermajority laws will go beyond the set listed in the Fundamental Law. A rule in the Transitional Provisions of the Fundamental Law allows Parliament to require in a cardinal law that any subject matter regulated by the Parliament must be approved by a qualified majority. This provision allows the government to put any policy area it would like beyond the reach of a future simple majority. This could well result in an arcane tangle of cardinal laws and qualified majority laws in the Hungarian legal system. Taken to an extreme, this Parliament could tie the hands of all future Parliaments in ways that are inconsistent with the principles of democratic rule.

---

48 Act CXCIV of 2011 on the Budget Council, and Basic Principles of Taxation and Pension.

Conclusions

As we have seen, the 2011 Hungarian Fundamental Law is not really a democratic constitution, if by a democratic constitution we mean one that upholds democratic principles, preserves checks and balances, provides room for future democratic decision making and encourages pluralistic consultation. This is hugely ironic. In 1989, Fidesz and the Alliance of Free Democrats joined together to put to the public a referendum on the structure of the presidency in the new constitutional order at that time. Both parties wanted to avoid a presidential system with its centralized power in order to enhance parliamentary government. The public agreed and the country adopted a parliamentary system in which the Parliament was the most powerful body of state.

Under the 2011 Fundamental Law, however, the façade of parliamentary government is just that—a façade. The appearance of parliamentarism and democratic institutions is a front for the reality of centralized executive control. When one traces out how power works in this new constitution, it belongs in the hands of the Fidesz party and in the hands of Viktor Orbán, the prime minister. Behind every institution and every law, one can see the influence of one party and one man. The conclusion seems inescapable that, in winning the 2010 elections with such a lopsided vote, Orbán's intention was to eliminate separation of powers. As we tried to show, the new constitutional order that consists of the Fundamental Law and the cardinal laws perfectly fulfills this plan: the new constitutional structure does not contain any meaningful separation of powers. The word "republic" has disappeared from the name of the country, too, and that may be the most telling sign of all. This new constitutional system properly guarantees neither fundamental rights nor checks and balances. Hungary, under this new Fundamental Law, however, formally keeps a "republic" as the form of government, but can no longer be described substantively as a republican state governed by the rule of law.

Between Revolution and Constitution: The Roles of the Hungarian Constitutional Court

Oliver W. Lembcke and Christian Boulanger

Juvenal's Question

There are questions which are themselves more important than their answers. In some cases, answers may even be downright undesirable, at least if they possess a definitive character. Such a case may be represented by the question ascribed to the Roman poet Juvenal: *Quis custodiet ipsos custodes?* ("Who will guard the guards themselves?") The aphorism comes from the *Satires*, where it refers to the problem of how the virtuousness of women can possibly be protected if the guardians of their virtue are themselves corrupt.[1] It has since gained significance in a political context. Today it represents first and foremost a challenge for constitutional courts. These institutions are handed the task of guarding the (tense) balance between the principles of the rule of law (including human rights) and democratic self-determination, both hallmarks of modern constitutionalism. That the "guardians of the constitution" find themselves exposed to Juvenal's question time and again (though in different variations) is doubtless a sign of the increased power of constitutional courts, gained at the expense of legislatures.

If classical doctrine viewed legislation as the site and expression of the people's sovereignty, modern constitutional history has substantially qualified the definitude of this relationship. Differentiating legislation into statutory and constitutional laws creates the preconditions for the hierarchization of those laws, and accordingly for the possibility of exerting control over the legislative power in the light of constitutional standards. It is generally constitutional courts, not legislatures,

[1] Iuvenalis, D.I. *Satires,* trans. Niall Rudd (Oxford: Clarendon Press, 1991), VI, 347–348.

which have profited from these developments. Their power to interpret and apply the constitution allows them to partake in the sovereignty of the state. And the more they are able to emerge as the sole—if only *de facto*—interpreter of the constitution, the larger their "corner of sovereignty" becomes.[2] The essential function of Juvenal's question therefore is to allow this participation in state sovereignty, along with its precarious democratic legitimacy, to come into view. For this reason, despite its literary overuse, it has lost none of its relevance. To the contrary: more than ever, constitutional court judges in liberal democracies are confronted with the challenge of justifying their judicial power before a critical (professional) public—always in the knowledge that the question of who will guard the guardians shall return precisely in the case of a powerful constitutional court.[3]

The relationship between power and the public sphere in the case of constitutional courts is in no way unilateral, however, nor is it confined only to public critique. Rather, the public is at the same time the medium in which a specific form of political power is produced: authority. Hannah Arendt recalled that the concept of authority (*auctoritas*) signifies the ability to "increase" (*augere*) the common good, and that this form of power is to be differentiated from that of *potestas*, which has its roots in the power of the will and is aimed at implementing binding decisions.[4] Taking this differentiation as a basis in the case of constitutional jurisprudence, it becomes clear that the function of a constitutional court is not to impose its will on others. Rather, its task is to demonstrate judgment in interpreting the constitution. Every such act of interpretation represents a chance for the court to revise and update the guiding principles which led to the founding of the political community in which it operates, and to make itself the representative of these fundamental concepts of order. The expectation is that the constitutional court will succeed in doing this, and when it does, its authority is confirmed in the fact of its recognition by all

---

[2] Böckenförde, E.-W. *Staat, Nation, Europa: Studien zur Staatslehre, Verfassungstheorie und Rechtsphilosophie* (Frankfurt am Main: Suhrkamp, 1999), 168.

[3] For the purpose of this paper, the term "constitutional court" refers to any court that has the power of invalidating laws or other normative measures on the basis that they contradict the constitution (including the Supreme Court of the United States or India).

[4] Arendt, H. *Macht und Gewalt* (Munich: Piper, 1994), 188.

who are subject to its judicial decision. Authority exists in the interplay between recognition and subordination; precisely for this reason, it is to be understood less as a lasting condition and more as a dynamic process, in which authority must continually be demonstrated through judgment within the medium of the public sphere.

This process, however, is prone to disruption. Typical examples include critiques that culminate in discussions about the acceptability of constitutional court verdicts, in which the self-evidence of the idea of being subordinated to court jurisdiction—even voluntarily—is eroded and the alternative, though it can no longer claim to be "constitutional," becomes palpable. A sustained disruption occurs when the discourse of legitimacy finds itself transformed at the level of the highest constitutional bodies into the discourse of sovereignty and compels an answer to Juvenal's question.[5] Such a state of tension introduces the looming threat of a decision—related to Carl Schmitt's logic of decisionism—about the hierarchy of the sources of legitimacy whose very duality forms the foundation of the democratic constitutional state, with consequences for the state's institutional framework. The precarious position of these constitutive principles finds its expression in the enthronement of a political sovereign who claims to speak for the people as the *pouvoir constituant*. This is precisely what happened in the Hungarian parliamentary election of 2010.

The Court's Authority

On paper, the Hungarian Constitutional Court is considered to be one of the most powerful constitutional courts in history. Until the passage of the new Hungarian constitution in 2011, the Court's abundance of responsibilities was extensive and, compared to the jurisdiction of courts in other countries, extraordinary.[6] This assessment

[5] Using the French Revolution as an example, Arendt has pointed to the corrosive effects discourses of sovereignty generally have on authority. Arendt, H. *On Revolution* (New York: Penguin, 2006).

[6] Brunner, G. "Structure and Proceedings of the Hungarian Constitutional Judiciary" in *Constitutional Judiciary in a New Democracy: The Hungarian Constitutional Court*, eds. Sólyom and Brunner (Ann Arbor: University of Michigan, 2000), 65.

applied particularly with regard to the realm of judicial review. Review of the courts, however, was not provided for. One of the most astonishing provisions was the so-called *actio popularis*—which fell victim to the most recent reforms to the Constitutional Court—whereby literally anyone, without any standing, could challenge before the Court the unconstitutionality of a legal norm, the Parliament's dereliction of its constitutional duties, or the violation of his constitutional rights.[7]

The history of the court's origins provides the explanation for these far-reaching powers. After opposition parties had been able to push through an acceptable constitution during roundtable discussions, they demanded the strongest and most easily mobilized court possible in order to protect the constitution—as well as political minorities.[8] The negotiations failed to reduce mistrust on either side. To the contrary: while opposition forces feared that the Hungarian Socialist Party would be incapable of abiding by the negotiated statutory and constitutional provisions in the wake of an electoral victory, the ranks of what had previously been the communist party were apprehensive of a victorious opposition that would put the former *nomenklatura* on trial.[9]

---

[7] Lurking behind the concept of allowing citizens to file suit against the government without further standing is the emancipatory idea of freeing Hungary from the juridical legacy of the communist regime as thoroughly as possible. Yet this legal concept has failed to develop into an exemplary model to be followed. At least in comparison to other European legal systems, the norm is that appellants must demonstrate that they have been directly affected by a certain action in order to be able to file a complaint. The German Constitutional Court has explicitly barred any *actio popularis*: BVerfGE 79, 1 (14).

[8] From the perspective of political theory, the developments which led to the establishment of the Hungarian Constitutional Court are evidence of the fruitfulness of Ginsburg's insurance theory, which suggests that constitutional courts are established by political actors in the course of drafting a constitution in order to secure their own positions of power. Ginsburg, T. *Judicial Review in New Democracies: Constitutional Courts in Asian Cases* (Cambridge, UK: Cambridge University Press, 2003).

[9] Regarding the roundtable negotiations, cf. Bozóki, A. *The Roundtable Talks of 1989: The Genesis of Hungarian Democracy* (Budapest: Central European University Press, 2002).

Fear and mistrust did not impede compromise, however, but rather gave rise to a downright pragmatic political praxis, the so-called "handshake tradition."[10] Not only did the Constitutional Court emerge from this tradition,[11] but it is also expressed in the fact that a great many central laws (e.g. laws pertaining to the establishment of the Constitutional Court, to media and to elections) were passed by the Parliament with a two-thirds majority.[12] Not least, this orientation toward general consensus is demonstrated by the parameters governing the change of regime itself, which occurred under the conditions of legal continuity. To cite but two examples of this, the 1989 constitutional amendments were passed according to the regular procedure of the old, non-democratic Parliament; and likewise, all laws from the communist era maintained their legal validity until they were abolished by the Constitutional Court. In short, the now "old" constitution may be understood as a consensus constitution, oriented toward the integration of political camps that were and are ideologically far apart. Yet this constitutional agreement was nothing more than a minimum consensus, one which could not disguise the fact that the different camps remained political enemies. In such a situation, the task of managing this minimum consensus fell to the Constitutional Court.

From the beginning, i.e. since January 1, 1990, the Hungarian Constitutional Court has acted as guardian of the balance of political forces as they existed at the time of the new republic's founding. Precisely during this first phase, however, it did not content itself with a "narrow" interpretation of its role, but rather documented its self-confidence and claim to power with a series of spectacular decisions. In a political stalemate, the Court used (and occasionally exploited) its

---

[10] Haraszti, M. "The Handshake Tradition: A Decade of Consensus Politics Bears Liberal Fruit in Hungary—But What Next?" in *Between Past and Future: The Revolutions of 1989 and Their Aftermath*, eds. Antohi, S. and V. Tismăneanu (Budapest: Central European University Press, 2000), 273.

[11] Part of the "deal" was an agreement about the procedure for electing the first five judges to the Constitutional Court. Two were chosen by the opposition, two by the government; the fifth was agreed upon by both parties.

[12] The tradition continued with an agreement made between the winner of the first election (the conservative Hungarian Democratic Forum) and the left-liberal opposition party (the Alliance of Free Democrats) in 1990, in order to attain the necessary two-thirds majority and thereby first be able to establish a viable legal framework.

broad jurisdiction to significantly shape Hungary's democratic transformation in a number of ways. Indeed, there was hardly any area in which the Court did not intervene. To mention just a few examples: the juridical reappraisal of the past, the redistribution of property in the wake of the expropriations of the communist era, the institutional configuration of Hungary's constitutional democracy, and the expansion of the sphere of the citizen as a fundamental right, in deliberate distinction to the state-socialist model of subordinating its subjects.[13]

The president who most shaped the Court, not only through his appointment but also intellectually, is László Sólyom.[14] That the Constitutional Court in its first eight years evolved into an active actor in Hungarian politics can essentially be traced back to his leadership role.[15] In the first 4–5 years, with self-confidence and an ambitious mission to use the Constitutional Court to steer Hungarian politics toward European constitutionalism,[16] he was able to win over his fellow judges in many cases—in part with the aid of a novel doctrine that borrowed from the constitutional jurisprudence of other countries.[17] In this way, the judges delayed or even put a stop to entire legislative projects put

---

13 Translations of the Constitutional Court's decisions during the period 1990–1998 are available in edited form. Brunner, G. and L. Sólyom, *Verfassungsgerichtsbarkeit in Ungarn* (Baden-Baden: Nomos, 1995). Sólyom, L. and G. Brunner, *Constitutional Judiciary in a New Democracy: The Hungarian Constitutional Court* (Ann Arbor: The University of Michigan, 2000).

14 One of the peculiarities of the Hungarian Constitutional Court was that the judges elected their president from within their own ranks. This rule has been removed in the Fundamental Law, however. The president of the Court is now determined by the Parliament.

15 See Babus for a lively portrait of the first chief justice. Babus, E. "The Superego of the Transformation. The First Eight Years of the Constitutional Court," *The Hungarian Quarterly* 40, no. 153 (1999): 3. Sólyom considered himself a founding father of the Hungarian Constitutional Court. Sólyom, L. "Introduction to the Decisions of the Hungarian Constitutional Court" in Brunner G. *Constitutional Judiciary in a New Democracy: The Hungarian Constitutional Court*, 5.

16 Boulanger, C. "Europeanisation through Judicial Activism? The Hungarian Constitutional Court's Legitimacy and the 'Return to Europe'" in *Spreading Democracy and the Rule of Law?* ed. Sadurski, Czarnota and Krygier (Dordrecht: Springer, 2006).

17 Dupré, C. *Importing the Law in Post-communist Transitions: the Hungarian Constitutional Court and the Right to Human Dignity* (Oxford: Hart, 2003).

forth by the then-ruling majority. Thus, for example, they derailed the first conservative government's reprivatization plans by invoking the principle of equality,[18] just as they thwarted the planned welfare reforms introduced by the coalition of Socialists and Free Democrats in the name of "acquired rights" and the formal category of "legal security."[19]

Sólyom's interventionist attitude in part garnered much sympathy for the Court among the public—for a long time, opinion polls declared it one of the most popular institutions in the country.[20] Yet alongside this recognition, the Court frequently elicited condemnation, particularly among legal experts, for its "activist" jurisprudence.[21] The concept of the "invisible constitution" sparked particularly sharp criticism. Sólyom conceived this concept as a system of constitutional doctrine that is intended to increase the argumentative rationality of individual decisions and to this end should not shy away from borrowing from the jurisdiction of constitutional courts in other modern constitutional states.[22]

---

[18] Decision 21/1990. (X. 4.)

[19] Decision 43/1995. (VI. 30.) For a critical perspective on welfare reform decisions, see Kis, J. *Constitutional Democracy* (Budapest, New York: Central European University Press, 2003), 285–295.

[20] Husz, D. "Intézmények presztízse 1989 és 1998 között" [The Prestige of Institutions between 1989 and 1998] in *Magyarország Évtizedkönyve, 1988–1998*, eds. Kurtán, S. and P. Vass (Budapest: Demokrácia Kutatások Magyar Központja Alapítvány, 1998), 821.

[21] Béla Pokol, the Constitutional Court's most famous critic, first introduced to the debate the much-discussed (particularly in the American context) concept of judicial activism (See, for example, Pokol B. "Aktivizmus és az Alkotmánybíróság" [Activism and the Constitutional Court] in *Magyarország Politikai Évkönyve 1992*, eds. Kurtán, Sándor, and Vass (Budapest: Demokrácia Kutatások Magyar Központja Alapítvány, 1993) 150–155.; Pokol, B. "The Constitutionality of Legislation" in *European Legal Cultures*, eds. Gessner, V. and A. Höland and Cs. Varga (Aldershot: Dartmouth, 1996) 451. For Pokol, such activism is "a greater departure from the text of the law". Pokol, B. *The Concept of Law. The Multi-Layered Legal System* (Budapest: Rejtjel, 2001), 78.

[22] Sólyom introduced the concept in a concurring opinion to the Constitutional Court's decision to abolish the death penalty [Decision 23/1990. (X. 31.)]. However, the "invisible constitution" was never employed by the Court again, which has to do in part with the concept's negative reception. See the concept from another perspective in Tribe, L.H. *The Invisible Constitution* (Oxford: Oxford University Press, 2008).

For critics, this concept like no other captured the Court's hubris in elevating itself above the will of the democratic legislature and shaping the constitution according to its own ideas.[23] Similar criticisms came from politicians, especially members of Parliament. It is unsurprising that the Court's interventions found little favor in the Parliament. By exercising its right of judicial review in a way that was politically "color blind," the Court demonstrated its independence; nonetheless, the impression in all political camps was that it showed too little respect to the democratic majority. An impression that was not without consequences, as the Parliament swapped out the first squad of judges after their second term of office in favor of candidates who tended to be more reserved.[24] Against this background, it becomes immediately clear why most of the Orbán government's attacks have been directed against course-setting changes in constitutional law made during Sólyom's term.[25]

---

[23] Sajó, A. "Reading the Invisible Constitution: Judicial Review in Hungary," *Oxford Journal of Legal Studies* 15 no. 2 (1995): 253.

[24] Scheppele, K. L. "The New Hungarian Constitutional Court," *East European Constitutional Review* 8, no. 4 (1999): 81.

[25] For the purposes of this chapter, the Constitutional Court's activity after 1998 can thus be disregarded. Gábor Halmai links the various eras of the Court through 2005 with the names of the presidents of the Court at those times. Sólyom's "activist" court was followed by the "passivist" court of 1998–2003 under János Németh. András Holló's brief presidency from 2003 to 2005 returned the Court to a moderate activism. Since that time, there have been two more presidents of the Court: Mihály Bihari from 2005 to 2008, and Péter Paczolay from 2008 through the present. Halmai, G. "The Transformation of Hungarian Constitutional Law from 1985 to 2005" in *The Transformation of the Hungarian Legal Order 1985–2005*, eds. Jakab, Takács, and Tatham (The Hague: Kluwer, 2007). As a general assessment, it is safe to say that the second part of the Sólyom era and the second decade of the Hungarian constitutional jurisprudence were less "activist" than the first years. Yet, the Court kept its role as the final guardian of the constitution, and repeatedly engaged in conflicts with the government. See Kis, *Constitutional Democracy*, 278–284. See also Erdei, Á. and A. Holló eds., *Selected Decisions of the Constitutional Court of Hungary (1998–2001)* (Budapest: Akadémiai Kiadó, 2005).

Revolution and Counterrevolution

The conflict between continuity and revolution was for Sólyom an issue essential to the Constitutional Court's work. For him, the key function of the Court consisted in "re-establishing the law's tarnished reputation;" the principle of the rule of law was "the fulcrum which will allow us to lever the old world out of its place."[26] In doing so, the formal side of the law—which in certain cases may disallow even what is politically desirable—must be taken into consideration, as the Court made clear with one of its most controversial decisions, in which it rejected the government's attempts to criminally prosecute human rights violations from the communist period.[27] At issue was, first and foremost, redress for government retaliation against and actual massacres of Hungarian citizens who had taken part in the anti-communist, anti-Soviet uprising of 1956, the statute of limitations for which crimes had according to prevailing law long since expired. In its decision,[28] the Court unanimously struck down the government's law, asserting that a constitutional state cannot be realized by unconstitutional means. Laws which ignore statutes of limitations that remain in effect and are formally undisputed violate the principle of legal certainty, which is derived from the rule of law. The real revolution, according to the Court, was Hungary's proclaiming itself a constitutional state after four decades of communist tyranny. This "constitutional revolution" could not be followed by any further "revolutionary justice;" the

[26] Cited in Babus, E. "The Superego of the Transformation. The First Eight Years of the Constitutional Court."

[27] See the detailed analyses by Brunner, G. and G. Halmai, "Die juristische Bewältigung des kommunistischen Unrechts in Ungarn" in *Juristische Bewältigung des Kommunistischen Unrechts in Osteuropa und Deutschland*, ed. Brunner, G. (Berlin: Berlin Verlag Arno Spitz, 1995); Halmai, G. and K.L. Scheppele "Constitutional Solutions to the Extra-Constitutional State," *Journal of Constitutional Law in Eastern and Central Europe* (1995): 179.; Tóth, G.A. "The Bitter Pills of Political Transition" in *The Transformation of the Hungarian Legal Order 1985–2005*, eds. Jakab, Takács, and Tatham (The Hague: Kluwer, 2007) 283. For a very critical assessment, see Józsa, Gy. *Aufarbeitung der kommunistischen Vergangenheit in Ungarn* (Cologne: Bundesinstitut für ostwissenschaftliche und internationale Studien, 1998).

[28] Decision 11/1992. (III. 5.)

Constitutional Court, as the guardian of constitutionalism, would see to that.[29]

As was to be expected, the decision was met with outrage by the parliamentary majority and even by parts of the public. The coalition refused to admit defeat and twice more introduced its bill in an altered form, ultimately pushing through a version based on international law. Regardless of how popular or unpopular this decision was at the time, it can be said with certainty that the Court's early verdicts alienated a large portion of the population who identified with the victims of the 1956 uprising.[30] When the Court ultimately allowed the prosecution of communist crimes in a limited form,[31] the conservative government was able to claim this as a victory; its persistence had paid off. The Court's veto has continued to gnaw at the collective memory of anti-communist Hungarians young and old, as an act of formalistic resistance against historical justice.

After Orbán was elected prime minister in 2010 having a two-thirds majority that could amend the constitution, he set into motion a comprehensive legislative machine in order to conduct his revolution from above. The scope of these legislative packages, Orbán asserted, would exceed even that of the legal reforms executed after the collapse of communism.[32] The two-thirds majority opened a window of opportunity for Orbán to enshrine his vision of a new Hungary in constitutional law without having to rely on compromises with the opposition. To be sure, they were "generously" invited to participate in the

---

29 See Sólyom, L. "Introduction to the Decisions of the Hungarian Constitutional Court," 36–37.

30 Of course, not everybody who had suffered under the repression and terror of that era was seeking revenge. For example, Árpád Göncz, then Hungarian president, had been sentenced to life imprisonment after 1956 and opposed the *ex post facto* legislation.

31 Decision 53/1993. (X. 13.) made way for the criminal investigation, on the basis of international law, of massacres that had occurred during the repression of the 1956 uprising. See Tóth, G. A. "The Bitter Pills of Political Transition."

32 "Orbán Says Government to Complete Wave of Legislation by End of Year; Changes 'greater in Scale' Than Those Following Collapse of Communism." http://www.politics.hu/20111214/orban-says-government-to-complete-wave-of-legislation-by-end-of-year-changes-greater-in-scale-than-those-following-collapse-of-communism/.

project, but very soon had to learn that the majority had no plans even to debate their objections.[33] A constitutional provision requiring a four-fifths majority to determine the basic features of a new constitution was eliminated early on, and no right of the opposition to have a substantial voice in the process was acknowledged, in marked contrast to earlier efforts to draft a constitution in the 1990s.[34] The new constitution, the result of a conversation the constituent party had only with itself, radically changes Hungary's constitutional identity. It prescribes not a neutral-constitutional republic but a historically-founded Christian-conservative community whose symbol is a "holy crown" from the 12th century middle ages. The constitution's Schmittian "decision" lies not only in the fact that it excludes a considerable portion of the Hungarian population who reject this constitutional identity from its introductory proclamation: "We, the members of the Hungarian nation, declare..." Its decisionist character consists also in the fact that the government made no effort (or rather, didn't dare) to subject it to a popular vote which might have shown it to be a constitution of the people. And so nothing remains but hollow pathos and the mere assertion of an ideologically homogenous nation.

Clash of Jurisdictions

Orbán won a clear victory in this battle. His powerless opposition can for the time being do nothing to oppose a national "counterrevolution" that was properly conducted, formally speaking, and legitimized by a decisive electoral victory, not least since the parliamentary majority elected a president who considered himself not an independent constitutional body but Orbán's proxy, and who signed without objection

---

33 After the government passed legislation to restrict the Constitutional Court's competences (see below), the opposition considered that a red line had been crossed and withdrew from a constitutional committee in which they initially had participated.

34 Hungary attempted to pass a new constitution in 1994–1997. The governing coalition of socialists and liberal democrats granted the opposition significantly more of a voice in the proceedings than they should have had according to the election results. Arato, A. "The Constitution-Making Endgame in Hungary," *East European Constitutional Review* 5 no. 4 (Fall 1996): 31–39.

every law the Parliament passed. The government's only remaining opponent is the Constitutional Court, which had proven the effectiveness of its power of judicial review in the past. It is thus little wonder that since Fidesz's electoral victory the Court has been in the crosshairs of the new government's drive for reform, with the stated goal of limiting the Court's influence. The result is a power struggle between two institutions, with both sides availing themselves of every means at their disposal. Orbán, a politician through and through, cleverly exploits the *kairos*, his chance to speak out against the Court as "the voice of the people." In turn, the Court, backed into a corner, musters what little means of defense it has to defy these attacks—at least symbolically—by invoking the highest values of the legal order. Yet this reveals one of the weaknesses of any constitutional court: it can do little to counter attacks from a government supported by a large—and in the case of Hungary, constitution-changing—majority. This is all the more true when the court is not in good standing with the public. Here the Hungarian Constitutional Court's weakness seems to have to do with power politics. Despite—or perhaps even because of—its brilliant start in the 1990s, it has been unable to find enduring support in Hungarian society.[35]

Strategies and instruments

The ruling majority initiated a number of measures to gain influence on the Court's decision making. Shortly after the election victory, the procedure for electing judges was changed. The Fidesz and Christian Democratic People's Party coalition replaced the old process, which granted the opposition a certain veto power, with a new rule that allowed them to push through their candidates at will. Shortly thereafter, the number of judges was increased to fifteen. In sum, seven justices have so far been elected by the majority to the court based on the new rules.[36] The government did not want to rely on the effects of

[35] Unlike, for example, the German Constitutional Court. Lembcke, O.W. *Hüter Der Verfassung: Eine institutionentheoretische Studie zur Autorität des Bundesverfassungsgerichts* (Tübingen: Mohr Siebeck, 2007).

[36] For a detailed analysis of these developments, see Kovács, K. and Tóth, G. A. "Hungary's Constitutional Transformation," *European Constitutional Law Review* 7 (2011): 183–203.

court packing alone, however. The institution itself had to be changed so that it would no longer prevent the majority in Parliament from ruling as it wished. Constitutional amendments served this goal by stripping the Court of its power of review in nearly all matters relating to the national budget and tax issues.

The immediate occasion for restricting the Court's jurisdiction was provided by the governing coalition's passage of a penalty tax on the overly high severance pay of public servants,[37] a decision that could count on large public support. The ruling coalition first passed a constitutional amendment designed to ensure the legality of a retroactive penalty tax, which could then be levied "if the income was given contrary to good morals."[38] This was followed by a law that imposed a 98 percent tax on all severance payments to public servants that were paid out after January 1, 2010 and exceeded two million forints (about €7,300 EUR). That this confiscatory, retroactive tax law was submitted to the Constitutional Court is as unsurprising as the fact that the Court overturned it.[39] What is striking is that the verdict was unanimous; even Judge István Stumpf, who had just been elected to the Court by the governing majority, affirmed the measure's unconstitutionality. The main thrust of the judges' ruling was that even under the new constitutional provision, the law was unconstitutional on the grounds that it taxed all severance payments without distinction, not simply those which offended good morals. Many of those affected had obtained their severances legitimately under to the then-current law and according to their employment contracts.[40]

From the government's point of view, the ruling read like an open declaration of war (familiar from the Sólyom era)—but one for which it

[37] Particularly scandalous were cases like that of the former personnel manager for Budapest's public transport company, who "had received severance pay in the amount of 100 million [forints], only to be rehired a short time later." Kispál, G. "Rechtsempfinden Versus Verfassung," *Budapester Zeitung*, November 2, 2010.

[38] Article 70/I(2) of the Constitution as of November 2010.

[39] Decision 184/2010. (X. 28.)

[40] Kovács, K. and Tóth, G. A. "Hungary's Constitutional Transformation," 92.

was prepared.[41] On the very same day, party whip János Lázár declared that the law would be passed again, though not before the Constitutional Court was stripped of its power to review regulations relating to the budget and tax and customs laws. The Court would not be allowed to review any provisions that could not also be the subject of a referendum. That Fidesz was ready to introduce a corresponding bill only a few hours later is a testament to the foresight brought to bear in this case. The bill was introduced with the explanation that the Constitutional Court's broad jurisdiction, which was "extraordinary compared to other countries," had been necessary in the first years following the fall of the communist system, as at that time there existed "a great need for the Court to assume a role in developing the law." In light of the "stabilization of the constitutional state," however, "this broad role is no longer appropriate at the present time."[42]

Various factors[43] may have contributed to the passage of a watered-down version of the constitutional amendment on November 16, 2010[44] Article 32/A(3) now specifies that the Constitutional Court

[41] If the governing coalition's aim had been limited to eliminating the previous government's disproportionately high severances, a simple revision of the planned legislation would have sufficed for this purpose. Among other things, this would have required defining more precisely the concept of income given "contrary to good morals," in order to differentiate between legitimate and illegitimate severances. This type of wording would very likely have been accepted by the Court, which had implicitly recognized the validity of the constitutional amendment despite its violation of the prohibition against retroactive legislation. Kovács, K. and Tóth, G. A. "Hungary's Constitutional Transformation," 19.

[42] Cited in "Befugnisse Des Verfassungsgerichts Beschränkt, Modifiziertes Strafsteuergesetz Beschlossen," *Hungarian Voice—Ungarn News Blog.* https://hungarianvoice.wordpress.com/2010/11/16/befugnisse-des-verfassungsgerichts-beschrankt-modifiziertes-strafsteuergesetz-beschlossen/.

[43] The government's proposal was met with a storm of indignation on the part of the opposition as well as that part of the public which was critical of the government. Yet even within the ranks of Fidesz and its coalition partner there were voices which advised against such a policy. With Hungary's presidency of the EU Council approaching, the government could have little interest in such bad press.

[44] Mayer, G. "Verfassungsgericht in Ungarn beschränkt," *Der Standard*, November 16, 2010. http://derstandard.at/1289608042835/Verfassungsgericht-in-Ungarn-beschraenkt.

can examine budgetary issues only if "the content of these statutes violates the right to life and human dignity, the right to the protection of personal data, the right to freedom of thought, conscience and religion or the right connected to Hungarian citizenship under Article 69 of the Constitution." As has already been correctly noted in the literature, searching for a legal logic that might link together and justify these criteria would be pointless; the conditions are politically motivated. Missing are those legal principles—such as the prohibition of discrimination or the right to property—on the basis of which the Constitutional Court had declared tax laws and other rules with financial implications to be unconstitutional in the past.[45]

The measures with which Fidesz is seeking to limit the influence of the Constitutional Court's jurisprudence are illustrative of the party's general strategy of remaking Hungary's political system with the aid of its constitution-changing majority. As State Secretary Mihály Varga explained the day after the verdict, it was not the policy that would have to be changed, but the Constitution. According to Varga, the Constitutional Court had found no fault with the tax itself, but because of formal rules had been forced to overturn it, thus preventing the relief to the national budget the tax would have brought. Therefore the time had come for these rules to be changed. The plan was put into action immediately. First, the special tax was once again enacted via another new constitutional amendment and legislation supported by it.[46] Even more importantly, however, the restrictions on the Court's jurisdiction did not remain temporary measures for the purpose of implementing specific policy goals, but rather were adopted with almost no changes into the new constitution Article 37(4). Laws and regulations pertaining to the national budget may furthermore be reviewed only with reference to a narrowly defined list of fundamental

[45] Decision 184/2010. (X. 26.) See Kovács, K. and G. A. Tóth, "Hungary's Constitutional Transformation," 194.

[46] The criterion that the income has been given contrary to good morals was removed from the constitution. In return, a five-year window was introduced during which period "special" retroactive taxes could be levied. A new law then decreed on this basis that all public sector severance packages over 3.5 million forints (about €18,000) be taxed at an additional 98 percent. Kovács, K. and G. A. Tóth, "Hungary's Constitutional Transformation," 192.

rights, though this restriction applies only to the substantive aspects of laws. Formal errors, i.e. those pertaining to "procedural requirements for the drafting and publication of such legislation," can still be subjected for review by the Constitutional Court without restriction. Literally, the measures are only temporary, i.e. "as long as state debt exceeds half of the Gross Domestic Product." As the level of Hungary's national debt is not expected to cross this 50 percent threshold any time soon, the limitations are here to stay in the foreseeable future. That this was not intended from the start is hard to believe not least because of the way in which this restriction of the Court's jurisdiction has been executed. It ultimately was made a top priority by Orbán, assisted by his party's own deliberate preparations and ready to implement his scheme even in the face of resistance.

The Court's past activism needed to be checked, and Fidesz had a favorable opportunity to do so. That its attacks on the Court led to a loss of prestige both at home and abroad was unpleasant, but this was consciously accepted by party strategists. Additionally, there were no political actors to be found who were able or willing to campaign on the Court's behalf. The opposition was nothing to worry about, the public was in part quickly neutralized as a threat by the popularity of harsh measures against the grifters of the unloved previous government, and the European Union was legally powerless. Moreover, having won this ground, Orbán's strategy was obviously to take the topic off the agenda. The constitutional solution is to be understood in this sense: the restrictions on judicial review are found not in Article 24, which enumerates the powers of the Constitutional Court, but in Article 37, under the rubric of "Public Finances." The rules concerning the Court's jurisdiction make no reference to these subsequent restrictions.

The (hidden) agenda

What may also not be transparent to outside observers is one of the essential principles encoded in the preamble to the new constitution from which Fidesz has drawn much of its energy in its quarrel with the Constitutional Court. Hungarians, the preamble claims, deny any statute of limitations for "the inhuman crimes committed against the Hungarian nation and its citizens under the national socialist and communist dictatorships."[47] Observance of the formal rule of law is thus robbed of its normative foundation, as was also the case in the verdicts of the Sólyom Court. If the legislative power cannot effect a lasting correction of the Constitutional Court's jurisdiction, the constituent power can. And the Orbán government leaves no doubt that this is its intention. Hungarians "do not recognize the communist constitution of 1949, since it was the basis of a tyrannical rule;" moreover, they "proclaim it to be invalid."

This explicit rejection of the 1949 Constitution may seem superfluous—it was ultimately replaced by the Constitution of 1989, and even that was over twenty years ago. In the worldview of the new Hungarian government, however, delegitimizing the 1989 Constitution is crucial, as is breaking with the strategy of promoting the fiction of its legality as represented by the Constitutional Court. The goal is not only to push the previous constitution—which formally still bore the title ("Act XX of 1949")—closer to its Stalinist predecessor, but also to delegitimize case law built on the foundation of the old constitution. Ultimately, according to the preamble, the 1990s are also included among "the decades in the twentieth century leading to moral decay" that must be overcome through a "spiritual and intellectual renewal." Other elements of the preamble, which according to the constitution itself is legally binding [Article R(3)], also point in this direction. In contrast to the Constitutional Court, which has invoked the principles of the universal rule of law, the preamble refers to Hungary's "historical constitution," which holds historically symbolic meaning for conservative Hungarian nationalists[48] but is utterly ambiguous in its normative content.

The preamble makes clear that it was not the roundtable negotiations which represent Hungary's vital new beginning. Instead, the "current liberty was born of our 1956 Revolution," the ideals of which would be realized only now, after twenty years that prolonged the "moral decay" that had been the result of the developments in the

[47] See also the introductory points 1–7 in the Transitional Provisions of the Fundamental Law in this volume.

[48] See for a critical analysis of the creation of this political symbolism at in the 19th century Bak, J. and A. Gara-Bak, "The Ideology of a 'Millennial Constitution' in Hungary," *East European Quarterly* 15, 3 (1981): 307. See also Sándor Radnóti's contribution in this volume.

20th century.[49] In other words, those who were (and are) "on the other side," particularly Socialists and Free Democrats, are not among the pillars of the new constitution. The drafters of the constitution thereby address that part of the population which believes, as former President of the Court Sólyom recently put it, that "the reason behind their current poor economic and social stations is that there never was a real regime change." Fidesz can thus sell its restriction of the Constitutional Court's power as part of a political program designed to restore the country's morals and correct the mistakes of the past. The battle over the Court has thus become a battle over how the past is interpreted.[50]

The Court's reaction

Initially the Constitutional Court reacted to the parliamentary majority's attacks against it by mobilizing the two legitimizing resources that remain at its disposal: the invocation of "Europe" on the one hand, and on the other of its monopoly on interpreting the constitution, whereby the Court furthermore does not shy away from taking recourse to the "invisible constitution" if it must. It is in this sense that one must understand a statement to the press, released by the Court in both Hungarian and English, in which the judges take objection to the government's intentions and point out that the Constitutional Court "is one of the most important institutions, which serves as a guarantee of the democratic state under the rule of law" and is responsible for "the protection of the Constitution, constitutionalism and the fundamental rights of the citizens."[51]

---

[49] Whether the 1990s are part of this "moral decay" remains unclear: The preamble proclaims the formation of the first Parliament in May 1990 as "the beginning of our country's new democracy and constitutional order," but the language of the preamble makes it clear that the constitutional drafters reject the constitutional and political heritage of the last two decades.

[50] This point is explicitly made by Sólyom. "Address by President László Sólyom to the International Conference Marking the 20th Anniversary of the Establishment of the Constitutional Court, Budapest, November 23, 2009." *The homepage of the Constitutional Court of the Republic of Hungary*. http://www.mkab.hu/index.php?id=laszlo_solyom__president_of_the_republic_of_hungary.

[51] See for this and the following quotations "Press Release on the Modification of the Constitutional Court's Fields of Competence." http://www.mkab.hu/index.php?id=press_release_on_the_modificiation_of_the_constitutional_court_s_fields_of_competence.

Its powers of review, the judges state, are comparable to those of other constitutional courts, and *ex post facto* review of legal norms requires that the Court's power "extend to all legal norms, irrespective of their subject-matter" and that the Court be "entitled to annul unconstitutional norms." That is to say, a judicial review process that would have different effects on different areas of the law is (exceedingly) constitutionally dubious. The judges furthermore insisted on addressing a structural weak point of the new government, namely the European context in which Hungary exists: "[T]he legislature has to reckon with the possibility of inspections carried out by the European Court of Human Rights and by the European Court of Justice even in areas excluded from constitutional review." In other words, Hungary's unilateral approach, which falls short of constitutional standards, could prove to be short-lived in light of the country's membership in both the Council of Europe and the European Union.

The Constitutional Court did not stop at these suggestions, however, as two subsequent cases demonstrate:

(1) In a decision regarding the constitutionality of statutory rules which would allow public servants to be fired without requiring that any reasons be given for the dismissal, the Court asserted the significance of European law. In its verdict,[52] it declared the statute to be unconstitutional to the extent that it concerned public officeholders. The judges conceded that it might be necessary to make it easier to dismiss public servants in order to increase the quality and efficiency of public administration. However, the dismissal of officeholders without reason—against the backdrop of European standards regarding employment law—would violate the constitutional law pertaining to the holding of public office.[53]

[52] Decision 8/2011. (II. 18.)

[53] The Constitutional Court suspended the verdict from taking effect until May 31, 2011, as it would have otherwise been impossible for officeholders to resign on their own in the absence of a statutory provision. A later Decision 29/2011. (IV. 7.) invalidated the law pertaining to the dismissal of public employees on similar grounds. However, the European Court of Human Rights holds that there has been a violation of the right to a fair hearing of a former governmental official dismissed from service, because the Constitutional Court decisions did not open the way for an effective remedy. *K.M.C. v. Hungary*, no. 19554/11, July 10, 2012.

(2) October brought the hotly anticipated verdict on the new draft of the so-called "98 percent law." At this time, the constitutional amendments were already in effect which prohibited the Court from reviewing laws of taxation on the basis of their compatibility with principles of equality, the rule of law or other criteria that normally play a role in "constitutional tax law." Despite this clear directive, the Court unanimously declared the law unconstitutional on the basis of the principle of human dignity outlined in Article 54(1), one of the few constitutional benchmarks for judging budget-related laws that yet remained. The judges argued that levying a further 98 percent tax upon income on which taxes had already been paid violated the human dignity of those affected. Amounts already collected would have to be repaid. The verdict, however, applied only to the period 2005–2010, which had been taxed retroactively.[54]

One could describe the legal argument that a retroactively applied tax is a violation of human dignity as "creative;" it certainly is not undisputed. Yet it expresses the Court's intention to assert certain constitutional principles—specifically: the prohibition against retroactive legislation and the principle of equal treatment under the law—against a positivistic reading of the constitution. The extraordinary circumstances required the Court to take a detour via the most universal standard of protection the constitution had to offer: human dignity. This strategy links up effortlessly with Sólyom's concept of the "invisible constitution," a coherent system of constitutional principles that does not conform to the changing constitutional priorities of political majorities, but rather exists independently,[55] and the application of which is decided by the Constitutional Court alone. In this sense, the Court's verdict on the constitutionality of the "98 percent law" strengthens its claim to sovereignty in interpreting the (invisible) constitution. But that was not the last word on the issue. According to the reports of various tax authorities, the verdict resulted in a loss of two to four million Euros. Speaking in Parliament, Fidesz party leader János Lázár claimed the decision was "damaging to Hungary's interests." Beyond that, the governing coalition's parliamentary representatives apparently

[54] Decision 37/2011. (V. 10.)

[55] Sólyom, L. "Introduction to the Decisions of the Hungarian Constitutional Court," 41–42.

did not find the content of the Court's argument worth criticizing. The law was simply passed again, with the difference that the 98 percent tax now applied only to severances that had been paid out after January 1, 2010.

During the final session in which the Constitutional Court handled cases on the basis of the old constitution, the Court declared Hungary's controversial religion law and parts of its internationally criticized media law, as well as parts of the government's trial reforms, to be unconstitutional.[56] This "last revolt"[57] of the Court occurred in opposition to vehement dissent from the newly-appointed Judge Béla Pokol.[58]

There is plenty of room for controversy on the question whether these acts of resistance earn the Constitutional Court the title of a defender of constitutionalism or, rather, as some observers claim, represent symbolic gestures meant to conceal its general failure to stand up against the illiberal politics of the government.[59] What is of interest here is that the conflict between the two institutions has a structural nature. It is not only their disparate and at times irreconcilable views in individual areas of politics which are at issue, however. From a theoretical perspective, the dispute between the Constitutional Court and the governing majority reflects a fundamental struggle for the future of liberal—read: constitutional—democracy. This is a clash of different ideas about the

---

[56] Decision 164/2011. (XII. 20.), Decision 165/2011. (XII. 20.), Decision 166/2011. (XII. 20.)

[57] "Letztes Aufbegehren: Verfassungsgericht in Ungarn Verurteilt Mediengesetz," *Pester Lloyd*, December 19, 2011. http://www.pesterlloyd.net/2011_51/51urteilmediengesetz/51urteilmediengesetz.html.

[58] Against the backdrop of his previous critiques, it is not surprising that his dissenting opinion espoused a "radical understanding of democracy" that emphasized the primacy of the Parliament. It remains to be seen whether Pokol will be able to get his way in the medium term.

[59] The Constitutional Court declared in 2011 that it does not have competence to review either the constitutionality of the constitution-making procedure or the substance of the constitutional amendments. Decision 61/2011. (VII. 13.) It is also noteworthy that it was the Venice Commission, and not the Constitutional Court, who reviewed and criticized *substantially* the 2011 cardinal acts on the churches (Venice Commission, *Opinion 664/2012*) and the judiciary (Venice Commission, *Opinion 663/2012*). See also the late Decision 33/2012. (VII. 17.) on the unconstitutionality of the lowering of the judicial retirement age.

relationship between the law and politics as well as about the legitimacy of democratic laws within a parliamentary system of government, with opposing consequences for the role of constitutional jurisprudence.

From the point of view of a modern constitutionalist, the Hungarian government's actions have ripped serious holes in the protection of basic rights.[60] Judge István Stumpf, elected to the Constitutional Court by the Fidesz majority, expressed this succinctly when he stated that the curtailment of the Court's jurisdiction had left "an open wound on the body of constitutional democracy."[61] Parliament can now act unconstitutionally without fear of being punished for having violated the Constitution. For proponents of a democratically legitimized parliamentary sovereignty, on the other hand, the Constitution does not possess some higher legitimacy but rather is merely a set of guidelines that can be changed by the will of the majority in Parliament. From this perspective, no "normative surplus," no "invisible constitution" that stands in opposition to democratic majorities can legitimately exist; and in this sense, a Parliament that passes laws according to existing rules cannot, by definition, act unconstitutionally.

The Majoritarian Quest for Sovereignty

"Hungary will be great again, / Worthy of its old, great honor!" With these lines from Sándor Petőfi's "National Song" (*Nemzeti dal*), Viktor Orbán effectively summed up the electoral goals of his party. A return to former greatness, i.e. in essence, a reclamation of the values that made Hungary strong, and an overcoming of the present lethargy of the state and society. In the words of the Fidesz leader, what was at stake was nothing less than a "revolution," a break with the present constitution, which was still "infected" by the era of communism and occupation, from which the entire country continued to suffer.

---

[60] This view is shared by the Venice Commission. See *Opinion 621/2011 on the new Constitution of Hungary* in this volume.

[61] This statement is obviously very close to Sólyom's point of view, coming from a Fidesz appointee. "Constitutional Court Annuls Church Law, Parts of Media, Criminal Law." http://www.politics.hu/20111220/constitutional-court-annuls-church-law-parts-of-media-criminal-law/.

According to Orbán, the election in April finally provided the long-awaited opportunity to bring together the nation and convert its will into political power. A pre-announced revolution, as it were. And real electoral success on April 11 only encouraged the new prime minister. In his view, it was not merely a decisive election, it was a "revolution in the polling booth," with a dual mandate from voters for their representatives: first, as a parliament, to form a government capable of action, and second, as a national assembly, to devise a new constitution.[62] At least two aspects of this interpretation of the will of the electorate are worth taking note of: first the concept of "revolution" itself, but also the sovereign interpretation that elevates an election to a revolutionary act. A synopsis of these two aspects will ultimately make clear the challenges currently facing the Constitutional Court's jurisdiction.

What revolution?

Like so many other political terms, the notion of revolution is overdetermined and thus at bottom requires a theoretical conceptualization. Yet even if one leaves these conceptual problems aside and instead wishes to understand revolution in perceptual, real-world terms, little remains to justify its use here.[63] There was no profound transformation of social structures or radicalization of ideological paradigms, nor did any epochal progress in the consciousness of freedom occur. Nor, for that matter, can a "revolutionary climate" be identified in which forms of collective effervescence experienced a subsequent authorization from which institutional structures of order emerged. The elections did in fact give the governing party the two-thirds majority needed to amend the constitution. Yet this outcome and the consequent opportunities for reshaping the political system were not only the result of overwhelming agreement among voters—the victors of the election received about 53 percent of the popular vote—but also a product of

---

62 In his ceremonial speech at Vörösmarty Square in Budapest on April 25, 2010, Orbán stated: "We... are a constituent assembly and parliament, which makes a new system at the same time."

63 For an overview of the various conceptions of revolution, see Lembcke, O.W. and F. Weber, eds. "Emotion und Revolution. Spurenlese zu einer Theorie der affektiven Grundlagen politischer Ordnungen," *Österreichische Zeitschrift für Politikwissenschaft* 39, no. 2 (2010): 171–186.

the existing framework of institutional order, first and foremost the right of suffrage and the way it functions to build majorities. In short, the concept of revolution invoked here was less socially justified than politically motivated. It referred not to actual groundbreaking change, but rather was employed in a sort of anticipation of the program the government intended to implement. When Orbán spoke of a national unity, of a "system of national cooperation,"[64] this was in no way an expression of real, already-existing relationships, but rather the imagining of a social future his politics are dedicated to realizing. His political program has drawn its legitimacy from the new government's symbolic representation of such a unity. It claims to shine a light on this absence of community and at the same time aspires to grant itself lasting validity. The ideal site for this is the Constitution—especially in the political landscape of Hungary, where negotiations over a new constitution failed in 1996. The Fidesz government's fixation on the constitutional question has been fueled significantly by the opportunity it has had to combine electoral success with remaking the constitution. The purpose is to achieve a double legitimization: the new order and its constitution are (additionally) legitimized by their symbolic break with communism, and this symbolism attains legal validity by the fact of "Hungarian" values attaining constitutional status.

The projection of revolution was intended to create room for two political projects of which Orbán and his men have made little secret. They want to increase both the government's capacity for action as well as the bonds between the state and society. These two goals give Orbán's vague talk of "national cooperation" a concrete form; what is essentially at issue is a politics of unity, of inclusion, that—as Carl Schmitt never tired of emphasizing—can be achieved only through exclusion. And the invocation of Schmitt is actually not as far-fetched as it may appear at first glance. Like Schmitt, the new Hungarian government is convinced that a "strong state" offers the best guarantee

[64] Orbán made this proclamation shortly after his electoral victory. Considering the term "national cooperation" more closely, its Orwellian dimension immediately becomes apparent. While "cooperation" connotes inclusion and an openness to dialogue, what is really meant here is the exclusion of everybody who does not subscribe to the ideological definition of "Hungary" promoted by Fidesz.

against the antagonistic pluralism of modernity, and like Schmitt, it understands unity to mean homogeneity, uniformity. This has consequences for its understanding of the constitution. According to this view, the 1989 Constitution not only bears the stigma of its legal continuity with the 1949 Constitution, it is moreover a patchwork of partisan political compromises and thus cannot claim to be an expression of the formative power of the people.

From Schmitt's perspective, this power of the people is not manifested in constitutional charters anyway. Rather, it reveals itself in the existence and strength of the state, not least in distinction to other states. The unity of the people in the state is the result of a political act that cannot be derived from any sort of content or precepts, but rather represents an existential and at the same time sovereign decision about the people's own destiny. It is a genuinely political act, according to Schmitt, because the establishment of such a unity is ultimately determined by no criteria other than the fact of the decision about its membership, in which friend is distinguished from enemy. At the same time, the decision reveals who speaks in the name of the people. Constitutional questions are thus always questions of sovereignty. They call into action that power which can in fact embody and—from the top down—implement the national unity of the people. The chutzpah with which the Hungarian government (re)interpreted its electoral victory as a revolutionary mandate reflects essential elements of Schmittian constitutional theory. This is seen, for example, in its specific understanding of national unity, which Orbán and his followers have conceived not only as uniformity within society on the basis of values but also as a quasi-identitary relation between the state and the people. Consequently, it is then the task of the government to further shape and consolidate national unity, including by means of creating a new constitution. The government's capacity for action and power of implementation are taken to be the credentials which legitimize the undertaking; Fidesz, too, seems to agree that constitutional questions are questions of sovereignty.

Nowhere is the dialectic link between sovereignty and legitimacy more clearly demonstrated than in the dual role of Parliament, which according to the will of the government is both law-maker and constitution-maker. One could say that, at least superficially, such democratic self-empowerment is part of the tradition of the French Revolution. Because the Third Estate constituted the entirety of the nation, it had not only the power but also the right to seize the reins of political self-determination, transform the gathering of the Estates-General into a National Assembly and thereby establish the foundations of France's new order. This is how history actually played out, in many essential ways following a script that had been written specifically for this purpose: *Qu'est-ce que le tiers état?*, the pamphlet that made its author Emmanuel Joseph Sieyès an overnight celebrity among the French revolutionaries. Undoubtedly, the rupture with the *ancien régime* was to be a complete and thorough one. At the same time, however, Sieyès introduced a distinction which continues to be relevant for modern constitutional theory and the practice of drafting constitutions, that between the *pouvoir constituant* and the *pouvoirs constitués*. The latter powers operate on the basis of a (legally) constituted order; the former has itself no prescribed form, but rather on behalf of the nation seeks out the appropriate practices which produce the system of political order in the first place—and its office ends the moment this work is completed. Mixing these two powers, according to Sieyès, threatens to abolish the qualities of responsibility and accountability inherent to the office, with the result of dissolving the bonds between nation and constituent power. If it represented the nation only symbolically, without itself being subject to the democratic decision-making process, this would be a characteristic of absolutism, of the old order, not the new.

The Hungarian government has ignored these considerations, not out of ignorance, but out of indignation. The time is past to distinguish between preparation and implementation in this constitutional process; even the raised quorums designed to compel inclusion of the opposition in the drafting of proposals are no longer seen as binding by the Fidesz government. This and other measures make abundantly clear the government's desire to seize uncontrolled freedom in reshaping the political order. Its intended parliamentization of the political system is to be understood in this light; the aim is to ensure and perpetuate the privilege of interpretation in constitutional questions that the heads of government have claimed for themselves with the support of their two-thirds majority in Parliament. In its classic Westminster variant, the parliamentary system of government distinguishes itself by keeping the number of players who hold veto power at a minimum. Political checks and balances are exercised within the framework of a temporal separation of powers; Election Day is Judgment Day, but in the interim the polity is ruled by a kind of temporary dictatorship of the majority.[65] Hungary introduced a parliamentary system after 1989, the "pure" realization of which, however, was restricted by the institutionalization of a constitutional court system equipped with broad and powerful jurisdiction. The parliamentarization of government that Fidesz has striven for with its drafting of a new constitution is thus primarily aimed at weakening the powers of the Constitutional Court, namely through its self-assured claim to be the true representative of the sovereignty of the people. This sort of Schmitt-oriented understanding of constitutional government leaves little room for a constitutional court that is independent of and able to assert itself against its political founders.[66] It is also a rejection of the balance between democratic self-determination and a constitutional rule of law that is characteristic of modern constitutionalism.

What is the Court's role?

Abolishing the right to bring constitutional lawsuits against the government without further standing is a cornerstone of Orbán's strategy of parliamentarization—and it has consequences for the role of constitutional jurisprudence, which had previously been defined by abstract review. Given the low hurdles for bringing an *actio popularis*, the Court was in a position to take an active role in reshaping the old socialist law, and in fact it did. At the same time, by acting in this capacity, it grew into the role of being the (only) effective opponent of a government backed by a parliamentary majority. The unitary nature of the political system has further reinforced this "politicization" of constitutional jurisprudence. In contrast to, say, German federalism, there are no other powerful veto players.

---

[65] In the classical case of United Kingdom, this temporary dictatorship of the majority is moderated by extra-legal balances, constitutional conventions, and a distinct political culture. See e.g. Dicey, A.V., *Introduction to the Study of the Law of the Constitution* (10th edn., London: MacMillan, 1961).

[66] In his debate with Hans Kelsen over the question of who ought to be guardian of the Weimar Constitution, Schmitt famously argued in favor of the president as opposed to a constitutional court.

The new political circumstances are to radically change these existing structures. Abstract *ex post facto* review can now be initiated only by the government, one-fourth of the members of Parliament, and the commissioner for fundamental rights [Article 24(2)(e)]. A remedy of constitutional complaint was introduced [Article 24 (2)(d)]. Considered in terms of comparative law, these amendments seem *prima facie* reasonable, particularly as the new requirements for demonstrating that one's rights have been directly violated could lead to a reduction in "querulous," frivolous complaints.[67] Given the current balance of political power, however, the new rules effectively mean that for now, Hungary's democratic opposition has no access to abstract judicial review. The socialists, the greens, and the new parliamentary group comprising the "democratic coalition" cannot bring before the court any issues demanding abstract review without cooperation from the extreme right-wing Jobbik. Given his chosen political identity, the president cannot be considered a co-guardian of the constitution at the present time. And the new office of the commissioner for fundamental rights, which has replaced the previous system of four ombudsmen, was staffed for a period of six years by the Fidesz-dominated Parliament. The prospects for regulating government policy by means of abstract judicial review will thus be bleak for years to come.

If the opposition had had a real say in the drafting of the constitution, it would never have agreed to these amendments in their existing form given these repercussions. The changes to the constitution effectively transformed Hungary from a multi-polar, liberal democracy into a majoritarian one; Fidesz made little secret of the fact that this was its intention. Orbán led the way by going on the offensive. Per one of his statements in October 2010: "Not the people's notion of justice should be changed, but the old rules which we come up against." The Constitutional Court was moreover to be thanked, Orbán continued, for bringing to the government's attention those measures which were necessary to fulfill the people's notion of justice but which the old constitution prohibited. The new constitution would resolve these con-

[67] In March 2011, Péter Paczolay, who has been president of the Court since 2008, stressed that the Court's position is to require appellants to demonstrate that they have been personally affected; furthermore, the direct access of citizens to the Constitutional Court remains desirable.

flicts. János Lázár, leader of the Fidesz parliamentary group, argued during the parliamentary debate over the law that the restriction "will not weaken the rule of law but strengthen democracy since it fulfills the will of the electorate." Justice Minister Tibor Navracsics defended the measures during a trip to Poland by pointing to countries such as Great Britain or the Scandinavian states that lack a constitutional court entirely, noting that no one would call those nations' democracies into question. Hungary has "only entered the next stage in development of democracy." Lázár ultimately came to the point in a 2010 radio interview, saying that "in extraordinary times, extraordinary means are necessary" and "meeting an election promise never weakens but strengthens democracy." Hungary must thus be rebuilt as a "majoritarian democracy… where there is no need for democratic brakes and counterweights, as in the last 20 years."[68]

These assertions make clear how closely tied Fidesz' electoral victory is to its "rival," i.e. constitutional jurisprudence, in the party's self-perception. The essence of these statements is that true democracy can at bottom only be obtained by reducing the jurisdiction and scope of influence of the once-powerful Hungarian Constitutional Court. What is overlooked, if not concealed, are the disintegrative effects of a model of competition based on political majorities—and in this case dominance—over a political culture which rests not on an evolving democratic consensus on "dos" and "don'ts" (particularly as relates to the governing majority), but on a tradition of mistrust among the various political camps. Political mistrust is typical of societies in transition where the break between the old political order and the foundations of its legitimacy has been severe and irreconcilable. This sort of rupture can be compensated for by, among other things, the establishment of (fictive) continuities of legality that supply processes and procedures for negotiation between the representatives of the antagonistic camps, as well as by prudent moderation through pragmatic compromises. A constitutional court can take on both functions, but it is then tasked with stimulating processes of learning that contribute to allowing a lived democratic praxis to emerge from those pragmatic compromises.

---

[68] Quotes are obtained from the archive of the Hungarian News Agency (MTI). English translation of MTI-news and information see at http://www.politics.hu.

In terms of intellectual history, the idea that a constitutional court can contribute to the emergence of such praxis, particularly under the conditions of regime change, may be traced back to the French Revolution. With his pamphlet *Qu'est-ce que le tiers état?* (1789), Sieyès not only forged the intellectual weapons of the Revolution, he also wracked his brain over how the long and grueling constitutional debate in France could come to an end. A new constitution would be designed to prevent abuses of power like those which occurred under the rule of Robespierre, where obsession with virtue soon escalated into Terror, and establish much longed-for stability.

Yet how can one bring a revolution to rest without betraying its goal? Sieyès attempted to a give a comprehensive answer to this question with his two Thermidor speeches (1795) before the Commission of Eleven. A key component of his conception lies in the idea of a multi-functional constitutional court, a *jury constitutionnaire* in part designed to neutralize disputes between the public powers as the court of the state and, as the court of the people, to protect the fundamental rights of individuals. Additionally, as the court of cassation, the *jury* is given the task of guarding the constitutionality of the political process. For Sieyès, the master of constitutional theory, this also includes precisely that dimension of politics which aims to constitutionalize its own rules of play. Thus according to Sieyès, changing the constitution—without which process a constitution is in danger of losing its open-ended, forward-looking character and ultimately its orienting force—also falls within the *jury*'s sphere of responsibilities. Its task is to recognize important challenges and prepare their normative adaptation by amending or adding to the constitution, in order to then subject them to a democratic decision made by the people and their representatives in Parliament.

What Sieyès developed on the drawing board of political theory is nothing less than a prototype of modern constitutional courts.[69] The organization of the process by which a constitution may be changed has particular significance for the development and stabilization of democratic structures in a politically-divided society. In terms of

[69] Developed in unitary France, Sieyès' conception lacks a sense for the disputes over federal jurisdiction that some see as the actual cradle of constitutional jurisprudence.

political theory, Sieyès' aim is to give form—to the greatest possible extent—to the might of the constituent power through the legally-regulated interactions of political institutions, in order to make its work a component of the political order. It is not the sovereignty of an extra-constitutional constituent power (*pouvoir constituant*) which attends to fundamental constitutional questions, but the authority of the highest constituted powers (*pouvoirs constitués*) under the guidance of the *jury constitutionnaire*. This could have been the role of the Hungarian Constitutional Court on that nation's path toward a new constitution. Now it is up to the Court to regain enough authority to remove the question of sovereignty from everyday democratic politics.

Governance, Accountability, and the Market

MÁRTON VARJU

This chapter investigates the provisions of the new Hungarian Fundamental Law on governance, accountability and the market. Its main contention is that the Fundamental Law largely failed to reflect on the changes experienced by European states, including Hungary, in the past decades affecting the relationship between the state and individuals, the modes and mechanisms of accountability, and the relationship between the state and the market. These changes emanated from processes, such as the emergence of the regulatory state following periods of deregulation, privatization and marketization,[1] the decline of government by control in delivering public policy and the parallel emergence of the managerial post-regulatory state,[2] and the contraction of the state following the economic and fiscal crisis after 2008.[3] The challenges of European market integration[4] and the demands of European and global governance[5] led to further significant changes in the functioning of the state in Europe.

The Fundamental Law, by choice, takes only a limited account of several contemporary developments and practices in organizing the

[1] Majone, G. "The Rise of the Regulatory State in Europe," *West European Politics* 17 (1994): 77.

[2] Scott, C. "Regulation in the Age of Governance: the Rise of the Post-Regulatory State" in *The Politics of Regulation*, Jordana, J. et al, eds. (Cheltenham: Edward Elgar, 2004), 145.

[3] The Fiscal Implications of the Global Economic and Financial Crisis, IMF Staff Position Note (2009) SPN/09/13.

[4] Armstrong, K. *Regulation, Deregulation, Re-regulation* (London: Kogan Page, 2000).

[5] Lee, S. and S. McBride, "Introduction: Neo-Liberalism, State Power and Global Governance" in *Neo-Liberalism, State Power and Global Governance*, Lee and McBride, eds. (Dordrecht: Springer, 2007), 1.

state, most of which are already present in Hungary. The dispersal of public powers among public and private actors, the availability of more responsive modes of governance other than law, the state functioning as mediator or facilitator in the policy process, the benefits of horizontal and cooperative, even network-like, relationships of governance between public and private actors, the increasing role of the market in the public sphere, or the accountability dilemmas of the regulatory and the post-regulatory state should warrant a reaction from a 21st century constitutional text. By no means do I intend to resolve the "fundamental mismatch"[6] between constitutions and newer paradigms of governance and accountability. Instead, I will engage in a criticism of the narrow understanding of governance, the narrow construction of public power and accountability, and the gaps in the constitutional regulation of the market in the Fundamental Law. The necessity for a broader constitutional understanding of governance and accountability is clearly indicated by the legal excesses and the accountability problems generated in the regulation of fiscal policy discretion and instituting a constitutional debt ceiling, one of our central issues.

In the following, I will attempt to provide a comprehensive account of the Fundamental Law's provisions on governance and accountability with specific regard to the implementation of contemporary ideas of governance and of new designs for accountability. The fiscal constitution, the rules and institutions introduced to control fiscal policy discretion, will be scrutinised extensively as an example in the Fundamental Law of experimenting with new governance and accountability. The chapter will close with a discussion on a related topic, the incomplete recognition and regulation in the Fundamental Law of the relationship between the state and the market.

A Constitution for Government or for Governance?

The Fundamental Law discharges its task of establishing a constitutional government in a series of core provisions. It incorporates the basic constitutional tenets of government and prescribes a system of

[6] De Búrca, G. and J. Scott, *New Governance, Law and Constitutionalism*, 5, http://www.ucl.ac.uk/laws/clge/docs/govlawconst.pdf.

government. Its principles include popular sovereignty, democratic legitimacy and the rule of law (Article B), and the separation of powers and the state's monopoly of coercion (Article C). Its primary method of governance includes generating legislation and legislative instruments and their subsequent enforcement by state institutions. The basic framework for law as the primary means of government is provided in Articles R-T on the legal system which establishes the hierarchy of the Fundamental Law over legislation and legislative instruments, determines the legal nature of the Fundamental Law and legislative tools, and regulates the fundamental conditions of legality for legislation and legislative instruments.

The system for government is introduced in the institutional provisions of the Fundamental Law in the part "The State" covering Parliament, the president of the republic, the Government, autonomous regulatory bodies, the Constitutional Court, the judiciary, the Prosecution Office, the commissioner for fundamental rights, and local governments. The regulation of state institutions follows the principle of separation of powers, and prescribes basic institutional provisions determining powers, tasks, terms of office and accountability. The rules and processes of government place the state in the center and affirm its institutional superiority in a hierarchical system of government. In the only visible process of government, rule making falls onto Parliament, Government, local governments and autonomous regulatory bodies, power for a preliminary scrutiny of legislation is given to the president of the republic, and the Constitutional Court discharges the task of constitutional review of legislation. Government determines the tasks, powers and structures of public authorities, the steering of public authorities is carried out by the responsible minister, public authorities and local governments are entrusted with the application and enforcement of rules, the judicial review of administrative action falls onto the judiciary, and maladministration may be subject to investigations by the commissioner for fundamental rights.

Based on the text, these provisions of the Fundamental Law should secure a constitutional government in Hungary. The disappointment comes from the inability of the Fundamental Law to recognize that the exercise of public powers and the development and delivery of public policy and the provision of public goods, beyond a hierarchical and state centered system and process of government, assumes more complex, inclusive and flexible arrangements for governance. It does not recognize a requirement of quality from government (a constitutional principle of good government), the availability of means of government other than law (e.g. procurement), or a requirement of an open and participatory process of policy making (a constitutional principle of open government and a definition of citizenship from the perspective of governance).

The concept of regulation of the Fundamental Law is painfully outdated. It envisions a monolithic and omnipotent state capable of delivering public policy by the means of law. Without questioning the importance of command and control regulation by law, the Fundamental Law could have offered a constitutional presence for other "techniques" of regulation, such as regulation by competition,[7] or self-regulation by private (economic) actors and other self-regulatory practices where private regulatory activity is coordinated or recognized by the state, such as co-regulation and meta-regulation.[8] The assumption in the constitutional text that the law corresponds to the public good and the public interest represents a rather naïve conception of law and regulatory activity ignorant of the obvious and documented failures of legal regulation.[9]

The Fundamental Law is not entirely silent about new modes of governance and the quality requirements of governance. The Budget Council in the fiscal constitution represents a new form of expert governance (Article 44). It also incorporates in the fundamental rights catalogue a right to good administration (Article XXIV) which refers to the right of individuals to a fair, impartial administrative procedure in a reasonable time, the duty of public authorities to give reasons, and the right to hold public authorities liable for damages caused by unlawful conduct. Access and participation of individuals is regulated in Article XXV including the right of individuals to submit petitions, complaints

[7] Daintith, T. "The techniques of government" in *The Changing Constitution*, Jowell, J. and D. Oliver, eds. (Oxford: Oxford University Press, 2004), 209–236, and Baldwin, R. and M. Cave, *Understanding Regulation* (Oxford: Oxford University Press, 1996), 35–39.

[8] Coglianese, C. and E. Mendelson, "Meta-Regulation and Self-Regulation" in *The Oxford Handbook of Regulation*, Baldwin, R. et al., eds. (Oxford: Oxford University Press, 2010), 148–149.

[9] Baldwin and Cave, *Understanding Regulation*, 35–39.

or proposals to public authorities. The only reference to good governance can be found in Article XXVI which when expanding on the gradual obligation of the state to utilize the benefits and advances of science and technologies mentions the aims of effectiveness of governance, improvement in the delivery of public services, transparency of public affairs and equal opportunities.

Beyond Articles XXIV-XXVI, including a rather narrow concept of good administration, and, as a result, of maladministration, and a promise of improving the quality of government, the Fundamental Law in its extensive general provisions could have recognized a subsidiarity principle advocating government closer to citizens, a principle of good governance referring to the quality of public services, public goods, legislation and administrative action, and a principle of a participatory policy process on all levels of government. The constitutional regulation of the legal system could have called for an effective, responsive and economical use of law in governance, supplementing a constitutional principle of better regulation. The few rules on the administrative state, such as the right to good administration (Article XXIV), could have been expanded to cover a broader idea of administrative justice beyond the requirements of a fair administrative process and effective remedies, to incorporate a broader understanding of good and bad administrative behavior, and to describe a more horizontal and cooperative relationship between public authorities and individuals, in particular, social and economic stakeholders. A clear constitutional obligation to measure the impact, efficiency and quality of regulatory and bureaucratic performance could have also found expression among these rules.

The provisions of the Fundamental Law on citizenship could have provided the constitutional basis for a new, enhanced relationship between the state and individuals. Disappointingly, Article G considers citizens as mere subjects of rights and obligations providing them a more reduced status than that of active contributors and partners in governance. This is compatible with the state-centered and hierarchical vision of public affairs dominating the Fundamental Law conceiving citizens as bystanders or spectators in the public arena where the traditional political and legal actors engage in the act of government. The Fundamental Law narrows citizens' access to the Constitutional Court, reduces the breadth of the ombudsman system, and delimits the availability of referendums. The right to good administration in Article XXIV contains only a right to a fair administrative process and offers little for the publicly engaged citizen. It would require an extremely liberal reading of Article O on the individual's obligation to contribute to attaining state and community tasks to regard it as a foundation of governance processes built on citizen participation and contribution. There is no indication that the Fundamental Law would recognize the multifaceted nature of citizenship which would distinguish between the statuses and actions of citizens as voters, clients, consumers, and interest- and stakeholders. It does not recognize citizens as capable of contributing to the democratic legitimacy of governance, as endowed with interests and information crucial for the governance process, as facilitators of accountability and transparency, and as partners in collaborative processes of governance.

The narrow language used by the Fundamental Law in relation to governance deprives Hungarian constitutionalism from valuable components. It misses the opportunity to define the nature, the means and the benchmarks of the process of governance. In general, it fails to bring citizens closer to the public arena, closer to government.

Accountability

Accountability is a concept central to modern constitutionalism. Principally, it refers to the ability to constrain public power by requiring government to give account of *and* account for its action or inaction. Accountability and its neighboring principles of openness and transparency should deserve a mention among the most fundamental building blocks of the Hungarian constitutionalism, the rule of law and democracy, which the new Fundamental Law failed to achieve. It does, however, incorporate the fundamental mechanisms of political and legal accountability.

Forms of political and legal accountability are regulated in the institutional provisions of the Fundamental Law. These include parliamentary scrutiny, committees and reports (Articles 1–7), parliamentary scrutiny and control of Government in European Union matters (Article 19), the responsibility of the prime minister and ministers (Articles 18, 20–22), the scrutiny of legislation by the president of the republic (Article 6), the constitutional review of legislation (Article 24), the judicial review of administrative measures and local government legislation (Article 25), criminal responsibility (Articles 25 and 29), investigations by the commissioner for fundamental rights (Article 30), and the scrutiny of local government legislation by the county-level representations of central government, named "government offices" (Article 32). Fiscal accountability, which gained recognition among the fundamental principles of Hungarian constitutionalism in Article N prescribing a balanced, transparent and sustainable budget management, is regulated extensively in the part dealing with public finances.

Legal and political accountability as regulated in the Fundamental Law would satisfy many readers. It suggests a comprehensive system of accountability under the rule of law of a state-centered order of government in which links of accountability are maintained between the organs of the state. These methods of accountability are not faultless,[10] and deserve separate scrutiny. Our analysis, however, focuses on a more generic deficiency of the Fundamental Law's system of accountability; that related to the constitutional regulation of new governance.

If we acknowledge that governance is in fact an inclusive process based on participation and contribution by a variety of public and private actors, accountability must also include elements of participation and communication and assume a deliberative and discursive relationship.[11] Horizontal structures of governance need to build on horizontal designs of deliberative democratic legitimacy between the state, citizens, consumers, information providers and stakeholders, which in turn requires horizontal forms of accountability. Furthermore, the diffusion in contemporary states of public power among public and

---

[10] The system of administrative justice under the Fundamental Law is rather narrow. It focuses on judicial review and a now hierarchically centralized ombudsman office. There is no indication that the Fundamental Law would recognize extending the system of non-judicial grievances and remedies against the state, or that its concept of justice would acknowledge negotiation or dispute resolution within the administrative state. A constitutional definition of administrative discretion and the relationship of accountability and administrative discretion could have enriched the good administration provisions of Articles XXIV-XXVI.

[11] Dowdle, M.W. "Public Accountability: Conceptual, Historical and Epistemic Mappings" in *Public Accountability*, Dowdle, ed. (Cambridge: Cambridge University Press, 2006), 12.

private actors (e.g. by means of privatization, or local community empowerment) requires broader modes of control and accountability which must go beyond "the relatively formal legal conception of constitutional controls."[12] While existing traditional modes of government require traditional forms of legal and political accountability and strong forms of bureaucratic accountability, in relation to new forms of governance (e.g. expert governance, or self-regulation) the Fundamental Law should have recognized qualitatively different methods of accountability.

The Fundamental Law acknowledges many elements of public accountability: elections, a professionalized bureaucracy, judicial review, openness and transparency. Its weak good governance principle, its limited vision of new governance and its even more reduced approach to regulation and regulatory qualities, such as responsiveness and gradual intervention,[13] however, question its ability provide the foundations of a genuinely comprehensive system of accountability. Market-based methods of public accountability, which rely on the pressure of competition and consumer demand, such as public procurement, are entirely avoided from the constitutional text. Methods of private accountability, such as private and public audits, disclosure obligations, quality management and quality control regimes, benchmarks, good practices, peer review, or interest generation, should have been given some form of constitutional recognition. The Fundamental Law should at least have attempted expressing the problem of accountability excesses and making the tradeoff between effective governance/administration and accountability.[14]

Lacking a comprehensive concept and system of public accountability is a genuine constitutional hiatus. The Fundamental Law already faces an accountability crisis having introduced a new form of expert governance in fiscal matters by the Budget Council without providing a convincing system of similarly novel accountability arrangements. The

---

[12] Scott, C. "Regulatory Governance and the Challenge of Constitutionalism" in *The Regulatory State*, Oliver, D. et al., eds. (Oxford: Oxford University Press, 2010), 19.

[13] Ayres, I. and J. Braithwaite, *Responsive Regulation* (Oxford: Oxford University Press, 1992).

[14] Bovens, M. *Public Accountability*, 5, www.qub.ac.uk/polproj/reneg/contested_meanings/Bovens_Public%20Accountability.connex2.doc.

participation of Hungary in different constructions of new governance and new accountability in the European Union, including the new EU Fiscal Stability Treaty,[15] should require recognition from the constitutional text. The drafters should have considered an "extended approach to accountability"[16] for the new constitutional order.

New accountability may find its way into constitutions by means of regulating principles and institutions. Accountability could have been granted a place among the "Foundations" of the Fundamental Law with references to alternative mechanisms of control and accountability. The narrow regulation of open government and transparency, as the right of access to information and a promise of an institution to enforce that right (Article VI), the reference to higher transparency in the obligation of the state to implement the achievements of science and technology (Article XXVI), and the random institutional provisions referring to transparency suggest a lower constitutional priority of these fundamental elements of accountability. The novel element of autonomous regulatory bodies in governance (Article 23) was introduced without addressing the long obvious accountability problems of agency regulation.[17] The only area where the drafters of the Fundamental Law made a visible effort to advance accountability is the regulation of the fiscal constitution.

The fiscal constitution

The fiscal provisions of the Fundamental Law[18] address the failure of governments to deliver (socially) optimal fiscal policy, the most obvious cause of which being the deficit bias of governments,[19] and

[15] Treaty on Stability, Coordination and Governance in the Economic and Monetary Union.

[16] Scott, C. "Accountability in the Regulatory State," *Journal of Law and Society* 27, 1 (2000): 42–43, 38.

[17] Graham, C. *Is there a Crisis in Regulatory Accountability?* Centre for the Study of Regulated Industries Discussion Paper No. 13, The Chartered Institute of Public Finance and Accountability (1995).

[18] Previous efforts include Act LXXV of 2008 on the prudent management of state resources and budgetary responsibility.

[19] Debrun, X. et al. "Independent Fiscal Agencies," *Journal of Economic Surveys* 23, 1 (2009): 44, 48–50.

provide a response to the deficit and debt problems arising from weak fiscal discipline and the misuse of fiscal policy discretion by delineating the legal (constitutional) boundaries of fiscal policy and establishing institutions and processes to control fiscal policy discretion.[20] From the international debate, it is not entirely clear that the introduction of both rule-based and institutional responses is necessary[21] and what their actual impact on fiscal decency may be,[22] the success of any constraint on fiscal policy discretion depending ultimately on the government's commitment to its original fiscal mandate.[23] In general, what is expected from the constitutional (legal rules) on fiscal policy is to discourage undesirable uses of fiscal discretion and introduce a commitment regime for governments to achieve optimal policy results.[24]

The framework for fiscal policy and fiscal accountability in the Fundamental Law regulates the budget and the budgetary procedure, introduced a ceiling for public debt, includes provisions on national assets, and establishes an institutional framework for the delivery of fiscal policy and accountability in fiscal policy. The general constitutional principles are included in Article N according to which fiscal policy must be based on the requirements of stability, transparency and sustainability. In achieving this, the primary responsibility rests on Parliament and Government with an obligation on the Constitutional Court, the judiciary, local government and state bodies to observe these principles in the course of their functioning.

---

[20] Debrun, X. and M.S. Kumar, *Fiscal Rules, Fiscal Councils and All That: Commitment Devices, Signalling Tools or Smokescreens?*, Banca d`Italia Workshop on Fiscal Policy: Current Issues and Challenges (2007), 479, http://www.bancaditalia.it/studiricerche/convegni/atti/fiscal_policy/Session%203/Debrun_Kumar.pdf.

[21] Debrun, X. *Democratic Accountability, Deficit Bias and Independent Fiscal Agencies*, IMF Working Paper 11/173 (2011), 9, "In principle, any high level legal norms effectively tying policy makers to ex-ante optimal policies could achieve the same theoretical result as an 'independent' institution with an adequately determined mandate."

[22] Debrun and Kumar, *Fiscal Rules*, 480, and Debrun et al., "Independent Fiscal Agencies," 66.

[23] Debrun et al., "Independent Fiscal Agencies," 75.

[24] Debrun et al., "Independent Fiscal Agencies," 47.

Transparency, a key element of fiscal accountability, is granted a crucial role in designing revenues and expenditures (Article 36(2)), executing the budget (Article 37(1)), the transfer (privatization) of national assets (Article 38(4)), and the payment of subsidies or monies arising out of a contract (Article 39(1)). Transparency is also emphasized in relation to the management of public monies and national assets, and information about it qualifies as information available for public disclosure (Article 39(2)). Public procurement is not identified as a key aspect of transparency in public spending. More importantly, in relation to the management of state or local government owned "business organizations," while subjected to the general fiscal policy requirements of lawful, practical and efficient management of public funds under Article 37(1), the constitutional requirement of transparency is deliberately missing (Article 38(5)), although transparency could apply if this provision is read together with Article 39(1).

Accountability attached to the fiscal transparency requirements is spelt out much less clearly. There is no constitutional regulation of approving the implementation of the budget, which received only a brief mention among Parliament's competences in Article 1(2)(c),[25] and its constitutional consequences. Compared with the grave consequences attached to the inability of Parliament to adopt a budget (Article 3(3)), this seems misbalanced. The institutional regulation of the State Audit Office provides for the core of fiscal accountability provisions in the Fundamental Law. The State Audit Office is empowered to monitor the lawfulness, practicality and efficiency of implementing the budget (Article 43). The elements of the general system for legal, political and bureaucratic accountability, regulated elsewhere in the Fundamental Law, are also applicable.

---

[25] According to the Constitutional Court, this provision being a mere description of competences is unjusticiable. Decision 15/1993. (III. 12.) and Decision 908/E/2009. (September 27, 2011). Decision 908/E/2009. also declared that the technical-legal aspects of public finances, such as the content of the balance, the means used administering the balance, the accounting of financial operations, or the application of accounting principles, are not constitutional questions. With fiscal discretion opened so wide and constitutional control kept so narrow, a more detailed constitutional regulation could have been warranted under Article N.

The rule based response: the debt ceiling

The problems of fiscal irresponsibility and the misuse of fiscal discretion are addressed in the Fundamental Law in the provisions on a constitutional debt ceiling and the related institutional and procedural arrangements. The debt ceiling is set at a 50 percent ratio of public debt and the GDP, and contains an obligation to reduce public debt and a constitutional limitation on increasing public debt.[26] It applies to Parliament and Government in the adoption and the execution of the budget, and prohibits assuming debts and financial obligations the result of which would bring public debt beyond the ceiling, or increase public debt while public debt is above the ceiling (Articles 36(4-5) and 37(2-3)).

Introducing a stringent constitutional debt ceiling, while it enhances the credibility of fiscal policy and indicates that fiscal responsibility is taken seriously, is not an entirely convincing legal and political response to fiscal problems as it suggests that a simple fiscal solution is possible in complicated times[27] and that the fiscal performance of governments can now be measured in a simple way.[28] Also, a debt ceiling alone may be insufficient to achieve fiscal discipline. It needs to be linked to a high level of fiscal transparency, noting that transparency alone may suffice for a committed government to achieve fiscal decency, and to an appropriately designed institutional framework. A complementary institutional response may be necessary to resolve the dilemma inherent in rule based responses, the demand for simple and

---

[26] There are clear obligations following from EU law (Article 126 TFEU) to manage national debt and deficit. Article 1 of Protocol 12 on the Excessive Deficit Procedure sets out the reference values referred to in Article 126(2) TFEU. These reference values are three percent for the ratio of the planned or actual government deficit to Gross Domestic Product at market prices; 60 percent for the ratio of government debt to gross domestic product at market prices. Hungary has been subject to an on-going excessive deficit procedure by the European Commission since July 2004 which culminated in the suspension of payments from the Cohesion Fund in March 2012.

[27] Debrun, *Democratic Accountability*, 3.

[28] Eichengreen, B. et al. *Public Debts: Nuts, Bolts and Worries* (Geneva: International Center for Banking and Monetary Studies, 2011), 22.

strict yet flexible constraints on fiscal policy discretion,[29] and to enforce the binding commitment of governments to fiscal discipline.[30] Governments must be genuinely committed to fiscal decency as the credibility of rule-based constraints, which may already be weakened by introducing an unfeasibly strict debt ceiling, may quickly evaporate. This was the case for the new Hungarian constitutional debt ceiling the credibility of which was practically annihilated by Act CXCVI of 2011 on the stability of public finances in Hungary which before the entry into force of the Fundamental Law suspended the application of the debt reduction obligation following from the debt ceiling until January 1, 2015 liberating the present Parliament from its constitutional obligations.

Apart from its temporary suspension, the most significant limitation of the debt ceiling in the Fundamental Law is that its regulation leaves the boundaries of fiscal policy discretion under its scope undefined. This weakens its credibility considerably leaving no indication in the current state when public debt exceeds the debt ceiling, apart from the prohibition of increasing public debt, concerning the timing and rationing of debt reduction.[31] On the one hand, this may allow for good maneuverability in delivering fiscal policy and avoids fiscal rules suffocating policy discretion.[32] On the other, it questions whether the debt ceiling would be able to constrain fiscal policy discretion and lead to achieving effective debt reduction. In these circumstances, the effective implementation of the debt ceiling will depend on the proper functioning of the related institutional and procedural arrangements and on the application of the said 2011 act on the stability of public finances regulating the implementation of the debt reduction obligation in the budgetary process.[33]

---

29 Debrun et al., "Independent Fiscal Agencies," 46 and Eichengreen, *Public Debts*, 22.

30 Debrun and Kumar, *Fiscal Rules*, 79.

31 Criticised in Várnay, E. "Közpénzügyek az Alkotmányban—az adósságfék" [Public finances in the constitution: the debt ceiling] *Jogtudományi Közlöny* 10 (2011): 483–495.

32 On the necessity of debt variability and fiscal flexibility, Danninger, S. *A New Rule: "The Swiss Debt Brake,"* IMF Working Paper 02/18 (2002): 7 and 13.

33 The key provision is Section 4(2) of Act CXCVI of 2011 on the stability of public finances in Hungary which provides that the increase in public debt compared to public debt in the previous fiscal year must not supersede the difference between 50 percent of the rate of real increase of inflation and

The regulation of exemptions allowed from the debt reduction obligation to accommodate unforeseen circumstances and events for the purpose of ensuring flexibility and responsiveness in fiscal policy may also prove problematic. Article 36(6) accepts that in case of a state of emergency (a "special legal order"), or when the economy suffers an enduring and significant relapse ("a significant and enduring national economic recession"),[34] national debt may be increased by the necessary degree.[35] The requirement of necessity represents a crucial boundary to fiscal discretion, made available to government under the exemptions, allowing public debt increases necessary to finance emergency relief operations or to reinstate the overall economic equilibrium. It is unclear, however, whether the necessity requirement would provide a justiciable principle of fiscal proportionality available before the Constitutional Court or ordinary courts to challenge the legal measures authorizing state borrowing or assuming other financial obligations.[36] On this basis, the necessity requirement under Article 36(6) would be alone for the government to assess indicating the availability of considerable fiscal policy discretion when resorting to the exemptions.

---

the GDP. It appears that Section 4(2), not forgetting that its implementation was suspended until January 1, 2015, leaves a considerable leeway in relation to the debt reduction obligation. In this light, the constitutional debt ceiling is more flexible and dynamic than originally expected reading the constitutional text, which is not necessarily a disadvantage. Ultimately, even with these provisions in place, debt reduction will depend on the political commitment of Hungarian governments.

34 In the meaning of Section 7 of Act CXCVI of 2011 a decrease in the real value of the GDP will constitute a significant and enduring recession; a rather liberal reading of the exemption clause allowing for a constitutionally uncomplicated departure from the obligations embedded in the debt ceiling.

35 "To the extent necessary to mitigate the consequences of the circumstances" and "to the extent necessary to restore the balance of the national economy."

36 The Hungarian provisions are similar to Article 115(1) of the Grundgesetz and the interpretation of those provisions by the German Constitutional Court, BVerfG, 2 BvF 1/04 (131). It is denied that a justiciable principle of fiscal proportionality would follow from the exemption or could be created under general constitutional principles, Siekmann, H. "The Burden of an Aging Society as a Public Debt, The Perspective of the German Constitutional Law and the Law of the EU," *European Public Law* 13, no. 3 (2007): 489–518.

The institutional framework

With broad fiscal policy discretion available under the debt ceiling in achieving debt reduction and under the exemptions from the debt reduction obligation, only the related institutional and procedural responses seem to be able to provide a safeguard against the abuse of fiscal policy competences by government. The creation of institutions called fiscal councils has been a popular solution for constraining fiscal discretion around the world entrusting them with the task of improving the transparency and predictability of public finances and strengthening the long-term orientation of fiscal policy.[37]

There are two major types of fiscal councils.[38] The first have the task of ensuring transparency by reporting publicly on budgetary developments and commenting on fiscal policy, and are staffed with independent experts. The second are endowed with genuine decision making powers in the budgetary process and are staffed with government officials and other political appointees. Debrun distinguishes between independent fiscal agencies which equipped with a clear mandate to enforce fiscal targets mimic the institutional standing of central banks on the fiscal side, and fiscal councils which lack a direct legal mandate over fiscal policy but are able to provide independent analysis and projections and a normative assessment of fiscal policy.[39]

The Budget Council of the Fundamental Law falls into the category of independent fiscal agencies; a unique constitutional development in the world where governments have so far refrained from introducing such stringent form of institutional constraint on fiscal policy.[40] The institutional brakes are provided in Article 44 which equips the Budget Council, entrusted with the task of monitoring the "feasibility" of the budget, with the power of preliminary endorsement of the budget. By exercising the power of endorsement, the Council ensures that

[37] Eichengreen, *Public Debts*, 29. Fiscal councils inform voters after assessing fiscal performance whether to sanction or reward government fiscal policy, and may be given competences to enforce compliance with fiscal rules, Debrun, *Democratic Accountability*, 11–12.

[38] Eichengreen, *Public Debts*, 30.

[39] Debrun et al., "Independent Fiscal Agencies," 45.

[40] Ibid., 73.

the budget in preparation complies with the debt ceiling and the debt reduction obligation. The full scope of the formal power of preliminary endorsement is determined in Act CXCVI of 2011 on stability of public finances. The veto power of the Council could be applied in relation to the adoption of the budget and any subsequent modification of the budget necessitated by the debt reduction obligation or by an enduring and significant relapse in the economy. The legal consequence of the Budget Council declining to endorse the budget is that Parliament is constitutionally prevented from passing the budget. This could lead to the fall of the government as under Article 3(3)(b), in case the budget for a given year is not accepted by March 31 of that year, the president of the republic may dissolve Parliament and order new elections. A further institutional brake is available in the jurisdiction reserved for the Constitutional Court to annul the budget on grounds that the procedural requirements in the constitutional text for adopting the budget have been violated (Article 37(4)).

The power of preliminary endorsement and the consequences of using those powers presents a serious challenge to the constitutional principle of democratic legitimacy. Restraining the competences of a democratically elected Parliament in fiscal policy matters by an independent expert body requires serious justification and that justification may only come from producing an output of socially optimal fiscal policy. The fall of government and the dissolution of Parliament in a fiscal crisis may also prove to be a politically irresponsible constitutional solution, questioned by the OECD whether it could ever be deployed constructively.[41] As a less radical but constitutionally more balanced alternative, the refusal of the Budget Council to endorse the budget could attract the legal consequence of an absolute or qualified majority vote instead of a majority decision in Parliament on the budget, as applied in the regulation of the Swiss debt brake.[42] This would sustain executive continuity and would provide increased legitimacy to the execution of the budget.

The independence of fiscal councils, based on the experiences of central bank independence, was seen as an essential condition to their

[41] OECD Economic Surveys: Hungary 2012, 17, www.oecd.org/eco/surveys/hungary.

[42] Article 159(3)(c) of the Federal Constitution of the Swiss Federation.

appropriate functioning as expert-knowledge based controls of fiscal discretion.[43] Independence could be ensured by placing importance on professional qualities when appointing the members of the council, determining its composition, granting longer and non-renewable periods of office for members, placing restrictions on the government's ability to remove members, establishing prohibitions on government interfering with or instructing the council, or establishing safeguards for its budgetary and institutional independence. The independence of the Budget Council is by and large provided for by the relevant constitutional rules. It is composed of three individuals, its president, the president of the Hungarian National Bank[44] and the president of the State Audit Office. The presidents of the Council and the National Bank are appointed by the president of the republic and the president of the State Audit Office is elected by two-thirds majority of Parliament for 12 years.[45] Formally, these provisions should guarantee the independence of the Budget Council from the executive.

A higher degree of independence for bodies endowed with public powers represents a serious challenge for the constitutional requirement of accountability. In such constructions, the "chain of command" and the hierarchical structure for delegating powers are broken.[46] Their task of constraining public policy discretion or delivering public policy following principles based on expert knowledge without being influenced by government and other public or private stakeholders makes the application of traditional forms of accountability nearly impossible. Bodies, such as the Budget Council, require experimental (reflexive,

43 Calmfors, L. and S. Wren-Lewis, "What should fiscal councils do?" *Economic Policy* 26, 68 (2011): 651, 668, and Eichengreen, *Public Debts*, 96. The crucial factors in their independence were identified as appointment by Parliament, a liberal mandate, the availability of sufficient data and information, excluding government interference with their work or resources, and appointment of members on the basis of their professional experience.

44 Under Article 41(1) of the Fundamental Law the National Bank of Hungary is the central bank of the country.

45 The latter criticized by the OECD as capable of undermining the political acceptability of the Budget Council in a political gridlock, OECD Economic Surveys: Hungary, 17.

46 Harrington, C. and Z. Umut Turem, "Accounting for Accountability in Neoliberal Regulatory Regimes" in ed. Dowdle, H.W., *Public Accountability*, 197–200.

spontaneous, hybrid)[47] regimes of accountability which may operate with soft, quality-focused mechanisms of accountability, such as peer review, benchmarking, or institutional competition.[48] The failure to determine how these independent bodies may be held to account is a severe constitutional omission.

The Fundamental Law does not assign a specific mechanism of accountability to the Budget Council. We find no *ex post* control procedures to verify that the use of powers by the Council was compatible with its mandate and which may offer the application of sanctions for deviations from the mandate. The aim of ensuring sustainable and optimal fiscal policy led to establishing an institutional arrangement in the Fundamental Law which created an accountability gap in the constitutional text. The Budget Council is endowed with the hard constitutional competence of preliminary endorsement, which may amount to a power of veto, for exercising which the Council cannot be held to account under the constitution.

The lack of accountability raises serious doubts regarding the legitimacy of delegating fiscal policy competences to the Budget Council.[49] In fact, the evident legitimacy and accountability problems of independent fiscal agencies, such as the Budget Council, should convince governments to refrain from introducing independent expert bodies with hard powers into the constitutional framework of fiscal policy.[50] The independence of the Council in itself is insufficient to remedy its legitimacy problems, and the failure to regulate its accountability on the constitutional level is a strong normative argument against its

[47] Scott, C. "Spontaneous Accountability" in Dowdle, *Public Accountability*, 190.

[48] Ibid.

[49] An "independent and impartial body with no electoral accountability would not only be a recipe for chaos: it would be profoundly undemocratic," by Lord Nolan, *R. (Alconbury Developments Ltd) v. Secretary of State for the Environment, Transport and the Regions* [2001] UKHL 23, para 60, referring to placing the controversial ministerial competence, exercised with a view to policy considerations, in the hands of an independent body.

[50] Introducing a strong impartial enforcer of fiscal rules is constitutionally impossible owing to the lack of democratic accountability, Debrun et al., "Independent Fiscal Agencies," 61. The power of the Budget Council is "beyond democratic considerations," "clearly excessive" in light of the Council's resource problems, and should be removed, OECD Surveys: Hungary, 51.

existence. The Budget Council may derive some legitimacy from its policy output or expert knowledge. However, if its legitimacy builds on these elements, the relevant arrangements for accountability must also include these qualitative factors, which considering the narrow vision of the Fundamental Law on accountability seems as an unachievable constitutional exercise in Hungary.

Ensuring the legitimacy and accountability of the Budget Council assumes a strong and clear constitutional mandate. The strength of the mandate is crucial as the delegation of fiscal policy competences are based on the contention that political representatives will harmfully distort fiscal policy[51] and that Parliament is unable to deliver optimal fiscal policy. The mandate must rely on a social consensus on what constitutes sound fiscal policy. In the absence of this, the Council's exercise of powers will not be legitimate. The clarity of the mandate is also essential for holding the Council to account. It should specify which competences are delegated and indicate the criteria for exercising the delegated competences.

The mandate provided in Article 44 for the Budget Council is rather rudimentary. It refers to the task of monitoring the feasibility of the budget and the enforcement of the debt ceiling. Assumedly, Article N on the requirement of a balanced, transparent and sustainable budget management provides a principle-based background for the Council's mandate. However, there is no further indication of a normative basis for the Council's accountability. Commentators pointed out that the Fundamental Law avoided defining fundamental issues, such as the Council's working competences, its power to monitor the implementation of the budget, its institutional background and institutional attachment to the policy process in government, and more importantly the criteria and substantive framework for its assessment of the budget.[52] The failure to include in the Fundamental Law specific rules of fiscal discipline other than the debt ceiling, for instance a constitutional obligation of multi-annual budgetary planning, means that the conceptual grounding of accountability on the basis of the current normative elements, especially Article N, is weak.

---

51 Debrun et al., "Independent Fiscal Agencies," 54.

52 Várnay, "Közpénzügyek," V.1. Not remedied reassuringly by Act CXCVI of 2011.

The accountability dilemmas associated with the Budget Council are related to the more general accountability problems of the Fundamental Law. It was argued above that new modes of governance, if acknowledged in constitutions, require new approaches in accountability. The Budget Council, an independent body entrusted with the task of delivering expert governance, is a peculiar addition to the state-centered system of government in Hungarian constitutionalism. Under a mandate to influence public policy with expert opinion and quality being the most significant benchmark of activities carried out under that mandate, the traditional forms of legal and political accountability will not be sufficient to hold the Budget Council accountable.

The question is whether the Fundamental Law is able to incorporate the desired new forms of accountability. Placing the accountability of the Budget Council to the international level, for instance by designing an accountability mechanism within the European Union framework, in the absence of the relevant international framework is only a theoretical possibility. Constitutions would have more difficulty accommodating other less formal international solutions, such as peer review by fiscal councils in other states or by international expert organizations (the IMF, or the OECD).[53] Expert peer review by independent domestic analysts or independent public policy organizations, the effectiveness of which depends on the transparency and publicity of the peer review process, would require considerable flexibility to achieve constitutional recognition. The most obvious solution is introducing a procedural instrument, such as a constitutional obligation of reporting to Parliament, or of providing sufficient reasons when the power of endorsement is used, which contributes to achieving accountability by increasing transparency and by requiring the Council to explain how and why it reached its decision.[54] Another solution could be empowering Parliament to depart with an absolute or qualified majority vote from the decision of the Council on the preliminary endorsement of the budget. This was mentioned earlier as a potentially less stringent consequence of the budget failing to meet the expectations of the Council than that offered in the Fundamental Law

[53] Calmfors and Wren-Lewis, "What should fiscal councils do?", 669.

[54] Act CXCVI of 2011 provides for a duty to give and publish reasons for Budget Council decisions.

and could serve for the Budget Council as a channel of accountability to Parliament.

Besides the accountability gap associated with the Budget Council, the fiscal constitution in the Fundamental Law suffers from another serious accountability problem. This is the conditional curtailment of the competences of the Constitutional Court in constitutional review which diminishes the possibility of holding fiscal legislation to account. Article 37(4) provides that until the national debt ratio is above the constitutional debt ceiling the Constitutional Court will only be allowed to review and annul acts of Parliament relating to the budget, on the implementation of the budget, on taxes, other revenues and customs duties, and local taxation on grounds that they infringe the fundamental right to life, human dignity, the protection of personal data, the freedom of thought, conscience and religion, or the provisions on citizenship.[55] Commentators pointed out that under prevailing constitutional practice the anxiety of government, which led to the curtailment of the competences of the Constitutional Court to interfere with measures introduced for the reduction of public debt, is unwarranted, as the jurisprudence of the Constitutional Court acknowledges a broad margin of appreciation of Parliament and Government in matters falling within fiscal policy.[56] The flexibility sought to be gained by reducing constitutional accountability, appears to have been available under the former, more complete system of constitutional review.

The conditional suspension of competences of the Constitutional Court, introduced with the intention to keep fiscal policy discretion by and large intact, read together with the broad fiscal policy discretion available under the debt ceiling indicates that the Fundamental Law in achieving debt reduction gave primacy to the instruments designed by Government and adopted by Parliament over competing constitutional values and requirements. In meeting the debt reduction obligation, fiscal policy discretion is granted immunity from constitutional consid-

---

[55] The provisions were already available in the 1989 Constitution (Article 32/A(2)), introduced by the reigning government as a widely criticized response to an unfavorable decision from the Constitutional Court which declared provisions of an act placing retroactively a 98 percent tax burden on certain benefits paid to civil servants "violating the sense of justice in society" unconstitutional. Decision 184/2010. (X. 28.)

[56] Várnay, "Közpénzügyek," VI.1.3.1.

erations which otherwise would be crucial in determining what would qualify as a correct policy response to achieve socially optimal fiscal policy. Lacking the possibility to subject fiscal policy to considerations of social equity and redistribution, expressed in the constitutional principles of non-discrimination, solidarity, private autonomy and protection of property rights, questions whether fiscal policy delivered under the new constitutional framework would be politically and socially optimal and acceptable.

The accountability gap in the fiscal constitution caused by Article 37(4) is not absolute. First, ordinary domestic courts, with the help of the EU Court of Justice, are not prevented from engaging in the review of fiscal legislation on the basis of European Union law, the law of the internal market and EU human rights in particular. Provided that the measure under challenge falls under the scope of EU law, its compatibility with the fundamental right to property and other fundamental rights available in the jurisprudence of EU courts, or enumerated in the EU Charter of Fundamental Rights can be subject to judicial scrutiny by Hungarian courts. Examining by ordinary courts whether Hungarian fiscal legislation lawfully interferes with the rights of traders in the internal market is strikingly similar to constitutional review by the Constitutional Court on the basis of the right to property and the freedom to pursue an economic activity.[57] Under the jurisprudence of the Constitutional Court, which excluded on jurisdictional grounds the constitutional review of domestic legislation in light of EU law,[58] recourse to the EU Charter of Fundamental Rights is not available before the Constitutional Court to circumvent the restrictions in Article 37(4).[59] Challenging fiscal legislation before the Constitutional Court on grounds of incompatibility with international human rights treaties, such as the European Convention on Human Rights, is a viable alternative, noting that the relevant competence of the Constitutional Court is reserved for applications from a restricted group of privileged applicants.[60]

---

[57] See, Snell, J. "Non-Discriminatory Tax Obstacles in Community Law," *International and Comparative Law Quarterly* 56 (2007): 339.

[58] Decision 29/2011. (IV. 7.) and Decision 72/2006. (XII. 15.)

[59] Decision 368/D/2010. (October 25, 2011).

[60] Ibid.

Moreover, the jurisdiction available under Article 37(4), if applied wisely by the Constitutional Court, could in principle achieve a certain level of constitutional accountability of fiscal legislation. The indication that despite its reduced jurisdiction the Constitutional Court could exert control on fiscal discretion comes from a ruling which held that "the retroactive taxation of a legal income, generated without infringing any laws, in a tax year which has ended, represents such a degree of public interference with an individual's autonomy that it lacks an acceptable reason, and thus, violates human dignity."[61] However, the recent jurisprudence of the Constitutional Court, proceeding in a new personal composition, indicates that a strict reading of Article 37(4) will be followed.[62] Legal certainty, general constitutional aims, the right to social security, the presumption of innocence, the right to good reputation, and non-discrimination were regarded as justiciable grounds outside the remit of Article 37(4).[63] The only avenue open is to apply the non-discrimination principle relating to natural persons under the right to respect for human dignity triggering the application of Article 37(4) to fiscal legislation.[64]

The new fiscal constitution of the Fundamental Law is not an entirely assuring development in Hungarian constitutionalism. Despite its generally progressive contribution, it generated a serious crisis in constitutional accountability and it is uncertain that the balance struck in the constitutional provisions between constraining and encouraging fiscal discretion would achieve the desired socially optimal fiscal policy. In the current state of public finances in Hungary, when the debt ceiling functions as a debt reduction obligation, the nearly untamed discretion of government in meeting that obligation questions whether the rule based response of the debt ceiling is capable of remedying the debt bias of governments. The new institution, the Budget Council may change the rules of the game using its hard competences but cannot succeed without a genuine commitment from government to achieve

---

[61] Decision 37/2011. (V. 10.)

[62] Decision 1618/B/2010. (October 3, 2011).

[63] Decision 225/B/2007. (September 27, 2011), Decision 1618/B/2010. (October 3, 2011), and Decision 379/B/2003. (October 18, 2011).

[64] The jurisprudence remains unsettled, see, Decision 3/B/2008. (October 25, 2011), Decision 744/B/2010. (October 11, 2011), and Decision 1428/B/2011. (October 25, 2011).

sustainable public finances. The double accountability gap in the fiscal constitution is another pressing problem. The Fundamental Law failed to introduce accountability arrangements for the Budget Council, an "independent fiscal agency" endowed with hard constitutional competences, and the conditional suspension of the Constitutional Court's jurisdiction in fiscal matters guarantees nearly complete immunity for fiscal policy action from judicial oversight.

The State and the Market

The constitutional relationship between the state and the market is perhaps the area in which a new constitution could have introduced significant improvements. In Hungary, the role of the state in the market and the role of the market in the state have been subject to significant changes. Many public services are offered by economic operators competing for consumers in the market, the market is relied upon to increase accountability in public purchasing, direct state involvement in the economy was rolled back through privatization, and state regulatory intervention in the market is being reduced by deregulation and is subjected to control by means of better regulation programs and regulatory impact assessment requirements. The majority of these changes were the direct consequences of Hungary's membership in the European Union.

The gradual reduction of the state's presence in the market, the complex tasks entrusted upon the state in regulating the market, and the marketization of the public sphere is a conceptual minefield for constitutions. The issue here is the ability of constitutional texts to capture the complex relationship between the state and the market and the novel means of market governance by the state. Constitutions may struggle with articulating that powers traditionally associated with the state are exercised by private actors, that the state is expected to rely on novel powers and means in steering the market, and that the constitutional requirements transparency and accountability are expected to be extended beyond the public domain. Crucially, the effective delivery of public policy in the market may require horizontal, collaborative relationships among stakeholders and relying on or making room for regulatory instruments beyond traditional command and control regulation, such as different forms of self-regulation.[65] Constitutional texts with a state-centered approach to governance and the dominance of law as an instrument of governance may have limited capacities in this regard.

The Fundamental Law struggles with providing an adequate constitutional definition of the relationship between the state and the market. Its provisions create a rather loose constitutional framework for the operation of the market and treat the constitutional conditions for state intervention in the market in a similarly untaxing manner. The relationship between the state and the market is only subject to a handful of general constitutional objectives and economically relevant fundamental rights. Arguably, constitutions may only be required to provide a general constitutional framework for the economy allowing that framework to be filled with the economic policy of governments and the legislative background for economic activities under that policy. However, considering the constitutional challenges arising from the transformation of the role of the state in the market and the role of the market in the state, which should affect the constitutional regulation of public powers, governance, transparency and accountability, a more advanced constitutional regulation of the market would be desirable.[66]

The economic constitution

The constitutional foundation of economic policy and discretion in delivering economic policy is provided in Article M of the Fundamental Law. In this fundamental constitutional principle, Hungary commits to an economy based on free enterprise and fair competition while, like the 1989 Constitution, the Fundamental Law subscribes to a free market agenda. In the jurisprudence of the Constitutional Court, the constitutional aim of a free market does not favor a concrete model of a market economy and indicate particular boundaries of state intervention. It would receive substantial constitutional protection only

---

[65] Mörth, U. "Introduction" in *Soft Law in Governance and Regulation. An Interdisciplinary Analysis,* Mörth, U. ed. (Cheltenham: Edward Elgar, 2004), 6.

[66] In the U.S. context see Sunstein, C.R. "Conclusion" in *After the Rights Revolution* (Cambridge, Massachusetts: Harvard University Press, 1993).

when attached to a fundamental right, such as the right to property or the freedom to pursue an economic activity, or when state intervention represents a radical departure from a market economy, such as reintroducing economic planning for the whole of the economy.[67] Only a general obligation for the state to maintain a market economy and monitor its functioning may be deduced from Article M.[68] The obligation in Article M to protect the economy and consumers from anti-competitive corporate activity and the general obligation to protect consumers provide a more exacting license for intervention in the economy, without establishing concrete constitutional boundaries for competition and consumer policy discretion. These indicate a broad constitutional mandate and a wide margin of appreciation for the state to regulate the economy.

Article M, by subjecting state intervention in the market to nearly unrestrained economic policy discretion, achieves little in defining the constitutional relationship between the state and the market. Beyond enabling market regulation to pursue diverse economic and social policy objectives, it fails to recognize the variety of forms the state may intervene in the market and the ways and extent the market has penetrated the public sphere. Article M assumes a clear divide between the public and the private and suggests a construction in which the state may regulate the market by traditional formal means subject to traditional formal mechanisms of accountability. It turns a blind eye to public powers being exercised by actors in the private sector, to the necessity to extend considerations of the public sphere to the private sector, such as transparency, public responsibility, accountability and justice, and to the necessity for the state to influence the market by using non-conventional means, such as organizing networks, or steering self-regulation.

In mapping the regulation of the market in the Fundamental Law, Article M needs to be read together with further constitutional provisions found it the catalogue of fundamental rights and freedoms. The key provisions are Article XII on the freedom to pursue an economic activity and Article XIII on the fundamental right to property. The catalogue of fundamental rights also includes elements regard-

---

[67] Decision 33/1993. (V. 28.), Decision 54/1993. (X. 13.) and Decision 21/1994. (IV. 16.)

[68] Decision 19/2004. (V. 26.)

ing state intervention in the market for the promotion and protection of non-market values. These include equality (Article XV), labor law and health and safety regulation (Article XVII), social security (Article XIX), human health (XX), the environment (XXI), human dignity and integrity in research and commerce (Articles II and III), privacy, personal data and good reputation (Article VI), freedom of the press, the electronic media and communications (Article IX), and freedom of research and education (Articles X and XI). Some of these fundamental entitlements introduce more detailed constitutional provisions directing state intervention, such as an agriculture free of GMO and access to food and water under the right to health, the prohibition on the importation of waste under the right relating to the environment, and an explicit social element in the market: access to public services and housing under Article XXII.

The fundamental right to property provides the classical boundaries of state intervention in the market.[69] It does not establish immunity for the market from state intervention as it recognizes the legitimacy of interferences with property rights in the public interest and allows for the most extreme form of intervention, the expropriation of private property in the public interest (Articles I and XIII). Its scope is also limited. While it may incorporate the protection of certain legitimate expectations, it does not extend to the protection of market interests, commercial opportunities, or prospective gains in the market.[70] In the Fundamental Law, the possibility of state interference in the public interest is reinforced by the clause in Article XIII on social responsibility associated with ownership. This latter provision may indicate a market economy built on private property in which communitarian interests are given constitutional priority in the Fundamental Law over individual autonomy expressed by property rights. From this, a constitutional foundation for state intervention for the protection of shared interests, such as environmental protection, energy sustainability,

---

[69] Van Banning, T.R.G. *The Human Right to Property* (Antwerp: Intersentia, 2002), 167 and Bratza, N. "The Implications of the HRA 1998 for Commercial Practice," *European Human Rights Law Review* 5 (2000): 6–7.

[70] From the jurisprudence of the European Court of Human Rights, *Anheuser-Busch Inc. v. Portugal*, no. 73049/01, January 11, 2007, para 63 and *Pine Valley Developments Ltd. and Others v. Ireland*, no. 12742/87, November 29, 1991, para 59.

health and safety, or corporate responsibility could be deduced. The constitutional balance shifting towards communitarian interests is also reflected in the partial suspension of the competences of the Constitutional Court in the constitutional regulation of the debt ceiling (Article 37(4)) which by excluding the constitutional review of fiscal measures on the basis of the right to property indicates a constitutional presumption provided in the Fundamental Law that the interest of public debt reduction overrides the ownership rights of individuals.

The prevailing constitutional jurisprudence offers little to supplement the constitutional provisions relating to economic policy discretion and state intervention in the market. There is no indication that the jurisprudence would have responded to the new developments in the relationship between the state and the market. The case law holds that intervention with property rights must be proportionate and serve the public interests[71] and that property rights are accorded an economic edge representing the foundation for private social and economic autonomy.[72] Property rights are also regarded as entitlements on assets derived from one's value-generating work (or other activity of economic value).[73]

Another constitutional benchmark for the regulation of the market by the state follows from the fundamental freedom to pursue an economic activity. In the constitutional jurisprudence, it refers to work and other economic activity, and enshrines a right to pursue or continue an activity of economic value available to challenge state regulation interfering with that particular economic activity.[74] The right to pursue a profession may receive constitutional protection as a form of ownership rights when the license to pursue a profession and the right of access to the income generated under that license provide the subject matter of the legal dispute.[75] The freedom to pursue an economic activity receives the same constitutional protection as other fundamental rights,[76] and its utility in restraining state intervention depends on

[71] Decision 27/1999. (IX. 15.)
[72] Decision 64/1993. (XII. 22.)
[73] Decision 43/1995. (VI. 30.)
[74] Decision 27/1999. (IX. 15.)
[75] Decision 28/2006. (VII. 26.)
[76] Decision 881/B/1991. (November 9, 1992) and Decision 54/1993. (X. 13.)

whether the legal provisions in question aim at the right of the individual to engage in an economic activity, or concern the institutional arrangements of economic activity and the market. While the rights of individuals receive more stringent constitutional protection, the institutional arrangements may only be subject to a light touch control which would be available in exceptional circumstances, or when attached to other constitutional provisions, such as non-discrimination.[77]

Public ownership is regulated in the Fundamental Law in a piecemeal fashion.[78] It includes the possibility of expropriating private property (Article XIII) and state stewardship of natural resources, such as forests, land and water (Article P). The jurisprudence reveals that state monopolies could be constitutionally acceptable,[79] but state ownership may not undermine competition in the market.[80] The fundamental changes affecting public ownership and the delivery of public services in contemporary European states are only represented in the conditional fundamental right of access to public services (Article XXII). It implies a constitutional recognition that public services can be provided by private economic operators subject to the obligation in public law to guarantee a universal access (on fair prices) to the services they provide. This provision alone, considering the Fundamental Law's narrow approach to governance and accountability, is insufficient constitutional regulation of the market of public services failing to recognize its specific governance and accountability considerations. Also, an exclusively rights based recognition of public services regulation focusing on the question of consumer access grants virtually unlimited discretion for the state to design the regulatory framework and determine public expenditure. In light of the relevant provisions of EU law, this discretion is much more limited than as it appears in the Fundamental Law, and there are strategic benefits to be gained by anchoring a more detailed set of regulatory principles in the constitutional text capable of safeguarding a Hungarian market of public services from European intervention.

---

[77] Decision 54/1993. (X. 13.)

[78] The Fundamental Law no longer contains a reference to the equal status of private and public ownership, a measure introduced in the 1989 Constitution (Article 9(1)).

[79] Decision 1814/B/1991. (September 14, 1994).

[80] Decision 469/B/1997. (April 14, 1998).

The Fundamental Law incorporates its most vigorous economic agenda and most detailed regulation of the relationship between the state and the market in the provisions on European integration. Article E speaks of a constitutional aim to promote European integration to achieve the freedom, well-being and security of European nations, and it establishes the constitutional foundations for Hungary's membership in the European Union. If approached from its actual impact, Article E implies that Hungary has adhered to the economic and public policy priorities of the European Union. The EU, with the internal market in its heart, follows a primarily market oriented agenda with legislation and public monies available to offset the unacceptable social, environmental, or ethical effects of market integration in Europe.[81] Article E is listed among the fundamental principles of Hungarian constitutionalism, and indicates a privileged constitutional position, beside the rule of law and democracy, for free trade, free economic migration, free enterprise, undistorted competition and private ownership, and a recognition that the state's autonomy in regulating the market has diminished, as they follow from the provisions of the EU Treaties.[82] Article E should be interpreted as imposing considerable limitations on domestic economic policy discretion under the Fundamental Law. It is also a source of conflict within the Fundamental Law capable of challenging the economic and social model embedded in other constitutional provisions.

The regulation in the Fundamental Law of the relationship between the state and the market is disappointing. The only comprehensive element is the constitutional aim of a market economy and the broad economic dimensions of the European integration principle. The remainder is fragmented, unprincipled in relation to restraining economic policy discretion, keeps quiet about the impact of EU membership on economic policy and regulation, and fails to recognize openly the market and competition as a form of governance in delivering pub-

---

[81] Schieck, D. "Re-embedding economic and social constitutionalism: Normative perspectives for the EU" in *European Economic and Social Constitutionalism after the Treaty of Lisbon*, Schieck, D. and U. Liebert and H. Schneider eds. (Cambridge: Cambridge University Press, 2011), 17.

[82] Armstrong, K. "Mutual Recognition" in *The Law of the Single European Market*, Barnard, C. et al., eds. (Oxford: Hart Publishing, 2002), 226.

lic policy.[83] The Fundamental Law appears as conceptually unprepared to recognize that the constitutional values of transparency and accountability may be secured by the market and competition and that the market and competition may be applied as means of governance to achieve economic and social policy objectives. Article M, containing the constitutional aim of a market economy, leaves it unspecified whether it should only be interpreted as imposing restrictions on state interference with the market, or also as determining when the state may resort to the market as a means of governance. As raised in connection with Article E and public services regulation, the constitutional regulation of economic policy discretion requires more and better expressed principles in the Fundamental Law.

Conclusions

The Hungarian Fundamental Law, despite some progressive elements, has not been successful in regulating the constitutional issues of governance and accountability and the relationship between the state and the market. It subscribes to a narrow vision of a hierarchical, order and control based system of governance and a matching framework for accountability. The experiment with new governance in the fiscal constitution generates serious constitutional problems as a matter of legitimacy and accountability, without immediate solutions being available under the Fundamental Law. Its regulation of the market and economic policy discretion leaves crucial questions unanswered and leaves the economic constitution exposed to European Union economic policy and regulation. A more coherent and clearer regulation and definition of key constitutional principles may provide a solution.

---

[83] On the latter see Scott, C. "Regulatory Governance," 27 and Donahue, J.D. "Market-Based Governance and the Architecture of Accountability" in *Market-Based Governance* Donahue, J.D. et al., eds. (Washington DC: Brookings Institution, 2002).

V. EUROPEAN PERSPECTIVES

No New(s), Good News?
The Fundamental Law and the European Law

ANDRÁS BRAGYOVA

Introduction

This paper intends to examine the effect of the Fundamental Law to the relationship between European Law (now Union law)[1] and Hungarian law. First, I would like to make a rather obvious but important distinction. The relationship of European law and Hungarian law includes two separate questions which should be carefully distinguished: first, the relationship of European law to Hungarian law; and second the relationship of Hungarian law to European law. These two questions are in no way symmetrical. The first is a question of European law, thus independent form Hungarian law, while the second is a question of Hungarian law (and does not concern European law). Of course, the Fundamental Law (as the former Constitution did) can regulate only the second question.

To begin with the most important contention, the Fundamental Law does not seem to announce any overriding change in the relationship of Hungarian law to European Law. On the other hand, for the reason set out above, the Fundamental Law has not changed the relationship of *European law to Hungarian law*. It did not alter the second aspect (the relation of Hungarian law to European law) either; although, as a matter of fact it could have done. Thus, it left intact, "as it is," the status of European law in Hungarian law at the constitutional level. Consequently, the substantive part of this paper is the same, as it were without the Fundamental Law.

---

[1] I shall use the two terms interchangeably as they are synonymous after the entry into force of the Lisbon Treaty.

I start with a textual analysis, comparing the old and the new texts. Then I will undertake a brief overview of the most important holdings of the Hungarian Constitutional Court about the status of European law in the Hungarian legal system. Next, I shall venture into prophecies about the impact of the Fundamental Law on the relationship between Hungarian law and European law. To anticipate my conclusion, I do not expect substantial change in the legal status of the European law in Hungarian legal system: it will be neither better, nor worse.

Preliminary Analysis

The 1989 Constitution as amended in 2003 contained a European (or integration) clause (Article 2/A). It was drafted as a compromise[2] between several views and proposals advanced by lawyers and politicians, differing in their more or less pro-European attitudes. As a result, it became, as in the adage attributed to Sieyes, short and obscure, thus leaving wide latitude to future interpreters. With all the understandable criticisms against the text, it served quite well the aim it wanted to achieve. It was sufficiently ambiguous and foggy to make possible a constitutional interpretation reasonably acceptable to a wide circle of Hungarians and satisfy at the same time the Union.

I shall begin with the comparison of the integration clauses as formulated in the Constitution and in the Fundamental Law. They read as follows:

1989 Constitution	*2011 Fundamental Law*
Article 2/A	*Article E*
(1) In order to participate in the European Union as a Member State, and on the basis of an international treaty, the Republic of Hungary may,	*(2) In order to participate in the European Union as a Member State, and on the basis of an international treaty, Hungary may, to the extent*

[2] About the drafting and the process of adoption see in particular Chronowski, N. *Integrálódó alkotmányjog* [Integrating Constitutional Law] (Pécs: Dialóg Campus, 2005). And see Dezső, M. and A. Vincze *Magyar alkotmányosság az európai integrációban* [Hungarian Constitutionalism in the European Integration] (Budapest: HVG-ORAC, 2006).

to the extent necessary to exercise the rights and fulfil the obligations set out in the founding treaties, exercise certain constitutional competences jointly with other Member States; these powers may be exercised separately through the institutions of the European Union.	*necessary to exercise the rights and fulfil the obligations set out in the founding treaties, exercise some of its competences deriving from the Fundamental Law jointly with other Member States, through the institutions of the European Union.*
	(3) The law of the European Union may stipulate generally binding rules of conduct subject to the conditions set out in paragraph (2).

The textual analysis shows, at the first sight at least, only slight dissimilarity between the two clauses. In fact, a great deal of the text in the Fundamental Law is identical to that of the Constitution. The text of Fundamental Law is obviously based on (or borrowed from) the Constitution. There are, however, differences too; and they are important since (one must suppose) they have been deliberately changed and therefore might reflect an attitude differing from the Constitution.

First, the Fundamental law omits the explicit reference to the supranational element of the Union ("through the institutions of the EU"). On the other hand, it retains the basic construction, i.e. the limited transfer of constitutional competences to the Union by virtue of the Constitution/ Fundamental law and on the basis of international treaties.[3]

Both the Constitution and the Fundamental Law contain a general declaration of commitment of the Hungarian state for European Unity (which obviously includes the European Union). The main question is, quite obviously, how far or to what extent the interpretation of the Integration Clause under the Constitution will remain unaffected by the new text (and the new context). If there will be a differ-

[3] The Hungarian text is a bit ambiguous both in the Constitution and in the Fundamental Law with respect to *the number* of the treaties. It can mean a single treaty or more treaties as well. This ambiguity can well be intentional, since Hungary became member of the EU by virtue of a single treaty (the Treaty of Accession), but by accepting this treaty it came to be bound by several treaties, i.e. the Founding Treaties and many others as part of the *acquis communautaire*. As a matter of fact, the only treaty voted upon by Parliament was the Treaty of Accession (with appendices).

ence of interpretation in the future, the text will be the tiniest factor in it; rather, the change of the hermeneutic context will have played a more important role.

The Constitution and the European Law

Prelude: The sugar surplus duty case

The first case decided by the Court pertaining to European Law[4] during the membership of Hungary in the European Union was characteristically a case about transitory measures in connection with the newcomers in the agriculture market.[5] The European Commission in several regulations imposed duties on surplus sugar imported to the accession states before accession in order to obtain the European export subsidies in a fraudulent (or speculative) manner. The legal basis of the regulation was the Treaty of Accession which empowered the institutions of the Community to adopt certain transitory measures before the entry into force of the Accession Treaty but became applicable only after its entry into force. The duties on sugar imported were imposed on surplus stocks of sugar which would entitle their exporters to subsidies under the European agrarian market regulations. In short, the duty imposed was aimed to prevent speculation and protect the community market. In accordance with the regulation, the Parliament adopted, in April 2004 a law to implement the Commission regulation which was due to enter into force on or after the day of accession. Since the sugar stocks subject to the duty were imported before the entry into force of the Accession Treaty and the stocks were subject to the duty as of May 1, the Law implementing the Commission regulation were suspect of being *ex post* legislation.

---

[4] I shall not discuss cases decided before the entry into the EU, but one surely deserves mention in a footnote: Decision 30/1998. (VI. 25.) on the Association Agreement with the European Union. In this case the Court made it clear that the transfer of law-making competence to EU organs is not allowed without a specific authorization in the Constitution.

[5] Decision 17/2004. (V. 25.)

In fact this was the opinion of the president of the republic who, availing himself of the constitutional powers under Article 26(2) of the Constitution, initiated *a priori* control of the law with Constitutional Court. They found the law unconstitutional on the grounds that it imposed the sugars stocks duty retroactively, thus violating the rule of law clause of the Constitution. The Court, although discussed in detail the community law background of the measure in question, found that the "question to be decided is not the validity or interpretation of the rules of the European Union, but the conformity with the Constitution of the Hungarian law adopted for the implementation of the regulation."[6]

The Court found the Law contrary to the Constitution on the ground of its retroactivity, since it imposed a duty to stocks existing before the envisaged entry into force of the law. As the quote above shows, the Court construed the case as if it had nothing to do with European law, arguing that a Hungarian law has to meet all the requirements of constitutionality under Hungarian law, irrespective of the fact that it implements European law.

Almost certainly this explains the criticisms the sugar decision reaped. Critics censured the (alleged or real) anti-union—that is parochial—attitude of the Court with respect to European law.[7] The court, however, expressly disclaimed to touch upon the position of European community law in Hungarian legal order, since the measures in question were enacted immediately before, though certainly in view of, the entry of Hungary into the Union. In any case, at the moment of the decision Hungary was already member of the EU, the law contained certain transitory provisions to eliminate the possibility of speculative deals in the agrarian (sugar) market in connection with the entry of the new states into the Union (Community).

---

6 Ibid.

7 See Sajó, A. "Learning Co-operative Constitutionalism the Hard Way: the Hungarian Constitutional Court Shying Away from EU Supremacy," *Zeitschrift für Staats- und Europawissenschaften* 2 (2004): 351.

The leading case: Sportingbet

The interpretation of the integration clause of the Constitution by the Constitutional Court in the *Sportingbet* case[8] essentially stated that the European law is not to be treated as international law within the meaning of Article 7(1) of the Constitution. Hence the Founding Treaties of the European Union—as modified by the Lisbon Treaty—are not "international treaties" for the purposes of the Constitution. This is, in fact, the adoption of the well-established view of European Court since 1963 (in the cases *Van Gend en Loos* and *Costa*). Famously, the Court stated that the Community (as it then was) and its law

> constitutes a new legal order of international law for the benefit of which the states have limited their sovereign rights... Independently of the legislation of the Member States, Community law therefore not only imposes obligations on individuals but is also intended to confer upon them rights, which become part of their legal heritage.[9]

And

[8] Decision 153/E/2005. (June 16, 2006). I call the case Sportingbet, since the Hungarian subsidiary of the company launched the complaint against a Hungarian law favoring the national gambling monopoly against EU competitors. The regulation, similar to that of several EU member states, was believed to be contrary to the community law, but the Commission hesitated to take action against non-complying states. Sportingbet thus sought legal remedy unavailable to it at the EU level. The name of company does not appear in the decision. It is interesting to note that in the meantime the European Court found that the German legal restrictions quite similar to the Hungarian were not violating Union law. See the cases *Winner Wetten GmbH v. Bürgermeisterin der Stadt Bergheim*, C-409/06; *Markus Stoss and Others v. Wetteraukreis and Kulpa Automatenservice Asperg GmbH and Others v. Land Baden-Württemberg*, C-316/07, C-358/07 to C-360/07, C-409/07 and C-410/07; *Carmen Media Group Ltd v. Land Schleswig-Holstein and Innenminister des Landes Schleswig-Holstein*, C-46/08.

[9] *Van Gend en Loos v. Nederlandse Administratis der Belastingen*, C-26/62, [1963] ECR 1.

> By contrast to ordinary international treaties, the EEC Treaty has created its own legal system which, on the entry into force of the Treaty, became an integral part of the member States and which their courts are bound to apply.
>
> By creating a community of unlimited duration having its own institutions, its own legal personality, its own legal capacity and capacity of representation on the international plane, and, more particularly, real powers stemming from a limitation of sovereignty and a transfer of powers the States to the Community, the member States limited their sovereign rights... and created a body of law which bind both their nationals and themselves.[10]

In other terms, by virtue of the sovereignty transfer clause of Article 2/A(1) the law-making powers under the Constitution—that is, that of Parliament or of the Government—are deemed to be replaced by the law-making of the organs of the Union. Thus, directly applicable norms of the European law are to be regarded sharing the same force of law (or legal validity) as the norms originating from Hungarian (autochthonous) sources of law. Consequently the law-making acts of the Union have by virtue of the Constitution the same effect as the sources (law-making facts) of the Hungarian law.

There are a few further consequences implied in this view. First, the norms of the European law (to the extent they are directly applicable in the Hungarian legal system) are valid in Hungarian law in the final analysis on the basis of the Hungarian constitution. The reason of their validity or binding force is the delegation (transfer of competence) contained in the Hungarian constitution. Thus, the Hungarian constitution allows the validity and the application of the norms of European Union Law in the Hungarian legal system. The ultimate basis of validity of the Union law in the Hungarian legal system is the Constitution.

Indeed the Court did not analyze in much detail the nature of the transfer of competences in the Constitution. Still the argumentation certainly leads to the conclusion that the transfer being made in the Hungarian constitution, from a constitutional point of view the European law, so far as it is applicable in any form in the Hungarian legal

---

10 *Costa v. ENEL*, C-6/64, [1964] ECR, 585, 593.

system and by its administrative or judicial organs, is ultimately Hungarian law—with all the due reservations as to its interpretation. Second, this means a *prima facie* priority of *application* for European law in Hungarian legal system but not a priority with respect to the validity of European norms. The first is an obligation of European law, while a reinforced priority in the validity could be conferred only by national constitutions (but not as matter of obligation under Union law).[11] However, third, a Hungarian law (legal norm) contrary to European law is not deemed unconstitutional for that matter. If there is a conflict (real or supposed) between Hungarian law and European law, ordinary courts of law are to clarify the situation by seeking preliminary ruling from the European Court.

Alternatively, the organs of the European Union (in particular the Commission) have the power to enforce European law, if the Hungarian legal order violates obligations under European law. Most importantly, the Constitutional Court has not been prepared to regard the violation of European Union law as *per se* unconstitutional. Thus, the Court does not assume—although does not expressly deny it either—that there is a *constitutional obligation* incumbent upon all organs of the state to apply European law. Or, if so, this obligation is (or used to be) based on the principle of the rule of law, rather than to Article 2/A(1) of the Constitution. On the other hand, the *Europarechtsfreundlichkeit* (or harmonious interpretation) is a constitutional value in Hungarian legal order. A constitutional value is a constitutionally preferred state of affairs in the legal system. It has a significant role to play if there are conflicting (in particular mutually exclusive) interpretations of the constitutional or sub-constitutional norms, since the constitutional value determines the preferred solution. Practically that means that in case of doubt the interpretive solution in conformity (or better in conformity) with European law should be chosen. The Europe-friendly interpretation entails the duty to opt for an interpretation or application of con-

[11] The difference between the two kinds of priority is often neglected although their separation is conceptually (if not practically) essential. An example of the non-distinction is found in Alter, K. *Establishing the Supremacy of European Law* (Oxford: Oxford University Press, 2001) and see *Principles of European Constitutional Law*, von Bogdandy, A. and J. Bast eds. (Portland: Hart, 2006).

stitutional as well as sub-constitutional (ordinary) law in conformity with European law, or, if necessary, to prefer a solution the least hurting European obligations. (See the water protection plan case.)[12]

Fourth, let us consider the inverse possibility: what happens when a norm of the European law is contrary to the Hungarian constitution? Although the question is rather theoretical, it must be said that the position of Hungarian Court implies the competence of the Constitutional Court to declare the norm of European law unconstitutional and therefore null and void. In case of the implementation of European law through internal law-making, thus by making rules of Hungarian law in conformity with European law—as in the case of directives—the extent of the constitutional control is in principle the same as for any Hungarian legal norm, the national (that is, member state) constitutional law governs the implementation of the directly inapplicable rules of European law (such as the directives) as to the law-making competence. Hence, a directive implemented in violation of the substantial or procedural constitutional rules applicable to law-making are liable to be found null and void. One example could be the violation of the constitutional requirement to give enough for preparation to apply the law or the prohibition of retroactive legislation. Nevertheless, the principle of Europe-friendliness applies so that if the declaration of unconstitutionality would hamper the fulfillment of obligations under European law, the Court will certainly leave time for the legislator for rectification. Such a result is practically acceptable but it leaves open a few key questions about the relationship of Hungarian and European law.

To sum up, the *Sportingbet* decision settled satisfactorily from the constitutional point of view the *direct applicability* of the European (then community) law in the Hungarian legal system satisfying the demands of European law. On the other hand, the nature and extent of the priority of the European law has remained, like in many other jurisdictions, less than clear. The reason is obvious: the priority of the European law is much more disputed concept and its understanding is sensibly different in constitutional law than in European law, not speak

[12] Decision 6/2011. (II. 3.) The Court in this case found a resolution of the Government unconstitutional on formal grounds, but drew the consequences only *pro futuro*, since the resolution implemented a Union measure on water management.

among jurists of in these fields. The priority question directly concerns the rank of European legal norms in national legal systems, which is a highly sensitive constitutional-political question. It is no surprise, then, that the legal nature and limits of the priority, if any, of European law against national law in the Hungarian legal system has remained much more obscure. Decisions of the Constitutional Court following *Sportingbet*, as we will see left the main questions the priority problem more or less open. This is particularly true of the Lisbon decision.

The EUIN decision

The Constitutional Court was faced, though indirectly in a sense, with the constitutional validity of the European Arrest Warrant[13] that occupied several constitutional courts of the continent.[14] It deserves mention even if technically at the time of its adoption did not relate European Community Law but to the then so-called Third Pillar—Cooperation in Justice and Security—of the Union. Now, after the entry into force of the Lisbon Treaty, it is a question of Union law. The case concerned the constitutionality of the Treaty extending the scope of application of the European Arrest Warrant to two non-EU states participating in the Schengen border-control regime, viz. Iceland and Norway. The ground of the unconstitutionality was Article 57(4) of the Constitution, i.e. the principle *nullum crimen sine lege*.

The Court had to decide about the constitutional validity of an act authorizing the Government and the president to accept the treaty concluded between Iceland and Norway on the one hand and the European Union and its member states participating in the Schengen regime on the other. The application of the president of the republic concerned the constitutionality of the obligation under the Treaty to deliver persons committed a crime under the law of the state requesting the delivery not being a criminal offense under Hungarian law. As mentioned, the president argued that the delivery of a person

[13] Agreement between the European Union and the Republic of Iceland and the Kingdom of Norway on the surrender procedure between the Member States of the European Union and Iceland and Norway. Council Decision, 2006/697/EC, June 27, 2006.

[14] Decision 32/2008. (III. 12.)

(or the possibility thereof) by virtue of an arrest warrant issued by a state for an action where the action is criminal offense but is not in Hungarian law violates the principle of *nullum crimen* and therefore unconstitutional.

The decision irrespective of its quite questionable reasoning—the principle of double incrimination has hardly anything to do with the *nullum crimen*—made it clear that (at least the fundamental) principles of the Hungarian constitution are stronger and thus must prevail over Union law (as it then was). It leaves slightly any doubt that the fundamental principles of the Hungarian constitution (like the *nullum crimen*) are to respected by the Hungarian legislator in the course of the implementation of the European Union law. Surely, the weight of the precedent is weakened by two factors. For one, the decision concerns a treaty concluded between the European Union and two non-member states albeit in strong connection with the Union law (Schengen and the European Arrest Warrant). Still, the subject matter was not directly applicable community law, and any member state could have opted out under Article 34 of the Treaty on European Union (as it then was). Second, with the entry into force of the Lisbon Treaty, the former Third Pillar became a full-fledged part of the Union law, thus the *ratio decidendi* of the case is not directly operative any more. (Moreover, in the meantime the Hungarian Constitution was modified in order to make the EUIN Treaty safe from constitutional point of view.)

The Lisbon Treaty Case

The Hungarian Constitutional Court availed itself of the opportunity to express its views on the Lisbon Treaty in a decision of 2010[15]—that is, *after* the entry into force of the Lisbon Treaty. This decision is curious and spurious on several grounds. First, it decided a question that was to be qualified at the moment of the decision for all practical purposes moot.

In addition, it is difficult to ascertain the legal norms the constitutionality of which was examined in the decision. The difficulty arises from the fact that the Hungarian Court examined the constitutionality of the Lisbon Treaty after its *entry into force*. Now, unlike the ill-

[15] Decision 143/2010. (VII. 14.)

fated Constitutional Treaty, the Lisbon treaty was not a wholly new text to replace the founding treaties of 1953/1957/1958 as modified and amended several times but a modification and amendment of the founding treaties. Due to this circumstance the Lisbon Treaty ceased to be an independent legal instrument as of December 1, 2009 (the day it entered into force), since it was incorporated into the founding treaties. Strictly speaking, we have now no Lisbon Treaty as such—in force, if one wishes—but the founding treaties (the Treaty on European Union, the Treaty on the Functioning of the Union and their many appendices, declarations etc.) *as amended and modified* by the Lisbon Treaty. For this reason one might find it curious to read a decision discussing the constitutional validity of an already non-existent treaty.

So, a decision after the entry into force of the Lisbon Treaty is a decision about the constitutionality of the Founding Treaties as they had been modified by the Lisbon Treaty, not simply on the constitutionality of the amendments introduced with the Lisbon Treaty. On this ground the better view would have been to dismiss the application for addressing a moot question *at the moment of the decision*, since the applicant questioned only the constitutionality of the Lisbon Treaty[16]—that is, the changes introduced by it into the founding treaties—but not the membership in the Union in general. Since there was no possibility any more to impede the entry into force of the Lisbon Treaty (as it had entered into force in the meantime), the only possibility would have been to withdraw from the Union under Article 50 of the Treaty on European Union, an option not envisaged in the application. These reservations aside, the decision set out a few principles about the limits of European Law in the Hungarian legal system left open in the previous decisions. Still, as a result it is not all more settled than it used to be before what are the inherent constitutional limits of the EU-membership in Hungarian law.

This lack of clarity is due, presumably, to the fact that the Hungarian Constitutional Court and constitutional doctrine, until recently firmly maintained that the constitution-amending power of Parliament

[16] To be precise, it challenged the constitutionality of the act *authorizing the acceptance* of the Lisbon Treaty. The result is, of course, the same.

is legally unlimited.[17] This principle being accepted, it is indeed very difficult, if not just impossible, to claim that there are constitutional-legal limits to the Union membership in Hungarian law. If the constitution may be amended or revised by the two-thirds majority of Parliament *ad libitum,* it is curious to argue that there are limitations imposed upon the amending power with respect to the Union. All that can be said on these grounds is that there are only *limited limits* under the constitution, as any restraint may be overridden by the constitutional revision. Thus, until the doctrine of unlimited amending power is not reversed or disavowed, there cannot be effective constitutional limits of EU membership in Hungarian law. As a matter of fact, one of the weaknesses of this decision is that it avoids this very issue and therefore in many respects appears to be dissatisfying.

The irony of the history is that a year later the Court was no longer in the position to avoid the issue of the limits of the amending power under the Constitution. The majority, if not unanimously, upheld the earlier view, with the not unimportant qualification that the Court has the power to review the regularity of the amending procedure, but dismissed the possibility of substantive control of constitutional amendments.[18] This view entails that there are at the moment no absolute constitutional limits to the transfer of constitutional powers to the Union.

Let me add at the end of the review of the case-law of the Court in EU matters that it left unsettled the question of the constitutional nature and conditions in the Hungarian legal order of the priority of European law.[19] Indeed, the Constitutional Court did not address the question of the existence of constitutional (i. e. constitution-based) obligation to recognize the primacy of the European (Union) law. The Court appears to analyze the priority of the European law in terms of the validity and binding force of the *directly applicable* Union law in the Hungarian legal system. This approach is, at least theoretically, unsat-

---

[17] Decision 1260/B/1997. (February 9, 1998).

[18] Decision 61/2011. (VII. 13.)

[19] For a recent comprehensive overview of the issue addressed here see Fazekas, F. and M. Varju "The reception of European Union law in Hungary: The Constitutional Court and the Hungarian judiciary," *Common Market Law Review* 48, no. 6 (2011).

isfactory and leaves open many issues regarding the constitutional position of the Union law in the Hungarian legal system.

The European Law in the Fundamental Law

As mentioned at the outset, the Fundamental Law, at least on the surface, does not appear to add anything to (or, for that matter, subtract from) the established practice of the Constitutional Court discussed above. The established case-law of the Constitutional Court, will probably continue to be the *acquis constitutionnel* under the Fundamental Law. At the very least every reasonable argument speaks for it. Still, a word of caution: at the moment we do not know anything but the text of the Fundamental Law. Since it does not seem to be much at variance to the Constitution still in force until January 1, 2012, it is reasonable to suppose that the interpretation of the integration clause will accordingly not deviate from the Constitution either. A few caveats, however, should be made.

As I suggested above, much will depend on the position of the Constitutional Court about the relationship between the Fundamental Law and the previous Constitution. There are many grounds to suppose and not less to support the thesis that the Fundamental Law is, technically speaking, a comprehensive modification of the Constitution, since the Fundamental law was adopted according to the rules governing the amendment of the Constitution (as stated in the Closing Provisions of the Fundamental Law). Hence it is reasonable to assume that the Court will in the interpretation of the Fundamental Law follow its own precedents under the Constitution. Still, at this moment the question is open and we must wait some time to see whether the prediction will prove correct.

Of course one might ask the question whether other provisions of the Fundamental Law could influence the interpretation of the European clause, in particular the reference to the historical constitution. One peculiar (if not to say unique) feature of the Fundamental Law is the provision on the interpretation of the Fundamental Law [Article R(3)]. It states that the provisions of the Fundamental Law shall be interpreted in accordance with their purpose, the National Avowal and the achievements of the historical constitution. Moreover, in Article

28 the Fundamental Law instructs the Courts of Law to construe the rules of law once again in accordance with their purpose and the Fundamental Law. It adds that in interpreting the Fundamental Law and the rules of law it shall be supposed that they serve a morally good and economically reasonable purpose in harmony with common sense and the common good.

I am inclined to believe that Article R will not be quite irrelevant in questions of European Law. The "achievements of our historical constitution" are surely not related to the European law and there is not slightest chance that it could shed any light on the interpretation of this particular clause. In addition, historically the European Union and its predecessors did not exist at all, let alone the membership of Hungary in the Union.

As we saw, the interpreter of the Fundamental Law is pretty well-furnished with directives to follow. A skeptic would argue that provisions of this type are definitely unable to guide, let alone to bind, the interpreter. It is well-established in legal theory that legal rules on the interpretation of the law could not bind the interpreter as long as the same interpreter construes the provisions on interpretation as any other rule of law. The power of interpretation is difficult to control. In any case, Article R makes it clear that the National Avowal is *not* a text of strictly legal nature, but rather a source of inspiration for the interpreter (whatever that means). The National Avowal mentions Europe several times. First, it mentions King Saint Stephen (r. A.D. 1000–1038) who "made our country a part of Christian Europe." Next, the National Avowal refers to the contribution of Hungarian people in defending Europe which is part of the Hungarian national mythology. Similar language is easy to find in the national conscience of many nations in Central and Eastern Europe. Third, the National Avowal states, quite surprisingly, that Hungarian national culture is a rich contribution to the diversity of an integrated Europe. The underlying philosophy may well not be quite profound but it does not lack clarity. It is essentially a nationalistic credo with strong emphasis on national values. Even the (relatively) universalistic reference to Christianity is collocated with a stress on the role of Christianity in preserving national identity. The other references to Europe also allude to national (i.e. collective) virtues: the defense of Europe and the Hungarian contribution to European culture.

With more than a bit of fantasy one could surmise a parallelism between the Habsburg Pragmatic Sanction (enacted by the Hungarian Diet in 1723)[20] which had been considered as the foundation of the historical constitution, and the present relationship to the European Union. The Pragmatic Sanction contained the famous *indivisibiliter ac inseperabiliter (undivided and inseparable)* clause on Austro-Hungarian relations that guaranteed the (relative) independence of Hungary within the framework of the Habsburg Monarchy and had been regarded as the main legal basis of the Austro-Hungarian Compromise in 1867. A possible "historical" argument could construe the legal position of Hungary in the European Union as a modern variant of the *indivisibiliter ac inseparabiliter* relationship well-known in the historical constitution.

According to the historical constitution, the Pragmatic Sanction was valid in Hungary (in the Lands of Saint Stephen's Crown) only with the consent of the Diet, contrary to the Hereditary Lands of the Habsburg Empire where such consent had not been required. If this is an "achievement of the historical constitution," as it surely is, it will be quite an easy play to interpret any provision on the transfer of the powers of the nation being contrary to the deepest-seated historical achievements of the historical constitution. In this way the historically inspired interpretation might be a forceful argument for anti-European constitutional construction of the Fundamental Law. Those familiar with the constitutional views of the radical right in Hungary will confirm that similar arguments are pretty frequent in those circles. This is an imaginary illustration of the possible use of the argument from the "historical constitution." Nevertheless, it illustrates its metaphorical (or even allegorical) and imprecise character. Its function at its best could be but ornamental. As such it is a matter of taste: some will like it, others not. However, it could become really dangerous if the reference to

---

[20] See in English: Marczali, H. *Hungary in the Eighteenth Century* (Cambridge: Cambridge University Press, 1910), 347 et seq. and see Evans, R. J. W. *Austria, Hungary, and the Habsburgs, c. 1683–1867* (Oxford: Oxford University Press, 2006), 13. The fundamental historical work remains Turba, G. *Geschichte des Thronfolgerechtes in allen Habsburgischen Ländern bis zur Pragmatischen Sanktion Kaiser Karls VI. 1156 bis 1732* (Vienna: Fromme, 1903). See also: Turba, G. *Die pragmatische Sanktion, mit besonderer Rücksicht auf die Laender der Stephanskrone* (Vienna: Manz, 1906).

a fictitious historical constitution replaces the serious and strict juristic analysis and argument. Still worse, it could have been taken seriously.

Another fact worth mentioning here is the underlying philosophy of the Fundamental Law. As the National Avowal shows, it contains a substantial element of nationalistic, not to say parochial, ideology. The question is, of course, how much it will influence the interpretation of the Fundamental Law, particularly in the field of European law. Even if there is no explicit ("textual") conflict between the essential idea of the European Union and the National Avowal (and sometimes the rest of the Fundamental Law) the tension is nevertheless palpable. The Union demands—indeed presupposes—that the member states renounce of the narrow self-centered national state constitutional philosophy. The Fundamental Law, on the contrary, quite explicitly follows a nationalistic political and constitutional philosophy. It is more than clear from the National Avowal. The idea of a self-contained national state is indisputably incompatible with the aim of European Unity also embraced by the Fundamental Law. The dominant underlying ideology of the Fundamental Law is clearly a kind of pseudo-historical nationalism, with a strong emphasis on national values.

On a less symbolic level the Fundamental Law fares slightly better. It contains, in the chapter entitled Foundations a general European unity clause[21] and the European Clause quoted above. The power given to the Union to establish general rules of behavior seems to be a reinforcement of the position of the Union law in the Hungarian legal system. On closer inspection, however, this is not necessarily the case. The European Clause is theoretically questionable and may eventually lead to serious problems. As we have seen above, Article E(3) states that Union law may establish binding rules of conduct subject to the conditions set out in paragraph (2). This text appears to recognize European law as a source of *Hungarian law.* If so, it is of doubtful value for the following reasons.

For one thing, the sources of Union law are not *sources of law* in Hungarian legal system. They are sources, according to the already quoted well-known statement of the European Court (which has been

[21] Article E(1): "In order to achieve the highest possible measure of freedom, well-being and security for the peoples of Europe Hungary shall contribute to the achievement of European unity."

persistently maintained since), that is the Community (now Union) legal order is a special legal order within international law. From this statement it follows that the Union law is not a "source of law" in the legal system of the member states but rather the Union legal order as such is in its applicable parts, as it were, incorporated into the legal system of the member states. This distinction is important. The incorporation into the legal system of member states means that the secondary sources of European law (or the Treaties themselves, in so far as they are directly applicable) are not "sources" of law in the legal systems of the member states. Rather, norms valid in the European law are valid and applicable norms in the legal system of the member states *because they are valid norms of the European law*. In no case can a court of a member state adjudicate the validity *under European law* of a norm of European law, as this is the exclusive jurisdiction of the European Court under Article 263 of the Treaty on the Functioning European Union. It is true that the Founding Treaties are the *final*, but not the *ultimate*, basis of validity (the rule of recognition) of the Union legal order and thus the legal system of the member states.

For this reason the Union law is not a self-containing legal system, but a legal order. That is, it has its own criteria of validity but the ultimate rule of recognition lies outside the legal order. A *legal system*, on the contrary, contains its own ultimate rule of validity. In other words, a legal system is closed as to its validity (including the change of the constitution) while ultimate criterion of the validity of a *legal order* is part of another legal order. In case of the Union law this is through the intermediary of the Founding Treaties: the constitutions of the member states.[22] According to this view, the Union law preserves its relative autonomy in its relationship towards the legal system of the member states, still being in last analysis dependent on their existence. The Union legal order is not part of the legal system of the member states, only a great number of its norms are integrated into them. In any case not all, since the institutional law, often called the "constitutional law of the Union," is by definition not applicable, and therefore is not part

[22] For an analysis of the EU legal system from the point of view discussed in the text, see van Roermund, B. "Jurisprudential dilemmas of European Law" in *Construing Legal Systems: European Union in Legal Theory,* ed. MacCormick, N. (Dordrecht, Boston, Mass.: Kluwer Academic, 1997), 27.

of the legal system of the member states. Most importantly, the union legal order has its own criteria of validity, only the ultimate rule of recognition is part of international law (and simultaneously of the constitutional law in the member states).[23]

The incorporation of the directly valid and applicable Union law into the Hungarian legal system entails that the examination of the validity (and interpretation in case of uncertainty) of the rules of European law is outside the reach of the Hungarian courts of law. As we have seen, this has been the position of the Hungarian Constitutional Court too. Now, the qualification "subject to the conditions set out in paragraph (2)" may suggest, that under the Fundamental Law, there are constitutional constraints as to the validity of the rules of European law in the Hungarian legal system. That formulation can be construed as empowering the Constitutional Court to examine whether a rule of the European law is *ultra vires* from the point of view of Hungarian constitutional law. In this reasoning the Court would retain the power to declare a rule of European law invalid or inapplicable in Hungarian law because it exceeds the powers transferred to the Union under the Fundamental Law. If it were so, it would have been a false understanding of nature of the transfer of competences to the Union.

From the point of view of the constitutional law the transfer of constitutional ("sovereign") powers, as the European clause itself makes it clear, is a transfer in conjunction and on equal footing with the other member states and on the basis of the Founding Treaties. If, as I believe, the term "on the basis of" means "in accordance with" the Treaties, then the interpretation and application of the Treaties, including the decision on the legal validity of the rules of Union law is within the exclusive jurisdiction of the European Court. Thus, any constitutional power given to a court of a member state to examine the validity of a rule of European law would be contrary to the very principle of the transfer of powers to the Union. A national constitutional court has no choice but to accept the European law valid and applicable within the national legal system according to the criteria of

---

[23] See Bragyova, A. "Az Európai Unióhoz való csatlakozás alkotmányjogi kérdései" [Constitutional aspects of the EU-accession] in Inotai, A. ed. *EU-tanulmányok* [EU-Studies] Vol. 1 (Budapest: Nemzeti Fejlesztési Hivatal, 2002), 1090.

validity and rules of interpretation as applied by the European Court. Still, under Hungarian law presumably, the Constitutional Court has two powers with regard to Union law. It may control the constitutionality of the treaty transferring constitutional powers to the organs of the Union before its entry into force *(a priori)* but not when it is already in force, when the powers have already been transferred to the Union.[24] Second, as the rules of European law are valid and therefore applicable in the Hungarian legal system just as the "original" norms of Hungarian law, they are subject to the substantive constitutional control like any norm valid in the legal system. The latter is a pretty unlikely case, especially in view of incorporation of the Charter of Fundamental Rights into the Treaty by virtue of Article 6(1) of the Treaty on European Union and the accession of EU to the European Convention on Human Rights, but it does not challenge the validity of the Union law according to its own criteria; on the contrary, it assumes the validity of the rule examined.

A few words are perhaps in place here about the European Charter of Human Rights and the European Convention on Human Rights to which the European Union shall accede, as mentioned above. They have hardly anything to do directly with the fundamental rights guaranteed in the Fundamental Law. Both the Charter and the Convention create (or can create) obligations only for the Union and ought to be implemented in the Union legal order, thus they apply to Union law. For this reason they have no direct influence as such to the legal system of the member states, since they are on this account, applicable only to the Union organs and to the states implementing Union law. (The European Court of Human Rights in the *Bosphorus* case[25] held that the Convention applies to states implementing European law.) Certainly, the joining of the European Convention and the Charter are responses to the not so indirect criticisms of the German Constitutional Court, above all, supplying in this way, to the satisfaction of many, an acceptable guarantee of fundamental rights within the Union legal order. In doing so, the Union law can maintain itself outside the reach of some

---

[24] I elaborated this point in connection with the Lisbon Treaty in my concurring opinion written in Lisbon Treaty Case. Decision 143/2010. (VII. 14.)

[25] *Bosphorus Hava Yollari Turizm Ve Ticaret Anonim Şirketi* v. *Ireland* [GC], no. 45036/98, June 30, 2005.

constitutional courts or other internal courts eager to protect fundamental rights in applying European law. In Hungary, as we have seen, there were no signs of such an intention, except perhaps the Sugar Surplus Duty case mentioned earlier. It is of course quite a different (and separate) question that European Convention is binding on all member states as an international treaty independently of the Union law.

A different, still unsettled, perhaps not even clearly raised, question bears upon the constitutional control of laws (norms) inextricably connected to Union law without being directly applicable as such. An obvious example is a law implementing a directive but any regulation with at least partly Union-law determined content (without being implementation of a directive).[26] The peculiarity in such case is that the legal rules examined are not sources of the European law but just ordinary sources of Hungarian law. For instance, the law restricting publicity of tobacco products and alcoholic beverages is a just a law and it could be found in violation of the freedom of commercial free speech. Its content is, however, an implementation of the Council Directive 2003/33/EC. In such cases the judicial self-restraint and the recognition of the constitutionally anchored value of the participation in the Union will lead to an acceptable solution.

There is one provision of the Fundamental Law which most probably violates the Union law; this is Article K stating that the Hungarian (it says "Hungary's") official currency is the forint (HUF, as abbreviated in the rest of the world). Rules about national currency are quite unusual in most constitutions, since the regulation of the constitutional power to coin money or issue currency is quite sufficient as it used to be the case in the Constitution. Moreover, it is a bit strange to fix in the constitution the denomination of the money unit in a country which, in the course of the 20th century alone, knew three different official currencies (viz. the *korona* until 1926, after that the *pengő*, and from 1946 the *forint*). The most alarming, however, is the manifest violation of the Founding Treaties in Article K. Undoubtedly, the official currency of the Union is the Euro as clearly stated in Article 3 (4) of the Treaty on European Union. In addition Article 136 of the Treaty

[26] Such a case was, however, mentioned in passing above in connection with the case concerning the *pro futuro* nullity of a Government resolution about water management.

on the Functioning of the Union calls member states not having as their national currency the Euro "derogation States" making it clear, like other provisions on common monetary policy do, that member states—except Britain and Denmark, which opted out at the outset in protocols attached to the Treaty of Maastricht (and later Sweden)—are under the legal obligation to adopt the Euro as national currency. No doubt, in practice the proviso is rather pointless, since the introduction of the Euro as the national currency of Hungary is a far cry at the moment. Thus, the violation of the Union law in an instrument of constitutional value is symbolic rather than anything else. Still, it is a worrying sign of the less than pro-European attitude in the spirit and letter of the Fundamental Law.

A recent event, the proposed modification of the Treaty on the Functioning of the Union in order to reinforce the monetary and fiscal union connection with the Euro-crisis and the corresponding proposals adopted at the session of the European Council on December 9, 2011, will almost inevitably be the first test-case for the Fundamental Law in European affairs. The steps taken for the new economic governance and the strengthening of the monetary and fiscal union are important for the Union as a whole. Hungary, being outside the Euro-zone, has a modest role to play in this process. For Hungarian constitutional law and practice the impact might be considerably greater. Clearly, the choice between the preservation of national sovereignty and the pro-federalist option will emerge once again.

It is worth mentioning here that the European Clause of the Fundamental Law allows (though probably does not make inevitable) a restrictive interpretation excluding the further "federalization" of the Union under the Fundamental Law.[27] I use the term in quotation marks, for it has a special meaning in the European context. The formulation in the Fundamental Law does not indeed mention the European institutions as objects of the transfer of powers. It remains open what conclusion can be drawn from this fact. One could certainly argue that the institutions of the Union derive their authority, at least in final analysis, from the member states via the Treaties, thus satisfying the Article E(2). A sort of "federalization," if it is ever to happen,

[27] According to the *Opinion on the Fundamental Law of Hungary* (see in this volume), only the restrictive interpretation is correct.

will need in each member state either the revision of the constitution or a new constitution. This is why the meaning of the clause remains symbolic rather than practically important.

It is worth adding that Article 29 of the Transitional Provisions of the Fundamental Law contains a curious provision, at variance, as it seems, to (but not only) European Law. It institutes a special tax, thus denominated, to cover the expenses incurred by any judgment or decision of the European Court of Justice, the Constitutional Court or other court of law obligating the Hungarian state to money payment not covered in the budget. In plain English, it means that Parliament has the power to impose special taxes on taxpayers as a punitive or retributive measure for a judgment (or "decision") of the European Court if it happens to condemn Hungary to pay. This is quite possible, in view of the controversial financial measures adopted by Parliament in the present legislative period (or, of course, earlier too). As a matter of fact, a judgment of the European Court handed down on July 28, 2011[28] establishing that Hungary violated its obligations under the VAT Directive of the Council of 2006 caused a significant gap in the budget. The outcome of the case was no surprise to the experts, so that the government ought to have been prepared to it in due course. Once again, this provision, having according to Article 31 of the same law the force of the Fundamental Law, reflects a peculiar attitude towards Union law and reinforces the impression created by the Fundamental Law proper. It is not indeed improved by the proviso that the rule remains in force only until the public debt in Hungary will be reduced to 50 percent of the GDP, since at present the debt ratio stands above 80 percent.

Conclusions

In this paper I argued that there is no reason to expect important changes in the constitutional position of the European law due to the entry into force of the Fundamental Law. However, as I pointed out above, the generally nationalist rhetoric of the Fundamental Law and its underlying philosophy and spirit (if any) is not particularly

[28] *European Commission v. Hungary*, C-274/10.

pro-European. Still, as far as the text and its probable interpretation is concerned there is nothing to suggest a change in the practice of constitutional regulation of the position of the European law in the Hungarian legal system.

Even if it is difficult to predict future developments, there are good reasons to assume that the relationship between European law and the Hungarian legal system (and still less *vice versa*) will not visibly change under the Fundamental law. On the other hand, the makers of the Fundamental Law missed an opportunity, not quite unintentionally as one might suppose, to clarify a few obscure points, let alone to reinforce the constitutional position of the European law in Hungarian legal system. The latter was certainly not their intention, given the rather limited sympathy of the constitution-amending two-thirds majority towards the European Union, especially its so-called federalist features.

The less *new* we have, the better it is.

Trees in the Wood: The Fundamental Law and the European Court of Human Rights

JEREMY MCBRIDE

Introduction

Many of the constitutional changes found in Hungary's new Fundamental Law relate—whether directly or indirectly—to rights and freedoms guaranteed by the European Convention on Human Rights ("the European Convention"). This chapter considers those changes from the perspective of the mandate given to the European Court of Human Rights ("the European Court") by the European Convention. Pursuant to this mandate, the European Court has a decisive role in the interpretation and application of all the rights and freedoms set out in Section I of the European Convention, as well as those in any Protocols ratified, which High Contracting Parties such as Hungary have undertaken to secure to everyone within their jurisdiction.[1] The European Court thus could be looked to as a forum in which the compatibility of Hungary's constitutional changes with European human rights standards—a matter of considerable controversy before and since the adoption of the constitutional changes—is not only contested but also resolved.[2] However, whether the changes themselves, rather than measures taken in purported reliance on them, can actually be subject to the scrutiny of the European Court will very much depend on certain

[1] Hungary has ratified all the Protocols adding rights to the European Convention, with the exception of Protocol No. 12 which embodies a general guarantee against discrimination.

[2] A non-judicial approach would be for Article 8 of the Statute of the Council of Europe to be invoked. This provision allows for the suspension of the rights of representation and the termination of membership of states which have seriously violated the obligation to collaborate sincerely and effectively in the realization of the aim of the Council of Europe as set out in Article 1.

jurisdictional and procedural requirements first being satisfied. As a result it is necessary to consider the implications of the changes for the observance of those requirements as much as for their compliance with the substantive provisions of the European Convention.

The various issues are thus addressed first through some consideration of the general relevance of constitutional provisions for both fulfillment and violation of the rights and freedoms in the European Convention. Then the potential for conflict between specific provisions in the Fundamental Law and these rights and freedoms is explored, focusing more on where the changes possibly give rise to obligations that run counter to those rights and freedoms rather than entail a lowering of the degree of constitutional protection that they are afforded. Finally the wider issue of the Fundamental Law's compliance with the principles of democracy and the rule of law underpinning the European Convention is examined.

Constitutions and the European Convention

Most of the High Contracting Parties have constitutional guarantees of many, if not all, of the rights and freedoms found in the European Convention. Many of them afford these rights and freedoms a quasi-constitutional status, whether as a result of the constitution giving ratified treaties a higher status than other laws or by establishing an interpretative approach that requires laws to be interpreted as far as possible in a manner consistent with the European Convention. Often a High Contracting Party has both a constitutional guarantee of rights and freedoms and a special status for treaties such as the European Convention.[3] Undoubtedly all these constitutional arrangements can, depending upon the interpretative approach actually adopted,[4] assist

[3] Hungary has been amongst them as the Constitutional Court took the view in Decision 4/1997. (I. 22.) that a parliamentary act transforming a treaty such as the European Convention has precedence over acts and other legal measures but it remains to be seen whether this view is maintained under the Fundamental Law.

[4] Not all courts of High Contracting Parties follow or even have regard to the case law of the European Court in interpreting and applying either their constitutional guarantees or provisions in the European Convention where it

the effective implementation of the European Convention and obviate the need for recourse to the European Court. However, there is no obligation under the European Convention that ratification should entail its provisions being incorporated into domestic law,[5] let alone being accorded some constitutional status, although the former has certainly been encouraged by the Council of Europe. Indeed the European Court does not even consider there to be a requirement that it should be possible to challenge the compatibility of particular legislative provisions, as opposed to specific acts and omissions, with the European Convention's rights and freedoms as part of the obligation under Article 13 to provide an effective remedy for any violation of them.[6] The approach to be adopted in implementing these rights and freedoms is thus a matter of choice for each High Contracting Party.[7]

As a consequence the removal or weakening of established constitutional guarantees of rights and freedoms[8] would not, any more than a failure to elevate provisions in the European Convention to the constitutional level, normally entail a breach of any obligation assumed through its ratification. However, such a step could be problematic in at least two circumstances. Moreover it could also accelerate the possibility of recourse to the European Court when it is alleged that certain rights and freedoms have been violated.

Certainly a removal or reduction in constitutional guarantees would be problematic if that meant that there was no other basis in domestic law for securing the rights and freedoms in the European Convention. However, while constitutional guarantees often enhance the protection of ordinary law and can ensure a more "appropriate" interpretation of that law, fulfillment of the obligations as a High Con-

---

has the force of law. Furthermore, the application of the European Convention's provisions can still be affected by a reluctance to regard them as self-executing despite being incorporated into domestic law.

5 See e.g. *Observer and Guardian v. United Kingdom*, no. 13585/88, November 26, 1991, at para 76.

6 See e.g. *James and Others v. United Kingdom*, no. 8793/79, February 21, 1986, para 85.

7 This also generally applies to the execution of judgments; see *Scordino v. Italy (no. 1)* [GC], no. 36813/97, March 29, 2006, para 233.

8 As well as of measures giving the European Convention a quasi-constitutional status.

tracting Party does not generally depend upon the existence of constitutional guarantees as there will be many detailed rules in ordinary law that give effect to the requirements of the European Convention. Indeed, without such detailed provisions, many of those requirements could not in practice be met. The lowering of constitutional protection for rights and freedoms is in most instances, therefore, unlikely to result in a breach of the fundamental obligation laid down in Article 1 of the European Convention or a violation of specific rights and freedoms.

A different view would, of course, need to be taken of a constitutional change that actually made it unconstitutional to comply with the requirements of the European Convention. Such a change would necessarily mean that the state concerned, contrary to Article 1, was no longer securing the rights or freedoms concerned to everyone within its jurisdiction. However, although this would be a serious breach of the undertaking made through ratification of the European Convention, it is probably not one that could be brought before the European Court other than by another High Contracting Party. This is partly because Article 1 is not included in the rights and freedoms in respect of which individual applications are authorized under Article 34 but mainly because the mere existence of a law (constitutional or other) is not normally sufficient to constitute someone as a victim of a violation of one of those rights and freedoms, as required by the latter provision.[9]

A constitutional prohibition on giving effect to an aspect of right or freedom under the European Convention would, in the event of an adverse ruling by the European Court, also be an impediment to the execution of the judgment as required by Article 46 since the appropriate general measure (the removal of the constitutional prohibition) and possibly individual measures (such as the quashing of a conviction) could not be undertaken without some constitutional amendment.[10]

---

[9] Exceptions have been recognized as existing in the case of legislative provisions creating offences contrary to rights and freedoms under the European Convention (e.g., *Dudgeon v. United Kingdom*, no. 7525/76, October 22, 1981) and where someone is a member of a class of people who risk being directly affected by the legislation concerned (e.g., *Burden v. United Kingdom* [GC], no. 13378/05, April 29, 2008).

[10] This problem does not so far appear to have arisen in practice.

However, the weakening of the level of constitutional protection for rights and freedoms—whether permissive or mandatory in character—is also likely to have implications for the need for those claiming to be a victim of a violation of rights and freedom under the European Convention to exhaust domestic remedies. This is because it would result in a potential argument that there was no longer any means of remedying the illegal violation. As a consequence resort to the European Court could be speedier in some cases, namely, those where the incompatibility is clear cut and not open to debate, since there would be no need to seek constitutional redress for the application of the measure that is the immediate cause of the alleged violation.

Specific Provisions in the Fundamental Law

The possibility that certain provisions in the Fundamental Law are in some way weaker than or even contrary to the European Convention is not something that can be conclusively established for the moment since they have yet to be interpreted and applied. Indeed it is possible that they will be given effect in a manner that does not directly conflict with or fall below the requirements of the European Convention as a consequence of the stipulation in Article Q(2) that "in order to comply with its obligations under international law, Hungary shall ensure that Hungarian law be in conformity with international law."

However, whether that is so may depend on the way "conformity" is understood and also the significance in practice of Articles R(3) and I(3) which respectively provide for a requirement that the provisions in the Fundamental Law be interpreted "in accordance with their purposes, with the Avowal of National Faith contained therein, and with the achievements of our historical constitution" and the possibility that a fundamental right "may be restricted... to protect a constitutional value." Moreover, the issue of compliance with the requirements of the European Convention will necessarily be to some extent opaque as the evolving interpretation of its provisions can lead to an expansion in the understanding of what these requirements entail. At the same time it must be recognized that, in so far as the provisions run counter to the way a European consensus on certain issues is currently being seen to develop, the conservative or regressive position being adopted by Hungary could have the effect of changing the course of that development.

Nonetheless there are certain provisions in the Fundamental Law which are undoubtedly framed in a manner suggesting that they either will not reach the level of protection required by the European Convention or will actually require conduct that is incompatible with the requirements of the latter instrument.

There are at least nine aspects of the Fundamental Law which appear to afford less protection than is required by the European Convention.

The first concerns the specification in the National Avowal that statutes of limitation are inapplicable "for inhuman crimes committed against the Hungarian nation and its citizens under the national socialist and communist dictatorships." Certainly the concept of "inhuman crimes" is not necessarily coterminous with the exception from the prohibition on retrospective criminal liability in Article 7 of the European Convention for acts or omissions which were at the time of their commission either offences under international law or criminal according to the general principles of law recognized by civilized nations even if not an offence under national law. As the case law of the European Court demonstrates, these exceptions respectively cover offences established under international law at a given point of time after the adoption of the European Convention or war crimes and crimes against humanity established as part of international law prior to its adoption.[11] They thus do not cover all conduct that might be regarded as reprehensible. Any attempt, therefore to rely on the National Avowal to expand criminal liability—whether through new legislation or the interpretation of existing limitation provisions—beyond this exception would clearly be contrary to the European Convention.[12]

Second, the grounds of prohibited discrimination in Article XV(2) do not include sexual orientation. This omission leaves the Fundamental Law ostensibly in the same position as Article 14 of the European Convention and Protocol No. 12, which also make no express refer-

[11] See e.g. *Korbely v. Hungary* [GC], no. 9174/02, September 19, 2008.

[12] It should be noted that Article XXVIII(4) and (5) is in similar terms to Article 7 of the European Convention and this may constrain the effect of the provision in the National Avowal.

ence to sexual orientation. However, it is a ground that is firmly established in the case law of the European Court[13] and the omission, when taken with both the specific inclusion of the much more recently recognized ground of disability in the list and the exclusion of the possibility of same-sex marriages in Article L(1), could be construed as excluding sexual orientation from the protection Article XV(2) notwithstanding the latter's "catch-all" ground of "other circumstances."[14]

Third, the fact that the freedom and diversity of the press is only stated in Article IX to be a right belonging to everyone—as it is in Article 10 of the European Convention—but a duty for Hungary while at the same time is to be found in a discrete paragraph from the one guaranteeing the freedom of every person to express opinions could lead to its application in a manner at odds with the approach of the European Court, which has repeatedly emphasized the fundamental role of the press in securing and maintaining the democratic process.[15]

Fourth, the provision for life imprisonment without parole in Article IV(2) would be incompatible with the prohibition on inhuman and degrading treatment in Article 3 of the European Convention in the event that this is interpreted as allowing such a penalty to be imposed regardless of the nature of the offence or the circumstances of the offender.[16]

Fifth, a conflict with the European Convention could result from the application of the provision in Article XXIII(6) for the denial of the right to vote for every person disenfranchised by a court for committing an offence or due to his or her limited mental capacity. This provision provides no criteria governing such disenfranchisement but it is clear from the case of *Hirst v. United Kingdom* that the European Court considers that laws that allow for automatic disenfranchisement are

---

13 See e.g. *Karner v. Austria*, no. 40016/98, July 24, 2003.

14 See also Kriszta Kovács's contribution in this volume.

15 See e.g. *Observer and Guardian v. United Kingdom*. See also the Opinion of the Commissioner for Human Rights on Hungary's media legislation in light of Council of Europe standards (https://wcd.coe.int/ViewDoc.jsp?id=1751289) and the OSCE Analysis (http://www.osce.org/fom/75990).

16 See *Kafkaris v. Cyprus* [GC], no. 21906/04, February 12, 2008 and *Vinter and Others v. United Kingdom*, nos. 66069/09 and 130/10 and 3896/10, January 17, 2012.

contrary to Article 3 of Protocol No. 1.[17] Indeed, following the *Hirst* case the European Court ruled in *Alajos Kiss v. Hungary* that losing the right to vote as a result of imposition of an automatic, blanket restriction of the franchise of those under partial guardianship is a violation of the Convention.[18]

Sixth, the protection from expulsion in Article XIV(2) is not as extensive as that required by the European Convention since this applies only to situations in which the person concerned faces the danger of a death sentence, torture or other inhuman treatment or punishment. Not only does this not include the risk of being subjected to treatment that is degrading but it also does not provide protection against expulsion where there is risk of an unjustified deprivation of liberty, an unfair trial or a violation of the right to freedom of thought, conscience and religion, all of which have been recognized by the European Court as requiring a High Contracting Party not to expose someone to such a risk through his or her deportation or expulsion.[19] The last of these risks ought to be satisfactorily addressed by the duty in the third paragraph of Article XIV to grant asylum to persons facing persecution for their religious persuasions[20] but the other two remain without any constitutional safeguard.

Seventh, the authorization in Article XIX for the nature and extent of social measures to be "determined by law in accordance with the usefulness to the community of the beneficiary's activity" is undoubtedly capable of excluding persons from adequate social protection notwithstanding their total destitution. As such this could result in violations of both the right to life and the prohibition on inhuman and degrading treatment under Articles 2 and 3 of the European Convention.[21]

---

[17] *Hirst v. United Kingdom (no. 2)* [GC], no. 74025/01, October 6, 2005. Reaffirmed in *Scoppola v. Italy (no. 3),* [GC], no. 126/05, May 22, 2012.

[18] *Alajos Kiss v. Hungary,* no. 38832/06, May 20, 2010. See also the opinion of the Venice Commission recommending the total abolition of voting restrictions for persons with mental disabilities (http://www.venice.coe.int/docs/2011/CDL-AD%282011%29045-e.pdf).

[19] See e.g. *Z. and T. v. United Kingdom* (dec.), no. 27034/05, February 28, 2006 and *Othman v. United Kingdom,* no. 8139/09, January 17, 2012.

[20] It is worth mentioning though that under Article XIV(3) non-Hungarian citizens shall be granted asylum only if neither their country of origin nor another country provides protection for them.

[21] See e.g. *Cyprus v. Turkey* [GC], no. 25781/94, May 10, 2001.

Eighth, the provision in Article 54(1) for the suspension or restriction of fundamental rights during special legal orders such as states of national crisis and states of emergency goes beyond the express terms of Article 15 of the European Convention in that no exception is made with regard to the prohibition of slavery or servitude but perhaps more importantly it allows for disregard of the condition in Article I(3) of the Fundamental Law that a restriction on a fundamental right should be only to "the extent that is absolutely necessary, proportionately to the objective pursued, and respecting the essential content of such fundamental right." As a consequence there is certainly a risk that this could lead to the disregard of the requirement in Article 15 that any measures in derogation of rights and freedoms under the European Convention should only be "to the extent strictly required by the exigencies of the situation."

Finally, the protection for the right to property does not seem as extensive as that under Article 1 of Protocol No. 1, notwithstanding the terms of Article XIII, since Article 37(4) does not permit this right to be the basis for challenging a range of financial and tax legislation as long as the state debt exceeds half of the Gross Domestic Product and the calculation of that debt is a matter for the legislature rather than any objective measure. Although financial measures will rarely conflict with the prohibition on expropriation and any way the European Court gives them a wide margin of appreciation, the fact that they can include those affecting pensions undoubtedly makes the risk of such a conflict greater.

Although the Fundamental Law seems to favor Christianity and already established religions both in the terms of the National Avowal and the provision in Article VII(2) for cooperation by the state with churches "for community goals," this does not necessarily entail those belonging to newer religions or those with no religious belief being put at any disadvantage. On its face there is, therefore, no risk of a violation of Article 9, taken alone or in conjunction with Article 14, of the European Convention or of Article 2 of Protocol No. 1. Nevertheless this is an area where practice that is incompatible with these provisions could be encouraged by the terms of the Fundamental Law and future developments will need to be subjected to close scrutiny and possible correction.[22] For instance, the act implementing Article VII of the

---

[22] See *Lautsi and Others v. Italy* [GC], no. 30814/06, March 18, 2011.

Fundamental Law has been found by the Venice Commission, despite embodying a liberal and generous framework for freedom of religion, to fall short of international standards in a number of crucial respects (recognition of a church, the de-registration of hundreds of previously recognized churches, and the unequal treatment of religious beliefs and communities).[23]

Attention will need to be paid to the actual application of the prohibition on belonging to political parties and engaging in political activities that affects the commissioner for fundamental rights and his or her deputies, judges, prosecutors and the members of the defense forces, the national security service and the police. Although such a bar in the case of the Hungarian police was upheld by the European Court,[24] it should be noted that its conclusion that the latter restriction did not breach the right to freedom of expression and association under Articles 10 and 11 of the European Convention was in part based on the fact that police officers continued to have the right "to expound election programs, promote and nominate candidates, organize election campaign meetings, vote in and stand for elections to Parliament, local authorities and the office of mayor, participate in referenda, join trade unions, associations and other organizations, participate in peaceful assemblies, make statements to the press, participate in radio or television programs or publish works on politics."[25] An extension of the effect of the prohibition for at least some of the categories of persons concerned as a result of constitutionalizing it would probably lead to a finding of a violation of Articles 10 and 11.

There seem to be at least five provisions in the Fundamental Law which could be construed as either requiring action contrary to or prohibiting compliance with the European Convention.

The first concerns the reduction in the retirement age for judges from 70 to 62 effected by Article 26(2), assuming that this is to be applied to serving judges and not future appointees. Such a change in the employment rights of the judges concerned necessarily entails an

---

23 Act CCVI of 2011 on the Right to Freedom of Conscience and Religion and the Legal Status of Churches, Denominations and Religious Communities. See, further, Renáta Uitz's contribution in this volume.

24 *Rekvényi v. Hungary* [GC], no. 25390/94, May 20, 1999.

25 Ibid., para 49.

abrogation of their civil rights—it is of no consequence that the contracts affected are ones with public servants since the case law of the European Court now treats these the same as other employment contracts[26]—and thus affect their possessions.[27] A violation of Article 1 of Protocol No. 1 could only be avoided if legislation provided for the judges to be properly compensated for the expropriation of their rights. In addition, the independence guarantee in Article 6 of the Convention could be a discrete ground of challenge to this provision, although it only a party to legal proceedings and not the judge would be in a position to invoke the requirement of judicial independence.

A second conflict could arise from several aspects of the formulation of the obligation to perform military service in Article XXXI. First, this obligation applies only to adult males, which may involve discrimination on grounds of sex as women increasingly serve in the armed forces of European countries.[28] Second, no exception is made from the obligation in respect of the capacity to serve, which could be contrary to the prohibition on inhuman and degrading treatment in Article 3 of the European Convention. Third, although account is purportedly taken of the position of those with conscientious objections, the exception made is only as regards the need to do armed service and this does not address the position of those whose conscientious objection is to the use of force as such (which unarmed service would still sustain) or a particular conflict. Fourth, no provision is made for conscientious objection in the obligation for every citizen to perform work for national defense. These latter two limitations run counter to the protection for conscientious objection under Article 9 of the European Convention where there is a serious and insurmountable conflict between an obligation and a person's conscience or belief and which Article 4(3)(b) does not preclude from applying even to military service itself.[29]

A third conflict, also involving Article 4 of the European Convention, might lie in the obligation in Article XII "to contribute to the

---

[26] See *Vilho Eskelinen and Others v. Finland* [GC], no. 63235/00, April 19, 2007. See also *K.M.C. v. Hungary*, no. 19554/11, July 10, 2012.

[27] See e.g. *Azinas v. Cyprus* [GC], no. 56679/00, April 28, 2004.

[28] *Karlheinz Schmidt v. Germany*, no. 13580/88, July 18, 1994.

[29] See *Batayan v. Armenia* [GC], no. 23459/03, July 7, 2011.

enrichment of the community through their work, performed according to their best abilities and possibilities" as this would seem to have the potential to require more than the exception to the prohibition on forced or compulsory labor for "any work or service which forms part of normal civic obligations."[30] The latter, on the other hand, could well cover the obligation in Article XVI(4) for adult children "to take care of their parents if they are in need."

A fourth conflict could stem from the specification in Article II that "the life of the fetus shall be protected from the moment of conception." Taken on its own, a provision for such protection is unlikely to be problematic but as an elaboration of the right to life it could lead to the conclusion that both abortion and in vitro fertilization (during which fetuses are destroyed) is not permitted. A prohibition on both of these would undoubtedly be incompatible with the right to respect for private life under Article 8 of the European Convention, particularly as the case law of the European Court has established that there is no European consensus as to when life begins.[31]

The potential for a fifth conflict lies in the stipulation in Article L(1) that marriage is "the union of a man and a woman" as this undoubtedly precludes the possibility of same-sex marriages. As such this is not incompatible with the current interpretation of the right to marry in Article 12 of the European Convention. Nevertheless this is an area in which the European consensus is moving towards not just extending protection to same-sex relationships but also to allowing those relationships to be institutionalized as marriage should that be the wish of the parties to them. Article L(1) would thus be an impediment to responding to any evolution in this direction by the case law of the European Court.

---

[30] See *Zarb Adami v. Malta*, no. 17209/02, June 20, 2006.

[31] See *Evans v. United Kingdom* [GC], no. 6339/05, April 10, 2007 and *A., B. and C. v. Ireland* [GC], no. 25579/05, December 16, 2010. See, further, Catherine Dupré's contribution in this volume.

The Impact on Democracy and the Rule of Law

It is not only the potential clash with particular provisions that calls into question the Fundamental Law's compatibility with the European Convention—there are certain aspects of it which could be regarded as running counter to the principles of democracy and the rule of law (including the independence of the judiciary), the fundamental importance of which the European Court has emphasized on many occasions.

The possible conflict with democracy comes particularly from the way in which the Fundamental Law provides for so much of elaboration of rights and freedoms and socio-economic policy to be governed by cardinal acts.[32] These acts must be adopted and can only be amended by a two-thirds vote of the members of Parliament present,[33] allowing a transient majority—which may either be the result of an exceptional electoral landslide or just the votes of those present on the day[34]—to give enhanced protection to the matters concerned. It is, of course, not inconsistent with democracy for some matters to be entrenched in this way. Indeed this is the basis for the constitutional protection of human rights but, as is clear from the application of the limitation clauses under the European Convention and the development of the doctrine of the margin of appreciation, the European Court recognizes that democracy entails considerable freedom of choice in the adoption of not only of social and economic policies but

---

[32] That is, in respect of the matters addressed by Articles G(1) and (4), I(4), l(3), VII(3), VIII(4), IX(3), XXIII(4), XXIX(3), XXXI(3), (4) and (6), 2(1) and (2), 4(2) and (5), 5(8), 7(3), 12(5), 17(4), 23(1), (2) and (4), 24(2)(g),(3)(c) and (5), 25(7), 26(1) and (2), 29(7), 31(3), 33(3), 35(1), (2) and (4), 38(2), 40, 41(1), (4) and (5), 42, 43(4), 44(5), 45(2) and (5), 46(6), 49(3)(c), 50(3), 51(1) and (4), 52(3), 53(1) and (2), 54(4).

[33] The veto given by Article 44(3) to the Budget Council over the adoption of the central budget goes well beyond constitutional provisions adopted or being considered in other European countries in the restrictions being imposed on the powers of the legislature with the aim of securing fiscal rectitude.

[34] This can be contrasted for the specification in Article S(2) of a two-thirds majority of all members of Parliament for the adoption of any amendment to the Fundamental Law itself.

also the balance to be achieved between rights or freedoms and other competing interests.[35]

Democracy is to an extent specifically required by the commitment given in Article 3 of Protocol No. 1 to the holding of free elections so as to ensure "the free expression of the opinion of the people in the choice of the legislature." This provision is, however, concerned more with the scope of the franchise, the regulations governing candidacy and the electoral process than the powers left to the legislature.[36] Moreover the European Court's primary concern with upholding democracy has been in cases where it has found inadmissible attempts by individuals and organizations to invoke rights and freedoms under the European Convention to undertake action that it considered anti-democratic in means or objective.[37] Nonetheless there are two possible bases on which the potentially excessive circumscription that could be effected through cardinal acts as to the choice open to future Parliaments could be challenged before the European Court.

The first would be to assert that this is incompatible with the prohibition on abuse of rights in Article 17 of the European Convention.[38] This is, however, a provision that has rarely been invoked against states—to which it applies as much as to individuals—and it has never resulted in any substantive discussion by the European Court, let alone an adverse ruling against a state. Nonetheless one member of the former European Commission of Human Rights did accept the argument that a totalitarian conspiracy involving a government rendered its dero-

---

[35] See *Handyside v. United Kingdom*, no. 5493/72, December 7, 1976, *Hatton v. United Kingdom* [GC], no. 36022/97, July 8, 2003 and *J A Pye (Oxford) Ltd and JA Pye (Oxford) Land Ltd v. United Kingdom* [GC], no. 44302/02, August 30, 2007.

[36] See e.g. *Aziz v. Cyprus*, no. 69949/02, June 22, 2004, *Tănase and Chirtoaca v. Moldova*, no. 7/08, November 18, 2008 and *The Georgian Labour Party v. Georgia*, no. 9103/04, July 8, 2008.

[37] See e.g. *Refah Partisi (The Welfare Party) and Others v. Turkey* [GC], nos. 41340/98, 41342/98, 41343/98 and 41344/98, February 13, 2003.

[38] Article 17 provides that "Nothing in this Convention may be interpreted as implying for any State, group or person any right to engage in any activity or perform any act aimed at the destruction of any of the rights and freedoms set forth herein or at their limitation to a greater extent than is provided for in the Convention."

gation under Article 15 impermissible under Article 17.[39] A challenge relying on the latter provision would undoubtedly need to be brought by a state as an individual might well have difficulty in demonstrating that the effect on them of the use of cardinal acts is sufficient to constitute them as a victim.

The second basis for a challenge—and one open more readily to individuals—might be an assertion that the limitations on particular rights and freedoms were not necessary in a democratic society. This is not something that can be assessed in the abstract as the concern here is whether a particular interference corresponds with a pressing social need and is proportionate to the legitimate aim being pursued. However, the inability to abandon certain limitations solely because they have been imposed by cardinal acts might make the argument that of those limitations are needed less compelling, especially if they are out of line with the position adopted by other European countries.

The possibility that the Fundamental Law might not be fully compatible with the requirements of the rule of law stems from several features in it. Undoubtedly legal certainty could well be imperiled both by the proclamation in the National Avowal of the invalidity of the communist 1949 Constitution without further clarification of the consequences of this and by the provision in Article I(3) for the "Acts"—a term that is not defined—to determine the rules for fundamental rights and obligations without any guidelines to govern their scope and elaboration or any indication whether these are the same as or in addition to the cardinal acts mentioned in various fundamental rights provisions.

Moreover the rule of law must be regarded as being seriously undermined by the fairly indefinite and extensive immunity from constitutional challenge, already noted, that has been given by Article 37(4) to a wide range of measures that could affect individual rights and obligations. Furthermore judicial independence—a *sine qua non* for the rule of law—is undoubtedly going to be affected not only by the sudden removal of the former head of the Supreme Court[40] and a significant number of judges through advancing the retirement age but also by the fact that the chief prosecutor and the head of the National Judicial Office may designate any case to a court at an equal level but

[39] The *Greek* case, 12 YB 1 (1969), at 102–103.
[40] Article 11(2) of the Transitional Provisions.

outside the normal court's jurisdiction,[41] as well as by the failure of the Fundamental Law to specify the different levels of courts and thus providing no constitutional protection against changes to them. Judicial independence could also be threatened by the fact that both the remuneration of judges and the grounds for their removal are left by Articles 25(7) and 26(1) to be defined by a cardinal act, without any assurance that the internationally recognized standards governing these matters will be observed. Furthermore the specification in Article 25(5) that "the organs of judicial self-government shall *participate* in the administration of the courts"[42] does not inspire much confidence that the courts will not be subject to the dictates of the executive.[43]

---

41 Articles 11(3) and 11(4) of the Transitional Provisions.

42 Emphasis added. See, further, Act CLXI of 2011 on the organization and administration of courts and Act CLXII of 2011 on the legal status and remuneration of judges.

43 The law implementing the lowering of the judicial retirement (but not the provision in the Fundamental Law) has been held by the Constitutional Court to violate judicial independence. Decision 33/2012. (VII. 16.) This ruling would probably not meet the standards for judicial independence in Article 6 of the European Convention since it would seemingly find a less sudden but still retroactive reduction in retirement age acceptable. Moreover, the ruling, although finding the law unconstitutional *ab initio*, did not invalidate the presidential orders dismissing judges pursuant to it and so dismissed judges unable to secure their reinstatement would still have claims for redress to advance in the European Court. One dissenting judge (Pokol) suggested that the case was inadmissible because the judges bringing it should first have gone to the labor courts which could then have referred the issue to the Constitutional Court. However, in *K.M.C. v. Hungary*, no. 19554/11, July 10, 2012, the European Court saw the prospect of such a reference as speculative and not a reason for finding that domestic remedies had not been exhausted in a case of a civil servant dismissed without any reasons for such action being given. It is improbable, therefore, that claims of violation of the European Convention for reasons not addressed by the Constitutional Court would be barred because a reference relating to them was not first sought from the labor courts. The European Commission has also sought a declaration from the EU Court of Justice that Hungary has failed to fulfill its obligation under Articles 2 and 6(l) of Council Directive 2000/78/EC as result of the lowering of the retirement age since this embodied differential treatment on grounds of age not justified by a legitimate purpose and, in any event, not appropriate or necessary for the achievement of the stated purpose; *European Commission v. Hungary*, C-286/12 (pending).

Some of the issues relating to judicial independence could well figure as elements in complaints that there has not been a fair trial since Article 6(1) of the European Convention requires cases to be determined by an independent tribunal. Furthermore, the enforced retirement of judges, as has been seen, will engage their right to property under Article 1 of Protocol No. 1. The latter right could also be breached if the annulment of the communist constitution actually had any impact on previously established rights and obligations. The need for special acts to determine rules for fundamental rights and obligations might also mean that the scope of rights are insufficiently defined or that limitations are insufficiently precise to satisfy the requirement of the European Convention that these be "prescribed by law" or "in accordance with the law" and thus constitute a violation of the rights and freedoms that it guarantees.

Despite these possibilities, the European Court would probably be much more comfortable if any challenge based on democracy and the rule of law was made through the political organs of the Council of Europe.[44]

Conclusion

What the European Court will actually make of the Fundamental Law if any of its provisions come before it clearly remains in the realm of speculation. Interpretation, inaction and inconclusive evidence can all result in nothing objectionable being established in the particular circumstances of a case. Indeed the fact that the European Court is charged with determining specific cases of alleged violations of the European Convention means that it can be unable, or even unwilling, to see the wood for the trees; a case in isolation will not always be recognized as embodying a systemic flaw. Nevertheless the provisions of the Fundamental Law and/or measures taken pursuant to them certainly have the potential for considerable argument as to whether the requirements of the European Convention are being satisfactorily implemented in Hungary. In view of the range of potential problems of

[44] Under Article 8 of the Statute of the Council of Europe; see n. 2.

compliance, it can be expected that issues arising from the implementation of the Fundamental Law could keep the European Court very busy for some time to come. This is all more regrettable since Hungary's efforts in the early 1990s to ensure that national law and practice complied with the European Convention before ratifying it were exemplary.

VI. APPENDIX

The Fundamental Law of Hungary[1]

[1] There are several English versions of the Fundamental Law.

An English translation of the draft text was presented to the European Union for the public hearing on the Hungarian Constitution (European Parliament, March 29, 2011). This translation proved to be misleading since it missed crucial elements of the original text. Hungarian human rights NGOs released a *Full list of mistakes and omissions of the English Version of the Hungarian draft Constitution* (http://tasz.hu/files/tasz/imce/list_of_all_the_omissions_and_mistranslations.pdf). Moreover, Hungarian Civil Liberties Union issued an alternative translation of the draft text (http://tasz.hu/files/tasz/imce/alternative_translation_of_the_draft_constituion.pdf).

Soon after the Hungarian Parliament adopted the Fundamental Law, the Hungarian Ministry of Public Administration and Justice made a first official English translation of the Fundamental Law, which was published on governmental websites, sent to international organizations and printed in a special issue of the official gazette. This version is also available in French and German languages (http://www.kormany.hu/en/news/the-new-fundamental-law-of-hungary). The analysis of the Venice Commission is based upon the first official English translation (see *Opinion 621/2011*, para 16).

Since the official translation was found to be misleading, Hungarian scholars decided to make a new one. (See Csink, Schanda, Varga eds., *The Basic Law of Hungary: A First Commentary*, Budapest-Dublin: Clarus Press, National Institute of Public Administration, 2012, 295.)

Meanwhile the Hungarian Ministry of Public Administration and Justice released a second, revised version of the English translation, which is published, e.g., on the website of the Hungarian Constitutional Court.

This volume contains the second official version of the text in American English with some explanatory footnotes added by the editor of this volume.

THE FUNDAMENTAL LAW OF HUNGARY

(25 April 2011)

God bless the Hungarians[2]

AVOWAL OF NATIONAL FAITH[3]

WE THE MEMBERS OF THE HUNGARIAN NATION, at the beginning of a new millennium, with a sense of responsibility for every Hungarian, declare the following:

We are proud that one thousand years ago our king, Saint Stephen, built the Hungarian State on solid foundations, and made our country a part of Christian Europe.

We are proud of our forbears, who fought for the survival, freedom and independence of our country.

We are proud of the outstanding intellectual achievements of the Hungarian people.

We are proud that our people have fought in defense of Europe over the centuries and, through their talent and industry, have enriched Europe's common values.

We recognize the role Christianity has played in preserving our nation. We value our country's different religious traditions.

We promise to preserve the intellectual and spiritual unity of our nation torn apart in the storms of the past century. The nationalities living with us form part of the Hungarian political community and are constituent parts of the State.

---

[2] This is the first line of the Hungarian national anthem.

[3] In other translations the preamble is named as *National Creed* or *National Avowal.*

We commit ourselves to cherishing and preserving our heritage, our unique language, the Hungarian culture, the languages and cultures of nationalities in Hungary, and the natural and man-made riches of the Carpathian Basin. Bearing responsibility for our descendants, we shall protect the living conditions of future generations by making prudent use of our material, intellectual and natural resources.

We believe that our national culture is a rich contribution to the diversity of European unity.

We respect the freedom and cultures of other peoples, and shall strive to cooperate with every nation of the world.

We hold that human existence is based on human dignity.

We hold that individual freedom can only unfold through cooperation with others.

We hold that the family and the nation provide the most important framework for our coexistence, and that our fundamental cohesive values are fidelity, faith and love.

We hold that the strength of a community and the honour of each person are based on work, an achievement of the human mind.

We hold that we are duty-bound to help the vulnerable and the poor.

We hold that the common goal of citizens and the State is to achieve the highest possible measure of well-being, security, order, justice and liberty.

We hold that democracy exists only where the State serves it citizens and administers their affairs in an equitable manner and without abuse or partiality.

We honor the achievements of our historical constitution and we honour the Holy Crown, which embodies the constitutional continuity of Hungary's statehood and the unity of the nation.

We do not recognize the suspension of our historical constitution due to foreign occupations. We declare that no statutory limitation applies to the inhuman crimes committed against the Hungarian nation and its citizens under the national socialist and communist dictatorships.

We do not recognize the communist constitution of 1949, since it was the basis of a tyrannical rule; therefore we proclaim it to be invalid.

We agree with the members of the first free Parliament, who proclaimed in their first decision that our current liberty was born of our 1956 Revolution.

We date the restoration of the self-determination of our State, lost on the nineteenth day of March 1944, from the second day of May 1990, when the first freely elected popular representation was formed. We shall consider this date to be the beginning of our country's new democracy and constitutional order.

We hold that after the decades in the twentieth century leading to moral decay, a spiritual and intellectual renewal is absolutely necessary.

We trust in a jointly-shaped future and the commitment of young generations. We believe that our children and grandchildren will make Hungary great again through their talent, perseverance and moral strength.

Our Fundamental Law shall be the basis of our legal order: it shall be a covenant among Hungarians past, present and future. It is a living framework expressing the nation's will and the form in which we wish to live.

We, the citizens of Hungary, are ready to found the order of our country upon the cooperation of the nation.

FUNDAMENTALS

Article A

The name of OUR COUNTRY shall be Hungary.

Article B

(1) Hungary shall be an independent, democratic State under the rule of law.
(2) Hungary, as to its form of government, shall be a republic.
(3) The source of public power shall be the people.
(4) The people shall exercise their power through their elected representatives or, in exceptional cases, directly.

Article C

(1) The functioning of the Hungarian State shall be based on the principle of the separation of powers.
(2) No one's activities shall be aimed at the acquisition or exercise of power by force, or at the exclusive possession of power. Everyone shall have the right and obligation to resist such attempts in a lawful way.
(3) The State shall have the right to use coercion in order to enforce the Fundamental Law and the rules of law.

Article D

Bearing in mind that there is one single Hungarian nation that belongs together, Hungary shall bear responsibility for the fate of Hungarians living beyond its borders, shall facilitate the survival and development of their communities, shall support their efforts to preserve their Hungarian identity, the application of their individual and collective rights, the establishment of their community self-governments, and their prosperity in their native lands, and shall promote their cooperation with each other and with Hungary.

Article E

(1) In order to achieve the highest possible measure of freedom, well-being and security for the peoples of Europe Hungary shall contribute to the achievement of European unity.
(2) In order to participate in the European Union as a Member State, and on the basis of an international treaty, Hungary may, to the extent necessary to exercise the rights and fulfil the obligations set out in the founding treaties, exercise some of its competences deriving from the Fundamental Law jointly with other Member States, through the institutions of the European Union.
(3) The law of the European Union may stipulate generally binding rules of conduct subject to the conditions set out in paragraph (2).
(4) The authorization for expressing consent to be bound by an international treaty referred to in paragraph (2) shall require the votes of two-thirds of all Members of Parliament.

Article F

(1) The capital of Hungary shall be Budapest.
(2) The territory of Hungary shall be divided into counties, cities or towns, and villages. In cities or towns districts may be formed.

Article G

(1) A child born to a Hungarian citizen shall be a Hungarian citizen by birth. A cardinal Act may specify other grounds for the origin or acquisition of Hungarian citizenship.
(2) Hungary shall protect its citizens.
(3) No one shall be deprived of his or her Hungarian citizenship acquired by birth or obtained in a lawful manner.
(4) The detailed rules for citizenship shall be laid down in a cardinal Act.

Article H

(1) In Hungary the official language shall be Hungarian.
(2) Hungary shall protect the Hungarian language.
(3) Hungary shall protect Hungarian sign language as a part of the Hungarian culture.

Article I

(1) The coat of arms of Hungary shall be a vertically divided shield with a pointed base. The left field shall contain eight horizontal bars of red and silver. The right field shall have a red background and shall depict a base of three green hills with a golden crown atop the higher central hill through which rises a silver patriarchal cross. The Holy Crown of Hungary shall rest on top of the shield.

(2) The flag of Hungary shall feature three horizontal bands of equal width coloured red, white and green from top to bottom as the symbols of strength, fidelity and hope, respectively.

(3) The anthem of Hungary shall be the poem *Himnusz* by Ferenc Kölcsey set to music by Ferenc Erkel.
(4) The coat of arms and the flag may also be used in other historically developed forms. The detailed rules for the use of the coat of arms and the flag, as well as the state decorations shall be laid down in a cardinal Act.

Article J

(1) The national holidays of Hungary shall be:
  a) the 15th day of March, in memory of the 1848-49 Revolution and War of Independence;
  b) the 20th day of August, in memory of the foundation of the State and King Saint Stephen the State Founder; and
  c) the 23rd day of October, in memory of the 1956 Revolution and War of Independence.
(2) The official state holiday shall be the 20th day of August.

Article K

The official currency of Hungary shall be the forint.

Article L

(1) Hungary shall protect the institution of marriage, understood to be the conjugal union of a man and a woman established by their voluntary decision, and the family as the basis of the nation's survival.
(2) Hungary shall support the commitment to have children.
(3) The protection of families shall be regulated by a cardinal Act.

Article M

(1) The economy of Hungary shall be based upon work which creates value, and upon freedom of enterprise.

(2) Hungary shall ensure the conditions of fair economic competition. Hungary shall act against any abuse of a dominant position and protect the rights of consumers.

Article N

(1) Hungary shall enforce the principle of balanced, transparent and sustainable budget management.
(2) Parliament and the Government shall have primary responsibility for the enforcement of the principle referred to in paragraph (1).
(3) In the course of performing their duties, the Constitutional Court, courts, local governments and other state organs shall be bound to respect the principle referred to in paragraph (1).

Article O

Everyone shall be responsible for their own self, and shall be bound to contribute to the performance of state and community tasks according to their abilities and possibilities.

Article P

Natural resources, in particular agricultural land, forests and the reserves of water, biological diversity, in particular indigenous plant and animal species, as well as cultural assets shall form the nation's common heritage; the State and every person shall be bound to protect, maintain and preserve them for future generations.

Article Q

(1) In order to establish and maintain peace and security and to achieve the sustainable development of humanity, Hungary shall strive to cooperate with all the peoples and countries of the world.
(2) In order to comply with its obligations under international law, Hungary shall ensure that Hungarian law be in conformity with international law.
(3) Hungary shall accept the generally recognized rules of international law. Other sources of international law shall become part of the Hungarian legal system by publication in rules of law.

Article R

(1) The Fundamental Law shall be the foundation of the legal system of Hungary.
(2) The Fundamental Law and the rules of law shall be binding on everyone.
(3) The provisions of the Fundamental Law shall be interpreted in accordance with their purposes, with the Avowal of National Faith contained therein, and with the achievements of our historical constitution.

Article S

(1) The President of the Republic, the Government, any parliamentary committee or any Member of Parliament may submit a proposal for the adoption of a new Fundamental Law or for any amendment of the Fundamental Law.
(2) For the adoption of a new Fundamental Law or any amendment thereof the votes of two-thirds of all Members of Parliament shall be required.
(3) The Speaker of Parliament shall sign the Fundamental Law or an amendment thereof and send it to the President of the Republic. The President of the Republic shall sign the Fundamental Law or the amendment thereof within five days of receipt and shall order its publication in the Official Gazette.
(4) The designation of the amendment of the Fundamental Law in its publication shall include the title, the serial number of the amendment and the date of publication.

Article T

(1) A generally binding rule of conduct shall be laid down in a rule of law which is adopted by an organ specified in the Fundamental Law as being competent to make law and which is published in the Official Gazette. A cardinal Act may determine different rules for the publication of local government decrees and for rules of law adopted during any special legal order.
(2) A 'rule of law'[4] shall mean Acts of Parliament (hereinafter referred to as 'Act' in the English translation), government decrees, decrees of the Prime Minister, decrees of Ministers, decrees of the Governor of the

[4] *Rule of law* is equivalent to *laws*.

National Bank of Hungary,[5] decrees of the head of an autonomous regulatory organ and local government decrees. In addition, decrees of the National Defense Council adopted during a state of national crisis and decrees of the President of the Republic adopted during a state of emergency shall also be rules of law.

(3) No rule of law shall be contrary to the Fundamental Law.

(4) 'Cardinal Act' shall mean an Act, the adoption or amendment of which requires the votes of two-thirds of the Members of Parliament present.

[5] *National* Bank is the central bank of Hungary. *Governor* of the National Bank is equivalent to *President* of the National Bank.

FREEDOM AND RESPONSIBILITY

Article I

(1) The inviolable and inalienable fundamental rights of MAN shall be respected. It shall be the primary obligation of the State to protect these rights.
(2) Hungary shall recognize the fundamental individual and collective rights of Man.
(3) The rules relating to fundamental rights and obligations shall be laid down in Acts. A fundamental right may only be restricted in order to allow the exercise of another fundamental right or to protect a constitutional value, to the extent that is absolutely necessary, proportionately to the objective pursued, and respecting the essential content of such fundamental right.
(4) Legal entities established by an Act shall also have the fundamental rights, and they shall also be bound by the obligations which, by their nature, apply not only to human beings.

Article II

Human dignity shall be inviolable. Every human being shall have the right to life and human dignity; the life of the fetus shall be protected from the moment of conception.[6]

Article III

(1) No one shall be subjected to torture, inhuman or degrading treatment or punishment, or be held in servitude. Trafficking in human beings shall be prohibited.
(2) It shall be prohibited to perform any medical or scientific experiment on human beings without their informed and voluntary consent.
(3) Practices aimed at eugenics, the use of the human body or its parts for financial gain, and the cloning of human beings shall be prohibited.

---

[6] This is a proper translation of the original "*magzat*." The first official English version, however, contains "*embryonic and fetal life.*" See Catherine Dupré's contribution in this volume.

Article IV

(1) Everyone shall have the right to liberty and to security of the person.
(2) No one shall be deprived of their liberty, except for reasons stipulated in an Act and only in accordance with the procedure stipulated in an Act. Life imprisonment without parole may only be imposed for the commission of a willful and violent criminal offence.
(3) Any person suspected of having committed a criminal offence and held in detention shall either be released or brought before a court within the shortest possible period of time. The court shall give a hearing to the person brought before it and immediately make a decision with a written reasoning either to release the person or to place him or her under arrest.
(4) Anyone whose liberty has been restricted without a well-founded reason or unlawfully shall have the right to compensation for the damage suffered.

Article V

Everyone shall have the right, as specified in an Act, to repel any unlawful attack against their person or property, or one that poses a direct threat to the same.

Article VI

(1) Everyone shall have the right to have their private and family life, home, communications and good reputation respected.
(2) Everyone shall have the right to the protection of their personal data, as well as to access and disseminate data of public interest.
(3) An independent authority set up by a cardinal Act shall supervise the enforcement of the right to the protection of personal data and of the right to access data of public interest.

Article VII

(1) Everyone shall have the right to freedom of thought, conscience and religion. This right shall include the freedom to choose or change one's religion or other conviction, and the freedom to manifest or abstain from manifesting, to practice or teach, either alone or in community with others, in public or in private, one's religion or other conviction through religious acts or ceremonies, or in any other way.

(2) The State and the churches shall operate separately.[7] Churches shall be autonomous. The State shall cooperate with the churches for the attainment of community goals.
(3) The detailed rules relating to churches shall be laid down in a cardinal Act.

Article VIII

(1) Everyone shall have the right to peaceful assembly.
(2) Everyone shall have the right to form and join organizations.
(3) Political parties may be formed and may operate freely on the basis of the right to association. Political parties shall participate in the formation and expression of the will of the people. Political parties shall not exercise public power directly.
(4) The detailed rules for the operation and financial management of political parties shall be laid down in a cardinal Act.
(5) Trade unions and other interest representation organizations may be formed and may operate freely on the basis of the right to association.

Article IX

(1) Everyone shall have the right to freely express their opinion.
(2) Hungary shall recognize and protect the freedom and pluralism of the press,[8] and ensure the conditions for freedom of information necessary for the formation of democratic public opinion.
(3) The detailed rules relating to the freedom of the press and to the organ supervising media services, press products and the infocommunications market shall be laid down in a cardinal Act.

Article X

(1) Hungary shall ensure the freedom of scientific research and artistic creation, the freedom of learning in the interest of enabling the acquisition of the highest possible level of knowledge, and, within the framework determined by an Act, the freedom of teaching.

---

[7] The original "*különváltan működnek*" means separated functioning of churches and state. The 1989 Constitution contained "*elválasztva*", which was a reference to the classical separation principle. See Renáta Uitz's contribution in this volume.

[8] The original "*sokszínűség*" means *diversity*. The Fundamental Law does not acknowledge explicitly the *pluralism* of the press.

(2) The State shall not have the right to decide on questions of scientific truth; only scientists shall have the right to evaluate scientific research.
(3) Hungary shall protect the scientific and artistic freedom of the Hungarian Academy of Sciences and the Hungarian Academy of Arts. Higher education institutions shall be autonomous in terms of the content and methods of research and teaching; their organisation and financial management shall be regulated by an Act.

Article XI

(1) Every Hungarian citizen shall have the right to education.[9]
(2) Hungary shall ensure this right by extending and generalising public education, by providing free and compulsory primary education, free and generally accessible secondary education, and higher education accessible to everyone according to their abilities, and by providing financial support as laid down in an Act to those receiving education.[10]

Article XII

(1) Everyone shall have the right to freely choose their job or profession, and to engage in entrepreneurial activities. Everyone shall have a duty to contribute to the enrichment of the community through their work, performed according to their abilities and possibilities.
(2) Hungary shall strive to create conditions ensuring that everyone who is able and willing to work has the opportunity to do so.

Article XIII

(1) Everyone shall have the right to property and succession. Property shall entail social responsibility.
(2) Property may only be expropriated in exceptional cases and in the public interest, in such circumstances and manner as stipulated by an Act; expropriation shall be accompanied by full, unconditional and immediate compensation.

---

[9] The original *művelődés* is a broader concept; it includes also participation in cultural activities.

[10] The original *közművelődés* includes institutions such as libraries, museums and the network of local cultural centers.

Article XIV

(1) Hungarian citizens shall not be expelled from the territory of Hungary and may return at any time from abroad. Foreigners staying in the territory of Hungary may only be expelled on the basis of a lawful decision. Collective expulsion shall be prohibited.
(2) No one shall be expelled or extradited to a State where he or she would be in danger of being sentenced to death, being tortured, or being subjected to other inhuman treatment or punishment.
(3) Non-Hungarian citizens – upon their request and if neither their country of origin nor another country provides protection for them – shall be granted asylum by Hungary if they are persecuted in their native country or in the country of their habitual residence for reasons of their belonging to a race, nationality or a particular social group, or for reasons of their religious or political convictions, or if they have a well-founded fear of such persecution.

Article XV

(1) Everyone shall be equal before the law. Every human being shall have legal capacity.
(2) Hungary shall guarantee the fundamental rights to everyone without any discrimination, in particular on grounds of race, color, sex, disability, language, religion, political or other opinion, national or social origin, property, birth or any other status.
(3) Women and men shall have equal rights.
(4) Hungary shall facilitate the realization of equal opportunity with special measures.
(5) Hungary shall take special measures to protect children, women, the elderly and persons living with disabilities.

Article XVI

(1) Every child shall have the right to the protection and care necessary for their proper physical, intellectual and moral development.
(2) Parents shall have the right to choose the upbringing to be given to their children.
(3) Parents shall have the obligation to take care of their children for as long as they are minors. This obligation shall include the provision of schooling for their children.
(4) Adult children shall take care of their parents if they are in need.

Article XVII

(1) Workers and employers shall cooperate with each other, with a view to ensuring employment and the sustainability of the national economy, as well as to other community goals.
(2) Workers, employers and their respective organizations shall have the right, in accordance with an Act, to conduct negotiations with each other and conclude collective agreements on the basis thereof, and to take collective action or hold strikes in order to defend their interests.
(3) Every worker shall have the right to working conditions respecting their health, safety and dignity.
(4) Every worker shall have the right to daily and weekly rest periods, and annual paid leave.

Article XVIII

(1) The employment of children shall be prohibited except for cases specified in an Act where their physical, intellectual or moral development is not endangered.
(2) Hungary shall ensure through special measures the protection of young people and parents in the workplace.

Article XIX

(1) Hungary shall strive to provide social security to all of its citizens. Every Hungarian citizen shall be entitled to assistance as laid down in an Act in the event of maternity, illness or disability, or if he or she becomes a widow(er) or an orphan, or loses employment owing to circumstances beyond their control.
(2) Hungary shall implement social security for the persons referred to in paragraph (1) and for other persons in need through a system of social institutions and measures.
(3) The nature and extent of social measures may be determined by an Act also in accordance with the usefulness to the community of the beneficiary's activities.
(4) Hungary shall contribute to ensuring a livelihood for the elderly by maintaining a unified state pension system based on social solidarity and by allowing for the operation of voluntarily established social institutions. The conditions of entitlement to state pension may be specified by an Act also in view of the requirement for increased protection for women.

Article XX

(1) Everyone shall have the right to physical and mental health.
(2) Hungary shall further the realization of the right laid down in paragraph (1) by an agriculture which is free of genetically modified organisms, by ensuring access to healthy food and drinking water, by organizing safety at work and healthcare provision, by supporting sports and regular physical exercise, as well as by ensuring the protection of the environment.

Article XXI

(1) Hungary shall recognize and enforce the right of every person to a healthy environment.
(2) A person who causes any damage to the environment shall be obliged, as specified in an Act, to restore it or to bear the costs of restoration.
(3) It shall be prohibited to import pollutant waste to Hungary for the purpose of disposal.

Article XXII

Hungary shall strive to ensure decent housing conditions and access to public services for everyone.

Article XXIII

(1) Every adult Hungarian citizen shall have the right to vote and to stand as a candidate in elections of Members of Parliament, local government representatives and mayors, and of Members of the European Parliament.
(2) Every adult citizen of another Member State of the European Union who is a resident of Hungary shall have the right to vote and to stand as a candidate in elections of local government representatives and mayors, and of Members of the European Parliament.
(3) Every adult person recognized as a refugee, immigrant or resident in Hungary shall have the right to vote in elections of local government representatives and mayors.
(4) A cardinal Act may subject the right to vote or its completeness to residence in Hungary, and it may prescribe additional criteria for eligibility to stand as a candidate in elections.

(5) In elections of local government representatives and mayors voters may vote in the locality of their residence or their registered place of stay. Voters may exercise their right to vote in the locality of their residence or their registered place of stay.
(6) Those disenfranchised by a court for a criminal offence or for limited mental capacity shall not have the right to vote and to stand as a candidate in elections. Citizens of other Member States of the European Union who are residing in the territory of Hungary shall not have the right to stand as a candidate in elections if – pursuant to a rule of law, judicial or other official decision of their State of citizenship – they have been excluded from the exercise of this right in their country.
(7) Everyone who has the right to vote in elections of Members of Parliament shall have the right to participate in national referenda. Everyone who has the right to vote in elections of local government representatives and mayors shall have the right to participate in local referenda.
(8) Every Hungarian citizen shall have the right to hold public office according their suitability, qualifications and professional competence. Public offices that shall not be held by members or officers of political parties shall be specified in an Act.

Article XXIV

(1) Everyone shall have the right to have their affairs handled impartially, fairly and within a reasonable time by the authorities. Authorities shall give reasons for their decisions in the manner laid down in an Act.
(2) Everyone shall have the right to be compensated, in the manner laid down in an Act, for any damage unlawfully caused by the authorities in the performance of their duties.

Article XXV

Everyone shall have the right to submit – either alone or jointly with others – a written petition, complaint or proposal to any organ exercising public power.

Article XXVI

The State shall strive to make use of the latest technical solutions and the achievements of science to make its functioning efficient, raise the standard of public services, improve the transparency of public affairs, and promote equality of opportunity.

Article XXVII

(1) Everyone staying lawfully in the territory of Hungary shall have the right to move freely and to freely choose their place of stay.
(2) Every Hungarian citizen shall have the right to enjoy the protection of Hungary during his or her stay abroad.

Article XXVIII

(1) Everyone shall be entitled to have any charge against him or her, or his or her rights and obligations in any litigation, adjudicated within a reasonable time in a fair and public trial conducted by an independent and impartial court established by an Act.
(2) No one shall be considered guilty until his or her liability under criminal law has been established by the final decision of a court.
(3) Everyone who is prosecuted shall have the right to defense at all stages of criminal proceedings. Defense counsels shall not be held accountable for opinions expressed while providing legal defense.
(4) No one shall be found guilty and subjected to punishment for an act that, at the time it was committed, was not a criminal offence under the law of Hungary or – within the sphere specified by an international treaty or a legal act of the European Union – under the law of another State.
(5) Paragraph (4) shall not exclude the prosecution and conviction of a person for an act which, at the time it was committed, was a criminal offence according to the generally recognized rules of international law.
(6) With the exception of extraordinary cases of legal remedy laid down in an Act, no one shall be prosecuted or convicted for a criminal offence for which he or she has already been finally acquitted or convicted in Hungary or – within the sphere specified by an international treaty or a legal act of the European Union – in another State according to law.
(7) Everyone shall have the right to seek legal remedy against decisions of the courts, authorities or other organs of public administration which infringe his or her rights or legitimate interests.

Article XXIX

(1) Nationalities living in Hungary shall be constituent parts of the State. Every Hungarian citizen belonging to a nationality shall have the right to freely declare and preserve his or her identity. Nationalities living in Hungary shall have the right to use their mother tongue, to use their

names in their own language individually and collectively, to foster their culture and to receive education in their mother tongues.

(2) Nationalities living in Hungary may set up local and national self-governments.

(3) The detailed rules relating to the rights of nationalities living in Hungary, as well as those relating to the election of their local and national self-governments, shall be laid down in a cardinal Act.

Article XXX

(1) Everyone shall contribute to the financing of common needs according to their capacity and to their participation in the economy.

(2) For persons raising children, the extent of contribution to covering common needs shall be determined by taking into consideration the costs of raising children.

Article XXXI

(1) All Hungarian citizens shall be obliged to defend their country.

(2) Hungary shall maintain a volunteer reserve system for national defense purposes.

(3) During a state of national crisis, or if Parliament decides so during a state of preventive defense, adult men of Hungarian citizenship residing in Hungary shall perform military service. If military service involving the use of arms runs counter to the conscience of the person liable to render military service, he shall perform unarmed service. The forms and detailed rules of the performance of military service shall be laid down in a cardinal Act.

(4) For the duration of a state of national crisis, adult Hungarian citizens residing in Hungary may be ordered, as laid down in a cardinal Act, to perform work for national defense purposes.

(5) For adult Hungarian citizens residing in Hungary civil protection obligation may be introduced, as laid down in a cardinal Act, in the interest of performing national defense and disaster management tasks.

(6) In the interest of the performance of national defense or disaster management tasks everyone may be obliged, as laid down in a cardinal Act, to perform economic and material services.

THE STATE

Parliament

Article 1

(1) HUNGARY's principal organ of popular representation shall be Parliament.

(2) Parliament shall

a) adopt and modify the Fundamental Law of Hungary;

b) adopt Acts;

c) adopt the central budget and approve its implementation;

d) authorize the expression of consent to be bound by international treaties falling within its tasks and competences;

e) elect the President of the Republic, the members and the President of the Constitutional Court, the President of the Curia, the Prosecutor General,[11] the Commissioner for Fundamental Rights and his or her deputies, and the President of the State Audit Office;

f) elect the Prime Minister, decide on any matter of confidence related to the Government;

g) dissolve representative bodies of local government which operate in a way that is contrary to the Fundamental Law;

h) decide on the declaration of a state of war and on the conclusion of peace;

i) make decisions related to any special legal order and to participation in military operations;

j) grant general amnesty;

k) perform other tasks and exercise other competences laid down in the Fundamental Law or in Acts.

Article 2

(1) Members of Parliament shall be elected by direct and secret ballot by citizens eligible to vote, on the basis of universal and equal suffrage, in elections which guarantee free expression of voters' will, in a manner laid down in a cardinal Act.

---

[11] *Prosecutor General* is equivalent to *Chief Prosecutor*.

(2) The participation in the work of Parliament of nationalities living in Hungary shall be regulated by a cardinal Act.
(3) The general election of Members of Parliament shall be held in the month of April or May of the fourth year following election of the previous Parliament, except for elections resulting either from Parliament dissolving itself or from it being dissolved.

Article 3

(1) The mandate of Parliament shall commence with its constitutive sitting, and shall last until the constitutive sitting of the next Parliament. The constitutive sitting shall be convened by the President of the Republic within thirty days of the elections.
(2) Parliament may declare its own dissolution.
(3) The President of the Republic may dissolve Parliament, and simultaneously set a date for new elections, if
   a) Parliament, when the mandate of the Government terminates, fails to elect the person proposed by the President of the Republic for Prime Minister within forty days of presentation of the first nomination; or
   b) Parliament fails to adopt the central budget for the current year by 31 March.
(4) Prior to dissolving Parliament, the President of the Republic shall ask for the opinions of the Prime Minister, the Speaker of Parliament and the leaders of the parliamentary fractions.
(5) The President of the Republic may exercise his or her right pursuant to point a) of paragraph (3) until Parliament elects a Prime Minister. The President of the Republic may exercise his or her right pursuant to point b) of paragraph (3) until Parliament adopts the central budget.
(6) The new Parliament shall be elected within ninety days of Parliament dissolving itself or of it being dissolved.

Article 4

(1) Members of Parliament shall have equal rights and obligations, they shall perform their activity in the public interest, and they shall not be given instructions in that respect.
(2) Members of Parliament shall be entitled to immunity and to remuneration ensuring their independence. A cardinal Act shall specify the public offices which shall not be filled by Members of Parliament, and may stipulate other cases of conflict of interests.

(3) The mandate of a Member of Parliament shall terminate
a) upon the completion of the term of Parliament;
b) upon his or her death;
c) upon the declaration of a conflict of interests;
d) upon resignation;
e) if the conditions necessary for his or her election no longer exist; or
f) if he or she has failed to participate in Parliament's work for one year.

(4) Parliament shall decide with a majority of two-thirds of the votes of the Members of Parliament present on the establishment of the fact that the conditions necessary for the election of a Member of Parliament no longer exist, on the declaration of a conflict of interests, and on the fact that a particular Member of Parliament has failed to participate in Parliament's work for one year.

(5) The detailed rules on the legal status and the remuneration of Members of Parliament shall be laid down in a cardinal Act.

Article 5

(1) The sittings of Parliament shall be open to the public. At the request of the Government or of any Member of Parliament, and with the votes of two-thirds of all Members of Parliament, Parliament may decide to hold a sitting *in camera*.

(2) Parliament shall elect the Speaker of Parliament, Deputy Speakers and recorders from among its members.

(3) Parliament shall establish standing committees consisting of Members of Parliament.

(4) In order to coordinate their activities Members of Parliament may establish parliamentary fractions in accordance with the conditions laid down in the Rules of Procedure.

(5) Parliament shall have a quorum if more than half of its members are present.

(6) Unless otherwise provided for by the Fundamental Law, Parliament shall adopt its decisions by a simple majority of votes of the Members of Parliament present. The Rules of Procedure may stipulate that certain decisions be adopted by a qualified majority.

(7) Parliament shall establish the rules of its operation and the order of its debates in its Rules of Procedure, which are to be adopted by a majority of two-thirds of the votes of the Members of Parliament present.

(8) The provisions ensuring regular sittings of Parliament shall be laid down in a cardinal Act.

Article 6

(1) The President of the Republic, the Government, any Parliamentary Committee, or any Member of Parliament may propose bills.

(2) Parliament may, upon a motion submitted before the final vote by the proponent of the bill, by the Government or by the Speaker of Parliament, send the adopted Act to the Constitutional Court for an examination of its conformity with the Fundamental Law. Parliament shall decide on the motion after the final vote. If the motion is adopted, the Speaker of Parliament shall send the adopted Act without delay to the Constitutional Court for an examination of its conformity with the Fundamental Law.

(3) The Speaker of Parliament shall sign the adopted Act within five days and send it to the President of the Republic. The President of the Republic shall sign the Act within five days of receiving it and order its publication. If Parliament has sent the Act to the Constitutional Court for an examination of its conformity with the Fundamental Law pursuant to paragraph (2), the Speaker of Parliament may only sign and send it to the President of the Republic if the Constitutional Court has not found any violation of the Fundamental Law.

(4) If the President of the Republic considers an Act or any of its provisions to be contrary to the Fundamental Law, and no examination pursuant to paragraph (2) has been conducted, he or she shall send the Act to the Constitutional Court for an examination of its conformity with the Fundamental Law.

(5) If the President of the Republic disagrees with an Act or any of its provisions and has not exercised his or her right pursuant to paragraph (4), prior to signing the Act he or she may return it once, together with comments, to Parliament for reconsideration. Parliament shall hold a new debate on the Act and decide again on its adoption. The President of the Republic may also exercise this right if the Constitutional Court has not found any violation of the Fundamental Law in the course of its examination conducted pursuant to Parliament's decision.

(6) The Constitutional Court shall decide on the motion pursuant to paragraphs (2) or (4) out of turn, but within thirty days at the latest. Should the Constitutional Court establish a violation of the Fundamental Law, Parliament shall hold a new debate on the Act in order to eliminate the violation.

(7) If the Constitutional Court does not establish any violation of the Fundamental Law in the course of the examination initiated by the President of the Republic, the President of the Republic shall sign the Act without delay and order its publication.

(8) The Constitutional Court may be requested to conduct another examination, pursuant to paragraphs (2) and (4), of the conformity with the Fundamental Law of an Act debated and adopted by Parliament pursuant to paragraph (6). The Constitutional Court shall decide on the repeated motion out of turn, but within ten days at the latest.

(9) If Parliament amends the Act returned due to any disagreement of the President of the Republic, the examination of its conformity with the Fundamental Law pursuant to paragraphs (2) or (4) may be requested only in relation to the amended provisions, or on the grounds that the procedural requirements laid down in the Fundamental Law for the making of the Act have not been complied with. If Parliament adopts the Act returned due to any disagreement of the President of the Republic with the text unamended, the President of the Republic may request the examination of its conformity with the Fundamental Law on the grounds that the procedural requirements laid down in the Fundamental Law for the making of the Act have not been complied with.

Article 7

(1) Members of Parliament may ask questions of the Commissioner for Fundamental Rights, of the President of the State Audit Office, of the Prosecutor General or of the Governor of the National Bank of Hungary about any matter within their competence.

(2) Members of Parliament may submit interpellations or questions to the Government or any of its Members about any matter within their competence.

(3) The inquiry activities of parliamentary committees and the obligation to appear before such committees shall be regulated by a cardinal Act.

National referenda

Article 8

(1) Parliament shall order a national referendum at the initiative of at least two hundred thousand citizens with voting rights. Parliament may order a national referendum at the initiative of the President of the Republic, the Government, or one hundred thousand citizens with voting rights. The result of a valid and conclusive referendum shall be binding on Parliament.

(2) National referenda may be held about any matter within the tasks and competences of Parliament.

(3) No national referendum may be held on
   a) any matter aimed at the amendment of the Fundamental Law;
   b) the central budget, the implementation of the central budget, central taxes, duties, contributions, customs duties, or the content of Acts determining the central conditions for local taxes;
   c) the contents of Acts on the elections of Members of Parliament, local government representatives and mayors, and Members of the European Parliament;
   d) any obligation arising from international treaties;
   e) personal matters and questions concerning the establishment of organizations within the competence of Parliament;
   f) the dissolution of Parliament;
   g) the dissolution of a body of local government representatives;
   h) the declaration of a state of war, state of national crisis and state of emergency, and on the declaration or extension of the state of preventive defense;
   i) any matter related to participation in military operations;
   j) the granting of general amnesty.

(4) A national referendum shall be valid if more than half of all citizens with voting rights have cast valid votes, and it shall be conclusive if more than half of those voting validly have given the same answer to a question.

The President of the Republic

Article 9

(1) The Head of State of Hungary shall be the President of the Republic, who shall embody the unity of the nation and be the guardian of the democratic operation of the state organization.

(2) The President of the Republic shall be the Commander in Chief of the Hungarian Defense Forces.

(3) The President of the Republic
   a) shall represent Hungary;
   b) may attend and take the floor at the sittings of Parliament;
   c) may propose bills;
   d) may initiate national referenda;
   e) shall set the date for general elections of Members of Parliament, local government representatives and mayors, and of Members of the European Parliament, and for national referenda;
   f) shall make decisions concerning a special legal order;
   g) shall convene the constitutive sitting of Parliament;

h) may dissolve Parliament;
i) may send Acts adopted by Parliament to the Constitutional Court to have their conformity with the Fundamental Law examined, or may return them to Parliament for reconsideration;
j) shall propose persons for the offices of Prime Minister, the President of the Curia, the Prosecutor General and the Commissioner for Fundamental Rights;
k) shall appoint professional judges and the President of the Budget Council;
l) shall confirm the appointment of the President of the Hungarian Academy of Sciences; and
m) shall determine the organization of his or her office.

(4) The President of the Republic shall
a) express consent to be bound by international treaties on the basis of authorization by Parliament;
b) accredit and receive ambassadors and envoys;
c) appoint Ministers, the Governor and Deputy Governors of the National Bank of Hungary, the heads of autonomous regulatory organs and university professors;
d) appoint university rectors;
e) appoint and promote generals;
f) award decorations, prizes and titles specified by an Act, and authorize the use of foreign state decorations;
g) exercise the right to grant pardon to individuals;
h) decide on matters of territorial organization falling within his or her tasks and competences;
i) decide on matters related to the acquisition and termination of citizenship;
j) decide on all matters assigned to his or her competence in an Act.

(5) The counter-signature of a Government Member shall be required for all actions and decisions of the President of the Republic under paragraph (4). An Act may provide that a decision assigned by an Act to the competence of the President of the Republic need not be countersigned.

(6) The President of the Republic shall refuse to comply with the obligations set out in points b) to e) of paragraph (4) if the conditions specified in rules of law have not been met or if he or she has well-grounded reasons to conclude that his or her compliance would lead to a serious disorder in the democratic operation of the state organization.

(7) The President of the Republic shall refuse to comply with those set out in point f) of paragraph (4) if such compliance would violate the values enshrined in the Fundamental Law.

Article 10

(1) Parliament shall elect the President of the Republic for five years.
(2) Any Hungarian citizen who has reached the age of thirty-five may be elected President of the Republic.
(3) The President of the Republic may be re-elected only once.

Article 11

(1) The President of the Republic shall be elected no sooner than sixty but no later than thirty days prior to the expiry of an incumbent president's mandate; should the incumbent President's mandate terminate prematurely, a new President of the Republic shall be elected within thirty days of such termination. The date for the election of the President of the Republic shall be set by the Speaker of Parliament. Parliament shall elect the President of the Republic by secret ballot.
(2) The election of the President of the Republic shall be preceded by nomination. For a nomination to be valid, the written recommendation of at least one-fifth of the Members of Parliament shall be required. Nominations shall be submitted to the Speaker of Parliament before the vote is ordered. Each Member of Parliament may recommend one candidate. If a Member of Parliament recommends more than one candidate, all recommendations of that Member shall be invalid.
(3) President of the Republic elected in the first round of voting shall be the person who receives a majority of two-thirds of the votes of all Members of Parliament.
(4) If the first round of voting is inconclusive, a second round shall be held. The two candidates receiving the highest and second highest number of votes in the first round may stand in the second round. If in the first round of voting there is a tie in the first place, those candidates may be voted for who have received the highest number of votes. In the event of a tied vote only for second place in the first round of voting, those candidates may be voted for who have received the highest and second highest numbers of votes. President of the Republic elected in the second round of voting shall be the candidate who – regardless of the number of those participating in the vote – receives the highest number of valid votes. Should the second round of voting also be inconclusive, a new election shall be held on the basis of new nominations.
(5) The voting procedure shall be completed within a period of no more than two consecutive days.
(6) The President-elect of the Republic shall enter office upon expiry of the previous President's mandate, or, should the previous President's

mandate have ended prematurely, on the eighth day following the announcement of the result of the election; prior to taking office the President-elect of the Republic shall take an oath before Parliament.

Article 12

(1) The person of the President of the Republic shall be inviolable.

(2) The office of President of the Republic shall be incompatible with any other state, social, economic or political office or mandate. The President of the Republic shall not pursue any other gainful occupation nor accept pay for other activities, with the exception of activities falling under copyright protection.

(3) The mandate of the President of the Republic shall terminate

a) upon expiry of his or her term of office;

b) upon his or her death;

c) if he or she is incapable of fulfilling his or her duties for over ninety days;

d) if the conditions necessary for his or her election no longer exist;

e) upon declaration of a conflict of interests;

f) upon his or her resignation; or

g) upon his or her removal from the office of the President of the Republic.

(4) Parliament shall decide with a two-thirds majority of the votes of Members of Parliament present to establish any condition of the President of the Republic preventing him or her of fulfilling his or her duties for over ninety days or on the absence of the conditions required for his or her election, or on the declaration of a conflict or interests.

(5) The detailed rules of the legal status of the President of the Republic, and his or her remuneration shall be laid down in a cardinal Act.

Article 13

(1) Criminal proceedings against the President of the Republic may be instituted only after the termination of his or her mandate.

(2) If the President of the Republic willfully violates the Fundamental Law, or willfully violates any Act in connection with the exercise of his or her official functions, or if he or she commits a willful criminal offence, one-fifth of all Members of Parliament may propose his or her removal from office.

(3) A majority of two-thirds of the votes of all Members of Parliament shall be required to start impeachment proceedings. Voting shall be held by secret ballot.

(4) The President of the Republic shall not exercise his or her powers in the period between the adoption of Parliament's decision to impeach and the conclusion of impeachment proceedings.
(5) The Constitutional Court shall have the competence to conduct the impeachment proceedings.
(6) If, as a result of its proceedings, the Constitutional Court establishes the responsibility of the President of the Republic under public law, it may remove the President of the Republic from office.

Article 14

(1) Should the President of the Republic be temporarily prevented from acting, or if his or her mandate terminates, the Speaker of Parliament shall perform the tasks and exercise the competences of the President of the Republic until he or she is no longer prevented from acting, or until the new President of the Republic takes office.
(2) The fact that the President of the Republic is temporarily prevented from acting shall be established by Parliament upon the motion of the President of the Republic, the Government or any Member of Parliament.
(3) While substituting for the President of the Republic, the Speaker of Parliament shall not exercise his or her rights as a Member of Parliament, and his or her duties as Speaker of Parliament shall be performed by the Deputy Speaker of Parliament designated by Parliament.

The Government

Article 15

(1) The Government shall be the general organ of executive power; its tasks and competences shall encompass all matters which are not expressly assigned by the Fundamental Law or a rule of law to the tasks and competences of another organ. The Government shall be answerable to Parliament.
(2) The Government shall be the principal organ of public administration; it may establish organs of state administration pursuant to Acts.
(3) Acting within its competence, the Government shall adopt decrees in matters not regulated by an Act, or on the basis of an authorization given by an Act.
(4) The decree of the Government shall not be contrary to any Act.

Article 16

(1) The members of the Government shall be the Prime Minister and the Ministers.
(2) By decree, the Prime Minister shall appoint one or more Deputy Prime Minister(s) from among the Ministers.
(3) The Prime Minister shall be elected by Parliament at the proposal of the President of the Republic.
(4) A simple majority of votes of all Members of Parliament shall be required to elect the Prime Minister. The Prime Minister shall take office immediately upon his or her election.
(5) The President of the Republic shall make his or her proposal pursuant to paragraph (3)
   a) at the constitutive sitting of the new Parliament, if the mandate of the Prime Minister has terminated with the formation of a newly-elected Parliament;
   b) within fifteen days of the termination of the mandate of the Prime Minister, if such termination is due to the Prime Minister's resignation from office, his or her death, the declaration of a conflict of interests, the absence of conditions required for his or her election, or the fact that Parliament has expressed its lack of confidence in the Prime Minister in a vote of confidence.
(6) If Parliament fails to elect the person proposed for the office of Prime Minister pursuant to paragraph (5), the President of the Republic shall make a new proposal within fifteen days.
(7) Ministers shall be appointed by the President of the Republic at the proposal of the Prime Minister. Ministers shall take office on the date designated in their deed of appointment or, in the absence thereof, immediately upon their appointment.
(8) The Government shall come into existence with the appointment of the Ministers.
(9) Members of the Government shall take an oath before Parliament.

Article 17

(1) The ministries shall be listed in an Act.
(2) Ministers without portfolio may be appointed to perform the tasks determined by the Government.
(3) The metropolitan and county government offices shall be organs of the Government with general territorial state administration competence.

(4) The provisions of a cardinal Act regarding the designation of ministries, Ministers or organs of public administration may be amended by an Act.
(5) The legal status of government officials shall be regulated by an Act.

Article 18

(1) The Prime Minister shall define the general policy of the Government.
(2) Ministers shall – within the framework of the general policy of the Government – autonomously direct the sectors of state administration within their competence and the organs subordinated to them, and shall perform the tasks assigned to them by the Government or the Prime Minister.
(3) Acting within their competence, Members of the Government shall adopt decrees, as authorized by an Act or a government decree, either autonomously or in agreement with other Ministers; such decrees shall not be contrary to any Act, government decree or decree of the Governor of the National Bank of Hungary.
(4) Members of the Government shall be answerable to Parliament for their actions, and Ministers shall be answerable to the Prime Minister. Members of the Government may attend and take the floor at sittings of Parliament. Parliament or a committee thereof may require Members of the Government to attend any of their sittings.
(5) The detailed rules of the legal status of members of the Government, their remuneration as well as the rules regarding the substitution of Ministers shall be laid down in an Act.

Article 19

Parliament may request information from the Government on the government position to be represented in the decision-making procedures of those institutions of the European Union which operate with government participation, and may take a stand on the draft placed on the agenda thereof. In the course of European Union decision-making, the Government shall act on the basis of the position taken by Parliament.

Article 20

(1) Upon termination of the Prime Minister's mandate, the mandate of the Government shall come to an end.
(2) The Prime Minister's mandate shall terminate
   a) upon formation of a newly-elected Parliament;

b) if Parliament adopts a motion of no-confidence against the Prime Minister and elects a new Prime Minister;
c) if Parliament expresses its lack of confidence in the Prime Minister by a vote of confidence initiated by the Prime Minister;
d) upon resignation;
e) upon his or her death;
f) upon the declaration of conflict of interests, or
g) if the conditions necessary for his or her election no longer exist.

(3) A Minister's mandate shall terminate
a) upon termination of the Prime Minister's mandate;
b) upon the Minister's resignation;
c) upon his or her dismissal; or
d) upon his or her death.

(4) Parliament shall decide on the establishment of the absence of the conditions necessary for the election of the Prime Minister or on the declaration of a conflict of interests by a two-thirds majority of the votes of Members of Parliament present.

Article 21

(1) One-fifth of all Members of Parliament may submit a written motion of no-confidence against the Prime Minister, together with the designation of a candidate for the office of Prime Minister.

(2) If Parliament supports the motion of no-confidence, it thereby expresses its lack of confidence in the Prime Minister, and simultaneously elects the person proposed for the office of Prime Minister in the motion of no-confidence. Such decision of Parliament shall require a simple majority of the votes of all Members of Parliament.

(3) The Prime Minister may propose a vote of confidence. Parliament expresses its lack of confidence in the Prime Minister if in the vote of confidence proposed by the Prime Minister a simple majority of all Members of Parliament do not support the Prime Minister's motion.

(4) The Prime Minister may propose that the vote on a motion submitted by the Government be simultaneously a vote of confidence. Parliament shall be deemed to have expressed its lack of confidence in the Prime Minister if it does not support the proposal submitted by the Government.

(5) Parliament shall decide on the question of confidence – either a motion of no-confidence or the Prime Minister's motion pursuant to paragraphs (3) or (4) – no sooner than three days, and no later than eight days from the submission of the motion.

Article 22

(1) From the termination of its mandate until the formation of a new government the Government shall exercise its powers as a caretaker Government, but shall not express consent to be bound by international treaties and may adopt decrees only on the basis of authorization provided for by an Act and in cases of urgency.

(2) If the mandate of the Prime Minister has terminated by resignation, or upon the formation of a newly-elected Parliament, the Prime Minister shall exercise his or her powers as a caretaker Prime Minister, but he or she shall not propose the dismissal of a Minister or the appointment of a new Minister, and may adopt decrees only on the basis of authorization provided for by an Act and in cases of urgency.

(3) If the mandate of the Prime Minister has terminated due to his or her death, to the declaration of a conflict of interests, to the absence of the conditions required for his or her election, or to the fact that Parliament has expressed its lack of confidence in the Prime Minister in a vote of confidence, the powers of the Prime Minister shall be exercised by the Deputy Prime Minister until a new Prime Minister is elected, with the limitations provided for in paragraph (2) hereof; should there be more than one Deputy Prime Minister, these powers shall be exercised by the First Deputy Prime Minister.

(4) A Minister shall exercise his or her powers as a caretaker Minister from the termination of the mandate of the Prime Minister until the appointment of a new Minister, or until the mandating of another member of the new Government for the temporary exercise of the relevant ministerial powers, but may adopt decrees only in cases of urgency.

Autonomous regulatory organs

Article 23

(1) Parliament may establish autonomous regulatory organs by a cardinal Act for the performance of certain tasks and the exercise of certain competences belonging to the executive branch.

(2) The head of an autonomous regulatory organ shall be appointed by the Prime Minister or, on the proposal of the Prime Minister, by the President of the Republic for the term specified in a cardinal Act. The head of an autonomous regulatory organ shall appoint his or her deputy or deputies.

(3) The head of an autonomous regulatory organ shall report annually to Parliament on the activities of the autonomous regulatory organ.

(4) As authorized by an Act, the head of an autonomous regulatory organ shall issue decrees within his or her competence as defined by a cardinal Act; such decrees shall not be contrary to an Act, a government decree, a prime ministerial decree, a ministerial decree or a decree of the Governor of the National Bank of Hungary. In issuing decrees, the head of an autonomous regulatory organ may be substituted for by the deputy he or she has designated in a decree.

The Constitutional Court

Article 24

(1) The Constitutional Court shall be the principal organ for the protection of the Fundamental Law.

(2) The Constitutional Court shall
- a) examine adopted but not yet published[12] Acts for conformity with the Fundamental Law;
- b) review, at the initiative of a judge, the conformity with the Fundamental Law of rules of law applicable in a particular case;
- c) review, on the basis of a constitutional complaint, the conformity with the Fundamental Law of the rules of law applied in a particular case;
- d) review, on the basis of a constitutional complaint, the conformity with the Fundamental Law of a judicial decision;
- e) review, at the initiative of the Government, of one fourth of all Members of Parliament or of the Commissioner for Fundamental Rights, the conformity of rules of law with the Fundamental Law;
- f) examine whether rules of law are in conflict with international treaties; and
- g) perform further tasks and exercise further competences laid down in the Fundamental Law or in a cardinal Act.

(3) The Constitutional Court,
- a) shall annul any rule of law or any provision thereof which is contrary to the Fundamental Law within its competence pursuant to points b), c) and e) of paragraph (2);

---

[12] I.e. *promulgated.*

b) shall annul any judicial decision which is contrary to the Fundamental Law within its competence pursuant to point d) of paragraph (2);
c) may annul any rule of law or any provision thereof which conflicts with an international treaty within its competence pursuant to point f) of paragraph (2); and shall determine other legal consequences as laid down in a cardinal Act.

(4) The Constitutional Court shall be a body composed of fifteen members, each elected for twelve years by Parliament with a majority of two-thirds of the votes of all Members of Parliament. Parliament shall elect, with a majority of two-thirds of the votes of all Members of Parliament, a member of the Constitutional Court who shall serve as its President until the expiry of his or her mandate as judge of the Constitutional Court. Members of the Constitutional Court shall not be members of a political party or engage in any political activity.

(5) The detailed rules of the competence, organisation and operation of the Constitutional Court shall be laid down in a cardinal Act.

Courts

Article 25

(1) Courts shall administer justice. The principal judicial organ shall be the Curia.

(2) The courts shall decide on
a) criminal cases, private law litigations and on other matters defined by an Act;
b) the legality of public administration decisions;
c) whether a local government decree is contrary to another rule of law and on its annulment;
d) the establishment of the failure of a local government to comply with its law-making obligation based on an Act.

(3) In addition to those specified in paragraph (2), the Curia shall ensure uniformity of the application of the law by the courts, and make decisions on the unity of law which shall be binding on the courts.

(4) The judicial system shall have a multi-level organization. Separate courts may be established for specific groups of cases, especially for litigation in public administration and labour matters.

(5) The organs of judicial self-government shall participate in the administration of the courts.

(6) An Act may provide that in certain types of litigation other organs may also conduct proceedings.
(7) The detailed rules of the organization and administration of courts and of the legal status of judges, and the remuneration of judges shall be laid down in a cardinal Act.

Article 26

(1) Judges shall be independent and only subordinated to Acts; they shall not be given instructions as to their judicial activities. Judges may only be removed from office for the reasons and in a procedure specified in a cardinal Act. Judges shall not be members of a political party or engage in any political activity.
(2) Professional judges shall be appointed – as laid down in a cardinal Act – by the President of the Republic. Only persons having reached the age of thirty years may be appointed judge. Except for the President of the Curia, the service relationship of judges shall terminate upon their reaching the general retirement age.
(3) The President of the Curia shall be elected by Parliament from among the judges for nine years at the proposal of the President of the Republic. The President of the Curia shall be elected by a two-thirds majority of the votes of all Members of Parliament.

Article 27

(1) The courts, unless otherwise provided by an Act, shall adjudicate in chambers.
(2) In certain cases and in a manner specified by an Act, lay judges shall also participate in the administration of justice.
(3) Only professional judges may conduct proceedings as a single judge in a case or act as the president of a chamber. In cases specified by an Act, court secretaries may also conduct proceedings within the competence of a single judge; in the course of the court secretary's relevant proceedings paragraph (1) of Article 26 shall apply.

Article 28

In the course of the application of law, courts shall interpret the text of rules of law primarily in accordance with their purposes and with the Fundamental Law. When interpreting the Fundamental Law or rules of law, it shall be presumed that they serve moral and economical purposes which are in accordance with common sense and the public good.

The Prosecution Service[13]

Article 29

(1) The Prosecutor General and the Prosecution Service shall contribute to the administration of justice by enforcing the punitive authority of the State. The Prosecution Service shall prosecute criminal offences, take action against other unlawful acts or omissions, and shall contribute to the prevention of unlawful acts.

(2) The Prosecutor General and the Prosecution Service shall, pursuant to the provisions of an Act,
   a) exercise rights in connection with investigations;
   b) represent public prosecution in court proceedings;
   c) supervise the legality of the execution of punishments;
   d) perform further tasks and exercise further competences specified in an Act.

(3) The organization of the Prosecution Service shall be headed and directed by the Prosecutor General, who shall appoint public prosecutors. With the exception of the Prosecutor General, the service relationship of public prosecutors shall terminate upon their reaching the general retirement age.

(4) The Prosecutor General shall be elected from among the public prosecutors for nine years by Parliament at the proposal of the President of the Republic. A majority of two-thirds of the votes of all Members of Parliament shall be required to elect the Prosecutor General.

(5) The Prosecutor General shall report annually to Parliament on his or her activities.

(6) Public prosecutors shall not be members of a political party or engage in any political activity.

(7) The detailed rules of the organization and operation of the Prosecution Service, of the legal status of the Prosecutor General and of public prosecutors, as well as their remuneration shall be laid down in a cardinal Act.

---

[13] In other translations, *Prosecutor's Office* or *Prosecution Office*.

The Commissioner for Fundamental Rights

Article 30

(1) The Commissioner for Fundamental Rights shall perform fundamental rights protection activities, his or her proceedings may be initiated by anyone.
(2) The Commissioner for Fundamental Rights shall inquire into those improprieties related to fundamental rights that come to his or her knowledge, or have those improprieties inquired into, and initiate general or specific measures to remedy them.
(3) Parliament shall elect the Commissioner for Fundamental Rights and his or her deputies for six years with the votes of two-thirds of all Members of Parliament. The deputies shall ensure the protection of the interests of future generations and of the rights of nationalities living in Hungary. The Commissioner for Fundamental Rights and his or her deputies shall not be members of a political party or engage in any political activity.
(4) The Commissioner for Fundamental Rights shall report annually to Parliament on his or her activities.
(5) The detailed rules relating to the Commissioner for Fundamental Rights and to his or her deputies shall be laid down in an Act.

Local governments

Article 31

(1) In Hungary local governments shall function for the administration of local public affairs and the exercise of local public power.
(2) Local referenda may be held, as laid down in an Act, on any matter within the tasks and competences of the local government.
(3) The rules relating to local governments shall be laid down in a cardinal Act.

Article 32

(1) In the management of local public affairs and within the framework of an Act, local governments
a) shall adopt decrees;
b) shall adopt decisions;
c) shall autonomously administer their affairs;

d) shall determine the rules of their organization and operation;
e) shall exercise rights of ownership with respect to local government property;
f) shall determine their budgets and autonomously manage their affairs on the basis thereof;
g) may engage in entrepreneurial activities using their assets and revenues available for this purpose, without jeopardizing the performance of their mandatory tasks;
h) shall decide on the types and rates of local taxes;
i) may create local government symbols, and institute local decorations and honorary titles;
j) may request information from a competent organ, initiate a decision, or express an opinion;
k) may freely associate with other local governments, set up associations for the representation of their interests, cooperate within their competence with local governments from other countries, and become members of international organizations of local governments; and
l) shall perform other tasks and exercise other competences laid down in an Act.

(2) Acting within their competence, local governments shall adopt local government decrees in order to regulate local social relations not yet regulated by an Act or when authorized to do so by an Act.

(3) Local government decrees shall not be contrary to other rules of law.

(4) Local governments shall send local government decrees to the metropolitan or county government office immediately after their publication. If the metropolitan or county government office finds that the local government decree or any of its provisions is contrary to a rule of law, it may apply to a court for a review of the local government decree.

(5) The metropolitan or county government office may apply to a court to establish the local government's failure to comply with its law-making obligation based on an Act. Should the local government fail to comply with its law-making obligation by the date fixed by the court in its decision establishing failure, the court shall order – upon the initiative of the metropolitan or county government office – that the local government decree necessary to remedy the failure be adopted by the head of the metropolitan or county government office on behalf of the local government.

(6) The property of local governments shall be public property which shall serve the performance of their tasks.

Article 33

(1) The tasks and competences of a local government shall be performed and exercised by its representative body.
(2) A local representative body shall be headed by the mayor. The president of the county representative body shall be elected by the county representative body from among its members for the term of its mandate.
(3) A representative body may elect committees and set up an office as laid down in a cardinal Act.

Article 34

(1) Local governments and state organs shall cooperate to achieve community goals. An Act may define mandatory tasks and competences for local governments. For the performance of their tasks and the exercise of their competences, local governments shall be entitled to receive proportionate budgetary and other financial means.
(2) An Act may prescribe that mandatory tasks of local governments be performed through associations.
(3) Apart from their local government tasks, the mayor and the president of a county representative body may, in exceptional cases, also perform tasks and exercise competences of state administration on the basis of an Act or of a government decree authorized by an Act.
(4) The Government shall ensure supervision of the legality of local governments through the metropolitan and county government offices.
(5) In the interest of preserving a balanced budget, an Act may prescribe that certain conditions be met, or that local governments obtain the approval of the Government, for local governments to contract a debt or undertake any other commitment of an extent defined by an Act.

Article 35

(1) Local government representatives and mayors shall be elected by direct and secret ballot by citizens eligible to vote, on the basis of universal and equal suffrage, in elections which guarantee free expression of the will of the voters, in the manner laid down in a cardinal Act.
(2) Local government representatives and mayors shall be elected for five years as laid down in a cardinal Act.
(3) The mandate of local representative bodies shall terminate on the day of the general elections for local government representatives and mayors. If elections cannot be held due to a lack of candidates, the mandate of the local representative body shall be extended until the day of

the interim elections. The mandate of mayors shall last until the election of the new mayors.

(4) Local representative bodies may declare their dissolution as laid down in a cardinal Act.

(5) At the motion of the Government – submitted after obtaining the opinion of the Constitutional Court – Parliament shall dissolve the representative body whose operation is contrary to the Fundamental Law.

(6) Upon a local representative body dissolving itself or upon it being dissolved, the mandate of the mayor shall also terminate.

Public finances

Article 36

(1) Parliament shall adopt an Act on the central budget and on the implementation of the central budget for each year. The Government shall submit the bill on the central budget and the bill on implementation thereof to Parliament by the deadline provided for in an Act.

(2) The bill on the central budget and the bill on implementation thereof shall contain state expenditures and revenues in the same structure, in a transparent manner and in reasonable detail.

(3) With the adoption of the Act on the central budget, Parliament shall authorize the Government to collect the revenues and effect the expenditures determined in the same.

(4) Parliament shall not adopt an Act on the central budget which would result in the state debt exceeding half of the Gross Domestic Product.

(5) As long as state debt exceeds half of the Gross Domestic Product, Parliament may only adopt an Act on the central budget which provides for state debt reduction in proportion to the Gross Domestic Product.

(6) Derogation from the provisions of paragraph (4) shall only be allowed during a special legal order and to the extent necessary to mitigate the consequences of the circumstances triggering the special legal order, or if there is a significant and enduring national economic recession, to the extent necessary to restore the balance of the national economy.

(7) If Parliament fails to adopt the Act on the central budget by the beginning of the calendar year, the Government shall be authorized to collect the revenues determined in the relevant rules of law and, within the framework of the appropriations determined in the Act on the central budget for the previous year, effect the pro-rata expenditures.

Article 37

(1) The Government shall implement the central budget in a lawful and expedient manner, with effective management of public funds and by ensuring transparency.

(2) With the exceptions specified in paragraph (6) of Article 36, no such debt or financial commitment may be assumed in the course of the implementation of the central budget as would allow the state debt to exceed half of the Gross Domestic Product.

(3) As long as the level of state debt exceeds half of the Gross Domestic Product, with the exceptions specified in paragraph (6) of Article 36, no such debt or financial commitment may be assumed in the course of the implementation of the central budget which would result in an increase, as compared to the previous year, of the ratio of state debt in relation to the Gross Domestic Product.

(4) As long as the level of state debt exceeds half of the Gross Domestic Product, the Constitutional Court may, within its competence pursuant to points b) to e) of paragraph (2) of Article 24, review the Acts on the central budget, on the implementation of the budget, on central taxes, on duties and on contributions, on customs duties, and on the central conditions for local taxes as to their conformity with the Fundamental Law exclusively in connection with the rights to life and human dignity, to the protection of personal data, to freedom of thought, conscience and religion, or in connection with the rights related to Hungarian citizenship, and it may only annul these Acts for the violation of these rights. The Constitutional Court shall have the right to annul without restriction Acts governing the above matters if the procedural requirements laid down in the Fundamental Law for the making and publication of such Acts have not been observed.

(5) The method for the calculation of state debt and the Gross Domestic Product, as well as the rules relating to the implementation of the provisions of Article 36 and of paragraphs (1) to (3) hereof shall be laid down in an Act.

Article 38

(1) The property of the State and of local governments shall be national assets. The aim of the management and protection of national assets shall be to serve the public interest, to satisfy common needs and preserve natural resources, and to take into account the needs of future generations. The requirements for preserving and protecting national

assets, as well as for the responsible management thereof, shall be laid down in a cardinal Act.

(2) The scope of the exclusive property and of the exclusive economic activities of the State, as well as the limitations and conditions of the alienation of national assets of outstanding importance for the national economy shall be determined by a cardinal Act with regard to the aims referred to in paragraph (1).

(3) National assets may be transferred only for purposes specified in an Act, with the exceptions specified in an Act, taking into account the requirement of proportionate values.

(4) Contracts for the transfer or utilization of national assets may be concluded only with an organization in which there is transparency of ownership structure, organization, and of the activities relating to the management of the transferred or utilized national assets.

(5) Business organizations in state or local government ownership shall manage their finances in a manner determined by an Act, autonomously and responsibly according to the requirements of legality, expediency, and effectiveness.

Article 39

(1) Only such organizations may receive subsidies or contractual payments from the central budget that have transparency of ownership structure, organization, and of the activities for which funding is to be used.

(2) Every organization managing public funds shall publicly account for the management of those funds. Public funds and national assets shall be managed according to the principles of transparency and clean public life. Data relating to public funds and national assets shall be data of public interest.

Article 40

In the interest of predictable contributions to common needs and of a secure livelihood for the elderly, the basic rules for the sharing of public burdens and for the pension system shall be determined in a cardinal Act.

Article 41

(1) The National Bank of Hungary shall be the central bank of Hungary. The National Bank of Hungary shall be responsible for monetary policy as laid down in a cardinal Act.

(2) The Governor and Deputy Governors of the National Bank of Hungary shall be appointed for six years by the President of the Republic.

(3) The Governor of the National Bank of Hungary shall report annually to Parliament on the activities of the National Bank of Hungary.

(4) As authorized by an Act, and within his or her competence as laid down in a cardinal Act, the Governor of the National Bank of Hungary shall issue decrees, which shall not be contrary to Acts. In issuing decrees, the Governor of the National Bank of Hungary may be substituted for by the Deputy Governor he or she has designated in a decree.

(5) The detailed rules of the organization and operation of the National Bank of Hungary shall be laid down in a cardinal Act.

Article 42

The rules relating to the organ supervising the financial intermediary system shall be laid down in a cardinal Act.

Article 43

(1) The State Audit Office shall be the organ of Parliament responsible for financial and economic audit. Within its competence as laid down in an Act, the State Audit Office shall audit the implementation of the central budget, the management of public finances, the utilization of public funds and the management of national assets. The State Audit Office shall carry out its audits according to the criteria of legality, expediency and effectiveness.

(2) The President of the State Audit Office shall be elected for twelve years by Parliament with a majority of two thirds of the votes of all Members of Parliament.

(3) The President of the State Audit Office shall report annually to Parliament on the activities of the State Audit Office.

(4) The detailed rules of the organization and operation of the State Audit Office shall be laid down in a cardinal Act.

Article 44

(1) The Budget Council shall be an organ supporting the legislative activity of Parliament; it shall examine whether the central budget is well-founded.

(2) The Budget Council shall take part in the preparation of the Act on the central budget as specified in an Act.

(3) In order to ensure compliance with the requirements set out in paragraphs (4) and (5) of Article 36, the prior approval of the Budget Council shall be necessary for the adoption of the Act on the central budget.

(4) The members of the Budget Council shall be the President of the Budget Council, the Governor of the National Bank of Hungary and the President of the State Audit Office. The President of the Budget Council shall be appointed for six years by the President of the Republic.
(5) The detailed rules of the operation of the Budget Council shall be regulated by a cardinal Act.

The Hungarian Defense Forces

Article 45

(1) Hungary's armed forces shall be the Hungarian Defense Forces. The core duties of the Hungarian Defense Forces shall be the military defense of the independence, territorial integrity and borders of Hungary, the performance of collective defense and peace-keeping tasks arising from international treaties, as well as the carrying out of humanitarian activities in accordance with the rules of international law.
(2) Unless otherwise provided for by an international treaty, Parliament, the President of the Republic, the National Defense Council, the Government or the competent Minister shall have the right to direct the Hungarian Defense Forces within the framework determined in the Fundamental Law and in a cardinal Act. The Hungarian Defense Forces shall operate under the direction of the Government.
(3) The Hungarian Defense Forces shall take part in the prevention of disasters, and the relief and elimination of their consequences.
(4) Professional staff members of the Hungarian Defense Forces shall not be members of a political party or engage in any political activity.
(5) The detailed rules of the organization, tasks, direction and control, and operation of the Hungarian Defense Forces shall be laid down in a cardinal Act.

The police and national security services

Article 46

(1) The core duties of the police shall be the prevention and detection of criminal offences, and the protection of public security, law and order and the order of state borders.
(2) The police shall operate under the direction of the Government.

(3) The core duties of the national security services shall be the protection of the independence and lawful order of Hungary, and the assertion of its national security interests.

(4) The national security services shall operate under the direction of the Government.

(5) Professional staff members of the police and the national security services shall not be members of a political party or engage in any political activity.

(6) The detailed rules of the organization and operation of the police and the national security services, the rules of the use of covert operative means and methods, as well as the rules relating to national security activities shall be laid down in a cardinal Act.

Decisions on participation in military operations

Article 47

(1) The Government shall decide on those troop movements of the Hungarian Defense Forces and of foreign armed forces which involve the crossing of borders.

(2) With the exception of the cases specified in paragraph (3) below, Parliament shall, with a two-thirds majority of the votes of Members of Parliament present, decide on the use of the Hungarian Defense Forces abroad or within Hungary, on their stationing abroad, as well as on the use of foreign armed forces within or departing from the territory of Hungary, or on the stationing of foreign armed forces in Hungary.

(3) The Government shall decide on the use of the Hungarian Defense Forces and of foreign armed forces referred to in paragraph (2) and based on a decision of the European Union or the North Atlantic Treaty Organization, or on other troop movements thereof.

(4) The Government – while simultaneously informing the President of the Republic – shall immediately report to Parliament any decision made in accordance with paragraph (3), or authorizing the participation of the Hungarian Defense Forces in peace-keeping missions or in humanitarian activities in foreign theatres of operation.

SPECIAL LEGAL ORDERS

Common rules for the state of national crisis and the state of emergency

Article 48

(1) Parliament shall

a) declare a state of national crisis and set up a National Defense Council in the event of the declaration of a state of war or an imminent danger of armed attack by a foreign power (danger of war);

b) declare a state of emergency in the event of armed actions aimed at subverting the lawful order or at the acquisition of exclusive power, or in the event of grave acts of violence committed with arms or objects suitable to be used as arms, capable of endangering life and property on a massive scale.

(2) For the declaration of a state of war, the conclusion of peace, or the declaration of a special legal order pursuant to paragraph (1), a majority of two thirds of the votes of all Members of Parliament shall be required.

(3) The President of the Republic shall have the power to declare a state of war, to declare a state of national crisis and set up the Defense Council, or to declare a state of emergency if Parliament is prevented from taking such decisions.

(4) Parliament shall be deemed to be prevented from taking such decisions if it is not in session and its convening is made impossible by insurmountable obstacles caused by lack of time or the events necessitating the declaration of a state of war, state of national crisis or state of emergency.

(5) The Speaker of Parliament, the President of the Constitutional Court and the Prime Minister shall unanimously determine that Parliament is prevented from acting and that the declaration of a state of war, a state of national crisis or a state of emergency is justified.

(6) As soon as Parliament is no longer prevented from acting, it shall at its first sitting review whether the declaration of a state of war, state of national crisis or state of emergency was justified, and decide on the legality of the measures taken. A majority of two-thirds of the votes of all Members of Parliament shall be required for such decision.

(7) During a state of national crisis or a state of emergency Parliament shall not dissolve itself, nor shall it be dissolved. During a state of national

crisis or a state of emergency no date shall be set for general elections of Members of Parliament, nor shall such elections be held; in such cases a new Parliament shall be elected within ninety days of the termination of the state of national crisis or state of emergency. If the general elections of Members of Parliament have already been held but the new Parliament has not yet had its constitutive sitting, the President of the Republic shall convene the constitutive sitting for a date within thirty days of the termination of the state of national crisis or state of emergency.

(8) If Parliament has dissolved itself or has been dissolved, it may be convened also by the Defense Council during a state of national crisis, or by the President of the Republic during a state of emergency.

The state of national crisis

Article 49

(1) The President of the Defense Council shall be the President of the Republic, and its members shall be the Speaker of Parliament, the leaders of parliamentary fractions, the Prime Minister, the Ministers and – with the right of consultation – the Chief of Staff of the National Defense Forces.

(2) The Defense Council shall exercise
   a) the powers delegated to it by Parliament;
   b) the powers of the President of the Republic;
   c) the powers of the Government.

(3) The National Defense Council shall decide on
   a) the use of the Hungarian Defense Forces outside or within Hungary, on their participation in peace-keeping missions, on their humanitarian activities in foreign theatres of operation, or on their stationing abroad;
   b) the use of foreign armed forces within or departing from the territory of Hungary, or their stationing in Hungary;
   c) the introduction of extraordinary measures laid down in a cardinal Act.

(4) The National Defense Council may adopt decrees with which it may – as laid down in a cardinal Act – suspend the application of certain Acts or derogate from the provisions of Acts, and take other extraordinary measures.

(5) Such decrees of the National Defense Council shall cease to have effect upon termination of the state of national crisis, unless Parliament extends their effect.

The state of emergency

Article 50

(1) The Hungarian Defense Forces may be used during a state of emergency if the use of the police and of the national security services should prove insufficient.
(2) During a state of emergency, if Parliament is prevented from acting, the President of the Republic shall decide on the use of the Hungarian Defense Forces pursuant to paragraph (1).
(3) During a state of emergency the extraordinary measures determined in a cardinal Act shall be introduced by decree of the President of the Republic. In his or her decree, the President of the Republic may – as laid down in a cardinal Act – suspend the application of certain Acts, derogate from provisions of Acts, and take other extraordinary measures.
(4) The President of the Republic shall inform the Speaker of Parliament without delay of any extraordinary measures introduced. During a state of emergency, Parliament – or if it is prevented from acting, the National Defense Committee of Parliament – shall remain continuously in session. Parliament – or if it is prevented from acting, the National Defense Committee of Parliament – shall have the power to suspend the application of the extraordinary measures introduced by the President of the Republic.
(5) Extraordinary measures introduced by decree shall remain in force for thirty days, unless their effect is extended by Parliament or, if it is prevented from acting, the National Defense Committee of Parliament.
(6) Such decrees of the President of the Republic shall cease to have effect upon termination of the state of emergency.

The state of preventive defense

Article 51

(1) In the event of a danger of external armed attack or in order to fulfill an obligation arising from an alliance, Parliament shall declare a state of preventive defense for a fixed period of time and simultaneously authorize the Government to introduce the extraordinary measures laid down in a cardinal Act. The period of the state of preventive defense may be extended.
(2) For the declaration or extension of the special legal order pursuant to paragraph (1), the votes of two-thirds of the Members of Parliament present shall be required.

(3) After having put forward a motion for the declaration of a state of preventive defense, the Government may, in a decree, introduce measures derogating from the Acts governing the operation of public administration, the Hungarian Defense Forces and law-enforcement organs, of which measures it shall continuously inform the President of the Republic and the competent permanent committees of Parliament. The measures introduced in this way shall remain in force until Parliament's decision on the declaration of a state of preventive defense, but for no longer than sixty days.
(4) During a state of preventive defense the Government may adopt decrees by which it may suspend the application of certain Acts, derogate from the provisions of Acts, and take other extraordinary measures as laid down in a cardinal Act.
(5) Such decrees of the Government shall cease to have effect upon termination of the state of preventive defense.

Unexpected attacks

Article 52

(1) In the event of an unexpected incursion of external armed groups into the territory of Hungary, until the decision on the declaration of a state of emergency or state of national crisis the Government shall – if necessary in accordance with the armed defense plan approved by the President of the Republic – take immediate action using forces proportionate to the gravity of the attack and prepared therefor, to repel the attack and defend the territorial integrity of Hungary with domestic and allied emergency air defense and aviation forces in order to protect lawful order, life and property, public order and public security.
(2) The Government shall inform Parliament and the President of the Republic without delay of the action taken pursuant to paragraph (1).
(3) In the event of an unexpected attack, the Government may introduce extraordinary measures laid down in a cardinal Act, and may adopt decrees with which it may – as laid down in a cardinal Act – suspend the application of certain Acts, derogate from the provisions of Acts, and take other extraordinary measures.
(4) Such decrees of the Government shall cease to have effect upon termination of the unexpected attack.

The state of danger

Article 53

(1) In the event of a natural or industrial disaster endangering life or property, or in order to relieve the consequences thereof, the Government shall declare a state of danger, and may introduce extraordinary measures laid down in a cardinal Act.
(2) During a state of danger the Government may adopt a decree with which it may – as determined in a cardinal Act – suspend the application of certain Acts, derogate from the provisions of Acts, and take other extraordinary measures.
(3) The decree of the Government pursuant to paragraph (2) shall remain in force for fifteen days, except if the Government – on the basis of an authorization from Parliament – extends the effect of the decree.
(4) The decree of the Government shall cease to have effect upon termination of the state of danger.

Common rules for special legal orders

Article 54

(1) Under a special legal order the exercise of fundamental rights – with the exception of the fundamental rights laid down in Articles II and III, and in paragraphs (2) to (6) of Article XXVIII – may be suspended or restricted beyond the extent defined in paragraph (3) of Article I.
(2) Under a special legal order the application of the Fundamental Law shall not be suspended and the operation of the Constitutional Court shall not be restricted.
(3) A special legal order shall be terminated by the organ empowered to introduce the special legal order if the conditions for its declaration no longer exist.
(4) The detailed rules to be applied under any special legal order shall be laid down in a cardinal Act.

CLOSING PROVISIONS

1. The Fundamental Law of Hungary shall enter into force on 1 January 2012.
2. Parliament shall adopt this Fundamental Law according to point a) of subsection (3) of Section 19[14] and subsection (3) of Section 24[15] of Act XX of 1949.
3. The transitional provisions related to this Fundamental Act shall be adopted separately by Parliament according to the procedure referred to in point 2 above.
4. The Government shall submit to Parliament the bills necessary for the implementation of the Fundamental Law.

*

We, Members of Parliament elected on 25 April 2010, being aware of our responsibility before God and man, and availing ourselves of our power to adopt a constitution, have hereby determined the first unified Fundamental Law of Hungary as above.

'May there be peace, freedom and concord.'

DR. PÁL SCHMITT	LÁSZLÓ KÖVÉR
President of the Republic	*Speaker of Parliament*

[14] I.e. Article 19.
[15] I.e. Article 24.

Transitional Provisions of the Fundamental Law[1]

[1] The Closing Provisions of the Fundamental Law state that transitional provisions shall be adopted separately by Parliament according to the rules of the Fundamental Law on constitution-making procedure, i.e., with two-thirds majority of the MPs. Based on this authorization, on December 30, 2011 Parliament enacted the Transitional Provisions of the Fundamental Law, which were promulgated by the President of the Republic next day and came into effect on January 1, 2012. Article 31 of this legal norm declares that the Transitional Provisions form a part of the Fundamental Law. See also the First Amendment of the Fundamental Law in this volume.

In fact, the Transitional Provisions consist of retrospective paragraphs, transitory norms and substantive amendments to the Fundamental Law.

TRANSITIONAL PROVISIONS OF THE FUNDAMENTAL LAW

THE TRANSITION FROM THE COMMUNIST DICTATORSHIP TO DEMOCRACY

We, Members of the Parliament—conscious that the constitutional order's secure functioning cannot stand on a solid foundation without acknowledging the past and the conclusions to which it leads; without naming the crimes committed against people, groups and society during communism and the perpetrators of these crimes; without condemning and prosecuting the perpetrators of these crimes with an emphasis on the responsibility of the leaders of the communist regime and at the same time the compensation of the victims of these crimes; without differentiating between democracy and dictatorship, right and wrong, and good and evil—state the following in order to facilitate the adoption of Hungary's first constitution according to the requirements of a rule of law state:

1. Communist dictatorship is incompatible with a state based on the rule of law and created by the will of the people through the first free elections in 1990. The current Hungarian rule of law state cannot be built on the crimes of the communist system.
2. The Hungarian Socialist Worker's Party and its legal predecessor (the state party) are responsible
   a. For eliminating, with the help of the Soviet Army, the democratic, multi-party effort of the post WWII years;
   b. For a legal system based on illegality and the exclusive use of power;
   c. For eliminating an economy based on the freedom of property and for indebting and permanently destroying the competitiveness of the economy;
   d. For subjecting Hungary's economy, military, foreign policy and human resources to foreign rule;
   e. For systematically destroying traditions based on European values and undermining the nation's identity;
   f. For depriving or seriously limiting fundamental rights of individual citizens and certain groups, specifically
      - For murdering, subjecting to foreign rule, unlawfully imprisoning, forcing into labor camps, torturing, and inhumanely treating people;

- For arbitrarily confiscating property from citizens and limiting their rights to private property;
- For completely depriving people of their freedom and subjecting their political opinions and expressions of will to state coercion;
- For negatively discriminating against people based on origin, worldview or political conviction and for obstructing their progress and self-fulfillment based on knowledge, diligence, and talent;
- For the self-serving intrusion of political and ideological grounds into education, cultural education, scientific life and culture;
- For creating and operating a secret police to illegally observe and influence people's personal lives;

g. For strangling in blood the October 1956 revolution in collaboration with Soviet troops, subsequently ruling based on fear and retribution and forcing 200,000 Hungarians to emigrate;
h. For causing a drop in Hungary's ranking among European nations and in world comparison;
i. For those public law crimes which were carried out for political reasons and which the justice system failed to prosecute for political reasons.

3. The Hungarian Socialist Worker's Party, its predecessors and the political organizations created in the communist ideology for their service were all criminal organizations, and their leaders are responsible without statute of limitations for maintaining a repressive system, violating rights, and betraying the nation.
4. The Hungarian Socialist Party shares the responsibility of the state party—through the continuity in party leadership that bridged the old and the new party—as the legal successor to the Hungarian Socialist Worker's Party, as the inheritor of the illegally amassed wealth and as the benefactor of the illegitimate advantages acquired during the transition.
5. Under the communist dictatorship, it was impossible to prosecute crimes involving the construction and maintenance of the system nor was it possible to do so—given that the constitutional transition did not break legal continuity—after the first free elections. The leaders of the dictatorship were never held responsible in a legal or moral manner. As the Fundamental Law comes into effect, there is now the possibility for delivering justice.
6. Every citizen who showed resistance to the communist dictatorship, who was unjustly prosecuted or was injured in his rights and human dignity by the servants of the communist dictatorship deserves recognition and moral compensation, as long as the person did not participate in these violations of the law.

7. The communist dictatorship systematically prompted the violation of the law, but the acts were perpetrated by individuals. For the living and future generations, the memory of the crimes committed must be preserved and the perpetrators must be named.

The Parliament and other Hungarian state bodies will base their actions on the above constitutional provisions.

Article 1

(1) The remuneration of communist leaders, granted by the State in statute, may be reduced according to degrees defined in law.
(2) The revenues from the reductions carried out in accordance with Paragraph (1) must be used for alleviating the injuries caused by the communist dictatorship and preserving the memory of its victims.

Article 2

(1) The statute of limitations cannot toll on a crime committed against Hungary or against individuals in the name or interest of the state party or with its consent during the communist dictatorship that were not prosecuted for political reasons by ignoring the penal code in effect at the time the crime was committed.
(2) The statute of limitations for a crime defined in Paragraph (1) will be set according to the penal code in effect at the time the crime was committed and will commence 1 January 2012 if the crime's statute of limitations passed before 1 May 1990.
(3) The statute of limitations for a crime defined in Paragraph (1) will be defined according to the penal code in effect at the time the crime was committed and will commence 1 January 2012 if the crime's statute of limitations passed between 2 May 1990 and 31 December 2011 and the perpetrator of the crime was not prosecuted.

Article 3

(1) In order to preserve the memory of the crimes committed in relation to communist crimes, a National Memorial Commission will be established.
(2) The National Memorial Commission will investigate the functioning of the communist dictatorship and the role of individuals and organizations who held the powers of the communist regime. The Commission will also report on its activities and publish its results.

Article 4

Discovering how the communist dictatorship functioned and securing society's sense of justice are both public interests. Those who held power during the communist dictatorship constitute public individuals. For the public interest, those who held power during the communist dictatorship must tolerate public statements (with the exception of deliberate and untrue statements) regarding their roles and their acts related to the communist dictatorship. Data on personal information in relation to these roles and acts may be revealed to the public.

TRANSITIONAL PROVISIONS PERTAINING TO THE COMING INTO EFFECT OF THE FUNDAMENTAL LAW

Article 5

The Fundamental Law does not impact previously adopted laws, administrative measures and other legal means of state administration, individual decisions, and duties assumed in international agreements.

Article 6

The legal successors to state bodies that served their tasks and jurisdiction according to Act XX of 1949 on the Constitution of the Republic of Hungary are bodies that serve their tasks and jurisdiction according to the Fundamental Law.

Article 7

References to the Republic of Hungary will remain in place according to the normative acts enacted before 31 December 2011, even after the enactment of the Fundamental Law goes into effect designating the country as Hungary, as long as the transition to the new national name set in the Fundamental Law cannot be completed according to the principles of responsible resource management.

Article 8

The coming into effect of the Fundamental Law does not impact—with the exceptions outlined in Articles 9–18—the mandate of elected and appointed officials of Parliament, the Government, local governments, and officials appointed or elected before the Fundamental Law comes into effect.

Article 9

a) Articles 3 and 4 of the Fundamental Law should apply to the mandate of the Parliament and Members of Parliament in office at the time the Fundamental Law comes into effect.

b) Articles 12 and 13 of the Fundamental Law should apply to the mandate of the President of the Republic in office at the time the Fundamental Law comes into effect.
c) Articles 20 and 21 of the Fundamental Law should apply to the mandate of the Government and members of the Government in office at the time the Fundamental Law comes into effect.
d) Article 27(3) of the Fundamental Law should apply to the mandate of judicial clerks serving at the time the Fundamental Law comes into effect.
e) Article 33(2) of the Fundamental Law should apply to the mandate of regional assembly presidents in office at the time the Fundamental Law comes into effect.
f) Article 35(3)–(6) of the Fundamental Law should apply to the mandate of local government representative bodies and mayors in office at the time the Fundamental Law comes into effect.

Article 10

The date of reference for Article 4(3)f) of the Fundamental Law is the date the Fundamental Law comes into effect.

Article 11

(1) The Curia is the legal successor in matters of adjudication to the Supreme Court and the National Justice Council and the President of the National Judicial Office is their legal successor in matter of administration of the courts. .
(2) The mandate of the President of the Supreme Court, the President and members of the National Justice Council end when the Fundamental Law comes into effect.
(3) In order to guarantee the right to trial within a reasonable timeframe, as provided in Article XXVIII(1) of the Fundamental Law, the President of the National Judicial Office may assign any case to a court at an equal level but outside the normal court's jurisdiction, if the caseload across courts is not balanced.
(4) In order to guarantee the right to trial within a reasonable timeframe, as provided in Article XXVIII(1) of the Fundamental Law, the Public Prosecutor, as the leader and manager of the Office of the Prosecutor based on Article 29 of the Fundamental Law, may assign any case to a court at an equal level but outside the normal court's jurisdiction, if the caseload across courts is not balanced. This does not impact

the right of the President of the National Judicial Office as granted in Paragraph (3) and the right of the prosecution to assign a case to any court within their jurisdiction.

Article 12

(1) If a judge reaches the general retirement age, defined in Article 26(2) of the Fundamental Law, before 1 January 2012, his or her term of service will end 30 June 2012. If a judge reaches the general retirement age, defined in Article 26(2) of the Fundamental Law, between 1 January 2012 and 31 December 2012, his or her term of service will end 31 December 2012.

(2) If a person is appointed by a specific government decision to serve as a mediator or arbitrator under Article 25(6) of the Fundamental Law, the person will be subject to the general retirement policy, outlined in Article 26(2) of the Fundamental Law, as of 1 January 2014.

Article 13

If a prosecutor reaches the general retirement age defined in Article 29(3) of the Fundamental Law before 1 January 2012, his or her term of service will end 30 June 2012. If a prosecutor reaches the general retirement age defined in Article 29(3) of the Fundamental Law between 1 January 2012 and 31 December 2012, his or her term of service will end 31 December 2012.

Article 14

(1) The minimum age requirement, defined in Article 26(2) of the Fundamental Law, must be applied to judicial appointments—except in cases defined in Paragraph (2) that are based on an application process that is announced after the Fundamental Law comes into effect.

(2) If the appointment takes place without a formal application process, the minimum age requirement must apply to judicial appointments made after the Fundamental Law comes into effect.

Article 15

The title of the Parliamentary Commissioner for Citizen Rights will change to Commissioner for Fundamental Rights when the Fundamental Law comes into effect. The Commissioner for Fundamental Rights is the legal successor to the Parliamentary Commissioner for Citizen Rights, the Parliamentary Commissioner for National and Ethnic Rights and the

Parliamentary Commissioner for the Rights of Future Generations. The serving Parliamentary Commissioner for National and Ethnic Minority Rights becomes the deputy to the Commissioner for Fundamental Rights and protects the rights of nationalities living in Hungary when the Fundamental Law comes into effect; the serving Parliamentary Commissioner for the Rights of Future Generations becomes the deputy to the Commissioner for Fundamental Rights and protects the rights of future generations when the Fundamental Law comes into effect; their mandate will end when the mandate of the Commissioner for Fundamental Rights ends.

Article 16

The mandate of the serving Commissioner for Data Protection ends when the Fundamental Law comes into effect.

Article 17

The title of President of a Regional Council becomes the President of the Regional Representative-body when the Fundamental Law comes into effect.

Article 18

The serving member of the Budget Council, appointed by the President of the Republic, becomes the President of the Budget Council when the Fundamental Law comes into effect.

Article 19

(1) The provisions of the Fundamental Law must be applied to pending cases as well as future cases—with the exceptions outlined in Paragraphs (2)-(5).

(2) Article 6 of the Fundamental Law must be applied beginning with the first Parliamentary session after the Fundamental Law comes into effect.

(3) The petitions filed by individuals who do not have the right to petition to the Constitutional Court under the Fundamental Law are terminated—unless the petitions come under the jurisdiction of an organization other than the Constitutional Court after the Fundamental Law comes into effect, in which case the petition may be transferred. An individual may file the petition again with the Constitutional Court based on the conditions outlined in cardinal act.

(4) Articles 38(4) and 39(1) of the Fundamental Law should be applied, as defined in law, to contracts and grants in effect 1 January 2012 and negotiations of contracts and grants in process when the Fundamental Law comes into effect.

(5) The third sentence of Article 70/E(3) of Act XX of 1949 on the Constitution of the Republic of Hungary, in effect 31 December 2011, should be applied according to the normative acts in effect 31 December 2011 to changes in the condition, nature or amount of pensions or the transformation of such pensions to other provisions until 31 December 2012.

Article 20

Articles 26(6), 28/D, 28/E, and 31(2)-(3) of Act XX of 1949 on the Constitution of the Republic of Hungary should be applied to cases ongoing at the time the Fundamental Law takes effect.

Article 21

(1) Parliament, in the cardinal Act on the Status of Churches, lists the recognized churches and defines the conditions for recognizing further churches. A cardinal Act may prescribe that recognizing an organization as a church should require that the organization be in existence for a given length of time with a certain number of members and that the State take into account the general historic traditions and societal support for the organization.

(2) Parliament, in a cardinal Act on Nationalities residing in Hungary, lists the recognized national minorities and defines the conditions for recognizing other nationalities. A cardinal Act may define the conditions for recognizing a national minority to include the length of time of residence in Hungary, the number of members of the group and the initiation of recognition of the minority group through application by a member of the minority group.

Article 22

(1) In applying Article 24(2)c) of the Fundamental Law, a constitutional complaint is a

(a) complaint submitted against a normative act that is already in effect that violates of the petitioner's rights guaranteed in the Fundamental Law and that is applied in a judicial decision, after the petitioner has exhausted all available legal remedies or no legal remedy is available, together with

(b) a complaint submitted against a normative act that violates the petitioner's rights guaranteed in the Fundamental Law, in an individual case with a direct effect and that is applied without a judicial decision, after the petitioner has exhausted all legal remedies or no legal remedy is available.

(2) Applying Article 24(2)d) of the Fundamental Law, a constitutional complaint is a complaint submitted in a case where a right guaranteed in the Fundamental Law is infringed by a judicial decision or by another judicial action that closes a case, after the petitioner has exhausted all available legal remedies or there are no legal remedies.

Article 23

(1) The first general elections for local government representatives and mayors after the Fundamental Law comes into effect will be held in October 2014. The general elections of local government representatives and mayors will be held the same day—with the exception of the first general elections after the Fundamental Law comes into effect—as the elections for representatives to the European parliament; the time between two subsequent general elections for local government representatives and mayors may differ from the period set in Article 35(2) in order to follow the general elections for representatives to the European parliament.

(2) The participation, in Parliament, of representatives of nationalities living in Hungary should be guaranteed, as defined in Article 2(2), in the work of the first Parliament elected after the Fundamental Law comes into effect.

Article 24

Fundamental Law coming into effect does not affect prior decisions—in accordance with Act XX of 1949 on the Constitution of the Republic of Hungary—of the Parliament or the Government on the deployment of the Hungarian Army in Hungary or abroad, deployment of foreign forces in or originating from Hungary or the decisions of the Hungarian Army on the deployment of Hungarian forces abroad or the deployment of foreign forces within Hungary.

Article 25

(a) The Fundamental Law's provisions on state of national crisis should be applied in case a state of national crisis is declared.

(b) The Fundamental Law's provisions on state of emergency should be applied if a state of emergency is declared as a result of armed acts that aim to overthrow the constitutional order or to acquire the exclusive use of power or to commit armed or non-armed violent acts that endanger *en masse* life or property.
(c) The Fundamental Law's provisions on state of extreme danger should be applied in case a state of national crisis is declared as a result of a natural disaster or industrial accident that endangers *en masse* life or property.
(d) The Fundamental Law's provisions on the state of preventive defense should be applied in case a state of preventive defense is declared.
(e) The Fundamental Law's provisions on unexpected attacks should be applied in case a situation emerges as defined in Article 19/E of Act XX of 1949 on the Constitution of the Republic of Hungary.
(f) The Fundamental Law's provisions on state of extreme danger should be applied if a state of extreme danger is declared.

Article 26

(1) If, when the Fundamental Law comes into effect, a person is barred from participating in public affairs by a final court judgment, the person does not have a right to vote under the Fundamental Law.
(2) If a person whose capacity is limited or restricted by being subject to guardianship on the basis of a final court judgment, the person does not have the right to vote until the guardianship is terminated by a court or until a court decision returns to the person the right to vote.

Article 27

Article 37(4) of the Fundamental Law should remain in force for Acts that were promulgated when the state debt to the Gross Domestic Product ratio exceeded 50% even if the ratio no longer exceeds 50%.

Article 28

(1) Article 12(2) of Act XX of 1949 on the Constitution of the Republic of Hungary, in effect 31 December 2011, should be applied in case of a transfer of local government property to the state or another local government until 31 December 2013.
(2) Article 44/B(4) of Act XX of 1949 on the Constitution of the Republic of Hungary, in effect 31 December 2011, remains in force until 31

December 2012. After 31 December 2011, a normative act authorized by an Act of Parliament may grant public administrative tasks and jurisdiction to a notary of a competent local government.

(3) A capital or regional government office may ask a court to decide whether a local government failed in its statutory obligation to deliver a decision. If the local government does not satisfy its statutory obligation to deliver a decision within the time frame set by a court, the court may order, based on the capital or regional government office's initiative, the head of the capital or regional government office to address the failure by issuing a decree in the name of the local government.

(4) Article 22(1) and (3)-(5) of Act XX of 1949 on the Constitution of the Republic of Hungary, in effect 31 December 2011, remains in force until the cardinal law as called for by Article 5(8) of the Fundamental Law comes in effect. Parliament will adopt the cardinal laws according to Articles 5(8) and 7(3) of the Fundamental Law before 30 June 2012.

(5) Until 31 December 2012 Parliament may require in a cardinal act that certain of its decisions be subject to a qualified majority.

Article 29

(1) As long as the public debt exceeds 50% of the Gross Domestic Product, if the Constitutional Court, the Court of the European Union, another court or other law applying that body's decision requires the state to pay a fine, and the Act on the central budget does not contain necessary reserves to pay the fine, and the amount of the fine cannot be allocated from the budget without undermining a balanced management of the budget or no other item from the budget may be eliminated to provide for the fine, a general contribution covering the common needs must be specified that relates in its name and content exclusively and explicitly to the above fine.

(2) Those who were illegally deprived of their lives or freedom based on political factors and saw the unjust damage to their property caused by the state prior to 2 May 1990 cannot be granted financial or other material compensation in a new compensation statute.

Article 30

(1) A Cardinal Act, as defined in Articles 41 And 42 of the Fundamental Law, may specify that a new organization assume the tasks and jurisdiction of the organization charged with Financial Supervisory Authority and the Hungarian National Bank. The President of the

Republic appoints the head of this organization according to Article 41(2) of the Fundamental Law.

(2) In the case defined in Paragraph (1), the vice-president of the new organization, with respect to the tasks on monetary policy and central banking, is the President of the Hungarian National Bank, in office at the time the Act on the new organization comes into effect, and the vice-president of the new organization, with respect to tasks on supervising the financial sector, is the President of the Financial Supervisory Authority, in office at the time the Act on the new organization comes into effect. The vice-presidents will remain in office until their terms as President expire. Once the mandate of the vice-president ends, the President of the Republic appoints new vice-president according to Article 41(2) of the Fundamental Law.

CLOSING PROVISIONS

Article 31

(1) The Transitional Provisions of the Fundamental Law (thereinafter: Transitional provisions) comes into effect 1 January 2012.

(2) Parliament adopts the Transitional Provisions based on Articles 19(3) a)and 24(3) of Act XX of 1949 on the Constitution of Republic of Hungary and with respect to Paragraph 3 of the Closing Provisions of Hungary's Fundamental Law. The Transitory Provisions form a part of the Fundamental Law.

(3) Hereby repealed are

a) Act XX of 1949 on the Constitution of the Republic of Hungary,

b) Act I of 1972 on the unified text of the Constitution of the People's Republic of Hungary and on the amendment to Act XX of 1949,

c) Act XXXI of 1989 on the amendment to the Constitution,

d) Act XVI of 1990 on the amendment to the Constitution of the Republic of Hungary,

e) Act XXIX of 1990 on the amendment to the Constitution of the Republic of Hungary,

f) Act XL of 1990 on the amendment to the Constitution of the Republic of Hungary,

g) the 25 May 2010 amendment to the Constitution,

h) the 5 July 2010 amendment to the Constitution,

i) the 6 July 2010 amendment to the Constitution,

j) the 11 August 2010 amendment to the Constitution,

k) Act CXIII of 2010 on the amendment to Act XX of 1949 on the Constitution of the Republic of Hungary,

l) Act CXIX of 2010 on the amendment to Act XX of 1949 on the Constitution of the Republic of Hungary,

m) Act CLXIII of 2010 on the amendment to Act XX of 1949 on the Constitution of the Republic of Hungary,

n) Act LXI of 2011 on the amendments to Act XX of 1949 on the Constitution of the Republic of Hungary to create certain necessary transitional acts in relation to the Fundamental Law.

o) Act CXLVI of 2011 on the amendment to Act XX of 1949 on the Constitution of the Republic of Hungary,

p) Act CLIX of 2011 on the amendment to Act XX of 1949 on the Constitution of the Republic of Hungary.

Article 32

In memory of its enactment, April 25th is designated as the day of the Fundamental Law.

DR. PÁL SCHMITT	LÁSZLÓ KÖVÉR
President of the Republic	*Speaker of Parliament*

First Amendment of the Fundamental Law[1]

[1] Parliament enacted the First Amendment on June 4, 2012. It was promulgated by the President of the Republic on June 18, and entered into force the next day.

The aim of Article 1(1) is to make clear that the Transitional Provisions form a part of the Fundamental Law. Previously several scholars questioned its normative and hierarchical status, because only the Transitional Provisions declared its own constitutional character, not the Fundamental Law. Following these arguments the commissioner for fundamental rights initiated a Constitutional Court review on conformity of the Transitional Provisions with the Fundamental Law.

Article 1(2), which was a late addendum to the bill at the very end of the parliamentary debate, secures that not only the remuneration of an incumbent president of the republic but also of former presidents shall be laid down in a cardinal act. This provision guarantees the stability of the resigned president Pál Schmitt's payment.

Article 2 repeals the provision that regulates possible merger of the Hungarian National Bank with the financial supervisory authority. The European Commission criticized earlier that the governor of the National Bank would become a simple deputy chairman of a new system, which would structurally encroach on his independence. (See the infringement proceeding initiated by the European Commission on January 17, 2012, IP/12/24.)

FIRST AMENDMENT OF THE FUNDAMENTAL LAW OF HUNGARY

Parliament, acting as a constitution-maker based on Article 1(2)a) of the Fundamental Law modifies the Fundamental Law as follows:

Article 1

(1) The Closing Provisions of the Fundamental Law shall be supplemented with the following point 5:
"5. The Transitional Provisions to the Fundamental Law (31 December 2011) adopted according to point 3 above form a part of the Fundamental Law."

(2) In Article 12(5) of the Fundamental Law the text part "the President of the Republic" shall be replaced with the text "the President of the Republic and the former President of the Republic".

Article 2

Article 30 of the Transitional Provisions to the Fundamental Law shall be repealed.

Article 3

(1) This Amendment to the Fundamental Law shall enter into force on the day after its promulgation.

(2) Parliaments adopts this Amendment to the Fundamental Law based on Articles 1(2)a) and S(2).

JÁNOS ÁDER
President of the Republic

LÁSZLÓ KÖVÉR
Speaker of Parliament

Bill on the Second Amendment of the Fundamental Law[1]

[1] The bill submitted by Justice Minister Tibor Navracsics on September 7, 2012 would change and amend the Transitional Provisions so that judges' term of employment can continue until age 65. Previously, the Constitutional Court held the law implementing the lowering the retirement age from 70 to 62 to violate the principle of judicial independence. Decision 33/2012. (VII. 16.) See more on this in Jeremy McBride's contribution in this volume. See also the case of *European Commission v. Hungary* (C-286/12) before the European Court of Justice.

The bill specifies that those over 62 may not hold senior posts in courts. Moreover, the provision that judges over 62 may not fill senior posts in courts does not apply to the president of the Curia and the head of the National Judicial Office.

Furthermore, Fidesz MP János Lázár submitted a bill with the same title (Second Amendment of the Fundamental Law) on September 18, 2012. This would amend the Transitional Provisions in order to introduce a voter registration requirement.

SECOND AMENDMENT OF THE FUNDAMENTAL LAW OF HUNGARY

Parliament, acting as a constitution-maker based on Article 1(2)a) of the Fundamental Law modifies the Fundamental Law as follows:

Article 1

(1) Article 12 of the Transitional Provisions of the Fundamental Law shall be supplemented with the following Paragraph (3):
"(3) No person could serve as a judge as long as he or she receives a public pension or an allowance that is due after the person reaches the retirement age."

(2) Article 12 of the Transitional Provisions of the Fundamental Law shall be replaced by the following:

"Article 12

(1) With the exception of the President of the Curia, the mandate of a judge shall be terminated after he or she completed the 65th year of his or her life.

(2) With the exception of the President of the Curia and the head of the central judicial administrative body, a person cannot serve

a. in a leadership position in the judiciary,
b. in a leadership position in the central judicial administrative body or,
c. in the agency that is charged with supervising the central judicial administrative body,

if he or she completed the 62th year of his or her life.

(3) No person could serve as a judge as long as he or she receives a public pension or an allowance that is due after the person reaches the retirement age.

(4) If a person is appointed by a specific government decision to serve as a mediator or arbitrator based upon an act under Article 25(6) of the Fundamental Law, the employment of the person shall be terminated as of January 1, 2014 if he or she completed the age defined

in Paragraph (1). Unless defined otherwise in an act, if this person reaches the age defined in Paragraph (1) before January 1, 2014 his/her employment shall be terminated on December 31, 2013.

Article 2

(1) Article 13 of the Transitional Provisions of the Fundamental Law shall be supplemented with the following Paragraph (2) while the text of Article 13 shall become Paragraph (1):

(2) "No person could serve as a prosecutor as long as he or she receives a public pension or an allowance that is due after the person reaches the retirement age."

(3) Article 13 of the Transitional Provisions of the Fundamental Law shall be replaced by the following:

"Article 13

(1) With the exception of the Prosecutor General, the mandate of a prosecutor shall be terminated after he or she completed the 65th year of his or her life.

(2) With the exception of the Prosecutor General, no person, aged over 62, shall serve in a leadership position in the prosecution.

(3) No person could serve as a prosecutor as long as he or she receives a public pension or an allowance that is due after the person reaches the retirement age."

Article 3

(1) This Amendment of the Fundamental Law – with the exception of Paragraph (2) – shall enter into force on November 1, 2012.

(2) Article 1(2) and Article 2(2) shall enter into force on January 1, 2013.

(3) Parliament adopts this Amendment of the Fundamental Law based on Articles 1(2)a) and S(2) of the Fundamental Law.

Opinion on the Fundamental Law of Hungary (Amicus Brief)[1]

Edited by ANDREW ARATO, GÁBOR HALMAI, JÁNOS KIS

Authors: Zoltán Fleck, Gábor Gadó, Gábor Halmai, Szabolcs Hegyi, Gábor Juhász, János Kis, Zsolt Körtvélyesi, Balázs Majtényi, Gábor Attila Tóth

[1] The Brief was submitted to the Venice Commission early June 2011. Available in English from the page of the Law and Public Affairs, Princeton University: http://lapa.princeton.edu/hosteddocs/amicus-to-vc-english-final.pdf; in Hungarian in *Fundamentum, Human Rights Quarterly* 1 (2011): 158–161.

On February 2012 another Brief was presented to the Commission *On the Transitional Provisions of the Fundamental Law and on the key cardinal laws* edited by Gábor Halmai and Kim Lane Scheppele. Available at http://lapa.princeton.edu/hosteddocs/hungary/Amicus_Cardinal_Laws_final.pdf. The authors of these amicus briefs are constitutional scholars that came together solely for the purpose of this task.

CONTENTS

1. INTRODUCTION

The Hungarian Parliament passed Hungary's Fundamental Law on April 18, 2011. The Fundamental Law, which enters into force on January 1, 2012, supersedes the previous constitution (hereinafter: 1989 Constitution), which, in keeping with the requirements of democratic constitutionalism during the 1989–90 regime change, comprehensively amended the first written Constitution of Hungary (Act XX of 1949). The drafting of the Fundamental Law took place without following any of the elementary political, professional, scientific and social debates. These requirements stem from the applicable constitutional norms and those rules of the House of Parliament that one would expect to be met in a debate concerning a document that will define the life of the country over the long term. The debate—effectively—took place with the sole and exclusive participation of representatives of the governing political parties. In its opinion approved at its plenary session of 25-26 March 2011, the Council of Europe's Venice Commission also expressed its concerns related to the document, which was drawn up in a process that excluded the political opposition and professional and other civil organizations. The document–according to the declaration set forth in Article B–seeks to maintain that Hungary is an independent, democratic state governed by the rule of law, and furthermore—according to Article E—that Hungary contributes to the creation of European unity; however, in many respects it does not comply with standards of democratic constitutionalism and the basic principles set forth in Article 2 of the Treaty on the Functioning of the European Union [hereinafter: TFEU].

This opinion addresses the procedural problems related to the drafting of the Fundamental Law, and those flaws in its content in relation to which the suspicion arises that they may permit exceptions to the European requirements of democracy, constitutionalism and the protection of fundamental rights, and, thus, that in the course of their application they could conflict with Hungary's international obligations.

2. THE QUESTIONABLE LEGITIMACY OF CONSTITUTION-MAKING SOLELY BY THE GOVERNING MAJORITY

The process leading to the adoption of Hungary's new constitution are to be analyzed from three points of view: formal legality, adherence to rules of preparation and the availability of the required social and political support.

1. The most important question is whether the adoption of the new constitution meets the requirement of legality, that is, whether or not the constitutional rules applying to the procedures for drafting and adopting a constitution have been met. As regards the legal basis of its creation, the Fundamental Law refers to two passages of the 1989 Constitution, which is still in force: Articles 19(3)a) and 24(3).

Pursuant to Article 19(3)a), the Parliament adopts the Constitution of the Republic of Hungary. Article 24(3) of the Constitution authorizes the two-third majority of Members of Parliament to change the constitution. This passage does not include a rule on the *drafting of the constitution.* This deficiency was recognized and corrected by Parliament in 1995 when the plan to adopt a new constitution was seriously considered for the first time after the comprehensive overhaul of the first written, state-socialist/communist, i.e.: one-party-dictated, 1949 Constitution in 1989. It was then that Article 24(5) of the Constitution was adopted. In view of the two-third majority of the governing coalition at the time, which was similar to that enjoyed by the government party today, this provision prescribed that as a first step in drafting the constitution Parliament is to adopt the regulatory principles of the new constitution in the form of a resolution of the House of Parliament by a four-fifth majority of Members of Parliament. To implement this constitutional norm, by amending the Standing Orders of Parliament, a house rule was adopted by the required majority regulating the process of preparation. The latter provision was deregulated by a four-fifth majority towards the end of that Parliament's term in 2007. At the same time, the rule stated in Article 24(5) of the 1989 Constitution remained in force. This made it clear that the preparation of the constitution necessitates the inclusion of the opposition into the preparatory process even in case of a two-third majority of the ruling parties at a later time. This guarantee was removed from the Constitution by the current government coalition by a two-third majority of Members of Parliament in July 2010. It in itself amounts to a constitutional violation that a law adopted by and requiring a four-fifth majority was annulled by a two-third majority—for which annulment no constitutional or political justification whatsoever was offered. However, the annulment of Article 24(5) has had other serious consequences, as well. It has divested opposition parties of their negotiating positions. It has made it clear that they are only to serve as a backdrop in the drafting of the new constitution. Furthermore, the Constitution has been left without a rule regulating the process of preparing the making of the new constitution.

2. Parliament sought to make up for the lack of such a norm concerning the preparation of the constitution by adopting the Parliamentary

Resolution 47/2010 (VI. 29.) pursuant to which an *ad hoc* Committee for the Preparation of the Fundamental Law was established. Of the 45 members of the ad hoc committee 30 were delegated by the governing parties. The committee introduced to Parliament a draft-resolution for the regulatory directives for Hungary's Constitution on December 20, 2010. Parliament has never read, discussed or voted on this draft-resolution. Instead, Parliament adopted the Parliamentary Resolution 9/2011 (III. 7.) on March 7, 2011 on the preparation of the new constitution. This was promulgated on March 9, that is, five days prior to the introduction of the bill on the new Fundamental Law to Parliament. The wording of this Resolution invites Members of Parliament to submit their bills amending the Fundamental Law until March 15, 2011. At the same time, diverging from the House's normal legislative and constitution-making procedures, the Resolution also states that any bill, which enjoys the support of half of any parliamentary faction—ipso facto—is to be read by Parliament. By doing so, the governing majority has acknowledged that the parliamentary minority is to be given a special status in the constitution-drafting procedure without however restoring or securing their negotiating positions in fact.

The bill which was ultimately submitted on March 14, 2011 and was signed by all Members of Parliament of the government's parties had been prepared by a three-person-committee appointed by the government and led by a member of the European Parliament who, consequently, does not have a seat in the Hungarian Parliament. At the same time, the Parliamentary Resolution (referred to supra) supplemented the House Standing Orders with regulations regarding the drafting of the new constitution. These regulations made it possible to diverge from the usual process of law-making and, so, to complete the Parliamentary discussion of the bill in nine calendar days.

It follows that, contrary to what would be expected of document shaping the country's life in the long run, the preparation of the new Fundamental Law has been carried out exclusively by the governing party coalition and in the absence of constitutional and parliamentary regulations and was not preceded by the necessary political, professional, scientific and social debates. Worries concerning the exclusion of the public and also opposition political forces, professional, scientific and other non-governmental organizations were expressed by the statement of the Venice Committee of the European Council passed at its plenary session on March 25-26, 2011.

3. The new Fundamental Law was only supported by the governing party alliance and was rejected by other parliamentary and extra-parliamentary parties. Public opinion was demonstrably in favour of a referendum to

at least decide on the adoption or rejection of the text. However, only a majority decision of Members of Parliament in session could have made possible the calling of such a referendum. This was rejected by the ruling parties. As a result, the new Fundamental Law has not gained the support of a sufficiently broad consensus of political parties nor has it received a direct confirmation by the electorate.

It is not surprising that the text of the new Fundamental Law is in many ways divisive which a considerable share of the population rejects. It is therefore foreseeable that not even the passing of time will endow it with the consensual support of Hungarian citizens subject to Hungarian law. Its legitimacy will remain doubtful.

3. THE FUNDAMENTAL LAW ON THE IDENTITY OF THE POLITICAL COMMUNITY

An important criterion for a democratic constitution is that everybody living under it can regard it as his or her own. The Fundamental Law breaches this requirement on multiple counts.

1. Its lengthy preamble, entitled National Avowal, defines the subjects of the constitution not as the totality of people living under the Hungarian laws, but as the Hungarian ethnic nation: "*We, the members of the Hungarian Nation...* hereby proclaim the following". A few paragraphs down, the Hungarian nation returns as "our nation torn apart in the storms of the last century." The Fundamental Law defines it as a community, the binding fabric of which is "intellectual and spiritual": not political, but cultural. There is no place in this community for the nationalities living within the territory of the Hungarian state. At the same time, there is a place in it for the Hungarians living beyond our borders.

The elevation of the "single Hungarian nation" to the status of constitutional subject suggests that the scope of the Fundamental Law somehow extends to the whole of historical, pre-Trianon Hungary, and certainly to those places where Hungarians are still living today. This suggestion is not without its constitutional consequences: the Fundamental Law makes the right to vote accessible to those members of the "united Hungarian nation" who live outside the territory of Hungary. It gives a say in who should make up the Hungarian legislature to people who are not subject to the laws of Hungary.

2. It characterizes the nation referred to as the subject of the constitution as a Christian community, narrowing even further the range of people

who can recognize themselves as belonging to it. "We recognize the role of Christianity in preserving nationhood," it declares, not as a statement of historical fact, but also with respect to the present. And it expects everyone who wishes to identify with the constitution to also identify with its opening entreaty: "God bless the Hungarians."

This text—the first line of the National Anthem—originated in 1823. At that time in Hungary, as in most countries of Europe, everybody proclaimed themselves publicly to be believers, even those who were not believers. A Hungarian today can look back on those words in this knowledge, if a non-believer. He or she can respect it as the legacy of a bygone age.

But, if it is written over the constitution almost 200 years later, then this entreaty to God is not a venerable tradition, but a new development. It expresses that the Hungarian state wishes to return to a previous state of affairs, in which the community that possessed the state still defined itself as a congregation of faithful Christians.

3. The name of the 1989 Constitution was "The Constitution of the Republic of Hungary". Its first Article reads thus: "Hungary shall be a republic." This statement means more than that the head of state does not live in the royal palace, and does not take office based on dynastic rules of succession. It simultaneously differentiates the new Hungarian democracy from the post-1949 People's Republic and the post-1920 Regency; from the communist dictatorship and the authoritarian regime of the interwar period. The new constitution, in contrast to this, is the "Fundamental Law of Hungary." The word "republic" is not included among the 509 words of its preamble; and only occurs once in the main text. Even here its meaning has been narrowed: it no longer says anything about the *intellectuality* of our political apparatus, but merely about the *form of government* ("Hungary's form of government shall be that of a republic").

This narrowing of meaning sends out a symbolic message. The Fundamental Law does not draw the historical dividing lines where the 1989 Constitution did. It claims that the "continuity" of Hungarian statehood lasted from the country's beginnings until the German occupation of the country on March 19, 1944, but was then interrupted only to be restored on May 2, 1990, the day of the first session of the freely elected Parliament. Thus it rejects not only the communist dictatorship, but also the Temporary National Assembly convened at the end of 1944, which split with the fallen regime. It rejects the national assembly election of December 1945. Today's democracy-watchers would classify the parliamentary election of December '45 as "partly free," adding that it was the freest in Hungary's entire history up until that time. It also rejects the progressive legislation of the National Assembly: the "little constitution" of the

Republic approved at the beginning of 1946, which the Round Table was able to draw on in '89; as well as the abolition of noble titles and the Upper House of Parliament.

At the same time, it spells out that: "We honour... the Holy Crown, which embodies the constitutional continuity of Hungary's statehood and the unity of the nation." This declaration is diametrically opposed to the republican ethos of 1946 and 1989. The crown symbolized the unity of the *nobility-centered conception of* nation, and the continuity of the *nobility-centered conception of the* constitution.

4. "We deny any statute of limitation for the inhuman crimes committed against the Hungarian nation and its citizens under the national socialist and communist dictatorships," continues the list of declarations. If "inhuman" crimes should be taken to mean war crimes and crimes against humanity, then the denial of a statute of limitations complies with effective international law—if it means something else however, then the Fundamental Law, in breach of the prohibition on retroactive effect, classifies as having no statute of limitations on criminal acts for which the limitation period has already expired. At the same time, it does not care to acknowledge that war crimes and crimes against humanity were committed not only by foreign occupying forces and their agents, but also between 1920 and 1944 by extreme right-wing "free troops" and the security forces of the independent Hungarian state, and not only against "the Hungarian nation and its citizens," but also against other peoples.

Neither does it care to acknowledge that the continuity of Hungary's statehood was not interrupted on March 19, 1944. Restrictions were placed on the government agencies' freedom to act, but they were not shut down. The Regent remained in his office, and the parliament sat and regularly passed those bills that were introduced by the government. The Hungarian state leadership did not declare the termination of legal continuity, but cooperated with the occupying powers.

The Fundamental Law only recognizes the (pre-1944) glorious pages of Hungarian history, but does not acknowledge the acts and failures that give cause for self-criticism. It only holds to account the—reputed or genuine—injuries caused to the Hungarian people by foreign powers, and does not wish to acknowledge the wrongs committed by the Hungarian state against its own citizens and other peoples.

It raises to a constitutional level the worst traditions of national self-glorification, self-pity and self-justification. Its view of history is anachronistic, Christian-nationalist kitsch; it is unacceptable to the non right-leaning part of the country and even elicits embarrassment from a section of the right wing.

4. CITIZENSHIP, VOTING RIGHTS, NATION: THE NEW BOUNDARIES OF THE POLITICAL COMMUNITY

1. Unlike most of the major changes enacted with the Fundamental Law, where the regulation of citizenship is concerned the substance that lies beyond the constitutional provisions is known: the separation of citizenship from place of residence and the principle of effectivity. The legislature has lifted the requirement to reside in Hungary in cases where a person can certify or "demonstrate the likelihood" that they are of Hungarian descent and/or descended from a Hungarian citizen, and that they have knowledge of the Hungarian language.

2. The new regulations on citizenship—in keeping with the fact that the Fundamental Law indicates as the source of constitutional authority, in place of the people, an ethnically-based "single" Hungarian nation (Article D)—serve to ethnicize, in the extreme, the procedure for obtaining citizenship. Although the extension of Hungarian citizenship to persons living abroad is not worded directly into the Fundamental Law, this step brings irreversible and far-reaching changes to the boundaries of the political community. This is because the Fundamental Law—correctly—prohibits a person from being deprived of their citizenship on any count (Article G(3)) and also elevates to constitutional level the principle under which Hungarian citizenship may be "inherited" without limitation, so the child of a Hungarian citizen is in every case a Hungarian citizen. In this way, the members of communities abroad who obtain Hungarian citizenship under the legislation will pass their Hungarian citizenship on from generation to generation, regardless of their place of residence (Article G(1)).

3. The new legislation raises serious concerns with respect to the ban on discrimination. On the one hand it should be noted that the principle of granting benefits on the grounds of ethnicity is applied in many other European states, and benefits founded on cultural proximity can usually be regarded as an accepted purpose for discrimination. On the other hand, however, the extent of the difference in treatment must be proportionate to this purpose. It is contentious that while the legislature does not expect a preferred applicant to even settle in Hungary, the main rule applied to the non-preferred group is that the applicant must live in Hungary for an *uninterrupted* period of eight years. This issue could be especially pertinent in light of the fact that Protocol No. 12 to the European Convention on

Human Rights also extends the ban on discrimination to rights above and beyond those set forth in the Convention, which means that it will also be applicable in the procedure for gaining citizenship. Hungary has not ratified the Protocol, but has signed it—and accordingly it may not approve any new legislation that runs counter to it. With this statutory amendment, Hungary has joined in the tendency, most typical of countries in the Balkan Peninsula, of treating the regulations on citizenship as a means of nation-building in the ethnic sense.

4. The new constitutional norms has failed to embed, into the regulations on citizenship, the existing European standards that already feature in the European Convention on Nationality, and which, due to Hungary's inertia, are not reflected in the Hungarian legislation to this day: the naturalisation procedure lacks all the guarantees of transparency, the authority is under no obligation to justify its decision, and there is no right to a judicial review.[2] In light of the new constitutional rules, this also means that the legal substance of the vaguely worded provision which, although it refers to "Hungarian descent," is ethnically charged based on political statements, remains uncertain, and unfathomable to the general public. Applying the law is the task of an apparatus created specifically for this purpose, which will implement the clearly espoused political intention to naturalise Hungarians living abroad—with no effective control, as described above.

5. According to the OSCE's Bolzano Recommendations: "States should refrain from taking unilateral steps, including extending benefits to foreigners on the basis of ethnic, cultural, linguistic, religious or historical ties that have the intention or effect of undermining the principles of territorial integrity [...] States may take preferred linguistic competencies and cultural, historical or familial ties into account in their decision to grant citizenship to individuals abroad. States should, however, ensure that such a conferral of citizenship respects the principles of friendly, including good neighbourly, relations and territorial sovereignty, and should refrain from conferring citizenship en masse, even if dual citizenship is allowed by the State of residence."[3]

Although these are primarily security-policy considerations, good neighbourly relations and the principle of sovereignty are also decisive factors. The granting of dual citizenship *en masse* fits in with plans of the

[2] European Convention on Nationality, Strasbourg, November 6, 1997. See Article 11 on the provision of written reasons for decisions, and Article 12 on the right to legal remedy.

[3] OSCE Bolzano Recommendations, points 10–12.

cross-border national unification of persons of the same ethnicity living in relatively high numbers close to the border, and as such it raises a number of problems, ranging from extraterritorialism, through discrimination, to the issue of good neighbourly relations.[4] While dual or multiple citizenship has become increasingly accepted in international practice, in certain contexts this solution, sacrificing the principle of territorial integrity in the name of strengthening ethnic identity, can lead to tensions.[5]

6. The extension of citizenship and voting rights, in view of its international consequences, should only be undertaken with particular caution, with a view to maintaining good neighbourly relations and respecting the principle of sovereignty. Due to the extraterritorial application, the holding of elections, in particular, will require bilateral consultation that did not take place in the course of the earlier legislative work.[6] Prior to the extension of voting rights, Slovakia and Ukraine reacted negatively to the mere granting of citizenship: people living in these countries are threatened with the loss of citizenship of their country of residence if they take the opportunity offered by the Hungarian statutory amendment.

7. The Fundamental Law leaves open the question of whether the right to vote is dependent on having a permanent address in Hungary, and it also makes no provision regarding precisely in what manner and in what form Hungarian citizens without a Hungarian place of residence will exercise their voting rights (Article XXIII(4)). The answer to this is probably not unconnected to what proportion of Hungarians living outside the country's borders eventually request naturalisation. The number of submitted applications currently stands at over 80,000. Given that the populations of Hungarian communities abroad amount to several million people, in the electoral system of a country with 10 million inhabitants the extension of

---

4 For the aspects involved, see the minority-themed publication of the Venice Commission, entitled: "The Protection of National Minorities by their Kin-State," Athens, June 7-8, 2002, CDL-STD(2002)032, *Science and technique of democracy* No. 32, D.

5 As the Venice Commission noted with regard to voting rights granted as a benefit to minorities: "A given mechanism may help to reduce tensions in one country, but create tensions in another." European Commission For Democracy Through Law, Report on Dual Voting for Persons Belonging to National Minorities, Strasbourg, June 16, 2008, Study No. 387/2006, para 7.

6 Regarding the cooperation obligation determined in bilateral treaties, see: The Protection of National Minorities by their Kin-State, Athens, June 7-8, 2002, CDL-STD(2002)032, Science and technique of democracy No. 32, especially footnote 15.

voting rights as described above could lead to substantial anomalies—consider, for example, the approval of the state budget with the supporting votes of representatives' of citizens who, at best, only bear the social and economic consequences of the decision in a limited extent. The detailed rules on the extension of voting rights abroad will greatly influence the quality of Hungarian democracy in the future.

5. THE RELATIONSHIP BETWEEN RIGHTS AND OBLIGATIONS

The Fundamental Law reshapes the relationship between rights and duties in contrast with the 1989 Constitution. This change will impact on the substantive rules of most of the Hungarian legal system (for example, the chapter on fundamental rights itself contains 18 passages pertaining to the legislation of new acts of Parliament) and the practice of political institutions, as well. Although fundamental rights and duties (Articles I-XXXI) were included in one chapter, the chapters called "National Avowal" and "Foundation" also contain principles concerning the enjoyment and exercise of rights as well as the fulfilment of duties. (The relevance of the "National Avowal" is based on Article R, which prescribes with mandatory force that the interpretations of provisions of the Fundamental Law are to be in harmony with the National Avowal's declarations.)

The relationship of rights and duties stated by the Fundamental Law is marked by a peculiar ambiguity. The description of a number of entitlements and duties follows the conception that shaped the 1989 Constitution as well. This is a liberal conception of law which has been developed and elaborated in modern constitutional democracies (e.g., Articles IV-VIII, XIV-XV, XXIII, XXIV, XXVI-XXVII, XXX-XXXI). However, the Fundamental Laws adds a number of rules which are incompatible with the liberal consensus of modern constitutions. This threatens to transform the structure of fundamental rights, as well. According to certain provisions of the Fundamental Law, and the general picture which they outline, the exercise of certain rights depends on the discharging of duties. As a result, they can no longer be regarded as inalienable individual rights. This ambiguity can be detected in the passage of the National Avowal according to which "individual freedom can only unfold in cooperation with others" (the article cataloguing fundamental rights also bears the title "Freedom and responsibility").

1. According to the modern conception, which the 1989 Constitution shares with conceptions of the world's constitutional democracies, and which has been shaped by Hungarian constitutional review, as well

everyone enjoys fundamental rights equally and the state is to protect everyone's rights equally. According to this conception, inalienable constitutional rights are entitlements which lay the groundwork for the duties of the state (and those of all other agents, as well). "It is the primary duty of the state to protect the inviolable and inalienable rights of human beings" (I.). That is, it is not for the state to decide what it will protect and what it will not. (Nor are human beings given these rights by the makers of the constitution.) A conception running counter to this manifests itself, however, in a number of passages in which the Fundamental Law makes the exercise of rights expressly dependent on the discharging of duties. For example, Article XII declares in one and the same passage everyone's right to choose one's employment and profession freely, and their duty to contribute to the welfare of the community by doing work in accordance with one's abilities and opportunities. This is unacceptable in a liberal democracy. The bearer of an inalienable right is free not only to choose among available opportunities for work, but also to refrain from work. The obligation to work is contrary to freedom. Moreover, since this passage includes a duty, it also empowers an entity (local government, authority) to oversee whether this duty is discharged.

2. Binding the exercise of inalienable human rights to the meeting of duties does not only undermine the internal structure of rights and duties (basically eliminating inalienable human rights), but is also objectionable in terms of its content. An analysis of the content of these duties reveals that the Fundamental Law is outdated. The 1989 Constitution was based on the equal recognition of individual and communal forms of life and a plurality of views regarding the good life. The Fundamental Law breaks with this tradition by including moral duties among the fundamental rights. It thereby selects those forms of the good life which it regards as morally valuable and worthy of constitutional protection. The Fundamental Law excludes the following components of the liberal constitutional conception: equal recognition of the plurality (freedom) of forms of life, the neutrality of (and tolerance by) the state and respect for personal autonomy.

By defining one man and one woman as the subjects of marriage (see Article L), the Fundamental Law creates a long-term constitutional obstacle to individual demands for extending the plurality of forms of partnership. Although, by doing so, it adopts the legal position of the Hungarian Constitutional Court, this measure will clearly hamper an eventual revision of existing legal interpretations. Article XIX on social rights and the social policies of the state entitle Parliament to place those citizens, who make use of welfare institutions, under an obligation to engage in "activities benefiting the community." The freedom of teaching and learning is subordinated to a definite goal, namely the acquisition of the highest possible form of knowledge (see Article X). Grown-up children incur a duty to look after parents who are in need (see Article XVI).

Although the subject of rights is the human being, even if their rights are communal (Article I), the new Constitution is in some of its passages anti-individualist. Rights do not necessarily serve to protect the autonomous interests of persons, but rather collective interests (which remain unspecified). In these passages, the new Constitution does not regard entitlements as the limits of collective (state) agency, but rather treats the interests of the collective as the source and at the same time limitation of rights. Thus the new Constitution identifies the foundations of the economy the freedom of enterprise *and* value-creating work (see Article M); the pursuit of individual welfare is coupled with duties owed to the collective (see Article O); the article on the freedom of property and inheritance admonishes to the "social responsibilities" of the owner (see Article XIII).

3. In addition to burdening citizens with duties, the Fundamental Law also restricts their rights (and, parallel to this, reduces the pertaining obligations of the state). The passage on equality does not include the prohibition of legal inequality or discrimination on the basis of sexual orientation (although it does include the same prohibition of discrimination of the handicapped). At the same time, protection is given to the life of the fetus from conception (see Article II). This can easily lead to the restriction of the autonomy of women in early stages of pregnancy, as well. Extending the right of self-defense to the protection of property broadens the private use of violence to a dangerous extent (see Article V).

In sum, the concept of law of the Fundamental Law reflects the intention of the Hungarian state not to remain neutral as regards the life and ideologies of its citizens. Furthermore, it seeks to restrict citizens' rights which undermines the value of these entitlements. This restrictive approach to rights presents a conception which is hardly defensible in a modern society based on the plurality of forms of life.

6. INTERVENTION INTO THE RIGHT TO PRIVACY

The Fundamental Law breaks with a distinguishing feature of constitutions of rule-of-law states, namely, that they comprise the methods of exercising public authority and the limitations on such authority on the one hand and the guarantees of the enforcement of fundamental rights on the other. Instead of this, the text brings several elements of private life under its regulatory purview in a manner that is not doctrinally neutral, but is based on a Christian-conservative ideology. With this, it prescribes for the members of the community a life model based on the normative preferences that fit in with this ideology in the form of their obligations towards the community. These values, which are not doctrinally neutral, feature as high up as the Fundamental Law's preamble entitled National Avowal:

"We recognise the role of Christianity in preserving nationhood."

"We hold that individual freedom can only be complete in cooperation with others." "We hold that the family and the nation constitute the principal framework of our coexistence, and that our fundamental cohesive values are fidelity, faith and love".

"Our Fundamental Law... expresses the nation's will and the form in which we want to live."

With particular regard to the fact that according to Article R the provisions of the Fundamental Law must also be interpreted in keeping with the National Avowal, and that according to Article I(3) fundamental rights may be restricted in the interest of protecting a constitutional value, this provision could serve as the basis for a restriction of fundamental rights.

Certain provisions of the Fundamental Law pertaining to fundamental rights intervene in questions of marriage and the family, the prohibition on same-sex marriage, and the protection of embryonic and fetal life, prescribing ideologically-based normative value preferences in private relationships.

1. According to Article L of the Fundamental Law:

"(1) Hungary shall protect the institution of marriage as the union of a man and a woman established by voluntary decision, and the family as the basis of the nation's survival.

(2) Hungary shall encourage the commitment to have children.

(3) The protection of families shall be regulated by a cardinal Act."

The Fundamental Law's conception of marriage – which, incidentally, follows the definition serving as the basis for the Constitutional Court's Decision 154/2008. (XII. 17.) AB on the constitutionality of registered domestic partnerships—corresponds roughly to the Catholic natural-law interpretation of marriage, which regards faithfulness, procreation and the unbreakable sanctity of the relationship between spouses as the most important elements of marriage. This constitutional regulation, founded on natural-law principles, protects those of the people's interests that not everyone attributes to themselves, and with which they do not necessarily wish to identify themselves and, thus, it breaches their autonomy. When defining marriage and evaluating the role of the family a modern, living constitution—especially a new Fundamental Law—should accommodate the changes to society that increase the range of choices available to the individual. This should have required the Fundamental Law to regulate the institution of marriage and family together with the fundamental rights guaranteeing the self-determination of the individual and the principle of equality.

2. With the constitutional ban on same-sex marriage the constitution-maker has ruled out the future ability of the Hungarian legislature, following the worldwide tendency, to make the institution of marriage available to same-sex couples. In keeping with this, Article XV of the Fundamental Law does not mention discrimination based on sexual orientation and gender identity in its list of prohibited forms of discrimination. This means that the Hungarian constitution-maker does not prohibit the state from supporting or negatively discriminating against a way of life—based on sexual orientation alone. This solution runs counter not only to the European Union's Charter of Fundamental Rights and the case law of the European Court of Justice (for the latest example see judgment C-147/08 in the case of Jürgen Römer v. Freie und Hansestadt Hamburg), but also to the provisions of Hungary's still effective Act CXXV of 2003 on the Promotion of Equal Treatment and Equal Opportunities.

3. According to Article II of the Fundamental Law: "Human dignity shall be inviolable. Every human being shall have the right to life and human dignity; embryonic and fetal life shall be subject to protection from the moment of conception." Apart from the Irish constitution of 1937, there is no other European constitution that protects embryonic and fetal life from the moment of conception. The Fundamental Law does not state explicitly that the embryo and fetus has a right to life, but it supports this interpretation by incorporating the phrase "embryonic and foetal life shall be subject to protection from the moment of conception" into the same sentence as the statement that "every human being shall have the right to life." In this way it prompts both the legislature, ordinary and Constitutional Court judges' interpretation of the law to restrict women's right to self-determination.

Uncertainties also arise with regard to the artificial reproduction procedures that have been widely permitted by the medical act of 1997. By necessity, the in-vitro fertilisation methods permitted by law entail the death of numerous embryos, either inside or outside of the womb. In view of the fact that the Fundamental Law does not differentiate between in-utero and in-vitro embryos, we have to conclude that they both enjoy the same constitutional protection. This could cause in-vitro fertilisation to become unviable.

It gives rise to considerable legal uncertainty if a country—like Hungary to this very day—which promotes various means of treating infertility, including in-vitro fertilisation and implantation and, which also permits research on embryos, prescribes in its Fundamental Law the constitutional protection of embryonic and fetal life from the moment of conception. This requirement could bring into question the constitutionality of artificial reproduction procedures and the compatibility of the new constitutional provision with international treaties ratified by the Republic of Hungary, including the Oviedo Convention on Human Rights and Biomedicine, approved by the Council of Europe.

All of these provisions breach the autonomy of individuals who do not accept the normative life models defined on the basis of the Fundamental Law's ideological values—as the preamble words it: "the form in which we want to live"—and they are capable of ostracising them from the political community.

7. STATE GOALS INSTEAD OF SOCIAL RIGHTS

The provisions of the Fundamental Law pertaining to social rights result in no dramatic change with respect to the protection of these rights, mainly because under the 1989 Constitution the Constitutional Court did not recognise the fundamental-right status of social provisions. Some of the provisions of the Fundamental Law (Articles XII, XIX and XX), reflecting the spirit of the Constitutional Court's judicial practice to date, make this even clearer than the previous text. At the same time, in certain places (e.g. Article XIX(3) and (4)), the wording contains new mandates and restrictions in line with current policies with which the constitution-maker attempts to prevent the new direction taken by social-policy measures from being declared unconstitutional and seeks to classify the solutions brushed aside by the current government as unconstitutional in the future.

1. Unlike the previous legislation, the Fundamental Law does not proclaim the right to work (which the Constitutional Court has also interpreted as no more than the state's obligation, not specified in any more detail, to pursue an employment policy), and, thus, the new provisions make it clear that the provision relating to creating work opportunities is only a state goal. A new element, however, is the prescription of an obligation to perform work to the best of the individual's ability and potential—which is rather hard to define by a court of law.

2. By prescribing the obligation for employees and employers to cooperate and by recording the objectives of such cooperation the Fundamental

Law, in contrast to the constitutional provision, places this process under constitutional protection; the wording, however, leaves room for uncertainty regarding the normative status of the provision. In line with Article 6 of the European Council's Social Charter and Article 28 of the EU Charter of Fundamental Rights, the Fundamental Law affords constitutional protection to the collective bargaining process. It is significant, however, that the Hungarian text—as opposed to the official English translation—avoids the term "strike," using instead the expression "work stoppage" ("munkabeszüntetés"; see, Article XVII). From the context, it appears that both parties in the bargaining process have this right, which thus permits the employer to prevent the performance of work (lock out). This was not an inference that could be made from the provisions of the 1989 Constitution. With respect to the regulation of the right to strike, a diminishing of the guarantees is marked by the fact that the related law is no longer subject to a two-thirds parliamentary majority.

The Fundamental Law contains no provisions on the constitutional protection of wages. (Article 70/B(2) of the 1989 Constitution sets forth the principle of equal pay for equal work, while 70/B(3) contains, with respect to the remuneration of work, a provision that still proclaimed the distribution principle of state socialism.)

3. The Fundamental Law, in keeping with the spirit of the Constitutional Court precedents, treats the creation of social security not as a right, but as a state goal. The wording of Article 70/E of the 1989 Constitution and some of the relevant Constitutional Court decisions, in principle, left open the opportunity for the right to social security to be interpreted as a fundamental right at some time in the future. Constitutional Court Decision 32/1998. (VI. 25.) even went as far as to outline, in abstract terms, the constitutional extent of the right to social security. The new text eliminates the opportunity for interpretations of this kind. The second sentence is virtually a word-for-word repetition of the second phrase of Article 70/E, but while this clearly only lists examples of those entitled to receive assistance, the new text can be interpreted as an exhaustive list of the entitled groups, from which it can be concluded, for example, that the state only needs to concern itself with creating social security for the groups included in the list (and not people unemployed through "their own fault," for example). Another change is reflected in the fact that the assistance to be provided is no longer of the extent "necessary for subsistence", but just the extent "determined by law."

Social insurance has been removed from among the means of creating social security, and only the system of social institutions and measures remains in the text. These provisions aim to ensure that there are no constitutional barriers to introducing measures to make benefits dependent on the performance of work or other activity regarded as socially beneficial, in keeping with the new social-policy approach.

The text rules out the reinstatement of the compulsory private pension funds regime, with the aim of this being to make it impossible, due to a conflict with the Fundamental Law, to re-introduce this previously tried social-policy solution, which is rejected by the present government.

8. LACK OF MARKET ECONOMY GUARANTEES

The passing of the Fundamental Law cannot be listed among the symbolic political acts. Restrictions, which are unacceptable in a state governed by rule-of-law also count as major interventions in the operation of the market. The success of the political steps serving the purpose of macroeconomic adjustment cannot be separated from the fate of the protection of fundamental rights. The protection of political freedoms and the survival of market-economy institutions are inseparable from each other. Taking a stand against this provocative invasion of the private sector by those in power is imperative both on moral and business grounds.

The Fundamental Law makes no mention of the fact that Hungary is a market economy. There is no doubt that the proclamation of the—still effective—1989 Constitution in this regard (see, Article 9(1): "The economy of Hungary shall be a market economy, in which public and private property shall be equal and be granted equal protection.") clearly has no normative effect, yet its omission is nevertheless revealing. The implication is that several provisions of the Fundamental Law are irreconcilable with the main expectations that represent the key features of a social market economy and, therefore, the constitution-maker has sought to resolve this conflict to the detriment of the market economy.

The purpose of this analysis is not to judge whether there is economic justification for the Fundamental Law to specify, at the level of detail found in Articles 36–37, the desirable level of state debt and the obligations and prohibitions that prevail in situations where this is not achieved. There is no doubt, however, that it should not be possible to waive protection of fundamental rights, even temporarily, citing the public finance problems of the state. The new Fundamental Law, on the other hand, does precisely that: based on Article 37(4), a private owner may only claim protection against state authority if the national economic indicators are relatively favourable. In a market economy it is unacceptable for the—reputed or genuine, rightful or indefensible—interests of the state to enjoy priority over protection of the right to property that underpins the freedom of those subject to law and for there to be no impartial forum to serve justice in a constitutional dispute between the state and the owner. While Article XIII(1) of the Fundamental Law highlights that "property shall entail social responsibility," it does not make it clear that the owner's fundamental right to protection from the state extends to the rights and privileges acquired in observance of the provisions of law. (The Parliament, in a fast-track amendment to the still effective 1989 Constitution, following approval of the Fundamental Law, made it clear that it interprets the protection of the right to property more narrowly: it does not apply to the acquired rights formerly obtained by those with pension entitlement). The "fading" of the concept of the market economy is also made apparent by the fact that while the Fundamental Law remains silent about the key principals of private autonomy and freedom of contract; it goes unreasonably far in referring the task of defining the state's exclusive property, and the issues of disposal over so-called national assets, to the authority of an act to be passed with a qualified majority of parliamentary representatives (with a so-called cardinal act; for this, see Article 38(2) of the Fundamental Law).

In summary it can be stated that the aim of the Fundamental Law is not to lay down the most important guarantees of the market economy, but rather to strengthen, by legal means, the political and economic power of the state and the party alliance with which it is intertwined.

9. FREEDOM OF CONSCIENCE, UNEQUAL RELIGIONS – COOPERATING CHURCHES, OPERATING SEPARATELY FROM THE STATE

Article VII of the Fundamental Law preserves the structure of Article 60 of the 1989 Constitution and appropriates a substantial part of its wording. Nevertheless, a stark difference can be demonstrated between the stances of the two constitutions towards freedom of conscience and religion.

1. The preamble to the Fundamental Law, which it is compulsory to take into consideration when interpreting the main text (see, Article R(3)), commits itself to a branch of Christianity, the Hungarian Roman Catholic tradition. According to the text of the preamble, "We are proud that our king Saint Stephen built the Hungarian state on solid ground and made our country a part of Christian Europe," the members of the Hungarian national recognise Christianity's "role in preserving nationhood," and honours the fact that the Holy Crown "embodies" the constitutional continuity

of Hungary's statehood. Besides the sacral symbols, this choice of ideology is reflected—inter alia—in the Fundamental Law's concept of community and its preferred family model (Article L), and its provision regarding the protection of embryonic and fetal life from the moment of conception (Article II).

The preamble, while giving preference to the thousand-year-old Christian tradition, states that "we value the various religious traditions of our county." The choice of words displays its model of tolerance, under which the various worldviews do not have equal status, although following them is not impeded by prohibition and persecution. It is however significant that the tolerance thus declared only extends to the various "religious traditions," but does not apply to the more recently established branches of religion, or to those that are new to Hungary, or to non-religious convictions of conscience.

This means that the Fundamental Law does not simply approve of the world view, religion, practices and cultural heritage of a portion of the country's citizens, but also states a position regarding the question of which world view and perception of life is true and correct, thereby according lower status to the rival doctrines and cultural practices. In other words, the Fundamental Law does not merely recognise the historical role of Christianity in the creation of the state, but also makes a commitment to its moral and political principles. Consequently it breaks with the solution applied in the 1989 Constitution, which remained neutral among the competing doctrinal approaches.

2. Article VII(1) of the Fundamental Law recognizes the freedom of conscience and religion and defines the main substantive elements of these: "This right shall include the freedom to choose or change religion or any other persuasion, and the freedom for every person to proclaim, refrain from proclaiming, profess or teach his or her religion or any other persuasion by performing religious acts, ceremonies or in any other way, whether individually or jointly with others, in the public domain or in his or her private life." Here the standard text essentially appropriates the working of Article 60(1)-(2) of the 1989 Constitution.

In a departure from this, however, Article VII(2) of the Fundamental Law proclaims: "The State and Churches shall operate separately. Churches shall be autonomous. The State shall cooperate with the Churches for community goals." The 1989 Constitution prescribed the "separation of the state and the church," while the new wording—employing a solution similar to that of the pre-1989 Hungarian constitution, describes "separate" operation. This seemingly insignificant semantic difference, however, sheds light on the passage about the "cooperation" between the state and the churches. This is because the Fundamental Law does not provide regarding cooperation between the state and associations, social, health-care and cultural institutions or between other non-governmental organisations. It only prescribes cooperation between other state organs, local governments and the state. (see, Article 34(1)).

The Fundamental Law's model of "separate, but cooperating" churches appropriates Hungarian constitutional court practice, under which the rules on public education, social and health-care and taxation may give preference to the "historical churches" over other churches, and the churches may be given an advantage over other institutions (associations, foundations). The incorporation of this approach into the Fundamental Law makes it far more difficult for this constitutional-court practice—which does not comply with the principle of equality—to change.

Another change brought by the Fundamental Law is that Article VII(3) requires a two-thirds majority of votes in order to change the detailed rules pertaining to the churches. The 1989 Constitution only protected freedom of conscience and religion from legislation passed with a simple parliamentary majority. Therefore, while a broad parliamentary consensus used to be needed in order to change the most important guarantees of fundamental rights, in the future the detailed rules pertaining to church institutions will not be amendable with a simple majority. The likely consequence of the new structure will be that, based on the authority of the Fundamental Law, in the near future the party with a two-thirds parliamentary majority will pass an Act on Churches that emphatically enshrines the "tolerated, but not treated as equal"-model for freedom of conscience, and the "separate, but cooperating" model pertaining to the churches.

10. WEAKENING OF THE PROTECTION OF FUNDAMENTAL RIGHTS

The decline in the level of protection for fundamental rights is significantly influenced not only by the substantive provisions of the Fundamental Law pertaining to fundamental rights, but also by the weakening of institutional and procedural guarantees that would otherwise be capable of upholding those rights that remain under the Fundamental Law. The most important of these is a change to the review power of the Constitutional Court, making it far less capable than before of performing its tasks related to the protection of fundamental rights. Added to this is the change in the composition of the Constitutional Court, taking place prior to the entry into force of the Fundamental Law, which will further impede it in fulfilling its function as protector of fundamental rights.

1. The considerable restriction on ex-post control has caused great controversy in Hungary and abroad, because the withdrawal of the right to review financial laws created a solution found nowhere else in the world, since there is no other institution functioning as a constitutional court whose right of review has been restricted based on the object of the legal norms to be reviewed. The constitutional court judges can only review these laws from the perspective of those rights (the right to life and human dignity, protection of personal data, freedom of thought, conscience and religion, or the right to Hungarian citizenship) that they typically cannot breach. The restriction remains in effect for as long as state debt exceeds half of what is referred to in the Hungarian text as "entire domestic product," the content of which is uncertain. Therefore, in the case of laws that are not reviewable by the court the requirement that the constitution be a fundamental law, and that it be binding on everyone, is not fulfilled. This also clearly represents a breach of the guarantees, set out in Title 2 of the TFEU, relating to respect for human dignity, freedom, equality and the respecting of human rights—including the rights of persons belonging to a minority.

With regard to the Constitutional Court's powers of *ex post* control, the effectiveness of the protection of fundamental rights is reduced not only by the limitation of their objective scope, but also by a radical restriction of the range of persons that may initiate a Constitutional Court review. This is due to the abolition of one of the peculiarities of the Hungarian regime change: the institution of the *actio popularis*, according to which a petition claiming ex post norm control may be submitted by anybody, regardless of their personal involvement or injury. Over the past two decades or more this unique institution has provided not only private individuals, but also non-governmental organizations and advocacy groups with the opportunity to contest in the Constitutional Court, for the public good, those legal provisions that they regard as unconstitutional. It could of course be argued that this institution has never existed in any other democratic state, but it has nevertheless undoubtedly contributed substantially to ensuring the level of protection of fundamental rights that has been achieved and which now diminishing.

Abstract *ex post* norm control, under Article 24(2)e) of the Fundamental Law, may in future only be initiated by the government, a quarter of the votes of Members of Parliament, or the Commissioner for Fundamental Rights. Given the balance of power in the current parliament, this makes any such petitions highly unlikely, since the government and the ombudsperson appointed by it are hardly about to make use of this opportunity, while a quarter of MPs' votes would assume a coalition between the two democratic opposition parties and the radical right-wing party, which supports the government.

The Fundamental Law also leaves open the question of whether the Constitutional Court, in relation to its restricted powers of *ex post* control, continues to have the right to annul legal provisions that are deemed to be unconstitutional. While Article 24(3) does mention the authority of annulment, it adds "or shall determine legal consequences set out in a cardinal act." In other words, it is conceivable that the cardinal Act on the Constitutional Court, to be passed at a later juncture, may not ensure the right of annulment.[7]

Without a knowledge of the cardinal Act on the Constitutional Court, it is also impossible to know the fate of the several hundred petitions that are already lying in the court's in-tray, submitted in the form of an *actio popularis* by private individuals entitled to do so prior to the entry into force of the Fundamental Law, but who will be subsequently divested of this right. Will the *ad malam partem* retroactive effect, so willingly applied by the present government in other cases, also come into play here with the result that the Constitutional Court does not pass judgement on previously submitted petitions?

2. As we have seen, private individuals or organisations may only turn to the Constitutional Court in future if they themselves are the victims of a concrete breach of law and this has already been established in a civil-administration or a final court decision. In this case, the legal remedy offered by the Constitutional Court will naturally only affect them. In other words, the extension of opportunities to submit constitutional complaints is no substitute whatsoever for the widely available right of private individuals and organisations to file petitions. Besides this, without any knowledge of the cardinal Act on the Constitutional Court, for the time being, the details of the extended constitutional complaints procedure, the precise conditions for initiating such a complaint, and the legal consequences, are unknown to us.

3. There is no doubt that the widely available opportunity to submit complaints could be beneficial to the judging of cases involving fundamental rights, and this has been the case in Germany, Spain and the Czech Republic. A prerequisite for this, however, is a Constitutional Court that is committed to fundamental rights and is independent from the government. The present government, on the other hand, has done all it can to prevent this since taking office in May 2010. This process began with the

[7] We note that in this respect the "official" English translation of the Fundamental Law is misleading, because it refers not to alternative legal consequences, as in the Hungarian text, but to "further" legal consequences.

alteration of the system for nominating constitutional court judges, giving the governing parties the exclusive opportunity to nominate and subsequently replace judges. The Fundamental Law, in a further weakening of the guarantees of independence, increased the number of Constitutional Court judges from eleven to fifteen, which—in view of the fact that one position is currently unoccupied—makes it possible to select five more new judges, after the two judges selected in May 2010, with their appointments lasting for a term of twelve years rather than the previous nine; in other words, for three parliamentary cycles. In future the president of the constitutional court, who has until now been elected for a term of three years by the judges, will be selected by Parliament for the duration of his/her time in office. These changes cannot wait until the entry into force of the Fundamental Law on January 1, 2012; rather, the president and the new members will be selected at the end of July based on an amendment to the existing constitution, passed in July 6, 2011.

11. JUDICIAL AUTONOMY WITHOUT GUARANTEES

1. The text of the Fundamental Law does not provide sufficient guarantee of judicial autonomy. The passages of the Fundamental Law pertaining to the administration of justice are missing a number of important guarantees and symbolic elements. These deficiencies permit changes to public law that could threaten the autonomy of the courts. Unlike the currently effective constitution, the Fundamental Law makes no mention of the judicial levels, and does not name the elements of the judicial system, and, thus, it gives authority to abolish the regional courts of appeal. It does not deal with the administration of the courts: even prior to 1997 the wording of Article 25(5), which mentions the participation of organs of judicial self-government in court administration, proved to be an insufficient guarantee in the face of excessively broad interpretations of government powers. The Fundamental Law, therefore, does not prevent the creation of an administration model in which there are no counterbalances to central governmental powers.

2. The classic constitutional principle of equality under the law is also missing from among the guiding principles pertaining to the operation of the judicial system.

A declaration that the courts are the protectors of constitution order, and of rights and lawful interests, is conspicuously absent from the Chapter on the courts. The wording that "[The] Courts shall administer justice" does not guarantee the courts' monopoly on administering justice. Thus, a classic element of the division of powers is also missing.

3. Article 28 of the Fundamental Law addresses the judicial interpretation of law, with a text that defies interpretation. The statement that judges should interpret legal norms not only in accordance with the Fundamental Law, but must also based on the assumption that they serve common sense, the public good and a moral and economic purpose, is obscure and therefore gives rise to legal uncertainty. Concerns relating to the interpretation of legislation are also raised by the section of the Fundamental Law that permits the restriction of fundamental rights on the basis of constitutional values, the substance of which is obscure. ("A fundamental right may be restricted to allow the exercise of another fundamental right or to defend any constitutional value to the extent absolutely necessary, in proportion to the desired goal and in respect of the essential content of such fundamental right.") This is particularly worrying given what has previously been said about the values enshrined in the preamble.

4. The renaming of the highest judicial level as the Curia enables the governing parties to use their two-thirds majority of Parliament to elect a new person in place of the president of the current highest judicial body, the Supreme Court, who was elected with a mandate lasting until 2015. The term of the new supreme judge, acceptable to the governing parties, is increased from six years to nine years by the Fundamental Law.

Immediately before the final vote, without any consultation or impact study, the text of the Fundamental Law came to include a new rule that changes, from one day to the next, the upper age limit for serving judges from 70 years to the general age of pension entitlement (currently 62 years). This amendment, chiefly due to the lack of preparation, professional grounding and the speed of its introduction, breaches the principles pertaining to the protection of the judges' status. After approving the Fundamental Law, the Parliament also passed a statutory amendment ordering a moratorium on the filling of vacated court judge positions, obviously in anticipation of changes to the appointment procedures. All of these measures endanger the continuity of the administration of justice and threaten to undermine confidence in its impartiality. The lowering of the age ceiling and the moratorium on appointments took place under circumstances in which the governing forces had given numerous signs of its mistrust of the judicial staff.

12. THE DEMOLITION OF 1989 CONSTITUTION'S OMBUDSPERSON MODEL

According to the 1989 Constitution, this institution is based on the conception of ombudspersons of equal rank. Its success is demonstrated by the fact that it has served as an example for the development of the ombudsman model of several countries undergoing democratic transformation. The 1989 Constitution specifies that Parliament can create ombudsman positions for the protection of any fundamental right, or interrelated fundamental rights, pertaining to sensitive social issues provided that their everyday violation threatens the freedom of citizens. Those rights which are given special protection in this way are excluded from the competence of the general ombudsperson. They are safeguarded by a specialized ombudsperson who pays them heightened attention. The government and public administration thus has to face a number of counterparts who are themselves independent from one another. The ombudspersons themselves are involved in this way in a kind of competition of autonomy. The scope of authority of the specialized ombudspersons can be broader than that given to the ombudsman of citizens' rights. It can also include special competencies required for enabling the exercise of the given right(s). That is, they do not only possess the standard scope of authority given to an ombudsperson. Among these, the scope of investigation by the ombudsperson for data protection and freedom of information and the ombudsperson for future generations also extends to the private sphere. Both ombudspersons can also function with authoritative powers. The institutions of the minority and data protection and freedom of information ombudspersons have also served as guarantees for the execution of pertaining directives of the European Union.

1. By abolishing specialized ombudspersons, the new Fundamental Law abandons the model of protecting fundamental rights described above. The details of the new regulation are inconsistent or remain unknown. All that the new Fundamental Law says about them is that Parliament will elect by two-third majority two vice ombudspersons "to protect the interests of future generations and the rights of ethnic groups living in Hungary."

2. According to the Article on fundamental rights "an independent authority, to be created by means of a cardinal act, will oversee the enforcement of the right to the protection of personal data and the right to access information of public interest" (Article VI(3)). Although it is difficult to know what exactly is meant by "independent authority," the most likely scenario is that the ombudsperson for data protection will become a government official. If this institution will not be given guarantees subsequently to safeguard it independence, then this new regulation may also conflict with the European Union directive for data protection (95/46/EC) which requires "complete independence" of the pertaining official procedures. As regards the level of data protection, it seems unlikely that a

government not always steadfastly committed to the transparency of the state and the protection of personal data is going to be efficiently controlled by a government authority. This will yield an absurd situation especially in the area of freedom of information where in each dispute the state is opposed by the "independent authority."

3. Replacing the specialized ombudsperson, in the future the vice ombudsperson in charge of the protection of the rights of ethnic groups will be chosen by Parliament by a two-third majority. Abolishing the position of an independent minority ombudsperson also concerns the requirements of the European Union directive 2000/43/EC. This because the Office for Equal Treatment, which handles cases of discrimination alongside the minority ombudsperson is not independent from the government. It is worth mentioning that although the Hungarian government has worked to prepare a framework decision on the Roma in the course of its Presidency of the European Union, the Fundamental Law is not in accordance with these efforts as the Roma minority is not explicitly mentioned among the target groups of positive discrimination. Article XV(5) states that "Hungary takes special measures to protect children, women, the elderly and the handicapped."

4. The Fundamental Law declares that the protection of the "interests of future generations" will be overseen by a vice ombudsperson elected by a two-third majority. This wording diverges from the current scope of authority of the ombudsperson as it does not refer to the right to a healthy environment. It is therefore unclear what function will be assigned to this vice ombudsperson's position. If this ombudsperson will really be put in charge of the protection of future generations, then it is questionable who still unborn persons, who are not legal persons, can file complaints at the office of the ombudsperson or even on what grounds ex officio inquiries will be possible.

5. The future of the statutorily created Complaints Committee for Law Enforcement, which was modelled on the institution of the collective ombudsperson, is unclear since the Fundamental Law contains no provisions regarding this issue. At present, the five members of this body are chosen for a period of six years by a two-thirds majority in Parliament upon the joint recommendation of the two Parliamentary Committees in charge of law enforcement and human rights, respectively. The scope of authority of this body is special insofar as it can be appealed to not only after all instances of public administration have been used. Rather, the investigation of this body forms part of the procedure, which is concluded by the decision by the Chief of the Police.

13. THE CONSTITUTIONAL ENTRENCHMENT OF POLITICAL PREFERENCES

It is one of the functions of constitutions to entrench in the form of entitlements or procedural rules those moral values which are shared by the overwhelming majority of society. Fundamental rights, the doctrine of division of powers and procedural order of decision-making in public matters have been traditionally regarded as such constitutionally entrenched values. By contrast, in countries resembling Hungary in their system of parliamentary governance most issues of public policy, especially economic and social policies, have been assigned to the competence and responsibility of the governing majority winning the elections.

At the time of the regime change, Parliament assigned the regulation of the politically most sensitive fundamental rights in the 1989 Constitution—including the right to form associations and the right to demonstrate, electoral rights, freedom of religion as well as rules concerning independent institutions, the military and law enforcement—to laws requiring a two-third majority. The reason for this step was that in a young democracy emerging from decades of dictatorship self-regulating instincts to exclude the abuse of power cannot be expected to function fully. The content of these two-thirds topics, however, have not concerned the fundaments of the operation of the executive or economic and social policies.

The new Fundamental Law regulates some issues which would have to be decided by the governing majority, while it assigns others to laws requiring a two-third majority. This makes it possible for the current government enjoying a two-third majority support to write in stone its views on economic and social policy. A subsequent government possessing only a simple majority will not be able to alter these even if it receives a clear mandate from the electorate to do so. In addition, the prescriptions of the Fundamental Law render fiscal policy especially rigid since significant shares of state revenues and expenditures will be impossible to modify in the absence of pertaining two-third statutes. This hinders good governance since it will make it more difficult for subsequent governments to respond to changes in the economy. This can make efficient crisis management impossible. These risks are present irrespective of the fact whether in writing two-thirds statutes the governing majority will exercise self-restraint (contrary to past experience). The very possibility created by the Fundamental Law to regulate such issues of economic and social policies by means of two-thirds statutes is incompatible with parliamentarism and the principle of the temporal division of powers.

1. As regards pensions, the Fundamental Law itself excludes the possibility that a subsequent governing majority create a funded pension scheme based on capital investment. Europe and the Western world in general will face serious demographic challenges in the coming decades. One possible response of public policy to this challenge is the partial transformation of the pay-as-you-go pension system to a funded pension scheme based on capital investment. Such a decision is to be preceded by a comprehensive social debate and assessment of the pros and cons of different public policy solutions. It is not compatible with the functions of the constitution that the current governing majority excludes the application of one of the available public policy solutions in the Fundamental Law without having been empowered by the electorate to do so. In addition, Article 40 of the Fundamental Law assigns the basic rules of the pension system to a cardinal act, which, as mentioned above, requires a two-third majority. It is impossible to know today to what extent this statute will regulate the pension system. In any case, the Fundamental Law makes it possible that the retirement age and other conditions of eligibility as well as the basis for calculating pensions will be modifiable only by a two-third majority. This prevents subsequent governments winning popular support at free elections to put in practice its own views of pension policy.

2. Article L of the Fundamental Law specifies that the regulation of family welfare support is also to be subject to two-thirds statutory regulation. Without knowing the text of the planned statute it is impossible to decide to what extent the governing majority intends to regulate this issue in the pertaining two-thirds statute. It is clear, however, that the pertaining prescriptions of the Fundamental Law creates the possibility that every detailed issue of the family welfare support will only be modifiable subsequently by a two-third majority. It is to be part of the ruling majority's social policy at any given time to settle questions such as the child's age limit until which motherhood support is paid, the eligibility conditions and amount of this support, or the eligibility of different family types for different kinds of support. Thus, in a parliamentary democracy there is no justification for writing in stone the views of the current government coalition in such a manner.

3. Article 40 of the Fundamental Law states that basic rules of taxation are to be determined by a fundamental statute, that is, one requiring a two-third majority. This prescription makes it possible that the currently ruling government coalition to set its own views in a two-third statute on tax policies, especially as regards the linear, flat tax and the exceptionally

high tax benefits for families. This could easily make it impossible that a subsequent government gaining power because of its promise to introduce progressive taxation realize its public policies based on the mandate received from voters.

4. In addition to the long-term fixing of preferences concerning economic and social policies, the governing parties can implement their very own personal preferences, too, in the appointment and replacement of the leaders of independent institutions. Parliament chose as president of the State Audit Office for 12 years and a head of the National Media and Telecommunications Authority for nine years former MPs of the bigger governing party. The chief prosecutor appointed for nine years is a former parliamentary candidate of the bigger governing party. Without any additional reason, the coming into force of the Fundamental Law makes it in itself possible that the governing parties nominate only their own candidates for the positions of five Constitutional Court judges, a new president of the Constitutional Court, the head of the ordinary judiciary, as well as new ombudspersons for six, nine and twelve years, respectively. Following the adoption of the Fundamental Law, a statute prohibits the president of the National Council of Justice, who, at the same time, is also the president of Hungary's Supreme Court, to appoint judges until the Fundamental Law comes into force. Clearly, the aim of this moratorium is that the head of the Curia, to be chosen for nine years on the basis of new Fundamental Law, should appoint the heads of the most important courts. This will result in the long-term entrenchment of personal preferences. This can undermine the adequate operation of independent institutions.

5. In a related development, the Fundamental Law gives the Budget Council the right to veto the state budget statute. Two of the three members of the Council were appointed by the ruling government coalition until at least 2019. At the same time, the Fundamental Law fails to define unequivocally what is covered by the Council's right to veto. In addition, it does not contain guarantees to exclude the abuse of the powers of this body. Such guarantees would be all the more required as the drafting of the budget is the competence and responsibility of the governing majority at any given time. This prerogative cannot be limited by a body which seems to be independent, but consists of appointees of an earlier government. This raises the possibility that in addition to—or even instead of—considerations regarding the sustainability of budgetary policies the Budgetary Council may be guided by preferences of public policy when exercising its veto right.

14. THE INTERNATIONAL COMPATIBILITY OF THE FUNDAMENTAL LAW

The Fundamental Law expresses its commitment to the international community and international law (Article Q) and also contains a Europe clause, forming the basis for cooperation with the EU (Article E), but with a content that is not entirely identical to that of the 1989 Constitution. According to the 1989 Constitution "[the] Republic of Hungary may exercise certain competences deriving from the Constitution in conjunction with the other member states; ... the exercise of these competences may be realized independently, through the institutions of the European Union" (Article 2/A(1)). The Fundamental Law rewrites this as follows: "Hungary may exercise some of its competences arising from the Fundamental Law jointly with other member states through the institutions of the European Union" (Article E(2)). The original rule permitted the Hungarian state to delegate certain powers to EU bodies in which it has no joint decision-making rights—the Fundamental Law does not allow this. It makes it possible to declare as unconstitutional the delegation of any competence to an EU institution if this results in termination of the nation state's consensual decision-making right. The current constitutional rule was made so as not to stand in the way of the EU's continued development along federal lines—the new underlying intent is to obstruct federalisation.

1. Article Q(1), unlike the currently effective Constitution, does not contain a renunciation of war and prohibition on the use of force, although in a positive manner it does list peace, security and sustainable development as aims in its cooperation with the nations and countries of the world. Article Q(2)-(3) provide with regard to the relationship between international law and Hungarian law, maintaining the requirement for harmony between them, the monist adoption of the generally accepted rules of international law, and the system of dualist transformation in the case of other sources of international law (treaties).

2. Based on Article 24(2)f), the Constitutional Court will continue to investigate whether laws breach international agreements; the Fundamental Law does not mention, however, who shall initiate procedures of this nature, and also makes no reference to the opportunity for an *ex officio* review. No mention is made of how harmony should be created if a Hungarian law breaches a generally accepted rule of international law. Where an international agreement is breached by a piece of legislation or constituent provision, the annulment of the latter two is only an option

(Article 24(3)c)). This weakens the requirement set out in Article Q(2), under which Hungarian laws must be in harmony with international law: it would have been more opportune to prescribe categorical annulment of such legislation, naming it as an exception due to a conflict with the EU's founding treaties.

3. Article E contains only one new rule in comparison to Article 2/A and Article 6(4) of the 1989 Constitution: namely that the law of the EU may stipulate a generally binding rule of conduct. This requirement, incidentally, also follows from the EU's founding treaties. The rule, however, still says nothing about requesting priority of application.

4. With respect to these constitutional norms, the international agreements continue to oblige Hungary to respect, protect and uphold the rule of law, democracy and fundamental rights. The above-mentioned provisions—since they relate to the effect that the laws governing nations have on Hungarian law—are valid in respect of the constitution (as prevailing at any time), and set requirements that broach no exceptions. Several provisions of the Fundamental Law, however, can also be interpreted as permitting exceptions to the aforementioned European requirements—pertaining to democracy, the rule of law and the protection of fundamental rights—and as such they could come into conflict with international commitments.

4.1. Article R(3), in respect of the Fundamental Law as a whole— including Articles E and Q—makes it compulsory to take the preamble and the achievements ("*acquis*") of the historical constitution into consideration for the purposes of interpretation. The preamble, which is, thus, granted normative status, only defines European unity in a cultural sense ("We believe that our national culture is a rich contribution to the diversity of European unity"), sees international cooperation in terms of nations (in contrast to the wording of Article Q), and its collectivist approach is not in keeping with the spirit of the European Convention on Human Rights and the Charter of Fundamental Rights. The substantive meaning of "the achievements of our historical constitution" is totally ambiguous; there is no legal-scientific consensus in Hungary regarding their precise nature, and it is by no means obvious whether it should be taken to include the precedents stemming from Constitutional Court's interpretation practice accumulated since the regime change, while it is also unclear which of the achievements are reconcilable with international commitments.

4.2. It also deserves a mention that the Fundamental Law—in contrast to Article 5 of the currently effective Constitution—does not express its constitutional recognition of the borders set out in the relevant international agreement.

4.3. It is problematic, from the perspective of the requirement of democracy, that the Fundamental Law does not clearly identify the political community as the community of citizens living subject to the laws of Hungary; accordingly it permits the naturalisation of Hungarians living abroad without their relocation, and raises the prospect that together with "extraterritorial" citizenship, they will also be given the right to vote.

Such enfranchisement does not comply with Articles 39–40 of the Charter of Fundamental Rights or with Article 20(2) of the TFEU. This is because it does not assure the citizens of other EU member states of the same conditions as Hungarian citizens in European Parliament and local authority elections, since for the former group must have a Hungarian place of residence, while in the case of Hungarian citizens this requirement does not apply.

The creation of democratic will is restricted by the fact that the Fundamental Law stipulates that many of the current government's public policy preferences, from family and tax policy to pensions policy, must be enshrined in cardinal acts, which could make it impossible for voters who are dissatisfied with today's government policy to achieve a change in the direction of government.

4.4. The principle of the rule of law is compromised by the fact that violating the Fundamental Law has no effective constitutional consequence or sanction, since in the case of legislation pertaining to public finances the restrictions on the Constitutional Court's right of review and annulment, with the exception of four areas of fundamental law, will remain in place for an indeterminate period. As a consequence of the restrictions on Constitutional Court review power, numerous fundamental rights (especially, e.g. the right to property, social rights, freedom of enterprise, the right to employment, the principle of non-discrimination) are weakened. In the governmental system of a parliamentary democracy, the institution of constitutional review, which serves as a counterbalance against parliamentary and the executive actions, is what guarantees the division of power and safeguards the sovereignty of the law (finally, the constitution). The closer this so-called "acting unit" is between the legislative and the executive branches, the broader the review power should be constitutionally ensured in order to maintain a healthy balance. Paradoxically, with the chosen solution the Fundamental Law also rules out the protection of its own public finance provisions by the Constitutional Court. Breaches of the constitutional rules pertaining to public finances are most likely to occur through precisely those laws on the budget, taxes etc., which the Constitutional Court is not even permitted to review in terms of their compliance with Articles 36–40. Thus, the section on public finances is less effective, and does not represent a full guarantee with regard to international financial obligations.

4.5. According to Article K of the Fundamental Law, Hungary's official currency is the forint. This new provision runs counter to the onus on member states to fulfil their obligations arising from the founding treaties of the European Union. In the Accession Treaty Hungary agreed to adopt the European Union's common currency, the euro, as and when it meets the conditions for doing so. In this case, it is not the member state that decides whether to join the euro, but the European Council. In other words, the Hungarian constitution-maker has no authority to provide with regard to the national currency.

Opinion on the New Constitution of Hungary[1]

European Commission for Democracy Through Law (Venice Commission)

[1] *Opinion 621/2011.* Adopted by the Venice Commission at its 87th Plenary Session (June 17–18, 2011) on the basis of comments by Christoph Grabenwarter (Member, Austria), Wolfgang Hoffmann-Riem (Member, Germany), Hanna Suchocka (Member, Poland), Kaarlo Tuori (Member, Finland), Jan Velaers (Member, Belgium).

Previously, the Venice Commission adopted its *Opinion 614/2011* on three legal questions arising in the process of drafting the new Constitution of Hungary (March 25–26, 2011). Subsequently, the Venice Commission issued *Opinion 662/2012* on the elections to Parliament (June 18, 2012), *Opinion 663/2012* on the judiciary, *Opinion 664/2012* on freedom of religion and the status of the churches (March 16–17, 2012), Opinion *665/2012* on the Constitutional Court (June 19, 2012), Opinion *668/2012* on the prosecution (June 19, 2012), and *Opinion 671/2012* on the nationality issues (June 19, 2012). In 2012 the Commission commenced to review more cardinal acts, i.e., freedom of information, family protection and the Transitional Provisions of the Fundamental Law.

I. INTRODUCTION

1. At its meeting of 26 March 2011 in Paris, the Monitoring Committee of the Parliamentary Assembly decided to ask the Venice Commission to provide an Opinion on the new Constitution of Hungary.

2. A working group of Rapporteurs was set up, composed of Ms Hanna Suchocka and Messrs Wolfgang Hoffmann-Riem, Christoph Grabenwarter, Kaarlo Tuori and Jan Velaers.

3. On 17–18 May 2011, the working group, accompanied by Mr Thomas Markert and Ms Artemiza Chisca of the Venice Commission Secretariat, travelled to Hungary in order to meet with representatives of the authorities, the political parties represented in the Hungarian Parliament, the Constitutional Court and the civil society. The Venice Commission wishes to thank them all for the discussions which took place on this occasion and the Hungarian authorities for the excellent organization of the visit.

4. The present Opinion, which is based on the comments provided by the rapporteurs, was adopted by the Venice Commission at its 87th Plenary Session in Venice from 17 to 18 June 2011.

A. Background information

5. The present Constitution of the Republic of Hungary was adopted on 20 August 1949. It is the country's first and only written Constitution, and Hungary is the only former Central and East-European country that did not adopt an entirely new Constitution after the fall of Communism.[2]

6. From 1988 on, the idea of preparing a new Constitution emerged in Hungary. The declared aim was to establish a multiparty system, parliamentary democracy and a social market economy. Due to time pressure, however, a new Constitution could not be drafted and the National Assembly adopted a comprehensive amendment to the 1949 Constitution (Act XXXI of 23 October 1989). The Preamble of the Constitution as

---

[2] See also the particular case of Latvia: On May 4, 1990 the Supreme Council of the Republic of Latvia declared Latvia independent and adopted articles 1, 2, 3 and 6 of the Constitution of 1922. The rest of the Constitution remained in abeyance until it was reviewed to fit the modern situation; the Constitution was fully reinstated by Latvia's parliament on July 6, 1993.

amended in 1989 states that the Constitution shall remain in force, as a temporary one, until the adoption of a new Constitution.[3]

7. Since 1989, the Constitution has been amended several times, including, due to the two-thirds majority held by the ruling coalition, more than ten times more recently.

8. When the current Hungarian Government came to power in 2010, the preparation and adoption of a new constitution was again put on the agenda and this became a major project for the current majority. A Body of National Consultation and an *Ad-Hoc* Parliamentary Constitution Drafting Committee have been set up for this aim. The *Ad-hoc* Parliamentary Committee was set up in June 2010 and started its work on 20 July 2010. It prepared a Concept Paper, which in the end was only considered to be a working document for the constitution-making process. Meanwhile, a Draft was prepared by FIDESZ/KDNP elected representatives and introduced before the Hungarian Parliament on 14 March 2011. It was adopted by the Hungarian Parliament with the votes of the FIDESZ/KDNP coalition on 18 April 2011 and signed by the President on Hungary on 25 April 2011. As indicated by its Closing Provisions, the new Constitution shall take effect on 1 January 2012. Transitional provisions are still to be adopted.

9. The Monitoring Committee of PACE on 26 March 2011 decided to request the Venice Commission for an opinion on the adopted Constitution.

B. Preliminary remarks

10. The Venice Commission has already provided its legal assistance to the Hungarian authorities in the context of the current constitutional process. In its Opinion CDLAD(2011)001 adopted at its 86th Plenary Session (Venice, 25–26 March 2011), it assessed, at the request of the Hungarian authorities, three legal questions having been raised in the process of drafting the new Constitution: the possible incorporation in the new

---

[3] "In order to facilitate a peaceful political transition to a state under the rule of law, realizing a multi-party system, a parliamentary democracy and a social market economy, the Parliament hereby establishes the text of the Constitution of our country—until the adoption of the new Constitution of our country."—The Constitution of the Republic of Hungary [Act XX of 1949 as revised and restated by Act XXXI of 1989].

Constitution of provisions of the EU Charter of Fundamental Rights (hereafter: the EU Charter), the role and significance of the preliminary review among the competences of the Constitutional Court and the role and significance of the *actio popularis* in *ex post* constitutional review. The Commission gave its legal opinion on these three specific issues and the most suitable options that, in its view, could be implemented in the Hungarian context, in the absence, at that time, of the draft of the new Constitution. The Commission notes in this context that the recommendations contained in this Opinion have been partly taken into account (see however § 122).

11. In its Opinion adopted in March 2011, the Venice Commission, in the light of the numerous concerns raised within the civil society over the lack of transparency of the process of the adoption of the new Constitution and the inadequate consultation of the Hungarian society, has also formulated a number of general comments with regard to this process. It criticized the procedure of drafting, deliberating and adopting the new Constitution for its tight time-limits and restricted possibilities of debate of the draft by the political forces, within the media and civil society. It took note with regret that no consensus had been possible—among political forces and within society—either over the process or the content of the future constitution.[4] In the light of the information received with regard to the final stage of debate and adoption of the new Constitution, the above-mentioned comments are still valid.

12. The Venice Commission wishes to underline that a constitutional culture which clearly separates constitutional issues from ordinary politics and sees the constitution as a commonly accepted framework for ordinary democratic processes -with their understandable and even healthy political disagreements—is a precondition for a fully successful and legitimate constitution-making process.

13. The Commission however notes that, while no genuine dialogue has been possible between the majority and the opposition during the debate and final adoption of the new Constitution, according to the information provided to the Venice Commission during its visit in May 2011, there will be co-operation between the majority coalition and the opposition in the preparation of the implementing legislation.

---

[4] See CDL-AD(2011)001, Opinion on three legal questions arising in the process of drafting the new Constitution of Hungary, § 16–19.

C. The object of the opinion

14. It is generally welcomed by the Venice Commission that former communist countries adopt a new and modern Constitution to create a new framework for society, guaranteeing democracy, fundamental freedoms and the rule of law.

15. When the Venice Commission evaluates a new Constitution, it primarily tries to check whether its provisions are in compliance with the European Convention on Human Rights (ECHR) and in line with the democracy and rule of law standards and fundamental values commonly shared by the member states of the Council of Europe.

16. The analysis below is based on the English translation of the adopted Constitution provided by the Hungarian Ministry of Public Administration and Justice and published on the official website of the Hungarian Government. The translation may not accurately reflect the original version in every point and, consequently, certain comments and omissions could be affected by problems of the translation.

17. The following comments are not meant to be an in depth study of the entire Constitution. They aim at providing substantial insights with regard to some selected points.

II. GENERAL REMARKS

18. Hungary has adopted a new Constitution which aims to meet the general features of a modern Constitution within the framework of the Council of Europe. In particular, the Venice Commission welcomes the fact that this new Constitution establishes a constitutional order based on democracy, the rule of law and the protection of fundamental rights as underlying principles. It notes that constitutions of other European States, such as Poland, Finland, Switzerland or Austria, have been used as a source of inspiration. A particular effort has been made to follow closely the technique and the contents of the ECHR and to some extent the EU Charter.

19. A special feature of the new Constitution of Hungary is that, while drawing on the above-mentioned standards, this Constitution contains a number of particular variations of European guarantees which can partly be found in a limited number of European constitutions. Most of them are linked to national traditions and identity. These are considered to be an

important factor in European Union law (Art. 6 TEU)[5] and also accepted under the ECHR. The Venice Commission considers in this respect that, while a number of these special guarantees may be seen as part of national constitutional autonomy, other guarantees must be analyzed in the light of European standards, above all the case law of the ECtHR (see comments under specific provisions of the Constitution).

20. The task might be more difficult in some cases due to sometimes unclear interrelations between its different provisions as well as to the fact that the constitutional text often relegates to cardinal (organic) laws the definition of the detailed rules applicable to the concerned matters (including fundamental rights, institutional settings, structural arrangements for the operation of the judicial power etc.).

21. More generally, while it represents a major step for the current ruling coalition and for Hungary, the adoption of the new Constitution in April 2011 appears to be, as confirmed by its text, only the beginning of a longer process of establishment of a comprehensive and coherent new constitutional order. This implies adoption or amendment of numerous pieces of legislation, new institutional arrangements and other related measures. To be fully successful, these processes should be based on the largest consensus possible within the Hungarian society.

A. Cardinal laws

22. The Constitution provides for an extensive use of cardinal laws to regulate in detail the most important society settings. It contains over 50 references to cardinal laws, including their definition in Article T § 4.[6] Cardinal laws should regulate *inter alia* issues or sectors such as: family policy (Article L) the designation of ministries and other public administration organs (Art. 17 § 4), the term of office and remit of the "Autonomous Regulatory Organs" (Art. 23, §§ 2, 4), the judiciary (Article 25 (7), the basic rules of public finances, public service provisions, pension system etc. (Art. 40), the State Audit Office (Art. 43 § 4), the Budgetary

---

[5] "Fundamental rights, as guaranteed by the European Convention for the Protection of Human Rights and Fundamental Freedoms and as they result from the constitutional traditions common to the Member States, shall constitute general principles of the Union's law." (Art.6.3).

[6] "Cardinal Acts shall be Acts of Parliament, the adoption and amendment of which requires a two-thirds majority of the votes of Members of Parliament present."

Council (Art. 44 § 4), the defense forces (Art. 45 §§ 2, 5), the police and the national security services (Art. 46 § 6), the rights of nationalities (Art. XXIX § 3) etc.

23. These cardinal laws, known in other legal systems as "organic laws," require a qualified majority of two thirds of the members of parliament present for their adoption and amendment. Their aim is to prevent too easy introduction of changes concerning matters related to the Constitution, which nevertheless are not of such fundamental importance as to be regulated by the Constitution itself. The requirement of a supermajority also underlines the need for a broad consensus in these fields. For instance, matters such as the elections or the rules of procedure of the parliament are often laid down in cardinal acts. Such organic laws are not a specific feature of the Hungarian constitution system, as other constitutions, e. g. in Albania[7], Austria[8], Croatia[9], France[10] and Montenegro[11], make also use of this possibility to regulate certain topics. Moreover, a comprehensive—though less broad—system of cardinal laws is already part of the current Hungarian Constitution.

24. This being said, the Venice Commission finds that a too wide use of cardinal laws is problematic with regard to both the Constitution and ordinary laws. In its view, there are issues on which the Constitution should arguably be more specific. These include for example the judiciary. On the other hand, there are issues which should/could have been left to ordinary legislation and majoritarian politics, such as family legislation or social and taxation policy. The Venice Commission considers that parliaments should be able to act in a flexible manner in order to adapt to new framework conditions and face new challenges within society. Functionality of a democratic system is rooted in its permanent ability to change. The more policy issues are transferred beyond the powers of simple majority, the less significance will future elections have and the more possibilities does a two-third majority have of cementing its political preferences and the country's legal order. Elections, which, according to Article 3 of the First Protocol to the ECHR, should guarantee the "expression of the opinion of the people in the choice of the legislator," would become meaningless if the legislator would not be able to change important aspects of the

[7] Art. 81 § 2.
[8] See inter alia. Art. 14 § 10, Art. 14 a § 8, Art. 30 § 2, Art. 37 § 2.
[9] See inter alia Art. 6, 7, 11, 23, 25, 27, 34.
[10] Art. 91 § 3.
[11] Art. 91 § 3.

legislation that should have been enacted with a simple majority. When not only the fundamental principles but also very specific and "detailed rules" on certain issues will be enacted in cardinal laws, the principle of democracy itself is at risk.[12] This also increases the risk, for the future adoption of eventually necessary reforms, of long-lasting political conflicts and undue pressure and costs for society. The necessity of a certain quorum may however be fully justified in specific cases, such as issues forming the core of fundamental rights, judicial guarantees or the rules of procedure of the Parliament.

25. While acknowledging that States enjoy a wide margin of appreciation in establishing the scope and level of detail of the constitutional provisions and of the different levels of domestic legislation, the Venice Commission considers that the subjects of cardinal laws, as prescribed by the new Hungarian Constitution, are far too many.

26. In addition, in view of this extensive use of cardinal laws, it is important to clearly distinguish these laws from other laws and the Constitution itself. The new Hungarian Constitution makes such a distinction in one aspect: cardinal laws require a two-thirds majority of the MPs present while a two-thirds majority of all MPs shall be applied with regard to the Constitution itself. As far as the substance is concerned, a sufficient justification for using this type of law is very often missing. The Commission would like to recall that, as stated in its March Opinion, "*as a rule, constitutions contain provisions regulating issues of the highest importance for the functioning of the state and the protection of the individual fundamental rights. It is thus essential that the most important related guarantees are specified in the text of the Constitution, and not left to lower level norms*" (§ 52).

---

[12] See in particular the following articles: L (3) on the protection of families; VII (3) on the detailed rules for Churches, VIII (4) on the detailed rules for the operation and financial management of political parties, IX on the detailed rules for the freedom of the press and the organ supervising media services, press products and the infocommunications market, XXIX (3), on the detailed rules for the rights of nationalities living in Hungary and the rules for the elections of their local and national self-governments, XXXI (3) on the detailed rules for military service; 38 (1) on the requirements for the preservation, protection and responsible management of national assets, 38 (2) on the scope of the State's exclusive properties and exclusive economic activities and the limitations and conditions of the alienation of national assets; 40 on the fundamental rules of general taxation and the pension system, and 41 on the monetary policy.

27. In conclusion, the Venice Commission recommends restricting the fields and scope of cardinal laws in the Constitution to areas where there are strong justifications for the requirement of a two-thirds majority.

B. Rules of interpretation

28. The Commission takes note with interest of the effort made by the Hungarian constitutional legislator to provide guidance with regard to the main principles, values and sources to be used for an adequate interpretation and application of the new Constitution. This effort is however hampered by a certain lack of clarity and consistency between elements, in different constitutional provisions, which are of relevance for the interpretation of the Constitution.

29. The concept of "historical constitution," used both in the Preamble and in Art. R, dealing specifically with the interpretation of the Constitution, brings with it a certain vagueness into constitutional interpretation. There is no clear definition what the "achievements of the historical constitution," referred to in Art. R, are.

30. Furthermore, it is regrettable that neither Art. R above-mentioned nor Art. 28, dealing with the courts' interpretative obligations, mentions Hungary's international law obligations, nor does the chapter on "Freedom and Responsibility" include any reference to international human rights instruments. In the dualistic model of the relations between international and domestic law, an important means to secure respect for international human rights treaties consists of the obligation, for courts and public authorities, to interpret constitutional provisions on fundamental rights and freedoms in light of human rights treaties. It is thus particularly important to derive such an obligation from Art. Q(2), according to which "*Hungary shall ensure harmony between international law and Hungarian law in order to fulfil its obligations under international law*." The obligation to interpret constitutional provisions in the light of international human rights treaties binding on Hungary concerns, inter alia, Art. I (3), which states that "*[a] fundamental right may be restricted to allow the exercise of another fundamental right or to defend any constitutional value to the extent absolutely necessary, in proportion to the desired goal and in respect of the essential content of such fundamental right*." This would for instance mean that eventual limitations should also be in harmony with the limitation clauses in the ECHR (see also comments under Article 28 below).

III. SPECIFIC REMARKS

A. Preamble

31. The Commission recalls that preambles have above all a political purpose and represent political declarations meant to stress the importance of the fundamental law, its principles, values and guarantees, for the state concerned and its population. As a consequence, they should also have a significant unifying function. In the absence of European standards in this area, the specific elements that are included in the Preamble depend on the will of the constitution-making authority.

32. The Preamble of the new Constitution indeed contains numerous national, historical and cultural references, such as to King Saint Stephen, the Christian tradition and the Hungarian culture and language. It would be difficult to neglect the importance, for Hungary, of these factors and their particular role in building and preserving the Hungarian state and nationhood. One can note, as far as the religious aspect is concerned, that while stressing the major role of Christianity in the history of Hungary, the Preamble also states that "*we value the various religious traditions of our country*." Such a statement is of key importance. It should be adequately taken into account in the future application and interpretation of the Constitution and should be extended to the protection of all religions, religious traditions and other convictions of conscience.

33. It should also be noted that, notwithstanding the strong emphasis put on the national element and the role of the Hungarian nation,[13] there has been an effort to find a balance, in the Preamble, between the national and universal elements: "*we believe that our national culture is a rich contribution to the diversity of European unity and we respect the freedom and culture of other nations, and shall strive to cooperate with every nation of the world*".

34. That being said, there are a number of statements and terms in the Preamble that might raise concern. These statements, terms and the underlying approach are all the more problematic as, according to Article R § 3[14] of the

[13] "We are proud that our people has over the centuries defended Europe in a series of struggles and enriched Europe's common values with its talent and diligence."

[14] "The provisions of the Fundamental Law shall be interpreted in accordance with their purposes, the National Avowal and the achievements of our historical constitution."

Constitution, the Preamble shall have a substantial influence on the interpretation of the entire Constitution and appears to be provided legal significance. Although preambles are usually seen as one of several means of interpretation of the Constitution, the reference to the Preamble in Article R § 3 may lead to problems in the Hungarian case since the Preamble's text lacks precision, which is essential for a legal text, and contains a number of potentially controversial statements. The reference to the "historical constitution" is quite unclear, since there have been different stages in the development of different historical situations in Hungary and therefore there is no clear and no consensual understanding of the term "historical constitution."

35. First, problems of legal nature may arise. This might be the case if the paragraph on the old 1949 Constitution is understood strictly in a technical way: "*We do not recognize the communist constitution of 1949, since it was the basis for tyrannical rule; therefore we proclaim it to be invalid.*" If this is meant to have legal consequences, it can only be read as leading to ex tunc nullity -otherwise it would have been sufficient to declare that the former Constitution was repealed. Ex tunc nullity of the former Constitution could lead to the result that all acts of state enacted under the former Constitution would lose their legal basis and will thus be invalid themselves. This may also be used as an argument for ignoring the rich case law of the Hungarian Constitutional Court which, although based on this "invalid" constitution, has played an important role in Hungary's development towards a democratic state governed by the rule of law. Even Constitutional institutions like the Parliament would lose their legitimacy and have to be seen as legally inexistent. This would lead to a legal paradox since an illegitimate or even non-existent Parliament cannot enact a new Constitution.

36. At the same time, the above-mentioned paragraph can be considered to be a political statement, statement which does not mean that all acts and laws based on the former constitution, especially since 1989, will become invalid. Rather, the expression can be regarded as drawing a clear line between the democratic system in place and the former communist regime. The 1949 Constitution was legitimized by the decision of Parliament and the amendments adopted since 1989 and the 1990 elections. This is clearly stated by the Preamble's text: "*We date the restoration of our country's self-determination, lost on the nineteenth day of March 1944, from the second day of May 1990, when the first freely elected body of popular representation was formed. We shall consider this date to be the beginning of our country's new democracy and constitutional order.*" Moreover, the new constitution in

its Closing provisions refers to the provisions of the present Constitution as the legal basis for the adoption of the Fundamental Law.[15]

37. The Commission has taken due note that, according to the Hungarian authorities met during its May visit to Budapest, the declaration of the invalidity of the 1949 Constitution should only be understood as a political statement. It nonetheless finds regrettable that such an important statement and an unfortunate internal contradiction has been retained in the Preamble without due regard to its potential legal and political implications. It trusts that the Constitutional Court of Hungary will provide clarity on this sensitive issue in the context of its future interpretation of the new Constitution. The adoption of transitional provisions is also an opportunity for providing legal clarity on this matter.

38. The Commission further considers that, while it is not uncommon that the Preamble to a Constitution or the chapter on the general principles includes provisions on the values underlying the Constitution, a Constitution should avoid defining or establishing once and for all values of which there are different justifiable conceptions in society. Such values, as well as their legislative implications, should be left to the ethical debates within society and ordinary democratic procedures, respecting at the same time the country's human rights and other international commitments.

39. It is also of particular importance that the constitutional legislator pays proper attention to the principle of friendly neighborly relations and avoids inclusion of extra-territorial elements and formulations that may give rise to resentment among neighboring states. In this respect, the Preamble seems to be premised on a distinction between the Hungarian nation and (other) nationalities living in Hungary. The Hungarian nation, in turn, also includes Hungarians living in other states. According to the Preamble, "*we promise to preserve the intellectual and spiritual unity of our nation torn apart in the storms of the last century.*" This statement implies obvious historical references and should be read in conjunction with Art. D, establishing Hungary's "*responsibility for the fate of Hungarians living beyond its borders.*" Such a wide understanding of the Hungarian nation and of Hungary's responsibilities may hamper inter-State relations and create interethnic tension (see also comments under Article D below).

---

[15] "Parliament shall adopt the Fundamental Law pursuant to Sections 19(3)a) and 24(3) of Act XX of 1949." (Closing provisions, paragraph 2).

40. The Preamble however continues by stating: "*the nationalities living with us form part of the political community and are constituent parts of the State.*" While this statement may be seen as an effort towards inclusiveness, it is also to be noted that the Preamble has been written in the name of "we the members of the Hungarian nation," intimating that members of the "nationalities living with us" are not part of the people behind the enactment of the Constitution. The Constitution should be seen as the result of the democratic will-formation of the country's citizens as a whole, and not only of the dominant ethnic group. Therefore, the language used could/should have been more inclusive (such as, for example "*We, citizens of Hungary*..."). It is, again essential, that a comprehensive approach is favored in the context of the interpretation of the constitutional provisions.

B. Foundation

Article D

41. The Venice Commission finds that the statement in Article D that "*Hungary shall bear responsibility for the fate of Hungarians living beyond its borders*" touches upon a very delicate problem of the sovereignty of states and, being a rather wide and not too precise formulation, might give reason to concerns. In particular, the Venice Commission finds unfortunate the use, in this context, of the term "responsibility". This term may be interpreted as authorizing the Hungarian authorities to adopt decisions and take action abroad in favor of persons of Hungarian origin being citizens of other states and therefore lead to conflict of competences between Hungarian authorities and authorities of the country concerned. Such action includes inter alia support to the "*establishment of their community self-governments*" or "*the assertion of their individual and collective rights.*"

42. The Venice Commission recalls that, while states may legitimately protect their own citizens during a stay abroad, as indicated in its Report on the Preferential Treatment of National Minorities by their Kin-State[16], "responsibility for minority protection lies primarily with the home-States." The Commission indeed added, in that report, that "kin-States also, lay a role in the protection and preservation of their kin-minorities, aiming at ensuring that their genuine linguistic and cultural links remain strong." It however considered that respect for the existing framework of minority protection, consisting of multilateral and bilateral treaties, must

[16] CDL-INF (2001) 19 Conclusions.

be held a priority. Unilateral measures by a State with respect of kin-minorities are only legitimate "if the principles of territorial sovereignty of States, *pacta sunt servanda*, friendly relations amongst States and the respect of human rights and fundamental freedoms, in particular the prohibition of discrimination, are respected." The Commission would also like to make reference in this respect to Article 2 of the Framework Convention for the Protection of National Minorities[17] (thereafter: the Framework Convention), to which Hungary is a Contracting Party. It this connection, it welcomes the provisions of Article Q of the new Constitution stressing the importance of ensuring "harmony" between international law and Hungarian law[18] and wishes to underline their importance.

43. As to the issue of "collective rights," it should be noted that, as indicated by the Explanatory Report of the Framework Convention, while "the rights and freedoms flowing from the principles of the Framework Convention may be exercised individually or in community with others," "no collective rights of national minorities are envisaged." This of course does not prevent Hungary, on its territory, to provide its own minorities with collective rights. Nevertheless, it is not up to the Hungarian authorities to decide whether Hungarians leaving in other States shall enjoy collective rights or establish their own self-governments.

44. The Venice Commission trusts that future interpretation of the Constitution and subsequent legislation and policies will be based on the interpretation of the said statement[19] as a commitment to support the Hungarians abroad and assist them, in co-operation with the States concerned, in their efforts to preserve and develop their identity, and not as a basis for extra-territorial decision-making. The Commission wishes to emphasize that, in their dialogue with the Commission's Rapporteurs, the Hungarian authorities have formally confirmed this narrow interpretation of the said statement.

---

[17] "The provisions of this framework Convention shall be applied in good faith, in a spirit of understanding and tolerance and in conformity with the principles of good neighborliness, friendly relations and co-operation between States."

[18] "(2) Hungary shall ensure harmony between international law and Hungarian law in order to fulfill its obligations under international law.

(3) Hungary shall accept the generally recognized rules of international law. Other sources of international law shall become part of the Hungarian legal system by publication in the form of legislation."

[19] "Hungary shall bear responsibility for the fate of Hungarian living beyond its borders."

Article H

45. The Venice Commission finds regrettable that Art. H, which regulates the protection of Hungarian language as the official language of the country, does not include a constitutional guarantee for the protection of the languages of national minorities. It however notes that Article XXIX guarantees the right to the use of these languages by Hungary's "nationalities" and understands this provision as implying also an obligation for the State to protect these languages and to support their preservation and development (see also the Preamble and Article Q of the Constitution).

Article L

46. Article L of the new Constitution contains a constitutional guarantee for the protection of the institution of marriage, which is defined as "the union of a man and a woman established by voluntary decision," as well as of the family "as the basis of the nation's survival." This definition of marriage has been criticized, as it might be interpreted as excluding the union of same sex couples.

47. The Venice Commission notes in this respect that, as the ECtHR held in its judgment of 24 June 2010, in the case of Schalk and Kopf v. Austria, "*although, the institution of marriage has undergone major social changes since the adoption of the Convention, the Court notes that there is no European consensus regarding same-sex marriage. At present no more than six out of forty-seven Convention States allow same-sex marriage*" (§ 58).

48. The Court further held, in § 105 of its judgment that "*[t]he Court cannot but note there is an emerging European consensus towards legal recognition of same-sex couples. Moreover, this tendency has developed rapidly over the past decade. Nevertheless, there is not yet a majority of States providing for legal recognition of same-sex couples. The area in question must therefore still be regarded as one of evolving rights with no established consensus, where States must also enjoy a margin of appreciation in the timing of the introduction of legislative changes. (see Courten, cited above; see also M. W. v. the United Kingdom (dec.), no. 11313/02, 23 June 2009, both relating to the introduction of the Civil Partnership Act in the United Kingdom)*"

49. Moreover, although not explicitly addressing the institution of traditional marriage, the EU Charter states in its Article 9: "The right to marry and the right to found a family shall be guaranteed in accordance with the national laws governing the exercise of these rights." Also, Article 23 of the United Nation International Covenant on Civil and Political Rights,

establishes that, "[t]he family is the natural and fundamental group unit of society and is entitled to protection by society and the State."[20] This Article further recognizes "[t]he right of men and women of marriageable age to marry and to found a family."[21]

50. In the absence of established European standards in this area and in the light of the above-mentioned case-law, the Commission concludes that the definition of marriage belongs to the Hungarian state and its constituent legislator and, as such, it does not appear to prohibit unions between same sex persons (although such unions cannot enjoy protection under the institution of marriage). The Commission notes in this context that registered same-sex civil partnerships enjoy legal protection (although within certain limits) in Hungary since 2009.

Article N

51. According to Art. N § 3, the Constitutional Court is obliged to respect the "principle of balanced, transparent and sustainable budget management." This statement seems to give the budget management priority with respect to a weighing of interests in cases of infringements of fundamental rights. The Venice Commission considers that financial reasons can bear on the interpretation and application of norms, but they are not as such sufficient to overcome constitutional barriers and guarantees. They must not in any way hamper the responsibility of the Court to scrutinize an act of state and to declare it invalid, if it violates the Constitution. (see further comments under *Article 24* below).

Article O

52. The provisions of Article O including an obligation for every person "to contribute to the performance of state and community tasks to the best of his or her abilities and potential" lack clarity, are too wide and may be difficult to apply. In particular, it is not clear either what kind of contribution could be imposed on "every person," nor who will decide on this or what the significance of "every person" is. One may also raise the question whether such an obligation can be extended to non-citizens and, if this is the case, what would be the consequences.

[20] International Covenant on Civil and Political Rights, art. 23, cl. 1, Dec. 16, 1966, 999 U.N.T.S. 171, [ICCPR], available at http://www2.ohchr.org/english/law/ccpr.htm#art23.

[21] Id. at art. 23, cl. 2.

Article R

(See comments under *Rules of interpretation* above)

Article T

53. A list of legislative acts by which generally binding rules of conduct can be established, as well as related publication rules (Article T (3) are provided by Article T of the Constitution. The list includes Acts of Parliament, government decrees, orders by the Governor of the national Bank of Hungary, orders by the Prime Minister, ministerial decrees, orders by autonomous regulatory bodies and local ordinances. In addition "legislation shall also include orders issued by the National Defense Council and the President of the Republic during any state of national crisis or state of emergency." Art. T (3) lays down that "no legislation shall conflict with the Fundamental Law." At the same time, Art. 23(2) stipulates that the decrees issued by autonomous regulatory bodies may not conflict with any act, government decree, any decree of the Prime Minister, ministerial decree or with any order of the Governor of the National Bank of Hungary. In other respects, the hierarchy of the enlisted legislative acts remains open.

54. The hierarchical relations between legislative acts are somehow complicated by the provisions on "special legal orders" empowering the National Defense Council (Art. 49(4)), the President (Art. 50(3)) and the Government (Art. 51(4), 52(3) and 53(2)) to "suspend the application of particular laws and to deviate from any statutory provision." This power is not limited by any explicit requirement of proportionality and should be adequately regulated by the relevant cardinal law.

55. Article T(4) defines "cardinal acts" as "[a]cts of Parliament, the adoption and amendment of which requires a two-thirds majority of the votes of Members of Parliament" (See related comments under *General Remarks* above).

C. Freedom and Responsibility
(Article I to XXXI)

a) General remarks

56. The Chapter "Freedom and Responsibility," laid down in Articles I to XXXI, regulates fundamental rights and has been partly built drawing on the structure of the EU Charter of Fundamental Rights and Freedoms.

57. The Commission recalls that the EU Charter places the individual and individual dignity at its heart. It notes at the same time the particular emphasis put by several parts of the Constitution on the citizens' responsibilities and obligations, which seems to indicate a shift of emphasis from the obligations of the state toward the individual citizens to the obligations of the citizens toward the community. In view of the vagueness of the relevant constitutional provisions, it would be advisable to specify obligations (and their legal consequences) such as:

> "Every person shall be responsible for his or herself, and shall be obliged to contribute to the performance of state and community tasks to the best of his or her abilities and potential." (Article O);
> "All natural resources, especially agricultural land, forests and drinking water supplies, biodiversity – in particular native plant and animal species – and cultural assets shall form part of the nation's common heritage, and the State and every person shall be obliged to protect, sustain and preserve them for future generations." (Article P).

58. The "Freedom and Responsibility" Chapter moreover seems to contain a collection of provisions of different legal nature. It covers fundamental principles and rights, so-called social rights as well as individuals' responsibilities. Fundamental rights are not restricted to individuals but also extended to communities[22] and "subjects of law established by an act". In the Commission's view, constitutions should provide a clear differentiation between principles, legal guarantees, freedoms and responsibilities and present them in a systematic order.

59. The new Hungarian Constitution relegates the task to determine "the rules for fundamental rights and obligations" to "special Acts" (Art. I § 3). The Constitution gives no guidelines for "special Acts" and does not specify nor restrict their scope. Since Articles II-XXI contain many vague terms, they could be considered as providing a margin of appreciation that is too wide in determining the content of these guarantees and the limits of the obligations by special Acts.[23] As a result of such a construction, there seems to be a risk that the constitutional provisions on freedom and

---

22 "(2) Hungary shall recognize the fundamental rights which may be exercised by individuals and communities."

23 "Special Acts" is the term used in the official translation of the Constitution received by the Venice Commission. In other translations, the term "legislative acts" is used.

responsibility might be eroded by special Acts. The Hungarian authorities are encouraged to make sure that, in the process of adoption/amendment of the relevant special acts, sufficient legal clarity and guarantees be provided for the effective enjoyment and protection of fundamental rights, in line with the applicable international standards. The Venice Commission stresses that the content of fundamental rights is a constitutional matter *par excellence*.

60. It is also essential to provide legal clarity, through the subsequent legislation, as far as restrictions of fundamental rights are concerned.[24] In addition, in so far the rights guaranteed in the Constitution are also guaranteed in international and European conventions on human rights ratified by Hungary, limitation clauses specified in these international instruments should also be fully respected. For example, Article 52 § 1 of the EU-Charter, contains *inter alia* the requirement that in a state under the rule of law, any restriction of a human right should be "provided for by law."[25]

b) Specific remarks

Article II

61. Article II of the Chapter "Freedom and Responsibility" stipulates that human dignity shall be inviolable. Furthermore, every human being shall have the right to life and human dignity, a right which can be found in any modern catalogue of fundamental human rights. As a special rule, Article II provides for the protection of embryonic and fetal life from the moment of conception.

62. This duty to protect may under certain circumstances come into conflict with Article 8 ECHR. Legislation regulating the interruption of pregnancy touches upon the sphere of private life of the woman concerned,

---

24 "A fundamental right may be restricted to allow the exercise of another fundamental right or to defend any constitutional value to the extent absolutely necessary, in proportion to the desired goal and in respect of the essential content of such fundamental right."

25 "Any limitation on the exercise of the rights and freedoms recognized by this Charter must be provided for by law and respect the essence of those rights and freedoms. Subject to the principle of proportionality, limitations may be made only if they are necessary and genuinely meet objectives of general interest recognized by the Union or the need to protect the rights and freedoms of others."

since whenever a woman is pregnant her private life becomes closely connected with the developing fetus.

63. According to the ECtHR case law, while the State regulations on abortion relate to the traditional balancing of privacy and the public interest, they must -in case of a therapeutic abortion -also be assessed against the positive obligations of the State to secure the physical integrity of mothers-to-be (ECHR judgment of 7. 2. 2006, Tysiac. / POL, no. 5410/03, § 107). Concerning Article 2 ECHR, the ECtHR is of the view that, in the absence of common standards in this field, the decision where to set the legal point from which the right to life shall begin lies in the margin of appreciation of the states, in the light of the specific circumstances and needs of their own population (ECtHR judgment of 8. 7. 2004 (GC), VO/. FRA, no. 53924/00, § 82).

64. At the same time, the preamble to the UN Convention on the Rights of the Child states "that, as indicated in the Declaration of the Rights of the Child, "the child, by reason of his physical and mental immaturity, needs special safeguards and care, including appropriate legal protection, before as well as after birth." Article 24, § 2 of this Convention requires moreover that "[s]tates take appropriate measures: "(d) To ensure appropriate pre-natal care for mothers."

65. However, this does not result in the recognition of an absolute right to life of the fetus. If Article 2 ECHR were held to cover the fetus, and its protection under this article were, in the absence of any express limitation, seen as absolute, an abortion would have to be considered as prohibited even where the continuance of the pregnancy would involve a serious risk to the life of the pregnant woman. This would mean that the unborn life of the fetus would be regarded as being of a higher value than the life of the pregnant woman (Commission decision of 13. 5. 1980, X./. UK, no. 8416/78, § 19).

66. In the light of the above, Article II of the Hungarian Constitution cannot be read as considering the life of the unborn child to be of higher value than the life of the mother and does not necessarily imply an obligation for the Hungarian State to penalize abortion. Weighing up the various, and sometimes conflicting, rights or freedoms of the mother and the unborn child is mandatory. Provided that such a balance of interests is met, the extension of the safeguards of Article II to the unborn child is in line with the requirements of the ECHR.

67. It is, at present, not clear how the Hungarian legislator will regulate abortion in the future. Concerns have been expressed that this provision might be used to justify legislative and administrative action restricting or even prohibiting abortion. For such a situation, the Venice Commission considers that the Hungarian authorities should pay particular attention to the ECtHR case law, including the recent judgment of 16 December 2010, in the case of A, B and C v. Ireland. In this judgment, the Court assessed that the Irish legislation struck "*fair balance between the right of the first and second applicants to respect for their private lives and the rights invoked on behalf of the unborn.*" In its judgment, the Court had *inter alia* taken into account that Ireland allows abortion where there is a risk to the life of the expectant mother.

68. The Venice Commission would like to add that, in the light of Protocol 6 ("Restriction of death penalty") and to Protocol 13 ("Complete abolition of death penalty") to the ECHR, both ratified by Hungary, and taking into account that the will of Hungarians authorities is to give high protection to human life, it is regrettable that neither Article II nor any other Article in the Constitution mentions explicitly the complete abolition of the death penalty.

Article IV

69. By admitting life imprisonment without parole[26], be it only in relation to the commission of willful and violent offences, Article IV of the new Hungarian Constitution fails to comply with the European human rights standards if it is understood as excluding the possibility to reduce, *de facto* and *de jure*, a life sentence. More specifically, it is only in line with Article 3 ECHR under certain conditions, as applied by the ECtHR in its case law. In its judgment of 12 February 2008 (Kafkaris v. Cyprus, no. 21906/04), the ECtHR summarized the case law as follows:

> *"97. The imposition of a sentence of life imprisonment on an adult offender is not in itself prohibited by or incompatible with Article 3 or any other Article of the Convention […].. At the same time, however, the Court has also held that the imposition of an irreducible life sentence on an adult may raise an issue under Article 3 […].*

---

26 "No person shall be deprived of his or her liberty except for statutory reasons or as a result of a statutory procedure. Life imprisonment without parole shall only be imposed in relation to the commission of willful and violent offences." (Article IV (2)).

98. In determining whether a life sentence in a given case can be regarded as irreducible the Court has sought to ascertain whether a life prisoner can be said to have any prospect of release. An analysis of the Court's case-law on the subject discloses that where national law affords the possibility of review of a life sentence with a view to its commutation, remission, termination or the conditional release of the prisoner, this will be sufficient to satisfy Article 3. The Court has held, for instance, in a number of cases that where detention was subject to review for the purposes of parole after the expiry of the minimum term for serving the life sentence, that it could not be said that the life prisoners in question had been deprived of any hope of release (see, for example, Stanford, cited above; Hill v. the United Kingdom (dec.), no. 19365/02, 18 March 2003; and Wynne, cited above). The Court has found that this is the case even in the absence of a minimum term of unconditional imprisonment and even when the possibility of parole for prisoners serving a life sentence is limited (see for example, Einhorn (cited above, §§ 27 and 28). It follows that a life sentence does not become "irreducible" by the mere fact that in practice it may be served in full. It is enough for the purposes of Article 3 that a life sentence is de jure and de facto reducible.

101. In reaching its decision the Court has had regard to the standards prevailing amongst the member States of the Council of Europe in the field of penal policy, in particular concerning sentence review and release arrangements […]. It has also taken into account the increasing concern regarding the treatment of persons serving long-term prison sentences, particularly life sentences, reflected in a number of Council of Europe texts (see paragraphs 68-73 above)."

70. In this regard, the Venice Commission refers to its previous comments stressing the particular significance of the interpretation of constitutional provisions on fundamental rights and freedoms in the light of human rights treaties binding on Hungary and related case-law, as it results from Article I (3) and Article Q(2) of the new Constitution (see related comments under *Rules of Interpretation* above).

Article VII

71. Article VII contains the right of freedom of thought, conscience and religion. According to its second paragraph, State and Churches shall be separate and Churches shall be autonomous. Furthermore, the State shall cooperate with the Churches for community goals.

72. Article 9 ECHR guarantees the freedom of thought, conscience and religion. That freedom entails, *inter alia*, freedom to hold or not to hold religious beliefs, and to practice or not to practice a religion (ECtHR judgment of 18. 2.1999 (GC), Buscarini and others ./. SMR, no. 24645/94, § 34). Article 9 ECHR applies not only to individuals but also to churches and religious communities. According to the ECtHR, the State shall act neutrally and impartially when organizing the exercise of different religious beliefs in order to uphold public security, religious harmony and tolerance in a democratic society. A separation between state and churches is an inevitable consequence of the rule of law, respect of human rights and the idea of democracy.

73. Mentioning the co-operation between churches and the State for community goals in Article VII does not constitute a State Church (although such systems exist in Europe), insofar as it is explicitly stipulated that churches shall be autonomous and separated from the state. The cooperation between state and churches can be seen as an additional value for the overall State policy in this field and may even strengthen the State's role as a neutral and impartial arbitrator and organizer. Furthermore, Article 17 TFEU[27] stipulates that the European Union shall maintain an open, transparent and regular dialogue with churches and non-confessional organizations. Also, as stated by the Venice Commission in its 2004 Guidelines for Review of Legislation Pertaining to Religion and Belief, "[l]egislation that acknowledges historical differences in the role that different religions have played in a particular country's history are permissible so long as they are not used as a justification for ongoing discrimination" (Chapter II.B.3). Against this background, Article VII is in line with Article 9 ECHR.

Article IX

74. The Venice Commission finds it problematic that freedom of the press is not formulated as an individual's right, but as an obligation of the state.

[27] "1.The Union respects and does not prejudice the status under national law of churches and religious associations or communities in the Member States.

2. The Union equally respects the status under national law of philosophical and non-confessional organizations.

3. Recognizing their identity and their specific contribution, the Union shall maintain an open, transparent and regular dialogue with these churches and organizations." (Treaty on the functioning of the European Union, Consolidated version, April 30, 2008, Article 17).

This freedom appears to be dependent on the will of the state and its willingness to deal with its obligation in the spirit of freedom. This construction has consequences for the substance, direction and quality of the protection, as well as for the chances for successful judicial review in cases of infringements of constitutional rights. Article IX is even more problematic since its paragraph 3 leaves the detailed rules for this freedom and its supervision to a cardinal Act—even without outlining the purposes, contents and restrictions of such a law. Once enacted, there will be no practical way for any further (simple) majority to change the act. The Commission suggests amending Article IX (and other norms on freedoms) in a way that explicitly makes clear that the constitutional guarantees contain individual rights.

Article XV

75. Article XV guarantees for all persons equal treatment before the law and states that special measures should be taken to promote effective implementation of this principle. Moreover, according to Article XV (2), "*Hungary shall ensure fundamental rights to every person without any discrimination on the grounds of race, color, gender, disability, language, religion, political or other views, national or social origin, financial, birth or other circumstances whatsoever.*"

76. Article XV lacks any mention of the prohibition of discrimination on the ground of sexual orientation. This however appears to be common to the majority of European Constitutions. In contrast, various international instruments, including the ICCPR (articles 2 and 26), the TFEU (article 19), and the Directive 2000/78/EC (the so-called "Employment Equality Directive"), as well as, more recently, the EU Charter (article 21§1), protect against discrimination on the ground of sexual orientation.

77. The Venice Commission would like to draw the attention of the Hungarian authorities to recent case law related to the meaning of the prohibition of discrimination, namely a recent judgment of 28 September 2010 (in the case of J.M. v. the United Kingdom), in which the ECtHR held (§54):

> "*54. As the Court's case-law establishes, for an issue to arise under Article 14 there must be a difference in the treatment of persons in relevantly similar situations, such difference being based on one of the grounds expressly or implicitly covered by that provision. Such a difference in treatment is discriminatory if it lacks reasonable and objective justification, that is to say it does not pursue a legitimate aim or if there is no reasonable relationship of proportionality between the means*

employed and the aim pursued. There is a margin of appreciation for States in assessing whether and to what extent differences in otherwise similar situations justify a different treatment, and this margin is usually wide when it comes to general measures of economic or social strategy (see most recently Carson and Others v. the United Kingdom [GC], no. 42184/05, § 61, 16 March 2010). However, where the complaint is one of discrimination on grounds of sexual orientation, the margin of appreciation of Contracting States is narrow (Karner, § 41, Kozak v. Poland, no. 13102/02, § 92, 2 March 2010). The State must be able to point to particularly convincing and weighty reasons to justify such a difference in treatment (E.B., § 91)."

78. Furthermore, in its recent judgment of 24 June 2010 in the case of Schalk and Kopf v. Austria, the ECtHR itself summarized this case law (see § 87[28]).

79. Article XV is an open-ended provision ("or other circumstances"). For that reason, the Hungarian Constitution might create the impression that discrimination on this ground is not considered to be reprehensible. The Venice Commission however proceeds from the assumption that the Hungarian Constitutional Court will interpret the grounds for discrimination in a manner according to which Article XV prohibits also discrimination on grounds of "sexual orientation." This is in line with the ECtHR case law, which regards "sexual orientation" as a prohibited distinctive feature under Article 14 ECHR, although the wording of Article 14 ECHR does not include this ground of discrimination.

---

[28] "87. The Court has dealt with a number of cases concerning discrimination on account of sexual orientation. Some were examined under Article 8 alone, namely cases concerning the prohibition under criminal law of homosexual relations between adults (see Dudgeon v. the United Kingdom, 22 October 1981, Series A no. 45; Norris v. Ireland, 26 October 1988, Series A no. 142; and Modinos v. Cyprus, 22 April 1993, Series A no. 259) and the discharge of homosexuals from the armed forces (see Smith and Grady v. the United Kingdom, nos. 33985/96 and 33986/96, ECHR 1999-VI). Others were examined under Article 14 taken in conjunction with Article 8. These included, inter alia, different age of consent under criminal law for homosexual relations (L. and V. v. Austria, nos. 39392/98 and 39829/98, ECHR 2003-I), the attribution of parental rights (Salgueiro da Silva Mouta v. Portugal, no. 33290/96, ECHR 1999-IX), permission to adopt a child (Fretté v. France, no. 36515/97, ECHR 2002-I, and E.B. v. France, cited above) and the right to succeed to the deceased partner's tenancy (Karner, cited above)."

80. It is important to note in this context that the Hungarian Act CXXV of 2003 on Equal Treatment and Promotion of Equal Opportunities forbids discrimination based on factors that include sexual orientation and sexual identity in the fields of employment, education, housing, health and access to goods and services.

Article XXIII

81. Article XXIII (6) of the new Constitution establishes that "a person disenfranchised by a court for committing an offence shall have no suffrage." The Venice Commission considers that the ECtHR case law[29] relating to Article 3 of Protocol No. 1 is of particular relevance for the subsequent interpretation and application of this constitutional provision.

Article XXIX

82. The Commission notes that, while the present Constitution asserts the State's obligation to ensure the fostering of the cultures of national and ethnic minorities, the use of their native languages, education in their native languages and the use of names in their native languages,[30] the basic provisions of the new Constitution dealing with the protection of Hungary's "nationalities" only make reference to the "respect" of the rights of citizens belonging to national minorities, without establishing any positive obligation on behalf of the State. The term "protect" is not used in relation to minority rights and the term "promote" is only mentioned in the Preamble in reference to "the cultures and languages of nationalities living in Hungary." It is true however that the Preamble includes a broader commitment of the State for the protection of its nationalities. The Venice Commission expects that the Hungarian authorities to make sure that such an approach will not result, in practice, in a diminution of the level of minority protection previously guaranteed in Hungary (see also comments under *The Commissioner for Fundamental Rights*).

[29] See in particular *Hirst v. the United Kingdom* (No. 2), no. 74025/01, Judgment of October 6, 2005, and *Frodl v. Austria*, no. 20201/04, Judgment of April 8, 2010.

[30] Article 68(2) 1949 Constitution of the Republic of Hungary, as amended.

Article XXXI

83. Article XXXI stipulates the duty of every adult male Hungarian citizen living in Hungary to perform military service and the possibility for those, whose conscience does not allow such a military service, to perform an unarmed service. Furthermore, every adult Hungarian citizen living in Hungary may be ordered to perform work for national defense purposes during a state of national crisis and to engage in civil protection for the purpose of national defense and disaster management.

84. The exception for conscientious objectors may raise a specific problem. While it is true that the ECHR leaves it to the member states to decide whether to establish any obligation to perform armed services, the obligation to perform unarmed service in Article XXXI has to be interpreted using a systematic approach. Unarmed services should be performed outside the army in order to avoid potential conflicts with Article 9 ECHR (the right to freedom of thought, conscience and religion). This would resemble regulations in other European states and their handling of armed and unarmed services.

85. Article 4 ECHR prohibits slavery, servitude and forced labor. Explicit exceptions are listed in § 3 and include, *inter alia*, any service of a military character or, in case of conscientious objectors in countries where they are recognized, service exacted instead of compulsory military service, as well as any service exacted in case of an emergency or calamity threatening the life or well-being of the community (see also comments under *Special legal orders* below).

86. In view of Article 4 ECHR, the compulsory performance of work for national defense purposes during a state of national crisis as stipulated in Article XXXI § 4 is in line with human rights standards. The duty of Hungarians to engage in civil protection for the purposes of national defense and disaster management lies within the scope of Article 4 § 3 ECHR as well. Situations that come naturally with the necessity of national defense, or disasters, can be seen as cases of "emergency or calamity."

87. In addition, Article XXXI § 5 of the Hungarian Constitution establishes that every person may be ordered to provide economic and financial services for the purpose of national defense and disaster management.

88. The provision of economic services can also be covered by the exception of Article 4 § 3, which exists for situations threatening the life or well-being

of the community. In contrast, the duty to provide financial services has to be considered under Article 1 Protocol no. 1 ECHR,[31] which provides for the right to the peaceful enjoyment of one's possessions. Public charges such as taxes can be regarded as an interference with Article 1 Protocol no. 1 ECHR. Such an interference can be justified, when a fair balance between the right to peaceful possession of property and the concerned public interest is struck.[32] Particular attention should therefore paid, in the practical implementation of Article XXXI § 5, to the respect of the said balance.

D. The State

89. The Venice Commission notes that the new Constitution maintains the current parliamentary system. It further notes that, in spite of the change of the country's name (from the Republic of Hungary to Hungary, Article A, "Foundation"), Hungary's present form of government—a republic, governed by the principles of democracy, rule of law and separation of power (as confirmed by the provision of the "Foundation" chapter—is maintained. Specific sections (although unevenly elaborated) are dedicated to the state powers, the main public institutions and their interrelations. The weakening of the parliamentary majority's powers and of the position of the Constitutional Court in the Hungarian system of checks and balances, as it results from the new Constitution, is for the Venice Commission a reason of concern.

Article 23 (Autonomous regulatory bodies)

90. Article 23 creates a power for the Parliament to establish autonomous regulatory bodies through a cardinal law. According to the Hungarian authorities, this provision has been adopted mainly to enable setting up the autonomous bodies that are required by EU legislation. Nevertheless, as its wording does not explicitly state this aim, one could see a risk that

---

[31] "Every natural or legal person is entitled to the peaceful enjoyment of his possessions. No one shall be deprived of his possessions except in the public interest and subject to the conditions provided for by law and by the general principles of international law.

The preceding provisions shall not, however, in any way impair the right of a State to enforce such laws as it deems necessary to control the use of property in accordance with the general interest or to secure the payment of taxes or other contributions or penalties."

[32] See in this respect ECtHR related case law, in particular ECtHR judgment of 18. 12. 1984, *Sporrong and Lönnroth./*.SWE,, no. 7151/75, § 73.

this instrument could be used (too extensively) as a way to curtail the parliament's powers.

Article 24 (The Constitutional Court)

91. Since 1990, the Constitutional Court has played a vital role in the Hungarian system of checks and balances. Moreover, the Venice Commission is pleased to note that the Court has gained international recognition through its case law.

92. Article 24 does not regulate in detail the mandate, organization and functioning of the Constitutional Court, leaving it the cardinal law to define more precisely the scope of its competences and related rules and procedures. In addition, further articles of the Constitution are relevant for the operation of the Constitutional Court (see related comments under *Rules of Interpretation*, *Public Finance*, etc.).

93. As far as the composition of the Court is concerned, the new Constitution increases the number of its members from 11 to 15 and prolongs their term of office from nine to twelve years. In addition, it transfers the election of its president from the Court to Parliament (by two-thirds majority) and prolongs his/her mandate to the entire duration of the mandate.

94. The Venice Commission acknowledges that election of the Constitutional Court's president by a political actor, and not by the Court itself, is a widely accepted phenomenon. It however notes that, according to the present Constitution of Hungary, the judges have elected the president from their own ranks, a system which is seen, in general, as a stronger safeguard for the independence of the Constitutional Court.

95. Regarding the duration of term of office of the Constitutional Court's judges, which is prolonged to twelve years, the Constitutional Court Act should preferably state that it is nonrenewable, to further increase the independence of the Constitutional Court Judges.[33]

---

[33] See CDL-AD (2009) 042, Opinion on Draft Amendments to the Law on the Constitutional Court of Latvia, § 14. See also CDL-INF(96) 2, Opinion 6/1995 Regulatory Concept of the Constitution of Hungary, § 15, stating: "to ensure that judges are completely independent of the bodies which elect them, it would be preferable if their term of office provided it is sufficiently long -were not renewable."

96. The Commission notes that further constitutional amendments to the Constitution still in force in Hungary—aiming to already introduce the above-mentioned changes to the number of judges of the Constitutional Court, their term of office and the election of the Court's president—are currently under discussion. The envisaged changes and the initiative to introduce them through an amendment to the present Constitution immediately after the enactment of the new Constitution have raised concerns within Hungarian society and represent a reason for concern for the Venice Commission also.

97. In the Commission's view, the above-mentioned changes in the composition and mode of election of the Constitutional Court must also be assessed in conjunction with the competences of the Court. On the one hand, the Venice Commission notes with satisfaction that the individual constitutional complaint has been introduced into the constitutional review system. On the other hand, in the light of the 2010 curtailment of the Court's powers,[34] confirmed by the new Constitution and of the recent developments mentioned in the previous paragraphs, the Commission is concerned that a number of provisions of the new Constitution may undermine further the authority of the Constitutional Court as a guarantor of constitutionality of the Hungarian legal order (see also related comments in § 51 above).

98. The Constitution imposes specific criteria for the management of the state budget as well as strict limitations to the State debt. Nevertheless, instead of giving the Constitutional Court full scope of control over the constitutionality of the budget and taxes legislation, it gives a special power of intervention in this domain to the new Budget Council. In line with the "veto power" of the Budget Council, the said curtailment of the powers of the Constitutional Court and which regards the budget, taxes and other financial legislation is conditional on the state debt exceeding

[34] See CDL-AD(2011)001, § 9. "As a result of a constitutional amendment in November 2010, a serious limitation of the competences of the Constitutional Court was introduced. According to this amendment, the Constitutional Court may assess the constitutionality of Acts related to the central budget, central taxes, stamp duties and contribution's, custom duties and central requirements related to local taxes exclusively in connection with the rights to life and human dignity, the protection of personal data, the freedom of thought, conscience and religion or with rights related to the Hungarian citizenship. Also, the Court may only annul these Acts in case of violation of the abovementioned rights."

50 % of the GDP. This will, however, be the case for the foreseeable future. This limitation of the Court's competences also covers the State Budget "implementation," which may expand even further the number and scope of acts that will not be subject of constitutional review. It is strongly recommended that the cardinal law regulating the competences, organization and operation of the Constitutional Court (as required by Article 24 § 5 of the new Constitution) provide all clarifications needed in this respect (see also related comments under *The Budget Council*).

99. In this context, the Commission recalls its remarks in its already mentioned Opinion of March 2011, on the role and functions of the Constitutional Court:

> *"a sufficiently large scale of competences is essential to ensure that the court oversees the constitutionality of the most important principles and settings of the society, including all constitutionally guaranteed fundamental rights. Therefore, restricting the Court's competence in such a way that it would review certain state Acts only with regard to a limited part of the Constitution runs counter to the obvious aim of the constitutional legislature in the Hungarian parliament "to enhance the protection of fundamental rights in Hungary".(§ 54; see also paragraphs 51-53).*

100. Article 6 § 8[35] may also be seen as a potential limitation to the authority of the Court. The Commission stresses in this respect that, to be referred to the Constitutional Court again, a law must differ substantially, in its wording, from the previously reviewed text. Otherwise, a second review is superfluous. The requirement of an expedited procedure in § 8 is also problematic. If the doubts regarding the constitutionality of a law have not been entirely dispelled through a different wording, the Court should be given sufficient time for a new deliberation. If from the Parliament´s view the adoption of the act is urgent, the Parliament can decide to adopt it without the objected provision and provide for a later amendment or amend the provision in a way that evidently takes into account all objections.

---

[35] "The Constitutional Court may be requested to re-examine the Act discussed and adopted by Parliament under Paragraph (6) for its conformity with the Fundamental Law under Paragraphs (2) and (4). The Constitutional Court shall decide on the repeated motion as soon as possible but no later than ten days from receipt."

101. As indicated above, the provisions of Article N § 3 of the new Constitution, impose the Constitutional Court the obligation to respect the "principle of balanced, transparent and sustainable budget management" in the course of performing its duties. The Commission wishes to understand this obligation as a requirement applicable to the administrative management of the Constitutional Court as a public institution, and not as an interpretation principle to be enforced in the context of its constitutional review task. In addition, it considers that this principle should not be applied in a way that adversely affects the financial autonomy and the overall independence of the Court in its functioning (see remarks on *Article N* above).

Articles 25 to 28 (Courts)

102. The new Constitution only establishes a very general framework for the operation of the judiciary in Hungary, leaving it to a cardinal law to define "the detailed rules for the organizations and administration of courts, and of the legal state and remuneration of judges" (Article 25 (7)). Although Article 26 (1) clearly stipulates that individual judges shall be independent and only subordinated to the law, a clear statement that courts constitute a separate power and shall be independent is missing. This however results from the general principle of separation of powers enshrined in Article C of the "Foundation" chapter. It is recommended that a clear reference to the principle of the independence of the judicial power and concrete guarantees for the autonomous administration of the judiciary be included in the relevant cardinal law.

103. During its visit to Budapest in May 2011, the Commission was informed that a far-reaching reform of the judiciary was under preparation in Hungary. Nevertheless, there is very limited information on this important reform in the Constitution and little knowledge within Hungarian society on its details.

104. This part of the Constitution also contains rather vague and general provisions. This entails a significant degree of uncertainty with regard to the content of the planned reform and gives reason to concern as it leaves scope for any radical changes. The Hungarian authorities are strongly encouraged to ensure that any future changes in the area of the judiciary and the envisaged reform as a whole are fully in line with the requirements of the separation of powers and the rule of law, and that effective guarantees are available for the independence, impartiality and stability of judges.

105. Provisions concerning the system of courts are of very general nature. Article 25 (4) only states that "the judiciary shall have a multi-level organization" and their detailed regulation is relegated to a cardinal law. In the absence of transitional provisions in the new Constitution, it is difficult to understand not only what "multi-level organization" means, but also whether all existing courts will be maintained and how the future structure will affect the status of judges.

106. It is also important to note that the new Constitution does not contain any reference to the National Council of the Judiciary, the body entrusted by the present Constitution (Article 50 §1) with the administration of the courts. It is therefore not clear whether this body will continue to exist, which solutions will be found to ensure adequate management of courts until the justice reform is effectively implemented and which mechanism will be put in place by the reform. The Venice Commission calls upon the Hungarian authorities to make sure that, whatever the chosen mechanism, strong guarantees will be provided for the independent administration of courts and no room for political intervention will be left.

107. According to Article 25 (1) of the new Constitution, the "Curia" (the Hungarian historical name for the Supreme Court), will be highest justice authority of Hungary. In the absence of transitional provisions and despite the fact that the election rules for its president remain unchanged in the new Constitution[36] a question arises: will this change of the judicial body's name result in replacement of the Supreme Court's president by a new president of the "Curia"? As to the judges, they "shall be appointed by the President of the Republic as defined by a cardinal Act." (Article 26 (2)). This also leaves of margin of interpretation as to the need to change (or not) the composition of the supreme body.

108. As stipulated by Article 26 (2), the general retirement age will also be applied to judges. While it understands that the lowering of the judge's retirement age (from 70 to 62) is part of the envisaged reform of the judicial system, the Commission finds this measure questionable in the light of the core principles and rules pertaining to the independence, the status and immovability of judges. According to different sources, this provision entails that around 300 of the most experienced judges will be obliged

[36] "The President of the Curia shall be elected from among its members for nine years by Parliament on the recommendation of the President of the Republic. The election of the President of the Curia shall require a two-thirds majority of the votes of the Members of Parliament" (Article 26 (4))."

to retire within a year. Correspondingly, around 300 vacancies will need to be filled. This may undermine the operational capacity of the courts and affect continuity and legal security and might also open the way for undue influence on the composition of the judiciary. In the absence of sufficiently clear information on the reasons having led to this decision, the Commission trusts that adequate solutions will be found, in the context of the reform, to address, in line with the requirements of the rule of law, the difficulties and challenges engendered by this measure.

109. Article 27 (3), stipulating that "In cases defined by law, court secretaries may also act within the competence of sole judges subject to Art. 26(1)," also lacks precision and creates ground for questions. Can the court secretary, who is not a judge, act as a judge? If this will be the case, this provision seems questionable from the perspective of the European standards relating to the status of judges. It is therefore essential that, in the context of the adoption of legislation to determine the specific "cases" referred to by Article 27 (3), the applicable standards are fully respected. In particular, clear mention should be made of the requirements to fulfill in order to discharge judicial duties and more general, of the conditions which should guarantee the competence, independence, and impartiality of judges and tribunals (cf Article 6 ECHR).

110. Article 28 seems to contain interpreting guidelines for courts, to be followed in the application of laws: "*In applying laws, courts shall primarily interpret the text of any law in accordance with its goals and the Fundamental Law. The interpretation of the Fundamental Law and other laws shall be based on the assumption that they serve a moral and economical purpose corresponding to common sense and the public benefit.*" The Commission understands that, since it is located in the section titled "Courts," this statement only aims at ordinary courts, excluding the Constitutional Court. In view of its rather general nature, it sees it more as a political declaration than as a constitutional interpretative directive. Nevertheless, the above-mentioned assumption should not be used, in the context of the interpretation of the Constitution, as a way to relativize, in the light of concrete moral and economic needs, the normative content of the Constitution.

Article 29 (Prosecution Services)

111. Compared to Chapter XI of the present Constitution, Article 29 of the new one reflects an evolution in the approach of the role of the prosecutor's office. While the present Constitution seems to establish, as a primary function of the Chief Public Prosecutor, the protection of the

rights,[37] the new Constitution focuses on the contribution of the Supreme Prosecutor and prosecution services to the administration of justice.

112. The Supreme Prosecutor and prosecution services shall: exercise rights in conjunction with investigations; represent public accusation in court proceedings; supervise the legitimacy of penal enforcement and exercise other responsibilities and competences defined by law (Article 29(2)). This approach is in line with the findings of the Venice Commission in its Report on European Standards as regards the Independence of the Judicial System[38]:

> *81. Further, in its Opinion on the Draft Law of Ukraine on the Office of the Public Prosecutor, the Venice Commission found that:*
> *"17. [...] The general protection of human rights is not an appropriate sphere of activity for the prosecutor's office. It should be better realized by an ombudsman than by the prosecutor's office"[39].*

113. The Constitution is very laconic as regards the legal status of prosecutors. It only regulates the prosecutors' appointment and the election of the Supreme Prosecutor, and refers to a future cardinal law for the detailed rules of the organization and operation of prosecution services, the legal status and remuneration of the Supreme Prosecutor and prosecutors (Article 29 (7)). There is no indication, in the constitutional provisions, of any particular changes that would affect the legal status of the prosecutors.

Article 30 (The Commissioner for Human Rights)

114. According to Article 30, one single Commissioner for Fundamental Rights will replace the previous four parliamentary commissioners (specialized ombudspersons), whose general responsibility will be to "protect fundamental rights." His or her deputies will be vested with the task to specifically

---

37 "The Chief Public Prosecutor and the Office of the Public Prosecutor of the Republic of Hungary shall ensure the protection of the rights of natural and legal persons as well as organizations without legal personality, and shall prosecute consistently any act which violates or endangers the constitutional order, security and independence of the country" (Article 51, § 1).

38 CDL-AD(2010)040, Report on European Standards as regards the Independence of the Judicial System: Part II the Prosecution Service, Venice, December 17–18, 2010.

39 CDL-AD(2009)048, Opinion on the Draft Law of Ukraine on the Office of the Public Prosecutor, Venice, June 12–13, 2009, emphasis added.

to "defend the interests of future generations and the rights of nationalities living in Hungary" (Article 30.2). As it results from Article VI.3, an independent authority in charge of supervising "the exercise of the right to the protection of personal data and the access to data of public interest" will replace the commissioner for personal data and freedom of information. While the detailed rules for the Commissioner for Fundamental Rights shall be established by separate act, no information is provided with regard to the future competences and functioning of the new data protection authority, nor reference is made to any related subsequent legislation.

115. The Venice Commission acknowledges that states enjoy a wide margin of appreciation with regard to such institutional arrangements, which depend to a large extent on the domestic specific situation. Moreover, one single ombudsperson or multiple ombudspersons may be more appropriate at different stages of the democratic evolution of states.[40] This being said, it considers it important that the above-mentioned re-organization does not entail a lowering of the existing level of guarantees for the protection and promotion of rights in the fields of national minority protection, personal information protection and transparency of publicly relevant information. More generally, it deems important to ensure that the decrease in the number of independent institutions does not have an negative impact on the Hungarian system of check and balances and its efficiency.

Articles 31-35 (Local governments)

116. Article 31 (1) of the new Constitution stipulates that "[I]n Hungary local governments shall be established to administer public affairs and exercise public power at a local level." Nevertheless, no explicit mention

[40] See CDL-AD(2007)020, Opinion on the possible reform of the Ombudsman Institution in Kazakhstan, Venice, June 1–2, 2007, § 25: " On balance, however, it would seem preferable to follow the third-named alternative in Kazakhstan, where the Ombudsman institution is presently in a stage of consolidation and development, and to organize the functions of the specialized ombudsperson within the overall institution of the national Ombudsman, by way of establishing a special department and/or appointing a deputy ombudsman for the special field. The special function presumably could then benefit directly from the status and legitimacy of the general Ombudsman, and the connection could in fact lend added strength and efficiency both to the special function and the national institution. If this approach is followed, it would be appropriate to have the deputy ombudsperson or head of department appointed either by the Ombudsman or by the appointing authority (Parliament/President) upon recommendation of the Ombudsman."

is made of the principle of local self-government. The Venice Commission recalls that the European Charter of Local Self-Government (CEAL), which is binding for Hungary, requires compliance with a minimum number of principles that form a European foundation of local democracy, including as a starting point the principle of local self-government.[41]

117. According to Article 2 of the CEAL, "the principle of local self-government shall be recognized in domestic legislation, and where practicable in the constitution." It is recommended that the cardinal law entrusted with the definition of local governments rules duly stipulate this and other important key principles laid down in the CEAL: the principle of subsidiarity, the principle of financial autonomy and that of adequacy between resources and competences, the legal protection of local self-government, the limits of the administrative supervision of local authorities. Adequate guarantees should be provided for their effective implementation.

118. With regard to local authorities' supervision, the new Constitution enables metropolitan or county government offices to adopt, upon court decision, local ordinances in cases of failure by the local authorities to introduce such acts under their "statutory legislative obligation" (Article 32 (5)). At present, the government supervises the lawful operation of local authorities and can only react to shortcomings by means of legal action, without being allowed to introduce local acts on their behalf. In the absence of more detailed rules, this provision might be problematic from the point of view of the principle of local self-government. According to Article 8.2 of the CEAL, "[a]ny administrative supervision of the activities of the local authorities shall normally aim only at ensuring compliance with the law and with constitutional principles. Administrative supervision may however be exercised with regard to expediency by higher-level authorities in respect of tasks the execution of which is delegated to local authorities." It is therefore recommended that the subsequent local self-government legislation provide clarity in this respect. In particular, a clear distinction should be established between, on the one hand, the local authorities' own competences and those delegated by the central government and, on the other hand, between the control of the local authorities' activities' legality and supervision of their decision's expediency.

[41] "Local self-government denotes the right and the ability of local authorities, within the limits of the law, to regulate and manage a substantial share of public affairs under their own responsibility and in the interests of the local population." (CEAL, Article 3 § 1).

119. Art. 35(5), allowing for Parliament's dissolution of local elected bodies on the ground of a violation of the Constitution, is also a source of concern. Such an important decision seems not to require a binding court decision and the role of the Constitutional Court in this context appears to be only of an advisory nature. It is recommended that the specific rules applicable in such situations, to be established by cardinal law (Article 35(4)), take duly into account the relevant principles of the CEAL and include guarantees to enable their respect.

Articles 36 to 45 (Public Finances)

The competence of the Constitutional Court

120. The Chapter on the Public Finances contains provisions which aim to bring about an improvement in the State finances. Specific restriction on the Parliament and Government budget-related decisions are set out in Art. 36 § 4, Art. 36 § 5, Art. 37 § 2-3.

121. The adoption of constitutional provisions which impose to maintain the state deficit below 50 % per cent of GDP, responds to a legitimate aim. Thus, it cannot be criticized in the light of international and European standards of democracy, human rights and the rule of law, on the condition that the laws implementing the budget—by raising taxes or by cutting the expenses of the state—comply with these standards.

122. From this perspective, serious concern has to be expressed as to Article 37 (4) of the new Constitution, which openly leaves breaches of the Constitution without a sanction by stating that the Constitutional Court's power to review is limited to the fields explicitly listed. Article 37 (4) reads as follows:

> "*(4) As long as state debt exceeds half of the Gross Domestic Product, the Constitutional Court may, within its competence set out in Article 24(2)b-e), only review the Acts on the State Budget and its implementation, the central tax type, duties, pension and healthcare contributions, customs and the central conditions for local taxes for conformity with the Fundamental Law or annul the preceding Acts due to violation of the right to life and human dignity, the right to the protection of personal data, freedom of thought, conscience and religion, and with the rights related to Hungarian citizenship […]*"."

123. In its March Opinion, the Venice Commission has already expressed its regrets with regard to this serious limitation of the competences of the

Constitutional Court introduced in November 2010 by constitutional amendment. In its view, such a limitation creates the impression that capping the national budget at 50% of the GDP may be considered to be such an important aim that it may even be reached by unconstitutional laws (see related comments under the chapter on the Constitutional Court).

124. It is important to note in this respect that the limited competence of the Court to assess whether a tax law violates "the right to life and human dignity, the right to the protection of personal data, freedom of thought, conscience and religion, and with the rights related to Hungarian citizenship" still allows the Hungarian Court to sanction potential abuses of the tax power. In a recent judgment dated 6 May 2011, the Court had to rule on a 98% tax law with a retroactive scope of five years. In its ruling, the Court held that "*[T]he retroactive taxation of a legal income, generated without infringing any laws, in a tax year which has ended, represents such a degree of public interference into an individual's autonomy that it lacks an acceptable reason, and thus, goes against human dignity…*"

125. Furthermore, as it results from the ECtHR case law,[42] tax laws fall within the ambit of Article 1 of the First Protocol of the ECHR. According to the ECtHR, a retroactive tax law imposing an excessive burden on the citizens can be considered to be a violation of Article 1 of the First Protocol of the ECHRM.[43]

126. In addition, to the extent that the words "the Acts on the State Budget and its implementation" in Article 37 (4) of the new Constitution also apply to laws cutting state expenses, the Venice Commission wishes to stress that, as indicated by the ECtHR case-law, the notion of "possessions" in Article 1 of the First Protocol covers all pecuniary rights, including welfare benefits, both of a contributory and of a non-contributory nature.[44]

---

[42] See e.g. ECtHR decision no. 19276/05, Allianz – Slovenská poist'ovna a.s. and Others v. Slovakia, November 9, 2010.

[43] ECtHR, *di Belmonte v. Italy*, June 16, 2010., appl. 72638/01; see also ECtHR *National & Provincial Building Society, Leeds Permanent Building Society and Yorkshire Building Society v. the United Kingdom*, judgment October 23, 1997, §§ 80-82. See also, on depriving private persons retroactively of their right to payment ECtHR, case *Pressos Compania Naviera SA and others v. Belgium*, judgment of November 20, 1995, Series A, no. 332

[44] See in particular the recent ECtHR judgment, *Plalam S.P.A. v. Italy*, May 18, 2010: § 36.

127. While the ECtHR recognized in a recent judgment that states dispose of a large margin of appreciation in this field,[45] this margin of appreciation is however not unlimited. On the one hand, the legislator will have to strike a fair balance between the demands of the general interest of the public and the requirements of the protection of the individual's fundamental rights, not imposing a disproportionate and excessive burden on certain private persons (Article 1, First Protocol). On the other hand, it will have to respect the principle of nondiscrimination: persons in analogous or relevantly similar positions may not be treated differently without an objective and reasonable justification (Article 14 ECHR). It is therefore essential, in states having opted for a constitutional court, that this court should be entitled to assess the compliance of all laws with the human rights guaranteed in the constitution, and especially with human rights of such a particular importance: the right not to be discriminated and the right not to be unduly deprived of its possessions.

The Budget Council

128. The establishment and the competences of the Budget Council, as well as its composition and the way it is established (Article 44(4)),[46] has a significant impact on the adoption of the State Budget and the Parliament's related power. This is of key importance for Parliament as, in addition to legislation, the Budget is the main instrument for parliamentary majority to express and implement its political programme. Article 44(3), interpreted in conjunction with Article 36(4)-(5), seems to grant the non-parliamentary Budget Council a "veto" power over Parliament's decision for the foreseeable future.

129. The adoption of the State budget is part of the core competence of the Parliament and usually its main exclusive privilege. Making its decision dependent on the consent of another authority—with limited democratic legitimacy, as none of the members of the Council is directly elected—is therefore problematic and might have a negative impact on the democratic legitimacy of budgetary decisions. Such decisions may be complicated further by the fact that the Council's composition will consist of members appointed by a previous majority. Moreover, apart from the general requirements stipulated in Article 36(4)-(5) previously quoted, the Constitution

---

[45] Idem, § 46.

[46] "The members of the Budget Council shall include the President of the Budget Council, the Governor of the National Bank of Hungary and the President of the State Audit Office. The President of the Budget Council shall be appointed for six years by the President of the Republic."

does not set up any condition for the "prior consent" of the Budgetary Council. The Venice Commission trusts that the Hungarian authorities will avoid a too rigid/restrictive interpretation of the "prior consent", and that this condition will be interpreted and implemented, as it results from Article 44 (1)-(2): as a "statutory contribution to the preparation of the State Budget Act" through "supporting Parliament's legislative activities and examining feasibility of the State Budget" (and not as an absolute power to block the adoption of the budget). As the compliance with the provisions of the Constitution—Article 36 (4)-(5), but also Article 44 (1)-(2)—is at stake, in any case the Constitutional Court should have the last word.

Levels of regulation

130. Several provisions of the Chapter on Public Finances refer to cardinal acts. These provisions are related to issues such as: general taxation and the pension system; the organization and operation of the National Bank National Bank and its responsibility for monetary policy; the organization and operation of the State Audit Office, the operation of the Budget Council.

131. As indicated before, there are no standards or precise criteria to determine the issues which should be regulated in the Constitution itself or in special majority acts. Nevertheless, the Commission considers to be in contradiction with the majority rule, which normally applies in a democracy, that the social, fiscal and financial policies of one political majority at a specific moment in time are cemented through a two third majority in the constitution or in cardinals laws. As a result, it will be particular difficult to translated the "free expression of the opinion of the people in the choice of the legislator" (Article 3, First Protocol to the ECHR), in future elections, in changes of these policies. The way in which the cardinal laws will be drafted is thus of key importance (see related comments under *Preliminary Remarks. Cardinal Laws*).

Articles 45 -46 (The Hungarian Defense Forces and the Police and National Security Services)

132. It is a Hungarian constitutional tradition that the issues of armed forces and police are regulated by the Constitution (see also chapter VIII of the present Constitution). In many countries, it is a matter of an ordinary law.

133. The Venice Commission notes that, in line with the main constitutional values referred to in the Preamble, the provisions of Article 45

clearly states the mains aims of the military defense of the country, namely Hungary's independence, territorial integrity and state borders. It is commendable that the constitutional provisions also open the way for common defense, peacekeeping tasks arising from international agreements.

Articles 48 to 54 (Special legal orders)

134. The provisions of Articles 48–54 are provided for a situation when normal functioning of the state's organs are seriously disturbed and it is impossible to make use of the regulations applicable to periods when such disturbances not exist. The Hungarian Constitution is not unique in regulating special legal orders in such a detailed way (see in this respect the Polish or the German Constitution).

135. The new Constitution sets out the conditions for the establishment of different types of special legal orders (the state of national crisis, the state of emergency; the state of preventive defense; unexpected attacks; the state of extreme danger) as well as specific conditions for the adoption of related extraordinary measures.

136. In order for special legal orders to be in line the European standards, certain specific conditions must indeed be fulfilled. The Constitution itself in its Article I (3) dealing with restrictions to fundamental rights states that "[A] fundamental right may be restricted to allow the exercise of another fundamental right or to defend any constitutional value to the extent absolutely necessary, in proportion to the desired goal and in respect of the essential content of such fundamental right."

137. In the light of the Venice Commission's conclusions in its Opinion concerning the Protection of Human Rights in Emergency Situations 46, this Chapter of the Hungarian Constitution appears to be generally in line with the European standards.

138. Increased clarity would be needed as to the scope of the cardinal law referred to in Article 50 (3), 51 (4), 52 (3), 53 (1-2). It is not entirely clear, from the wording of these provisions, whether the cardinal law only relates to "any extraordinary measure" or also—what would be advisable—to the suspension of the application of particular laws and the deviation from any statutory law. The general wording of Article 54 (4) seems to confirm this wider interpretation: "The detailed rules for any special legal order shall be defined by a cardinal 46 CDL(2006)015, § 35 and § 38. Act." When the relevant cardinal law is adopted or amended following

to the requirements of the Constitution, this aspect should clarified and the scope of the law defined accordingly.

139. The Commission also notes that, according to Article 54 (1), "[In] a special legal order, the exercise of fundamental rights may be suspended or restricted beyond Article I (3), except for the fundamental rights set out in Articles II and III, and Article XXVIII (2)-(5)." As Hungary is also bound by Article 15 of the ECHR and by Article 4 of the ICCPR, special legal orders will also have to comply with the provisions of these articles (see also comments under *Article T* above).

Closing provisions

140. As previously indicated, the reference in second paragraph of the Closing Provisions to the 1949 Constitution seems to be in contradiction with the statement, in the Preamble, by which the Hungarian 1949 Constitution is declared as invalid. The Venice Commission tends to interpret this apparent inconsistency as a confirmation of the fact that the said statement does not have legal significance. Nevertheless, it is recommended that this is specifically clarified by the Hungarian authorities. The adoption of transitional provisions (as required by the third paragraph of the Closing Provisions), of particular importance in the light of the existence, for certain provisions of the new Constitution, of possibly diverging interpretations, could be used as an excellent opportunity for providing the necessary clarifications. This should not be used as a means to put an end to the term of office of persons elected or appointed under the previous Constitution.

IV. CONCLUSIONS

141. The adoption of a new Constitution, aiming to consolidate Hungary as democratic state based on the principles of separation of powers, protection of fundamental rights and the rule of law, is a commendable step.

142. The Venice Commission welcomes the efforts made to establish a constitutional order in line with the common European democratic values and standards and to regulate fundamental rights and freedoms in compliance with the international instruments which are binding for Hungary, including the ECHR and the recent EU Charter. It notes that the current parliamentary system and the country's form of government—the republic—have been maintained. The Commission is pleased to note the introduction of the individual constitutional complaint in the Hungarian system of constitutional review.

143. The Venice Commission notes that the recommendations it formulated, in March 2011, following the authorities' request for assistance on specific legal issues raised in the constitutional process, have been partly taken into account.

144. By contrast, it is regrettable that the constitution-making process, including the drafting and the final adoption of the new Constitution, has been affected by lack of transparency, shortcomings in the dialogue between the majority and the opposition, the insufficient opportunities for an adequate public debate, and a very tight timeframe. The Commission hopes that the adoption of implementing legislation will be a more transparent and inclusive process, with adequate opportunities for a proper debate of the numerous major issues that are still to be regulated. It calls upon to all parties involved to adopt, beyond their political background and orientations, an open and constructive approach and effectively cooperate in this process.

145. The significant number of matters relegated, for detailed regulation, to cardinal laws requiring a two-thirds majority, including issues which should be left to the ordinary political process and which are usually decided by simple majority, raises concerns. Cultural, religious, moral, socio-economic and financial policies should not be cemented in a cardinal law.

146. The limitation of powers of the Constitutional Court on taxation and budgetary matters and the prominent role given to the Budget Council in the adoption of the State budget, represent further sensitive issues that have raised concern in the light of their potential impact on the functioning of democracy.

147. In addition, a rather general constitutional framework is provided for key sectors, such as the judiciary and further important society settings. This is also a source of concern, as it may have an impact on the quality and level of guarantees and protection available and on the effective implementation of the standards applicable to the sectors concerned. Guarantees for the main principles pertaining to such important matters are usually enshrined in the Constitution, especially when major reforms are planned, as it is the case for the Hungarian judiciary. The provisions relating to life imprisonment without parole could raise issues of compatibility with international norms that are binding on Hungary and the related case-law.

148. With regard to the constitutional protection of fundamental rights, the Commission considers that more precise indications should be

provided by the Constitution as to their content and stronger guarantees for their effective protection and enjoyment by individuals, in line with the international human rights instruments to which Hungary is a Contracting Party. The Venice Commission recalls that, as indicated in its March 2011 Opinion,[47] "*as a rule, constitutions contain provisions regulating issues of the highest importance for the functioning of the state and the protection of the individual fundamental rights. It is thus essential that the most important related guarantees are specified in the text of the Constitution, and not left to lower level norms.*"

149. The relevance of the Preamble for the Constitution's interpretation and some potentially problematic statements and terms contained therein have also gave reason to questions and would call for adequate clarification by the Hungarian authorities. This include the wording on the protection of the rights of Hungarians abroad contained in the Preamble and other related provisions of the new Constitution, which may be found problematic and engender concern in the framework of inter-state relations.

150. The Venice Commission trusts that adequate clarifications and responses—fully in line with the applicable standards—to the concerns mentioned before, will be provided in the context of the future interpretation and application of the new Constitution or by amending the Constitution where necessary. The preparation and adoption of cardinal and other implementing laws is an opportunity in this respect. The Venice Commission stands ready to assist the Hungarian authorities in this process upon their request.

[47] CDL-AD(2011)001, § 52.

Bibliography

Ackerman, B. *We the People, Transformations,* Vol. 2. Cambridge, Mass.: Harvard University Press, 1998.

Alter, K. *Establishing the Supremacy of European Law.* Oxford: Oxford University Press, 2001.

Andorno, R. "Human Dignity and Human Rights as a Common Ground for a Global Ethics." *Journal of Medicine and Philosophy* (2009): 1–18.

Antohi, S. and V. Tismăneanu eds. *Between Past and Future: The Revolutions of 1989 and Their Aftermath.* Budapest: Central European University Press, 2000.

Arato, A. *Civil Society, Constitution and Legitimacy.* Lanham: Rowman and Littlefield, 2000.

———. "Constitution-Making as a Learning Process: Andrew Arato's model of post-sovereign constitution-making: editor's introduction." *South African Journal on Human Rights: Constitution-Making as a Learning Process* 1, no. 26 (2010): 1–18.

———. *Constitution Making under Occupation: the Politics of Imposed Revolution in Iraq.* New York: Columbia, 2009.

———. "Democratic Constitution Making and Unfreezing the Turkish Process." *Philosophy and Social Criticism* 36, no. 3–4 (2010): 473–487.

———. "Post-Sovereign Constitution-Making in Hungary: After Success, Partial Failure, and Now What?" *South African Journal on Human Rights: Constitution-Making as a Learning Process* 1, no. 26 (2010): 19–44.

———. "The Constitution-Making Endgame in Hungary." *East European Constitutional Review* 5, no. 4 (1996): 31-39.

Arato, A. and Z. Miklósi, "Constitution Making in Hungary 1989–1996" in *Framing the State in Times of Transition: Case Studies in Constitution Making,* eds. Miller, L. E. and L. Aucoin, Washington DC.: United States Institute for Peace, 2010.

Arendt, H. *Macht und Gewalt.* Munich: Piper, 1994.

———. *On Revolution.* New York: Penguin, 2006.

Armstrong, K. "Mutual Recognition" in *The Law of the Single European Market,* eds. Barnard, C. et al., Oxford: Hart Publishing, 2002.

———. *Regulation, Deregulation, Re-regulation.* London: Kogan Page, 2000.

Ayres, I. and J. Braithwaite, *Responsive Regulation.* Oxford: Oxford University Press, 1992.

Babus, E. "The Superego of the Transformation. The First Eight Years of the Constitutional Court." *The Hungarian Quarterly*, 153 (1999): 3–11.

Bagehot, W. *The English Constitution.* 2nd Edition. Boston: Little, Brown, and Company 1873.

Bak, J.M. and A. Gara-Bak, "The Ideology of a 'Millennial Constitution' in Hungary." *East European Quarterly* 3 (1981): 307–323.

Bak, J.M. and P. Banyó and M. Rady eds. *The Laws of the Medieval Kingdom in Hungary*, Vol. 5. Idyllwild, CA: Charles Schlacks, Jr. and Budapest: Central European University Press, 2008.

Baldwin, R. and M. Cave, *Understanding Regulation.* Oxford: Oxford University Press, 1996.

Balogh, M. "Regnum et sacerdotium. Állam és egyház történetileg változó viszonyai Magyarországon" [Regnum et sacerdotium, The historically changing relations of church and state in Hungary]. *Vallástudományi Szemle* 6, no. 4 (2010): 9–24.

Bárd, P. "The Hungarian Constitutional Court Decision on Euthanasia. A Half Hearted Ruling, Case Study of the Decision 22/2003. (IV. 28.) of the Hungarian Constitutional Court." *Revue de Justice Constitutionnelle Est-Européenne* 4 (2004): 105–121.

Bauböck, R. "Stakeholder Citizenship and Transnational Political Participation: A Normative Evaluation of External Voting." *Fordham Law Review* 75, no. 5 (2007): 2393–2447.

Bauböck, R. and A. Liebich, eds. "Is There (Still) an East-West Divide in the Conception of Citizenship in Europe?" *EUI Working Papers*, RSCAS no. 19, Florence: European University Institute, 2010.

Bence, Gy. "Barátsággal váltunk el" [We parted in friendship] Philosopher György Bence on Fidesz, the nature of the political parties and the crown. *Népszabadság*, January 15, 2000.

Bibó, I. "A békeszerződés és a magyar demokrácia" [The peace treaty and the Hungarian democracy] in *Válogatott tanulmányok* [Selected studies], Vol. 2. Budapest: Magvető, 1986.

Böckenförde, E.-W. *Staat, Nation, Europa: Studien zur Staatslehre, Verfassungstheorie und Rechtsphilosophie.* Frankfurt am Main: Suhrkamp, 1999.

Boulanger, C. "Europeanisation through Judicial Activism? The Hungarian Constitutional Court's Legitimacy and the 'Return to Europe'" in *Spreading Democracy and the Rule of Law?* eds. Sadurski, W., A. Czarnota and M. Krygier, Dordrecht: Springer, 2006.

Bozóki, A. ed. *The Roundtable Talks of 1989. The Genesis of Hungarian Democracy.* Budapest: Central European University Press, 2002.

Bragyova, A. "Az Európai Unióhoz való csatlakozás alkotmányjogi kérdései" [Constitutional aspects of the EU-accession] in *EU-tanulmányok* [EU-Studies], Vol. 1. ed. Inotai, A., Budapest: Nemzeti Fejlesztési Hivatal, 2002.

———. "Equality and Constitution" in *The Constitution Found? The First Nine Years of the Hungarian Constitutional Review on Fundamental Rights,* ed. Halmai, G., Budapest: INDOK, 2000.

Bratza, N. "The Implications of the HRA 1998 for Commercial Practice." *European Human Rights Law Review,* 5 (2000).

Brunner, G. "Structure and Proceedings of the Hungarian Constitutional Judiciary" in *Constitutional Judiciary in a New Democracy: The Hungarian Constitutional Court,* eds. Sólyom, L. and G. Brunner, Ann Arbor: University of Michigan, 2000.

Brunner, G. and G. Halmai, "Die juristische Bewältigung des kommunistischen Unrechts in Ungarn" in *Juristische Bewältigung des Kommunistischen Unrechts in Osteuropa und Deutschland,* ed. Brunner, G., Berlin: Berlin Verlag Arno Spitz, 1995.

Brunner, G. and L. Sólyom, *Verfassungsgerichtsbarkeit in Ungarn.* Baden-Baden: Nomos, 1995.

Buda, P. "Állam és egyház: A polgári átalakulás eredményeinek leépítése" [State and church: Demolishing the achievements of civic reforms]. *Fundamentum* no. 2 (2001): 127–142.

Burgogne-Larsen, L. ed. *La dignité saisie par les juges en Europe* [Dignity applied by judges in Europe]. Bruxelles: Bruylant, 2010.

Burke, E. *Reflections on the French Revolution.* London: J. M. Dent & Sons Ltd., New York: E. P. Dutton & Co. Inc., 1951 [1910].

Calmfors, L. and S. Wren-Lewis, "What should fiscal councils do?" *Economic Policy* 26, no. 68 (2011): 649-695.

Choudhry, S. ed. *Constitutional Design for Divided Societies: Integration or Accomodation?* Oxford: Oxford University Press, 2008.

Christiano, T. "Authority and Democracy." *Journal of Political Philosophy* 12, no. 3 (2004): 266–290.

———. *The Constitution of Equality.* Oxford: Oxford University Press, 2008.

Chronowski, N. *Integrálódó alkotmányjog* [Integrating Constitutional Law]. Pécs: Dialóg Campus, 2005.

Cieslar, A. and A. Nayer, and B. Smeesters, *Le droit à l'épanouissement de l'être humain au travail, Métamorphoses du droit social* [The right to self-fulfillment in the work place. Transformations of Labour Law]. Bruxelles: Bruylant, 2007.

Coglianese, C. and E. Mendelson, "Meta-Regulation and Self-Regulation" in *The Oxford Handbook of Regulation,* eds. Baldwin, R. et al., Oxford: Oxford University Press, 2010.

The Constitution Unit at the School of Public Policy of the University College of London, *Checks and Balances in a Single-Chamber Parliament: A Comparative Study.* London: University College, 1998.

Csink, L. and B. Schanda and A.Zs. Varga eds., *The Basic Law of Hungary: A First Commentary.* Budapest-Dublin: Clarus Press, National Institute of Public Administration, 2012.

Daintith, T. "The techniques of government" in *The Changing Constitution,* eds. Jowell, J. and D. Oliver, Oxford: Oxford University Press, 2004.

Danninger, S. *A New Rule: "The Swiss Debt Brake."* IMF Working Paper 02/18 (2002).

Debrun, X. *Democratic Accountability, Deficit Bias and Independent Fiscal Agencies*, IMF Working Paper 11/173 (2011).

Debrun, X. and M.S. Kumar, *Fiscal Rules, Fiscal Councils and All That: Commitment Devices, Signalling Tools or Smokescreens?* Banca d'Italia Workshop on Fiscal Policy: Current Issues and Challenges (2007).

Debrun, X. and D. Hauner and M. S. Kumar, "Independent Fiscal Agencies." *Journal of Economic Surveys* 23, no. 1 (2009): 44-81.

De Tissot, O. "Pour une analyse juridique du concept de dignité du salarié" [A legal analysis of the concept of the employee's dignity]. *Droit Social* (1995): 972–977.

Dezső, M. and A. Vincze, *Magyar alkotmányosság az európai integrációban* [Hungarian Constitutionalism in the European Integration]. Budapest: HVG-ORAC, 2006.

Dicey, A.V., *Introduction to the Study of the Law of the Constitution,* 10th edition. London: MacMillan, 1961.

Di Ciommo, M. *Dignità umana e Stato costitutional, la dignità umana nel costituzionalismo europeo, nella Costituzione italiana e nelle jurisprudenze europee* [Human dignity and constitutional state, human dignity in European constitutionalism, in the Italian constitution and in European case law]. Firenze: Passigli Editore, 2010.

D'Oliveira, H. "Nationality and the European Union after Amsterdam" in *Legal issues of the Amsterdam Treaty*, eds. O'Keeffe, D. and P. M. Tworney, Oxford and Portland, Oregon: Hart Publishing, 1999.

Donahue, J.D. "Market-Based Governance and the Architecture of Accountability" in *Market-Based Governance,* eds. Donahue, J.D. et al. (Washington, DC: Brookings Institution, 2002).

Dorsen, N. and M. Rosenfeld and A. Sajó, and S. Baer, *Comparative Constitutionalism, Cases and Materials,* 2th edition. St. Paul, MN.: West, 2010.

Dowdle, M.W. "Public Accountability: Conceptual, Historical and Epistemic Mappings" in *Public Accountability,* ed. Dowdle, M.W. (Cambridge: Cambridge University Press, 2006).

Ducreux, M-E. "Emperors, Kingdoms, Territories: Multiple Versions of the Pietas Austriaca?" *The Catholic Historical Review* 97, no. 2 (2011): 276–304.

Duncan, C. *Civilising rituals inside public art museums.* London and New York: Routledge, 1995.

Dupré, C. *Importing the Law in Post-communist Transitions, The Hungarian Constitutional Court and the Right to Human Dignity.* Oxford: Hart Publishing, 2003.

Durham C. and S. Ferrari eds. *Laws on Religion and the State in Post-Communist Europe.* Leuven: Peeters, 2004.

Dworkin, R. *Law's Empire.* Oxford: Hart Publishing, 1998.

———. *Taking Rights Seriously.* London: Duckworth, 1977.

Eckhart, F. *A Szentkorona-eszme története* [A history of the Holy Crown doctrine]. Budapest: Magyar Tudományos Akadémia, 1941.

Eichengreen, B. et al. *Public Debts: Nuts, Bolts and Worries.* Geneva: International Center for Banking and Monetary Studies, 2011.

Elkins, Z., T. Ginsburg, J. Melton, *The Endurance of Constitutions.* Cambridge: Cambridge University Press, 2009.

Engel, P. *Beilleszkedés Európába, a kezdetektől 1440-ig* [Adaptation to Europe, from the beginnings to 1440]. Budapest: Háttér, 1990.

Erdei, Á. and A. Holló eds., *Selected Decisions of the Constitutional Court of Hungary (1998–2001).* Budapest: Akadémiai Kiadó, 2005.

Evans, R.J.W. *Austria, Hungary, and the Habsburgs, c. 1683–1867.* Oxford: Oxford University Press, 2006.

Fazekas, F. and M. Varju, "The reception of European Union law in Hungary: The Constitutional Court and the Hungarian judiciary." *Common Market Law Review* 48, no. 6 (2011): 1945-1984.

Feischmidt, M. "A kettős állampolgárságról" [On dual citizenship]. *Kisebbségkutatás*, 1 (2005): 30-33.

Ferejohn, J. and P. Pasquale, "The Law of Exception: A Typology of Emergency Powers." *International Journal of Constitutional Law* 2 (2004): 210–239.

Fillitz, H. *Die Schatzkammer in Wien. Symbole abendländischen Kaisertums.* Salzburg und Wien: Residenz, 1986.

Fletcher, G.P. "Human Dignity as a Constitutional Value." *University of Western Ontario Law Review* 22 (1984): 171–182.

Forró, G. "Kettős állampolgárság: készülnek az ügyfélfogadásra [Dual citizenship: getting ready for applicants]." *Krónika.ro*, September 20, 2010.

Gál, K. "The Hungarian Legislation on Hungarians Living in Neighboring Countries" in *The Protection of National Minorities by their Kin-State,* Science and technique of democracy, no. 32, Strasbourg: Council of Europe, 2002.

———. "The Hungarian Legislation on Hungarians Living in Neighbouring Countries" in *The Hungarian Status Law: Nation Building and/or Minority Protection,* eds. Kántor, Z. et al., Sapporo: Slavic Research Center, Hokkaido University, 2004.

Gant, T. *A Szent Korona amerikai kalandja 1945–1978* [The American adventure of the Holy Crown]. Debrecen: Kossuth Egyetemi Kiadó, 1997.

Gárdos-Orosz, F. "Constitutional Rights: Horizontal Effect and Anti-Discrimination Law in Hungary." *Acta Juridica Hungarica* 49, no. 1 (2008): 111-136.

Ginsburg, T. *Judicial Review in New Democracies: Constitutional Courts in Asian Cases.* Cambridge, UK: Cambridge University Press, 2003.

Goodin, R.E. and C. List, "Special Majorities Rationalized." *British Journal of Political Science* 36 (2006): 213–24.

Graham, C. *Is there a Crisis in Regulatory Accountability?* Centre for the Study of Regulated Industries. Discussion Paper No. 13, The Chartered Institute of Public Finance and Accountability (1995).

Granville, A. *Working a Democratic Constitution: The Indian Experience.* New Delhi: Oxford University Press, 1999.

Grünwald, B. *A régi Magyarország 1711–1825* [Old Hungary 1711–1825]. Budapest: Osiris, 2001.

Häberle, P. *Das Menschenbild im Verfassungsstaat* [The Image of Man in the Constitutional State], 4th edition. Berlin: Duncker und Humblot, 2008.

———. *Europäische Verfassungslehre* [European Constitutional Doctrine]. Baden-Baden: Nomos, 2009.

———. "Gott im Verfassungstaat" [God in the Constitutional State] in *Rechtsvergleichung im Kraftfeld des Verfassungsrechts* [Comparative Law in the field of constitutional law], ed. Häberle, P., Berlin: Duncker und Humblot, 1992.

———. *The Principle of Respect for Human Dignity.* Strasbourg: Council of Europe Publishing, 1999.

Habermas, J. "Das utopische Gefälle, das Konzept der Menschenwürde und die realistische Utopie der Menschenrechte" [The Utopian Gradiant, The Concept of Human Dignity and the Realistic Utopia]. *Blätter für Deutsche und Internationale Politik* 8 (2010), 43–53.

———. *Legitimation Crisis,* trans. McCarthy, C. Boston: Beacon Press, 1975.

Halász, I. "A kettős állampolgárság mint a magyar nemzetpolitika eszköze?" [Dual Citizenship as a Tool of the Hungarian Nation-policy?] *Regio: kisebbség, politika, társadalom* 15 (2004): 18–35.

———. "Választások és kisebbségek 2010. A 2010. évi közép-európai választások tapasztalatai kisebbségi szemszögből" [Elections and minorities 2010. The experiences of Central-European elections of 2010 from the viewpoint of the minorities]. *Pro Minoritate* (Spring 2011): 111-121.

Halmai, G. "Birth and Death—A Constitutional Approach. Constitutional Court on Abortion and Euthanasia." *Revue de Justice Constitutionnelle Est-Européenne* 4 (2004): 87–104.

———. "Referendum and Representative Democracy." *Fundamentum* no. 5 (2008): 5–21.

———. "The Hungarian Approach to Constitutional Review: The End of Activism? The First Decade of the Hungarian Constitutional Court" in *Constitutional Justice, East and West, Democratic Legitimacy and Constitutional Courts in Post-Communist Europe in a Comparative Perspective*, ed. Sadurski, W., The Hague: Kluwer Law International, 2002.

———. "The Transformation of Hungarian Constitutional Law from 1985 to 2005" in *The Transformation of Hungarian Legal Order 1985–2005*, eds. Jakab, A., P. Takács and A. Tatham, The Hague e.a.: Kluwer Law International, 2007.

Halmai, G. ed. *The Constitution Found? The First Nine Years of Hungarian Constitutional Review of Human Rights.* Budapest, INDOK, 2000.

Halmai, G. and K.L. Scheppele, "Constitutional Solutions to the Extra-Constitutional State." *Journal of Constitutional Law in Eastern and Central Europe* 2, no. 2 (1995): 179-197.

Hamilton, I.R. *The Taking of the Stone of Destiny.* Moffat: Lochar Publishing, 1991.

Haraszti, M. "The Handshake Tradition: A Decade of Consensus Politics Bears Liberal Fruit in Hungary—But What Next?" in *Between Past and*

Future: The Revolutions of 1989 and Their Aftermath, eds. Antohi, S. and V. Tismăneanu, Budapest: Central European University Press, 2000.

Harrington, C. and Z. Umut Turem, "Accounting for Accountability in Neoliberal Regulatory Regimes" in *Public Accountability*, ed. Dowdle, M.W., Cambridge: Cambridge University Press, 2006.

Héas, F. "Observations sur le concept de dignité appliqué aux relations du travail" [Observations on the concept of dignity as applied to work relationships]. *Le Droit Ouvrier* 746 (2010): 1–8.

Hogan, G. "How Catholic was the Constitution?" (paper presented at *The Constitution at 70*, Trinity College Dublin Centre for Law and Democracy), June 8–9, 2007.

Hogan G., G. Whyte, and J. M. Kelly: *The Irish Constitution*. London, Butterworths, 1994.

Hóman, B. and Gy. Szekfű, *Magyar történet* [A History of Hungary], Vol. II. Budapest: Királyi Magyar Egyetemi Nyomda, 1936.

Husz, D. "Intézmények presztízse 1989 és 1998 között" [The Prestige of Institutions between 1989 and 1998] in *Magyarország Évtizedkönyve, 1988–1998*, eds. Kurtán, S. and P. Vass, Budapest: Demokrácia Kutatások Magyar Központja Alapítvány, 1998.

Iordachi, C. *Country Report: Romania*. Florence: European University Institute, 2010.

Iuvenalis, D. I. *Satires*, trans. Rudd, N. Oxford: Clarendon Press, 1991.

Jackson, E. *Medical Law. Texts, Cases and Materials*. Oxford: Oxford University Press, 2010.

Jakab, A. *Az új Alaptörvény keletkezése és gyakorlati következményei* [The evolution and practical consequences of the new Fundamental Law]. Budapest: HVG ORAC, 2011.

———. "Die Euthanasieentscheidung des ungarischen Verfassungsgerichts vom 28 April 2003" [The Hungarian constitutional ruling on euthanasia of April 28, 2003]. *OsteuropaRecht* 50 (2004): 31–40.

Jakab, A. ed. *Az Alkotmány kommentárja* [Commentary to the Hungarian Constitution], 1–3. Budapest: Századvég, 2009.

Joerges, Ch. and N.S.L. Ghaleigh eds. *The Darker Legacies of Law in Europe*. Oxford: Hart Publishing, 2003.

Józsa, Gy. *Aufarbeitung der kommunistischen Vergangenheit in Ungarn*. Cologne: Bundesinstitut für ostwissenschaftliche und internationale Studien, 1998.

Kántor, Z. et al., eds. *The Hungarian Legislation on Hungarians Living in Neighbouring Countries*. Sapporo: Slavic Research Center, Hokkaido University, 2004.

Kantorowicz, E. H. *The King's Two Bodies. A Study in Medieval Political Theology*. Princeton, N.J.: Princeton Univerity Press, 1957.

Karpat, J. "Corona regni Hungariae im Zeitalter der Arpaden" (1937) in *Corona regni. Studien über die Krone als Symbol des Staates im späteren Mittelalter*, ed. Hellmann, M., Weimar: Hermann Böhlaus Nachf., 1971.

———. "Die idee der heilegen Krone Ungarns in neuer Beleuchtung" (1943–44) in *Corona regni. Studien über die Krone als Symbol des Staates im späteren Mittelalter*, ed. Hellmann, M., Weimar: Hermann Böhlaus Nachf., 1971.

Keating M. *The Independence of Scotland, Self-Government and the Shifting Politics of Union.* Oxford: Oxford University Press, 2009.

Kelsen, H. *General Theory of Law and State,* trans. Wedberg, A. Cambridge, Mass.: Harvard University Press, 1945.

Kis, J. "Alkotmányozás - mi végre?" I-III. [Why Constitution-making?] *Élet és Irodalom*, 55, no. 12, 13, and 14 (2011).

———. "A rendszerváltást lezáró alkotmány" ["Constitution closing the transition"]. *Népszabadság* August 19, 1994.

———. "Between Reform and Revolution." *East European Politics and Society* 12, no. 2 (1998): 300–389.

———. *Constitutional Democracy.* Budapest: Central European University Press, 2003.

Kispál, G. "Rechtsempfinden Versus Verfassung" *Budapester Zeitung*, November 2, 2010.

Kommers, D. *The Constitutional Jurisprudence of the Federal Republic of Germany.* Durham: Duke University Press, 1997.

Koselleck, R. "A kora újkor elmúlt jövője" [The past future of the early modern age] in *Elmúlt jövő. A történeti idők szemantikája* [The past future. A semantic of historical times], Koselleck, R. Budapest: Atlantisz, 2003.

Kovács, K. and G.A. Tóth, "Hungary's Constitutional Transformation." *European Constitutional Law Review* 7 (2011): 183–203.

Kovács, M. and J. Tóth, "Kin-state responsibility and ethnic citizenship: The Hungarian case" in *Citizenship Policies in the New Europe*, eds. R. Baubock, B. Perchinig, and W. Sievers, Amsterdam: Amsterdam University Press, 2010.

Kovács, M. and S. Pogonyi, and Z. Körtvélyesi, *The Politics of External Kin-State Citizenship in East Central Europe.* Florence: European University Institute, 2010.

Küpper, H. "Das zweite Abtreibungsurteil des ungarischen Verfassungsgerichts" [The Second abortion ruling of the Hungarian Constitutional Court]. *OsteuropaRecht* (1999): 155–169.

Lábady, T. "Constitutional protection of privacy: Protection of marriage and the family, right to privacy." *Acta Juridica Hungarica* 45-46, nos. 1–2 (1995–1996): 23-35.

Lee, S. and S. McBride, "Introduction: Neo-Liberalism, State Power and Global Governance" in *Neo-Liberalism, State Power and Global Governance,* eds. Lee, S. and S. McBride, Dordrecht: Springer, 2007.

Lembcke, O.W. *Hüter Der Verfassung: Eine institutionentheoretische Studie zur Autorität des Bundesverfassungsgerichts.* Tübingen: Mohr Siebeck, 2007.

Lembcke, O.W. and F. Weber, eds. "Emotion und Revolution. Spurenlese zu einer Theorie der affektiven Grundlagen politischer Ordnungen." *Österreichische Zeitschrift für Politikwissenschaft* 39, no. 2 (2010): 171–186.

Linz, J. J. "Presidential or Parliamentary Democracy: Does it Make a Difference?" in *The Failure of Presidential Democracy,* Linz, J.J. and A. Valenzuela, Baltimore: Johns Hopkins University Press, 1994.

Maatsch, A. *Ethnic Citizenship Regimes. Europeanization, Post-war Migration and Redressing Past Wrongs*, Palgrave Politics of Identity and Citizenship Series. London: Palgrave Macmillan, 2011.

MacCormick, N. ed. *Construing Legal Systems: European Union in Legal Theory*. Dordrecht, Boston, Mass.: Kluwer Academic, 1997.

Madison, J. "The Federalist No. 10" in *The Federalist Papers*, Hamilton, A. and J. Madison and J. Jay, New York: Bantam, 1982.

Majone, G. "The Rise of the Regulatory State in Europe." *West European Politics* 17, no. 3 (1994): 77-101.

Majtényi, B. *A nemzetállam új ruhája* [The nationstate's new cloth]. Budapest: Gondolat, 2007.

Majtényi, B. "'Vár állott, most kőhalom'—Alaptörvény és irodalom" ['Castle stood, a ruin now'—Fundamental Law and literature]. *Fundamentum* no. 4 (2011): 97–105.

Majtényi, L. and Z. Miklósi eds. *És mi lesz az alkotmánnyal?* [And what will be with the constitution?]. Budapest: Eötvös Károly Intézet, 2004.

Marczali, H. *Hungary in the Eighteenth Century*. Cambridge: Cambridge University Press, 1910.

Maurer, B. *Le Principe de Respect de la Dignité Humaine et la CEDH* [The principle of respect for human dignity and the European Convention on Human Rights]. Paris: La documentation française, 1999.

Mayer, G. "Verfassungsgericht in Ungarn beschränkt." *Der Standard*, November 16, 2010.

McClellan, A. *Inventing the Louvre. Art, Politics, and the Origins of the Modern Museum in Eighteenth Century Paris*. Cambridge: Cambridge University Press, 1994.

McCrudden, C. "Institutional Discrimination." *Oxford Journal of Legal Studies* 2, no. 3 (1982): 303-367.

McHarg, A. and D. Nicolson, "Justifying Affirmative Action: Perception and Reality" in *Debating Affirmative Action: Conceptual, Contextual and Comparative Perspectives*, eds. McHarg, A. and D. Nicolson, Oxford: Blackwell, 2006.

Medjouba, F. and J. Stefanelli, and M. Sánchez, *The Rights and Responsibilities of Citizenship*. London: British Institute of International and Comparative Law, 2008.

Mörth, U. "Introduction" in *Soft Law in Governance and Regulation. An Interdisciplinary Analysis*, ed. Mörth, U., Cheltenham: Edward Elgar, 2004.

Müller, J-W. *Constitutional Patriotism*. Princeton, NJ: Princeton University Press, 2007.

Navracsics, T. "A New Constitution for Hungary: Locking in the Values of the 1989–1990 Transition, At Last" *The Wall Street Journal*, April 19, 2011.

Nussbaum, M. and A. Sen, eds. *The Quality of Life*. Oxford: Clarendon Press, 1993.

O'Neal, P. "Presidential Power in Post Communist Europe: The Hungarian Case in Comparative Perspective." *Journal of Communist Studies* 9, no. 3 (1993): 177–201.

Orgad, L. "The Preamble in Constitutional Interpretation." *International Journal of Constitutional Law* 8 (2010): 714–738.

Paczolay, P. "Judicial Review of the Compensation Law in Hungary." *Michigan Journal of International Law* 13 (1992): 806-831.

Paczolay, P. ed. *Twenty Years of the Hungarian Constitutional Court.* Budapest: Constitutional Court of the Republic of Hungary, 2009.

Paine, T. "Rights of Men" in *The Great Works of Thomas Paine*, Vol. II. New York: D. M. Bennett Liberals and Scientific Publishing House, 1878.

Parragi, M. "A magyar állampolgársági jog és a külföldön élő magyarság" [The Hungarian Law of Citizenship and The Hungarians Living Abroad]. *Kisebbségkutatás*, 1 (2000): 37–50.

Pildes, R. "The Theory of Political Competition." *Virginia Law Review* 85, no. 8 (1999): 1605–1626.

Plomer, A. *The Law of Ethics and Medical Research.* London: Cavendish, 2007.

Pokol B. "Aktivizmus és az Alkotmánybíróság" [Activism and the Constitutional Court] in *Magyarország Politikai Évkönyve 1992*, eds. Kurtán, S. and P. Vass, Budapest: Demokrácia Kutatások Magyar Központja Alapítvány, 1993.

———. *The Concept of Law. The Multi-Layered Legal System.* Budapest: Rejtjel, 2001.

———. "The Constitutionality of Legislation" in *European Legal Cultures*, eds. Gessner, V. and A. Höland, and Cs. Varga, Aldershot: Dartmouth, 1996.

Przeworski, A. *Democracy and Market: Political and Economic Reforms in Eastern Europe and Latin America.* New York: Columbia University Press, 1991.

Ragazzi, F. and K. Balalovska, "Diaspora Politics and Post-Territorial Citizenship in Croatia, Serbia and Macedonia." *CITSEE Working Paper Series*, no. 18. Edinburgh: University of Edinburgh, 2011.

Rava, N. *Country Report: Serbia.* Florence: European University Institute, 2010.

Rawls, J. *A Theory of Justice.* Cambridge: Belknap Press of Harvard University Press, 1971.

———. *Political Liberalism.* New York: Columbia University Press, 2005.

Raz, J. *Between Authority and Interpretation: On the Theory of Law and Practical Reason.* Oxford: Oxford University Press, 2009.

———. *Practical Reason and Norms.* Princeton, NJ: Princeton University Press, 1990.

Romsics, I. *A trianoni békeszerződés* [The peace treaty of Trianon]. Budapest: Osiris, 2001.

Rugási, Gy. "Szellemképek. Töredékek a közelmúlt vallástörténetéből" [Apparitions. Fragments from the religious history of the recent past]. *Holmi* 11 (2000): 1331-1345.

Sadurski, W. ed. *Constitutional Justice, East and West, Democratic Legitimacy and Constitutional Courts in Post-Communist Europe in a Comparative Perspective.* The Hague: Kluwer Law International, 2002.

Sadurski, W. and A. Czarnota and M. Krygier eds. *Spreading Democracy and the Rule of Law?* Dordrecht: Springer, 2006.

Sarajlić, E. *Country Report: Bosnia and Herzegovina.* Florence: European University Institute, 2010.

Sajó, A. "A 'kisegyház' mint alkotmányjogi képtelenség" ['Small church' as a constitutional non-sense]. *Fundamentum* no. 2 (1999): 87–98.

———. "Learning Co-operative Constitutionalism the Hard Way: the Hungarian Constitutional Court Shying Away from EU Supremacy." *Zeitschrift für Staats- und Europawissenschaften* 2, no. 3 (2004): 351-371.

———. "Reading the Invisible Constitution: Judicial Review in Hungary." *Oxford Journal of Legal Studies* 15, no. 2 (1995): 253-267.

Schanda, B. *Magyar állami egyházjog* [Hungarian State Church Law]. Budapest: Pázmány Péter Katolikus Egyetem Kánonjogi Posztgraduális Intézet - Szent István Társulat, 2000.

———. *Religion and Law in Hungary.* The Hague: Kluwer, 2011.

———. "Religion and State in the Candidate Countries to the European Union: Issues concerning Religion and State in Hungary." *Sociology of Religion* 64, no. 3 (2003): 333–348.

Scheppele, K.L. "The New Hungarian Constitutional Court." *East European Constitutional Review* 8, no. 4 (1999): 51-87.

Schieck, D. "Re-embedding economic and social constitutionalism: Normative perspectives for the EU" in *European Economic and Social Constitutionalism after the Treaty of Lisbon,* eds. Schieck, D. and U. Liebert and H. Schneider eds. Cambridge: Cambridge University Press, 2011.

Schieck, D. and U. Liebert and H. Schneider eds. *European Economic and Social Constitutionalism after the Treaty of Lisbon.* Cambridge: Cambridge University Press, 2011.

Schima, S. "Focus: Freedom of Religion in Austria." *Vienna Journal on International Constitutional Law* 3, no. 3 (2009): 199–209.

Schleicher, D. "'Politics as Markets' Reconsidered: Natural Monopolies, Competitive Democratic Philosophy and Primary Ballot Access in American Elections." *Supreme Court Economic Review* 14 (2006), 1–26.

Schmitt, C. *Legality and Legitimacy,* trans. Seitzer J. Durham: Duke University Press, 2004.

Schramm, P.E. *Kaiser Königen und Päpste. Gesammelte Aufsätze zur Geschichte des Mittelalters,* Band IV. Stuttgart: Anton Hiersemann, 1970.

Schwartz, A. "Patriotism or Integrity? Constitutional Community in Divided Societies." *Oxford Journal of Legal Studies,* 31, no. 3 (2011): 503-526.

Scott, C. "Regulation in the Age of Governance: the Rise of the Post-Regulatory State" in *The Politics of Regulation,* eds. Jordana, J. et al., Cheltenham: Edward Elgar, 2004.

———. "Regulatory Governance and the Challenge of Constitutionalism" in *The Regulatory State,* eds. Oliver, D. et al., Oxford: Oxford University Press, 2010.

———. "Accountability in the Regulatory State." *Journal of Law and Society* 27, no. 1 (2000): 38-60.

Siekmann, H. "The Burden of an Aging Society as a Public Debt. The Perspective of the German Constitutional Law and the Law of the EU." *European Public Law* 13, no. 3 (2007): 489–518.

Snell, J. "Non-Discriminatory Tax Obstacles in Community Law." *International and Comparative Law Quarterly* 56, no. 2 (2007): 339–370.

Sólyom, L. and G. Brunner eds. *Constitutional Judiciary in a New Democracy: The Hungarian Constitutional Court.* Ann Arbor: University of Michigan Press, 2000.

Stolz, J. "Angoissée par son déclin démographique, la Hongrie renvoie les mères au foyer" [Anxious about her demographic decline, Hungary sends mothers back home] *Le Monde,* January 6, 2011.

———. "A Gyöngyöspata, vitrine de l'extrême droite" [At Gyöngyöspata, show case of the far right]. *Le Monde,* August 16, 2011.

———. "La Hongrie 'a besoin de chaque vie'" [Hungary 'needs every single life']. *Le Monde,* May 20, 2011.

Sunstein, C.R. *After the Rights Revolution. Reconceiving the Regulatory State.* Cambridge, Mass.: Harvard University Press, 1993.

Szabó, Y. "Work for Benefits?" *The Hungarian Quarterly* 191 (2008): 89-94.

Szathmáry, B. *Fejezetek az állami vallás- és egyházjogból, Tanulmányi segédlet az V. évfolyamos joghallgatók számára* [Chapters from state religion and church law, Study aid for 5th year law students]. Budapest: Károli Gáspár Református Egyetem, 2006.

Szemere, B. *Naplóm* [My diary], Vol. I. Pest: Ráth Mór, 1869.

Széchenyi, I. *Válogatott művei* [Selected works], II. Budapest: Szépirodalmi, 1991.

Taylor, J. A. *British Monarchy, English Church Establishment, and Civil Liberty.* Westport, Conn.: Greenwood Press, 1996.

Tóth, E. and K. Szelényi, *A magyar Szent Korona. Királyok és koronázások* [The Hungarian Holy Crown. Kings and coronations]. Budapest: Kossuth, 2002.

Tóth, G.A. "The Bitter Pills of Political Transition" in *The Transformation of Hungarian Legal Order 1985–2005,* eds. Jakab, A. and P. Takács and A. Tatham, The Hague: Kluwer Law International, 2007.

———. "Unequal Protection: Historical Churches and Roma People in the Hungarian Constitutional Jurisprudence." *Acta Juridica Hungarica* 51, no. 2 (2010): 122-135

Tóth, J. "Kettős állampolgárságot népszavazással?" [Dual Citizenship via referendum?]. *Fundamentum,* no. 2 (2004): 88–96.

Tóth, J. and Z. Körtvélyesi, "Naturalisation in Hungary: Exclusion by Ethnic Preference." *Open Citizenship* 2, no. 1 (2011).

Tribe, L.H. *The Invisible Constitution.* Oxford: Oxford University Press, 2008.

Turba, G. *Die pragmatische Sanktion, mit besonderer Rücksicht auf die Laender der Stephanskrone.* Vienna: Manz, 1906.

———. *Geschichte des Thronfolgerechtes in allen Habsburgischen Ländern bis zur Pragmatischen Sanktion Kaiser Karls VI. 1156 bis 1732.* Vienna: Fromme, 1903.

Twining, Lord E. *A History of the Crown Jewels of Europe.* London: B. T. Batsford, 1960.

Uitz, R. "Aiming for State Neutrality in Matters of Religion, The Hungarian Record." *University of Detroit Mercy Law Review* 83 (2006): 761–788.

Várnay, E. "Közpénzügyek az Alkotmányban—az adósságfék" [Public finances in the constitution: the debt ceiling]. *Jogtudományi Közlöny* 10 (2011): 483–495.

van Banning, T.R.G. *The Human Right to Property*. Antwerp: Intersentia, 2002.

van Roermund, B. "Jurisprudential dilemmas of European Law" in *Construing Legal Systems: European Union in Legal Theory*, ed. MacCormick, N., Dordrecht, Boston, Mass.: Kluwer Academic, 1997.

von Bogdandy, A. "The European Constitution and European Identity: Text and Subtext establishing a Constitution for Europe." *International Journal of Constitutional Law* 3 (2005): 295–315.

von Bogdandy, A. and J. Bast, eds. *Principles of European Constitutional Law*. Portland: Hart, 2006.

von Bogyay, T. "Über die Forschungsgeschichte der heiligen Krone" in *Insignia Regni Hungariae. I, Studien zur Machtsymbolic des mittelalterlichen Ungarn*, ed. Lovag, Zs. Budapest: 1983.

Waldron, J. *Law and Disagreement*. Oxford: Oxford University Press, 1999.

Weber, M. *Economy and Society*, trans. Fischoff, E. at al, Roth, G. and C. Wittich, eds. New York: Bedminster Press, 1968.

Weinrib, L. "Human Dignity as a Rights-Protecting Principle." *National Journal of Constitutional Law* 17 (2004): 325–345.

Wetzel, T. "Eddig mintegy 160 ezren éltek a könnyített honosítás lehetőségével" [So far 160,000 persons took the opportunity to naturalize under the preferential rules]. *Vajdaság Ma*, November 5, 2011.

Table of Cases

Council of Europe, European Court of Human Rights

European Union, European Court of Justice

Contributors

ANDREW ARATO is Dorothy Hart Hirshon Professor in Political and Social Theory at the New School for Social Research, New York and Invited Professor in the College de France, Paris. He taught at École des hautes études, and Sciences Po, Paris, and the Central European University, Budapest, had a Fulbright teaching grant to Montevideo, and was Distinguished Fulbright Professor at the Goethe University, Frankfurt, as well as invited professor at the Law School of the University of Toronto. Arato has served as a consultant for the Hungarian Parliament on constitutional issues (1995–1997), and as U.S. State Department Democracy Lecturer and Consultant on Constitutional issues in Nepal (2007) and Zimbabwe (2010). His most recent publications are *Civil Society and Political Theory* (1992), *Civil Society, Constitution and Legitimacy* (2000), and *Constitution Making under Occupation: The Politics of Imposed Revolution in Iraq* (2009).

MIKLÓS BÁNKUTI is Senior Research Specialist in the Law and Public Affairs Program at Princeton University. His research focuses on constitutional and legal reform in Hungary. He graduated with a Master in Public Affairs from Princeton University and holds undergraduate degrees in finance and economics. He has also worked as an analyst with the International Energy Agency and subsequently as a finance associate with the Clinton Foundation.

CHRISTIAN BOULANGER is Political Scientist and Legal Sociologist working at the Forum Transregional Studies in Berlin. Before joining the Forum, he helped founding the Law and Society Institute at Humboldt-Universität zu Berlin. His research interests include the transformation of the legal field in post-Communist societies, comparative constitutional and judicial studies, law and development, and the sociology of punishment from a comparative perspective.

ANDRÁS BRAGYOVA is Judge at the Constitutional Court of Hungary and Professor of Constitutional Law at the University of Miskolc. Since 1977 he has been researcher in the Institute of Legal Sciences of the Hungarian Academy of Sciences in Budapest. He was recurrent visiting professor at the Central European University, Department of Political Science. Professor Bragyova has published books and essays on constitutional law and theory, the philosophy of law and international law in Hungarian, English and other languages.

CATHERINE DUPRÉ is Senior Lecturer in Law at the University of Exeter. She started working on Hungarian constitutional law at the European University Institute, Florence in 1998. She has been a lecturer at the University of Birmingham and the University of Wales, Aberystwyth. She is currently developing a research project on the connections between the concept of human dignity and European constitutionalism, for which she was awarded a Research Fellowship from the Leverhulme Trust (2010–2011). She is the author of *Importing the Law in Post-communist Transitions: The Hungarian Constitutional Court and the Right to Human Dignity* (2003).

RONALD DWORKIN is Frank Henry Sommer Professor of Law and Philosophy at New York University. He is the 2007 recipient of the Holberg International Memorial Prize. He has been Professor of Jurisprudence at Oxford and Fellow of University College since 1969. He clerked for Judge Learned Hand, was associated with a law firm in New York and was a professor of law at Yale University Law School from 1962–1969. Professor Dworkin's books include *Taking Rights Seriously* (1977), *A Matter of Principle* (1985), *Law's Empire* (1986), *A Bill of Rights for Britain* (1990), *Life's Dominion* (1993), *Freedom's Law* (1996), *Justice in Robes* (2006), and, most recently *Justice for Hedgehogs* (2011). His forthcoming book, *Religion Without God*, is based on his 2011 Einstein Lectures.

GÁBOR HALMAI is Professor of Law and Director of the Institute of Political and International Studies at the Eötvös Loránd University, Budapest. Since 2003 he has been the national director of the European Masters Program in Human Rights and Democratization in Venice. Between 2007–2010 he was member of the EU Fundamental Rights Agency's Management Board based in Vienna. Professor Halmai's primary research interests are comparative constitutional law and human rights. He has published several books, articles, and edited volumes on these topics. His forthcoming book is on constitutional law, human rights, and globalization.

JÁNOS KIS is Professor of Political Science and of Philosophy at the Central European University, Budapest, and Distinguished Global Professor at the New York University, Department of Philosophy. He was a leading member of the democratic opposition to the communist regime and the first chairman of the Alliance of Free Democrats, Hungary's liberal party. He took an active part in the process of the transition to democracy in 1989/90. He withdrew from politics in 1991. Before 1989 he translated among other things, works of Rousseau, Fichte, and Kant. He taught at the École des Hautes Études en Sciences Sociales, Paris, in 1983, and at the New School for Social Research, New York, in 1988/89. His books include *Towards an East European Marxism* (with György Bence, 1978), *L'Égale Dignité: essai sur les fondements des droits de l'homme* (1989), *Politics in Hungary: For a Democratic Alternative* (1989), *Constitutional Democracy* (2003), *Politics as a Moral Problem* (2009).

ZSOLT KÖRTVÉLYESI is Assistant Professor at the European Studies Department at Eötvös Loránd University, Budapest and SJD student at the Comparative Constitutional Law Program of the Central European University where he obtained an MA degree in Nationalism Studies (2009). He has published several articles on nationality, minority rights, data protection, property rights, and freedom of assembly.

KRISZTA KOVÁCS is Senior Adviser of the Hungarian Constitutional Court, and Liaison Officer of the Venice Commission, Council of Europe. In 2000/2001 she was a visiting research fellow at the Human Rights Institute of the Columbia Law School. Between 1996 and 1998 she worked at the Constitutional and Legislative Policy Institute (an affiliate institution of CEU). She has published several articles on constitutional law, human rights and discrimination including a monograph on equality.

OLIVER W. LEMBCKE is Guest Professor of Political Science at Helmut Schmidt University, Hamburg. His research interests include political theory, legal philosophy, and comparative politics. Professor Lembcke is editor of *Zeitgenössische Demokratietheorie* (with Ritzi & Schaal, 2012) and the author of *Hüter der Verfassung. Eine institutionentheoretische Studie zur Autorität des Bundesverfassungsgerichts* (2007). He is also author of articles and book chapters, including *Balancing Law and Politics: The Contribution of Political Theory* (2011) and *Emmanuel Joseph Sieyès: Political Writings* (with Florian Weber, 2012).

JEREMY MCBRIDE is a barrister practicing from Monckton Chambers, London and a visiting professor at Central European University. He is also the Chairperson of the Scientific Committee of the European Union's Agency for Fundamental Rights and acts as an expert on human rights law for the Council of Europe. He is the editor of *Butterworths Human Rights Cases* and co-founder and Chair of INTERIGHTS (the International Centre for the Legal Protection of Human Rights). He was formerly Reader in International Human Rights Law at the University of Birmingham.

ZOLTÁN MIKLÓSI teaches political philosophy at the Department of Political Science of Central European University. Having pursued studies at the New School University of New York, he obtained his doctorate in philosophy at Eötvös Loránd University, Budapest in 2005. Working as an expert for Freedom House from 2000 to 2002, he served as one of the main authors of the 2001 and 2002 country reports on Hungary. He is research coordinator for the Eötvös Károly Institute. His main research interests include theories of justice, political obligation and especially the intersection of the two. He has published in these areas both in English and Hungarian.

SÁNDOR RADNÓTI is Professor of Aesthetics at Eötvös Loránd University, Budapest. He is an art-philosopher and literary critic. Deeply involved in the Samizdat movement in Communist Hungary, his academic career began only after the 1989 democratic transition. His previous books and essays include the relationship between mysticism and poetry, the cultural philosophy of Walter Benjamin, the aesthetic reconstruction of the views of certain significant art-historians, and treatises that studied the theoretical position of practical criticism and the concept of style.

KIM LANE SCHEPPELE is the Laurance S. Rockefeller Professor of Sociology and Public Affairs in the Woodrow Wilson School and the University Center for Human Values as well as Director of the Program in Law and Public Affairs, Princeton University. From 1994–1998, Scheppele did research at the Constitutional Court of Hungary and taught at both the Eötvös Loránd University, Budapest and at Central European University, where she was a founding director of the Program in Gender and Culture. She was John J. O'Brien Professor of Comparative Law at the University of Pennsylvania School of Law. Her many publications have appeared in law reviews and social science journals in English, Russian, French and Hungarian. Her forthcoming book is *The International State of Emergency: The Rise of Global Security Law* (2013).

GÁBOR ATTILA TÓTH is Associate Professor at the University of Debrecen, Faculty of Law; he is also Lecturer at the László Rajk College of Advanced Studies, Budapest. In 2010 he was a DAAD Research Fellow at the Humboldt University, Berlin. Between 2000–2010 he served as Adviser (from 2007 as Senior Adviser) to the Constitutional Court of Hungary. Gábor Attila Tóth was co-founder and program director of the Hungarian Civil Liberties Union. He was awarded a fellowship from the Invisible College, Budapest and a scholarship from Helsinki Committee, Warsaw. He has published several books, articles, and edited volumes on matters of constitutionalism and human rights both in English and Hungarian.

RENÁTA UITZ is Professor and Chair of the Comparative Constitutional Law program at Central European University, Budapest. Her research covers issues in transition to democracy, constitutionalism and fundamental rights. Freedom of religion together with church-state relations is one of her long-held intellectual interests. Her books are *Constitutions, Courts and History* (2005) and *Freedom of Religion in European Constitutional and International Case Law* (2007). She is editor (with András Sajó) of *Constitutional Topography: Values and Constitutions* (2010).

MÁRTON VARJU is member of the Institute of European Public Law at the University of Hull and research associate at the Centre for Law and Ethics in Biomedicine, Central European University, Budapest. He has also held teaching position at the University of Debrecen. He has been teaching European Union law, European Union governance, public law, and regulation for a number of years. He has coordinated major projects in university communications and e-learning.

Index

A

B

C

D

E

F

G

H

P

Q

R

For Product Safety Concerns and Information please contact our EU
representative GPSR@taylorandfrancis.com Taylor & Francis Verlag GmbH,
Kaufingerstraße 24, 80331 München, Germany

Batch number: 10703950

Printed by Printforce, the Netherlands